SolidWorks® 2009 Bible

Matt Lombard

WILEY

Wiley Publishing, Inc.

SolidWorks® 2009 Bible

Published by
Wiley Publishing, Inc.
10475 Crosspoint Boulevard
Indianapolis, IN 46256
www.wiley.com

Copyright © 2009 by Wiley Publishing, Inc., Indianapolis, Indiana

Published by Wiley Publishing, Inc., Indianapolis, Indiana

Published simultaneously in Canada

ISBN: 978-0-470-25825-5

Manufactured in the United States of America

10 9 8 7 6 5 4 3 2 1

For general information on our other products and services or to obtain technical support, please contact our Customer Care Department within the U.S. at (877) 762-2974, outside the U.S. at (317) 572-3993 or fax (317) 572-4002.

Library of Congress Control Number: 2008942699

This work is dedicated to my grandparents, Earl "Boots"
Woods and Mildred "Mid" Woods, who taught me that the
value of hard work goes beyond the numbers on a paycheck.

About the Author

Matt Lombard holds a mechanical engineering degree from Rochester Institute of Technology in Rochester, New York. Matt has worked as a design and manufacturing engineer in the medical and microelectronics industries. Currently, through his company Dezignstuff, he works mainly as a consumer product modeling consultant and technical writer.

Before becoming an engineer, Matt went to music school for two years and performed with the Navy band for four years. He still plays in local community groups for fun. Having grown up in the Adirondack Mountains of northeastern New York, he now calls the Shenandoah Valley of Virginia home.

Credits

Senior Acquisitions Editor
Stephanie McComb

Project Editor
Jade L. Williams

Technical Editor
Ricky Jordan

Copy Editor
Lauren Kennedy

Editorial Manager
Robyn Siesky

Business Manager
Amy Knies

Senior Marketing Manager
Sandy Smith

Vice President and Executive Group Publisher
Richard Swadley

Vice President and Executive Publisher
Bob Ipsen

Vice President and Executive Publisher
Barry Pruett

Project Coordinator
Kristie Rees

Graphics and Layout Technicians
Ana Carillo
Andrea Hornberger
Sarah Philippart

Quality Control Technician
Caitie Kelly

Media Development Project Manager
Laura Moss

Media Development Associate Producer
Angela Denny

Media Development Assistant Project Manager
Jenny Swisher

Proofreading and Indexing
Christopher M. Jones
Valerie Haynes Perry

Contents at a Glance

Contents

Contents

Contents

Contents

Part III: Working with Assemblies 395

Chapter 12: Building Efficient Assemblies. 397

Contents

Contents

Contents

Part IV: Creating and Using Libraries   525

Chapter 17: Using Hole Wizard and Toolbox 527

Contents

Contents

Contents

Part VI: Using Advanced Techniques   753

Chapter 26: Modeling Multi-bodies 755

Contents

Contents

Contents

Part VIII: Appendixes   993

Appendix A: Implementing SolidWorks 995

Contents

Contents

Acknowledgments

The ideas that go into a book of this size do not all originate with a single individual. Research for many of the topics was done at user group meetings, SolidWorks Corporation's discussion forums, and SolidWorks Customer Portal, as well as the blogs and Web sites of many individuals. I would like to thank all of the individuals who have posted to the public forums or blogs. Many of these people have knowingly or unknowingly contributed to my SolidWorks education, as well as that of many other SolidWorks users around the world.

Welcome to the SolidWorks 2009 Bible. This book has been written as a desk reference for beginning and intermediate SolidWorks users. SolidWorks is such an immense software program that trying to cover all of its functions is an extremely ambitious undertaking, and I know that a few have been left out. Because of the scope of the topic, I have limited the book to covering the basic SolidWorks package, without the Office, Office Professional, or Office Premium add-ins, although I have devoted half of a chapter to Toolbox.

About This Book

You will find enough information here that the book can grow with your SolidWorks needs. I have written tutorials for most of the chapters with newer users in mind, because for them, it is most helpful to see how things are done in SolidWorks step by step. The longer narrative examples give more in-depth information about features and functions, as well as the results of various settings and options.

I have included an extensive appendix covering the Tools, Options settings. This offers an in-depth explanation of each option, including both System Options and Document Properties. This appendix uses special symbols to identify items that are new for SolidWorks 2007 or that affect file size or speed.

How This Book Is Organized

This book is divided into eight parts.

Part I: SolidWorks Basics

This part explores basic concepts and terminology used in SolidWorks. You need to read this section if you are new to the software and especially if you are new to 3D modeling or parametric history-based design.

Part II: Building Intelligence into Your Parts

This part takes a deeper look at creating parametric relations to automate changes.

Part III: Working with Assemblies

Part III delves into assembly modeling in it various aspects, from efficiency to in-context modeling.

Part IV: Creating and Using Libraries

Part IV helps you understand how to build and manage libraries of various types with an eye toward upgrading versions, best practice and reusing data when possible.

Part V: Creating Drawings

This part examines the functionality within the 2D drawing side of the software. Whether you are creating views, making tables or customizing annotations, this chapter has something for everyone.

Part VI: Using Advanced Techniques

This part examines several types of advanced techniques, such as surface modeling and multi-body modeling. This is information you won't find in other SolidWorks books, explained here by some one who uses the functionality daily.

Part VII: Working with Specialized Functionality

Specialized functionality such as sheet metal, weldments, plastics and animation requires detailed information. Part VII includes these topics because they are key to unlocking all of the power available in SolidWorks.

Part VIII: Appendices

The appendices in this book cover a range of ancillary data from how to implement the software to a detailed and complete list of the available options. The Tools⇨Options list in Appendix B is one of those things that distinguishes this book from others available. You need to know where to find settings, and this appendix has it all.

Icons Used in This Book

This book uses a set of icons to point out certain details in the text. While they are relatively self-explanatory, here is what each of these icons indicates:

NOTE Notes highlight useful information that you should take into consideration, or an important point that requires special attention.

TIP Tips provide you with additional advice that makes the software quicker or easier to use.

CAUTION Caution icons warn you of potential problems before you make a mistake.

NEW FEATURE The New Feature icon highlights features and functions that are new to SolidWorks 2009.

CROSS-REF Cross-Ref icons point out where you can find additional information about a topic elsewhere in the book.

ON the CD-ROM This icon points you toward related material on the book's CD.

The *SolidWorks 2009 Bible* is unique in its use of these two icons:

BEST PRACTICE Best practice icons point out recommended settings or techniques that are safe in most situations.

PERFORMANCE Performance icons elaborate on how certain settings, features, or techniques affect rebuild speed or file size.

These icons point out and describe techniques and settings that are either recommended or not recommended for specific reasons. Best Practice is usually considered to be very conservative usage, where the stability of the parametrics and performance (a euphemism for *rebuild speed*) are the ultimate goals. These two aspects of SolidWorks models are usually weighed against modeling speed (how long it takes you to create the model).

Best Practice and Performance recommendations need to be taken seriously, but you should treat them as guidelines rather than as rules. When it comes right down to it, the only hard and fast rule about SolidWorks is that there are no hard and fast rules. In fact, I believe that the only reason to have rules in the first place is so that you know when you can break them. Parametric stability and modeling speed are not always the ultimate goals, and are often overridden when workaround techniques are used simply to accomplish a geometric goal.

Because not everyone models with the same goals in mind, a single set of rules can never apply for everyone. You must take the best practice suggestions and apply them to your situation using your own judgment.

My point of view while writing this book has been that of someone who is actually using the software, not of someone trying to sell ideas, nor of someone trying to make the software look good, or even that of an academic trying to make a beautiful argument. I try to approach the software objectively as a tool, recognizing that complex tools are good at some things and not so good at others. Both kinds of information (good and not-so-good) are useful to the reader. Pointing out negatives in this context should not be construed as criticizing the SolidWorks software, but rather as preparing the reader for real-world use of the software. Any tool this complex is going to have imperfections. Hopefully some of my enthusiasm for the software also shows through and is to some extent contagious.

Terminology

An important concept referred to frequently in SolidWorks is *design intent*. As a practical matter, I use the phrase *design for change* to further distinguish design intent from other design goals.

The reader needs to be familiar with some special terminology before continuing. In many cases, a SolidWorks vernacular or slang is used when the official terminology is either not descriptive enough or, as is sometimes the case, has multiple meanings. For example, the word *shortcut* has multiple meanings in the SolidWorks interface. It is used to describe right mouse button menus as well as hotkeys. As a result, I have chosen not to use the word shortcut and instead substitute the words *RMB* and *hotkey*.

I frequently use RMB to refer to Right Mouse Button menus, or other data that you access by clicking the right mouse button on an item. The word *tree* refers to the list of features in the FeatureManager. Also, command and option names are referred to using all initial capitals, even when SolidWorks does not use the same capitalization. For example, the setting Single Command Per Pick is listed in Tools ⇨ Options as Single command per pick. I do this to help the reader distinguish command names from other general text.

Differences are frequently found between the names of features on toolbars and the names in the menus or PropertyManager titles. In these cases, the differences are usually minor, and either name may be used.

Most functions in SolidWorks can work with either the object-action or the action-object scenarios. These are also called *pre-select* and *select*, respectively. For example, the Hole Wizard is one tool for which pre-selection is definitely recommended because a difference in functionality is seen between pre-selection and selection. The Fillet feature shows no difference between using pre-selection and selection, although for some fillet options such as face fillet, pre-select is not enabled. Most features allow pre-selection, and some functions, such as inserting a design table, require pre-selection. Although you cannot identify a single rule that covers all situations, *most* functions accept both.

Frequently in this book, I have suggested enhancement requests that the reader may want to make. This is because SolidWorks development is driven to a large extent by customer requests, and if a large number of users converge on a few issues, then those issues are more likely to be fixed or changed. Again, the enhancement request suggestions are not made to criticize the software, but to make it better. I hope that several of you will join me in submitting enhancement requests.

SolidWorks is an extremely powerful modeling tool, very likely with the best combination of power and accessibility on the MCAD market today. This book is meant to help you take advantage of its power in your work and even hobbyist applications. If I could impart only a single thought to all readers of this book, it would be that with a little curiosity and some imagination, you can begin to access the power of SolidWorks for geometry creation and virtual product prototyping. You should start with the assumption that there is a way to do what you are imagining, and that you should be open to using different techniques.

For AutoCAD users making the transition to SolidWorks, you should simply forget everything you know about AutoCAD, because most of it, except for the most general geometric concepts, will not apply to SolidWorks, and will often simply confuse you.

Whoever you are, I hope that you find insight deeper than simply "what does this button do?" in this book. I hope that you will find an intuition for thinking like the software. Jeff Ray, CEO of the SolidWorks Corporation has said that the goal is to make the software as "intuitive as a light switch." While most people will agree that they have some work left to achieve that particular goal, I believe that approaching the interface intuitively, rather than attempting to remember it all by rote, is the best method. Good luck to you all.

Contacting the Author

You might want to contact me for some reason. Maybe you found an error in the book, or you have a suggestion about something that you think would improve it. It is always good to hear what real users think about the material, whether you like it or thought it could be improved.

The best way to contact me is either through email or through my blog. My email address is matt@dezignstuff.com. You will find my blog at http://dezignstuff.com/blog. On the blog you can leave comments and read other things I have written about the SolidWorks software, CAD, and engineering or computer topics in general. I encourage you to also leave feedback on websites where you might have purchased the book. For example, Amazon allows customers to review books, and book reviews are always beneficial.

If you want to contact me for commercial help with a modeling project, the email address above is the best place to start that type of conversation.

Thank you very much for buying and reading this book. I hope the ideas and information within its pages help you accomplish your professional goals.

Part I

SolidWorks Basics

If you are a new SolidWorks user, the chapters of Part I are essential. I recommend reading these chapters in order, since the material in each chapter builds on the material of the previous chapter.

If you are an existing SolidWorks user but new to the post 2009 releases, I strongly recommend Chapters 2 and 5. Even if you are a very experienced user, I recommend Chapter 5. The visualization techniques are things we all use on a constant basis in the software, and picking up even a small tip can add to your productivity dramatically.

Chapter 1

Introducing SolidWorks

I f you are coming to SolidWorks from Inventor, Solid Edge, or another program in that class, you will find SolidWorks to be very familiar territory, with a similar if not identical design philosophy. SolidWorks also shares a lot of underlying structure with Pro/ENGINEER, and if you are coming from that product, there will be some relearning, but much of your training will be transferable.

If you are coming from 2D AutoCAD, CADKEY, or MicroStation, SolidWorks may at first cause a bit of culture shock for you. However, once you embrace feature-based modeling, things will go more easily. As you will see, SolidWorks, and in fact most solid modeling in general, is very process-based.

Regardless of how you arrived here with this *SolidWorks Bible* in your hand, here you are. Together we will progress through basic concepts to advanced techniques, everyday settings, and subtle nuances. This book will serve as your tutor and desk reference for learning about SolidWorks software.

This chapter will familiarize beginners with some of the tools available to make the transition, and with some of the basic facts and concepts that you need to know to get the most out of SolidWorks.

If all you want to do is to start using the software, and you are not concerned with understanding how or why it works, you can skip directly to Chapter 4 for sketches or Chapter 5 to start making parts, assemblies, and drawings. Of course, I recommend getting a bit of background and some foundation.

IN THIS CHAPTER

Starting SolidWorks for the first time

Identifying different types of SolidWorks documents

Understanding feature-based Modeling

Understanding history-based Modeling

Sketching with parametrics

Understanding Design Intent

Editing Design Intent

Working with associativity

Tutorial: Creating a part template

Starting SolidWorks for the First Time

SolidWorks has many tools for beginning users that are available when the software is installed. A default installation presents you with several options when the software is started the first time. Following is a catalog of these options and how to get the most benefit from them.

If you plan to go to formal SolidWorks reseller-based training classes, it is a very good idea to go through some of the tutorials mentioned in this section first; this way you are prepared to ask educated questions and have a leg up on the rest of the class. You will get more out of the training with the instructor if you have seen the material once before.

SolidWorks License Agreement

It is useful to be familiar with what this document says, but the agreement does not have any bearing on learning how to use the software other than the fact that it allows for a Home Use License. Many users find this part of the license agreement, shown in Figure 1.1, helpful. The primary user of the license at work is also allowed to use the license at home or on a portable computer. This is often a good option for learning, additional practice or completing the design of the deck or soapbox derby car. If your business uses floating licenses, the rules are somewhat different. Contact your reseller for details. In any case, select Accept to get past the License Agreement page.

FIGURE 1.1

The SolidWorks License Agreement

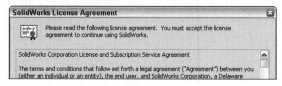

Welcome to SolidWorks

The Welcome to SolidWorks screen, shown in Figure 1.2, is the next thing to greet you. This helps you establish what type of tools you would like to see in the interface and gives you some help options. You may not get the chance to see this dialog box if someone else, for example an IT person, has installed and done an initial test on your software for you.

Quick Tips

Quick Tips enables balloons with tips to help you get started with several tasks. For example, the first Quick Tip you see may be this one, shown in Figure 1.3. When you begin to create your first document in SolidWorks, a Quick Tip helps guide you on your way.

FIGURE 1.2

FIGURE 1.2

Welcome to SolidWorks screen

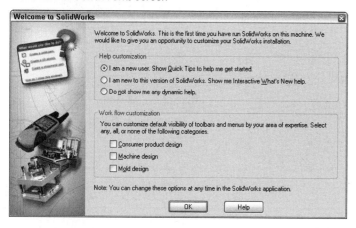

FIGURE 1.3

New SolidWorks Document Quick Tip

As you begin working, Quick Tips displays a box, shown in Figure 1.4, at the lower-right corner of the Graphics Window that offers context-sensitive help messages. As you work with the software, these messages change to remain relevant to what you are doing.

You can turn Quick Tips on or off using the small square on the Status Bar in the lower-right corner, as shown in Figure 1.5. You can turn the Status Bar itself on or off in the View menu; however, the Status Bar serves many useful purposes, even for advanced users, so I recommend you leave it turned on. You can also turn off Quick Tips in the Help menu by selecting Quick Tips. The on/off setting is document-type sensitive, so if you turned Quick Tips off in part mode, you will need to do it again for assemblies and drawings, as well. Quick Tips are a great way to get going or to get a little refresher if it has been a while or several versions have gone by since you last saw the software, but you shouldn't need them forever.

FIGURE 1.4

The main Quick Tip window

FIGURE 1.5

Turning Quick Tips on or off

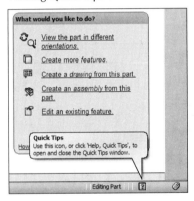

The first time you create a document, you will be prompted to select units for your default templates, as shown in Figure 1.6. This is an important step, although you can make changes later if needed. SolidWorks stores most of the document-specific settings in document templates, which you can set up with different settings for each type of document — parts, assemblies, and drawings. More information on part and assembly templates can be found later in this chapter. Drawing Templates are described in detail in Chapter 20.

The main significance of this default template unit option is not so much the units as the dimensioning standard that is selected. ISO (International Organization for Standardization) and ANSI (American National Standards Institute) standards use different methods of projecting views. ISO is typically a European standard and uses First Angle Projection, while ANSI is an American standard and uses Third Angle Projection. The standard projection used throughout this book is Third Angle.

FIGURE 1.6

Default template units selection

Units and Dimension Standard

Select the initial settings for the default templates:

Units:

IPS (inch, pound, second)

Dimension standard:

ANSI

NOTE: These settings can be changed for individual templates or documents in Tools, Options, Document Properties.

[OK]   [Cancel]   [Help]

The difference between Third and First angle projections can cause parts to be manufactured incorrectly if those reading the prints (or making the prints) do not catch the difference or see that there is some discrepancy. Figure 1.7 demonstrates the difference between the two projection types. Make sure to get the option correct. If someone else, such a computer specialist who is not familiar with mechanical drafting standards, initially sets up SolidWorks on your computer, you will want to verify that the default templates are correct.

FIGURE 1.7

Differences between First (left) and Third (right) angle projections

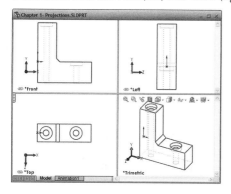
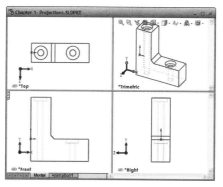

Notice that the icons in the View Orientation drop down are arranged in a Third Angle projection fashion. This might be confusing for people accustomed to using First Angle.

Another setting affecting projections that you will want to check is found at Tools ⇨ Options, Display/Selection ⇨ Projection type for four view viewport. This does not follow the dimensioning standard selected for the default templates or the country in which the software is installed.

Online documentation

Several types of online documentation are available to help SolidWorks learners along their path. A great place to start is with the SolidWorks Resources tab of the Task Pane (on the right side of the screen). This is the first tab in the list with the Home icon. The Getting Started section of the SolidWorks Resources tab is shown in Figure 1.8.

FIGURE 1.8

Getting Started on the SolidWorks Resources tab of the Task Manager

Tutorials

Following the link in the Help menu to the Online Tutorials leads you to a list of tutorials on subjects from sheet metal to macros, in parts assemblies, and drawings. These tutorials are certainly worth your time, and will build your skills and knowledge of basic functionality. This *SolidWorks Bible* distinguishes itself by going into far more detail and depth about each function, adding information such as best practice, performance considerations, and cautionary data, and acting as a thorough desk reference. The purpose of this book is not really to duplicate all of the resources for beginners, but to take the information into far more depth and detail, and answer the "why" questions instead of just the "how" questions.

What's New

With every release, SolidWorks publishes a What's New document to help you keep up to speed with the changes. This is typically a PDF file with accompanying example files. If you have missed a version or two, reading through the What's New files can help get you back on track. Again, don't expect a lot of detail or interface screen shots, but it should at least introduce the basic changes.

Moving from AutoCAD

In the Help menu is a selection called Moving from AutoCAD. This is intended to help transitioning users acclimate to their new surroundings. Terminology is a big part of the equation when making this switch, and figures prominently in the Moving from AutoCAD help file.

Likely the most helpful tools in Moving from AutoCAD are the Approach to Modeling and Imported AutoCAD Data sections. This information is useful whether you are coming to SolidWorks from AutoCAD or another CAD package.

Online User's Guide

The Online User's Guide is the traditional Help file. You can use either the Index or Search capabilities to find what you are looking for. The Online User's Guide contains screen captures and animations, sample files, and even a separate API (programming) help file. Frankly, it is not incredibly detailed, and often skips over important facts like what you might use a certain function for, or what the interface looks like, or even where you might find the command in the first place. The SolidWorks documentation is set to get some upgrades, so it remains to be seen if this is really an improvement or not. Meanwhile, this *SolidWorks Bible* fills in most of the gaps in information about the standard version of the software.

Tip of the Day

SolidWorks Tip of the Day is displayed at the bottom of the SolidWorks Resources tab of the Task Pane. Cycling though a few of these or using them to quiz coworkers can be a useful skills-building exercise.

Hardcopy documentation

Hardcopy documentation has regrettably dwindled from all software companies. Software manufacturers often claim that keeping up with the changes in print is too much work and inefficient. Still many users prefer to have a physical book in their hands, to spread out on the desk next to them; to earmark, highlight, and mark with post-its; and take notes in, as evidenced by you holding this book at this moment. Hardcopy documentation has an important role to play in the dissemination of information, even in a highly dynamic electronic age. The following items are still provided in hardcopy format.

- The Quick Start pamphlet acts as a rough outline for issues from installation to getting help. It is approximately ten pages and contains information that complete new users need to know.

- The Quick Reference Guide is a fold-out card that has reminders of some of the symbols displayed in the FeatureManager and other locations, as well as some of the default hotkeys and customization options.

Identifying SolidWorks Documents

SolidWorks has three main data type files. However, there are additional supporting types that you may want to know if you are concerned with customization and creating implementation standards. Table 1.1 outlines the document types.

TABLE 1.1

Document types

Design Documents	Description
.SLDASM	SolidWorks Assembly File Type
.SLDDRW	SolidWorks Drawing File Type
.SLDPRT	SolidWorks Part File Type
Templates and Formats	**Description**
.asmdot.	Assembly Template
.asmprp	Assembly custom properties tab template
.drwdot	Drawing Template
.drwprp	Drawing custom properties tab template
journal.doc	Design Journal Template
.prtdot	Part Template
.prtprp	Part custom properties tab template
.sldbombt	BOM Template (table-based)
.sldtbt	General Table Template
.slddrt	Drawing Sheet Format
.sldholtbt	Hole Table Template
.sldrevtbt	Revision Table Template
.sldwldtbt	Weldment Cutlist Template
.xls	BOM Template (Excel-based)
Library Files	**Description**
.sldblk	Blocks
.sldlfp	Library Part File
Styles	**Description**
.sldgtolfvt	Geometric Tolerance Style
.sldsffvt	Surface Finish Style
.sldweldfvt	Weld Style
Symbol Files	**Description**
gtol.sym	Symbol file allows you to create custom symbols
swlines.lin	Line Style definition file allows you to create new line styles
Others	**Description**
.btl	Sheet Metal Bend Table
calloutformat.txt	Hole Callout Format File

Others	Description
.sldclr	Color Palette File
.sldreg	SolidWorks Settings File
.sldmat	Material Database
.sldstd	Drafting standard
.swb, swp	Macros, Macro Features
.txt	Custom Property File, Sheet Metal Bend Line Note File
.xls	Sheet Metal Gauge Table

Saving your setup

If you have taken time to set up a computer and then need to reinstall SolidWorks, move to another computer, or duplicate the setup for another user, you need to copy out the files you have used or customized. All these files are located by default in different folders within the SolidWorks installation directory. Chapter 2 deals with interface settings and creating a registry settings file to copy to other computers or use as a backup, but that does not address also copying the files of various types that also comprise an installation customization.

BEST PRACTICE Especially when you are doing complex implementations that include templates for various types of tables or customized symbol files, it is important to have copies of these files in a location other than the default installation folder. Uninstalling SolidWorks or installing a new version will wipe out all of your hard work. Use the Tools ⇨ Options ⇨ File locations to locate these files in separate library folders that can be on the local hard drive or on a network location.

Templates

I have included some of my part and assembly templates on the CD-ROM for you. Copy these files to the location specified at Tools ⇨ Options ⇨ File Locations ⇨ Document Templates.

When you begin to create a new document, and the New SolidWorks Document dialog box gives you the option to select one of several files to start from, those files are templates. Think of templates as "start parts" that contain all of the document-specific settings for a part (Tools ⇨ Options ⇨ Document Properties). The same concept applies to assemblies and drawings. Templates generally do not have any geometry in them (although it is possible).

TIP The Novice interface for the File, New SolidWorks Document dialog box only allows you to select default templates. The Advanced interface allows you to select any available template.

As shown in Figure 1.9, several tabs can be displayed on the advanced interface. Each of these tabs is created by creating a folder in the template directory specified in Tool ⇨ Options.

FIGURE 1.9

The Novice and Advanced interfaces for the New SolidWorks Document dialog

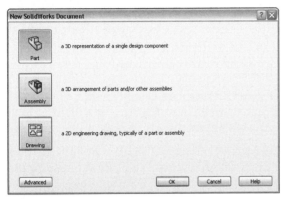

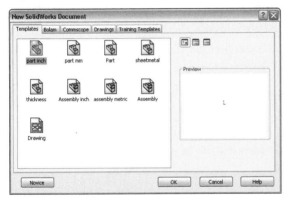

Using multiple document templates

Using multiple templates enables you to start working from multiple starting points, which is an advantage in many situations such as:

- Standardization for a large number of users
- Working in various units
- Preset materials
- Preset custom properties
- Parts with special requirements, such as sheet metal or weldments
- Drawings of various sizes with formats (borders) already applied
- Drawings with special notes already on the sheet

CROSS-REF Drawing templates and formats are complex enough that I cover them in a separate chapter. Chapter 20 Automating Drawings – The Basics discusses the differences between templates and formats and how to use them to your best advantage. This chapter addresses part and assembly templates.

Depending on your needs, it might be reasonable to have templates for metric and inch part and assembly, templates for steel and aluminum, and templates for sheet metal parts and for weldments, if you design these types of parts. If your firm has different customers with different requirements, you might consider using separate templates for those customers. Over time, you will discover the types of templates you need, because you will find yourself making the same changes over and over again.

To create a template, open a document of the appropriate type (part or assembly), and make the settings you wish the template to have; for example, units are one of the most common reasons to make a separate template, but in fact any of the Document Property settings is fair game for a template, from the dimensioning standard used to image quality settings.

CROSS-REF Document Property settings are covered extensively in Appendix B.

Some document specific settings are not contained in the Document Properties dialog box. Still, these settings are saved with the template. Settings that fall into this category are the View menu entity type visibility options and the Tools ⇨ Sketch Settings options.

Custom Properties are another piece of the template puzzle. If you use or plan to use BOMs (bills of materials), PDM (product data management), or linked notes on drawings, you need to take advantage of the automation options available with custom properties. Setting up custom properties is covered in detail in Chapter 20.

Also, the names of the standard planes are template specific. For example, the standard planes may be named Front, Top, and Side; or XY, XZ, and ZY; or Plane1, Plane2, and Plane3; or North, Plan, and East; or Elevation, Plan, and Side for different uses.

Locating templates

The templates folder is established at Tools ⇨ Options ⇨ File Locations ⇨ Document Templates. This location may be a local directory or a shared network location. Multiple folders may be specified in the list box, each of which corresponds to a tab in the New Document's Advanced interface.

Once all of the Document Properties, custom properties, and other settings are set to your liking and you are ready to save the file as a template, click File ⇨ Save As and in Files of Type, select Part Templates. SolidWorks prompts you to save the template in the first folder listed in the File Locations list. You can create assembly templates in the same way, but changing the settings for an assembly document.

You can also create additional tabs on the New SolidWorks Document dialog box can also be created by making subfolders in the main folder specified in the File Locations area. For example, if your File Locations list for Document Templates looks like Figure 1.10, then your New dialog will look like Figure 1.11.

FIGURE 1.10

Tools ➪ Options ➪ File Locations list

FIGURE 1.11

New SolidWorks Document dialog box

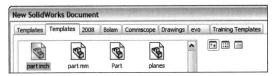

Adding subfolders to either of the locations listed in File Locations results in additional tabs in the New dialog, as shown in Figures 1.12 and 1.13.

FIGURE 1.12

Additional subfolders added to a File Locations path

FIGURE 1.13

Resulting tabs in New SolidWorks Document dialog box

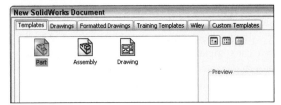

Default templates

Default templates are established at Tools ➪ Options ➪ Default Templates. The default templates must be in one of the paths specified in File Locations. Figure 1.14 shows the Default Templates settings.

FIGURE 1.14

Tools ➪ Options ➪ Default Templates settings

These templates will be used for operations (such as File Import and Mirror Part) where SolidWorks does not prompt for a template.

Parts
D:\library\Custom Templates\part inch.prtdot

Assemblies
D:\library\Custom Templates\Assembly inch.asmdot

Drawings
D:\library\Custom Templates\Drawings\inch B.drwdot

◉ Always use these default document templates
○ Prompt user to select document template

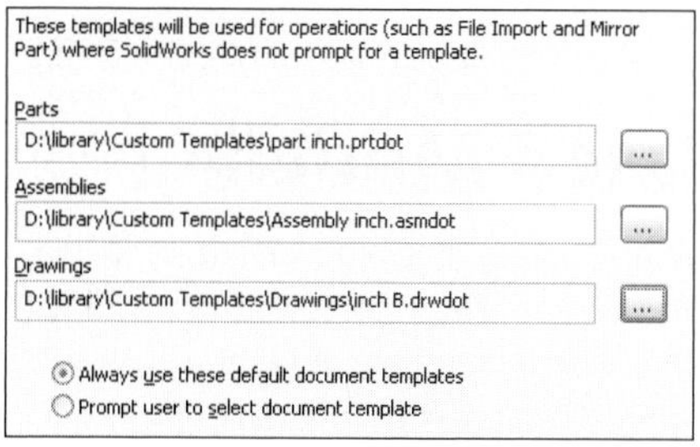

The Default Template option, Always use these default document templates Prompt user to select document template, applies to situations when a template is required by an automatic feature in the software such as an imported part, or a mirrored part. In this situation, depending on the setting selected, the system either automatically uses the default template or the user is prompted to select a template.

PERFORMANCE Allowing the software to apply the default template automatically can have a great impact on speed. This is especially true in the case of imported assemblies, which would require you to manually select templates for each imported part in the assembly if the Prompt user... option is used.

Sharing templates

If you are administering an installation of a large number of users, or even if there are just a couple of users working on similar designs, shared templates are a must. If every user is doing what she thinks best, you may get an interesting combination of conflicting ideas, and the consistency of the company's documentation may suffer. Standardized templates cannot make users model, assemble, and detail in exactly the same way, but they do start users off on the same foot.

To share templates among several users, create a folder for templates on a commonly accessible network location, preferably with read-only access for users and read-write permissions for administrators. Then point each user's File Locations and Default templates to that location. Access problems due to multiple users accessing the same files do not arise in this situation because templates are essentially copied to create a new document, not used directly.

CAUTION One of the downfalls of this arrangement is that if the network goes down, users no longer have access to their templates. This can be averted by also putting copies of the templates on the local computers; however, it has the tendency to undermine the goal of consistent documentation. Users may tend to use and customize the local templates rather than use the standardized network copies.

CAD administration and organizing any group of people on some level always comes down to trusting employees to do the right thing. There is no way to completely secure any system against all people trying to work around the system, so you must rely on having hired people you can train and trust.

Understanding Feature-Based Modeling

There is some terminology that you need to come to grips with before diving into building models with SolidWorks. Notice that I talk about "modeling" rather than "drawing," or even "design." This is because SolidWorks is really virtual prototyping software. Whether you are building an assembly line for automotive parts or designing decorative perfume bottles, SolidWorks can help you visualize your geometrical production data in the most realistic way possible without actually having it in your hand. This is more akin to making a physical model in the shop than drawing on paper.

"Feature-based" modeling means that you build the model by incrementally identifying functional shapes, and applying processes to create the shapes. For example, you can create a simple box by using the Extrude process, and you can create a sphere by using the Revolve process. However, you can make a cylinder by using either process, by revolving a rectangle or extruding a circle. You start by visualizing the 3D shape, and then apply a 3D process to a 2D sketch to create that shape. This concept on its own is half of what you need to know to create models with SolidWorks.

Figure 1.15 shows images of simple feature types with the 2D sketches from which they were created.

Many different feature types in SolidWorks enable you to create everything from the simplest geometry shown previously to more complex artistic or organic shapes. In general, when I talk about modeling in this book, I am talking about *solid* modeling, although SolidWorks also has a complete complement of surfacing tools. I will discuss the distinction between solid and surface modeling in Chapter 27.

Table 1.2 lists some of the most common features that you find in SolidWorks, and classifies them according to whether they always require a sketch, a sketch is optional, or they never require a sketch.

FIGURE 1.15

Simple extruded and revolved features

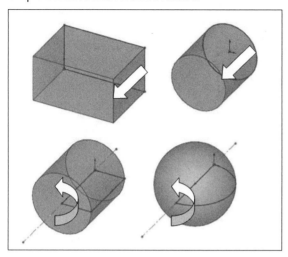

TABLE 1.2

Feature Types

Sketch Required	Sketch Optional	No Sketch (Applied Features)
Extrude	Loft	Fillet
Revolve	Sweep	Chamfer
Rib	Dome	Draft
Hole Wizard	Shape	Shell
Wrap	Deform	Flex

In addition to these features, there are other types of features that create reference geometry (such as curves, planes, and axes, surface features (covered in Chapter 27), and specialty features for techniques like weldments (Chapter 31), plastics/mold tools (Chapter 32), and sheet metal (Chapters 29 & 30).

Understanding History-Based Modeling

In addition to being feature-based, SolidWorks is also history-based. To show the process history, there is a panel to the left side of the SolidWorks window called the *FeatureManager*. The FeatureManager keeps a list of the features in the order in which you have added them. It also enables you to reorder items in the tree (in effect, to change history). Because of this, the order in which you perform operations is important. For example, consider Figure 1.16. This model was created by the following process, left to right starting with the top row:

1. Create a sketch.

2. Extrude the sketch.

3. Create a second sketch.

4. Extrude the second sketch.

5. Create a third sketch.

6. Extrude Cut the third sketch.

7. Apply fillets.

8. Shell the model.

If the order of operations used in the previous part were slightly reordered (by putting the shell and fillet features before Step 6), the resulting part would also look slightly different, as shown in Figure 1.17.

Figure 1.18 shows a comparison of the FeatureManager design trees for the two different feature orders. You can reorder features by dragging them up or down the tree. Relationships between features can prevent reordering; for example, the fillets are dependent on the second extruded feature, and cannot be reordered before it. This is referred to as a Parent/Child relationship.

CROSS-REF Reordering and Parent/Child relationships are discussed in more detail in Chapter 11, Editing and Evaluation.

ON the CD-ROM The part used for this example is available in the material from the CD-ROM, named Chapter 1 — Features.SLDPRT. Parts on the CD-ROM exist for both 2007 and 2009 versions.

The order of operations, or *history*, is important to the final state of the part. For example, if you change the order so that the shell comes before the extruded cut, the geometry of the model changes, removing the sleeve inside instead of the hole on top. You can try this for yourself by opening the part indicated previously, dragging the Shell1 feature in the FeatureManager, and dropping it just above the Cut-Extrude1 feature.

NOTE You can only drag one item at a time in the FeatureManager. So you may drag the Shell, and then drag each of two fillets, or you could just drag the Cut feature down the tree. Alternatively, you can put the shell and fillets in a folder and drag the folder to a new location.

Reordering is limited by parent-child relationships between dependent features.

FIGURE 1.16

Features used to create a simple part

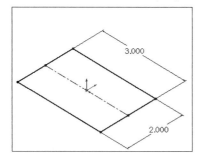

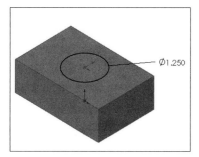

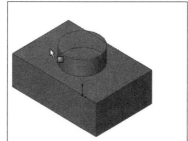

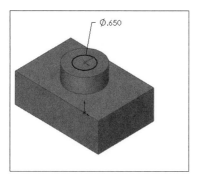

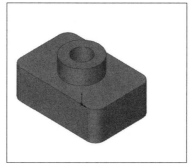

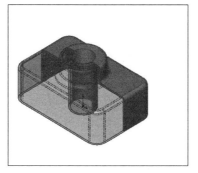

FIGURE 1.17

Using a different order of features for the same part

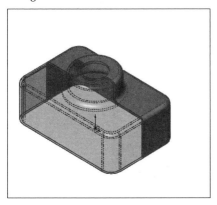

FIGURE 1.18

Compare the FeatureManager design trees for the parts shown in Figure 1.16 and Figure 1.17.

CROSS-REF You can read more about reordering folders in Chapter 11, Editing and Evaluations.

In some cases, reordering the features in the FeatureManager may result in geometry that might not make any sense; for example, if the fillets are applied after the shell, they might break through to the inside of the part. In these cases, SolidWorks gives an error that helps you to fix the problem.

In 2D CAD programs where you are just drawing lines, the order in which you draw the lines does not matter. This is one of the fundamental differences between history-based modeling and non-history-based drawing.

Features are really just like steps in building a part; the steps can either add material or remove it. However, when you make a part on a mill or lathe, you are only removing material. The FeatureManager is like an instruction sheet to build the part. When you reorder and revise history, you change the order of operations and thus the final result.

Sketching with Parametrics

You have already seen that sketching is the foundation that underlies the most common feature types. You will now find that sketching in parametric software is vastly different from drawing lines in 2D CAD.

Dictionary.com defines the word *parameter* as "one of a set of measurable factors . . . that define a system and determine its behavior and [that] are varied in an experiment." SolidWorks sketches are parametric. What this means to you as a SolidWorks user in a practical sense is that you can create sketches that change according to certain rules, and maintain relationships through those changes. This is the basis of parametric design. It extends beyond sketching to all of the types of geometry you can create in SolidWorks.

In addition to 2D sketching, SolidWorks also makes 3D sketching possible. Of the two methods, 2D sketches are by far the more widely used. You create 2D sketches on a selected plane, planar solid, or surface face, and use them to establish shapes for features such as Extrude, Revolve, and others. Relations in 2D sketches are often created between sketch entities and other entities that may or may not be in the sketch plane. In situations where other entities are not in the sketch plane, the out-of-plane entity is projected into the sketch plane in a direction that is normal to the sketch plane. This does not happen for 3D sketches.

You use 3D sketches for the Hole Wizard, routing, and weldments, among other applications such as complex shape creation.

CROSS-REF   For more information on 3D sketching, please refer to Chapter 31.

For a simple example of working with sketch relations in a 2D sketch, consider the sketch that is shown in Figure 1.19. The only relationships between the four lines are that they form a closed loop that is touching end to end, and one of the corners is coincident to the part origin. The small square icon near the origin shows the symbol for a *coincident* sketch relation. The setting to enable or disable these sketch relation symbols is found at View ⇨ Sketch Relations.

If you drag any of the unconstrained corners (except for the corner that is coincident to the origin), the two neighboring lines will follow the dragged endpoint, as shown in Figure 1.20. Notice the ghosted image left by the original position of the sketch. This is helpful when experimenting with changes to the sketch because you can see both the new and the old states of the sketch. The setting to enable or disable this ghosted position is found at Tools ⇨ Options ⇨ Sketch ⇨ Ghost Image On Drag.

FIGURE 1.19

A sketch of four lines

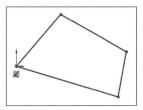

FIGURE 1.20

Dragging an endpoint

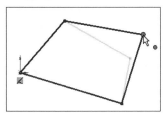

If you add a parallel relation between opposing lines, they now act differently, as shown in Figure 1.21. A parallel relation is added by selecting the two lines to be made parallel and selecting Parallel from the PropertyManager panel. You can also select the Parallel relation from the context bar that pops up in the graphics window when you have both lines selected.

CROSS-REF You can read more about the PropertyManager in Chapter 2, Navigating the SolidWorks Interface..

FIGURE 1.21

Dragging an endpoint where lines have relations

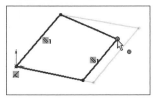

Next, a second parallel and a horizontal relation are added, as shown in Figure 1.22. If you are following along by re-creating the sketch on your computer, you will notice that one line has turned from blue to black.

FIGURE 1.22

Horizontal and parallel relations are added.

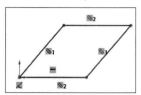

The colors represent sketch states. It may be impossible to see this in the black and white printing of this book, but if you are following along on your own computer, you can now see one black line and three blue lines. Sketch states include Underdefined, Overdefined, Fully Defined, Unsolvable, Zero Length, and Dangling.

- **Blue: Underdefined**. The sketch entity is not completely defined. You can drag a portion of it to change size, position, or orientation.

- **Red: Overdefined**. This can mean a number of things, but it is usually caused by conflicting relations or dimensions. For example, if a line has both horizontal and vertical relations, it becomes overdefined because one of the relations is satisfied, while the other is not.

- **Black: Fully Defined**. The sketch entity is fully defined by a combination of sketch relations and dimensions. A sketch cannot be fully defined without being connected in some way to something external to the sketch, such as the part origin or an edge. Multiple external entities may be used, as appropriate. (The exception to this rule is the use of the Fix constraint, which, although effective, is not a recommended practice.)

- **Pink: Unsolvable**. The difference between pink and red is that red conflicts with another relation but is in a potentially correct location, whereas pink conflicts with another relation, but is not able to move to a correct location, generally because of another red entity.

- **Yellow: Zero Length**. Solving the sketch relations would result in a zero-length entity; for example, this can occur where an arc is tangent to a line, and the centerpoint of the arc is also coincident to the line.

- **Brown: Dangling**. The relation has lost track of the entity to which it was connected.

There can be entities with different states within a single sketch. Also, endpoints of lines can have a different state than the rest of the sketched entity. For example, a line that is sketched horizontally from the origin has a *coincident* at one endpoint to the origin, and the line itself is *horizontal*. As a result, the line and first endpoint are black, but the other endpoint is underdefined because the length of the line is not defined. Sketch states are indicated in the lower-right corner of the graphics window and also in the status bar. You can see that dragging one corner allows only the lines to move in certain ways, as shown in Figure 1.23.

FIGURE 1.23

Sketch motion is becoming more constrained.

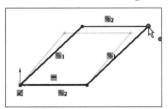

In addition to sketch relations. dimensions applied using the Smart Dimension tool are also part of the parametric scheme. If you apply an angle dimension (by clicking the two angled lines with the Smart Dimension tool) about the origin and try dragging again, as shown in Figure 1.24, you see that the only aspect that is not locked down is the length of the sides. Notice also that when the angle dimension is added, another line turns black.

FIGURE 1.24

Open degrees of freedom can be dragged.

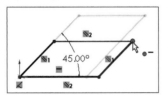

Finally, adding length dimensions for the unequal sides completes the definition of the sketch, as shown in Figure 1.25. At this point, all lines have turned black. This is the state that we call "fully defined." Between the dimensions and sketch relations, there is enough information to re-create this sketch exactly.

BEST PRACTICE It is considered best practice to fully define all sketches. However, there are times when this is not practical. When you create freeform shapes, generally through the use of splines, these shapes cannot easily be fully defined, and even if they are fully defined, the extra dimensions are usually meaningless, because it is impractical to dimension splines on manufacturing drawings.

It is the idea of reacting to change that is of most concern regarding parametric sketching. There are other factors that can also drive the sketch, such as equations, other model geometry that is external to the sketch, and even geometry from another part in an assembly, as you shall see later.

FIGURE 1.25

The fully defined sketch cannot be dragged, and there are no degrees of freedom.

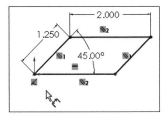

Understanding Design Intent

"Design Intent" is a phrase that you will hear SolidWorks users use a lot. I like to think of it as "design for change." Design Intent means that when you put the parametric sketch relations together with the feature intelligence, you can build models that react to change in predictable ways.

An example of Design Intent could be a statement in words that describes general aspects that help define the design of a part, such as "This part is symmetrical, with holes that line up with Part A, and thick enough to be flush with Part B." From this description, and the surrounding parts, it is possible to re-create the part in such a way that if Part A or Part B changes, the part being described updates to match.

Some types of changes can cause features to fail or sketch relations to conflict. In most situations, SolidWorks has ample tools for troubleshooting and editing that allow you to either repair or change the model. In these situations, it is often the Design Intent itself that is changing.

BEST PRACTICE When editing or repairing relations, it is considered best practice to edit rather than delete. Deleting often causes additional problems further down the tree. Many users find it tempting to simply delete anything that has an error on it.

Editing Design Intent

Design Intent is sometimes thought of as a static concept that controls changing geometry. However, this is not always the way things are. Design Intent itself often changes, thus requiring the way in which the model reacts to geometric changes to also change. Fortunately, SolidWorks has many tools to help you deal with situations like this.

View, Sketch Relations

To see the sketch relations is one of the most obvious tools necessary for visualizing existing Design Intent. You can show or hide icons that represent the relations using the menu selection View, Sketch Relations. When shown, these relations appear as a small icon in a small colored box in the graphics area next to the sketch entity. Clicking on the icon highlights the sketch elements involved in that relation. Refer to Figures 1.19 through 1.25 for examples of these relations.

 View, Sketch Relations is an excellent candidate for use with a hotkey, thus allowing you to easily toggle the display on and off.

CROSS-REF For more information on creating and managing hotkeys, see Chapter 2, Navigating the SolidWorks Interface.

You can use the sketch relation icons that are visible on the screen to delete relations by selecting the icon and pressing Delete on the keyboard. You can also use them to quickly tell the status of sketch relations by referring to the colors defined earlier.

Display/Delete Relations

 You can find the Display/Delete Relations tool on the Sketch toolbar or by selecting a sketch entity in an open sketch. The sketch status colors that were defined earlier also apply here, with the relations appearing in the appropriate color. (Relations are not shown in blue or black, only the colors that show errors, such as red, yellow, pink, and brown.) This tool also allows you to group relations by several categories:

- All in This Sketch
- Dangling
- Overdefining/Not Solved
- External
- Defined in Context
- Locked
- Broken
- Selected Entities

In the lower Entities panel, you can also replace one entity with another, or repair dangling relations.

CROSS-REF You can read more about repairing dangling entities in Chapter 11.

Suppressed sketch relations

Suppressing a sketch relation means that the relation is turned off and not used to compute the position of sketch entities. Suppressed relations are generally used in conjunction with configurations.

 Configurations are dealt with in detail in Chapter 10.

Working with Associativity

Associativity in SolidWorks refers to links between documents, such as a part that has an associative link to a drawing. If the part changes, the drawing updates as well. Bi-directional associativity means that the part can actually be changed from the drawing. One of the implications of this is that you do not edit a SolidWorks drawing by simply moving lines on the drawing; you must change the model, which causes all views of the part or assembly to update correctly.

Other associative links include using base parts, where one part is inserted as the first feature in another part. This might be the case when you build a casting. If the part is designed in its "as cast" state, it is then inserted into another part where machining operations are performed by cut features and the part is transformed into its "as machined" state. This technique is also used for plastic parts where a single shape spans multiple plastic pieces. A "master part" is created and split into multiple parts that could, for example, become a mouse cover and buttons.

One of the most important aspects of associativity is file management. Associated files are kept connected by filenames. If a document name is changed, and one of the associated files does not know about the change, then the association between the files can become broken. For this reason, you should use SolidWorks Explorer to change names of associated files. There are other techniques that work, as well as some techniques that you should avoid.

BEST PRACTICE It is considered poor practice to change filenames, locations or changing the name of a folder in the path of documents that are referenced by other documents with Windows Explorer. Links between parts, assemblies, and drawings can be broken in this way. Using SolidWorks Explorer or a Product Data Management, or PDM, application is the preferred method for changing filenames.

 Refer to Appendix A, Implementing SolidWorks, for more detailed suggestions for file management techniques.

Tutorial: Creating a Part Template

This simple tutorial steps you through making a few standard part templates for use with inch and millimeter parts and some templates for a couple of materials, as well.

1. Select from the menu Tools, Options ➪ System Options ➪ File Locations, and select Document Templates from the Show folder for list.

2. Click the Add button to add a new path to a location outside of the SolidWorks installation directory; for example, D:\Library\Templates.

3. Click OK to dismiss the dialog and accept the settings.

4. Select File ⇨ New from the menu.

5. Create a new Part document, selecting any template if using the Advanced interface.

6. Select from the menu Tools ⇨ Options ⇨ Document Properties ⇨ Detailing.

7. Make sure the ANSI standard is selected.

8. Change to the Units page.

9. Change the unit system to IPS, inches, with 3 decimal places, using millimeters as the dual units, with 2 decimal places. Set angular units to Degrees with 1 decimal place.

10. Change to the Grid/Snap page.

11. Turn off Display grid.

12. Change to the Image Quality page.

13. **Move the slider 2/3 of the way to the right, so it is closer to High.** Make sure the Save tessellation with part document option is on.

14. Click OK to save the settings and exit the Tools, Options dialog.

15. RMB (right mouse button) on the Materials entry in the FeatureManager, and select 1060 Alloy from the list.

16. From the menu select File ⇨ Properties, and click the Custom tab.

17. **Add a property called material of type Text.** In the Value / Text Expression column, click the down arrow and select Material from the list. Notice that the Evaluated Value shows 1060 Alloy.

18. **Add another property called description and give it a default value of Description.** At this point, the window should look like Figure 1.26.

FIGURE 1.26

Setting up Custom Properties

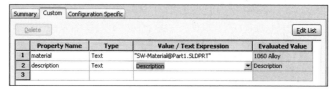

19. Click OK to close the Summary Information window.

20. Change the names of the standard planes by clicking them twice slowly or clicking once and pressing F2. Rename them to **Front**, **Top**, and **Side**, respectively.

21. Ctrl-select the three planes from the FeatureManager, RMB and select Show.

22. From the View menu, make sure that Planes is selected.

23. RMB on the Front plane and select Insert Sketch.

24. Select the Line tool and click and drag anywhere to draw a line.

25. Select the Smart Dimension tool and click on the line, then click in space in the Graphics Window to place the dimension. If you are prompted for a dimension value, press 1 and click the checkmark, as shown in Figure 1.27.

FIGURE 1.27
_____

Drawing a line and applying a dimension

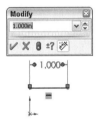

26. Press Esc to exit the Dimension tool and RMB on the displayed dimension and select Link Value.

27. Type thickness in the Name box, and click OK.

28. Press Ctrl+B (rebuild) to exit the sketch, select the sketch from the FeatureManager, and press Delete on the keyboard.

NOTE This exercise of creating the sketch and deleting it was done only to get the link value "thickness" entered into the template. Once this is done, every part made from this template that uses an Extrude feature will have an option box for Link to Thickness, which allows you to automatically establish a thickness variable for each part you create. This is typically a sheet metal part feature, but it can be used in all types of parts.

29. Click File ⇨ Save As and then select Part Template from the drop-down list. Ensure it is going into your template folder by giving it an appropriate name and clicking Save.

30. Edit the material applied to change it from 1060 Alloy to Plain Carbon Steel, and save as another template with a different name.

31. Change the primary units to millimeters with 2 places, and save as a third template file.

32. Exit the file.

Summary

Product development is about design, but it is even more about change. You actually design something once, but you may modify it endlessly (or it may seem that way sometimes). Similarly, SolidWorks is about design, but it really enables change. Think of SolidWorks as virtual prototyping software that allows you to change your prototype rather than having to make a new one. Virtual prototypes will never completely replace physical models, but they may reduce your dependence on them to some extent.

SolidWorks is also about reusing data. Associativity allows you to model a part once and use it for Finite Element Analysis (FEA), creating 2D drawings, building assemblies, creating photorealistic renderings, and so on. When you make changes to the model, your drawing is automatically updated, and you don't have to reapply FEA materials and conditions or redo the rendering setup. Associativity saves you time by reusing your data. Associativity and change driven by feature-based and history-based modeling can take some getting used to if you have had limited exposure to it, but with some practice, it becomes intuitive and you will see the many benefits for enabling change. Parametric sketching and feature creation help you to maintain Design Intent and also adjust it as necessary.

Chapter 2

Navigating the SolidWorks Interface

I n this chapter, you learn how to effectively identify, use, and customize the various aspects of the SolidWorks 2009 interface. In the 2008 release, Solidworks made some drastic changes to the interface. If you are familiar with older versions of the software, you may want to take a moment to acquaint yourself with some of the changes.

The interface changes in 2009 intend primarily to clean up the work area. With each release, the software provides more features and functions, and the previous interface scheme could not accommodate the space required for all these functions. The new interface scheme attempts to put the tools you need where you need them, when you need them.

Some of the changes are controversial, so in this chapter I present options for people who like to work differently from the way assumed by the new changes.

Settings control many aspects of the SolidWorks interface. These settings are covered in detail in Appendix B. Each interface element that is identified in Figure 2.1 is explained in greater detail in its own section of this chapter.

Once you have mastered the various interface elements and customized your SolidWorks installation, working with the software becomes much more efficient and satisfying. You may find that you can only master the interface with a lot of experience. The interface is complex, and can be daunting. Many existing users may find aspects of it in this book that they were not aware of even though they have been to training and used the software for years.

FIGURE 2.1

Elements of the SolidWorks interface

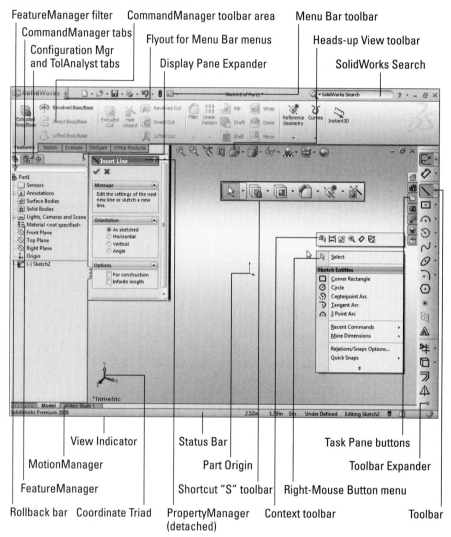

Identifying Elements of the SolidWorks Interface

The major elements of the SolidWorks interface are the graphics window, where all of the action takes place, the FeatureManager, which is the list of all the features in the part, the PropertyManager, where most of the data input happens, and the CommandManager/Toolbars, where you access most of the commands in the software. Of these, I cover the CommandManager/Toolbars first.

Using the CommandManager and toolbars

The CommandManager has been a controversial element of the interface since its introduction several releases ago, and especially since it was drastically revamped in SolidWorks 2008. SolidWorks has chosen to use the most radical options possible for the default install, so many users are turned off by its unwieldy initial appearance. If you are using SolidWorks 2009, I ask that you give the CommandManager a chance, because it saves interface space, groups related commands, and offers many customization options.

The changes to the CommandManager in the 2008 release are half completed. In my opinion, the changes started in 2008 do not make much sense until they are finished in 2009. If you use either the 2009 or 2007 interface first and then try to use 2008, this becomes obvious.

The CommandManager resembles in some respects the Microsoft (MS) Ribbon interface found in Office 2007 applications. SolidWorks did not do a strict implementation of the MS Ribbon, because SolidWorks wanted to add more customizability. A far more complete array of interface configuration possibilities await you with SolidWorks 2009. In this section of the chapter I will show you how to make the 2009 CommandManager work for you, or how to use regular or flyout toolbars to effectively replace it.

CommandManager

The CommandManager is an area of the interface that you can use to save space traditionally used by toolbars. The main mission of the CommandManager is to enable you to have easy access to all toolbars, and even access to customized groups of icons not available on a single default toolbar, without cluttering the entire screen with toolbars.

The CommandManager accomplishes this by using small tabs under the left end of the toolbar area to allow you to switch the toolbar that appears. Figure 2.2 shows the CommandManager in customize mode, showing all of the tabs available in a default setup. To get the CommandManager into customize mode, right-click on one of the Command Manager tabs and select Customize CommandManager. Alternatively, you can select Tools ⇨ Customize through the pull-down menus.

NOTE To access the pull-down menus in a default setup, place the cursor over the SolidWorks logo or the small flyout triangle to the right of it in the upper-left corner of the SolidWorks window. Figure 2.1 shows the flyout for pull-down menus. To keep the menu in that position, click on the push pin on the right end of the flyout menu bar.

FIGURE 2.2

Customizing the CommandManager

Customizing the CommandManager

Notice the last tab along the bottom of the CommandManager on the right. If you wanted to add a custom tab, you would just right-click this tab and select the toolbar you want to add. You can also select to add a blank tab and populate it with individual buttons. Figure 2.3 shows a detail of the menu options after right-clicking on the tab.

FIGURE 2.3

Adding tabs to the CommandManager

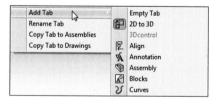

To add individual buttons, first find the button you want to add in the Tools, Customize dialog, in the Commands tab, then switch the CommandManager to the tab you want to add the button to, and drag the button from the Customize dialog to the CommandManager. You can remove buttons from the CommandManager by dragging them into the blank graphics window area.

Docking the CommandManager

In SolidWorks 2009, you can undock the CommandManager and leave it undocked, pull it to a second monitor, or dock it vertically to the left or right. To undock it, click and drag on any non-toolbar button area of the CommandManager, such as around the border. To re-dock an undocked CommandManager or to change its docking location, drag it onto one of the docking stations around the screen. Figure 2.4 shows the CommandManager undocked.

FIGURE 2.4

The undocked CommandManager

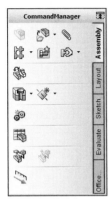

The small box with the arrows in it in the upper right hand corner of the undocked CommandManager is the Auto Collapse option. In the condition it is shown, the undocked CommandManager will not collapse, but if you click it, the arrows go away, and the entire CommandManager acts like a big fly-out toolbar. This can be very handy because it saves a lot of space on the screen, but at the same time it requires additional mouse movement to open it up. This is the common trade-off in this interface – you can trade screen space for additional mouse movement or clicks. This Auto Collapse option is only available with the undocked CommandManager.

 The PropertyManager is also undockable, and behaves the same way as the CommandManager with the docking stations, Auto Collapse and fly-out behavior.

Mixing CommandManager with toolbars

To put a toolbar inline with the CommandManager, either on the top row or vertically on the left or right, drag the toolbar to either the right end or the bottom of the CommandManager. A space on that row or column will open up. The amount of space that opens up depends on tab with the longest set of icons, even if that tab is not showing. To increase the amount of space available for a toolbar on the same row as a CommandManager, enter Customize CommandManager mode by right clicking on a tab and selecting Customize CommandManager. Then cycle through the available tabs, looking to see which one has the most icons. Remove or rearrange icons from the tab with the most. This makes more room for toolbars to the right of the CommandManager.

To get the most out of this arrangement, it is best if you turn off the text and the option to use only icons for large and small buttons. You can turn off the text by clicking the right-mouse button, selecting CommandManager, and deselecting the Use Large Buttons with Text icon.

Tabs and document types

SolidWorks remembers which tabs to show on a per document type basis. This means that when you are working on a part document, you will have one set of tabs. When you switch to an assembly document, you will see a different set of tabs. The same goes for drawings. Notice that in Figure 2.3 you see in the right mouse button menu the options Copy Tab To Assemblies and Copy Tab To Drawings. This makes it easier to set up customizations that apply for all document types.

Changing the appearance of the CommandManager

For an element of the interface that is supposed to save space, the default settings for the CommandManager surely take up a lot of it! When many users see the CommandManager for the first time, they ask how to turn off the text.

You can turn off the text in one of two ways. The easiest way is to right-click in the CommandManager and deselect Use Large Buttons with Text, as shown in Figure 2.5.

FIGURE 2.5

Adding or removing text from the CommandManager buttons

Another way to remove text from the CommandManager is to remove it only from selected icons. To do this, first enter the customize mode (Tools ➪ Customize or right-click on a CommandManager tab and select Customize CommandManager), and then right-click a button in the CommandManager and change the Show Text setting, as shown in Figure 2.6. The Show Text option is only available when Use Large Buttons With Text is enabled.

FIGURE 2.6

Changing the text setting for individual buttons in the CommandManager

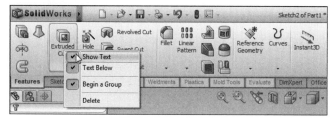

Notice also that the text by default goes to the right side of the icon, but using the RMB menu you can put the text beneath the icon. With these options and some patience to go through the entire interface, you can almost totally customize the appearance and function of your CommandManager.

The most streamlined and space-efficient way to set up the CommandManager is to turn off the text. This arrangement is shown in Figure 2.5, in the lower image. Notice that the CommandManager without text takes up the same amount of height as a normal toolbar, with the added room for the tabs at the bottom. The text can be useful for new users or features that you do not commonly use. Also notice that with the text turned off, you have room for more toolbar space at the end of the CommandManager.

The final setting for the CommandManager appearance is the size of the icons. This is an option that has changed back and forth from 2007 to 2008 and now again in 2009. With the 2009 release, you again have control over the size of the icon images in the CommandManager, This setting is found in the Customize dialog box (Tools ➪ Customize), and is shown in the upper-right side of Figure 2.7. The difference between large and small icons is shown in the lower part of the figure.

FIGURE 2.7

Setting large icons

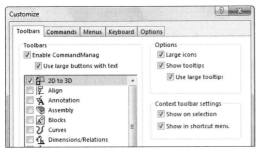

This setting applies to all of the toolbar icons except the Menu Bar and the RMB and Context Bar icons. The setting does apply to the S shortcut toolbar which I discuss later in this section. Large icons can be useful on displays with very high resolution, in particular on laptops where the screen itself may be small but the resolution is very high. All of the screen shots in this book are taken with the Large Icons option turned on for improved visibility. There is often a small difference between the appearance of the large and small icons.

Limitations

The CommandManager in the 2008 release had many limitations, including that it could not be undocked, and would not allow other toolbars on the same row. The 2009 release fixes these limitations, but a couple of items still remain.

If you undock the CommandManager, you cannot reorient the tabs horizontally. They remain vertical. Also, you cannot place multiple rows of toolbars on the same row as a CommandManager using large buttons with text. And you cannot dock the CommandManager to the bottom of the SolidWorks window. Another minor limitation is that although 2009 allows you to place toolbars at the right end of the CommandManager, it does not allow you to place them to the left of the CommandManager like you could in 2007.

These are relatively minor limitations which remain, and they could be resolved between the time this is printed and the time you read it.

Using toolbars

The point of the CommandManager is to allow you to get away from using regular toolbars, with the main goal being space savings. Unfortunately, when you save one thing, you usually wind up giving up something else. In the case of the CommandManager, the thing that you give up is mouse travel and clicks. You may find yourself clicking frequently back and forth between the Sketch and Features tabs. For this reason, in my interface setup, I put the Sketch toolbar vertically on the right, and remove it from the CommandManager. This allows me to see the Sketch and Features toolbars at the same time, and greatly reduces clicking back and forth between the tabs.

Toolbars may be turned on or off in several ways. To turn them on, right-click in a toolbar area, and you will be presented with a list of all the toolbars in SolidWorks. You can turn them on or off from here. Another way to do this is to use the Customize dialog (Tools ➪ Customize or the Customize option near the bottom of the RMB toolbar list). Yet another way is through the menus at View ➪ Toolbars.

Heads-up View toolbar

The Heads-up View toolbar is a new interface element in SolidWorks 2008 and is found along the middle of the top edge of the graphics window. Figure 2.8 shows the default arrangement of the Heads-up View toolbar, and it is shown in relation to the rest of the interface in Figure 2.1.

FIGURE 2.8

The Heads-up View toolbar

This toolbar is limited to only the icons of the View or Standard Views toolbars. You can customize this toolbar by right-clicking on it and selecting or deselecting the tools you want to have on it. The only way to turn it off is to remove all of the icons from it. If you have multiple document windows or multiple view ports showing, the Heads-up View toolbar will only show in the active window or view port. This toolbar often overlaps with other interface elements when several windows are tiled or if the active window is not maximized. It can run into the PropertyManager if it is pulled out of the FeatureManager, as well as the ConfirmationCorner or the Task Pane.

CROSS-REF Chapter 3, Working with Sketches, deals with the ConfirmationCorner in more detail.

Menu Bar Toolbar and Menu

The Menu Bar also has new functions in SolidWorks 2009. The first is the Menu Bar Toolbar. It is found just to the right of the SolidWorks logo on the title bar of the SolidWorks window. By default, it contains most of the elements of the Standard toolbar, and it is available even when no documents are open. It uses mostly flyout toolbar icons, so again it follows the trend of saving space at the expense of an extra click. This toolbar can be customized in the same way as normal toolbars in the Customize dialog under the Commands tab. Again, this toolbar cannot be turned off, but you can remove all of the icons from it.

NOTE In the same way that you could run the SolidWorks 2009 interface from just the CommandManager without any additional toolbars, you could do the same with just the Menu Bar Toolbar, customizing it with all flyout toolbars. The main advantages of this toolbar are that it is visible when no documents are open, and that it makes use of otherwise wasted space. You might set up the interface for a 12 inch normal aspect display laptop very differently from that of a desktop unit with a 24 inch wide screen.

There is also a Menu Bar Menu, which is hidden by default. The SolidWorks logo in the upper left of the SolidWorks window or the small triangle next to the logo serve as a flyout to expand the main SolidWorks menus. The menus can be pinned in place using the pushpin shown at the right end of the menus in Figure 2.9. When the menu is pinned, the toolbar moves to the right to accommodate it.

FIGURE 2.9

The Menu Bar Toolbar and Menu

Notice that on low resolution or non-maximized SolidWorks windows, you can run into some space problems if the Menu Bar Menu is pinned open. The SolidWorks window in Figure 2.9 is maximized at 1024 × 768 resolution, which is a common resolution when using digital LCD projectors or small notebook computers. The changes in the SolidWorks interface need to be examined with display size in mind. You might consider having different sets of settings for using a laptop at a docking station with a large monitor, using the laptop with a small monitor, or using the computer with a low resolution digital projector.

Flyout toolbar buttons

SolidWorks has implemented flyout toolbars that save space by putting several related icons on a flyout. For example, the Rectangle tool now has several different ways to make a rectangle, with a tool for each, and they are all on the rectangle flyout.

You can see all of the available flyouts in the Tools ➪ Customize menu, on the Commands tab, in the first listing in the window, Flyouts.

The purpose for flyouts is primarily to save toolbar space when several tools are closely related. SolidWorks has set up flyouts in two configurations: fly-outs that always maintain the same image for the front button (such as the Smart Dimension fly-out) and fly-outs that use the last used button on the front of the fly-out (such as the Rectangle fly-out). You can expand the flyout by clicking the arrow associated with the flyout button. You will find three different kinds of flyouts in SolidWorks: Toolbar flyouts, Add-in flyouts, and Similar function flyouts.

Toolbar flyouts are listed in Tools ➪ Customize ➪ Commands, and are listed from 2D to 3D through the Weldments toolbar. After Weldments in the list the fly-outs are Similar Function fly-outs. You can change the order of the items in the flyouts by changing the order of the items in the toolbars. Just display the original toolbar and use Tools ➪ Customize to reorder it to your liking. These toolbars will always have the same icon on the top. For example, if you use the Reference Geometry flyout to access the Axis command, the image for the Plane icon will remain on top. The image on top is considered to be the most commonly used function of that group of tools, and so remains on top.

Add-in flyouts, such as the eDrawing flyout, are controlled by that add-in and again keep the same icon always on top.

The flyouts used for tools of similar function are split between using the most recently used tool icon on top and keeping a consistent icon on top. The only tools that appear to follow the latest icon method are the Sketch Entities tools. Sketch Tools and other flyouts use a hard-coded top image.

Context toolbars

Context toolbars are toolbars that appear in the graphics window when you right-click or left-click on something. When you right-click, a context toolbar appears at the top of the RMB menu, and shows the functions that SolidWorks deems the most commonly used functions. This is a static list, and does not change as you use the buttons. These functions are removed from the actual RMB menu, and are replaced with only the toolbar icon in a toolbar above the abbreviated RMB menu, as Figure 2.10 shows.

An identical toolbar appears when you select (left-click) an item on screen. When this toolbar appears with a left-click, the rest of the RMB menu does not appear. Tooltips are available if you do not recognize the icons on the toolbar.

For reference, the icons in the toolbar atop the RMB menu shown in Figure 2.10 are in order from the upper-left: Edit Feature, Edit Sketch, Suppress, Rollback, Select Other, Create Sketch, Hide Body, Zoom To Selection, Normal To, and Appearance Callout. Notice that these selections do not reappear in the main menu.

FIGURE 2.10

Right-click context toolbar

These context toolbars are not editable, but you can turn them off, and put the RMB menus back to a more familiar configuration. To turn off either right click or left click, or both, context toolbars, click Tools ➪ Customize and use the options on the right side of the main Toolbars tab, as shown in Figure 2.11.

FIGURE 2.11

Context toolbar settings

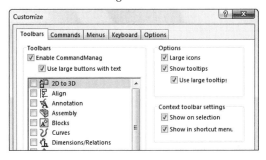

I personally find that the RMB context bars are distracting because they force you to read icons and text at the same time, as well as search a two-dimensional list of icons and a one-dimensional list of text. To me, this is just too confusing. I turn these off so that the RMB menus look like they always did.

However, I do find left click context bars useful for things like Hide Sketch, Edit Feature, Edit Sketch, Appearance Callout, sketch relations, and so on. When I use the RMB menus, I'm looking for a more general function. When using the left click context bars, I'm looking for something specific that I know is there. In Figure 2.11, Show on selection simply refers to the left click toolbar, and Show in shortcut menu refers to the RMB menu.

The purpose of the context toolbars is to save space by condensing some commands into a toolbar without text instead of a menu with icons and text. The left and right click toolbars are the same, but they work differently. The left click context toolbar fades as you move the cursor away from it and becomes darker as you move the cursor toward it. Once it fades past a certain point, you cannot get it back, except if you have Ctrl-selected multiple entities. The context toolbar does not appear until you release the Ctrl key. To get a context menu to show up again after it has faded, you can just move the cursor back to approximately where the toolbar would have been and press Ctrl again. This works only for multiple selection menus where Ctrl was used to multi-select. The functionality is probably a bug, or unintentional in any case, or else it would also work somehow for single selections.

Shortcut "S" toolbar

The Shortcut toolbar is also known as the "S" toolbar because by default it is accessed by pressing the S key. This toolbar can be customized for each document type, so it can have different content for parts, assemblies, and drawings. To customize the S toolbar, right-click on it when it is active and click the Customize from the menu, as shown in Figure 2.12.

FIGURE 2.12

The Shortcut "S" bar

Many people claim to have customized the S toolbar to such an extent that they have been able to remove all other toolbars from their interface. This is possibly true if you typically use a limited number of sketch entities, sketch relations, and feature types, or make extensive use of flyouts on the S toolbar, but if you tend to work in several corners of the software (say, surfacing, sheet metal, and plastic parts), you may need some additional toolbar space. It is completely believable to have access to most of the software's function with the S toolbar and either the Menu Bar Toolbar or the CommandManager. CommandManager by far gives you the most flexibility, but it also requires the most space, and conceivably more setup time as well.

The S key shortcut may conflict with a customization you have done, depending on how your software was installed. To change the S toolbar key to another character or to reassign it, follow the directions for creating and maintaining hotkeys later in this chapter in the section on customization. It is referenced as the Shortcut Bar in the Tools ➪ Customize ➪ Keyboard list.

Tooltips

One way to learn about the individual icons is to use the Tooltips that appear after you hover your cursor over an icon for a few seconds. Tooltips come in two varieties: large and small. Large Tooltips show the name of the tool, along with a brief description of what it does. Small Tooltips show only the tool's name. To change the Tooltip display from large to small, or to turn off the Tooltip display altogether, you can use the Tools ⇨ Customize menu option, as shown in the upper-right corner of Figure 2.11. In addition to the Tooltip balloons, tips also appear in the status bar at the bottom of the screen when the cursor is over an icon. Figure 2.13 shows a comparison between large and small Tooltips.

FIGURE 2.13

SolidWorks uses large Tooltips by default, although it can also show small Tooltips.

NOTE   The Tools ⇨ Customize menu option is inactive unless a SolidWorks document is open. To access Tools, Customize, first open a SolidWorks part, assembly, or drawing. Tools, Customize is different from the Customize Menu option that is found in all SolidWorks menus. The Customize Menu option is discussed later in this chapter.

Managing toolbars

After all of that, if you still feel you need to work with standard toolbars, it is easy to move, turn on and off, and add icons to toolbars. It is important to remember that different document types retain different toolbar settings; for example, the toolbars that you see with a part open are different from the toolbars that you see for drawings.

When you are working on parts, it is important to have both the Sketch and the Features toolbars active. When you are working on a drawing, you will never use the Features toolbar, but you will frequently use the Sketch toolbar. Likewise for assemblies, you may want to display some additional toolbars and eliminate others. For this reason, when you change from a part document to a drawing document, you may see your display adjust because the changing toolbars increase or decrease the amount of space that is required.

BEST PRACTICE   It is best practice to set up the toolbars for each document type so that they take up the same amount of space—for example, two rows on top and one column to the right. This way, changing between document types is not so jarring, with the graphics area resizing for each change.

Moving Toolbars

To move a toolbar, you can click with the cursor at the double bar on the left end of the toolbar, as shown in Figure 2.14. The cursor changes to a four-way arrow, and you can then drag the toolbar where you want it. Toolbars dock either vertically or horizontally. You can resize undocked toolbars so that they have rows and columns. This arrangement is typically used with the Selection Filter toolbar, which is often left undocked and compressed into a block that is three or four columns wide.

Double bars enable you to move toolbars.

If the SolidWorks window is not wide enough for the toolbar to fit entirely in the screen, double arrows like those shown in Figure 2.15 display at the end of the truncated toolbar. When you click the double arrows, a flyout toolbar appears with the missing icons, as shown in Figure 2.16.

A truncated toolbar showing double arrows

You can display a truncated toolbar by clicking the double arrows.

Flyout toolbars

You can use any toolbar as a flyout toolbar. Figure 2.17 shows the list of all flyout toolbars, which is exactly the same as the list of *all* toolbars. Flyout toolbars are a nice space-saving feature for tools that you use infrequently, but frequently enough to want to avoid going through the menus. To use a toolbar as a flyout, select it from the Flyout Toolbars list and drag it onto an existing toolbar. It displays with an arrow to the right. Clicking the arrow causes all of the tools to scroll out temporarily until you click either a toolbar icon or anything else.

To add icons to a flyout toolbar, temporarily show the regular toolbar that corresponds to the flyout toolbar, and add icons to the regular toolbar. When you are done adding or removing icons, turn off the regular toolbar; the changes are applied to the flyout.

FIGURE 2.17

The Flyout Toolbars are on the Commands tab in the Customize dialog box

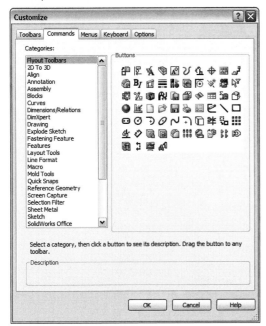

TIP If you want to create a separate toolbar, you can commandeer an existing one for your own purposes. For example, because I do not use the Tools toolbar, I have removed all of the regular icons from it and replaced them with relevant flyout toolbars, which I do use extensively. This allows me to consolidate space, and not have unused icons on my toolbars.

Full Screen mode

Full Screen mode enables you to quickly toggle the display so that only the graphics window and the Task pane display; the FeatureManager, menus, toolbars, and status bar are all hidden. Alternatively, you can hide just the FeatureManager or the toolbars.

In Full Screen mode, you can still access the menus by clicking the cursor along the top border of the window.

- To toggle to Full Screen mode, press the F11 key.
- To toggle the toolbar display, press the F10 key (see Figure 2.18).
- To toggle the FeatureManager display, press the F9 key.

FIGURE 2.18

The SolidWorks window with all toolbars hidden using the F10 key

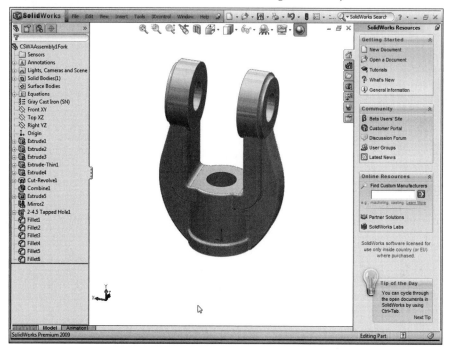

Workflow customization

When you first install and run the SolidWorks software, the SolidWorks Welcome screen shown in Figure 2.19 offers you the option to customize the interface using one of three preset option packages. Special menu and toolbar settings are made for Consumer product design, Machine design, or Mold design. After the software is initially installed, you only see this screen once, but you can change all of the options in other places, including the Options tab of Tools⇨Customize.

The three workflow customizations affect the interface as follows:

- Consumer product design adds the Surfaces toolbar to the CommandManager.
- Machine design adds Sheet Metal and Weldments toolbars to the CommandManager.
- Mold design adds Surfaces and Mold Tools toolbars to the CommandManager.

Similar changes are made to the menus to hide or show menu selections as appropriate. You can find more information about hiding and showing menu items later in this chapter.

If you want to select a different option after the initial setup, you can go to Tools⇨Customize⇨Options, where you can specify a different choice. Figure 2.20 shows the Options tab of the Customize dialog box.

FIGURE 2.19

The Welcome to SolidWorks screen

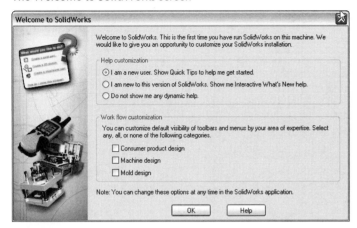

FIGURE 2.20

The Options tab of the Customize dialog box, where you can select a different workflow customization

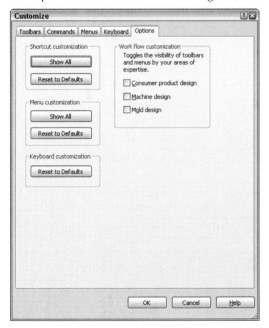

Menus

Everyone has his or her own style of working. For example, some people like to use menus and others do not. Some like to use hotkeys and others like the mouse. An example of a tool that does not have a toolbar equivalent is View ⇨ Modify ⇨ Section View, which is used to change the active section view's settings.

The most frequently used menu items are in the View, Insert, and Tools menus. All of the menus shown in this section have all of the possible selections turned on. As a result, the View menu in Figure 2.21 may contain options that are not available on your computer. Customizing menus is covered later in this chapter. Figure 2.21 also shows the Insert and Tools menus, along with an image of a menu with the Customize Menu mode activated.

The View menu is used primarily for turning on or off the visibility of entity types such as planes, sketches, or temporary axes. You can also do this by using hotkeys or by putting extra items on the View toolbar.

FIGURE 2.21

Popular menus

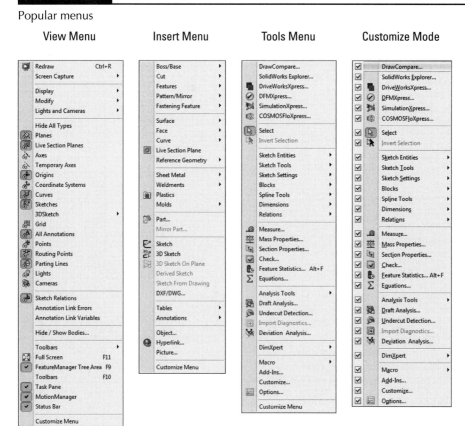

The Insert menu is used mostly for creating feature types for which you do not have a toolbar icon on the screen. For example, although the Move Face tool is only on the Mold Tools toolbar, it has many uses aside from mold design. You can find the Move Face tool at Insert ⇨ Face.

The Tools menu is used primarily for sketch entities or tools for which you have no icon on the screen. Several other commonly used tools, such as Measure, Equations, Customize, and Options, are also available in this menu.

You can customize menus by adding or omitting items. By using the Customize Menu option at the bottom of any menu—including shortcut (right mouse button) menus—you can remove items from any menu by clearing the check boxes next to tools that you do not use. To bring back the removed items, you can either go back to the Customize Menu or go to Tools ⇨ Customize ⇨ Options and click the Reset to Defaults buttons for menu and shortcut customization.

NOTE Be careful not to confuse this Customize Menu selection with the Customize... menu selection on the Tools menu. Figure 2.21 shows the Tools menu being customized.

The Tools ⇨ Customize ⇨ Options dialog box, shown in Figure 2.21, contains the Shortcut (right mouse button) menu and Menu customization options. These options enable you to show all of the menu items for both types of menus in a single stroke. By default, some items are hidden in various menus. Keyboard customization is discussed later in this chapter. Keyboard shortcuts are generally referred to as *hotkeys*.

NOTE SolidWorks terminology for Shortcut Menus, Alt-key (accelerator keys) shortcuts, the Shortcut "S" bar, and Shortcuts/Keyboard customization is slightly confusing because of these overlapping, yet unrelated, terms. For this reason, I will refer to Shortcut Menus as RMB (right mouse button) menus from here on, because this is the standard terminology among SolidWorks users. Shortcuts are also generally referred to as *hotkeys* among users. The Shortcut Bar will be referred to as the "S" Toolbar, and the Alt shortcuts will be called Alt-keys.

Cursors

SolidWorks cursors are context-sensitive, and change their appearance and function depending on the situation. Sketching cursors display a pencil and the type of sketch entity that you are presently sketching. Sketch cursors also display some dimensional information about the entity that you are sketching, such as its length or radius. Sketch cursor feedback is necessary for fast and accurate sketching.

CROSS-REF To learn more about sketch cursor feedback, see Chapter 3, Working with Sketches.

The Select cursor changes, depending the item over which you move it. Cursor symbols also help to remind you when selection filters are active. The cursor is frequently available as an OK button. For example, after selecting edges for a Fillet feature, the RMB functions as an OK button. Figure 2.22 shows various cursors and their significance.

FIGURE 2.22

Various SolidWorks Cursors

Select	OK selection	Select sketch plane	Sketch line

FeatureManager and PropertyManager windows

The FeatureManager window is the panel to the left of the screen that shows an ordered list of features describing how the part was built. SolidWorks users spend a fair amount of time using the FeatureManager to edit or inspect models. Figure 2.23 shows the FeatureManager for a simple model.

FIGURE 2.23

The FeatureManager for a simple model

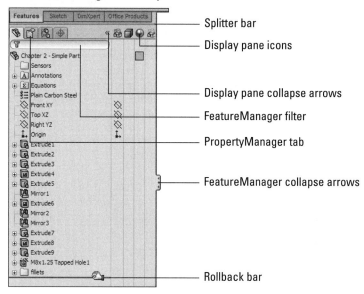

- Splitter bar
- Display pane icons
- Display pane collapse arrows
- FeatureManager filter
- PropertyManager tab
- FeatureManager collapse arrows
- Rollback bar

Using the FeatureManager

There is a splitter bar at the top of the FeatureManager that enables you to split the FeatureManager window into two windows, so that you can display the FeatureManager and another window, such as the PropertyManager. Small arrows in the middle of the right separator can collapse the FeatureManager to increase screen space. (The F9 key also collapses or opens the FeatureManager. Refer to Figure 2.23).

Display pane

You can open the Display pane flyout from the FeatureManager by using the double arrows at the top-right corner. The Display pane helps you to visualize where appearances or hidden bodies have been applied in a part document and additional functions in an assembly document. The display pane is helpful when looking for colors that are applied to the model at some level other than the part level.

 Appearances are covered in more detail in Chapter 5, Using Visualization Techniques.

Rollback bar

The Rollback bar at the bottom of the FeatureManager enables you to see the part in various states of history. Features can be added while the rollback bar is at any location. The model can also be saved while rolled back.

FeatureManager Filter

One of the most useful elements of the FeatureManager is the FeatureManager Filter. The Filter resides at the top of the FeatureManager. If you type text in the filter, SolidWorks will search feature names, descriptions, comments, tags, and dimension names for text matching the string, and only show matching features in the window. This also works in assemblies, where you can filter for part names or document properties. The filter is very useful for quickly finding parts, features, mates, or anything else that shows up in the part or assembly FeatureManager. I think it is one of the most useful enhancements in recent releases.

Using the PropertyManager

The PropertyManager is where you go to set most of the feature parameters, and where you edit properties of selected items such as sketch elements. You can manually switch to the PropertyManager using the tabs on the top of the Display panel, or allow it to pop up automatically when your input is needed. The left-most tab in the row of icons is the FeatureManager tab, the second from the left is the PropertyManager tab, the second from the right is the ConfigurationManager tab, and the right most tab is the TolAnalyst. Other icons may also appear in this area for drawings, or if you have add-ins such as PhotoWorks or SolidWorks Simulation (formerly COSMOS) turned on. The ConfigurationManager tab appears with more detail in Chapter 10, and the TolAnalyst tab appears again in Chapter 23.

One of the benefits of putting dialog boxes in the PropertyManager is that it saves a lot of space on the screen. On the other hand, you will often need to make a selection from the FeatureManager at the same time that the PropertyManager pops up and takes its place. This automatic pop-up behavior is controlled by a setting in the Tools ➪ Options ➪ System Options ➪ General ➪ Auto-show PropertyManager.

My favorite option for dealing with the PropertyManager is to detach it from the FeatureManager so that you can see them side by side instead of one or the other. The detachable PropertyManager is new in SolidWorks 2009. To detach it, drag the icon from the tabs out into the graphics area and release. Once detached, the PropertyManager can be moved to a second monitor, floated within the SolidWorks window, or docked. To put it back in its place under the FeatureManager, just drag it back on top of the FeatureManager, allow it to snap into place, and release it.

If you do not like the detachable PropertyManager, you can use either the splitter bars to put the FeatureManager on top and the PropertyManager beneath, or use the flyout FeatureManager. When creating or editing a feature, you can access the flyout FeatureManager by double-clicking the name of the feature at the top of the PropertyManager. The flyout FeatureManager is displayed just to the right of the regular FeatureManager, in the main graphics window, and is transparent to allow you to see the model through it. The various ways of combining the FeatureManager and PropertyManager are shown in Figure 2.24.

FIGURE 2.24

The detached PropertyManager, the flyout FeatureManager, and the split FeatureManager

Detached PropertyManager

Flyout FeatureManager

Split Feature Manager

Task pane

By default, the Task pane sits to the right of the SolidWorks screen, although you can undock it entirely. If you want to keep it open, click the pushpin in the upper-right corner of the pane. The Task pane is shown in Figure 2.25.

FIGURE 2.25

The Task pane

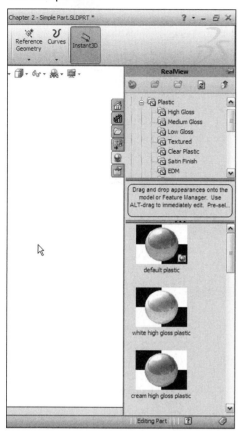
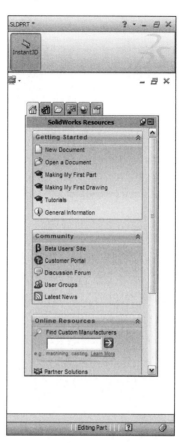

The Task pane is the home for several panels:

- **SolidWorks Resources.** These are useful links for templates, tutorials, tech support, news, GlobalSpec search, Tip-of-the-Day, and other resources.

- **Design Library.** This includes locally stored libraries, Toolbox, and 3D Content Central. This tab also contains "SolidWorks Content" which consists of additional library resources that can be downloaded directly from the Task Pane.

- **File Explorer.** This is a Windows Explorer–like interface that you can use to browse for files.

- **SolidWorks Search.** If you have installed the Windows Desktop Search with SolidWorks 2007 and indexed your files, you can perform searches that include filename and custom properties.

- **View Palette.** This palette allows you to visually select views and drag them onto a drawing sheet.

- **RealView.** This allows you to select appearances and scenes for your SolidWorks documents.

- **Custom Properties**. New functionality in 2009 enables you to create a custom interface that goes inside this Task Pane tab that will help you enter custom property data quickly, easily and accurately.

- **Recovered documents.** After a crash, auto recovered documents are listed in this special purpose Task Pane tab.

Status bar

The status bar is a non-intrusive way in which SolidWorks communicates information back to the user. It is located at the bottom of the screen, and you can enable it from the View menu. Figure 2.26 shows the status bar in action.

FIGURE 2.26

The status bar showing a Tooltip for the Sketch Circle tool

| Sketches a circle. Select the center of the circle, then drag to set its radius. | -1.995in 0.364in 0in Under Defined Editing Sketch2 |

The status bar can display the following information, indicators, and icons:

- Progress as parts, assemblies, or drawings load

- Tooltips for commands

- Measurements

- Sketch status for an active sketch

- In-context editing

- Suspend Automatic Rebuilds

- Icons that allow you to turn Quick Tips off or on

- Sheet scale for drawings

- Cursor position for drawings and sketches

- Whether you are editing the sheet, sheet format, or view of a drawing

Tags

Tags work like document properties, except that they do not need a property name; they just use a value. A tag could be considered simply a keyword that you can associate with a part in an assembly or even a feature in a part. Tags can be searched by SolidWorks Explorer or by the FeatureManager Filter. You can assign tags by clicking the yellow tag icon on the status bar in the lower right-hand corner of the SolidWorks window. Figure 2.27 shows a tag being added to a feature.

FIGURE 2.27

FIGURE 2.27

Adding a tag to a feature

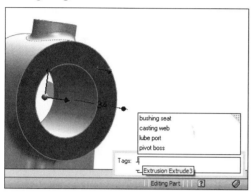

Quick Tips

Quick Tips appear in the pop-up window in the lower-right corner of the graphics window. They can change as you work so that they are sensitive to the context in which you are working. They are a great way for new users or infrequent users to learn or be reminded of the next steps available to them. You can activate and deactivate Quick Tips using the question mark icon in the lower-right corner of the SolidWorks window on the status bar. Figure 2.28 shows the Quick Tips window in action.

FIGURE 2.28

Quick Tips in action

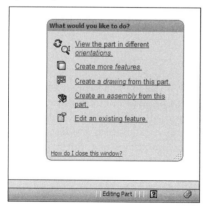

2D Command Line Emulator

This is a tool specifically for people who are coming to SolidWorks from AutoCAD. As the name suggests, it adds a command line to the bottom of the SolidWorks window that works like the AutoCAD command line in most respects. The available commands are somewhat limited compared to those that are available in AutoCAD. This tool only functions in the 2D sketch mode, on a drawing sheet, or in a drawing view; it does not work in a 3D sketch. The 2D Command Line Emulator is shown in Figure 2.29.

FIGURE 2.29

The 2D Command Line Emulator in action

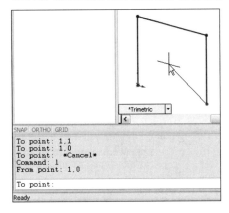

Available sketch tools in the 2D Command Line Emulator include Align, Arc, Array, 'Cal, Chamfer, Chprop, Circle, 'Color, Copy, DDcolor, Dim, Dist, Ellipse, Erase, Exit, Extrude, Fillet, 'Grid, Line, List, Massprop, Mirror, Move, Offset, 'Ortho, 'Osnap, 'Pan, Plot, Point, Polygon, Qsave, Rectangle, 'Redraw, 'Redrawall, Revolve, Rotate, Save, Saveas, 'Snap, Spline, Trim, U (undo), 'Units, 'View, and 'Zoom. Commands that are preceded by an apostrophe (') can be used as transparent commands, without exiting an active command. Notice that even the cursor changes to crosshairs.

BEST PRACTICE The best way to learn a new software package is to embrace the new way, not to cling to the old way. Although you may find the 2D Command Line Emulator more comfortable to work with, you will not achieve the same results as you will with the SolidWorks default sketching mode. For example, the resulting sketch entities created using the 2D Command Line Emulator are not constrained in any way, and the endpoints do not even merge. You can turn off the 2D Command Line Emulator by going to Tools ➪ Add-ins.

Making the Interface Work for You

As engineers and designers, we all like to tinker with things to optimize efficiency and to apply our personal stamp. When the SolidWorks software is installed, the interface is functional, but not optimal. In recent new releases, the new features in SolidWorks tend to use the most radical options available as the out-of-the-box defaults. In the previous pages, I have discussed managing and customizing toolbars and menus. In the remainder of this chapter, I discuss more about customizing the interface, and suggest some strategies that you might use to help customize your work environment.

Customizing colors

You need to be aware of a few things before you change all of the standard colors in the SolidWorks interface to whatever strikes your fancy. The first is that SolidWorks does not automatically alter text color to contrast with your background. As a result, if you set the background to black, and the text is black, you won't be able to see the text. This may seem obvious to some people, but AutoCAD automatically changes text color to contrast with the viewport background, and so AutoCAD users may take this functionality for granted.

Default selection colors

Between the 2007 and 2008 releases, SolidWorks changed some of the default colors used in the interface. However, not all users will see these changes immediately. Since the software was initially released in 1995, the color for selected items has been green. Users have based their color selections for part colors on this default, generally avoiding the green color so selections could be seen more easily.

Starting with the 2008 release, the selection color is now blue. But this is only the case if you have a new computer without a prior installation of SolidWorks on it. If your computer already has an earlier version of SolidWorks, you will continue with the green selection color even in 2008, but if you put 2008 or later on a computer that never had a version of SolidWorks, you will get the blue selection color.

Does it really matter whether the selection color is green or blue? No. What does matter is interface predictability and consistency. The color default selection color changing from one to another without any pressing need qualifies as random change, and I don't believe it positively impacts software usability. If the color change has a negative effect on your use of the software, be aware that you can change it back if you like. How to make the changes is described in this section.

With the introduction of RealView, the selection appears to glow in addition to changing colors. RealView is hardware driven visualization technology in SolidWorks that has grown in scope over the course of a couple of releases. RealView is described in more detail in Chapter 5, Using Visualization Techniques.

All of the interface colors are controlled at Tools ⇨ Options ⇨ Colors. The selection color in particular is set at Selected Item 1, as shown in Figure 2.30.

FIGURE 2.30

Changing interface colors

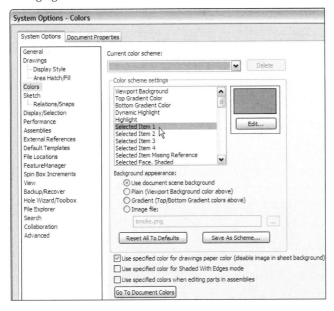

Notice that you can set a color scheme. I recommend that if you want to change the colors used in the interface, you save the settings as a color scheme so that the scheme can be re-created easily later or handed off to another computer. Color schemes are stored in the Windows registry, not as separate files. To transfer color settings to another computer, you will need to either use the Copy Settings Wizard or manually copy data from the Windows registry.

Before making changes, you might consider saving your initial settings as a separate scheme so you can get back to them if you need to.

CAUTION **Making changes to the Windows registry can adversely affect software installation and hardware performance. You should not attempt changes to the registry unless you know exactly what you are doing.**

Background options

Some colors should be avoided for the background, or you should at least make some other changes if you choose these colors. Black is used with fully defined sketches, dimensions, FeatureManager text, and annotations. Blue backgrounds can mask the underdefined sketch color. Bright green backgrounds can cause problems with seeing selected items. Bright red, aside from being a terrible color to stare at all day, also does not contrast well with some of the red highlights and error colors.

You might say that whatever color background you select, it makes items or features difficult to see. For this reason, many users choose a gradient background, which allows you to pick colors where items are always visible on one half of the screen or the other. Staring at a white screen all day can be uncomfortable for your eyes, so pick colors that allow you to see everything with "reasonable" contrast, yet are not glaringly bright. Very high contrast is hard on the eyes, and low contrast may make it difficult to distinguish items on the screen.

You have to consider what the purpose of the background is. Some people doing presentations may want the background to be attractive while otherwise staying out of the way. Others may only need the background to contrast with whatever is in front of it in a way that does not strain your eyes. For writing a book, the background generally needs to be white to match the page. No one scheme will suit all needs.

In addition to colors and gradients, you can use an image as the graphics window background. This gives you a wider range of customization capabilities, and several sample images are already available in the default settings.

RealView also adds some capabilities with *scenes*. Scenes can be applied from the RealView tab on the Task Pane. RealView offers three different types of scenes: Basic, Studio, and Presentation. Of these, I find the Studio scenes to be the best when I need something of that sort. RealView, along with scenes, is described in more detail in Chapter 5.

Customization strategies

You can easily customize many aspects of the SolidWorks interface, including:

- Toolbars
- Menus
- Background colors or images
- PropertyManager skins
- Task pane location
- Hotkeys
- Macros
- Custom application programming

Whether or not you should customize each of the previous items depends partially on how much time and energy you have to spend, as well as how much money you are ready to dedicate in the case of custom programming.

Hotkey approaches

Some of us old-timers prefer to use the keyboard over the mouse. If your hand-eye coordination is as bad as mine, you may also choose this approach. I can type without looking at the keyboard, but when I use the mouse, it takes me a few seconds to aim at an icon and hit it accurately. This means that I customize SolidWorks to use as many hotkeys as possible, and remove icons from the interface if I have them on a hotkey. Unfortunately, my memory is as bad as my eyesight, and so remembering 75 hotkey commands is a bit of a problem. I admit to having a printed list of hotkeys taped to the side of my monitor. While I know that needing to read the list to find a particular hotkey defeats most of the purpose of using them in the first place, I just accept it as a learning aid. This is a self-solving problem, because the hotkeys that I use the most are the ones that I learn most quickly.

I generally do not advocate trying to standardize a hotkey scheme across multiple users, unless the users all agree to it. The underlying reason for writing a section entitled "Hotkey approaches" is that everyone remembers things differently in the first place.

Any command that I use more than a few times an hour is worth assigning to a hotkey. I like to use alliteration when assigning keys to help with my faulty memory. Most-frequently used commands are assigned single-letter hotkeys, and less-frequently used commands are assigned combinations. Thus, Tools Options is linked to O, Measure to M, Select Vertex to Shift+V, and Curve Projected to Ctrl+J (Ctrl+P is the Windows standard for the Print command). Other people like to group keys into easy-to-reach combinations, and so the Q, W, A, S, Z, and X keys are often assigned first for right-handed mouse users.

Organizing hotkeys

Hotkeys are assigned and organized in the Tools ➪ Customize ➪ Keyboard dialog box, as shown in Figure 2.31. This interface enables you to see all of the hotkeys (called *shortcuts* in the list) easily. If you try to enter an existing hotkey, SolidWorks issues a prompt, telling you that the key is assigned to another command and what the command is, and asking you if you want to clear the other instance of the hotkey and make the new one active. You can also print out or copy to the Clipboard a list of only commands that use hotkeys.

Because the list of commands is so long, a Search function is available, and a drop-down arrow makes only the commands from a selected menu visible. The list of commands is organized by menu name, and the menus are listed as they occur in the interface. Fortunately, here on the Keyboard tab, SolidWorks allows you to sort using the column headers to list the menus, commands, or hotkeys in alphabetical order, simply by clicking the column header. This is a highly usable interface, one of my favorite interface changes in the last several releases.

FIGURE 2.31

Tools ⇨ Customize ⇨ Keyboard — the hotkey interface

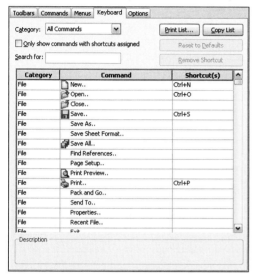

Using the keyboard

Moving between the mouse and the keyboard can be bothersome and time-consuming. In addition to the hotkey approach, you can use another keyboard method to save time. Many users become adept at using the Alt-key combinations to invoke menu items. Most menu items in Windows applications contain a single underlined letter.

To access a top-level menu, you can hold down the Alt key and press the underlined letter for that menu, and then just press an underlined letter in the menu to access specific commands. This technique enables you to navigate most of the interface without using the mouse. For example, to exit SolidWorks, instead of using the mouse to click the red X in the upper-right corner, you could press Alt+F, X. In Figure 2.32, you can see that the F in File is underlined, as is the X in Exit.

NOTE The SolidWorks documentation terminology becomes further confusing when talking about Alt-keys (accelerator keys). It says that the general class of keys is called shortcuts, which can be either accelerator keys or keyboard shortcuts. How these are distinguished from shortcut menus and shortcut toolbars is not clear. Again, for the purposes in this book, I refer to the shortcut menus as *RMB* (right mouse button) menus, accelerator keys as *Alt-keys,* and keyboard shortcuts as *hotkeys,* which is more in line with standard usage than the documented terminology.

FIGURE 2.32

Accelerator Keys in the File menu

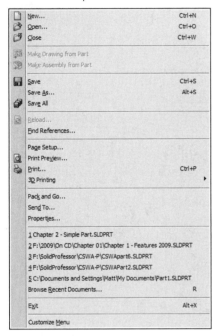

You may potentially run into conflicts when using Alt-keys. A combination of Alt + another keyboard key is a valid use of a hotkey combination. If you use any Alt hotkey combinations, it is likely that you have seen a conflict like this. In cases of conflict, the hotkey combination seems to gain priority over the Alt-key accelerator.

Fewest number of icons

In order to maximize valuable space on the monitor, many SolidWorks users strive to minimize the number of toolbar icons on the screen, or confine it to two rows of toolbars. You can do this by using the CommandManager, flyout toolbars, the "S" toolbar, right click toolbars, and hotkeys, and removing unused icons, as well as the other techniques discussed here.

Having an uncluttered workspace is definitely a plus, but having easy access to commands is the real purpose of an interface in the first place. You need to strike a balance between too much and not enough. The more kinds of work you do in SolidWorks, the more tools you will need to have available. If you only create relatively simple machined parts and drawings, you will need fewer tools available than someone who does complex plastic part assemblies with rendering and animation.

Device approaches

If you have never used a Spaceball or equivalent view-manipulation device, you should consider it. They are wonderful devices and do far more than just spin the view. Most of the devices also have several programmable buttons that you can link to menu items. They can move drawing views, parts within assemblies, and even manipulate selected objects in other Office applications and Web browsers.

Portions of the 2009 edition of this book have been written on a Tablet PC. A tablet might not be ideal for long periods of SolidWorks usage, but I use it regularly for presentations and even modeling when I really want to get the feel of drawing a line by hand, The stylus is not quite as intuitive as a pencil, but it is less of an impediment to the tactile feel of actual drawings than a clunky mouse.

Macros

Macros are short snippets of programming code that have a particular function. Most macros are small and intended for simple tasks that are repeated many times, such as changing selected dimensions to four decimal places or zooming the screen so that it is sized 1:1 (actual size). Macros may be recorded, written from scratch, or a combination where you record a particular action to be used as a starting point and then embellish it manually from there. Recorded macros may not always record the parts of the action that you want to make into a macro, but you can edit them manually to include anything that you can program with VISTA (Visual Studio Tools for Applications), which is included with the base SolidWorks package at no extra cost.

To access macros by using hotkeys, follow these steps:

1. **Make a folder in your SolidWorks installation directory called "macros."**
2. **Copy macros into this folder.**
3. **Start (or restart) SolidWorks.**
4. **Go to Tools ➪ Customize ➪ Keyboard.**
5. **Scroll to the bottom of the list under the Macros category, and assign hotkeys as you would for standard SolidWorks commands.**

Whether you are skilled at writing or recording macros, or you are just using macros collected from other people, they can be huge time-savers and offer functionality that you would not otherwise be able to access. Many of my accumulated macros have been made obsolete by that functionality being incorporated directly into SolidWorks.

Saving custom interface settings

Once you have set up your menus and toolbars, worked out all of the custom colors, figured out your hotkey usage, and connected your macros, you don't want to lose these settings when you reinstall the software or move to a different computer. Another user may want to share your settings, or you may want to transfer them to your home computer (for modeling the new deck or the doghouse, of course). Fortunately, these settings are very portable.

You can use the Copy Settings Wizard to save these settings out to a file. Access the wizard through Start ➪ Programs ➪ SolidWorks 2009 ➪ SolidWorks Tools ➪ Copy Settings Wizard. This creates a file with an *.sldreg file extension. You can restore settings by double-clicking this file on a computer that has SolidWorks installed on it.

NOTE   You may need to have administrator access to your computer to apply a SolidWorks registry file.

The SolidWorks settings are actually Windows registry settings. The file that is saved by the wizard is just a registry file that has a different extension to prevent it from being applied too easily. Saved-out Windows registry files have a *.reg file extension, and are integrated into the registry by simply double-clicking them. If you are not familiar with the Windows registry, you should not make direct changes, because even small changes can cause serious problems with your operating system, installed software, or even hardware. The settings that are saved out by the Copy Settings Wizard are safe to transfer between computers. In order for the Copy Settings Wizard to work, you need to have Administrator-level access to your computer. The Copy Settings Wizard is shown in Figure 2.33.

FIGURE 2.33

The Copy Settings Wizard

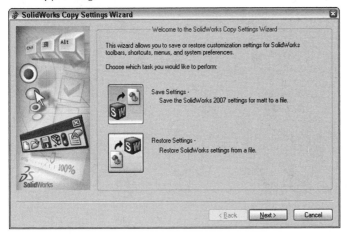

Working with multiple document windows

In SolidWorks, as in other areas of life, things can become chaotic. You may sometimes have the luxury of working on a single part at a time, but more often, you will find yourself with several documents open at once. This is a common situation for most users. Fortunately, SolidWorks has several methods for dealing with "information overload," to help you sort through it all.

Window management

Like most other Windows applications, SolidWorks can arrange the open document windows in one of several ways that are available through the Window menu (see Figure 2.34):

- **Cascade.** Most useful for accessing documents that are to be edited one by one.

- **Tile Horizontally.** Most useful for wide and short parts.

- **Tile Vertically.** Most useful for tall, narrow parts, or documents where you want to compare items in the FeatureManager.

- **Arrange Icons.** When windows are minimized to icons, this menu selection arranges the icons neatly, starting in the lower-left corner of the window.

FIGURE 2.34

The Window menu

The images in Figure 2.35 are meant to show the arrangement of the windows, not the content of the windows. Also remember that you can use the F9 key to close the FeatureManager, the F10 key to remove the toolbars to create extra interface space when arranging several windows in the graphics window and the F11 key to remove portions of the interface and allow you to work full screen.

Changing windows

You can use several techniques to change from one window to another. By clicking on the Window menu, you can view a list of open document windows (refer to Figure 2.34). You can then select the desired window directly from this menu. If more than a few windows are open, a More Windows option appears at the end of the list, as shown in Figure 2.36. Clicking on this option brings up a separate window that enables you to select from the complete list.

When a smaller number of windows are open, a simpler way to change windows is to press Ctrl+Tab. This is a Windows standard technique that also works in other Office applications. Ctrl+Tab takes you in one direction in the list of open windows, and Ctrl+Shift+Tab takes you in the opposite direction through the list. Starting with the 2008 release, Ctrl+Tab brings up the Open Documents interface (see Figure 2.36). This enables you to visually select the document that you want to open.

Additionally, the R hotkey by default opens the Recent Documents dialog, similar to the Recent Documents list in the File menu. This can also be accessed via the File menu if necessary. The Recent Documents dialog is shown in Figure 2.37.

FIGURE 2.35

Window Arrangements: Cascade, Tile Horizontally, and Tile Vertically

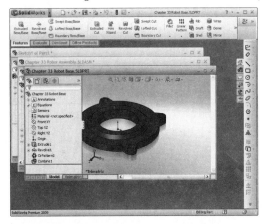

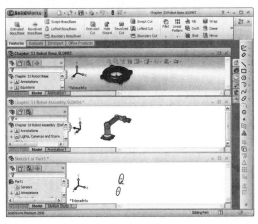

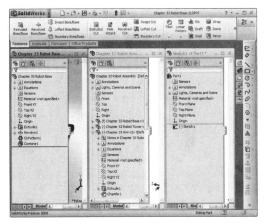

FIGURE 2.36

The Open Documents dialog

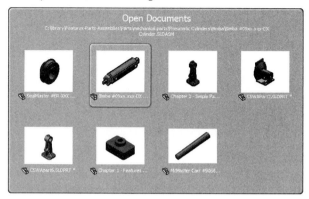

FIGURE 2.37

The Recent Documents dialog

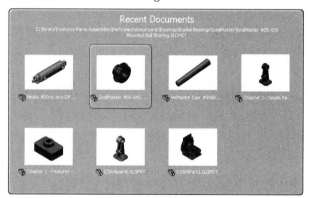

Tutorial: Getting to Know the Interface

By this point, you really have not learned much about making parts, assemblies, and drawings in SolidWorks, but you have learned quite a bit about using the interface. In this tutorial, you get some hands-on practice at manipulating the interface. This tutorial is intended to reinforce the following skills:

- Adding and removing toolbars
- Adding and removing toolbar buttons
- Adding and removing items from drop-down and RMB menus

- Setting up the CommandManager
- Setting up hotkeys
- Linking a hotkey to a macro
- Changing interface colors

Copy the existing settings

Regardless of what your initial settings are, you do not want to lose them. Before you start to make changes to your system, you should save out the existing settings to a file from which they can be recovered. You can do this using the Copy Settings Wizard, as shown in Figure 2.38.

FIGURE 2.38

The Copy Settings Wizard

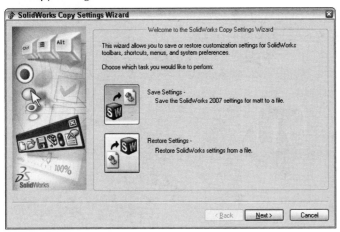

To use the Copy Settings Wizard, follow these steps:

1. **Close SolidWorks.**
2. **Click Start ⇨ Programs ⇨ SolidWorks 2009 ⇨ SolidWorks 2009 Tools ⇨ Copy Settings Wizard.**
3. **Select Save Settings, and click Next.**
4. **Enter a location and a name for the file.**
5. **Select the items that you would like to save.** For the purposes of this tutorial, make sure that the following options are selected: Keyboard Shortcuts, Menu Customization, Toolbar Layout, and All Toolbars.
6. **Click Finish.** Browse to the location where you saved the file and make sure that it is there.

Set all interface items to their default settings

You can set the interface back to the default settings using one of two methods. The first method, editing the Windows registry, may not be available to all users. It requires Administrator access to your computer and a good familiarity with Windows.

 **Editing the Windows registry can be dangerous if you make a mistake. Do not attempt this method is you have any doubts about what you are doing.**

To set SolidWorks back to its default settings, follow these steps:

1. Close SolidWorks.
2. Click Start ⇨ Run.
3. Type regedit, and click OK.
4. Browse to `HKEY_CURRENT_USER\Software\SolidWorks\SolidWorks 2009` or the appropriate folder for the version that you are using.
5. To return all settings in SolidWorks back to default, rename the entire SolidWorks 2009 folder to include "(old)" at the end of the filename.
6. Close the Registry Editor.
7. The folder is re-created when SolidWorks starts up again, and is populated with default values. If you need to get the previous folder back, you can delete the new one and rename the old one to remove the " (old)" from the name.

The second method, which is less risky but less complete, is to go to the main locations and use the tools provided to return settings to their defaults. Restart SolidWorks and create a new blank document (you cannot display the Customize dialog box without a document open). To access the resets for the interface, do the following:

1. Click Tools ⇨ Options ⇨ General ⇨ Reset, and go to the bottom-left area of the dialog box.
2. Click Tools ⇨ Customize ⇨ Toolbars ⇨ Reset, and go to the bottom-left area of the dialog box.
3. Click Tools ⇨ Customize ⇨ Menus ⇨ Reset All, and go to the right side of the dialog box.
4. Click Tools ⇨ Customize ⇨ Keyboard ⇨ Reset to Defaults, and go to the upper-right area of the dialog box.
5. Click Tools ⇨ Customize ⇨ Options; there are three Reset to Defaults buttons along the left side of the dialog box.

Customizing the CommandManager

Now that you have restored the default settings, you can begin customizing the interface with the CommandManager. To do this, open a part document or create a new one, then RMB click anywhere on the CommandManager, and deselect the Use Large Buttons with Text option, as shown in Figure 2.39. When you have done this, the check mark should no longer appear in front of the option.

FIGURE 2.39

Deselect the Use Large Buttons with Text option.

Next, add some toolbars to CommandManager, as follows:

1. **RMB click the CommandManager tabs, and select Customize CommandManager.**
2. **Click (left-click) on the New Tab icon at the right end of the CommandManager tabs and select Surfaces, Sheet Metal and Annotations. Turn off the Sketch tab by right clicking it and selecting Hide Tab.** The new tab icon is shown in Figure 2.40.

FIGURE 2.40

Adding tabs to the CommandManager

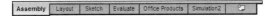

3. **In the Customize dialog, enable the Large Icons option.**
4. **Turn the Sketch toolbar on, but not inside the CommandManager, use the Toolbars tab of the Customize dialog.** Dock the Sketch toolbar to the right side of the window.
5. **Turn on the Standard Views toolbar and drag it to the right end of the CommandManager.** Now drag a couple of buttons off of it, such as the bottom, or left, or back views.
6. **On the Commands tab of the Customize dialog, select the Flyouts entry, and drag any Standard Toolbar type of flyouts from the Customize dialog to the Menu Bar Toolbar.** Figure 2.41 shows this step in action.
7. **Turn off the Customize dialog, and right-click on the Heads-up View toolbar**
8. **Turn off the tools that you will not use on the Heads-up View toolbar, and click outside of the menu when you are done.**
9. **Run your cursor over the main menu flyout and use the pushpin to pin the menu open**.
10. **Go to Tools ➪ Customize ➪ Options and click both Show All buttons for Shortcut Customization and Menu Customizations.** This removes the double arrows at the bottoms of RMB menus. This setting is shown in Figure 2.42.

FIGURE 2.41

Adding flyouts to the Menu Bar Toolbar

FIGURE 2.42

Removing truncated menus

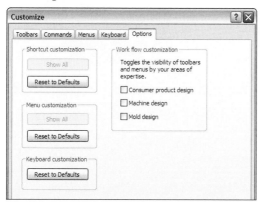

11. While still in Tools ⇨ Customize, change to the Toolbars tab and turn off the Context Toolbar Settings ⇨ Show On Selection option to disable the left click context toolbars, or disable the Show In Shortcut Menu to put the RMB menus back to their pre-2008 state (all entries in menu use text).

12. Click and drag the PropertyManager tab (second tab from the left) from the FeatureManager, and dock it just to the right of the FeatureManager under the CommandManager tabs. The display should now look like Figure 2.43.

FIGURE 2.43

The customized SolidWorks interface

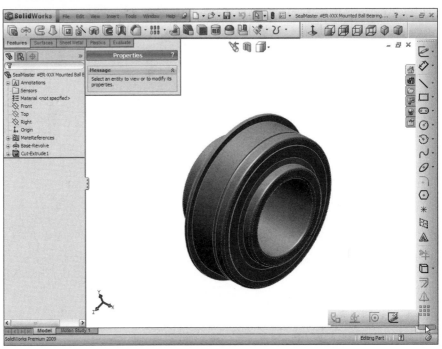

The small flyout in the lower-right corner of Figure 2.44 is the remainder of the Sketch toolbar that does not fit on the screen. This screen shot was taken on a 12-inch monitor with large icons at 1024 × 768 resolution. At such a low resolution, long toolbars do not fit on the screen, and the remaining icons are activated by the two small arrows at the end of the toolbar.

Customizing menus

If you always do the same types of work, or more importantly, *never* do certain types of work, then you might consider customizing some menus to remove items that you never use. Customization applies to both the main drop-down menus and the context-sensitive RMB menus. To customize a menu, follow these steps:

1. **Click Insert ⇨ Customize Menu. Note that Customize Menu is different from Customize.**

2. **Turn off the menu items Sketch from Drawing, DXF/DWG, Object, Hyperlink, and Picture (see Figure 2.44).** Click anywhere outside of the list to close it.

3. **Click the Insert menu to ensure that the deselected items have been removed.**

4. **RMB click the Right plane in the FeatureManager.**

FIGURE 2.44

Customizing the Insert menu

5. **Select Customize Menu.**

6. **Turn off Section View.** Click anywhere outside of the list to close it.

7. **RMB click the Right plane to verify that Section View has been removed.**

Change interface colors

This tutorial does not depend on RealView capabilities, but later work will. To find out if your computer is RealView capable, check your video card and driver version against the list on the SolidWorks Web site. On the main page of the site, follow the link for Video Cards.

Before starting this tutorial, make sure the RealView icon is disabled. You can turn off RealView at View ➪ Display ➪ RealView Graphics.

CROSS-REF For more information on RealView graphics, see Chapter 5.

Edit the colors used in the interface:

1. **Go to Tools ➪ Options ➪ Colors.** Make sure the "Plain (Viewport Background color above)" option is turned on.

2. **Change the Viewport Background color, first in the Color Scheme Settings list, to a light gray color, then click OK and make sure the setting was applied.**

3. Go back to Tools ⇨ Options ⇨ Colors, and click the Save As Scheme button, and save the color scheme as Plain Gray.

4. Now enable the "Gradient" option, and set the top and bottom gradient colors (second and third in the top list). Click OK and see how you like the gradient display. Adjust the colors until you are happy with them.

5. Go back to Tools ⇨ Options ⇨ Colors and click the Save As Scheme button, and save the color scheme as Gradient. Figure 2.45 shows the Tools ⇨ Options ⇨ Colors dialog box.

FIGURE 2.45

The Colors settings

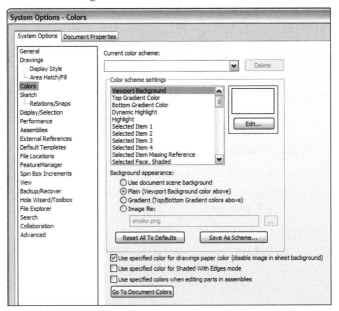

6. Use the Current Color Scheme drop-down list at the top to change the color schemes between the newly saved schemes,

Adding hotkeys

For many users, hotkeys are an integral part of the everyday experience of using SolidWorks. You can easily assign hotkeys and manage the assignments by following these steps:

1. Click Tools ⇨ Customize ⇨ Keyboard.

2. In the Search For text box, type Options.

3. Click in the Shortcut column, and type O.

4. Click again in the Search For text box, and type Customize.

5. Click in the text box next to the Tools ⇨ Customize entry and press Ctrl+C. Answer no to the question of whether you want to reassign the hotkey. Press Ctrl+T instead.

6. Click OK to exit the Customize dialog box.

7. Press the O key to bring up Tools ⇨ Options. Click OK to exit.

8. Press Ctrl+T to bring up Tools ⇨ Customize. Click OK to exit.

9. Press Alt+F, and then press X to exit SolidWorks.

Combining macros with hotkeys

Macros are covered in Chapters 34 and 35, but the following steps show you how to link a macro to a hotkey:

ON the CD-ROM You can use the macro called rectangle.swp, located on the CD-ROM.

1. **Find your SolidWorks installation directory.** By default, this directory is C:\Program Files\SolidWorks.

2. **Create a folder called Macros in the SolidWorks directory and put the rectangle. swp macro in it.**

3. **Start SolidWorks.**

4. **Create a new blank part document.**

5. **Press Ctrl+T to access the Customize dialog box.**

6. **Click the Keyboard tab.**

7. **In the Search For text box, type** rectangle.

8. **Click in the Shortcut column next to the listing with the Category of Macros, and press R.**

9. **Click OK to exit the Customize dialog box.**

10. **Press R.** The rectangle macro runs and draws a sketch rectangle on the Front plane, centered on the origin.

11. **Press Ctrl+S to access the Windows standard hotkey for the Save command.** Name the part **rectangle.sldprt** and save it to a workspace directory.

12. **Press Alt+F and then X to exit SolidWorks.**

The use of Alt-keys and hotkeys is somewhat exaggerated in this tutorial, but it is intended to get you used to working with them.

Summary

The SolidWorks interface is very busy and can be daunting. You can access most functions multiple ways, which can be liberating because it offers options, but it also adds to the confusion because there is so much to remember. You do not need to know every way to do everything; you only need to know the best way for you. After using this book to find the various ways of using the interface, just develop the way that is most comfortable for you and stick with it.

Be aware that every couple of releases, SolidWorks changes the interface, and often, they use the most radical options available as the new defaults. Keep a copy of your settings file with you so that you can restore settings or you can take your settings to another computer quickly if you need to.

Chapter 3

Working with Sketches

So far in this book, you have looked mainly at concepts, settings, and setup, which is necessary but pretty mundane business. However, here you begin to learn how to control parametric relationships in sketches. Then in later chapters, you begin to build models, simple at first, but gaining in complexity and always demonstrating new techniques and features that build your modeling vocabulary. Beyond this, you will move into putting the parts together into assemblies, which helps to make the "pretty pictures" look like something useful. Finally, you use the parts and assemblies to create drawings.

This chapter deals mainly with sketches in parts. However, you will be able to apply many of the topics I cover here to assemblies. Some related topics, such as Layout sketches, have functionality that is exclusive to assemblies and are covered in the assemblies chapter.

Several basic facts about sketches may be helpful before you start. While a part may have many sketches, only one sketch can be open at a time. This is due in part to the history-based nature of the software; every entry in the FeatureManager tree must be edited in the position in which it exists in the tree.

While you can create both 2D and 3D sketches, you will use 2D sketches most of the time. When referring to a generic *sketch*, a 2D sketch is always assumed. You will use 3D sketches in specific situations, and they will be explicitly called for when needed.

CROSS-REF I discuss 3D sketches in detail in Chapter 31.

When you open a sketch, several tools become available, specifically all of the sketch entities and tools. Conversely, there are several things that you cannot do *until* you open a sketch. For example, you cannot apply a Fillet feature while a sketch is open. Open sketches and selection filters are two very common sources of frustration for new users. Several indicators exist to let you know when you are in Sketch mode:

IN THIS CHAPTER

Opening a sketch

Identifying sketch entities

Inferencing in sketch

Exploring sketch settings

Using sketch blocks

Tutorial: Learning to use sketch relations

Tutorial: Using blocks and belts

- The title bar of the SolidWorks window displays the text Sketch X of Part Y.
- The lower-right corner of the status bar displays the text Editing Sketch X.
- The Confirmation Corner displays a sketch icon in the upper-right corner of the graphics window.
- The Sketch toolbar button now displays the text Exit Sketch and is pressed in.
- The red sketch Origin displays.
- If you are using the grid, it displays only in Sketch mode.

While most users find the sketch grid to be annoying or distracting, when teaching, I've always used the grid to remind students when they are in Sketch mode. If you find that you forget or would like a visual cue, the sketch grid is a useful, if less than fashionable, option.

Opening a Sketch

Several methods exist to open new sketches in SolidWorks:

- Click a sketch entity toolbar button from the Sketch toolbar; SolidWorks prompts you to select a sketch plane. When you select the plane, the sketch opens.
- Preselect a plane or planar face and then click either a sketch entity button or the Sketch button.
- Use the left-mouse button to click context toolbar — click a face or plane and select the Sketch icon.
- Right-mouse button click a plane or planar face and select Insert Sketch. Planes can be selected from either the graphics window or the FeatureManager.

You can open existing sketches in several ways:

- Right-click a sketch in the FeatureManager or graphics window, and select Edit Sketch.
- Select a sketch from the FeatureManager or graphics window, and click the Sketch button on the Sketch toolbar.
- Left-click a sketch or feature and click the Edit Sketch icon from the context toolbar
- Double-click a sketch with the Instant 3D tool active.

Identifying Sketch Entities

The first step in creating most SolidWorks parts is a sketch. This will usually be a 2D sketch, although you can also use 3D sketches. A 2D sketch is simply a collection of 2D lines, arcs, and other elements that lie together on a plane; it usually also contains relations and/or dimensions between the entities so that the sketch can automatically adjust to changes because each sketch entity understands its function.

SolidWorks sketch entities include many types, some of which you will use all of the time, and some of which you may not use, even if you spend years working with the software. Here I will identify each entity type so that you see it at least once and know that it is available if you need it at some point.

The Sketch toolbar

In the following section, I identify the default buttons on the Sketch toolbar first, followed by the rest of the entities that you can access through Tools ➪ Customize ➪ Commands ➪ Sketch.

 Sketch opens and closes sketches. You may notice that the name of the button changes depending on if the sketch is open or closed. If you preselect a plane or planar face and then click the Sketch button, SolidWorks opens a new sketch on the plane or face. If you preselect a sketch before clicking the Sketch button, SolidWorks opens this sketch. If you preselect an edge or curve feature before clicking the Sketch button, SolidWorks automatically makes a plane perpendicular to the nearest end of the curve from the location you picked. If you do not use preselection, and only click the Sketch tool with nothing selected, SolidWorks prompts you to select a plane or planar face on which you want to put a new sketch, or an existing sketch to edit.

 3D Sketch opens and closes 3D sketches with no preselection required. 3D sketch is covered in more detail in Chapter 31.

 Smart Dimension can create all types of dimensions used in SolidWorks, such as horizontal, vertical, aligned, radial, diameter, angle, and arc length. You can create dimensions in three ways, as shown in Figure 3.1:

- By selecting a line and placing the dimension
- By selecting the endpoints of the line and placing the dimension
- By selecting a pair of parallel lines and placing the dimension

Selecting the line is the easiest and fastest method. Selecting parallel lines on the ends is not recommended because if you delete either of the selected lines, the dimension is also deleted, although sometimes this method is necessary.

You can use the first and second techniques for the angled line shown in Figure 3.1 to create any of the three dimensions shown. To accomplish this task, drag the cursor while placing the dimension until the witness lines snap to the orientation you want.

TIP To lock the orientation of a dimension while moving the cursor to place the actual dimension value, click the right-mouse button. To unlock it, just click the right-mouse button again. The right-mouse button cursor shows a lock or unlock icon when this functionality is available.

In this case, the third technique locks you into the horizontal orientation because of the orientation of the selected lines.

FIGURE 3.1

Selection options for linear Smart Dimension

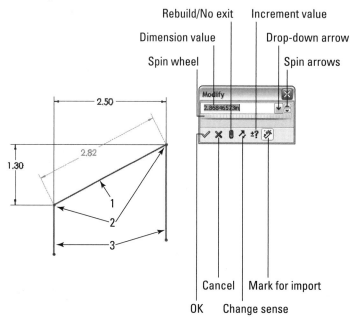

NOTE In some situations you may run into lines that appear to be parallel, but are not exactly so. This will cause you to get an angle dimension where you want a linear dimension. Here, you can select one of the lines and one endpoint. SolidWorks requires parallelism to a high precision, and situations like this can happen if the angular measurement is off in the second or third decimal place, measuring in degrees. Imported 2D drawings and reverse engineered 3D models can be particularly susceptible to this type of error.

CAUTION When you select lines to establish a dimension instead of endpoints, both of the lines gain an implied parallel relation that prevents them from moving as you might predict. In the example shown in Figure 3.1, neither of the end lines can be angled unless you remove the dimension.

Another issue that arises for adding dimensions to lines is that if you delete either of the lines, the dimension is also deleted. This is not true for the first and second techniques, where as long as the endpoints remain, the dimension also remains.

You can change Smart Dimension values in several ways. The most direct way is to directly key in a value such as 4.052. The software assumes document units unless you key in something specific. You could also key in an expression, even with mixed units, such as 8.045/2+.125 or 25.4+.625 in. Starting in SolidWorks 2009, you can also key in negative dimensions, which functions the same as the Change Sense button in the Modify box.

Another way to put a value into the Modify box is to click the down arrow to the right of the value field, and select either to use an equation to calculate a value or a Link Value. A Link Value is like a variable name to which you can assign a value. You can link multiple dimension values to that Link Value. In sheet metal parts, the default Link Value of Thickness is used, so that if you change the thickness in one feature, it will change for all the sheet metal features.

To the right of the drop-down arrow is a pair of up and down "spin" arrows that allow you to change the value in the Modify box by a set increment amount. The increment can be set in Tools ➪ Options ➪ System Options ➪ Spin Box Increments. You can also store multiple increment values in the Increment Value icon on the Modify box.

The final way to change the value in the Modify box is by using the wheel underneath the value field. The wheel uses the default increment value. Holding down Ctrl while using the wheel multiplies the increment by 10, and holding down Alt while using the wheel divides the increment by 10.

- **Radial.** You create the dimension by selecting an arc and placing the dimension. If you want a radial dimension of a complete circle, you must Right-click the dimension after you create it, select Properties, and deselect the Diameter Dimension option, as shown in Figure 3.2.

FIGURE 3.2

The Dimension Properties interface

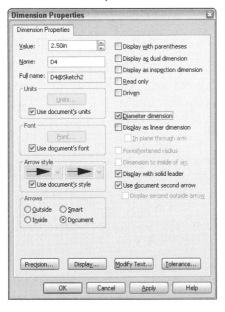
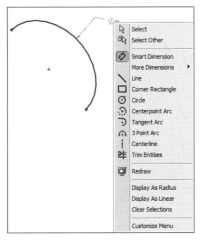

■ **Diameter.** You can create the dimension by selecting a complete circle and placing the dimension. If you want a diameter dimension for an arc, use the right-mouse button menu or Dimension Properties dialog box and select the Diameter Dimension option.

NOTE Along with the Radial and Diameter dimensions, you may also want to dimension between arcs or circles, from tangent or nearest points. To do this, use the Smart Dimension tool with the Shift key to select the arcs near the tangent points. Alternatively, to change a dimension from a center-to-center dimension to a max-to-max dimension, you can drag dimension attachment points to tangent points or use the dimension properties.

■ **Angle.** You can create the angle dimension in one of two ways. If the angle to be driven is between two straight lines, simply select the two straight lines and place the dimension. If you are creating an included angle dimension for an arc where there are not necessarily any straight lines drawn, then with the Smart Dimension tool active, first select the vertex of the angle, and then the two outlying points, as shown in Figure 3.3.

FIGURE 3.3

Creating an included angle dimension

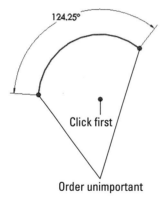

■ **Arc Length.** You can create the dimension by selecting an arc and its endpoints with the Smart Dimension tool.

 Line creates straight lines using one of two methods:

■ **Click-Click.** Used for drawing multiple connected end-to-end lines. Click-and-release the left-mouse button to start the line; each click-and-release ends the previous line and starts a new one. Double-click, press Esc, or deselect the Line tool to end.

■ **Click-Drag.** Used to draw individual or unconnected lines. Click, drag, and drop. The first click initiates the line, and the drop ends it.

Alternate methods for drawing lines include horizontal, vertical, angle, and infinite lines. The interface for these options displays in the PropertyManager, as shown in Figure 3.4.

- **Horizontal, Vertical.** These settings require you to select a starting point, and an ending vertical or horizontal position. There does not seem to be any compelling reason for you to use this instead of the regular line command.

- **Angle.** Enables you to specify an angle and drag a line at this angle. Again, I can find no compelling reason to use this tool.

- **Infinite Lines.** SolidWorks parts have a working space limited to 1000 meters on a side, centered on the Origin. Infinite lines extend well beyond this, although you cannot draw or dimension a regular line outside of this box. I have not come across a compelling use for this feature.

FIGURE 3.4

The Insert Line PropertyManager interface

NOTE The Add Dimensions option exists in several sketch entity PropertyManagers. This option adds Smart Dimensions to the newly sketched entities. The option is only shown in the sketch entity PropertyManager if the setting at Tools ➪ Options ➪ Sketch ➪ Enable On Screen Numeric Input On Entity Creation is turned on.

The on screen numeric input is not the same as the Input Dimension Value function, and in fact overrides that option. You can not input dimension values when using the Add Dimensions in conjunction with click-drag sketching. It appears to be intended for click-click drawing only, so that you can enter values between clicks.

Corner Rectangle creates a rectangle by clicking one corner and dragging to the diagonal corner. This action creates four lines with Horizontal and Vertical sketch relations, as appropriate. The Corner Rectangle is also available as a flyout icon that also makes available a Centerpoint Rectangle, a 3 Point Corner Rectangle (rectangle at an angle), and a 3 Point Center Rectangle, as well as the Parallelogram, Figure 3.5 shows the flyout and all the icons on the flyout, along with the PropertyManager for the Rectangle, which also allows you to switch types of rectangle easily.

FIGURE 3.5

The Rectangle flyout with associated icons

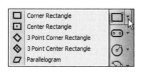
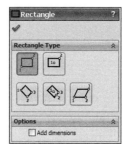

Notice also the Add Dimensions box in the PropertyManager. Clicking this box while creating a rectangle causes the software to add dimensions aligned with the sides of the rectangle. This option is also available for lines, arcs, and circles.

Note that this option used in conjunction with the Enable On-Screen Numeric Input On Entity Creation setting, found at Tools ➪ Options ➪ Sketch, can make creating sketch entities to the correct size immediately much easier.

Circle creates a circle using one of two methods, which are available from either the flyout icon or the Circle PropertyManager:

- **Center Creation.** Click the center of the circle and drag the radius. The Circle PropertyManager calls this function *center creation*.

- **Perimeter Creation.** To create a circle using this technique, you must select the Perimeter Creation option from the Circle PropertyManager window after clicking the Circle tool. There is also a separate Perimeter Creation toolbar button, and a menu selection for Tools, Sketch Entities, Perimeter Circle. This only creates tangent relations with other entities in the current sketch, and so if you are building a circle from model edges or entities in other sketches, you need to apply the relations manually. SolidWorks calls these functions *perimeter creation*.

  - **Tangent to Two Entities.** Start the circle with the cursor near one line in the sketch. A Tangent symbol appears by the cursor with a yellow background. Click and drag the diameter to the second tangent entity, where a similar cursor symbol should appear. Release the mouse button and Right-click the green check mark icon. This process is shown in Figure 3.6.

  - **Tangent to Three Entities.** Use the same process for Tangent to two entities, but omit the Right-click of the green check mark icon. After dropping on the second tangent, drag again to the third tangent entity.

FIGURE 3.6

Creating a perimeter creation circle

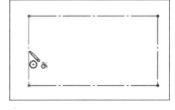
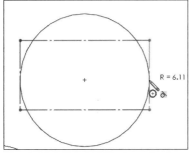

R = 6.11

 Centerpoint Arc creates an arc by clicking the center, dragging the radius, and then clicking and dragging the included angle of the arc. The first two steps are exactly like the Center-Radius circle.

 Tangent Arc creates an arc tangent to an existing sketch entity. Depending on how you move the cursor away from the end of the existing sketch entity, the arc can be tangent, reverse tangent, or perpendicular, as shown in Figure 3.7.

Another way to create a tangent arc is to start drawing a line from the end of another sketch entity, and while holding the left mouse button, to press the A key, or to return the cursor to the starting point and drag it out again. This second method can be difficult to master, but it saves time when compared to any of the techniques for switching sketch tools.

 3 Point Arc creates an arc by first establishing endpoints, and then establishing the included arc, as shown in Figure 3.8. Again, this tool also works using the Click-Click or Click-Drag methods.

 Sketch Fillet creates a sketch fillet in one of two ways. You can either select the endpoint where the sketch entities intersect, or you can select the entities themselves, selecting the portion of the entity that you want to keep. Figure 3.9 illustrates both techniques. The Sketch Chamfer tool is on the same flyout as the Sketch Fillet by default, and works much in the same way.

FIGURE 3.7

Using the Tangent Arc feature

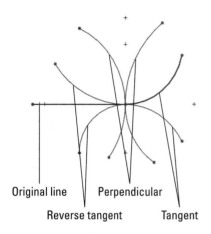

Original line | Perpendicular

Reverse tangent | Tangent

FIGURE 3.8

Creating a three point arc

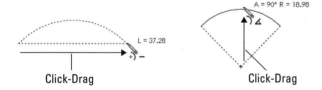

Click-Drag   Click-Drag

FIGURE 3.9

Creating a sketch fillet

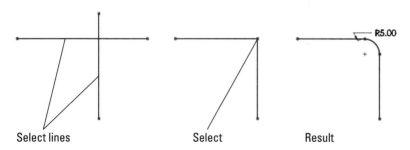

Select lines   Select   Result

Sketch Fillets

While the Sketch Fillet tool is easy to use, applies immediately, and may align with your way of working in a 2D program, it is not considered best practice to use sketch fillets extensively. Some reasons for this include:

- Large changes in the size or shape of the rest of the sketch can make the fillets cause the feature built from the sketch to fail.

- SolidWorks (and other parametric programs as well) often has difficulty solving tangent arcs in some situations. You may see them flip tangency or go around 270° instead of just 90°. Using a lot of fillets in a sketch can often cause trouble.

- If you want to remove the fillets temporarily, there is no good way to do this if you have used sketch fillets.

- Sometimes feature order requires that other features, such as draft, come before the fillet.

- Sometimes a 2D fillet simply cannot create the required geometry.

Fillet features are the preferred method for creating rounds and fillets. The same can be said for chamfers. Still, sometimes you need to use tangent arcs in sketches. You will have to decide for yourself which way works best for you.

 Centerline follows the same methods as regular lines, and is also called a *construction line* in some cases. Other construction entities such as construction circles are not available directly, but you can create them by selecting the For Construction option in the PropertyManager for any entity.

 Spline draws a freeform curve. Splines may form either a single closed loop or an open loop. In either case the spline is not allowed to cross itself. You can draw a spline by clicking each location where you want to add a control point. Figure 3.10 identifies the elements of a spline. The detail image shows the structure of a spline handle.

Splines are used mainly for freeform complex shapes in 2D and 3D sketches, although you can also use them for anything that you would use other sketch elements for. If you need more information on splines and complex shape modeling, refer to the *SolidWorks Surfacing and Complex Shape Modeling Bible* (Wiley, 2008).

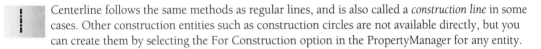 Point creates a sketch point. Aside from limited cases of lofting to a point or using a point as a constraint sketch in a Fill feature, sketch points are usually used for reference or for the location of the centerpoint of Hole Wizard features.

You can also use the sketch point as a virtual sharp. If two sketch entities do not actually intersect because of a fillet or chamfer, selecting the two entities and clicking the Point tool creates a point at the location where they would intersect if they were extended. This is useful for dimensioning to the sharp. Virtual sharp display is controlled by a Document Property setting described in more detail in Appendix B.

FIGURE 3.10

The structure of a spline and a spline handle

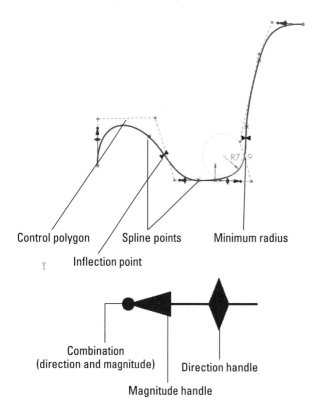

Control polygon / Spline points Minimum radius

Inflection point

Combination
(direction and magnitude) Direction handle

Magnitude handle

 3D Sketch Plane creates a plane in a 3D Sketch. I discuss 3D Sketches in more detail in Chapter 31. By sketching on planes within a 3D sketch, you get most of the benefits and usage of 2D sketches, and you do not have to deal with history between sketches. Before committing too much work to this course, you should look into some of the shortcomings of 3D Planes. The planes are treated just like another entity in the 3D sketch, which means you can assign sketch relations to them, but it also means that they can move around within the sketch like sketch entities.

 Add Relation displays a PropertyManager window that allows you to apply sketch relations. This interface appears to be obsolete because it is easier to simply select sketch items and apply relations via the context toolbar or in the PropertyManager window that appears automatically when you select them; however, there are some subtle workflow-related reasons for using this tool.

Two advantages exist to using the Add Relations dialog over simply selecting sketch entities and adding relations. When the Add Relation PropertyManager is active, you do not need to use the Ctrl key to select multiple entities. You also do not need to clear a selection before making a new selection for the next relation. These two reasons sound minor, but if you have a large number of sketch relations to apply, the workflow goes much more smoothly using this tool than the default method.

 Display/Delete Relations enables you to look through the relations in a sketch, and sort them according to several categories. From this window, you can delete or suppress relations and replace entities in relations.

 Quick Snaps flyout allows you to quickly filter types of entities that sketch elements will snap to when you move or create them. To access the tools, click the drop-down arrow to the right of the toolbar button.

 Mirror Entities mirrors selected sketch entities about a single selected centerline, and applies a Symmetric sketch relation. There is also a Dynamic Mirror function that is described later in this chapter.

 Convert Entities converts edges, curves, and sketch elements from other sketches into entities in the current sketch. When edges are not parallel to the sketch plane, the Convert Entities feature projects them into the sketch plane. Some elements may be impossible to convert, such as a helix, which would produce a projection that overlaps itself. Sketch entities created using Convert Entities get an On Edge sketch relation.

 Offset Entities works like the Convert Entities feature, except that it offsets the sketch to one side or the other of the projection of the original edge, sketch, or curve. Figure 3.11 shows the interface for this command.

The options available in the Offset Entities interface are as follows:

- **Add Dimensions.** Constrains offset sketch entities. Instead of the On Edge relations, Offset Entities creates an Offset sketch relation that cannot be recreated manually.

- **Reverse.** Changes the direction of the offset.

- **Select Chain.** Selects continuous end-to-end sketch entities.

- **Bi-directional.** Offsets to both sides simultaneously.

- **Make Base Construction.** If you are offsetting sketch entities within the active sketch, this option converts the original sketch entities to construction sketch geometry.

- **Cap Ends.** Is available only when you have selected the Bi-directional option. Capping the ends with arcs is an easy way to create a slot from a sketch of the centerline. This function works with all sketch entities, and so it is not limited to straight slots. Figure 3.12 shows examples of the Cap Ends option.

 The Offset Entities command may fail if the offset distance is greater than the smallest radius of curvature, and you are attempting to offset to the inside of the arc.

FIGURE 3.11

The Offset Entities interface

FIGURE 3.12

The results of using offset entities cap ends

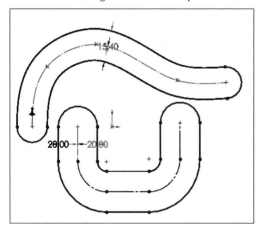

In addition to the bi-directional offset with capped ends, SolidWorks also has slot sketch entities for straight and curved slots, which you can find covered later in this chapter. Composite slots (made of a combination of straight and curved sections) still require the offset method.

Trim Entities is actually several functions rolled into one, and it is an extremely powerful tool for editing sketches. Trim Entities allows several methods for trimming, as well as extending and deleting sketch entities. Figure 3.13 shows the PropertyManager interface for this function.

FIGURE 3.13

The Trim Entities interface

- **Power Trim.** Trims by dragging a cursor trail over multiple entities. The entities that you drag the cursor over are trimmed back to the next intersecting sketch entity. Each time you trim an entity, a red box is left behind that remains until you trim the next entity. If you backtrack with the cursor and touch the red box, this trim is undone. This option is best used when you need to trim a large number of entities that are easy to hit with a moving cursor. Figure 3.14 shows the Power Trim feature in action.

  You can also use power trim to extend sketch entities along their paths by dragging the endpoints. Regular dragging can also change the position or orientation of the rest of the entity, but by using the Power Trim feature, you affect only the length.

FIGURE 3.14

The Power Trim feature in action

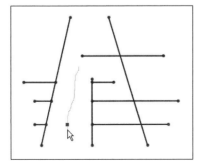

- **Corner.** Trims or extends two selected entities to their next intersection. When you use the Corner option to trim, the selected portion of the sketch entities is kept, and anything on the other side of the corner is discarded. Figure 3.15 shows two ways that the Corner option can work.

FIGURE 3.15

Using the Corner option

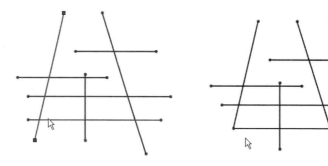

- **Trim Away Inside.** Trims away selected entities inside a selected boundary. The boundary may consist of a pair of sketch entities or a model face (edges of the face are used as the boundary). Only entities that cross both selected boundaries (or cross the closed loop of the face boundary twice) can be trimmed. This option does not trim a closed loop such as a circle, ellipse, or closed spline.
- **Trim Away Outside.** Functions exactly like the Trim Away Inside option, except that sketch entities outside of the boundary are discarded. The Trim Away Inside and Outside option are illustrated in Figure 3.16.

FIGURE 3.16

Using the Trim Away Inside and Outside options

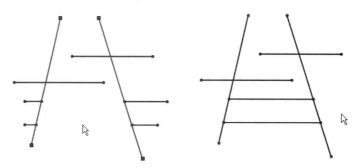

■ **Trim to Closest.** This is the default setting. Clicking on a sketch entity will:

  ■ Trim it back to the next entity if there is only one crossing entity.

  ■ Trim between two crossing entities if there are more than one.

  ■ Delete the entity if there are no crossing entities.

In all cases, the selected section of the entity is removed. The Trim to Closest option can also extend by dragging one entity to another; if an intersection is possible, the first entity is extended to the second entity. Figure 3.17 illustrates how the Trim to Closest option functions.

FIGURE 3.17

Using Trim to Closest to extend

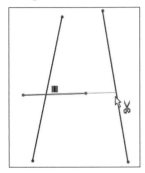

Construction Geometry toggles between regular sketch entities and construction entities. Construction sketch entities are not used to create solid or surface faces directly; they are only used for reference   for example, revolve centerlines, extrude and pattern directions, and so forth. Be careful with the icon for this function, because it looks almost identical to the No Solve Move icon, especially as printed here in gray scale.

The Stretch sketch tool is intended for use in sketches where there are enough dimensions to make a particular change difficult by changing dimensions only. It is similar in purpose and use to the AutoCAD Stretch function because it was loosely modeled after the AutoCAD functionality. Stretch allows you to specify a change that will change several dimensions simultaneously. Figure 3.18 shows the initial, intermediate, and final states of the sketch being stretched.

TIP   **The main ideas to remember with the Stretch tool are that it is used to stretch dimensioned lines, and that you need to select the lines that will lengthen or shorten as well as the lines that will move. Because if this, selecting entities for Stretch is best done with the right-to-left window selection, which also selects any items that the selection box crosses. (Left-to-right window selection only selects items that are completely within the selection box.)**

FIGURE 3.18

Using the Stretch sketch tool

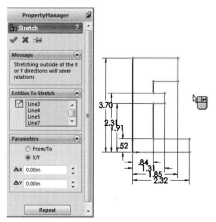
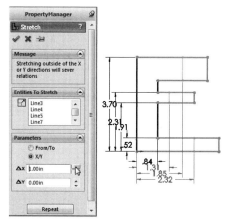

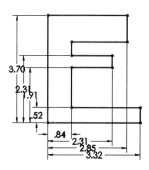

CAUTION Figure 3.18 shows the X/Y option being used, but if you use the From/To option, be aware that it may delete some sketch relations along the way.

The Move, Rotate, Copy and Scale sketch tools operate on selections within a sketch. You can use these tools with pre- or post-selection methods. These tools delete existing sketch relations when necessary to accomplish the task. For example, if you want to move a rectangle connected to the origin, the Move tool will delete the Coincident relation between the sketch endpoint and the origin. If you want to rotate a rectangle, the Rotate tool will delete all of the horizontal and vertical relations on the entities being rotated. This operation may result in a completely underdefined sketch. SolidWorks does not warn you that sketch relations are being deleted.

If you use the Scale tool on a fully defined sketch, SolidWorks will scale the position of the selected entities, deleting sketch relations if necessary to do so, but no dimensions will be scaled or deleted.

 Be careful when using these sketch tools. They can delete sketch relations without warning.

These sketch tools were originally put in the software to avoid some of the complexities and limitations of the Modify Sketch tool, which can also move, copy, rotate, and scale sketches. Figure 3.19 shows the simple interface for the Move Entities command. Select the entities to move in the upper box, and the method to move them below.

FIGURE 3.19

The Move Entities interface

 Select is usually used to turn off the previous command.

 Grid/Snap is used to open the Grid/Snap section of Tools ➪ Options ➪ Document Properties.

 Parallelogram can be used to draw a parallelogram (adjacent sides are not perpendicular, but opposite sides are parallel), draw the first side of the parallelogram in the same way as the first side of the rectangle, then drag the second side; setting the angle as well as the length.

 Polygon creates a regular *n*-sided polygon in the same way as a circle. Click the center and drag the radius. You need to set the number of sides in the PropertyManager before clicking in the graphics window.

 Ellipse is created by clicking the center, dragging one axis, and then dragging the other axis.

 Partial Ellipse is created by clicking the center, dragging one axis, dragging the other axis, and then clicking and dragging the included angle of the partial ellipse. The Partial Ellipse feature works like the centerpoint arc.

Parabola is created by clicking the location for the Focus, and then dragging the position of the Apex. You then click and drag the included angle of the parabola, as shown in Figure 3.20. This is a rarely used sketch entity and is often difficult to control with sketch relations or dimensions.

FIGURE 3.20

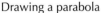

Drawing a parabola

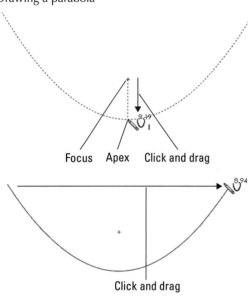

Spline on Surface is used in 3D sketches to draw a freeform spline on any 3D surface. The Spline on Surface feature can cross face boundaries as long as the faces are at least tangent (ideally curvature continuous) across the edge. Spline on Surface can be used to trim surfaces or create split lines.

Sketch Text creates editable text in sketches using TrueType fonts installed in your Fonts folder. Some fonts produce sketches that are unusable for solid features, due to violating sketch rules with overlapping or zero thickness. You need to be careful which fonts you select, but I have had success with a wide variety of fonts I have found on the Internet. Sketch Text may be dissolved into lines and arcs so that you can edit them manually. Dissolve is available on the right-mouse button menu. Figure 3.21 points out the key elements of the Sketch Text interface.

Intersection Curve, in 2D sketches, creates sketch entities where the sketch plane intersects selected faces. In 3D sketches, the Intersection Curve sketch tool creates sketch entities where any types of selected faces intersect. This can be an extremely useful tool in many situations.

FIGURE 3.21

The Sketch Text interface

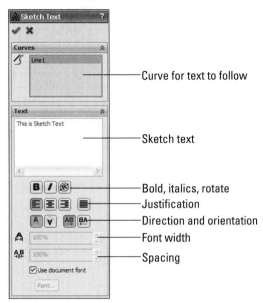

———— Curve for text to follow

———— Sketch text

———— Bold, italics, rotate
———— Justification
———— Direction and orientation
———— Font width
———— Spacing

 Face Curves applies the underlying U-V isoparameter mesh to a selected face. It is most commonly used as an evaluation tool for complex surfaces, but you can also use it to create curves to rebuild faces. Accepting the results by clicking OK creates a separate 3D sketch for each spline. Figure 3.22 shows the original surface and the results of using face curves on a complex lofted surface.

FIGURE 3.22

Using face curves on a complex surface

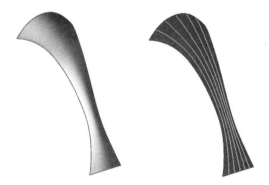

Extend extends a sketch entity up to its next intersection with another sketch entity. This is not to be confused with the Extend for surface entities.

 Split Entities splits a sketch entity into two segments. You can also delete it later to rejoin the entity back into a single segment. Closed loop entities require at least two split points.

 Dynamic Mirror can be used when you preselect a centerline, and Dynamic Mirror is turned on. Any new sketch entity that you draw is automatically mirrored to the other side of the centerline. The ends of the mirror line have hatch marks on them to remind you that you have mirroring turned on.

 Linear Sketch Pattern creates a one- or two-directional pattern of sketch entities. You can define spacing and angles. Figure 3.23 shows the interface and the results of this function.

FIGURE 3.23

The Linear Sketch Pattern interface

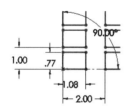

 Circular Sketch Pattern creates a circular pattern of sketch entities.

BEST PRACTICE You should use sketch patterns as little as possible. For much the same reasons that fillet features are preferred over sketch fillets, pattern features are also preferred over sketch patterns. Sketch patterns are not as editable or as flexible as feature patterns. They solve slowly, especially when you pattern a lot of entities. Best practice is to avoid sketch patterns unless there is no alternative.

Make Path is intended to help create machine-design motion in sketches; in particular, cam type motion. Although it is helpful, you do not need to make a block of the cam first. You can then Right-click the block and select Make Path. A tangent relation to a path enables a follower to roll around the entire perimeter.

 Modify Sketch is one of my favorite sketch tools, but it has been falling out of favor in more recent versions of SolidWorks because of the improvement of tools such as Move Sketch. The Modify Sketch feature is flexible and powerful, and enables you to move, rotate, and scale the sketch, as well as mirror about a horizontal or vertical axis or about both axes simultaneously. Figure 3.24 shows the interface, which consists of a dialog box, a special Origin, and a context-sensitive cursor.

FIGURE 3.24

The Modify Sketch interface

Both the left- and right-mouse buttons have special functions, which change when the cursor is moved over the three knots on the special Origin. The right-mouse button allows you to mirror or rotate the sketch, and the left mouse button, or LMB, allows you to move the Origin or move the sketch.

This function has some limitations when you use it with sketches that have external relations. Certain functions may be disabled, or a warning message may appear, saying that you need to remove external relations to get a particular function to work correctly.

 No Solve Move enables the moving of sketch entities without solving any relations in the sketch. If you select this option and you move an entity with relations that would otherwise not allow it to move (such as a collinear relation), then you are prompted with a choice to either delete the existing relation and continue or to copy the entity without the relation. As mentioned earlier, be careful with the icon for this function, since it looks almost identical to the Construction Geometry icon, especially as printed here in gray scale.

 Sketch Picture is a picture that is placed in the sketch, lies on the sketch plane, and is listed in the FeatureManager indented under the sketch. The sketch picture may be suppressed independently from the rest of the sketch, and when the sketch is hidden, the picture is not visible. You can easily move, resize, and rotate sketch pictures, as well as apply a transparent background color to them. Sketch Pictures are usually used for tracing over or as a planar decal without the need for PhotoWorks. Figure 3.25 shows the controls for manipulating the Sketch Picture feature.

FIGURE 3.25

The Sketch Picture interface

 Equation Driven Curve is a sketch spline driven by an equation, as shown in Figure 3.26. This sketch entity type was added in SolidWorks 2009. You only need to put the right-hand side of the equation into the box; for example, in an equation such as $y = x^2+4*x$, you would only enter the x^2+4*x portion, of course making sure to use standard notation for all math operators. The x1 and x2 values are the low and high limits of the value set, and the Transform simply moves the function from the 0,0 origin to the location where you need it to go.

  Straight Slot and Curved Slot draw slots of a given width and length with full rounds on the ends. All of the slot sketch entities can be seen in the PropertyManager shown in Figure 3.27. If you need to draw a composite slot, or a slot with multiple entities, you will need to use the bi-directional sketch offset with capped ends mentioned earlier.

The Dimensions/Relations toolbar

The Dimensions/Relations toolbar has a few tools that you have already seen, but as the name suggests, it also contains tools that will either help you to create or investigate dimensions and sketch relations. Figure 3.28 shows the default toolbar, but in the following pages, you look at all of the available tools that are available through Tools ➪ Customize ➪ Commands ➪ Dimensions/Relations.

FIGURE 3.26

Equation Driven Curve PropertyManager

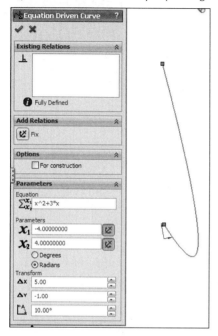

FIGURE 3.27

PropertyManager for the slot sketch entities

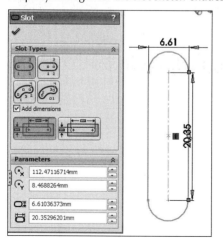

FIGURE 3.28

The Dimensions/Relations toolbar

- Smart Dimension. Gives the user the ability to dimension the sketch entity as you sketch.

- Horizontal Dimension. Applies a dimension to a sketch entity that drives the horizontal distance between the endpoints.

- Vertical Dimension. Works like a horizontal dimension but vertically.

- Baseline Dimensions. Creates dimensions only in *drawing* documents. Baseline Dimensions are different from most of the dimension tools that you find on the Dimensions/Relations toolbar in that they can create driven dimensions on view geometry, or driving dimensions on sketch geometry in a drawing, but cannot be used on sketch geometry in parts. Baseline Dimensions start from a single reference; then as you select additional references, additional dimensions are stacked (see Figure 3.29).

FIGURE 3.29

Baseline Dimensions on a drawing

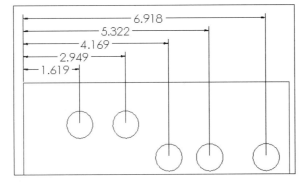

- Ordinate Dimensions. Driving dimensions where a set of ordinate dimensions originate from a common zero point. To use these dimensions, simply click a zero location, place the zero dimension, and then click additional points. The dimensions are placed and are automatically aligned to the rest of the dimensions.

If a line is *not* selected as the zero reference entity, the Ordinate Dimension feature defaults to a Horizontal Ordinate.

You can remove Ordinate Dimensions from the common alignment by Right-clicking the dimension and selecting Break Alignment. Ordinate Dimensions will jog automatically if SolidWorks senses that the dimensions are getting too close to one another. You can also jog them manually. After you create the Ordinate Dimension set, you can add to it by accessing the Add to Ordinate command through the right-mouse button menu. All of these options for Ordinate Dimensions are shown in Figure 3.30.

FIGURE 3.30

Options for Ordinate Dimensions

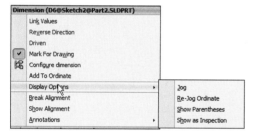

Not all of the listed options are available in the model sketch environment; some are available only in drawings.

 Horizontal and Vertical Ordinate Dimensions have the same function as the regular Ordinate Dimensions, except that they only drive horizontal and vertical dimensions, respectively.

 Chamfer Dimension is another type of dimension that is only driven and only applied in drawing documents. It works by first selecting the chamfered edge and then selecting the angle reference edge. It produces dimensions like the one shown in Figure 3.31.

 Automatic Relations toggles to enable or disable the automatic creation of sketch relations while sketching. This toggle is also available through Tools ➪ Sketch Settings ➪ Automatic Relations. Automatic relations help you to create intelligent sketches with less manual intervention. Although using them takes a little practice, it is well worth the effort.

As with any automatic function, there are times when automatic relations will do things that you do not expect or want. While you are sketching, it is recommended that you watch the cursor and the relations that it automatically applies.

FIGURE 3.31

Applying a chamfer dimension

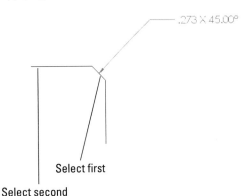

While sketching, symbols appear on the cursor to show that a relation will automatically be created. These symbols have a yellow background, and will apply horizontal, vertical, coincident, tangent, parallel, and perpendicular relations. Figure 3.32 shows two situations where automatic relations are applied—a horizontal and a tangent relation.

FIGURE 3.32

Some automatic relations that appear on the cursor

> **NOTE** Although Scan Equal shows up in the list of available tools, it never becomes active, and its functionality has been absorbed into the Fully Define Sketch tool.

Inferencing in Sketch

Although Inferencing and Automatic Relations are often confused, even by experienced SolidWorks users, these functions are not the same. *Inferencing* refers to the blue dotted lines that display in Sketch mode when the cursor aligns with endpoints, centerpoints, or the Origin. Inferencing does not create sketch relations, with one exception. If the cursor is aligned to one side of the endpoint of another line, and you draw a horizontal line, then an automatic Coincident relation is applied between the line and the endpoint. This also holds true if the cursor starts above or below the point and you draw a vertical line.

When the cursor displays a small sketch relation symbol with a yellow background, this means that an automatic relation is going to be applied. If the relation symbol has a white background, the relation is inferenced, but not applied as an actual sketch relation. The symbols with the blue (the color may also be green in SolidWorks 2008 or later) background are relations that have been applied to existing sketch entities. The symbols look the same, regardless of background color. Be aware that differences in versions and differences in color schemes can cause these colors to be different on your system.

The following are the symbols for the various inferences, automatic relation cursors, and applied sketch relations shown in Table 3.1. The difference between the three types is simply the background colors: white, yellow, and blue, respectively.

TABLE 3.1

Symbols

	Along X		Along Y		Along Z
	At Intersection of Two Faces		Coincident		Collinear
	Concentric		Coradial		Equal
	Equal Curvature		Fix		Horizontal
	Intersection		Midpoint		Offset
	On Edge		On Surface		Parallel
	Perpendicular		Pierce		Symmetric
	Tangent		Vertical		Display/Delete Relations
	Fully Define Sketch				

The Fully Define Sketch interface uses sketch relations and dimensions to fully define the active sketch. It allows you to select what types of sketch relations and dimensions will be used to do this. Figure 3.33 shows the Fully Define Sketch interface. Be careful of this icon because it looks almost identical to the Sketch icon.

FIGURE 3.33

The Fully Define Sketch interface

If you are familiar with older versions, the Fully Define Sketch function was formerly called Auto Dimension, and has absorbed the functionality of Scan Equal and Add Relations. This function is very useful when used with imported data. If you do not like the automatic dimensioning scheme, you can at least take advantage of the automatic sketch relations.

BEST PRACTICE   While the Fully Define Sketch function can clearly save you a lot of time dimensioning parts on a drawing, it does not necessarily use the best dimensioning practice for manufacturing drawings. This tool is best used in situations when baseline and ordinate dimensions are appropriate.

Exploring Sketch Settings

In addition to sketch tools, another important aspect of controlling sketches is sketch settings. Sketch settings are found in two different locations. The first location is at Tools ⇨ Options ⇨ Sketch. In this chapter, I cover the settings found at the second location, Tools ⇨ Sketch Settings. These settings mainly affect sketch relations.

CROSS-REF   The sketch settings at Tools ⇨ Options ⇨ Sketch are discussed in detail in Appendix B. They mainly affect sketch display issues, and have some overlap with Tools ⇨ Sketch Settings. Automatic Relations is covered in depth in the Dimensions/Relations toolbar section.

Automatic Solve is turned on by default. As you make changes to a sketch by adding relations or changing dimensions, SolidWorks automatically and immediately updates the sketch to reflect the changes. When the Automatic Solve setting is turned off, these changes are deferred until you exit the sketch or turn the Automatic Solve setting back on. The setting can be useful to prevent intermediate solutions (for example, when half of the changes are made) that may cause problems with the sketch, and when you are confident that the outcome will be correct. It is a rarely used option, and you could probably exist just fine without even knowing this option was there at all.

If you import a large drawing from the DXF or DWG formats, these drawings import as sketch entities into either a SolidWorks sketch or a drawing. SolidWorks may automatically turn off the Automatic Solve setting for performance (speed) reasons on files of this type.

Enable Snapping is turned on by default. It enables the cursor to snap to the endpoints of existing sketch entities to help you make cleaner sketches. When you turn this setting off, Automatic Relations is also disabled (although the icon for the setting remains depressed, Automatic Relations are not created). Holding down the Ctrl key while sketching disables snapping. Holding down the Ctrl key while dragging sketch entities will function like copying sketch geometry. No Solve Move is discussed in the Sketch toolbar section.

Detach Segment on Drag is turned off by default. When you turn this setting on, the Detach Segment on Drag feature enables you to pull a single sketch element away from a chain of elements. For example, if you have a rectangle and you want to detach one of the lines from the rest of the rectangle, without using this setting, you would have to draw extra geometry and then trim and delete lines in order to release the endpoints.

BEST PRACTICE It is recommended that you leave this setting off. Turn it on only when you need it, and then immediately turn it off again. This setting can be hazardous for everyday use, because it enables you to simply drag sketch elements that may be otherwise fully defined.

Override Dims on Drag is off by default. When you turn this setting on, it enables you to drag fully defined sketch geometry, and the dimensions will update to match the dragged size. This is another setting that you should use sparingly. It can be useful for doing concept work, but you should leave it off when working with production data for obvious reasons.

NOTE Combining Override Dims on Drag with Instant3D (formerly Move/Size Features) can be very handy for concept work.

Using Sketch Blocks

Sketch blocks are collections of sketch entities that can be treated as a single entity. You can use sketch blocks in parts, assemblies, and drawings. To create a sketch block, select a group of sketch entities and click the Make Block button on the Blocks toolbar, or select Tools ⇨ Blocks ⇨ Make. Preselection is not necessary, you can also select the entities after you invoke the command.

Blocks may be internal to a particular document, or they may be saved as an external file. The externally saved block may be linked to each document where it is used, so that if the block is changed, it updates in the documents where it is used.

You can use blocks in conjunction with the Make Path function mentioned earlier in this chapter to create functional layouts for mechanisms. You can also use blocks in an assembly to build parts in-context. Refer to Chapter 12 for a more in-depth examination of the assemblies aspects of blocks in SolidWorks.

The following is a description of the various tools that are available on the Blocks toolbar:

- **Make Block.** Creates a sketch block from selected sketch entities. You can position a manipulator to denote the insertion point for the block. Blocks may attach at any entity endpoint, but the insertion point follows the cursor.

- **Edit Block.** Enables you to edit an existing block as if it were a regular sketch.

- **Insert Block.** Allows you to select from a list of open blocks or browse to a location where blocks are stored. You can edit the insertion point by using the Edit Block function.

- **Add/Remove.** Allows you to add or remove sketch entities from the block without deleting them from the sketch while editing a block.

- **Rebuild Block.** Allows changes to a block to be reflected in any external relations without exiting the block. For example, if you have a block in a sketch, and a sketch line is coincident to one of the endpoints in the block, you may edit the block such that the referenced endpoint moves. As a result, the line in the sketch will not move until you either exit the block or use the Rebuild Block function.

- **Save Block/Save Sketch As Block.** Saves a selected block to an external file (with the *.sldblk extension), or saves the selected sketch as a block.

- **Explode Block.** Removes all of the sketch entities from a block and brings them into the current sketch.

- **Belt/Chain.** Enables you to make a belt or chain around a set of pulleys. Each pulley must be a block. After activating the command (by right-clicking on a sketch or block), you can select each pulley and use the arrow on the pulley to switch the side of the pulley to which the belt goes. You can also compensate for the thickness of the belt (this is important when both sides of the belt are in contact with pulleys), and drive the pulley arrangement using the length of the belt. Figure 3.34 shows the Belt/Chain dialog box.

FIGURE 3.34

The Belt/Chain dialog box

Tutorial: Learning to Use Sketch Relations

While it is useful to read through the definitions and functions of all of the sketch entities, tools, and relations, using your mouse to create is what this is all about. This tutorial makes sure that you get to know all of the major functions in SolidWorks sketches. Almost every part that you build will start with a sketch, so this is a skill worth mastering. Follow these steps to learn about sketch relations:

1. **Open a new part using a template that you set up in the Template tutorial from Chapter 1.** If you do not have this template, there is one provided for you on the CD-ROM named `BibleInchTemplate.prtdot`. Copy it to your templates folder and use it to create a new part. You may also use a SolidWorks default template.

2. **Select the Front plane in the FeatureManager, and click the Sketch button on the Sketch toolbar.** Click the Line tool from the Sketch toolbar.

3. Move the cursor near the Origin; the yellow Coincident symbol appears.

4. **Draw a line horizontal from the Origin.** Remember that there are two ways to sketch the line: Click-Click or Click-Drag. Make sure that the line snaps to the horizontal and that there is a yellow Horizontal relation symbol. The PropertyManager for the line should show that the line has a Horizontal relation. Also notice that the line is black, but the free endpoint is blue (after you hit Esc twice to clear the tool, then clear the selection). This means that the line is fully defined except for its length. You can test this by dragging the blue endpoint.

5. **Click the Smart Dimension tool on the Sketch toolbar, use it to click the line that you just drew, and place the dimension.** If you are prompted for a dimension, type **1.000.** If not, then double-click the dimension; the Modify dialog box appears, enabling you to change the dimension. The setting to prompt for a dimension is found at Tools ⇨ Options ⇨ General, Input Dimension Value.

6. **Draw two more lines to create a right triangle to look like Figure 3.35.** If the sketch relations symbols do not show in the display, turn them on by clicking View ⇨ Sketch Relations. You may want to set up a hotkey for this, because having sketch relations is useful, but often gets in the way. Note that the sketch relation symbols may also be green, depending on how your software is installed.

FIGURE 3.35

Draw a right triangle.

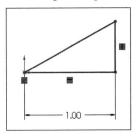

---

7. **Drag the blue endpoint of the triangle.** Dragging endpoints is the most direct way to change the geometry. Dragging the line directly may also work, but this sometimes produces odd results. The sketch leaves a ghost when dragging so that you can see where you started. Note that the setting for leaving a ghost when dragging a sketch is found at Tools ⇨ Options ⇨ Sketch, Ghost Image On Drag.

8. **Click the Smart Dimension tool, and then click the horizontal line and the angled line.** This produces an angle dimension. Place the angle dimension and give it a value of 30°.

9. **Click the Sketch Fillet tool, set the radius value to 0.10 inches, and click each of the three endpoints.** Where the 1.000-inch dimension connects to the sketch, SolidWorks has created *virtual sharps*. Figure 3.36 shows the sketch at this point. You may now want to turn off the Sketch Relations display because the screen is getting pretty busy. You can find this setting at View ⇨ Sketch Relations.

FIGURE 3.36

The resulting sketch after you perform Step 9

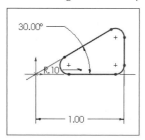

10. **Draw a line starting from the midpoint of the angled line.** The midpoint should highlight when you move the cursor close to it. Draw the line perpendicular to the angled line. A dotted yellow line appears, showing where the perpendicular lies. When you follow this line, the yellow perpendicular symbol appears on the cursor. Make this line approximately .25 inches long. Feedback on the cursor also shows the length of the line as you draw it.

11. **Draw two more lines ending at the endpoint of the sketch fillet, as shown in Figure 3.37.** Use the Inferencing lines to line up the second angled line with the end of the arc.

12. **Click the Trim tool from the Sketch toolbar.** Make sure that the Trim option is set to Closest. Click the angled line of the triangle between the two lines sketched in Step 11. This trims out that section, and makes the sketch a single closed loop. A warning may appear because you have a Midpoint relation to the line being trimmed, and you no longer want this relation, but you want the lines to intersect at their endpoints. Select Yes at the prompt.

FIGURE 3.37

The resulting sketch after you perform Step 11

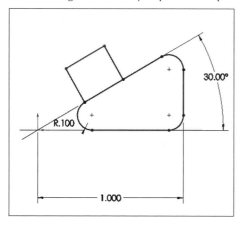

13. **Click the Smart Dimension tool.** Use it to create aligned dimensions on the short line (.25 inches) and one of the long lines (.125 inches). You may now want to reorganize some of the dimensions if the display is becoming crowded.

14. **At this point, two of the lines should be blue, but it may not be clear why they are not defined.** Select one of the blue lines and drag it. Notice that what changes is the arc nearest the Origin. This changes in a way that is not useful for this part. To lock this line where it needs to be, select the blue line nearest the Origin and the centerpoint of the arc nearest the Origin, and give them a Coincident relation in the PropertyManager. The result is a fully defined sketch, as shown in Figure 3.38.

15. **Save the part with the name** `Sketch Relations Tutorial.sldprt`. Close the part.

FIGURE 3.38

The resulting sketch after you perform Step 14

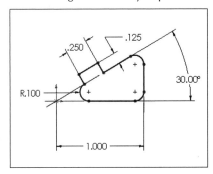

Tutorial: Using Blocks and Belts

Sometimes I am amazed at the things that can be done in SolidWorks, even with fairly simple tools. This is one of those times. If you design machines, then this tutorial will have some extra meaning for you. If you do not design machines, then these are still valuable tools to have in your toolbox ready to use in various situations. Follow these steps to learn about using Blocks and Belts.

1. **Open a new part with inches as the units.**

2. **Draw a sketch on the Front plane as shown in Figure 3.39, with four lines connected to the Origin.** Exit the sketch and rename it Layout Sketch, either by clicking twice on the name of the feature in the FeatureManager or by selecting it and pressing F2.

3. **Open a second sketch on the Front plane, and draw a circle centered on the Origin with a 6-inch diameter.**

FIGURE 3.39

The layout sketch

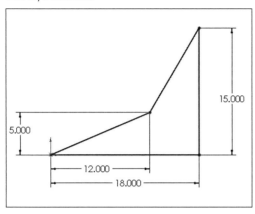

4. Inside the circle, draw a Centerpoint rectangle centered on the Origin.

5. Select two adjacent sides of the rectangle and make an Equal sketch relation between them (this makes the rectangle into a square).

ON the CD-ROM The CD-ROM for Chapter 2 contains a macro that automatically draws a rectangle that is centered on the Origin.

6. **Click the Smart Dimension tool, and apply a 1.000-inch dimension to one side of the square.** Turn off the Smart Dimension tool by clicking it again on the toolbar or pressing Esc.

7. **If the Blocks toolbar is not active, then activate it and select Make Block.** You can also access this command through Tools ➪ Block ➪ Make.

8. **Window select the circle and the square by clicking and dragging a box that includes all of the items in the sketch.** The PropertyManager to the left displays a circle and five lines that are to be made into a block.

9. **Expand the Insertion Point panel in the PropertyManager.** This causes a blue manipulator Origin to appear in the graphics window. Click this Origin and drag it onto the center of the circle. Then click the green check mark icon to exit the Make Block dialog box. This is shown in Figure 3.40.

10. **The items in the block now turn gray.** Click anywhere on the block and drag it out of the way. Then drag the center of the circle and drop it on the part Origin.

11. **Click the Insert Block tool on the Blocks toolbar.** Place the block on the opposite sharp corner of the layout sketch.

FIGURE 3.40

Creating a block

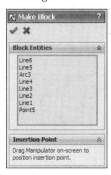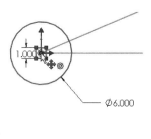

12. **Create another block that is identical to the first one, except that it has a diameter of 3 inches instead of 6 inches.** You can do this by selecting the first block, clicking Edit Block from the toolbar, and copying (window select and Ctrl+C). Then exit the Edit Block and paste (Ctrl+V) in the regular sketch. Make sure to also change the insertion point for this second block to the center of the circle.

13. **Insert a second instance of this second block, and make sure that both of them have the center of the circle at the two remaining intersection points of the four-sided shape of the layout sketch.** At this point, your sketch should look like Figure 3.41.

FIGURE 3.41

Block placement

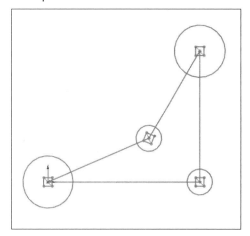

14. **Click the Belt/Chain tool on the Blocks toolbar.** Select the blocks in counterclockwise order, starting at the Origin. On the last pulley, you will have to click the arrow to get the belt to go the correct way around the pulley.

15. **Make sure that the Engage Belt option is selected.** This allows you to make the pulleys move in the same way that they would in a real belt-driven mechanism.

16. **Click the Use Belt Thickness option, and assign .25 inches for the thickness.** The belt should be offset from the pulleys.

17. **Click the green check mark icon.**

18. **Click and drag one of the corners of the square in a pulley.** All of the pulleys should turn as if this were a real mechanism. The ratios are also observed because the small pulleys rotate faster than the large ones.

19. **Save this part as** `Blocks and Belts Tutorial.sldprt`. **Exit the part.**

Summary

Sketching in SolidWorks is something that you will do almost every time you open the software. There are a lot of automated functions available that you can allow to do much of the work for you. You also have a lot of control to make changes manually. Remember that the best way to create most sketches is to make use of automatic relations when you can, sketch the approximate shape that you want to make, then either drag it to pick up automatic relations, add dimensions, or add relations manually.

The options for creating intelligent relationships that establish your design intent, as well as SolidWorks' capabilities in laying out mechanisms, is only limited by your imagination. The more familiar you become with the tools in your toolbox, the more of a craftsman you can become with this software.

Chapter 4

Creating Simple Parts, Assemblies, and Drawings

W hen you begin to build a model in SolidWorks, there are a few things to consider before you start. If you spend some time considering what you are doing first, then it will benefit you later in the process. Good modeling practice is based on robust design intent, which just means that you build a part that can adapt easily to changes. This section begins with questions that you need to ask.

Beginning to create simple parts will help you understand techniques used in more complex modeling projects. Learning on simple tools and then expanding your skills helps you to understand best practice issues, which makes you a better contributor to a team environment.

Discovering Design Intent

By asking questions about the part's function before you start modeling or designing, you can create a model that will be easier to edit, easier to properly place into an assembly, easier to detail in drawings, and easier for other SolidWorks users to understand when someone else has to work on your models. Sometimes you will be able to find answers for the questions, and other times not. Whether you are doing the modeling for someone else, or doing the design and modeling for yourself may make a difference in how you approach the modeling task.

The purpose of these questions is to help you establish design intent. The term *design intent* is a statement of how the part functions and how the model reacts to modeling changes.

It may help if you try to put the design intent into words to help you focus on what is important in the design. An example of a statement of design intent might be: "This part is symmetric about two planes, is used to support a 1.00" diameter shaft with a constant downward load of 150 pounds using a bronze bushing, and is bolted to a plate below it." This does not give you enough information to design the part, but it does give you information about two surfaces that are important (a hole for the bushing and the bottom that touches the mounting plate), as well as some general size and load requirements. The following questions can help you develop the design intent for your own projects.

Is the part symmetrical?

Symmetry is an important aspect of design intent. Taking advantage of symmetry can significantly reduce the time needed to model the part. Symmetry can exist on several levels:

- Sketch symmetry
- Individual feature symmetry
- Whole-part symmetry
- Axial symmetry (a revolved part)
- "Almost" symmetry (the whole part is symmetrical, except for a few features)
- Left and right symmetrical versions of the part
- The assembly may be symmetrical

What are the primary or functional features?

This is probably the most important question. Primary or functional features include how the part mounts or connects to other parts, motion that it needs to accommodate, and additional structure to support loads.

Often it is a good idea to create a special sketch as the first feature in the part that lays out the functional features. This could be as simple as a straight line to denote the bottom and a circle to represent the position and size of a mating part, or as complex as full outlines of parts and features from all three standard planes. This technique is called a *layout sketch*, and it is an important technique in both simple and complex parts. You can use layout sketches for anything from simply drawing a size-reference bounding box to creating the one point of reference for all sketched features in the part. You can use multiple layout sketches if a single sketch on one plane is not sufficient.

In what ways is the part likely to change?

When the marketing department gets out of their meeting at 4:45 pm, what changes do you need to be prepared for so that you can still be out the door by 5:00 pm? No one expects you to be able to tell the future, but you do need to model in such a way that your model easily adapts to future changes. As you gain experience with the software, and you keep this idea in mind, then you will develop some instincts for the type of modeling that you do.

What is the manufacturing method?

Modeling for the casting process is very different from modeling for the machining process. When possible, the process should be evident in your modeling. There are times when you will not know which process will be used to create the part when you start to create a model. If you are simply making an initial concept model, then you may not need to be concerned about the process. In these cases, it may or may not be possible to reuse your initial data if you need to make a detailed cast part from your non-process-specific model. Decisions like this are usually based on available time, how many changes need to be made, and a determination of the risk of making the changes versus not making the changes, as well as which decision will cost you the most time in the long run.

Sometimes it makes sense to allow someone else to add the manufacturing details. A decision like this depends on your role in the organization, and your experience with the process compared with that of other people downstream in the manufacturing process. For example, if you are not familiar with the Nitrogen Gas Assist process for molding polypropylene, and you are modeling a part to be made in that process, you might consider either soliciting the help of a tooling engineer or passing the work on to someone else to add engineering detail.

BEST PRACTICE As engineers, we are typically perfectionists. However, there always needs to be a balance between perfection and economy. Achieving both simultaneously is truly a rare event. Still, you should be aware that problems left by the designer for other downstream applications to solve (such as machining, mold making, and assembly) also have an impact on the time and cost of the project.

The best practice in this case is a judgment call. When faced with assembling a model sloppily or remodeling it perfectly, I usually choose to remodel because doing it the second time is always faster. Also, if additional changes are required, then you do not need to struggle with the sloppily assembled model. You can easily copy sketches from one part to another, while keeping the old part open as you build the new part. As a result, you may be surprised how quickly things go.

Will there be secondary operations?

When working with any manufacturing process, some secondary processes are generally required. For example, if you have a cast part, then you may need to machine the rough surface to create a flat face in some areas. You may also need to ream or tap holes. In plastic parts, you may need to press in threaded inserts.

There are some special tools in SolidWorks that you can use to document secondary operations:

- A technique called *Configurations* in SolidWorks allows you to create different versions of a part. For example, one configuration may have the features for the secondary operations suppressed (turned off), and showing just the part as cast, while the other configuration shows the part as machined.

CROSS-REF Chapter 10 discusses configurations and feature suppression in depth.

■ A technique called *Insert Part* allows you to use one SolidWorks part as the starting point for a second part. For example, the as-cast part has all of the features to make the part, but it is inserted as the first feature in the as-machined part, which adds the cuts required by the machining process.

Will there be other versions?

Sometimes there are size-based versions of parts that have to be created or versions based on additional features. If these are fairly simple, they can also be handled with configurations, but you need to plan this flexibility in advance.

Creating a Simple Part

In this section, I'll show you how to build the simple part shown in Figure 4.1. While the shape is simple, the techniques used and discussed here are applicable to a wide variety of real-world parts.

FIGURE 4.1

A simple machined part

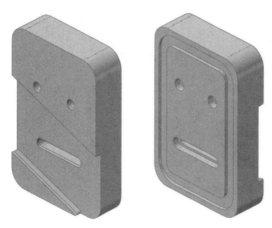

Where to start?

When you start creating a new part from a template and are confronted with the blank screen with only the part Origin showing, the question of where you should begin first comes to mind. Of course, it depends on the shape and function of your part, but for the time being, you can assume that you are working with the rectangular part (refer to Figure 4.1).

The first feature that you create should be positioned relative to the Origin. Whether there is a corner of a rectangle that is coincident to the Origin, the rectangle is centered on the Origin, or dimensions are used to stand the rectangle off from the Origin at some distance, you need to lock the first feature to the Origin.

When working with a simple part, the entire part can be described as rectangular or cylindrical. In these cases, it is easy to know where to start: you simply draw a rectangle or a circle, respectively. On complex parts, it may not be obvious where to start, and the overall part cannot be said to have any simple shape. In cases like these, it may be best to select *the* (or *a*) prominent feature, mounting location, functional shape, or focus of the mechanism. For example, if you were to design an automobile, what would you designate as the 0,0,0 Origin? The ground may be a reasonable location, or the plane of the centers of the wheels. Much of the automotive industry uses the center of the end of the crankshaft in the engine as the assembly Origin. That may seem arbitrary, but as long as everyone working on the vehicle agrees, it is as good a location as any. With that in mind, it seems logical to start the rectangular part by sketching a rectangle. Select the Top plane, and sketch a rectangle centered on the part Origin.

Symmetry

The next decision is about part symmetry. This part is not completely symmetrical, and so modeling a quarter of it and mirroring the entire model twice is not going to be the most effective technique. Instead, you should build the complete part around the Origin, and mirror individual features as appropriate. To start with this type of symmetry, you need to sketch a rectangle centered on the Origin. The centered rectangle is something that you will create frequently. In SolidWorks versions prior to 2008, there was no Centerpoint Rectangle sketch entity; you had to draw a rectangle and manually center it with construction geometry.

Figure 4.2 shows two common techniques for centering a rectangle on the Origin when you have to do it manually. You can use the sketch relation symbols to identify the relations that have been applied to this sketch.

FIGURE 4.2

Centered rectangle on the Origin

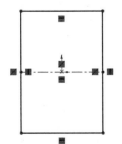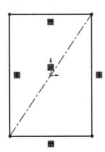

 To make a rectangle work like a square, use an Equal sketch relation on two adjacent sides. This only requires a single dimension to drive the size of the square.

Beginning with the rectangle that you sketched in the previous section, apply one horizontal dimension (4.00 inches) and one vertical dimension (6.00 inches). The sketch is fully defined at this point because both the size and position of the rectangle have been established.

BEST PRACTICE If you are dimensioning a horizontal line, the best way to do it is to simply select the line and place the dimension. Selecting the line endpoints can also work, but selecting the vertical lines on either side of the horizontal lines is not as robust. The problem is that if you use this third method, deleting either of the vertical lines causes the dimension to also be deleted. In the first two dimensioning methods, dimensions are not deleted unless you remove one of the endpoints, which requires deleting two lines: the horizontal line and one of the vertical lines.

Make it solid

Next, click Extrude from the Features toolbar, or click Insert ➪ Boss/Base ➪ Extruded. In the Direction 1 panel, select Mid Plane as the end condition. SolidWorks takes the distance that you entered and extrudes it symmetrically about the sketch plane. Enter **1.00 inch** as the distance.

Extrude Feature Options

The Extrude feature is one of the staples of SolidWorks modeling. Depending on the type of modeling that you do, the Extrude feature may be one of your main tools.

The Extrude interface

From

The From panel establishes where the Extrude feature starts. By default, SolidWorks extrudes from the sketch plane. Other available options are:

- **Surface/Face/Plane.** The extrude begins from a surface body, a face of a solid, or a reference plane.

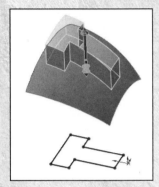

Extruding from a surface

CROSS-REF Surface features are discussed in detail in Chapter 27.

- **Vertex.** The distance from the sketch plane to the selected vertex is treated as an offset distance.
- **Offset.** You can enter an explicit offset distance, and you can also change the direction of the offset.

Direction 1 and Direction 2

Direction 1 and Direction 2 are always separated by 180 degrees. Direction 2 becomes inactive if you select Mid Plane for the end condition of Direction 1. The arrows that display in the graphics window show a single arrow for Direction 1 and a double arrow for Direction 2. For the Blind end condition, which is described next, dragging the arrows determines the distance of the extrude.

Each of the end conditions is affected by the Reverse Direction toggle. This toggle simply changes the default direction by 180 degrees. You need to be careful when using this feature, particularly when using the Up to end conditions, because if the entity that you are extruding up to is not in the selected direction, then an error results.

Following is a brief description of each of the available end conditions for the Extrude feature:

- **Blind.** Blind in this case means an explicit distance. The term is usually used in conjunction with holes of a specific depth, although here it is associated with a boss rather than a hole.

continued

continued

- **Up to Vertex.** In effect, Up to Vertex works just like the Blind end condition, except that the distance is parametrically controlled by a model vertex or sketch point.

- **Up to Surface.** Up to Surface could probably be better named *Up to Face*, because the end does not necessarily have to be an actual surface feature. This end condition may display a warning if the projection of the sketch onto the selected face extends beyond the boundary of the face. In that case, it is advisable to knit several faces together into a surface body and to use the Up to Body end condition.

- **Offset from Surface.** By default, Offset from Surface extrudes until it reaches a specified distance from a selected surface. There are two methods for determining the type of offset and one to determine direction.

    - The default offset method behaves as if the selected surface were offset radially, so that a surface with a 4-inch radius and a 1-inch offset would give a curvature on the end of the extrude of a 3-inch radius.

    - The second method, called Translate Surface, behaves as if the surface were *moved* by the offset distance.

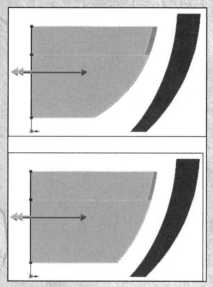

Offset from surface using the default and Translate Surface options

    - Reverse Offset refers to when the offset stops short of the selected face or when it goes past it.

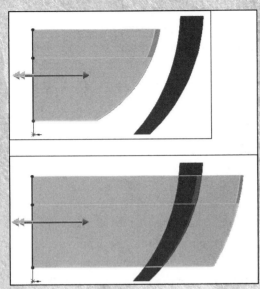

The Reverse Offset option

- **Up to Body.** The Up to Body end condition is very useful in many situations, especially when receiving the error message, "The end face cannot terminate the extrusion," from the Up to Face end condition.

- **Mid Plane.** The Mid Plane end condition eliminates the Direction 2 options and divides the extrude distance equally in both directions, so that if you specify a 1.00-inch Mid Plane, then SolidWorks extrudes .50 inches in one direction and .50 inches in the other direction.

- **Through All.** The Through All end condition is available only when there is already solid geometry existing in the part. When used for an extruded boss (which adds material), it extrudes to the distance of the farthest point of the solid model in a direction perpendicular to the sketch plane. When used for a cut, it simply cuts through everything.

- **Up to Next.** Up to Next extrudes the feature until it runs into a solid face that completely intercepts the entire sketch profile. If a portion of the sketch hangs over the edge of the face, the extrude feature will keep going until it runs into a condition that matches that description, which may be the outer face of the part in the direction of the extrusion.

By default, the Direction of Extrusion is normal to the sketch plane, but you can also select a linear entity such as an edge or axis as the direction. All of the end-condition options are still available when you manually define the Direction of Extrusion as something other than the default.

continued

continued

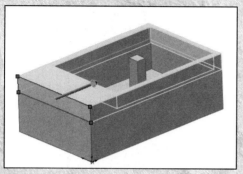

The Up to Next end condition used with a Cut extrude

You can also assign a draft option to an extrusion as it is created, and you can control the draft separately for Direction 1 and Direction 2.

BEST PRACTICE When dealing with molded or cast parts, certain types of features, such as draft, fillets, and shells, are often the targets of users trying to assign best practices. This is partially because using draft, fillets, and shells is very much like playing Rock, Paper, Scissors; you can never really win this game except by luck. Arranging the features in the correct order so that the model is efficient and achieves the desired results is challenging and resistant to definition by rules that apply in most situations. It is usually best to apply draft as a separate feature rather than using it in the definition of the Extrude feature. It is also best to apply draft after most of the modeling is done, but before you apply the cosmetic fillets and before using the shell feature.

Thin Feature

The Thin Feature panel is activated by default when you try to extrude an open loop sketch (a sketch that does not fully enclose an area). The end-condition options remain the same, but what changes is that the feature applies a thickness to the sketch elements, in the manner of a sheet metal, thin-walled plastic part, or a rib. The Thin Feature panel of the Extrude PropertyManager, along with a representative thin feature extrusion.

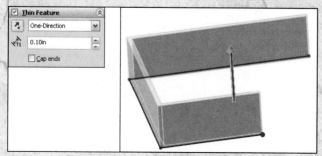

The Thin Feature panel and a thin feature extrusion

The Cap Ends option is available only when you specify a Thin Feature to be created from a closed loop sketch. This creates a hollow, solid body in a single step. You can also use Thin Features with cuts, and they are very useful for creating slots or grooves.

Contour Selection

SolidWorks works best when the sketches are neat and clean, when nothing overlaps, and when there are no extra entities on closed loops. However, when you need to use a sketch that does not meet these criteria, you can use an alternative method called Contour Selection.

Contour Selection enables you to select enclosed areas to for features, regardless of how many normal sketch rules the rest of the sketch violates.

BEST PRACTICE It is my opinion that this feature was introduced into SolidWorks only to keep up with other CAD packages, not because it is a great feature. I do not recommend using Contour Selection on production models. It is useful for creating quick models, but the selection is too unstable for any data that you may want to rely on in the future. The main problem is that if the sketch changes, the selected area may also change, or SolidWorks may lose track of it entirely.

Instant 3D

Starting in Solidworks 2008, SolidWorks introduced functionality called Instant 3D. Instant 3D allows you to drag sketches to create extrusions and to drag model faces to change the size and location of features. The function largely replaces and expands on the older functionality called Move/Size Features. Figure 4.3 shows the arrows added by Instant 3D, which are the handles that you pull on to create a solid from a sketch or edit an existing feature. Notice also that you can make cut features with Instant 3D. In fact, you can change a boss feature into a cut. I'm sure this is a neat sales demo trick, but I'm not aware of any practical application of changing a boss into a cut.

One of the attractive things about Instant 3D is that it allows you to make changes to parts quickly without any consideration for how the part was made. For example, the cylindrical part was made from a series of extrudes, with a hole cut through it with draft on the cut feature. The flat faces can be moved, and the cylindrical faces offset. SolidWorks, behind the scenes, figures out which sketches of which features have to be edited, which saves you time searching the FeatureManager. As you work through more complex parts, you will see how handy this can be at times. You can activate or deactivate Instant 3D using the icon on the Features toolbar.

NOTE When combined with the sketch setting Override Dims On Drag, Instant 3D can be a powerful concepting tool, even on fully dimensioned sketches.

Instant 3D also offers a tool called Live Section. Live Section allows you to section a part with a plane, and you can drag the edges of the section regardless of which features the edges belong to. To activate Live Section, right-click on a plane that intersects the part, and select Live Section.

FIGURE 4.3

Using Instant 3D and Live Section

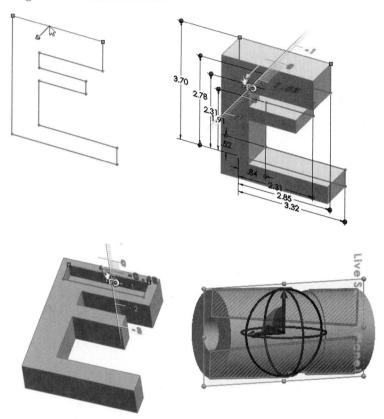

Making the first extrude feature

By centering the sketch on the Origin and extruding by using a Mid Plane end condition, the initial block is built symmetrically about all three standard planes, with the part Origin at the center. In many parts, this is a desirable situation. It enables you to create mirrored features using the standard planes, and also helps you to assemble parts together in an assembly later, when parts must be centered and do not have a hard face-to-face connection with other parts. Figure 4.4 shows the initial feature with the standard planes.

FIGURE 4.4

An initial extruded feature centered on the standard planes

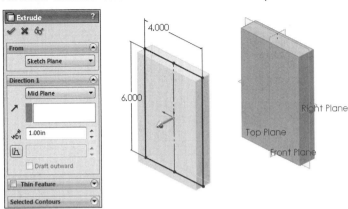

> **NOTE**   When you create a feature from a sketch, SolidWorks hides and absorbs (consumes) the sketch under the feature in the FeatureManager, so you need to click the plus sign next to the feature to see the sketch in the tree. You can right-click the sketch in the FeatureManager to show it in the graphics window.

The next modeling step is to create a groove on the back of the part. How is this feature going to be made? You can use several techniques to create this geometry. List as many techniques as you can think of, whether or not you know how to use them. Later, I will go through which techniques work and which do not.

> **TIP**   One of the secrets to success with SolidWorks, or indeed any tool-based process, is to know several ways to accomplish any given task. By working through this process, you gain problem-solving skills as well as the ability to improvise when the textbook method fails.

Figure 4.5 shows multiple methods for creating the groove. From the left to the right, the methods are a thin feature cut, a swept cut, and a nested loop sketch.

Another potential option could include a large pocket being cut out, with a boss adding material back in the middle. Each one of these is most appropriate in different situations. The thin feature cut is probably the fastest to create, but also probably the least commonly used technique for a feature of this type. Most users tend to use the nested loop option (one loop inside another).

FIGURE 4.5

Methods for creating the groove

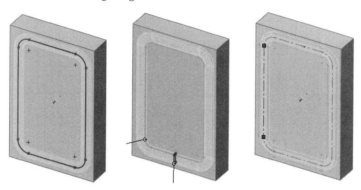

Relative size or direct dimensions?

You can control the size of the rectangle as an offset from the edges of the existing part or you could drive the dimensions of the rectangle independently. Again, this depends on the type of changes you anticipate. If the groove will always depend on the size of the part then the decision is easy. If the groove changes independently from the part, you will need to recreate relations within the sketch to reflect different design intent. To create a groove, you can create a rectangle by offsetting the block shape, and use sketch fillets to round the corners.

Creating the offset

There is one more thing to consider before you create the sketch. What should you use to create the offset: the actual block edges or the original sketch? The answer to this is a Best Practice type issue.

BEST PRACTICE When creating relations that need to adapt to the biggest range of changes to the model, it is best to go as far back in the model history as you can to pick up those relations. In most cases, this means creating relations to sketches rather than to edges of the model. Model edges can be fickle, with the use of fillets, chamfers, and drafts. The technique of relating features to driving layout sketches and reference geometry is called *horizontal modeling*, and it helps you create models that do not fail through the widest range of changes.

This best practice tip will become more significant the first time you create a feature built from model edges, and then make changes that break relations.

To create the offset for your part, follow these steps:

1. **Open a sketch on the face of the part.** To create the offset, expand the Extrude feature by clicking the plus icon next to it in the FeatureManager so that you can see the sketch. Regardless of how it displays here, this sketch appears before the extrude in the part history. RMB (right mouse button) click the sketch and select Show.

TIP You can view individual sketches and reference geometry entities such as planes from the RMB menu. The global settings for the visibility of these items are found in the View menu. You can access these items faster by using the View toolbar, or by linking the commands to hotkeys.

2. **Next, RMB click the sketch in the graphics window and click Select Chain.** This selects any non-construction, end-to-end sketch entities. Click Offset Entities on the Sketch toolbar. Offset to the inside by .400 inches. Apply .500-inch sketch fillets to each of the corners.

3. **Click Extruded Cut on the Feature toolbar.** By default, the extruded cut will cut away everything inside the closed profile of the sketch. Look down the FeatureManager window and click the check box on the top bar of the Thin Feature panel. Make the cut Blind, .100 inch. The Thin Feature type should be set to Mid Plane with a width of .400 inches. The PropertyManager and graphics window should look like Figure 4.6.

FIGURE 4.6

Creating the groove

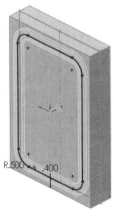

Sketch techniques

Although the next two features could be more easily and efficiently created by using a cut, I will create them as two extrudes. The main point here is to show some useful sketch techniques, rather than optimum efficiency. Begin with the part from the previous section and follow these steps:

1. **Open a new sketch on the large face opposite from the groove.** Draw a rectangle picking up the automatic coincident relation to one corner and then dragging across the part and picking up another coincident to the edge on the opposite side. Figure 4.7 shows the rectangle before and after this edit.

> **TIP** If you want to continue using the recommended best practice mentioned earlier of making relations to sketches rather than model edges, here are a few tips. In some situations (such as the current one) the sketch plane is offset from the sketch that you want to make relations to, and so the best bet is to use the Normal To view. The next obstacle is making sure that automatic relations pick up the sketch rather than the edge, and so you can use the Selection Filter to only select sketch entities.

2. **Delete the Horizontal relation on the line that is not lined up with an edge.** This enables you to drag it to an angle or apply the dimensions shown.

3. **Extrude sketch to a depth of 0.25 inch.**

FIGURE 4.7

Edits to a rectangle

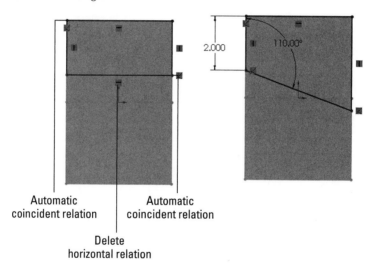

Automatic coincident relation

Automatic coincident relation

Delete horizontal relation

You can delete the Horizontal relation by selecting the icon on the screen. As a reminder, you can show and hide the sketch relation icons from the View menu. You can check to ensure that the relations were created to the sketch rather than the model edges by clicking the Display/Delete Relations button on the Sketch toolbar, clicking the relation icon to check, and expanding the Entities panel in the PropertyManager. The Entities box shows where the relation is attached to, as shown in Figure 4.8. In this case, it is a point in Sketch1. Without custom programming, there is no way to identify items in a sketch by name, but you already know which point it is; you just needed to know whether it was in the sketch or on the model.

FIGURE 4.8

The Display/Delete Relations dialog box

4. **The second sketch trick involves the use of a setting.** Before you try this, go to Tools ➪ Options ➪ Sketch, and ensure that Prompt To Close Sketch is turned on; then click OK to close the dialog box.

5. **Open another new sketch on the same face that was used by the last extrusion.** Draw an angled line across the left and bottom sides of the box, with the dimensions shown in Figure 4.9. In this case, for this technique to work, the endpoints of the line have to be coincident with the model edges rather than the sketch entities.

   This line by itself constitutes an open sketch profile, meaning that it does not enclose an area, and has unshared endpoints. Ordinarily, this results in a Thin Feature, as described earlier, but when the endpoints are coincident with model edges that form a closed loop, and the setting mentioned previously is turned on, SolidWorks automatically gives you the option of using the model edges to close the sketch. This saves several steps when compared to selecting, converting, and trimming manually.

6. **Click the Extrude tool on the Features toolbar.** Answer Yes to the prompt, and double-click the face of the previous extrusion. SolidWorks automatically uses the face that you double-clicked for an Up to Surface end condition. This is a simple way of linking the depths of the two extrusions automatically. Again, this entire operation could have been handled more quickly and efficiently with a cut, but these steps demonstrate an alternative method, which in some situations may be useful.

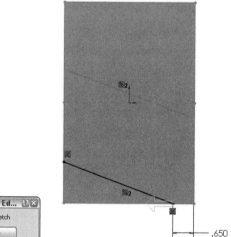

FIGURE 4.9

Using the prompt to close a sketch setting

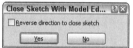

Hole Wizard

The next features that you will apply are a pair of counterbored holes. SolidWorks has a special tool that you can use to create common hole types, called the Hole Wizard. The Hole Wizard helps you to create standard hole types using standard or custom sizes. You can place holes on any face of a 3D model or constrain them to a single 2D plane or face. A single feature created by the Hole Wizard may create a single or multiple holes, and a feature that is not constrained to a single plane can create individual holes originating from multiple faces, non-parallel, and even non-planar faces (holes may go in different directions). All holes in a single feature that you create by using the Hole Wizard must be the same type and size. If you want multiple sizes or types, then you must create multiple features.

To apply counterbored holes to your part, follow these steps:

1. **Select the face that the groove feature was created on, and click the Hole Wizard tool on the Features toolbar.** Then set the hole to Counterbored, set the type to Socket Head Cap Screw, the size to one-quarter, and the end condition to Through All, as shown in Figure 4.10.

2. **Next, click to select the Positions tab at the top of the PropertyManager.** This is where you place the centerpoints of the holes using sketch points. It is often useful to create construction geometry to help line up and place the sketch points.

FIGURE 4.10

The Hole Wizard Hole Specification interface

CAUTION When you select a face to create a 2D Hole Wizard hole, SolidWorks always creates a sketch point at the location where you selected the planar face, and then activates the Point sketch tool. If you click anywhere in the graphics window with the Point tool active, you place additional points, which are used to create additional holes. If those points are off of the solid model, they may cause errors. To exit the Point tool, just press Esc.

3. **Draw two construction lines, horizontally across the part, with Coincident relations to each side.** Select both lines and give them an Equal relation. The point of this step is to evenly space holes across the part without dimensions or equations.

TIP Although several methods exist to make multiple selections, a box or window selection technique may be useful in this situation. If the box is dragged from left to right, then only the items completely within the box are selected. If the box is dragged from right to left, then any item that is at least partially in the box is selected.

TIP SolidWorks displays an error if you try to place a sketch point where there is an existing sketch entity endpoint. If you build construction geometry in a sketch and want to place a sketch point at the end of a sketch entity, then you have to create the sketch point to the side where it does not pick up other incompatible automatic sketch relations, and then drag it onto the endpoint.

4. **Place sketch points at the midpoint of each of the construction lines.** If there is another sketch point other than the two that you want to make into actual holes, then delete the extra points. Dimension one of the lines down from the top of the part, as shown in Figure 4.11. All of the sketch relation icons display for reference. Click OK to accept the feature once you are happy with all of the settings, locations, relations, and dimensions.

FIGURE 4.11

Placing the centerpoints of holes

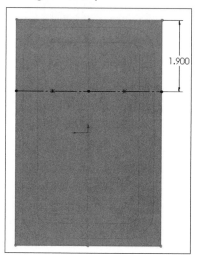

1.900

Cutting a slot

The Hole Wizard does not specifically allow you to cut slots, nor is there a Slot feature. However, SolidWorks has Slot sketch entities or you can use one of the following methods to cut a slot:

- **Use one of the Slot sketch tools.** SolidWorks has straight and arc slot options on the sketch toolbar.

- **Explicitly drawing the slot.** Draw a line, press A to switch to the Tangent Arc tool, draw the tangent arc, press A to switch back to the Line tool, and so on. Although you can press the A key to toggle between the line and arc functions, you can also toggle between a line and a tangent arc by returning the cursor to the line/arc first point.

- **Rectangle and arcs.** Draw a rectangle, place a tangent arc on both ends, and then turn the ends of the rectangle into construction entities.

- **Thin Feature cut.** As you did earlier with the groove, you can also create a Thin Feature slot, although you need to follow additional steps to create rounded ends on it.

- **Offset in Sketch.** By drawing a line, and using the Offset with Bi-directional, Make Base Construction, and Cap Ends settings, it is easy to create a slot from any shape by drawing only the centerline of the slot.

- **Library feature.** A library feature can be stored and can contain either simple sketches or more complex sets of combined features. The library feature is a good option for the counterbored slot used in this example. Library features are discussed in depth in Chapter 19.

Hole Wizard: Using 2D versus 3D Sketches

Hole Wizard holes use either a 2D or a 3D sketch for the placement of the hole centers. You can define the centers by simply placing and dimensioning sketch points. The 3D sketch type is used by default, with the 2D sketch type only being used when you select a planar face *prior* to clicking the Hole Wizard tool.

BEST PRACTICE I want to emphasize the importance of preselecting a flat face before starting the Hole Wizard. If you do not intend to put holes in different directions or on different levels, you should get in the habit of *always* preselecting a flat face before starting the Hole Wizard.

Because the 3D placement of holes seems so much more flexible, why would anyone want to use the 2D placement method? 3D sketches have several limitations with respect to dimensioning and sketch relations. Recent releases of SolidWorks have added relations such as Midpoint and Equal to 3D sketches, which are an improvement over previous versions, but still do not make the 3D sketch as usable as a 2D sketch in the end.

CROSS-REF Three-dimensional sketches are discussed in Chapters 17 and 31. Chapter 17 also gives a more detailed description of the Hole Wizard. Chapter 22 has additional information on the display of threads.

The following image shows a part with various types of holes created by the Hole Wizard, including counterbored, countersunk, drilled, tapped, and pipe-tapped holes. The part is shown in section view for clarity; however, the drilled hole is not shown in the figure.

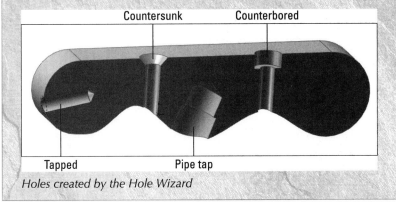

Holes created by the Hole Wizard

To cut slots in your part, follow these steps:

1. **In this case, use the Straight Slot option.** Slots are easiest to create with the click-click method rather than click-drag. Click near where you want the center of one end of the slot. Click again for the center of the other end; then click a third time for the width/end radius. The Slot PropertyManager is shown in Figure 4.12.

NOTE Using the Add Dimensions option in the Slot PropertyManager can help you size the slot more quickly. This does not require the Enable On Screen Numeric Input option to be turned on.

2. **From this sketch, create an extruded cut that extrudes up to the surface of the counterbore in the holes.** The through hole for the counterbored slot is also a slot, and so you can use the same technique.

FIGURE 4.12

Creating a slot

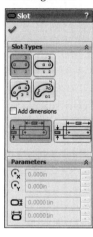
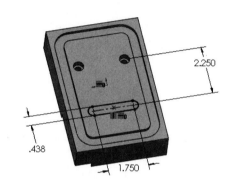

3. **Open a sketch on the bottom of the previous slot, and draw a straight slot.** You can create a cut using the Through All end condition.

TIP Picking up relations automatically may seem difficult at first, but with some practice, it becomes second nature. When trying to find the center of an arc, the centerpoint is usually displayed and is easy to select. However, when making a relation to an edge, the centerpoint does not display by default. To display it, hold the cursor over the arc edge for a few seconds; a marker that resembles a plus sign inside a circle will show you where the center is, thus allowing you to select it with a sketch tool and pick up the automatic relations.

In Figure 4.13, the first centerpoint has already been referenced, and the cursor is trying to find the centerpoint of the other end of the slot.

Applying automatic relations to a circular edge

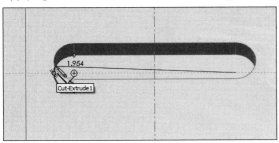

Fillets and chamfers

As mentioned earlier, it is considered a best practice to avoid using sketch fillets when possible, using feature fillets instead. Another best practice guideline is to put fillets at the bottom of the design tree, or at least after all of the functional features. You should not dimension sketches to model edges created by fillets unless there are no better methods available. There are too many ways, and reasons, to change sketches to make other features, especially important features, dependent on them. Several chapters could be written just about fillet types, techniques, and strategies in SolidWorks. Chapter 7 deals with more complex fillet types.

BEST PRACTICE Do not dimension sketches to model edges that are created by fillets. While the previous best practice about relations to sketch entities instead of model edges was a mild warning, you must heed this one more carefully.

To add fillets and chamfers to your part, follow these steps:

1. **Initiate a Fillet feature, and select the four short edges on the part.** Set the radius value to .600 inches. Click OK to accept the Fillet feature.

TIP When selecting edges around a four-sided part, the first three edges are usually visible and the fourth edge is not. You can select invisible edges by expanding the Fillet Options panel of the Fillet PropertyManager, and selecting the Select Through Faces option. When you have a complex part with a lot of hidden edges, this setting can be bothersome, but in simple cases like this, it is useful. Figure 4.14 shows this option in action.

2. **Apply chamfers to the edges of the angled slot through the part, as indicated in Figure 4.15.** Make the chamfers .050 inches by 45 degrees.

   Chamfers observe many of the same best practices as fillets.

FIGURE 4.14

Selecting an edge through model faces

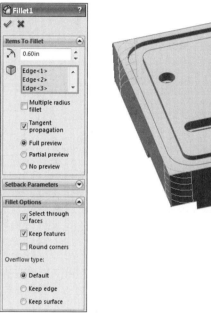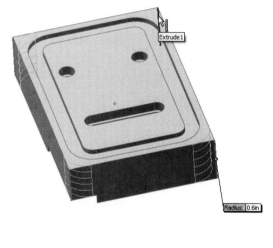

TIP Feature order is important with features like chamfers and fillets because of how they both tend to propagate around tangent edges. Although you can turn this setting off for both types of feature, it is best to get the correct geometry by applying the features in order.

CROSS-REF The Fillet Xpert, which helps you to manage large numbers of overlapping fillets by automatically sorting through feature order issues, is discussed in detail in Chapter 27.

3. **Select the four edges that are indicated for fillets in Figure 4.15.** Apply .050-inch-radius fillets.

4. **Apply a last set of .050-inch chamfers to the back side of the counterbores and slot.**

The finished part is simple, but you have learned many useful techniques along the way. In the rest of this chapter, you will put the part together with other parts to form an assembly and then create a quick 2D drawing of the part and the assembly to document the design.

FIGURE 4.15

Edges for Fillet and Chamfer features

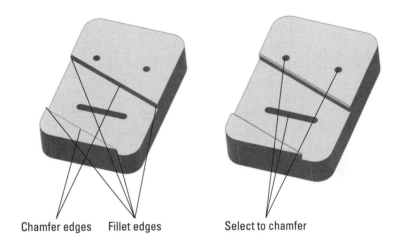

Chamfer edges   Fillet edges   Select to chamfer

Tutorial: Creating a Simple Assembly

Up to this point, you have been learning about how to create geometry, or parts. Assemblies involve organizing that geometrical data to represent real products or parts of products. Assemblies can be complex or simple. They can be structured in a single level or use many subassemblies. Assemblies can be static or allow Dynamic Assembly Motion. Relationships in the assembly can also drive part geometry.

This part of this chapter serves as an introduction to some of the basic functions and main features of assemblies. Because all of the geometry creation is done in the part document, most of what goes on in the assembly document has to do with organizing that geometry in space.

CROSS-REF Chapters 12 to 16 discuss various aspects of assemblies in greater detail.

The following pages describe common techniques that are used in assemblies. The part created earlier in this chapter is assembled with some additional parts that have already been created. The main point here is to give you a basic understanding of the assembly functions that exist and how they work, before exploring various aspects of the software in greater detail in Part II. To create a simple assembly, follow these steps:

ON the CD-ROM This tutorial uses parts called Chapter4Frame.sldprt and Chapter4Screw.sldprt from the CD-ROM, in the material for Chapter 4.

1. **From the CD-ROM, open the part named** `Chapter5Frame.sldprt`. With the part open, click the Make Assembly From Part/Assembly button on flyout toolbar under the New button in the title bar. If you have not made a custom template for assemblies, use the default assembly template that installed with SolidWorks. Move the cursor to the assembly Origin, where the cursor changes to indicate that the part Origin will be lined up with the assembly Origin. If the Origin is not visible on the screen, use the View ⇨ Origins menu selection to turn it on.

   The first part that you insert into an assembly has a Fixed constraint applied to it. This constraint is indicated by the (f) in front of the name of the part in the FeatureManager. Figure 4.16 shows the placement preview and cursor from step 1, as well as the FeatureManager after the part has been added.

FIGURE 4.16

Placing a part in a new assembly

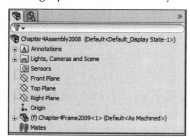

CROSS-REF   **The Frame part is a weldment. Information important to Weldments is discussed in detail in Chapters 31, and 26. Weldments are multi-body parts.**

2. **Open the part that you created in the previous tutorial.** If you do not have it, then you can open a prebuilt copy from the CD-ROM materials for Chapter 4. Once you open the part, change to the assembly window.

TIP   **You can press Ctrl+Tab to change between open documents, and Alt+Tab to change between open applications. These are Windows conventions that are not exclusive to SolidWorks.**

3. **From the assembly menus, click Insert ⇨ Component ⇨ Existing Part/Assembly.** This displays the PropertyManager, as shown in Figure 4.17. Select the machined part from the selection box and click in an open space in the graphics window to place it.

   Newly placed parts in the assembly (except for the very first part) are completely undefined in terms of position or location. Instead of the (f) symbol, for Fixed, the newly placed part displays a (-) symbol, which means Underdefined. You can change a Fixed part to underdefined by selecting Float in the RMB menu. Figure 4.17 also shows the FeatureManager with the new part in it. It is a little confusing that (f) stands for Fixed when the opposite condition, Float, also starts with an f.

FIGURE 4.17

The Insert Component interface

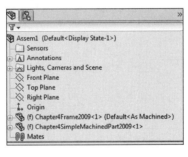

 NOTE Parts in an assembly are positioned relative to one another with mates. Mates are in many ways similar to sketch relations.

4. **Click the Mate button from the Assembly toolbar.** The mate options that are not grayed out are available with the current selection. For example, in Figure 4.18, the corresponding faces of the weldment and the machined part are selected, and these faces can be mated coincident, parallel, perpendicular, at a distance, or at an angle.

TIP You can move a part in an assembly by clicking the part and dragging it with the LMB (left mouse button). It follows whatever mates you have applied to it. To rotate a part that does not have any mates applied to it, drag the part with the RMB. The MMB still rotates the view.

FIGURE 4.18

Mate options

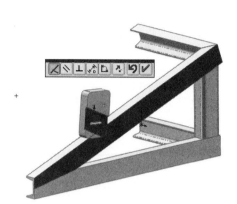

5. **Select the Coincident mate, and then the faces as shown in the figure.** If the machined part is turned as it is in Figure 4.18 (so that it interferes with the welded frame if the selected surfaces touch), then click the Flip Mate Alignment button on the popup toolbar or toggle the Mate Alignment buttons in the PropertyManager. Close the popup toolbar by clicking the green check mark icon.

BEST PRACTICE In contrast to sketch relations, most assembly mates have alignment orientation. Flat faces can be coincident in one of two orientations separated by 180 degrees. The same is true of concentric relations, as well as others. SolidWorks orients a part to the closest orientation that works. This means that it is often best to preposition parts to make it easier for the software. This usually involves some combination of rotating the view and rotating the part.

6. **Select the top angled face of the angled frame member and the corresponding flat face of the machined part.** Figure 4.19 shows which faces to select. Make these faces coincident. In this case, the parts are already in the correct orientation, and so there is no need to preposition them. Click the green check mark icon to accept the mate.

7. **One more mate is required to fully define the position of the machined part.** Drag the part and verify that it slides up and down the angled weldment member. Find the two tapped holes in the weldment and slide the machined part so that the holes appear in the counterbored slot. Ideally the holes should be symmetrical with the part, but the slot was created to allow room for adjustment.

Selecting mating faces

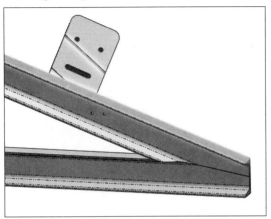

8. **Expand the machined part in the FeatureManager and select its Front plane.** From the View menu, turn on the display of temporary axes, and Ctrl-select the temporary axes in the centers of the threaded holes in the frame, as shown in Figure 4.20. Select the Symmetric mate on the Advanced Mates panel. Turn off the display of temporary axes when the mate is complete.

9. **Through the menus or Assembly toolbar, click Insert Component, and use the Browse button to find the existing** `Chapter4Screw.sldprt` **part on the CD-ROM, or on your hard drive if you have copied it there.**

10. **Notice that this part behaves differently in certain situations.** For example, when the cursor is over empty space, it is attached to the centroid of the part, but when the cursor is over a flat or cylindrical face, the part snaps to that face. This is because the part uses a Mate Reference, enabling planar and cylindrical faces to automatically get Coincident and/or Concentric mates when the part is dropped on them.

11. **Make sure that the Push Pin feature is activated in the Insert Component PropertyManager, and then drop the part at the bottom of each counterbored hole.** The part automatically gets Concentric and Coincident mates. Figure 4.21 illustrates the location where you should drop the part. Click OK to accept the part placement.

12. **You need to place two more screws in the assembly, but these ones cannot be auto-matically mated; you need to do this manually.** Copy two instances of the screws. To copy a screw, Ctrl-drag the part either from the graphics window or from the FeatureManager and drop it into the graphics window.

13. **Position the part and the view so that you can see the cylindrical body of the screw and the cylindrical face of the threaded hole in the C-channel.** With the Mate function active, select both faces and click OK. Repeat the process for the other screw and hole.

FIGURE 4.20

Creating a Symmetric mate

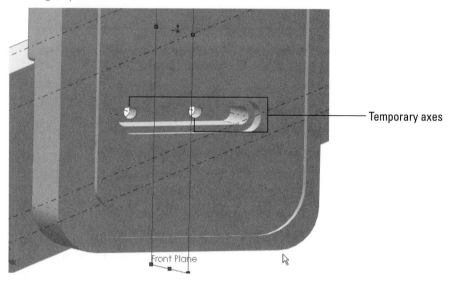

Temporary axes

FIGURE 4.21

Using a Mate Reference

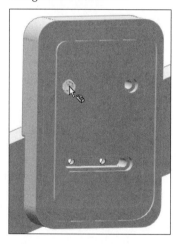

14. Now click the underside of the screw head and the counterbored surface of the slot, make sure that they will be coincident, and click OK. Repeat the process for the other screw.

15. Save and close the assembly.

This is a quick overview of the basic assemblies' functionality, which is expanded on in later chapters.

Tutorial: Making a Simple Drawing

If you are coming to SolidWorks from a dedicated 2D software, you will be creating drawings very differently from what you may be used to. In 2D design software, you draw each view individually, and when a change occurs, you have to go back through the views and ensure that each view is updated appropriately. In 2D, views are sometimes created sparingly because they are difficult to create and to update. This includes view types such as Isometric views, complex sections, and views projected at non-orthogonal angles.

In SolidWorks, drawing views are almost free, being simply projected from the 3D model. Updates are made in the model, and all views update automatically from there. You can handle dimensions in a couple of ways, either using the dimensions that you used to create the model, or placing new dimensions on the drawing (best practice for modeling is not necessarily the same as best practice for manufacturing drawings). To make a simple drawing, follow these steps:

1. **Press the New button from the Standard toolbar, or click File ⇨ New. From the New SolidWorks Document window, select the Drawing template.** The template contains all of the document-specific settings.

2. **After selecting the drawing template, the Sheet Format/Size dialog box displays, as shown in Figure 4.22.** Select the D-Landscape sheet size, as well as the format that automatically associates with that sheet size, and click OK. If the Model View PropertyManager appears, click the red X icon to exit.

3. **Before creating any views on the drawing, set up some fields in the format to be filled out automatically when you bring the part into the drawing. RMB click anywhere on the drawing sheet (on the paper), and select Edit Sheet Format.**

4. **Zoom in to the lower right-hand corner of the drawing.** Notice that there are several variables with the format $PRPSHEET:{Description}. These are annotations that are linked to custom properties. Some of them have properties with values (such as the Scale note), and some of the properties do not have values (such as the Description).

 5. **Add an annotation in the Drawn row, in the Date column.** You can add annotations by clicking Insert ⇨ Annotations ⇨ Note, or by activating the Annotations toolbar in the CommandManager and clicking the Note button. Type today's date as the text of the note.

CAUTION If you are using a SolidWorks default template and a circle appears around your note, then use the Text Format PropertyManager that appears when you are creating a note, expand the Border panel, and change the Circle option to None.

FIGURE 4.22

The Sheet Format/Size dialog box

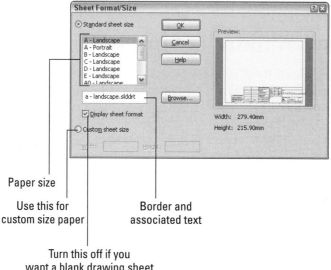

Paper size

Use this for
custom size paper

Border and
associated text

Turn this off if you
want a blank drawing sheet

6. **Add another note, this time to the Name column.** Do not type anything in the note, but use the Link to Properties button in the Note PropertyManager to create a link to a custom property. In the Link to Property dialog box, click the Model in View Specified option in Sheet Properties. Type **user** in the drop-down text box below the option. This now accesses a custom property in a part or assembly that is put onto this drawing and called "user," and will put the value where the note is placed.

7. **To return to Edit Sheet mode (out of Edit Format mode), select Edit Sheet from the RMB menu.** A little text reminder message appears in the lower-right corner on the status bar to indicate whether you are editing the Sheet or the Format.

8. **From the Drawings toolbar, select the Standard 3 View button, or through the menus, click Insert ⇨ Drawing View ⇨ Standard 3 View.** If the Chapter4SimpleMachinedPart document does not appear in the list box in the PropertyManager, then use the Browse button to select it. When you click the OK button, the three drawing views are created.

9. **Drawing views can be sized individually or for each sheet.** The Sheet Properties dialog box in Figure 4.23 shows the sheet scale. If this is changed, all of the views on the sheet that use the sheet scale are updated. If you select a view and activate the Drawing View PropertyManager, you can use the Scale panel to toggle from Use Sheet Scale to Use Custom Scale.

CAUTION In the United States, drawings are traditionally made and understood using the Third Angle Projection, which is the ANSI (American National Standards Institute) standard. In Europe, drawings typically use First Angle Projection, which is the ISO (International Organization for Standardization) standard. If you are not careful about making and reading your drawings, then you could make a serious mistake. There are times when in the United States, the SolidWorks software will install with ISO standard templates, which will project views using First Angle Projection. When using a template that you are unfamiliar with, it is a good idea to check the projection method. To do this, RMB click the drawing sheet and select Sheet Properties. The Type of Projection setting appears in the top middle of the dialog box, as shown in Figure 4.23. This dialog box looks similar to the Sheet Format/Size dialog box, but it has some additional options, including the projection type.

FIGURE 4.23

First-angle versus third-angle projections

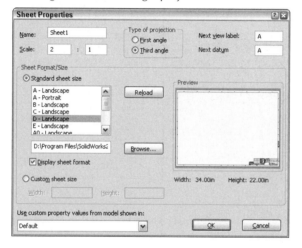

10. To create an Isometric view, activate the Drawings toolbar in the CommandManager, and click the Projected View button. Then select one of the existing views, and move the cursor at a 45-degree angle. If you cannot place the view where you would like it to go, then press the Ctrl key to break the alignment, and place the view where you want it.

11. You can change the appearance of the drawing view in several ways.

   ■ View ➪ Display ➪ Tangent Edges with Font uses phantom line type for any edge between tangent faces.

   ■ View ➪ Display ➪ Tangent Edges Removed completely removes any tangent edges. This is not recommended, especially for parts with a lot of filleted edges, because it generally displays just the outline of the part.

- **Shaded** or **Wireframe** modes can be used on drawings, accessed from the View toolbar.

- **Perspective** views must be saved in the model as a named view and placed in the drawing using the view name.

- **RealView** drawing views are not available on a drawing except by capturing a screen shot from the model and placing this screen shot in a drawing. The same applies to PhotoWorks renderings.

12. **Look at the custom properties that you created in the title block.** The date is there because you entered a specific value for it, but the Name field is not filled in. This is because there is no User property in the part. RMB click the part in one of the views and select Open Part. In the part window, click File ⇨ Properties, and in the Property Name column, type the property name **user**, with a value of your initials, or however your company identifies people on drawings. The Properties dialog box, also called Summary Information, is shown in part in Figure 4.24.

The Custom Properties entry table

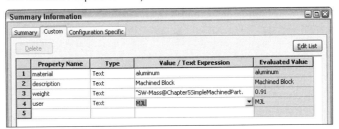

CROSS-REF When used in models and formats, Custom Properties are an extremely powerful combination, especially when you want to automatically fill in data in the format, in a BOM, or a PDM (Product Data Management) product. These topics are discussed in more detail in Chapters 20 and 24.

13. When you flip back to the drawing (using Ctrl+Tab), the Name column now contains the value of your initials.

14. **Click the Section View button on the Drawings toolbar.** This activates the Line command so that you can draw a section line in a view. When sketching, a line can go either on the Sheet or in a view. This is similar to the distinction between the Sheet and the Format. To make a section view, the section line sketch must be in the view. You will know that you are sketching in a view when a pink border appears around the view. You may also use Lock View Focus from the RMB menu to manually lock view focus.

15. Bring the cursor down to the circular edge of the slot to activate the center point of the arc. Once the center point is active, you can use the dotted inference lines to ensure that you are lined up with the center. Another option is to manually create sketch relations. Turning on temporary axes displays center marks in the centers of arcs and circles. Figure 4.25 shows the technique with the inference lines being used. Draw the section line through the slot, and then place the section view.

FIGURE 4.25

Creating a section view

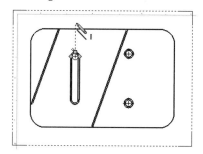

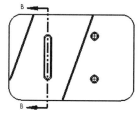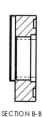

SECTION B-B

16. As mentioned earlier, you can use two fundamentally different methods for dimensioning drawings:

■ **Model Items** imports the dimensions used to build the SolidWorks model and uses them on the drawing. These dimensions are *bi-directionally associative*, meaning that changing them on the drawing updates the model, and changing them on the model updates them in the drawing. On the surface of things, this sounds too good to be true, and it is. The potential problems are that you might not model things the way you would dimension them for the shop. You have to answer several questions for yourself such as do the leader lines go to the right locations or can they be moved and the dimensions usually come in in such a way that they require quite a bit of moving them around.

■ **Reference (driven) Dimensions** can be applied to the drawing view directly. These are only associative in one direction, meaning that they measure what is there, but they do not drive the size or position of the geometry. All changes must be made from the model. Again, on the face of things, this appears to be redundant and a waste of time, but in my personal estimation, by the time you finish rearranging dimensions, checking to ensure that you have everything you need, and hiding the extraneous dimensions, you are usually far better off using reference dimensions.

BEST PRACTICE Users have strong opinions on both sides of this issue. The best thing for you to do is to use both methods and decide for yourself.

17. **If you choose to use the Model Items approach, you can do this by clicking Insert ➪ Model Items.** Then specify whether the dimensions should come from the entire model or just a selected feature. You also need to ask whether the dimensions should come into all views or just the selected one, and whether you want just a certain type of dimension, annotation, or reference geometry.

18. **Once the dimensions are brought in, you need to move some of them from one view to another, which you can do by Shift-dragging the dimension from the old location to the new location.** Ctrl-dragging predictably copies the dimension. You can move views by dragging an edge in the view.

Sheet versus Sheet Format

With new and even experienced users, there is some confusion around the Sheet versus Sheet Format issue. Part of the confusion is due to SolidWorks terminology. SolidWorks names the two items Sheet and Sheet Format. In this book, I simply use the terms *Sheet* and *Format*, to avoid linking the two items with a common first name. It would be better yet if *Format* were changed to *Border* or *Title Block* so that the name more closely matched the function. (The confusion goes deeper for longtime users because there was a time around SolidWorks 98 when templates as we know them did not exist, and what is now called the Format was called the Template, which is why templates have the file extension *.slddrt [DRawing Template]).

In a SolidWorks drawing, you are either editing the sheet or the format. When editing the sheet, you can perform actions such as view, move, and create views, but you cannot select, move, or edit the lines and text of the drawing border. When editing the format, you can edit the lines and text that make up the drawing border, but the drawing views disappear.

Often, users save a template that already uses a format, and save themselves some time by selecting everything all at once when they first select the drawing template for a new drawing.

While you cannot change templates after you create a document, you can swap formats, and change sheet sizes.

Summary

Part I, "SolidWorks Basics," has laid the foundation for the more detailed information that will follow. In the chapters in Part I, I have tried to give recommendations and answer questions that help you to develop an intuition for how SolidWorks software operates, which is the most crucial kind of knowledge when troubleshooting a modeling or editing problem.

This chapter has glossed over many of the important details in order to give you a quick overview of the basic functionality in SolidWorks for the three main data types: Parts, Assemblies, and Drawings. Later chapters expand on this information significantly.

Chapter 5

Using Visualization Techniques

In SolidWorks software, visualizing geometry is very important. In fact, visualization of 3D data is part of the overall mission of the software. Consequently, the visualization tools are very powerful. I remember first running SolidWorks and all of the things I could do to actually see how parts in an assembly fit together. When I used AutoCAD, the visualization was all in my head. I had to imagine what the 3D looked like given the 2D views. SolidWorks takes it so much further than just being able to see things in 3D; you can look at some parts of an assembly in wireframe while others are transparent and others are opaque. You can see a part with a reflective appearance. You can create section views in parts and assemblies to visualize internal details.

I hope that this chapter fills in some important capabilities in your SolidWorks toolbox and at the same time provides some of the awe and wonder that we sometimes get to experience while using incredible 3D tools to do actual work. I will start with the simple and pass through to some more advanced visualizations tools and techniques. If I sound a little enthusiastic about this topic, it is because visualization is the part of this software that really brings my imagination to life. It can be the source of real inspiration and allows me to communicate geometrical ideas with other people.

Manipulating the View

One of the most important skills in SolidWorks is manipulating the view. This is something users do more frequently than any other function in SolidWorks, and so learning to do it efficiently and effectively is very important, whether you look at it as rotating the model or rotating the point of view around the model. The easiest way to rotate the part is to hold down the middle mouse button (MMB) or the scroll wheel, and move the mouse. If your mouse does not have a middle button or a scroll wheel that can be used as a middle mouse button, then you can use the Rotate View icon on the View toolbar or the Heads-up View toolbar.

TIP Some mouse drivers change the middle button or scroll-wheel settings to do other things. Often, you can disable the special settings for a particular application if you want SolidWorks to work correctly and still use the other functionality. For example, the most common problem with mouse drivers is that when the model gets close to the sides of the graphics window and the scroll bars engage, the middle mouse button suddenly changes its function. If this happens to you, you should change the function of the middle mouse button to Middle Mouse Button from its present setting.

Arrow keys

The arrow keys enable you to rotate to the following views:

- **Arrow.** Rotate 15 degrees. To customize this setting, use Tools ⇨ Options ⇨ View.
- **Shift-arrow.** Rotate 90 degrees
- **Alt-arrow.** Rotate in a plane flat to the screen
- **Ctrl-arrow.** Pan

Middle mouse button

The middle mouse (MMB) button or scroll wheel has several uses in view manipulation:

- **MMB alone.** Rotate
- **Click or hover on edge, face, or vertex with MMB, and then drag MMB.** Rotate around selected entity.
- **Ctrl-MMB.** Pan
- **Shift-MMB.** Zoom
- **Double-click MMB.** Zoom to fit
- **Scroll with wheel.** Zoom in or out. To reverse direction of the zoom setting, use Tools ⇨ Options ⇨ View.
- **Alt-MMB.** Rotate in a plane flat to the screen

Using the View toolbars

The View toolbar, shown as the top image in Figure 5.1, contains the tools that you need to manipulate the view in SolidWorks. Not all of the available tools are on the toolbar by default, but I have added them here for this image. To customize your own View toolbar, you must use Tools ⇨ Customize and change to the Commands tab. Then select the View toolbar, and either drag items from the Customize dialog to the View Toolbar to add them, or from the View Toolbar into the empty graphics area to remove them. You can use these tools with part and assembly models but not drawings.

The Heads-up View toolbar is also shown in Figure 5.1. This toolbar was added to SolidWorks with the 2008 release. You can customize this toolbar by right-clicking on it. An interface will appear that enables you to select the items you want displayed on the toolbar. To finish, click outside of the interface, in the graphics window. You cannot add items that are not on the list that pops up. You cannot turn the Heads-up View toolbar off, but you can remove all of the toolbar buttons from it. All of these items from both the View and Heads-up View toolbars are also available on the View menu.

FIGURE 5.1

The View toolbar

Scrollbars and splitters

An option exists to add scrollbars and view pane splitters to the graphics window. SolidWorks 2007 had these interface elements, but they were removed in the 2008 release and then added back when SolidWorks discovered that users do indeed use them. This option is located at Tools ➪ Options ➪ Display/Selection. This selection will be grayed out if any SolidWorks documents are open (so you must close all SolidWorks documents to change it). When you zoom in such that the part/assembly/drawing is partially off the screen, the scrollbars will activate, allowing you to scroll up and down as well as left and right to pan the view.

The splitters enable you to split the main graphics window into multiple view ports. The options are two ports horizontally, two ports vertically, or four view ports. The splitter bars are located at the intersection of the scrollbars in the lower right-hand corner of the graphics window. Of course, you can also use the icons on the Standard Views toolbar for splitting the view into two vertical ports, two horizontal ports, or four ports.

Once a viewport has been split, you can remove the split either with the toolbar icons or by double-clicking the split border. If the view has been split into four, you can set it back to a single viewport by double-clicking the intersection of the horizontal and vertical port borders.

Figure 5.2 shows the scrollbars the splitters and the Standard Views toolbar with all of the view port tools. Notice the cursor in the lower right over one of the splitters.

FIGURE 5.2

Scrollbars and splitters

Using the Magnifying Glass

A new visualization aid introduced in SolidWorks 2009 is the Magnifying Glass. You can invoke it by pressing G, and dismiss it when you select something or when you press Esc. You can change the hotkey it is associated with by going to Tools ⇨ Customize ⇨ Keyboard. Magnifying Glass is listed in the Other category. The Magnifying Glass is intended to magnify a small area of the view to enable you to make a selection.

The magnified area follows your cursor as it moves, and you can zoom in and out by scrolling the MMB. Ctrl-dragging keeps the magnifying glass centered on the cursor. Pressing Alt creates a section view parallel to the view, and scrolling with Alt pressed moves the section plane further away or closer. Figure 5.3 shows the magnifying glass in operation, cutting a section view through a part.

FIGURE 5.3

Using the magnifying glass

> **NOTE** The intended purpose of the magnifying glass is to select small items. You may use it to inspect things, but remember it will disappear as soon as you select something.

Clicking the Triad axes

The Triad is the multicolored coordinate axes in the lower-left corner of the SolidWorks graphics window. You generally use it passively, to see how the view is oriented, and to get X, Y, Z reference directions for features that need it.

However SolidWorks 2009 adds functionality that allows you to make active use the Triad instead of just passive use. When you click on any axis, the view orients such that you are looking straight down that axis of the part. Clicking on the same axis a second time rotates the view 180 degrees. When you are in a named view, a little box in the lower-left corner shows the name of the view. This includes standard named views and custom named views. Anything that shows up in the View Orientation box (accessed by spacebar) displays a name in the corner. Figure 5.4 shows the Triad and the named view box in the lower-left corner.

The Triad and named view box

By Shift-clicking an axis of the triad, the view is rotated 90 degrees from the original orientation. Alt-clicking rotates the view around the clicked axis by the view rotation increment set in Tools ➪ Options ➪ View, which is 15 degrees by default. Using Ctrl in conjunction with any of these causes the view to rotate in the opposite direction. So if Shift-click makes the view rotate against the right hand rule about the clicked axis, Ctrl+Shift-click makes the view rotate with the right hand rule.

Using the View Tools

- **Zoom To Fit.** Resizes the graphics window to include everything that is shown in the model. You can also access this command by pressing the F key, or double MMB clicking.

- **Zoom To Area.** When you drag the diagonal of a rectangle in the display area, the display resizes to fit it. The border size around the fit area is fixed, and cannot be adjusted.

- **Zoom In/Out.** Drag the mouse up or down to zoom in or out, respectively. You can also access this command by holding down the Shift key and dragging up or down with the MMB. The hotkey Z or Shift+Z works for Zoom Out and Zoom In respectively. The percentage of the zoom is a fixed amount, and cannot be adjusted.

■ **Zoom To Selection.** Resizes the screen to fit the selection. You can also access this command from the right mouse button, or RMB, on the FeatureManager. For example, if you select a sketch from the FeatureManager, right-click and select Zoom to Selection, the view positions the sketch in the middle of the screen and resizes the sketch to match the display. The view does not rotate with Zoom to Selection.

TIP There is a reciprocal function that enables you to find an item in the tree from graphics window geometry. If you right-click a face of the model, then you can select Go To Feature in Tree, which highlights the parent feature.

■ **Rotate View.** Enables you to orbit around the part or assembly using the left mouse button (LMB). You can also access this command by using the MMB without the Toolbar icon.

■ **Pan.** Scrolls the view flat to the screen by dragging the mouse. You can also access this command by holding down the Ctrl key and dragging the MMB without using the Toolbar icon, or with Ctrl+Arrow.

■ **3D Drawing View.** Enables you to rotate the model within a drawing view to make selections that would otherwise be difficult or impossible. This is of no use in part and assembly models.

■ **Standard Views flyout toolbar.** The Standard Views toolbar will be discussed later in this chapter. The flyout enables you to access all of the Standard Views tools. This button is also called the View Orientation flyout, depending on where you see it.

■ **Wireframe.** Displays the model edges without the shaded faces. No edges are hidden.

■ **Hidden Lines Visible (HLV).** Displays the model edges without the shaded faces. Edges that would be hidden are displayed in a font.

■ **Hidden Lines Removed (HLR).** Displays the model edges without the shaded faces. Edges that are hidden by the part are removed from the display.

■ **Shaded with Edges.** The model is displayed with shading, and edges are shown using HLR. Edges can either be all a single color that you set in Tools ➪ Options ➪ Colors (typically black), or they can match the shaded color of the part.
Tools ➪ Options ➪ Document Properties ➪ Colors is where you find the document specific setting to use the same color for shaded and wireframe display, which becomes very useful in an assembly when all of the parts shown in wireframe are the same color as they are when they are shaded, instead of all being black.

■ **Shaded.** The model is displayed with shading, and edges are not shown.

■ **Shadows in Shaded Mode.** When the model is displayed shaded, a shadow displays "under" the part. Regardless of how you rotate the model, when Shadows are initially turned on, the shadow always starts out parallel to the standard plane that is closest to the bottom of the monitor. As you rotate the model, the shadow moves with it. If Shadows are turned off and then back on again, they again display parallel to the standard plane that is closest to the bottom of the monitor.

■ **Section View.** Sections the display of the model. Figure 5.5 shows the Section View command at work. You can use up to three section planes at once. Solid and surface models as well as assemblies can be sectioned. You can use the spin boxes, enter numbers manually, or drag the arrows that are attached to the section planes to move the section through the model. Section planes can also be rotated by dragging the border of the plane.

FIGURE 5.5

The Section View tool

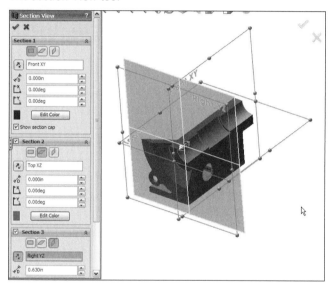

Clicking the check mark icon in the Section View PropertyManager enables you to continue working with the sectioned model, although you may not be able to reference edges or faces that are created by the section view. It is only a displayed section; the actual geometry is not cut.

Section Views can be saved to either the View Orientation box or to the Annotation View folder, which allows section views to be reused on the drawing. Annotation Views are described in more detail in Chapter 22.

 ■ **RealView.** Creates a more realistic reflective or textured display for advanced material selections. This feature does not work with all graphics hardware, so check the SolidWorks Web site to see if it supports your hardware. An entire section of this chapter is devoted to the various tools available with RealView graphics.

■ **Appearances.** Appearances allows you to apply colors, textures and materials to faces, bodies, features, parts and components. This functionality replaces the old colors and textures interfaces. The following toolbar buttons are not on the View toolbar by default, but you can add them if you want:

■ **Camera View.** Views the model through a Camera. You can use Cameras for:

■ Viewing the model from a particular point of view.

■ Creating renderings with perspective and depth-of-field (focus) blur; this feature is only available when PhotoWorks is added in.

■ Animating the position and target of the point of view in an animation; this feature is only available when Animator is added in.

Camera Views

Cameras are created through the RMB menu on the Lights and Cameras folder in the FeatureManager, as shown in Figure 5.6. When you add a Camera, an interface displays in the PropertyManager, as shown in Figure 5.7.

FIGURE 5.6

Adding a new Camera

In this interface, you can position the Camera object by dragging the triad, and you can resize the Field of View box by dragging the border. In the graphics window, you can use the left panel to target and position the Camera, while the right panel shows the view through the Camera.

The Depth of Field panel of the Camera PropertyManager is not shown, because it requires that PhotoWorks be added in. Depth of field can make objects outside of the focus area slightly out-of-focus, which can greatly add to the realism of renders.

FIGURE 5.7

Camera options and interface

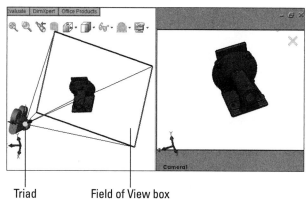

Triad   Field of View box

There are three methods to switch the graphics window to the Camera view:

- Through the View Orientation dialog box (accessed through the spacebar)
- Through the View Orientation popup (in the lower-left area of the graphics window)
- Through the RMB menu on the Camera in the Lights and Cameras folder in the FeatureManager

When you switch the view to the Camera view, the regular Rotate View command does not function. Rotating the view means moving the Camera. You can move the Camera by editing the Camera properties and reposition the Camera by dragging the triad, or by using the Turn Camera tool to rotate the view while looking through the Camera

 ■ **Turn Camera.** Allows you to rotate the view when looking through the Camera without editing the Camera properties. You must be looking through the camera and it must be unlocked for this to work. Dragging with the MMB does the same thing if the camera is unlocked.

 ■ **Draft Quality HLR/HLV.** Toggles between low-quality (draft) and high-quality edge HLR or HLV display. This affects display speed for complex parts or large assemblies. When in draft-quality mode, edge display may be inaccurate.

 ■ **Perspective.** Displays the model in perspective view without using a Camera. If you want to create a perspective view on a drawing, you must create a custom view in the View Orientation dialog box with Perspective turned on. Perspective can be adjusted through

View➪ Modify➪ Perspective by adjusting the relative distance from the model to the point of view. Relative distance is measured by the size of the bounding box of the model, and so if the model fits into a box roughly 12 inches on a side, and the perspective is set to 1.1, then the point of view is roughly 13 inches from the model. For more accurate perspective, you can use a Camera.

 ■ **Curvature.** A geometrical analysis tool that applies a color gradient to the part, based on the local curvature. You can also apply curvature display to individual surfaces through the RMB menu. With some hardware, curvature display can take more time to generate for complex models.

 **Settings in Tools ➪ Options ➪ Performance can greatly affect rebuild speed if curvature display data is regenerated for each part rebuild. You should leave this setting at the default setting, which is Only On Demand.**

 ■ **Zebra Stripes.** Another geometrical analysis tool that helps you to visualize the quality of transitions between faces across edges. Zebra Stripes simulates putting a perfectly reflective part in a room that is either cubic or spherical and where the walls are painted with black-and-white stripes. In high-end shape design, surface quality is measured qualitatively by using light reflections from the surface. Reflecting stripes makes it easier to visualize when an edge is not smooth.

The three cases that Zebra Stripes can help you identify are as follows (see Figure 5.8):

■ **Contact.** Surfaces intersect at an edge, but are not tangent across the edge. This condition exists when stripes do not line up on either side of the edge.

■ **Tangency.** Surfaces are tangent across an edge, but have different radius of curvature on either side of the edge (non-curvature continuous). This condition exists when stripes line up across an edge but the stripe is not tangent across the edge.

■ **Curvature Continuity.** Surfaces on either side of an edge are tangent and match in radius of curvature. Zebra Stripes are smooth and tangent across the edge.

In Figure 5.8, the Zebra Stripes in example A do not match across the edge labeled A at all. This is clearly the non-tangent, contact-only case. Example B shows that the stripes match in position going across the indicated edge, but they change direction immediately. This is the tangent case. Example C shows the stripes flowing smoothly across the edge. This is the curvature continuous case.

You can use the remaining icons in the View toolbar to toggle the display of various types of entities from reference geometry to sketches.

Consider using hotkeys to toggle the display of my favorite items to hide and show. I use T for Temporary Axes, P for Planes, R for Origins, and so on.

FIGURE 5.8

Zebra Stripes

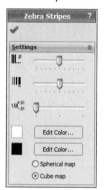
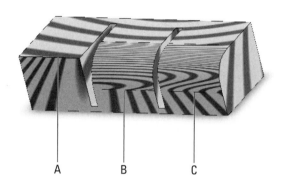

A   B   C

View Orientation

You can activate the View Orientation box by pressing the spacebar. View Orientation, shown in Figure 5.9, keeps all named views, saved section views, and standard views. Tools in the box also enable you to update standard views to the current view or to reset standard views to their defaults. Be aware of another toolbar button on the View toolbar that has the name View Orientation.

FIGURE 5.9

The View Orientation dialog box

The Standard Views flyout is called either Standard Views or View Orientation, depending on where you see it. The View Orientation dialog box contains the following controls:

- **Push Pin.** Keeps the dialog box active.

■ **New View.** Creates a new custom-named view.

■ **Update Standard Views.** Sets the current view to be the new Front view; all other views update relative to this change. This also updates any associated drawing views, but does not move any geometry or change plane orientation.

■ **Reset Standard Views.** Resets the standard views so that the Front view looks normal to the Front plane (Plane1, XY plane).

■ **Previous View** (undo view change). You can access this tool using the default hotkey Shift+Ctrl+Z.

View Orientation can also be manipulated from two other locations: the Standard Views toolbar, which is discussed later in this chapter, and the spacebar View Orientation popup, shown in Figure 5.10. This function allows you to select the orientation or the arrangement of viewports. The popup also displays any existing Cameras, which are described earlier in this section.

FIGURE 5.10

The View Orientation popup

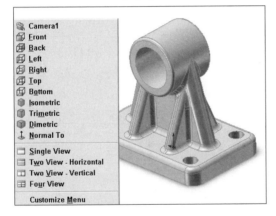

The Standard Views toolbar

I have already mentioned the Standard Views flyout on the View toolbar, but here I will describe the tools that it contains in detail. Figure 5.11 shows the Standard Views toolbar in its default configuration.

FIGURE 5.11

The Standard Views toolbar

By default, the Standard Views toolbar contains the View Orientation button, a tool from the View toolbar. The View Orientation button is discussed in detail earlier in this section.

Normal To has three modes of operation:

- **First Mode.** Click a plane, planar face, or 2D sketch. When you click Normal To, the view reorients normal to the selected plane, face, or sketch, and zooms to fit the model in the view. This method is shown in Figure 5.12.

FIGURE 5.12

The result of using Normal To on the end rib angled face

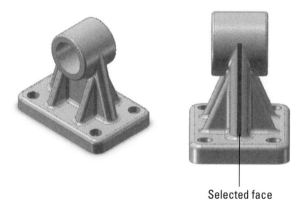

Selected face

- **Second Mode.** Click Normal To a second time. The view rotates 180° to display the opposite direction.
- **Third Mode.** After making the first selection, Ctrl-select another planar entity. The view is normal to the first selection and the second selection is rotated to the top. This method is shown in Figure 5.13.

FIGURE 5.13

Using Normal To with Second Selection to define the top

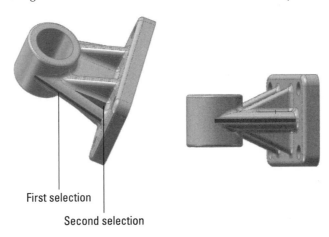

First selection

Second selection

Annotation views

Annotation views enable you to group annotations that were made in the 3D model into views that will be used on the drawing. They can be displayed under the Annotations folder in the FeatureManager for parts and assemblies. Annotation views can be created either automatically, when 3D annotations are added, or manually. An Unassigned Items annotation view acts as a catchall for annotations that are not assigned to any particular views. In the 3D model, you can use the views to reorient the model and display annotations. As mentioned earlier, annotation views can also capture a model section view to be shown in a drawing view. The Annotation views are shown for the Chapter5SampleCasting part in Figure 5.14.

FIGURE 5.14

Annotations views for Chapter5SampleCasting.sldprt

Understanding RealView

RealView is a hardware-driven set of visualization tools that help make the SolidWorks display look more realistic, adding reflections, reflected backgrounds, and shadows. RealView is intended to help the user to apply advanced effects to 3D models. The fact that RealView is hardware-driven means that not all video cards that are certified to work with SolidWorks also work with RealView. You need to check on the SolidWorks Web site to see what level of RealView your graphics card supports. A link to the video card testing site should be available from the SolidWorks home page, www.solidworks.com.

The SolidWorks 2008 version made a big change in the implementation of RealView, and the hardware support changed greatly with that release as well. Hardware that worked well for RealView in SolidWorks 2007 may not work for all of the RealView features in 2008.

In some situations, you can use RealView instead of PhotoWorks. In these cases, RealView acts as a real-time renderer. The main advantages that PhotoWorks holds over RealView are improved antialiasing control, improved shadow control, indirect illumination, global illumination, caustics, and effects such as depth of field from a camera.

You can even use RealView as a diagnostic tool for smooth joints between surfaces because RealView appearances apply a reflective surface to a part and then also apply a reflective background. This is essentially what the Zebra Stripes functionality is doing, but Zebra stripes applies a specific reflective background to make examining curvature continuity across edges more straight-forward.

You can turn RealView on or off by using the golden globe icon shown by default on the Heads-up View toolbar. If this icon is grayed out, then your system is not equipped with an appropriate RealView-capable graphics card. Generally, you need an nVidia 500 series or higher to get RealView capabilities. NVS series cards are not 3D cards and will not enable RealView. Some ATI FireGL cards may also work.

RealView basic components

RealView consists of:

- **Appearances.** Controls colors, textures, reflectivity, optical properties
- **Scenes.** Controls the background image and reflectivity image

If you are familiar with previous versions of SolidWorks, Appearances in the 2009 release completely take the place of the Colors functionality, even if you do not have RealView-capable video card.

Figure 5.15 shows the contents of the RealView tab in the Task Pane, as well as the callout that appears when you drop an appearance onto a part. The callout enables you to select if you want the appearance applied to the face, body, part, or assembly level.

FIGURE 5.15

Using the Appearances tab on the Task Pane to apply appearances

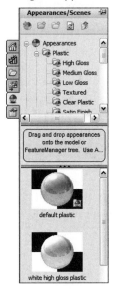

Applying appearances

Appearances starting in the 2009 release encompass colors and textures. Another way of saying that is that colors and textures have been rolled into appearances for 2009. To apply an appearance, use the Task Pane at the right of the graphics window, and click the Appearances tab. Figure 5.15 shows this. Then select an appearance from the list, and drag it onto the part where you would like to apply it. You can do this either in the part window or in the assembly window. A small popup will appear and present you with options for what to apply the appearance to, which is either the face, feature, body, or part.

If you are familiar with SolidWorks 2008 or prior, the way you work with color in SolidWorks 2009 is different. The Color icon is no longer the main means of changing the color of a part. Starting with the 2009 release, you use appearances. Appearances also enable you to change colors. To change the color of an applied appearance, use the Appearance Callout icon on the RMB menu, select the level you want to apply the color to (face, body, feature, part), and then select the color from the Appearance PropertyManager. Figure 5.16 shows the Appearance PropertyManager.

Appearance overrides

One of the things that confuse many users about applying an appearance is that it can be applied on many levels, and may override or be overridden by other appearances. This means that in a part, an appearance may be applied to a face, a feature, a body, or the entire part. There is a specific hierarchy to this system of overrides: part, body, feature, face, component, and automatic color changes.

FIGURE 5.16

The Appearance PropertyManager

When you apply an appearance at the level of the part (the name of the part shows in the Color and Optics PropertyManager), any other entity color will override it. You can assign Solid or Surface bodies an appearance that overrides the part appearance. Some color changes are automatic; for example, when you are editing parts in the context of an assembly, they can temporarily change colors or become transparent, which overrides everything else.

For complex surfaces, surface transition quality is often measured by reflections, and so setting up a reflective model can be key to finding shape imperfections. In lieu of reflective RealView materials, using lights with specularity can help you evaluate curved surfaces, although it is generally not useful for flat faces.

Other entity colors

You can color other entities in addition to the 3D shaded model. Curve entities (such as a helix or projected curve) can be colored in addition to sketches with the Edit Sketch Or Curve Color tool. You can only view sketch colors when the sketch is closed and shown, because when the sketch is open, the entity colors have special significance indicating the sketch status.

NOTE The Edit Sketch Or Curve Color works for sketches and limited curve features. It works for all curve features except for projected curves. Also, preselection does not work with this tool.

The Display pane

The Display pane flies out from the right side of the FeatureManager and displays a quick list of which entities have colors, materials, or textures assigned. It also shows hidden parts or bodies for assemblies and multibody parts. The Display pane is shown in Figure 5.17. You may notice that it does not display colors for faces, and it does not enable you to change anything from the Display pane; it just keeps and displays the record of where the color or optical properties were assigned. I revisit the Display pane in Chapter 12 to show you how it is used in assemblies.

FIGURE 5.17

The Display pane in action

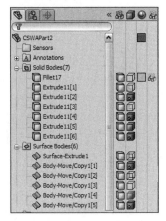

Automatic colors

The settings found at Tools ⇨ Options ⇨ Document Properties ⇨ Colors can be used to automatically color certain types of features with specific colors. For example, all Shell features can be colored red as they are created.

Using Display States

One of the most commonly used and powerful visualization aids available in SolidWorks is the Display States functionality (see Figure 5.18). Display States is simply the ability to show parts shaded, shaded with edges, wireframe, HLR (hidden lines removed), or HLG (hidden lines in gray).

FIGURE 5.18

Display States in an assembly

CROSS-REF Chapter 14 deals with Display States in more detail.

Using Edge Settings

Earlier in this chapter I discussed the Shaded with Edges display style. Some people think that this makes the parts look "cartoony." I agree, especially when the default black edges are used, but the display improves when the edge color matches the shaded part color. In any case, sometimes this method is necessary to see the breaks between faces, especially fillets.

Taking this one step further, you can also make use of the tangent edge settings. These settings are found in the View ⇨ Display menu. The settings are:

- **Tangent Edges Visible.** Tangent edges are displayed as solid lines, just like all other edges

- **Tangent Edges as Phantom.** Displays tangent edges in a phantom line font

- **Tangent Edges Removed.** Displays only non-tangent edges

The tangent edges removed setting leaves parts looking like a silhouette. I prefer the phantom setting because I can easily distinguish between edges that will actually look like edges on the actual part, and edges that only serve to break up faces on the model. The tangent edges visible setting conveys no additional information, and is the default setting. Figure 5.19 shows a sample part with all three settings.

FIGURE 5.19

Samples of the tangent edge settings

Tutorial: Visualization Techniques

Visualization is a key factor when working with SolidWorks software. Whether it is for a presentation of your design to customers or management or simply checking the design, it is important to be able to see the model in various ways. This tutorial guides you through using several tools and techniques.

1. **If the part named** `Chapter5Sample.sldprt` **is not already opened, then open it from the CD-ROM.** If it is open and changes have been made to it, then click File ➪ Reload ➪ OK.

2. **Practice using some of the controls for rotating and zooming the part.** In addition to the View toolbar buttons, you should also use Z and Shift+Z (Zoom Out and In, respectively), the arrow keys, and the Ctrl-, Shift-, and Alt-arrow combinations.

3. **Use the MMB to select a straight edge on the part, and then drag with the MMB.** This rotates the part about the selected entity. Also apply this technique when selecting a vertex and a flat face.

4. **Select the name of the part at the top of the FeatureManager.**

5. **Click the Appearance button from the Standard toolbar.**

6. **Click the color you want in the Favorite panel.** The model should change color. If you click and drag the cursor over the colors, the model changes color as you drag over each new color. You can also drag appearances from the Task Pane. Figure 5.20 shows interfaces for both methods.

7. **If the Color panel is not expanded, click the double arrows to the right to expand it.** Select the colors you want from the continuous color map. Again, click and drag the cursor to watch the part change color continuously.

8. **Create a swatch. In the Favorite panel, select the Create New Swatch button and call the new swatch color file** `BibleColors`.

9. **Select a color from the Color Properties continuous map; the Add Selected Color button becomes active.** Clicking the button adds the color to the swatch palette. You can add several colors to the palette to use as favorites later on.

> **TIP** You will be able to access these colors again later by selecting `BibleColors` from the drop-down list in the Favorite panel. You can transfer the colors to other computers or SolidWorks installations by copying the file `BibleColors.slddclr` from the `<SolidWorks installation directory>\lang\english` folder (or the equivalent file for your installed language).

10. **In the Appearance panel, move the Transparency slider to the right, and watch the part become transparent.**

11. **To prevent the Appearance window from closing after every change, click the push-pin at the top of the window.**

12. **Click the green check mark icon to accept the changes; note that with the push-pin icon selected, the window remains available.**

13. **Expand the flyout FeatureManager in the upper-left corner of the graphics window, as shown in Figure 5.21, so that all of the features in the part are visible.**

14. **Select the features Extrude1, Fillet7, and Fillet6 from the FeatureManager so that they are displayed in the Selection list of the Appearances window.** Select a color from the BibleColors swatch palette that you have just created.

15. **Click the check mark icon to accept the changes and clear the Selection list.**

16. **Select the inside face of the large cylindrical hole through the part, and assign a separate color to the face.**

FIGURE 5.20

The Color and Optics interface elements

FIGURE 5.21

The Flyout FeatureManager

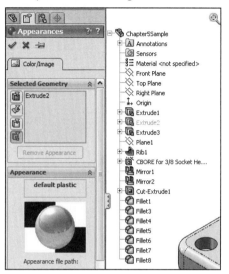

17. **Click the check mark icon to accept the changes, and click the red X icon to exit the command.**

18. **Expand the Display pane (upper-right area of the FeatureManager).** You should see color and transparency symbols for the overall part, and color symbols for three features. There is no indication of the face color that is applied.

19. **Remove the colors.** Open the Appearances window again, re-select the three features (Extrude1, Fillet7, and Fillet6), and click the Remove Color button below the Selection list. Do the same with the colored face. Return the part transparency to fully opaque.

20. **Click the check mark icon to accept the changes.**

21. **Change the edge display to Shaded (without edges).** Then change to a Wireframe mode. Finally, change back to Shaded With Edges.

22. **Now select View ⇨ Display ⇨ Tangent Edges as Phantom.** Figure 5.22 shows the difference between Tangent Edges Visible, as Phantom, and Removed settings.

FIGURE 5.22

Tangent Edge display settings for a shaded model

TIP Using the Tangent Edges as Phantom setting is a quick and easy way to look at a model to determine whether or not face transitions are tangent. It does not help to distinguish between tangency and curvature continuity; you need to use Zebra Stripes for that.

23. **Switch back to Shaded display.**

24. **If you do not have a RealView-capable computer, then skip this step.** Ensure that the RealView button in the View toolbar is depressed. RMB click the Material folder in the FeatureManager. Select Edit Material, and then select Steel, AISI 304. Rotate the part. Notice that the finish is semi-reflective. Click the check mark icon to accept the change.

25. **Turn the part over, select the bottom face, and apply an Appearance from the Task Pane. In the top panel, expand Appearances, Metals, Steel, and then select Wrought Steel. Apply the appearance just to the bottom face.** The rest of the part should retain the semi-reflective surface, as shown in Figure 5.23. Click the check mark icon to accept the change.

FIGURE 5.23

Applying a material to a part

26. **Click the Section View button on the View toolbar.** Drag the arrows in the middle of the section plane back and forth with the cursor to move the section dynamically through the part, as shown in Figure 5.24.

FIGURE 5.24

A section view

27. **Click the check box next to the Section 2 panel name, and create a second section that is perpendicular to the first.**

28. **Click the green check mark icon to accept the section.** Notice that while in the Section View PropertyManager, the RealView material does not display, but once you close the dialog box, RealView returns.

Summary

Visualization is a key function of the SolidWorks software. It can either be an end to itself if you are showing a design to a vendor or client, or it can be a means to an end if you are using visualization techniques to analyze or evaluate the model. In both cases, SolidWorks presents you with a list of tools to accomplish the task. The tools range from the analytical to the cosmetic, and some of the tools have multiple uses.

Part II

Building Intelligence into Your Parts

The chapters of Part II take you beyond the basic modeling tools to start taking advantage of the parametric options within SolidWorks. Chapter 6 acquaints you with the entire breadth of sketching tools and techniques available in SolidWorks. Chapter 7 assists you in finding the right tool for the right job. Chapter 8 debunks some myths about patterning and mirroring and helps you establish good design practices. The equations in Chapter 9 are, of course, one of the quintessential strengths of parametric modeling tools. Chapter 10 introduces the concept of Configurations, which will help you model variable driven models more quickly and efficiently. Chapter 11 sums it all up with what I consider to be the most important information in the book (editing), and helps you decide if your model is "good enough" through evaluation.

Chapter 6

Getting More from Your Sketches

Previous chapters have described the basic tools for sketching. This chapter takes you to the next level, preparing you to be able to use more advanced tools, editing and manipulating sketches, and working with sketch text, sketch pictures, and sketch colors. At the end of this chapter, with a little practice to help the information sink in, you should feel like you master the topic of sketching, and you should be able to handle almost any problem that is thrown at you.

Editing Sketch Relations

When I was teaching SolidWorks reseller classes, I frequently told my classes, "Delete is not an edit option." In time, you will find that this is good advice, even if you don't agree with it now. There are times to use the Delete command, but you should use it only when it is really necessary. In my own work, I sometimes go to extreme lengths to avoid deleting sketch entities, often just to stay in practice, but also because deleting sketch entities, or even features in a part, increases the likelihood that sketch or mate relationships will be broken.

The main reason for avoiding Delete in a sketch is that when you are editing a sketch that has other features that are dependent on it, the dependent features may lose their references, or *go dangling*. Because of this, even when you can use the Delete command instead of editing, it is still a good practice to edit instead. Deleting relations is not as critical as deleting sketch entities, unless the relations are referenced by equations or design tables.

BEST PRACTICE Before deleting sketch entities, try to understand what types of relationships the change will affect downstream. Be sure to consider other sketch relationships within the current part, mates and in-context relations in the assembly, and things of this nature. In fact, it is best to have all of this in mind when you are creating relationships to begin with. Try to make relations to the most stable entities available, which usually means sketches and reference geometry entities as high up in the tree as possible.

Display/Delete Relations

Display/Delete Relations is your primary tool when dealing with sketch relations. It is particularly useful to sort relations by the various categories that are shown in Figure 6.1.

FIGURE 6.1

The Display/Delete Relations PropertyManager

Sketch relations in the Display/Delete Relations dialog box can be divided into the following categories:

- **All in this sketch.** Shows all of the relations in the active sketch.

- **Dangling.** Shows only the dangling relations. Dangling relations appear in a brownish-green or olive color, and represent relations that have lost one of the entities that drives the relation. You can repair dangling relations by selecting the entity with the dangling relation, and then dragging the red dot onto the entity to which it should have the relation.

- **Overdefining/Not Solved.** Overdefined relations are any set of conflicting or redundant instructions that are given to a sketch entity, and appear in red. For example, if a line is collinear with an edge and also vertical, but the edge itself is not vertical, then both the collinear and vertical relations appear in red.

  The Not Solved condition often accompanies Overdefined. Not Solved typically refers to a dimension or relation that cannot be applied because of the conflict. The lower-right corner of the screen and the status bar show flags warning that the sketch is overdefined, as shown in Figure 6.2.

When an overdefined situation exists, all of the relations and dimensions in a sketch may often become overdefined. This can look like a daunting task to repair, when the entire problem is caused by a single relation. Do not automatically delete everything. Instead, try deleting or suppressing the last dimension or relation that was added, or a single relation that looks suspect. It is also a good idea to delete red relations before deleting yellow ones. Yellow simply means conflict, while red means a condition that cannot be applied. You can suppress a dimension by setting it to Driven in the right-mouse button menu, and you can suppress relations in the Display/Delete Relations PropertyManager.

FIGURE 6.2

An overdefined sketch

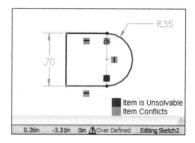

- **External.** External relations connect with an entity outside the active sketch. This includes the part Origin, or any model edges. The term *external relations* is also sometimes meant to signify any relations outside of the part.

- **Defined in Context.** Any relation between features in one part in an assembly and another part is considered an in-context relation.

- **Locked.** External relations (outside the part) may be locked or broken to increase speed and to lock out parametric changes. There is no advantage of breaking relations rather than locking them. Both are ignored, but locked relations can be unlocked; broken relations can only be deleted.

- **Broken.** See Locked.

- **Selected Entities.** Sketch relations are shown only for the selected sketch entities.

CROSS-REF In-context design, also called *top-down*, as well as locked and broken relations, is covered in detail in Chapter 16.

CAUTION Some of the relations listed in the Display/Delete Relations dialog box may be colored to signify the state of the relation. Unfortunately, colored relations are typically placed at the top of the list to attract attention, but when you select them, they are always gray, and so the advantage of color-coding is defeated. The only way around this is to select a relation other than the first one in the list. If there is only one relation in the list, you cannot see the state color.

Also be aware that the field backgrounds for the relation symbols are different depending on your installation of the software. If you install SolidWorks 2008 or later on a computer that has never had a version of SolidWorks on it before, you will get the new 2008 default colors. If you install SolidWorks 2008 on a computer that has had SolidWorks 2007 on it, you will get the old SolidWorks 2007 colors. The colors affected by this difference include the select highlight color, dynamic highlight, and sketch relation symbol background colors.

A setting in Tool ⇨ Options controls the display of errors. You can select Tools ⇨ Options ⇨ Featur eManager to find an option called Display Warnings, where you can choose Always, Never, and All but Top Level. When a sketch contains sketch relations with errors, they display as warning signs on the sketch, and will propagate to the top level of a part or assembly if you have chosen the Always option.

SketchXpert

The SketchXpert, shown in Figure 6.3, can help you to diagnose and repair complex sketch relation problems. The Diagnose button at the top creates several possible solutions that you can toggle through using the forward and backward arrow buttons in the Results panel. The Manual Repair button displays all of the relations with errors in a window and allows you to delete them manually.

By selecting the option at the very bottom of the dialog box, you can make the SketchXpert display any time that a sketch error occurs. To display the SketchXpert manually instead of automatically, you can access it by right-clicking in a sketch.

FIGURE 6.3

The SketchXpert dialog box

Copying and Moving Sketch Entities

SolidWorks offers several different tools to help you move sketch entities around in a sketch. In SolidWorks, it is usually recommended to keep the sketch as simple as you can, and to create patterns using feature patterns rather than sketch patterns. The following section discusses the main tools for moving and copying sketch entities.

Move entities

Move entities enables you to move selected sketch entities by either selecting From and To points, or by typing in XY coordinates for the move. When the Keep Relations option is off, this tool automatically detaches sketch segments whose endpoints are merged, as shown in Figure 6.4. If Keep Relations is on, SolidWorks moves the entities and tries to maintain the sketch relations and merged points. All of these tools have a pushpin icon in the interface, which allows you to use them many times when the pushpin icon is pushed in; they are deactivated after one use if the pushpin icon is not pushed in.

FIGURE 6.4

Using the Move tool

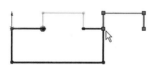

Rotate entities

Rotate entities rotates selected entities in a sketch in the same way that Move entities works. You can drag the angle or type it in manually. The green check mark icon is on the right-mouse button, as shown in the cursor display in Figure 6.5.

The Keep Relations option does not actually keep any relations — it deletes the Horizontal and Vertical relations in the sketch, as shown in Figure 6.5 — but it does keep the merged endpoints, as shown in the right-most image of Figure 6.5. This can be useful, especially considering how many sketch relations it would take to make a sketch move like this naturally.

FIGURE 6.5

Using the Rotate tool

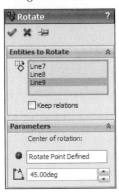
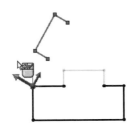
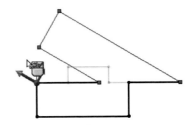

Copy entities

The Copy Entities tool works exactly like the Move Entities tool, except that it copies instead of moving.

Scale entities

Scale entities is one of those functions probably best left alone. This is because the results appear erratic and unpredictable, particularly if there are dimensions on the sketch. This tool works on a selection of entities, particularly on an isolated selection that is not connected to other entities in the sketch. The PropertyManager for the Scale Entities tool is shown in Figure 6.6.

FIGURE 6.6

The Scale PropertyManager

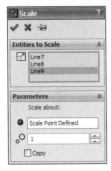

Modify Sketch

The Modify Sketch tool has been available in SolidWorks for a long time, but it has been super-seded by some of the newer tools mentioned previously. However, it still has some unique functionality that is not covered by any other sketch tool. Modify sketch works on the entire sketch rather than on selections from the sketch, and it works best if there are no external relations between sketch entities and anything outside the sketch. It can also work on a sketch without the sketch being active. While most feature and tool interfaces have been moved to the PropertyManager, Modify sketch still uses a dialog box that floats in the graphics window, as shown in Figure 6.7.

FIGURE 6.7

The Modify Sketch dialog box

Scale about

The scaling function in the Modify Sketch tool enables you to scale about either the part Origin or the Moveable Origin. The Moveable Origin is the black origin symbol with knobs on the ends of the axes and at the intersection. The Moveable Origin can be moved and even snapped to entities that are internal or external to the sketch.

Translate

The Translate function of the Modify Sketch tool enables you to click and drag to move the entire sketch, or to select a point and move it to a specific set of coordinates that you type in. If the sketch is dragged onto an external entity and picks up an automatic relation, then a message may appear that you can now use Modify sketch only for rotating the sketch because there is an external relation.

Rotate

The Rotate function of the Modify Sketch tool enables you to position the Moveable Origin to act as the center of rotation, and to either type in a rotation angle or drag with the right-mouse button to rotate, as indicated by the cursor.

Mirroring

When you place the cursor over the knobs on the Moveable Origin, the cursor symbols change to indicate the functionality of the right-mouse button. These cursors are shown in action in Figure 6.8. The cursors enable mirroring about X, Y, or both simultaneously.

FIGURE 6.8

The Modify Sketch tool cursors

> **NOTE** The Modify Sketch tool is still one of my favorite sketch editing tools to use because it is straightforward and doesn't do anything unexpected. It was also an original SolidWorks development, not a tool meant to duplicate existing AutoCAD functionality like some of the previously mentioned sketch tools.
>
> The one thing about Modify Sketch that many people find unsettling is that the red sketch origin moves and rotates along with the rest of the sketch. Once you make peace with the fact that you can't use the red sketch origin for much anyway, this becomes unimportant.

Copy and paste

Probably the simplest way to copy sketch entities in a sketch is to select the entities and use Ctrl+C and Ctrl+V or one of the many other methods available for this purpose (such as the right-mouse button menu, the Edit menu, and Ctrl+dragging).

In addition to copying selected entities within an active sketch, you can also select a sketch from the FeatureManager and copy or paste it to a selected plane or planar face. This creates a new sketch feature in the FeatureManager that has no relation to the original, although it does maintain internal dimensions and relations. (External relations are not copied with the sketch.) This is particularly useful when setting up certain types of lofts that use several profiles that can be created from a single copied profile. Copying and pasting is a fast and effective method of putting sketches on planes.

Simple drag

If a selected set of sketch entities has no external relations, then you can select it as a group and move it without distorting or resizing the sketch. For best results with this, avoid dragging end points.

Derived sketch

A derived sketch is a parametrically linked copy. The original parent and derived sketches do not need to have any geometrical relation to one another, but when the parent sketch is changed, the dependent derived copy is updated to stay in sync.

To create a derived sketch, you can select a plane or planar face, Ctrl-select the sketch of which you want to make the parametric copy, and then click Insert ⇨ Derived Sketch.

When you create a derived sketch, you cannot change its shape; it works like a block of a fixed shape driven by the parent. However, you can change the position and orientation of the derived sketch. Figure 6.9 shows a derived sketch and its parent. Modify Sketch is a great tool to use for manipulating derived sketches that don't have any relations to things outside the sketch, especially for mirroring or rotating.

FIGURE 6.9

A derived sketch and its parent

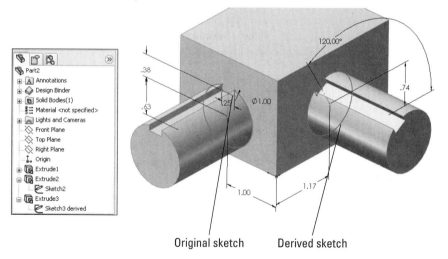

Original sketch   Derived sketch

Using Sketch Pictures

Sketch pictures are images that are placed in a sketch on a sketch plane. You can size and rotate the images, give them a transparent background, trace over them, and suppress them. They display as a child of the sketch. Image types that you can use as sketch pictures are BMP, GIF, JPEG, TIFF, PNG, PSD and WMF.

To bring a picture into a sketch, the sketch must first be active. Click Sketch Picture on the Sketch toolbar (it is not there by default, and so you may need to drag it onto the Sketch toolbar from the Tools ➪ Customize ➪ Commands dialog box). You can also access this command through the menus at Tools ➪ Sketch Tools ➪ Sketch Picture. You cannot use sketch pictures in assembly sketches, but they can be shown in a part sketch in an assembly.

To change the size of a sketch picture, you can double-click it and drag one of the handles around the outside of the image. When the picture comes into the sketch, it is usually too big, having been sized at a ratio of 1 pixel to 1 mm. To size a picture accurately, you should include a ruler or an object of a known size in the image. If you cannot do this, the next best thing is to guess the size. Draw a line in your sketch and dimension it to approximately the size of something that is recognizable in the image, and then move the image by clicking and dragging it to lay the dimensioned sketch entity as close over the object in the image as possible.

You can rotate and mirror images, as well, using the Sketch Picture PropertyManager. Images are opaque, and you cannot see the model through them, but at the same time, you also cannot see the images through the model. They are like a flat piece of paper that is pasted to the model or hanging in space.

You can add transparency to images, either by selecting a color or by using the built-in transparency in the image file. When you select a color to be transparent, you will also need to turn up both the Matching Tolerance and the Transparency value sliders, which are by default set to their minimum values.

CAUTION   Starting in 2007 and as late as early releases of SolidWorks 2009, if a Sketch Picture has had transparency applied to it, and you double-click the picture, SolidWorks automatically bumps you into the eyedropper mode, which is selecting a color to be transparent. A single extra click in this mode can make a mess of your Sketch Picture transparency settings by changing the selected transparency color.

Sketch pictures cannot be shown on a drawing associatively. The only way to do this is to capture an image of the sketch picture that is being shown in the model, and putting this image in the drawing. PhotoWorks does not use sketch pictures, either, and PhotoWorks Decals are a separate item altogether.

TIP   Although the most common use for the sketch picture is as a tracing guide, you can use it for a wide variety of other purposes. For example, any sort of logo, decal, or display that is on a flat surface can be shown as a sketch picture.

BEST PRACTICE   Best practice for using sketch pictures is to put them into a separate sketch near or at the top of the FeatureManager. Even though you can have sketch entities in a Sketch Picture sketch, I prefer to keep them in separate sketches. This is because when you use the sketch entities for an extrude or a loft guide curve, this sketch will be consumed under that feature, which means that the image becomes buried somewhere in your model, rather than being easily accessible at the top of the FeatureManager.

Three views

When building a model from images, it is often helpful to have three or more images from orthogonal views, similar to re-creating a part from a 2D drawing. If you have a left and a right view, it may be a good idea to put them on planes that are slightly separated so that the images are not exactly on top of one another, which makes them both hard to see. Putting them on slightly offset planes means that one will be clearly visible from one direction, and the other visible from the other direction.

Each sketch picture must be in a separate sketch. Figure 6.10 demonstrates the use of multiple sketch pictures to trace the outline of a vehicle, with the partially complete model shown with the images.

FIGURE 6.10

Using multiple sketch pictures

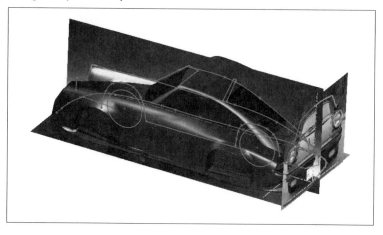

Additionally, you can put multiple sketch pictures inside a single sketch if you want to do that. Both images show up in the FeatureManager, and both can be displayed at the same time, although you may have difficulty if you want to put them on top of one another.

Perspective

When taking digital photographs to be used as sketch pictures in SolidWorks, you have to consider the effects of perspective on the image. Perspective can make it difficult to size items in the foreground or background. You should be aware of this, as well as that objects at different distances from the camera will appear at distorted sizes. If you are taking the pictures that will be used as sketch pictures, you can minimize the effects of perspective by standing farther away from the object and using zoom on the camera if possible.

Sharp edges

When you are drawing a sketch of an object, you are usually drawing theoretically sharp corners of the model. Real parts usually have rounded corners, and so you may have to use your imagination to project where the 3D surfaces would intersect at an edge minus the fillets.

When you are reverse-modeling a part from images, you are not using an exact science. It is better than not being able to put pictures into the sketch, but there is nothing about it that can be considered precise.

Auto Trace

Auto Trace is an add-in that you can turn on via the Tools ➪ Add-ins menu. Auto Trace is intended to trace between areas of contrast in Sketch Pictures, creating sketch entities. To use Auto Trace, make sure the add-in is activated. Activating the Auto Trace add-in activates a set of arrows at the top of the Sketch Picture PropertyManager. There is nothing to identify the functionality with the Auto Trace name. Figure 6.11 shows the Sketch Picture and Auto Trace PropertyManagers. The sliders for the Auto Trace functionality do not point out which end is high and which is low.

FIGURE 6.11

Sketch Picture and Auto Trace PropertyManagers

Auto Trace prefers solid blocks of black and white in the Sketch Pictures. To achieve this, you may need to use image processing software and reduce your picture to a two color (black and white) bitmap, TIF, or PNG image. Even if this pre-processing gives perfect results, don't expect much from Auto Trace.

I can't imagine a situation in which I would either use this myself or recommend anyone else to use it. In all cases, including idealized demonstration images or those in which traced images would be of the most benefit to the user such as logos with complex curvature, I believe it would be faster and more accurate to just do the tracing manually, even it means using splines.

Using Sketch Text

Sketch text uses TrueType fonts to create text inside a SolidWorks sketch. This means that any TrueType font that you have can be converted to text in solid geometry; this includes Wingdings and symbol fonts. Keep in mind that some characters in certain fonts do not convert cleanly into SolidWorks sketches. Sketch text still has to follow the rules for sketching and creating features such as closed contours, as well as not mixing open and closed contours.

You can make sketch text follow a sketch curve; to space it evenly along the curve, you can control character width and spacing, as well as overall size by specifying points or actual dimensions. Sketch text can also be justified right, left, centered and evenly, as well as reversed, rotated, and flipped upside down. Figure 6.12 shows the Sketch Text PropertyManager and some of the possible uses of sketch text.

The icons in the Sketch Text PropertyManager are fairly self-explanatory, other than the Rotated Text option, which rotates individual letters, and not the whole string of text.

You can use the Sketch Text tool multiple times in a single sketch to make pieces of text with different properties. Each string of text has a placement point located at the lower left of the text. This point can be given sketch relations or dimensions to locate the text.

If the text overlaps in places, as shown in Figure 6.12, you can correct this in a couple of ways. First, you can extrude it with the Merge option turned off so that each letter is created as a separate solid body. You can also explode sketch text so that it becomes simply lines and arcs in a sketch, which you can edit the same as any other sketch. You could also adjust the Width Factor and Spacing settings.

FIGURE 6.12

Examples of sketch text

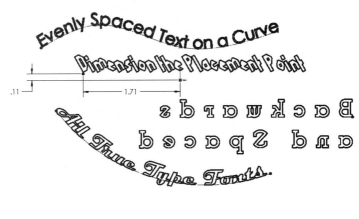

Using Colors and Line Styles with Sketches

Custom colors and line styles are usually associated with drawings, not sketches; in fact, they are most valuable when used for drawings. In sketches, this functionality is little known or used, but is still of value in certain situations.

Color Display mode

In drawings, you can use the Color Display Mode button to switch sketch entities on the drawing between displaying the assigned line or layer color and displaying the sketch status color. It has exactly the same effect here in part and assembly sketches.

When you press the button, the sketch state colors are used. When the button is not pressed, any custom colors that you have applied to the sketch entities will display. If the button is not pressed and you have not applied colors to the entities, then the default sketch state colors are used.

You can use sketch colors for emphasis, to make selected sketch entities stand out, or to make sketches with various functions immediately distinguishable. Color Display mode only has an effect on an active sketch. Once a sketch is closed, it returns to the gray default color for inactive sketch entities.

Line color

 Line color enables you to assign color to entities in an active sketch. Whether the assigned color or the default sketch status colors are used is determined by the Color Display Mode tool.

Edit sketch or curve color

 You can use the Edit Sketch Or Curve Color tool to assign color to an entire sketch. The color that you assign to sketches in this way displays only when the sketch is inactive, instead of the default gray color. They also follow the toggle state of the Color Display Mode button. For example, if the Color Display Mode button is depressed, then inactive sketches display as gray. When the Color Display Mode button is not pressed, then inactive sketches display in any color that you have assigned by using the Edit Color tool.

Line thickness and line style

 The Line Thickness and Line Style tools function independently from the Color Display Mode button, but they are still used only when the sketch is active. As soon as a sketch that contains entities with edited thickness and style is closed, the display goes back to the normal line weight and font.

To assign a thickness or a style, you can select the sketch entities to be changed, press the button, and select the thickness or style. Although a single sketch entity may have only a single thickness or style, you can use multiple thicknesses or styles within a single sketch. Figure 6.13 shows a sketch with the thickness and style edited.

CROSS-REF Line thickness and line styles are covered in more detail in the discussion of drawings in Chapter 20.

FIGURE 6.13

A sketch with edited line thickness and line style

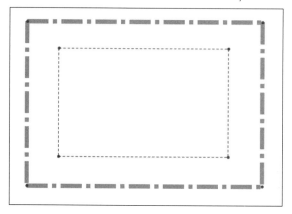

Using Other Sketch Tools

SolidWorks has a lot of functionality that crosses between multiple topics. The following tools could be placed in other sections of the book, but I have placed them here because they will help you work with and control 2D sketches in SolidWorks. Almost everybody who opens the SolidWorks software at one time or another has to use a sketch, so these tools could be applied by a wide swath of users.

RapidSketch

As the name suggests, RapidSketch is meant to help you rapidly create a number of sketches on different planes. As you move a sketch cursor over flat faces of a model, the faces highlight to indicate that you can start a new sketch there.

The workflow with this tool is that you start in one sketch, with an active sketch tool, move the cursor over another plane or face without exiting the first sketch, and start sketching the entity on the new plane.

The only real down side of using RapidSketch is that if you sketch on a particular plane or face where other planes or faces might be visible in the background, SolidWorks might interpret certain selections as trying to change sketch planes. To get back to a previous sketch, deactivate the current sketch tool (for example by using Esc) and double-click the previous sketch you want to get back to. To move to a later sketch, use the normal sketch exiting techniques.

Sensors

You can add Sensors in the SolidWorks FeatureManager for parts and assemblies by right-clicking on the Sensors folder and selecting Add Sensor. You can find the Sensors folder at the top of the FeatureManager. If you cannot find the Sensors folder, go to Tools ➪ Options ➪ FeatureManager, and make sure the Sensor folder is set to Show.

Figure 6.14 shows the Sensor PropertyManager. You can create sensors for measurements, simulation data, or mass properties. The reason I have included Sensors in this chapter is because of the measurements, which allow you to select a dimension, and set a range of values or criteria for which you want to be notified. The dimension can be a driving (black) sketch dimension, or a driven (gray) dimension on a sketch, or even a driven dimension placed directly on solid geometry.

The second image shows what happens when a sensor finds a condition that you asked it to notify you about.

In addition to turning Sensor alarms on or off, you can also suppress Sensors when no longer needed or to improve performance.

Sensors are a great way to keep an eye on particular values such as wall thickness or clearance between parts. Any value you want to monitor but don't drive directly can be monitored with a Sensor.

FIGURE 6.14

The Sensor PropertyManager

Meta data for sketches

Meta data in SolidWorks is non-geometrical text information. Meta data is particularly helpful as keywords in searches, and also in PDM applications. If you don't make use of meta data within your CAD documents, it can be easy to forget that it is there at all.

The sources for storing meta data in SolidWorks files are:

- Sketch and feature names
- Sketch and feature comments (access comments via the right-mouse button menu)
- Custom Properties
- Design Binder documents
- Tags for features (located on Status Bar in the lower-right corner)

Meta data searches can be particularly useful in large assemblies or parts with long lists of features that you need to access for various reasons. You can conduct searches for meta data through the FeatureManager Filter at the top of the FeatureManager. The Advanced Search function in assemblies can also search meta data sources. SolidWorks Explorer is a good first level data management solution that can search, display and edit meta data and previews. Windows Explorer can also search properties and tags.

Construction geometry

In SolidWorks, the only construction geometry that can be created directly is the construction line. All other sketch entities can be converted to construction geometry by selecting the Construction Geometry option within the sketch entity's PropertyManager or by using the Construction Geometry toggle toolbar button.

SolidWorks terminology is inconsistent, because it sometimes refers to construction lines as centerlines. The two are really the same thing. Centerlines are used for revolved sketches and mirroring, but there is no difference between a centerline and a construction line in SolidWorks.

Construction geometry is useful for many different types of situations. I use it frequently for reference sketch data. You can make sketch relations to construction geometry, and can use it for layout sketches or many other purposes limited mainly by your needs and imagination.

Tutorial: Editing and Copying

This tutorial guides you through some common sketch relation editing scenarios and using some of the Copy, Move, and Derive tools. Follow these steps to learn about editing and copying sketches:

1. **Open the part named** `Chapter6 Tutorial1.sldprt` **from the CD-ROM.** This part has several error flags on sketches. In cases where there are many errors, it is best to roll the part back and go through the errors one by one.

2. **Drag the rollback bar from just after the last fillet feature to just after Extrude3.** If Extrude3 is expanded so that you can see Sketch3 under it, then drop the rollback bar to after Sketch3. If a warning message appears, telling you that Sketch3 will be temporarily unabsorbed, then select Cancel and try the rollback again. Figure 6.15 shows before and after views for the rollback.

3. **Edit Sketch3 and turn off the Sketch Relations display (View ⇨ Sketch Relations).** Relations with errors will still be displayed. Click Display/Delete Relations on the toolbar (the Eyeglasses tool), and set it to All in This Sketch. Notice that all of the relations conflict, but only one is unsolvable: the Equal Radius relation. This appears to be a mistake because the two arcs cannot be equal.

4. **Delete the Equal Radius relation.** The sketch is still not fixed.

5. **Click the green check mark icon to close the Display/Delete Relations PropertyManager.**

6. **Right-click the graphics window and select SketchXpert. Then click Diagnose.**

7. **Using the double arrows in the Results panel, toggle through the available solutions.** All of the solutions except one remove sketch relations. Accept the one solution that removes the dimension. Some versions of SolidWorks may not have any solutions that remove the dimension. If this happens to you, use the Manual Repair option, and delete the dimension. When you are done, click the green check mark icon to exit the SketchXpert. The sketch no longer shows errors in the graphics window, but it still does in the FeatureManager.

FIGURE 6.15

Rolling the part back to Extrude3

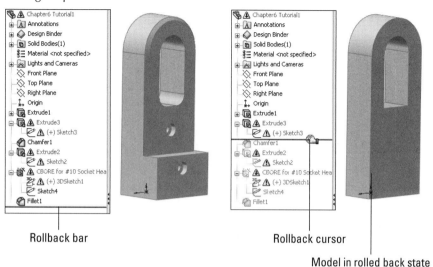

Rollback bar

Rollback cursor

Model in rolled back state

8. **Close the sketch.** Notice that the error flag does not disappear until the sketch has been repaired and closed.

9. **Use the rollback bar to roll forward to after Extrude2 and Sketch2.** Figure 6.16 shows the tooltip message that appears if you place the cursor over the feature with the error. With time, you will begin to recognize the error messages by a single keyword or even by the shape of the message text. This message tells you that there is a *dangling* relation — a relation that has lost one of the entities.

10. **Edit the sketch. (See Figure 6.17).** If you show the Sketch Relation icons again, the errors will be easier to identify. When you use Display/Delete Relations (Tools ⇨ Relations ⇨ Display/Delete Relations), the first two Coincident relations appear to be dangling. Clicking the relation in the Relations panel of the Display/Delete Relations PropertyManager shows that one point was connected to a line and the other point was connected to a point.

11. **Click the name of the dangling entity in the Entities panel of the PropertyManager; then click the vertex indicated in Figure 6.17 in the Replace box at the bottom.** When you have fixed the errors, exit the sketch and confirm that the flag is no longer on Sketch2.

    An easier way to repair the dangling relation is to click on the dangling sketch point once. It will turn red. Next drag the point onto an entity that you want to reattach the relation to.

12. **Drag the rollback bar to just before CutExtrude1. Edit 3DSketch1.** This sketch is overdefined. If the Sketch Relations are not on at this point, then turn them on again.

FIGURE 6.16

The Error tooltip

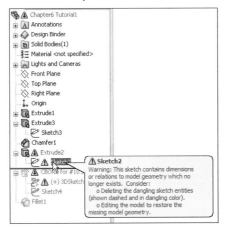

TIP Because this is a task that you will perform many times, this is a good opportunity to set up a hotkey for this function. As a reminder, to set up a hotkey, go to Tools ⇨ Customize ⇨ Keyboard, and in the Search box, type relations. In the Shortcut column for this command, select a hotkey to use.

13. **Double-click one of the relation icons; the Display/Delete Relations PropertyManager appears.** Notice that one of the sketch relations is a Fixed relation. Remove the Fixed relation, and exit the sketch.

14. **Right-click anywhere in the FeatureManager and select Roll To End.**

15. **Click CutExtrude1 in the FeatureManager so that you can see it in the graphics window, and then click a blank space to deselect the feature.**

16. **Ctrl-drag any face of the cut feature, and drop it onto another flat face.** The Ctrl-drag function copies the feature and the sketch, but the external dimensions and relations become detached. This will only work if Instant3D is turned off.

17. **Click Dangle in response to the prompt.** This means that you will have to reattach some dangling dimensions rather than re-creating them. Edit the newly created sketch, which now has an error on it.

18. **Two of the dimensions that went to external edges now have the olive dangling color.** Select one of the dimensions; a red handle displays. Drag the red handle and attach it to a model edge. Do this for both dimensions. The dimensions update to reflect their new locations. Exit the sketch and verify that the error flag has disappeared.

19. **Expand CutExtrude1, and select Sketch5 under it.** Ctrl-select a flat face on the model other than the one that Sketch5 is on. In the menu, select Insert ⇨ Derived Sketch. You are put into a sketch editing the derived sketch.

FIGURE 6.17

Fixing dangling errors

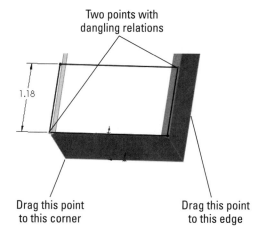

Two points with
dangling relations

1.18

Drag this point
to this corner

Drag this point
to this edge

20. **The sketch is blue, and so you should be able to resize it, right?** No, it doesn't work that way. You can test this by dragging the large circle; it only repositions the sketch as a unit.

21. **Dimension the center of the large circle to the edges of the model.**

22. **Drag the smaller circle, and notice that it swivels around the larger circle.** Create an angle dimension between the construction line between the circle centers and one of the model edges. Notice that the sketch is now fully defined.

23. **Exit the sketch, and look at the name of the derived sketch in the FeatureManager.** The term *derived* appears after the name, and the sketch appears as fully defined.

24. **Right-click the sketch and select Underive Sketch.** Notice that the sketch is now underdefined. The Underive command removes the associative link between the two sketches.

Tutorial: Controlling Pictures, Text, Colors, and Styles

This tutorial guides you through some of the miscellaneous functions in sketches, and shows you what they are used for and how they are used. Follow these steps to learn how to control these items:

1. **Open a new part using a template with inches as units.** Open a sketch on the Front plane, and draw a construction line starting from the origin 12 inches down (negative Y) away from the Origin.

2. **Insert a sketch picture in this sketch.** Use Sketch Picture 1.tif from the CD-ROM for Chapter 6.

3. **Resize the image so that the endpoints of the construction line are near the centers of the holes on the ends of the part.** To move the image, just double-click it first, and then drag it. To resize it, drag the corners.

4. **In the Transparency panel of the Sketch Picture PropertyManager, select the Eyedropper tool and click in the white background of the image.** Make sure that the color field next to the Eyedropper tool changes to white.

5. **Slide the Transparency and Matching Tolerance sliders all the way to the right, or type** 1.00 **in the number boxes.**

6. **Close the sketch, and rename it** Sketch Image Front View.

7. **Put the image Sketch Picture 2.tif, also from the CD-ROM, on the Right plane, and resize it to fit with the first image.** Center it symmetrically about the Origin. Also set the transparency to the same setting as the first image.

8. **Open a new sketch, also on the Front plane, and draw two circles to match the features on the ends.** Extrude them using a Mid Plane extrusion to match the image in the other direction (about 2.5 inches), as shown in Figure 6.18.

FIGURE 6.18

Using sketch pictures

9. **Open another new sketch on the Front plane and draw the tangent lines to form the web in the middle of the part.** Close the sketch to make a solid extrusion. Extrude this part .5 inches Mid Plane.

10. **Open a new sketch on the face of the large flat web that you created in the previous step, and offset the arc edge of the larger circular boss by 2.1 inches.**

11. **Change the arc to a construction arc and drag its endpoints to approximately the position shown in Figure 6.19.** The endpoints of the arc are blue after you drag them. Give them a Horizontal relation, and then dimension them.

Creating an offset arc

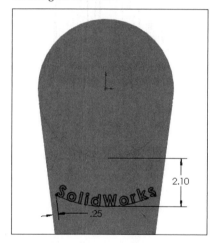

12. **Click Tools ➪ Sketch Entities ➪ Text to initiate the creation of sketch text.**

13. **Select the construction arc to go into the Curves window.**

14. **In the Text window, type** SolidWorks. Select the Full Justify option.

15. **Deselect the Use Document Font option, click the Font button, and then set the Units to .50 inches.** Click the Bold button to make the text thicker. Click OK to exit the dialog box. Click the green check mark icon to exit the sketch text, and then exit the sketch.

16. **Extrude the text to a depth of .050 inches with 3 degrees of draft.** The part at this point resembles Figure 6.20.

PERFORMANCE Sketch Text is a real performance killer. The more text that you use, the longer it takes to extrude. Draft on the extrusion adds to the time required.

FIGURE 6.20

Creating extruded text

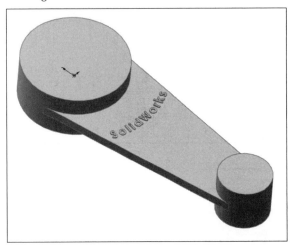

17. Select the flat face on the other side of the part from where you just extruded the text, and open a sketch.

18. Select the face and click the Offset button to make a set of sketch entities offset to the inside of the face by .50 inches. Remember that you may have to reverse the offset to get it to work properly.

19. Turn on the Line Format toolbar (right-click any toolbar other than the CommandManager and select Line Format).

20. Select all of the sketch lines, and change their color using the Line Color tool. Change the line thickness and the line style using the appropriate tools. The sketch now looks something like Figure 6.21.

21. When you click the Color Display Mode tool, the colors return to regular sketch colors. When you exit the sketch, the line weight and style also return to normal.

FIGURE 6.21

Using line thickness and line style

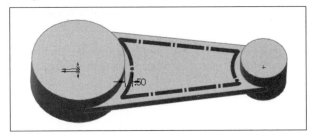

Tutorial: Using Meta Data

If you integrate the use of meta data into your company's modeling process, your SolidWorks models can be a resource for much more than just geometrical data. In this tutorial, discover the hidden treasure of extra information stored as meta data in this model.

1. **Open the part from the CD-ROM called** `Chapter 6 - Dial Cover.sldprt`.

2. **Check the Custom Properties in this file by going to File ⇨ Properties.** Notice the Thickness and Process properties in particular. All of the meta data entry interfaces are shown in Figure 6.22.

FIGURE 6.22

Meta data entry interfaces

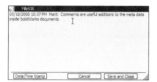  

3. **Add a Custom Property with the Property Name Material, type Text, and value ABS.**

4. **Check the Comments in this part.** Notice that a Comments folder exists near the top of the FeatureManager. Inside it is a list of the features for which I have written comments.

5. **Add a Comment by right-clicking on the VarFillet3 feature, selecting Comment fly-out arrow, clicking the Add Comment option, clicking the Date/Time Stamp button, and adding a comment that uses the word Blend.**

6. **Check the Tags for the part by clicking the small yellow tag in the lower right-hand corner of the Status Bar, then click on any feature, and double-click in the Tags interface box.**

7. **Add a Tag by selecting the Cut-Extrude1 feature and adding the tag pilar.**

8. **Right-click on any item in the FeatureManager and select Go To from the options.**

9. **Type 37 in the box and click the Find Next button.** The FeatureManager should highlight a feature near the bottom of the tree named Fillet37.

10. **Left-click on Fillet37 in the Feature Manager and select the Zoom To Selection tool.** Zoom to Selection is a magnifying glass with an equal sign in it. The display zooms and pans to a fillet on one end of the part.

11. **Right-click on a face of Fillet37 on the model and select Go To Feature (In Tree), which will select and scroll if necessary the FeatureManager to show Fillet37.** This sequence of tools shows the importance and interdependence of feature names and the actual geometry.

12. **Enter the word** Thickness **in the filter at the top of the FeatureManager.** Figure 6.23 shows the result. Notice how quickly the results appear. Notice also that the meta data item that caused the feature to show in the list can be shown in a tooltip by hovering the mouse over the feature.

FIGURE 6.23

Using the FeatureManager Filter to search for meta data

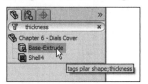

13. **Click the X at the right end of the filter to restore the FeatureManager to its original state, and type the word Pilar instead. Now filter for "Thermoform."**

Summary

Many tools that are available in sketches are not commonly shown in the most popular sources of information, including official training manuals. The difference between a good CAD tool and a great communication tool can be some of these minor functions that just make life a little easier, or the presentation or editing of data a little better. When you explore the capabilities of SolidWorks, it usually rewards you with functionality that is not immediately obvious.

Chapter 7

Selecting Features

henever I do a woodworking project, the most frustrating part of the job is to envision a result, but not be able to accomplish it because I do not have the tools to get it done; worse yet is to actually have the tools but either not understand how to use them or not even realize that I have them. Getting the job done is so much more satisfying when you use the right tools and get the job done right — not just so that it looks right, but so that it really is right.

I see users run into the same issues with SolidWorks. SolidWorks offers so many "tools in the toolbox" that it is sometimes difficult to select the best one, especially if it is for a function that you do not use frequently.

This chapter helps you to understand how each feature functions and offers situations when they are best applied or avoided.

IN THIS CHAPTER

Identifying when to use which tool

Creating curve features

Filleting

Selecting a specialty feature

Tutorial: Bracket casting

Tutorial: Creating a wire-formed part

Identifying When to Use Which Tool

I am always trying to think of alternate ways of doing things. It is important to have a backup plan, or sometimes multiple backup plans, in case a feature doesn't perform exactly the way you want it to. As you progress into more complex features, you may find that the more complex features are not as well behaved as the simple features. You may not be able to get away with just doing blind extrudes and cuts with simple chamfers and fillets for the rest of your career. And even if you could, who would want to?

As an exercise, I often try to see how many different ways a particular shape might be modeled, and how each modeling method relates to manufacturing methods, costs, editability, efficiency, and so on. You may also want to try this approach for fun or for education.

This chapter helps you identify which features to use in which situations, and in some cases which features to avoid. As SolidWorks grows more and more complex, and the feature count increases with every release, understanding how the features work and how to select the best tool for the job becomes ever more important. If you are only familiar with the standard half-dozen or so features that most users use, your options are limited. Sometimes simple features truly are the correct ones to use, but using them because they are the only things you know is not always the best choice.

Extrude

 Extruded features can be grouped into several categories, with extruded Boss and Cut features at the highest level. With the use of Instant3D, extruded bosses can be transformed into cuts. It is unclear what advantage this has in real world modeling, but options are options. As a result the names of newly created extrude features are simply Extrude1 where they used to be Extrude-Boss1 or Extrude-Cut1.

The "Base" part of the Extruded Boss/Base is a holdover from when SolidWorks did not allow multibody parts, and the first feature in a part had special significance that it no longer has. This is also seen in the menus at Insert ➪ Boss/Base. The Base feature was the first solid feature in the FeatureManager, and you could not change it without deleting the rest of the features. The introduction of multibody support in SolidWorks has removed this limitation.

CROSS-REF   **Multibody parts are covered in detail in Chapter 26.**

Solid Feature

In this case, the term *solid feature* is used as an opposite of *thin feature*. This is the simple type of feature that you create by default when you extrude a closed loop sketch. A closed loop sketch fully encloses an area without gaps or overlaps at the sketch entity endpoints. Figure 7.1 shows a closed loop sketch creating an extruded solid feature. This is the default type of geometry for closed loop sketches.

Thin Feature

The Thin Feature option is available in several features, but is most commonly used with Extruded Boss features. Thin features are created by default when you use an open loop sketch, but you can also select the Thin Feature option for closed loop sketches. Thin features are commonly used for ribs, thin walls, hollow bosses, and many other types of features that are common to plastic parts, castings, or sheet metal.

Even experienced users tend to forget that thin features are not just for bosses, but can also be used for cuts. For example, you can easily create grooves and slots with thin feature cuts.

FIGURE 7.1

A closed loop sketch and an extruded solid feature

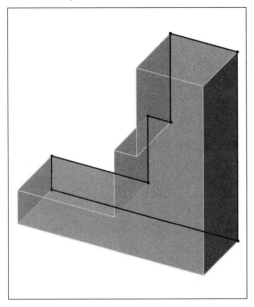

Figure 7.2 shows the Thin Feature panel in the Extruded Boss PropertyManager. In addition to the default options that are available for the Extrude feature, the Thin feature adds a *thickness* dimension, as well as three options to direct the thickness relative to the sketch: One-Direction, Mid-Plane, and Two-Direction. The Two-Direction option requires two dimensions, as shown in Figure 7.2.

FIGURE 7.2

The Thin Feature interface

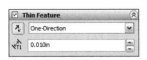 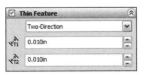

Thin feature sketches are typically simpler than closed loop sketches, which usually means that they are more robust through changes. You can create the simplest cube from a single sketch line and a thin feature extrude. However, because they are more specialized in some respects, they are not as flexible when the design intent changes. For example, if a part is going to change from a constant width to a tapered or stepped shape, thin features do not handle this kind of change. Figure 7.3 shows different types of geometry that are typically created from thin features.

FIGURE 7.3

Different types of geometry created from thin features

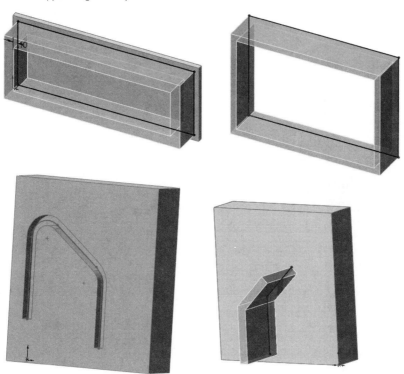

Sketch types

I have already mentioned several sketch types, including closed loop and open loop. Closed loop sketches make solid features by default, but you can also use them to make thin features. Open loop sketches make thin features by default, and you cannot use them to make solid features.

Sketch contours

 Sketch Contour is an option that is used in other competing CAD packages and that SolidWorks has adopted, probably more to match features in the competing software than to create a better way of doing things. In my opinion, using sketch contours promotes sloppy work, although in some cases, they act as valid time savers.

In general, sketch contours enable you to select enclosed areas where the sketch entities themselves actually cross or otherwise violate the usual sketch rules. One of these conditions is the self-intersecting contour.

BEST PRACTICE SolidWorks works best with well-disciplined sketches that follow the rules. As a result, if you plan to use sketch contours, then you should make sure that it is not simply because you are unwilling to clean up a messy sketch.

When you define features by selecting sketch contours, they are more likely to fail if the selection changes when the selected contour's bounded area changes in some way. It is best practice to use the normal closed loop sketch when you are defining features. Contour selection is best suited to "fast and dirty" conceptual models, which are used in very limited situations for production models.

As shown in Figure 7.4, there are several types of contour selection.

FIGURE 7.4

Types of contour selection

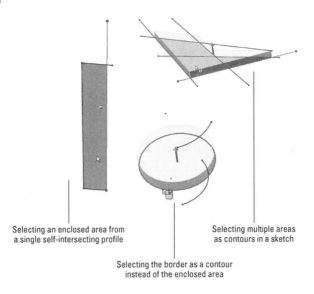

Selecting an enclosed area from
a single self-intersecting profile

Selecting multiple areas
as contours in a sketch

Selecting the border as a contour
instead of the enclosed area

3D sketch

You can make extrusions from 3D sketches, even 3D sketches that are not planar. While not necessarily the best way to do extrudes, this is a method that you can use when needed. You can establish direction for an extrusion by selecting a plane (normal direction), axis, sketch line, or model edge.

When you make an extrusion from a 3D sketch, the direction of extrusion cannot be assumed or inferred from anything — it must be explicitly identified. Extrusion direction from a 2D sketch is always perpendicular to the sketch plane unless otherwise specified.

Non-planar sketches become somewhat problematic when you are creating the final extruded feature. The biggest problem is how you cap the ends. Figure 7.5 shows a non-planar 3D sketch that is being extruded. Notice that the end faces are, by necessity, not planar, and are capped by an unpredictable method, probably a simple Fill surface. This is a problem only if your part is going to use these faces in the end; if it does not, then there may be no issue with using this technique. If you would like to examine this part, it is included on the CD-ROM as `Chapter 7 Extrude 3D Sketch.sldprt`.

FIGURE 7.5

Extruding a non-planar 3D sketch

If you need to have ends with a specific shape, and you still want to extrude from a non-planar 3D sketch, then you should use an extruded surface feature rather than an extruded solid feature.

One big advantage of using a 3D sketch to extrude from is that you can include profiles on many different levels, although they must all have the same end condition. So if you have several pockets in a plate, you can draw the profile for each pocket at the bottom of the pocket, and extrude all the profiles Through All, and they will all be cut to different depths.

3D sketches also have an advantage when all the profiles of a single loft or boundary are made in a single 3D sketch. This enables you to drag the profiles and watch the loft update in real time.

CROSS-REF Surfacing features are covered in detail in Chapter 27. Chapter 4 contains additional details on extrude end conditions, thin features, directions, and the From options. Chapter 31 also has more information on 3D sketches.

Instant 3D

Instant 3D is a function that was added in SolidWorks 2008, and largely replaces the Move/Size Features function. Instant 3D is not a complete replacement of Move/Size Features — it has some limitations that the older function does not have — but it also adds new functionality that did not exist before. This topic follows the Extrude feature because one of the functions of Instant 3D is to help you create extruded bosses and cuts quickly.

Instant 3D also allows you to edit other types of features and sketches by simply dragging handles in the graphics window, instead of editing numbers in a dialog box.

Creating extrudes with Instant 3D

Instant 3D allows you to select a sketch or a sketch contour and drag the Instant 3D arrow to create either a blind extruded boss or cut. The workflow when using this function requires that the sketch must be closed. Instant 3D cannot create a thin feature, and any sketch or contour that it uses must be a closed loop. Sketches must also be shown (not hidden) in order to be used with Instant 3D.

NOTE Even though the words "Instant 3D" suggest that you should be able to instantly create 3D geometry from a sketch that you may have just created, you do have to close the sketch first to get instant functionality.

Figure 7.6 shows Instant 3D arrows for extruding a solid and the ruler to establish blind extrusion depth. These extrusions were done from a single sketch with three concentric circles, using contour selection.

Even after you create an extruded boss, you can use Instant 3D to drag it in the other direction to make an extruded cut. When you do this, the symbol on the feature changes, but the name does not.

Prior to SolidWorks 2008, SolidWorks automatically assigned the name Boss-Extrude1 to an extruded boss. In SolidWorks 2008 and later, the default is simply Extrude1. If your second feature is a cut, SolidWorks names that feature Extrude2. So in the automatic naming conventions, SolidWorks no longer distinguishes between bosses and cuts.

If you have a sketch that requires contour selection — for example, the three concentric circles used in Figure 7.6, after the first feature is created from the sketch — SolidWorks automatically hides the sketch, and to continue with Instant 3D functionality using additional contours selected from that sketch, you will have to show the sketch again. This interrupts the workflow and makes using this functionality less fluid than it might otherwise be. I only mention it here so that you are aware of what is happening when the sketch disappears and the Instant 3D functionality disappears with it.

FIGURE 7.6

Creating features with Instant 3D

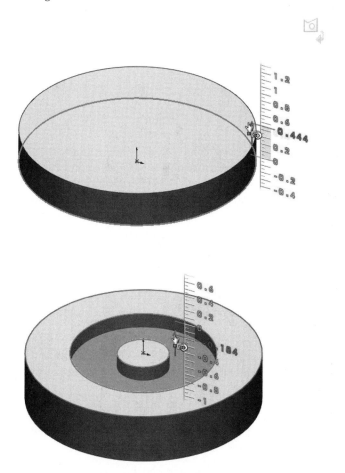

Notice the boss extrude symbol next to the hand in Figure 7.6. This enables you to switch the type of feature you are creating with Instant 3D. If geometry already exists in the part, and you drag a new feature into the existing solid, SolidWorks assumes you want to make a cut. But maybe what you are really trying to make is a boss that comes out the other side of the part. These heads-up display icons enable you to do this. Options include boss, cut, and draft. The draft option enables you to add draft to a feature created with Instant 3D.

While Instant 3D can only create extruded bosses and cuts, it can edit revolves. If you create a revolved feature revolving the sketch say 270°, the face created at the angle can be edited by Instant 3D dragging.

Editing geometry with Instant 3D

Instant 3D enables you to edit 2D sketches and solid geometry. You can also edit some additional feature types using Instant 3D such as offset reference planes. It can neither create nor edit surface geometry or 3D sketches in some situations. To edit solid geometry, click on a face, and an arrow appears. Drag the arrow, and SolidWorks automatically changes either the sketch or the feature end condition used to create that face. If a dimensioned sketch was used to create that face, SolidWorks will not allow you to use the Instant 3D arrow to move or resize the face. An option exists that enables Instant 3D changes to override sketch dimensions at Tools ➪ Sketch Settings ➪ Override Dims On Drag.

CAUTION Be careful with the Override Dims On Drag option. If you accidentally drag a fully defined sketch, this setting enables SolidWorks to completely resize the sketch. For working conceptually, it can be a great aid, but for final production models, you may do better to turn this off.

Instant 3D offers different editing options depending on how a sketch is selected.

- **A sketch is selected from the graphics window.** The pull arrow appears, enabling you to create an extruded boss or cut.

- **A sketch is selected from the FeatureManager.** If the sketch has relations to anything outside of the sketch, the sketch is highlighted with no special functionality available. If no external relations exist, a box with stretch handles enable scaling the sketch, and a set of axes with a wing enables you to move the sketch in X or Y or X and Y. Figure 7.7 shows this situation.

FIGURE 7.7

Sketch scaling and moving options with Instant 3D

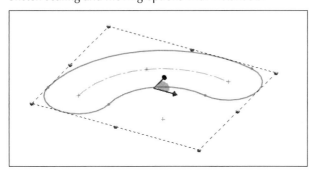

When Instant 3D is activated, double-clicking a sketch in either the FeatureManager or on a sketch element in the graphics window opens that sketch. While you are in a sketch, if you double-click with the Select cursor in blank space in the graphics window, you close the sketch. This only works for 2D sketches; 3D sketches can be opened, but not closed this way.

Revolve

Like all other features, revolve features have some rules that you must observe when choosing sketches that can be used to create a revolve:

- Draw only half of the revolve profile (draw the section to one side of the centerline).
- The profile must not cross the centerline.
- The profile must not touch the centerline at a single point. It can touch along a line, but not at a point. Revolving a sketch that touched the centerline at a single point would create a point of zero thickness in the part.

You can use any type of line or model edge for the centerline, not just the centerline/construction line type.

End conditions

There are three Revolve end conditions:

- **One-Direction.** The revolve angle is driven in a single direction.
- **Two-Direction.** The revolve angle can be driven in two independent directions.
- **Mid-Plane.** The revolve angle is divided equally in opposite directions.

There is no equivalent for Up to Vertex, Up to Next, Up to Surface, or Up to Body with the Revolve feature.

Contour selection

Like extrude features, revolve features can also use contour selection; as with the extrude features, I recommend that you avoid using contours for production work.

Loft

Many users struggle when faced with the option to create a loft or a sweep. Some overlap exists between the two features, but as you gain some experience, it becomes easier to choose between them. Generally, if you can create the cross-section of the feature by manipulating dimensions of a single sketch, then a sweep might be the best feature. If the cross-section changes character or severely changes shape, then a loft may be best. If you need a very definite shape at both ends and/ or in the middle, then a loft is a better choice because it allows you to explicitly define the cross-section at a point. However, if the outline is more important than the cross-section, then you should choose a sweep. If the path between ends is important, choose a sweep. If the ends themselves are more important and you just want to blend from one end to the other, then the loft is the better choice.

Both types of features are extremely powerful, but the sweep has a tendency to be fussier about details, setup, and rules, while the loft can be surprisingly flexible. I am not trying to dissuade you from using sweeps, because they are useful in many situations. However, in my own personal modeling, I probably use about ten lofts for every sweep. For example, while you would use a loft or combination of loft features to create a complex laundry detergent bottle, you would use the sweep to create a raised border around the label area.

Lofts are an example of *interpolated* geometry. That is to say that the loft is outlined by creating several loft sections and guide curves, and then the software interpolates the face geometry in between the sections. A good example of this is to put a circle on one plane and a rectangle on an offset plane and then loft them together. This arrangement is shown in Figure 7.8. The transition between shapes is the defining characteristic of a loft, and is also the reason for choosing a loft instead of another feature type. Lofts can create both Boss features and Cut features.

FIGURE 7.8

A simple loft

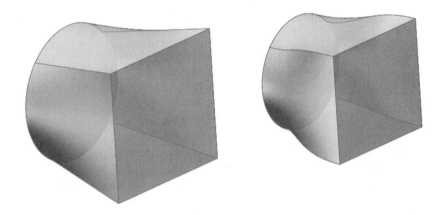

The two-profile loft with default end conditions always creates a straight transition, which is shown in the image to the left. A two-point spline with no end tangency creates a straight line in exactly the same way. By applying end conditions to either or both of the loft profiles, the loft's shape is made more interesting, as seen in the image to the right in Figure 7.8. Again, the same thing happens when applying end tangency conditions to a two-point spline: it goes from being a straight line to being more curvaceous, with continuously variable curvature. The Loft PropertyManager interface is shown in Figure 7.9.

FIGURE 7.9

The Loft PropertyManager

Entities that you can use in a loft

For solid lofts, you can select faces, closed loop 2D or 3D sketches, and surface bodies. You can use sketch points as a profile on the end of a loft that comes to a point or rounded end. For surface lofts, you can use open sketches and edges in addition to the entities that are used by solid lofts.

Some special functionality becomes available to you if you put all the profiles and guide curves together in a single 3D sketch. In order to select profiles made in this way, you must use the SelectionManager, which is discussed later in this chapter.

The Sketch Tools panel of the Loft PropertyManager enables you to drag sketch entities of any profile made in this way while you are editing or creating the Loft feature, without needing to exit and edit a sketch.

CAUTION While this sort of functionality may be attractive for a lot of reasons, it may not be the best way. Unless you are dealing with the simplest of geometry and sketch relations, 3D sketches — and more specifically 3D sketch planes — are simply not up to the task. The specific problem is sketch relations. I discuss 3D sketches in more detail in Chapter 31.

The similarities between lofts and splines

The words *loft* and *spline* come from the shipbuilding trade. The word *spline* is actually defined as the slats of wood that cover the ship, and the spars of the hull very much resemble loft sections. With the splines or slats bending at each spar, it is easy to see how the modern CAD analogy came to be.

Lofts and splines are also governed by similar mathematics. You have seen how the two-point spline and two-profile loft both create a straight-line transition. Next, a third profile is added to the loft and a third point to the spline, which demonstrates how the math that governs splines and lofts is also related to bending in elastic materials. Figure 7.10 shows how lofts and splines react geometrically in the same way that bending a flexible steel rod would react (except that the spline and the loft do not have a fixed length).

FIGURE 7.10

Splines, lofts, and bending

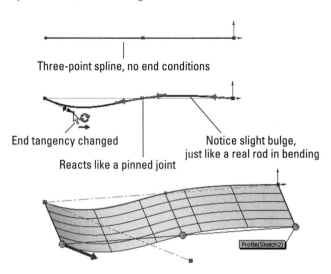

Three-point spline, no end conditions

End tangency changed

Reacts like a pinned joint

Notice slight bulge,
just like a real rod in bending

Profile(Sketch2)

With this bit of background, it is time to move forward and talk about a few of the major aspects of Loft features in SolidWorks. It is probably possible to write a separate book that only discusses modeling lofts and other complex shapes. This has in fact been done. The SolidWorks Surfacing and Complex Shape Modeling Bible (Wiley, 2008) covers a wide range of surfacing topics with examples in far greater detail. In this single chapter, I do not have the space to cover the topic exhaustively, but coverage of the major concepts will be enough to point you in the right direction.

The need for surfaces

In this chapter, I deal exclusively with solid modeling techniques because they are the baseline that SolidWorks users use most frequently. Surfaces make it easier to discuss complex shape concepts because surfaces are generally created one face at a time, rather than by using the method with solid modeling that creates as many faces as necessary to enclose a volume.

From the very beginning, the SolidWorks modeling culture has made things easier for users by taking care of many of the details in the background. This is because solids are built through automated surface techniques. Surface modeling in itself can be tedious work because of all the manual detail that you must add. Solid modeling as we know it is simply an evolutionary step that adds automation to surface modeling. The automation maintains a closed solid boundary around the volume.

Because surfaces are the underlying building blocks from which solids are made, it would make sense to teach surfaces first, and then solids. However, the majority of SolidWorks users never use surfacing, and do not see a need for it, and so surface functions are generally given a lower priority.

CROSS-REF   Refer to Chapter 27 for surfacing information.

Loft end constraints

Loft end conditions control the tangency direction and weighting at the ends of the loft. Some of the end constraints depend upon the loft starting or ending from other geometry. The optional constraints include the following:

None

The direction of the loft is not set by the None end constraint, but the curvature of the lofted faces at the ends is zero. This is the default end constraint for two-section lofts.

Default

The Default end constraint is not available for two-section lofts, only for lofts with three or more sections. This end constraint applies curvature to the end of the loft so that it approximates a parabola being formed through the first and last loft profiles.

The SolidWorks help file makes a special point to explain the difference between the None and Default end constraints, but the Default help makes it look as if it works with only two profiles, when in fact it does not.

Tangent to Face

The Tangent to Face end constraint is self-explanatory. This end constraint may fail or cause unwanted ripples or puckers in the part if profiles that are adjacent to one another or touch at an edge are lofted together. The Tangency to Face option includes a setting for tangent length. This is not a literal length dimension, but a relative weighting, on a scale from 0.1 to 10. The small arrow to the left of the setting identifies the direction of the tangency. Usually, the default setting is correct, but there are times when SolidWorks misidentifies the intended tangency direction, and you may need to correct it manually.

The Next Face option is available only when lofting from an end face where the tangency could go in one of two perpendicular directions. This is shown in Figure 7.11.

Apply to All refers to applying the Tangent Length value to all the tangency-weighting arrows for the selected profile. When you select Apply to All, only one arrow displays. When you deselect it, one arrow should display for each vertex in the profile, and you can adjust each arrow individually.

Curvature to Face

The difference between tangency and curvature is that tangency is only concerned with the direction of curvature immediately at the edge between the two surfaces. Curvature must be tangent and match the radius of curvature on either side of the edge between surfaces. This is often given many names, including curvature continuity, c2, and others. Lofted surfaces do not usually have a constant radius; because they are like splines, they are constantly changing in local radius.

Direction Vector

The Direction Vector end constraint forces the loft to be tangent to a direction that you define by selecting an axis, edge, or sketch entity. The angle setting makes the loft deviate from the direction vector, as shown in Figure 7.11. The curved arrows to the left identify the direction in which the angle deviation is going.

FIGURE 7.11

Examples of end constraints

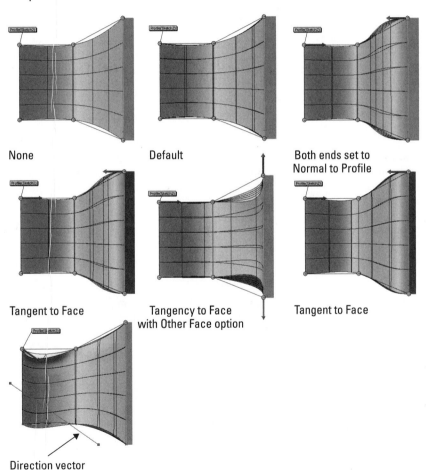

None

Default

Both ends set to
Normal to Profile

Tangent to Face

Tangency to Face
with Other Face option

Tangent to Face

Direction vector

Isoparameter U-V lines

The mesh or grid shown in the previous images appears automatically for certain types of features, including lofts. The grid represents *isoparameter* lines, also known as NURBS mesh or U-V lines. This mesh shows the underlying structure of the faces being created by the feature. If the mesh is highly distorted and appears to overlap in places, then it is likely that the feature will fail.

You can show or hide the mesh through the right-mouse menu when editing or creating a Loft feature, unless the SelectionManager is active. In this case, you can see only SelectionManager commands in the right-mouse button menu. In addition, planar faces do not mesh, only faces with some curvature.

Guide curves

Guide curves help to constrain the outline of a loft between loft profiles. Although it is best to try to achieve the shape you want by using appropriately shaped and placed loft profiles, this is not always possible. The most appropriate use of guide curves for solid lofts is at places where the loft is going to create a hard edge, which is usually at the corners of loft profile sketches. Guide curves often (but not always) break up what would otherwise be a smooth surface, and you should avoid them in these situations, if possible.

BEST PRACTICE Do not try to push the shape of the loft too extremely with guide curves. Use guide curves mainly for tweaking and fine-tuning rather than coarse adjustments. Use loft sections and end constraints to get most of the overall shape correct. Pushing too hard with a guide curve can cause the shape to kink unnaturally.

Although guide curves can be longer than the loft, they can not be shorter. The guide curve applies to the entire loft. If you need to apply the guide curve only to a portion of the loft, then split the loft into two lofts, one that uses the guide curve, and the other that does not. The guide curve must intersect all profiles in a loft.

If you have more than one guide curve, the order in which they are listed in the box is important. The first guide curve helps to position the intermediate profiles of the loft. It may be difficult or impossible to visualize the effects of guide-curve order before it happens, but remember that it does make a difference, and depending on the difference between the curves, the difference may or may not be subtle.

Guide curves are also used in sweeps, which I address later in this chapter. Figure 7.12 shows a model that is lofted using guide curves. The image to the left shows the sketches that are used to make the part. There are two sketches with points; you can use points as loft profiles. The image in the middle shows the Loft feature without guide curves, and the one to the right is the part with guide curves. If you would like to examine how this part is built, you can find it on the CD-ROM with the filename Chapter 7 Guide Curves.sldprt.

FIGURE 7.12

A loft with and without guide curves

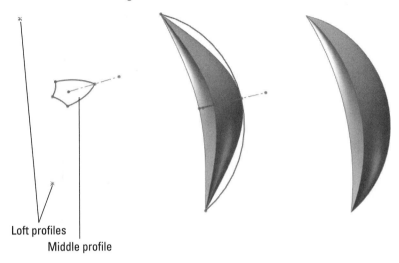

Loft profiles

Middle profile

Centerline lofts

The Centerline panel of the Loft PropertyManager is used to set up a Centerline loft. You can use the Centerline of a loft in roughly the same way that you use a sweep path. In fact, the Centerline loft resembles a sweep feature where you can specify the shape of some of the intermediate profiles. Centerline lofts can also create intermediate profiles. You may prefer to use a centerline loft instead of either a sweep or a regular loft because the profile may change in ways that the Sweep feature cannot handle, and the loft may need some guidance regarding the order of the profiles or how to smooth the shape between the profiles.

I cover sweep features later in this chapter. If you are creating a centerline loft, then you may want to examine the sweep functionality as well.

You can use centerlines simultaneously with guide curves. While guide curves must touch the profile, there is no such requirement for a centerline; in fact, the centerline works best if it does not touch any of the profiles.

The slider in the Centerline Parameters panel enables you to specify how many intermediate sections to create between sketched profiles.

SelectionManager

The SelectionManager simplifies the selection of entities from complex sketches that are not necessarily the clean, closed loop sketches that SolidWorks works with most effectively.

The SelectionManager has been implemented in a limited number of features. Selection options in the SelectionManager include the following:

- **OK.** Accepts the selection. This feature is also available on the right-mouse button menu.

- **Cancel.** Quits the SelectionManager

- **Clear All.** Clears the current selection set

- **Push Pin.** Keeps the SmartSelection window available, even when it is not required for sketch entity selections

- **Select Closed Loop.** You can select two different types of loops with this tool:
  - A parametric closed loop in a 2D or 3D sketch
  - A parametric loop of edges around a surface

- **Select Open Loop.** Selects a chain (end-to-end sketch entities)

- **Select Group.** Selects entities individually. If you click the Propagate symbol, all tangent edges are selected.

- **Select Region.** Works like the Contour Selection described earlier in this chapter.

- **Standard Selection.** Disables special functions of the SelectionManager. This feature works like a regular selection tool.
- **Auto OK Selections.** Becomes enabled when you use the Push Pin. This feature works for closed and open loop selection.

Loft options

You can choose from the following Loft options, as shown in Figure 7.13:

FIGURE 7.13

Loft options

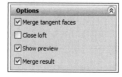

- **Merge tangent faces.** Model faces that are tangent are merged into a single face. This is done behind the scenes by converting profiles into splines, which make approximations but are smoother than sketches with individual tangent line and arc entities.

- **Close loft.** A closed loop is made of the loft. At least three loft profiles must exist in order to use this option. Figure 7.14 shows a loft where the Close Loft option is used, and the loft sections are shown. This model is on the CD-ROM with the filename `Chapter 7 – Closed Loft.sldprt`.

FIGURE 7.14

A closed loft

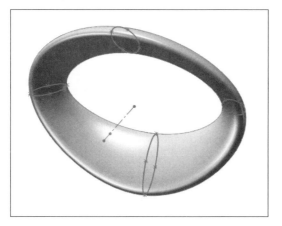

- **Show preview.** This turns the preview of the Loft feature on or off, if the feature is not going to fail. All of the following loft preview options are system options, and remain on until you turn them off.

  - **Transparent/Opaque Preview** is available from the right-mouse button menu when you edit a loft, if the SelectionManager is not active.

  - **Mesh Preview** is also available on the same right-mouse button menu.

  - **Zebra Stripe Preview** is also available on the same right-mouse button menu, and is covered in more depth in Chapter 11.

- **Merge result.** Merges the resulting solid body with any other solid bodies that it may contact.

Sweep

The Sweep feature uses more than one sketch. A sweep is made from a profile (cross-section) and a path, and can create a boss or a cut feature. If you want, you can also use guide curves. Sweeps can run the gamut from simple to complex. Typical simple sweeps are used to create wire, tubing, or hose. More complex sweeps are used for creating objects such as bottles, involutes, and cork-screws.

The main criteria for selecting a sweep to create a feature are that you must be able to identify a cross-section and a path. The profile (cross-section) can change along the path, but the overall shape must remain basically the same. The profile is typically perpendicular to the path, although this is not a requirement.

Simple sweep

An example of a simple sweep is shown in Figure 7.15. The paper clip uses a circle as the profile, and the coiled lines and arcs as the path.

FIGURE 7.15

A simple sweep feature

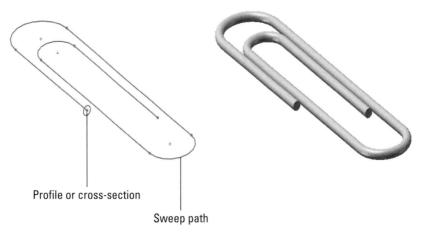

Profile or cross-section

Sweep path

Simple sweeps such as that shown in Figure 7.15 essentially set up SolidWorks to create geometry from simpler features such as Extrude and Revolve. If you look at the faces, you can see that they are created from straight lines and arcs, which lend themselves well to extrudes and revolves.

Sweep with guide curves

More complex sweeps begin to control the size, orientation, and position of the cross-section as it travels through the sweep. When you use a guide curve, several analogies can be used to visualize how the sweep works. The cross-section/profile is solved at several intermediate positions along the path. If the guide curve does not follow the path, the difference between the two is made up by adjusting the profile. Consider the following example. In this case, the profile is an ellipse, the path is a straight line, and there are guide curves that give the feature its outer shape. Figure 7.16 shows all these elements and the finished feature.

FIGURE 7.16

A sweep with two guide curves

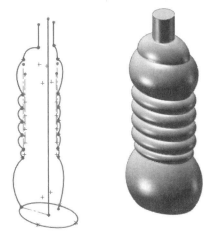

ON the CD-ROM The part shown in Figure 7.16 is on the CD-ROM with the filename `Chapter7 Bottle.sldprt`.

The sweep with guide curves does not create extrudes and revolves, although you can use simple lines and arcs with this feature. The changes in the cross-section are created from a more complex feature type, namely a loft. The PropertyManager for the Sweep function includes an option for Show Sections, which in this case creates almost 200 intermediate cross-sections. These sections are used to create a loft. You can think of complex sweeps as an automated setup for an even more complex loft. It is helpful to envision features such as this when you are troubleshooting or setting up more complex sweeps. If you open the part mentioned previously from the CD-ROM, you can edit the Sweep feature to examine the sections for yourself.

In most other published SolidWorks materials that cover these topics, sweeps are covered before lofts because many people consider lofts the more advanced topic. However, I have put lofts first because understanding them is necessary before you can understand complex sweeps, as complex sweeps really are just lofts.

Pierce relation

The Pierce sketch relation is the only sketch relation that applies to a 3D out-of-plane edge or curve without projecting the edge or curve into the sketch plane. It acts as if the 3D curve is a length of thread and the sketch point is the eye of a needle, where the thread pierces the needle eye. The Pierce relation is most important in the Sweep feature when it is applied in the profile sketch between endpoints, center points, or sketch points and the guide curves. This is because the Pierce relation determines how the profile sketch will be solved when it is moved down the sweep path to create a new intermediate profile.

Figure 7.17 illustrates the function of the Pierce relation in a sweep with guide curves. The dark section on the left is the sweep section that is sketched. The lighter sketches to the right represent the intermediate profiles that are automatically created behind the scenes.

FIGURE 7.17

The effects of the Pierce relation

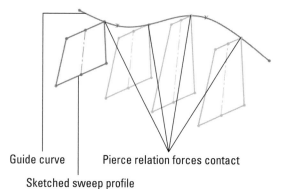

Guide curve | Pierce relation forces contact

Sketched sweep profile

Figure 7.17 shows what is happening behind the scenes in a sweep feature. The sweep recreates the original profile at various points along the path. The guide curve in this case forces the profile to rebuild with a different shape. Pierce constraints are not required in simple sweeps, but when you start using guide curves, you should also use a pierce.

If you feel that you need more profile control, but still want to create a sweep-like feature, try a centerline loft. The centerline acts like a sweep path that doesn't touch the profiles, but unlike a sweep you can use multiple profiles with it.

Figure 7.18 shows a more complicated 3D sweep, where both the path and the guide curve are 3D curves. I cover 3D curves toward the end of this chapter, and so you can refer ahead to these features to understand how this part is made.

FIGURE 7.18

A 3D sweep

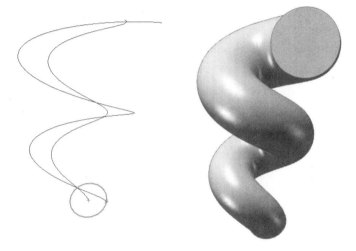

The part shown in Figure 7.18 is on the CD-ROM with the filename `Chapter 7 3D Sweep.sldprt`.

This part is created by making a pair of tapered helices, with the profile sketch plane perpendicular to the end of one of the curves. The taper on the outer helix is greater than on the inner one, which causes the twist to become larger in diameter as it goes up.

To make the circle follow both helices, you must create two pierce relations, one between the center of the circle and a helix, and the other between a sketch point that is placed on the circumference of the circle and the other helix. This means that the difference in taper angles between the two helices is what drives the change in diameter of the sweep.

Cut Sweep with a solid profile

The Cut Sweep feature has an option to use a solid sweep profile. This kind of functionality has many uses, but is primarily intended for simulating complex cuts made by a mill or lathe. Figure 7.19 shows a couple of examples of cuts you can make with this feature. The part used for this screen shot is also on the CD-ROM.

Cuts you can make with the Cut Sweep feature using a solid profile

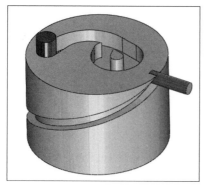

The solid profile cut sweep has a few limitations that I need to mention:

- It uses a separate solid body as the cutting tool, so you have to model multibodies
- The path must start at a point where it intersects the solid cutting tool body (path starts inside or on the surface of the cutting tool)
- The cutting tool must be definable with a revolved feature
- The cutting tool must be made of simple analytical faces (sphere, torus, cylinder, and cone; no splines)
- You cannot use a guide curve with a solid profile cut (cannot control alignment)
- The cut can intersect itself, but the path cannot cross itself

You can create many useful shapes with the solid profile cut sweep, but because of some of the limitations I've listed, some shapes are more difficult to create than others. For these shapes you might choose to use regular cut sweep features. Figure 7.20 shows an example of a cam-like feature that you may want to create with this method, but may not be able to adequately control the cutting body.

FIGURE 7.20

Controlling a cam cut may be a challenge

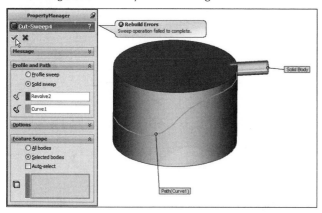

Creating Curve Features

Curves in SolidWorks are often used to help define sweeps and lofts, as well as other features. Curves differ from sketches in that curves are defined using sketches or a dialog box, and you cannot manipulate them directly or dimension them in the same way that you can sketches. Functions that you are accustomed to using with sketches often do not work on curves.

TIP When you come across a function that does not work using a curve entity, but that works on a sketch (for example, making a tangent spline), then it may help to use the Convert Entities feature. Converting entities on a helix into a 3D sketch creates a spline that lies directly on top of the helix and allows you to make another spline that is tangent to the new spline.

The following types of curves can be defined in SolidWorks:

- Helix/tapered helix/variable helix/spiral
- Projected curve
- Curve through XYZ points
- Curve through reference points
- Composite curve

You can find all the curve functions on the Curves toolbar or through the menus at Insert ➪ Curve.

Helix

The Helix curve types are all based on a circle in a sketch. The circle represents the starting location and diameter of the helix. Figure 7.21 shows the PropertyManagers of the Constant Pitch and Variable Pitch helix types.

FIGURE 7.21

The Helix PropertyManager

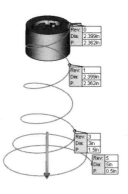

You can create all the helical curve types by specifying any combination of total height, pitch, and the number of revolutions. The start angle is best thought of as a relative number. It is difficult to predict where zero degrees starts, and this depends on the relation of the sketch plane to the Origin. The start angle cannot be controlled outside of the PropertyManager, and cannot be driven by sketch geometry. The term *pitch* refers to the straight-line distance along the axis between the rings of the helix. Pitch for the spiral is different and is described later.

Tapered Helix

The Tapered Helix panel in the Helix PropertyManager enables you to specify a taper angle for the helix. The taper angle does not affect the pitch. If you need to affect both the taper and the pitch, then you can use a variable pitch helix. Figure 7.22 shows how the taper angle relates to the resulting geometry.

Variable Pitch Helix

You can specify the variable pitch helix either in the chart or in the callouts that are shown in Figure 7.23. Both the pitch and the diameter are variable. The diameter number in the first row cannot be changed, but is driven by the sketch. In the chart shown, the transition between 4 and 4.5 revolutions is where the pitch and diameter both change.

FIGURE 7.22

The tapered helix

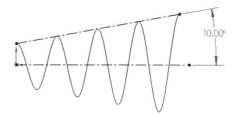

FIGURE 7.23

The variable pitch helix

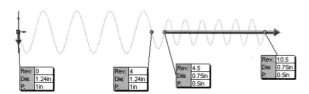

	Rev	Dia	P
1	0	1.24in	1in
2	4	1.24in	1in
3	4.5	0.75in	0.5in
4	10.5	0.75in	0.5in
5			

Spiral

A spiral is a flattened (planar) tapered helix. The pitch value on a spiral is the radial distance between revolutions of the curve.

Projected curve

Many users have difficulty envisioning the concept of the projected curve. The two options available for projected curves are:

- Sketch Onto Face
- Sketch Onto Sketch

These names can be misleading if you do not already know what they mean. In both cases, the word *sketch* is used as a noun, not a verb, and so you are not actively sketching on a surface; instead, you are creating a curve by projecting a sketch onto a face.

Sketch Onto Face

The Sketch Onto Face option is the easiest to explain, and so I will describe this one first. With this option set, the projected curve is created by projecting a 2D sketch onto a face. The sketch is projected normal (perpendicular) to the sketch plane. This is like extruding the sketch and using the Up To Surface end condition. The sketch can be an open or closed loop, but it may not be multiple open or closed loops, nor can it be self-intersecting. Figure 7.24 shows an example of projecting a sketch onto a face to create a projected curve.

FIGURE 7.24

A projected curve using the Sketch Onto Face option

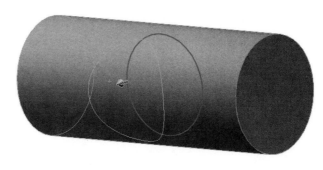

Sketch Onto Sketch

This is the concept that most frequently causes difficulty for users. The Sketch Onto Sketch Projected Curve option can be visualized in a few different ways.

Reverse 2D drawing visualization method

One way is to think of it as being the reverse of a 2D drawing. In a 2D drawing, 3D edges (you can think of the edges as curves) are projected onto orthogonal planes to represent the edge from the Front or Top planes. The Sketch Onto Sketch projection takes the two orthogonal views, placed on perpendicular planes, and projects them back to make the 3D edge or curve. This is part of the attraction of the projected curve, because making 3D curves accurately is difficult if you do it directly by using a tool such as a 3D sketch spline; however, if you know what the curve looks like from two different directions, then it becomes easy. Figure 7.25 illustrates this visualization method.

When you think of describing a complex 3D curve in space, one of the first methods that usually comes to mind is describing it as a 2D curve from perpendicular directions, exactly in the same way as you would if you created projected drawing views from it. From this, it makes sense to see the creation of the curve as the reverse process, drawing the 2D views first, from which you can then create the 3D curve.

Intersecting surfaces visualization method

A second method used for visualizing Sketch On Sketch projected curves is the intersecting surfaces method. In this method, you can see the curve being created at the intersection of two surfaces that are created by extruding each of the sketches. This method is shown in Figure 7.26.

FIGURE 7.25

The reverse 2D drawing visualization method for projected curves

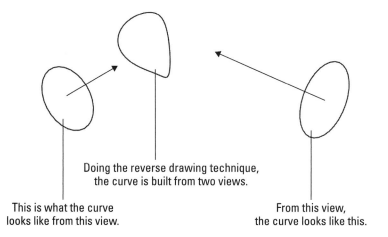

Doing the reverse drawing technique,
the curve is built from two views.

This is what the curve
looks like from this view.

From this view,
the curve looks like this.

FIGURE 7.26

Using intersecting surfaces to visualize a Sketch on Sketch projected curve

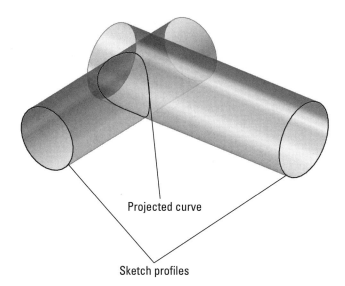

Projected curve

Sketch profiles

Curve Through XYZ Points

The Curve Through XYZ Points feature enables you to either type in or import a text file with coordinates for points on a curve. The text file can be generated by any program that makes lists of numbers, including Excel. The curve reacts like a spline, and so the teeter-tottering effect may be noticeable, especially because you cannot set end conditions or tangency. To avoid this effect, it may be a good idea to overbuild the curve by a few points on each end.

If you import a text file, the file can have an extension of either *.txt or *.sldcrv. The data that it contains must be formatted as three columns of X-, Y-, and Z-coordinates using the document units (inch, mm, and so on), and the coordinates must be separated by comma, space, or tab. Figure 7.27 shows both the Curve File dialog box displaying a table of the curve through X, Y, and Z points, and the *.sldcrv Notepad file. The file can be read from the Curve File dialog box by using the Browse button, but if you manually type the points, then you can also save the data out directly from the dialog box. Just like any type of sketch, this type of curve cannot intersect itself.

FIGURE 7.27

The Curve File dialog box showing a table of the curve through X, Y, and Z points, and a Notepad text file with the same information

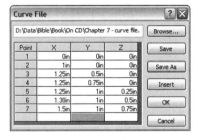
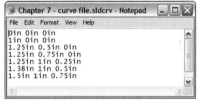

Curve Through Reference Points

The Curve Through Reference Points feature creates a curve entity from selected sketch points or vertices. The curve can be an open or closed loop, but a closed loop requires that you select at least three points. You cannot set end conditions of the curve, and so this feature works like a spline in the same way as the XYZ curve.

The most common application of this feature is to create a simple two-point curve across the opening of a surface feature to close the opening by using a surface feature such as Fill, Boundary, or Loft.

Composite curve

The composite curve joins together multiple curves, edges, or sketches into a single curve entity. The part shown in Figure 7.28 was created by using a composite curve to join together a 3D sketch, variable pitch helix, and a projected curve. You can also use model edges with the composite curve. The curve is shown on half of the part; the rest of the part is mirrored.

Composite curves overlap in functionality with the Selection Manager to some extent. In some ways the Composite Curve is nicer because you can save a selection in cast the creation of the feature that uses the Selection Manager fails (if you can't create the feature, you can't save the selection). On the other hand, Composite Curves don't function the same way that a selection of model edges do for settings like tangency and curvature.

FIGURE 7.28

A part created from a composite curve

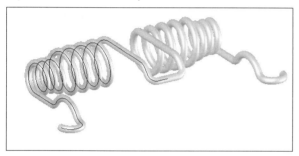

Split lines

Split lines are not exactly curves; they are really just edges that split faces into multiple faces. Split lines are used for several purposes, but are primarily intended to split faces so that draft can be added. They are also used for creating a broken-out face for a color break or to create an edge for a hold line fillet, which I discuss later in this chapter.

There are some limitations to using split lines. First, they must split a face into at least two fully enclosed areas. You cannot have a split line with an open loop sketch where the ends of the loop are on the face that is to be split; they must either hang off the face to be split or be coincident with the edges. Second, nested loops or multiple closed loops are not allowed, nor are self-intersecting sketches. If you need to do something with a sketch of one of these types, then you may be able to accomplish the same thing using multiple split-line features. If you want to create multiple stripes across a face, the best option may be to create an open loop sketch with many S-shaped zigzags.

One result of all these limitations is that it becomes difficult to make split lines using sketch text or other complex sketches. There are several ways of bypassing these limitations, such as copying the surfaces with Knit or Offset at zero distance and then trimming the surface with the sketch, or creating a very shallow solid extrude (although this can be very detrimental to rebuild and graphics speed).

As an alternative, you might consider using the Wrap feature with the Scribe option for situations where a split line has to go around a cylindrical or conical object. Split lines can also be created by Spline On Surface 3D sketch with the Intersection option in the Split line feature.

CAUTION A word of caution is needed when using split lines, especially if you plan to add or remove split lines from an existing model. The split lines should go as far down the tree as possible. Split lines change the face IDs of the faces that they split, and often the edges as well. If you roll back and apply a split line before existing features, you may have a significant amount of cleanup to do. Similarly, if you remove a split line that already has several dependent features, then many other features may also be deleted or simply lose their references.

Equation Driven Curve

The Equation Driven Curve is not really a curve feature, it is a sketch entity. It specifies a spline inside a 2D sketch with an actual equation. Even though this is a spline based sketch entity, it can only be controlled through the equation, and not by using spline controls.

Figure 7.29 shows the Equation Driven Curve PropertyManager along with a sample spline. If you want to put the toolbar button on your toolbar, look for it in the Sketch page of Tools ➪ Customize ➪ Commands.

FIGURE 7.29

Creating an Equation Driven Curve

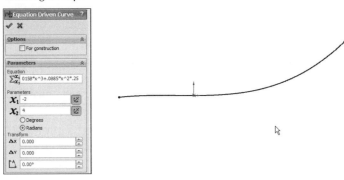

Use regular mathematical notation and order of operations to write the equation. X1 and X2 are for the beginning and end of the curve. Use the transform options at the bottom of the PropertyManager to move the entire curve in X, Y or rotation. To specify X = f(Y) (instead of Y = f(X)), use a 90 degree transform.

Filleting

SolidWorks offers very powerful filleting functions. Many filleting options are available, but most of them are relatively little used or even known. In fact, most users confine themselves to the Constant Radius or Variable Radius fillets. The following section describes all the available fillet types and options:

- Constant Radius Fillet
  - Multiple Radius Fillet
  - Round Corners
  - Keep Edge/Keep Surface
  - Keep Feature
- Variable Radius Fillet
- Face Fillet
  - Curvature Continuous Fillet
  - Face Fillet with Help Point
  - Single Hold Line Fillet
  - Double Hold Line Fillet
  - Constant Width Fillet
- Full Round Fillet
- Setback Fillet
- Setback Fillet with Variable Radius

Figure 7.30 shows the Fillet PropertyManager. There are other options that affect preview and selection of items, and these options are discussed in this section.

FIGURE 7.30

The Fillet PropertyManager

The Fillet feature comprises various types of functionality. Simple fillets on straight and round edges are handled differently from variable-radius fillets, which are handled differently from the single or double hold line fillet or setback fillets. Once you click the OK button to create a fillet as a certain type, you cannot switch it to another type. You can switch types before you click OK.

Creating a constant radius fillet

Constant radius fillets are the most common type that are created if you select only edges, features, or faces without changing any settings. When applying fillets in large numbers, you should consider several best-practice guidelines and other recommendations that come later in this chapter.

There are still some long-time users who distinguish between fillets and rounds (where fillets add material and rounds remove it). SolidWorks does not distinguish between the two, and even two edges that are selected for use with the same fillet feature can have opposite functions; for example, both adding and removing material in a single feature.

Selecting entities to fillet

You can create fillets from several selections, including edges, faces, features, and loops. Edges offer the most direct method, and are the easiest to control. Figure 7.31 shows how you can use each of these selections to more intelligently create fillets on parts.

> **TIP** To select features for filleting, you must select them from the FeatureManager. The Selection Filter only filters edges and faces for fillet selection. You can select loops in two ways: through the right-click Select Loop option, or by selecting a face and Ctrl-selecting an edge on the face.

> Another option for selecting edges in the Fillet command is the Select Through Faces option, which appears on the Fillet Options panel. This option enables you to select edges that are hidden by the model. This can be a useful option on a part with few hidden edges, or a detrimental option on a part where there are many edges due to patterns, ribs, vents, or existing fillets. You can control a similar option globally for features other than fillets at Tools ⇨ Options ⇨ Display/Selection, Allow Selection In HLR and Shaded Modes.

Faces and Features selections are useful when you are creating fillets where you want the selections to update. In Figure 7.32, the ribs that are intersecting the circular boss are also being filleted. If the rib did not exist when the fillet was applied, but was added later and reordered so that it came before the Fillet feature, then the fillet selection automatically takes the rib into account. If the fillet used edge selection, then this automatic selection updating would not have taken place.

FIGURE 7.31

Selection options for fillets

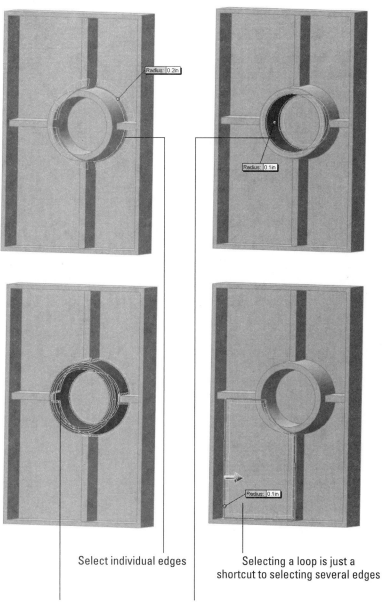

Select individual edges

Selecting a loop is just a
shortcut to selecting several edges

Selecting a feature fillets
all the edges
that touch the feature

Selecting a face fillets all
edges around the face

Tangent propagation

By default, fillets have the Tangent Propagation option turned on. This is almost always a good choice, although there may be times when you want to experiment with turning it off. Tangent propagation simply means that if you select an edge to fillet, and this edge is tangent to other edges, then the fillet will keep going along tangent edges until it forms a closed loop, the tangent edges stop, or the fillet fails.

If you turn off Tangent Propagation, but there are still tangent edges, then you may see different results. One possible result is that it could fail. One of the tricks with fillet features is to try to envision what you are asking the software to do. For example, if one edge is filleted and the next edge is not, then how is the fillet going to end? Figure 7.32 shows two of the potential results when fillets are asked not to propagate, whether or not to tangent edges. The fillet face may continue along its path until it runs off of the part or until the feature fails.

FIGURE 7.32

Turning off the Tangent Propagation option

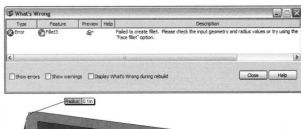

TIP This may sound counter-intuitive, but sometimes when fillet features fail, it may be useful to turn off propagation and make the fillet in multiple features. There are times when creating two fillets like the one shown in Figure 7.32 will work when making the same geometry as a single feature will not. This may be due to geometry problems where the sharp edges come together and are eliminated by the fillet.

BEST PRACTICE In general, fillets should be the last features that are applied to a model, particularly the small cosmetic or edge break fillets. Larger fillets that contribute to the structure or overall shape of the part may be applied earlier.

Be careful of the rock-paper-scissors game that you inevitably get caught up in when modeling plastic parts and deciding on the feature order of fillets, draft, and shell. Most fillets should come after draft, and large fillets should come before the shell. Draft may come either before or after the shell, depending on the needs of the area that you are dealing with on the part. In short, there is no single set of rules that you can consistently apply and that works best in all situations.

Dealing with a large number of fillets

Figure 7.33 shows a model with a bit of a filleting nightmare. This is a large plastic tray that requires many ribs underneath for strength. Because the ribs may be touched by the user, the sharp edges need to be rounded. Interior edges need to be rounded also for strength and plastic flow through the ribs. Literally hundreds of edges would need to be selected to create the fillets if you do not use an advanced technique.

FIGURE 7.33

A plastic tray with a large number of fillets

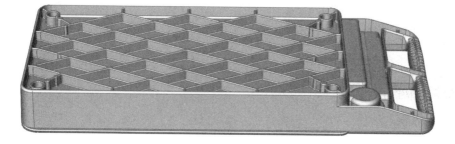

Selecting entities

Some of the techniques outlined previously, such as face and feature selection, can be useful for quickly filleting a large number of edges. Another method that still selects a large number of edges, but is not as intuitive as the others, is window selection of the edges. To use this option effectively, you may want to first position the model into a view where only the correct edges will be selected, turn off the Select Through Faces option, and use the Edges Selection filter.

Fillet Xpert

The Fillet Xpert is a tool with several uses. One of the functions is the ability to select multiple edges. A part like the one shown in Figure 7.33 is ideal for this tool. To use the Fillet Xpert, click the Fillet Xpert button in the Fillet PropertyManager. Figure 7.34 shows this. When you select an edge, the Fillet Xpert presents a pop-up tool bar giving you a choice of several selection options. Notice that Figure 7.34 shows the majority of the edges selected that are needed for this fillet.

FIGURE 7.34

Using the Fillet Xpert selection technique

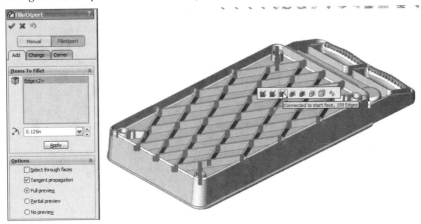

The Fillet expert is also a tool that automatically finds solutions to complex fillet problems, particularly when you have several fillets of different sizes coming together.

The Corner tab of the Fillet Xpert enables you to select from different corner options, which are usually the result of different fillet orders. To use the Corner Xpert, make sure the Fillet Xpert is active; then click on the corner face, and toggle through the options.

Using preview

I like to use the fillet preview. It helps to see what the fillet will look like, and perhaps more important, the presence of a preview usually means that the fillet will work.

Unfortunately, when you have a large number of fillets to create, the preview can cause a significant slowdown. Turning it off or using the Partial Preview are both possible options. Partial Preview shows the fillet on only one edge in the selection, and is much faster when you are creating a large number of fillets.

PERFORMANCE For rebuild speed efficiency, you should make fillets in a minimum number of features. For example, if you have 100 edges to fillet, it is better for performance to do it with a single fillet feature that has 100 edges selected rather than 100 fillet features that have one edge selected. This is the one case where creating the feature and rebuilding the feature are both faster by choosing a particular technique (usually if it is faster to create, it rebuilds more slowly).

BEST PRACTICE Although creation and rebuild speed are in sync when you use the minimum number of features to create the maximum number of fillets, this is not usually the case. (There had to be a downside.) When a single feature has a large selection, any one of these edges that fail to fillet will cause the entire feature to fail. As a result, a feature with 100 edges selected is 100 times more likely to fail than a feature with a single edge. Large selection sets are also far more difficult to troubleshoot when they fail than small selection sets that fail.

Using folders

When you have a large number of fillet features, it can be tedious to navigate the FeatureManager. It is therefore useful to place groups of fillets into folders. This makes it easy to suppress or unsuppress all the fillets in the folder at once. Separate folders can be particularly useful if the fillets have different uses, such as fillets that are used for PhotoWorks models and fillets that are removed for FEA (Finite Element Analysis) or drawings.

Multiple Radius Fillet

The Multiple Radius Fillet option in the Fillet PropertyManager enables you to make multiple fillet sizes within a single fillet feature. Figure 7.35 shows how the multiple radius Fillet feature looks when you are working with it. You can change values from the callout flags or in the PropertyManager.

FIGURE 7.35

Using the Multiple Radius Fillet option

 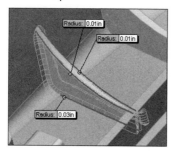

This may seem like an attractive way to group several fillets into as small a space on the FeatureManager as possible, but I cannot think of a single reason that would drive me to use this option. While there may be a small performance benefit to condensing several features into one, there are many more downsides that adversely affect performance:

- Loss of control of feature order
- A single failed fillet causes the whole feature, and thus all the fillets, to fail
- Troubleshooting is far more difficult
- Smaller groups of fillets cannot be suppressed without suppressing everything
- You cannot change the size of a group of fillets together

BEST PRACTICE While this may be more personal opinion than best practice, I believe that there are good reasons to consider using techniques other than single features that contain a lot of fillets, or single features that drive fillets of various sizes. Best practice would lean more toward grouping fillets that have a similar use and the same size. For example, you may want to separate fillets that break corners on ribs from fillets that round the outer shape of a large plastic part.

Another consideration is feature order when it comes to the fillet's relationship to draft and shell features. If the fillets are all grouped into a single feature, then controlling this relationship becomes impossible.

Round Corners

The Round Corners option refers to how SolidWorks handles fillets that go around sharp corners. By default, this setting is off, which leaves fillets around sharp corners looking like mitered picture frames. If you turn this setting on, the corner looks like a marble has rolled around it. Figure 7.36 shows the resulting geometry from both settings.

FIGURE 7.36

The Round Corners option, both on and off

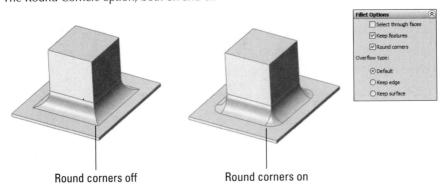

Round corners off   Round corners on

Keep Edge/Keep Surface

The Keep Edge/Keep Surface toggle determines what SolidWorks should do if a fillet is too big to fit in an area. The Keep Edge option keeps the edge where it is and tweaks the position (not the radius) of the fillet to make it meet the edge. The Keep Surface option keeps the surfaces of the fillet and the end face clean; however, to do this, it has to tweak the edge. There is often a tradeoff when you try to place fillets into a space that is too small. Sometimes it is useful to try to visualize what you think the result should look like. Figure 7.37 shows how the fillet would look in a perfect world, followed by how the fillet looks when cramped with the Keep Edge option and how it looks when cramped with the Keep Surface option.

FIGURE 7.37

The Keep Edge option and the Keep Surface option

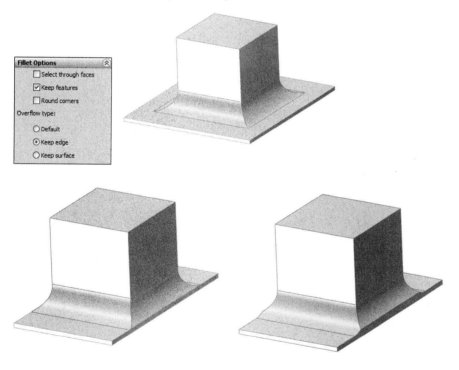

The Default option chooses the best option for a particular situation. As a result, it seems to use the Keep Edge option unless it does not work, in which case it changes to the Keep Surface option.

Keep Feature

The Keep Feature option appears on the Options panel of the Fillet PropertyManager. By default, this option is turned on. If a fillet completely surrounds a feature such as a hole (as long as it is not a through hole) or a boss, then turning off the Keep Feature option removes the hole or boss. When Keep Feature is on, the faces of the feature trim or extend to match the fillet, as shown in Figure 7.38.

The Keep Feature option, both on and off

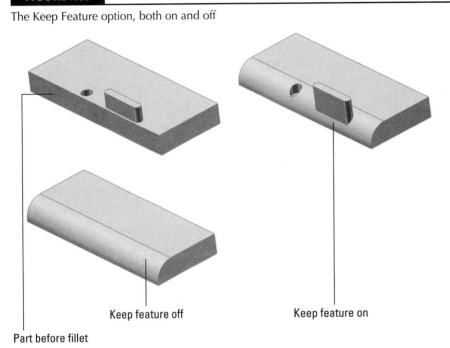

Part before fillet

Keep feature off

Keep feature on

Creating variable radius fillets

Variable radius fillets are another powerful weapon in the fight against boring designs; they also double as a useful tool to solve certain problems that arise. Although it is difficult to define exactly when to use the variable radius fillet, you can use it when you need a fillet to round an edge, and it has to change in size to fit the available geometry.

BEST PRACTICE It may be easier to identify when *not* to use a variable radius fillet. Fillets are generally used to round or break edges, not to sculpt a part. If you are using fillets to sculpt blocky parts, unless you are actively trying to make blocky parts with big fillets, then you may consider another approach using complex modeling, which will give the part a better shape and make it more controllable. Other options exist that give you a different type of control, such as the double hold line fillet.

In some ways, variable radius fillets function like other fillets. For example, they offer propagation to tangent edges and preview options.

Applying the values

When you first select an edge for the variable radius fillet, the endpoints are identified by callout flags with the value *unassigned*. A preview does not display until at least one of the points has a radius value in the box. You can also apply radius values in the PropertyManager, but they are easier to keep track of using the callouts. Figure 7.39 shows a variable radius fillet after the edge selection, after one value has been applied, and after three values have been applied. To apply a radius value that is not at the endpoint of an edge, you can select one of the three colored dots along the selected edge. The preview should show you how the fillet will look in wireframe display.

FIGURE 7.39

Assigning values to a variable radius fillet

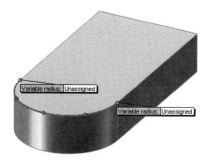

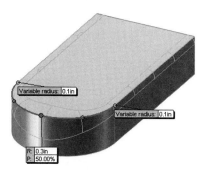

By default, the variable radius fillet puts five points on an edge, one at each endpoint, one at the midpoint, and one each halfway between the ends and middle. If you want to create an additional control point, there are three ways to do this:

- Ctrl-drag an existing point
- Select the callout of an existing point and change the P (percentage) value
- Change the Number of Instances value in the Variable Radius Parameters panel of the PropertyManager

If you have selected several edges, and several unassigned values are on the screen, then you can use the Set Unassigned option in the PropertyManager to set them all to the same value. The Set All option sets all radius values to the same number, including any values that you may have changed to be different than the rest. Figure 7.40 shows the Variable Radius Parameters panel.

FIGURE 7.40

The Variable Radius Parameters panel of the Fillet PropertyManager

Another available option with the variable radius fillet is that you can set a value of zero at an end of the fillet. You need to be careful about using a zero radius, because it is likely to cause down-stream problems with other fillets, shells, offsets, and even machining operations. You cannot assign a zero radius in the middle of an edge, only at the end. If you need to end a fillet at a particular location, you can use a split line to split the edge and apply a zero radius at that point. Figure 7.41 shows a part with two zero-radius values.

Straight versus smooth transitions

Variable radius fillets have an option for either a straight transition or a smooth transition. This works like the two-profile lofts that were mentioned earlier in this chapter. The names may be somewhat misleading because both transitions are smooth. The straight transition goes in a straight line, from one size to the next, and the smooth transition takes a swooping S-shaped path between the sizes. The difference between these two transitions is demonstrated in Figure 7.42.

Other reasons to use the variable radius fillet

Variable radius fillets use a different method to create the fillet geometry than the default constant radius fillet. Sometimes using a variable radius fillet can make a difference where a constant radius fillet does not work. This is sometimes true even when the variable radius fillet uses constant radius values. It is just another tool in the toolbox.

FIGURE 7.41

Zero radius values in the variable radius fillet

FIGURE 7.42

Straight versus smooth transitions of a variable radius fillet

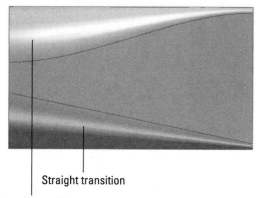

Straight transition

Smooth transition

Face fillet

Face fillets may be the most flexible type of fillet because of the range of what they can do. Face fillets start as simply an alternate selection technique for a constant radius fillet and extend to the extremely flexible double hold line face fillet, which is more of a blend than a fillet.

Under normal circumstances, the default fillet type uses the selection of an edge to create the fillet. An edge is used because it represents the intersection between two faces. However, there can sometimes be a problem with the edge not being clean, or being broken up into smaller pieces, or any number of other reasons causing a constant radius fillet using an edge selection to fail. In cases like this, SolidWorks displays the error message, "Failed to create fillet. Please check the input geometry and radius values or try using the 'Face Fillet' option."

Users almost universally ignore these messages. In the situation shown in Figure 7.43, the Face Fillet option suggested in the error message is exactly the one that you should use. Here the face fillet covers over all the junk on the edge that prevents the fillet from executing.

FIGURE 7.43

A face fillet covering a bad corner

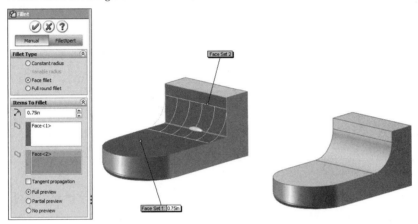

Face fillets are sometimes amazing at covering over a mess of geometry that you might think you could never fillet. The main limitation on fillets of this type is that the fillet must be *big* enough to bridge the gap. That's right, I said *big* enough. Face fillets can fail if they are either too small or too large. Figure 7.44 shows a complex fillet situation that is completely covered by a face fillet.

FIGURE 7.44

A face fillet covering complex geometry

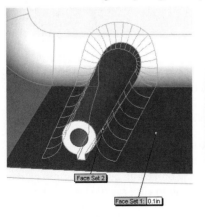
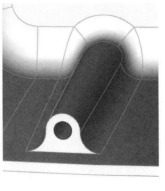

Continuous curvature face fillets

Curvature continuity refers to the quality of a transition between two curves or faces, where the curvature is the same or continuous at and around the transition. The best way to convey this concept is with simple 2D sketch elements. When a line transitions to an arc, you have non-continuous curvature. The line has no curvature, and there is an abrupt change because the arc has a specific radius.

NOTE Radius is the inverse of curvature, and so $r = 1/c$. For a straight line, $r = \infty$, in which case $c = 0$.

To make the transition from $r = \infty$ to $r = 2$ smoothly, you would need to use a variable radius arc if such a thing existed. There are several types of sketch geometry that have variable curvature, such as ellipses, parabolas, and splines. Ellipses and parabolas follow specific mathematical formulas to create the shape, but the spline is a general curve that can take on any shape that you want, and you can control its curvature to change smoothly or continuously. Splines, by their very definition, have continuous curvature within the spline, although you cannot control the specific curvature or radius values directly.

All of this means that continuous curvature face fillets use a spline-based variable-radius section for the fillet, rather than an arc-based constant radius. Figure 7.45 illustrates the difference between continuous curvature and constant curvature. The spikes on top of the curves represent the curvature ($1/r$, and so the smaller the radius, the taller the spike). These spikes are called a *curvature comb*.

FIGURE 7.45

Using curvature combs to evaluate transitions

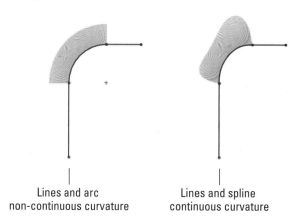

Lines and arc
non-continuous curvature

Lines and spline
continuous curvature

Notice how in Figure 7.46, the curvature comb immediately jumps from no curvature to the constant arc radius, but the spline image ramps up to a curvature that varies.

Face fillets with Help point

The Help point in the Face Fillet PropertyManager is a fairly obscure option. However, it is useful in cases where the selection of two faces does not uniquely identify an edge to fillet. For example, Figure 7.46 shows a situation where the selection of two faces could result in either one edge or the other being filleted (normally, I would hope that both edges would be filleted). The fillet will default to one edge or the other, but you can force it to a definite edge using the Help point.

FIGURE 7.46

Using a Help point with a face fillet

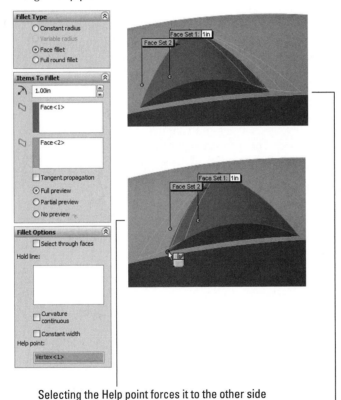

Selecting the Help point forces it to the other side

Face fillet defaults to the right side

In some cases, the Help point is ignored altogether. For example, if you have a simple box, and select both ends of the box as selection set 1, and the top of the box as selection set 2, then the fillet could go to either end. Consequently, assigning a Help point will not do anything in this case, because multiple faces have been selected. The determining factor is which of the multiple faces is selected first. If this were a more commonly used feature, the interface for it might be made a little less cryptic, but because this feature is rarely, if ever, used, it just becomes a quirky piece of trivia.

Single hold line fillet

A single hold line fillet is a form of variable radius fillet, but instead of it being defined using the variable radius fillet type, it is created using the face fillet. Rather than the radius being driven by specific numerical values, it is driven by a hold line, or edge, on the model. The hold line can be an existing edge, forcing the fillet right up to the edge of the part, or it can be created by a split line, which enables you to drive the fillet however you like. Figure 7.47 shows these two options, before and after the fillets. Notice that these fillets are still arc-based fillets; if you were to take a cross-section perpendicular to the edge between filleted faces, it would be an arc cross-section with a distinct radius. However, in the other direction, hold line fillets do not necessarily have a constant radius, although they may if the hold line is parallel with the edge between faces.

FIGURE 7.47

Single hold line fillets

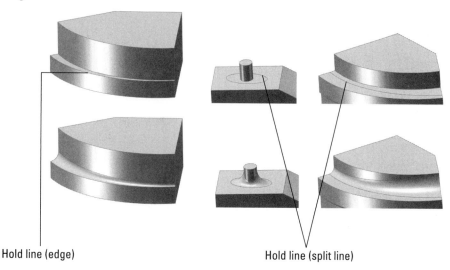

Hold line (edge)   Hold line (split line)

You can select the Hold line in the Fillet Options panel of the Face Fillet PropertyManager, as shown in Figure 7.48. The top panel, Fillet Type, is available only when the feature is first created. When you edit it after it has been created, the Fillet Type panel does not appear. As a result, you cannot change from one top level type of fillet to another after it has been initially created.

The PropertyManager interface for the hold line face fillet

Double hold line fillet

There are times when a single hold line does not meet your needs. The single hold line controls only one side of the fillet, and in order to control both sides of the fillet, you must use a double hold line fillet. SolidWorks software does not specifically differentiate between the single and double hold line fillets, but they are radically different in how they create the geometry. When both sides of the fillet are controlled, it is not possible to span between the hold lines with an arc that is tangent to both sides unless you were careful about setting up the hold lines so that they are equidistant from the edge where the faces intersect. This means that the double hold line fillet must use a spline to span between hold lines, as shown in Figure 7.49.

To get this feature to work, you need to use the Curvature Continuous option in the Fillet Options panel. Remember that this option creates a spline-based fillet rather than an arc-based fillet, which is exactly what you need for a double hold line fillet. This makes the double hold line fillet more of a blend than a true fillet. Figure 7.50 shows examples of the double hold line fillet.

FIGURE 7.49

A double hold line uses a spline, not an arc.

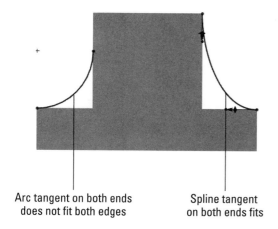

Arc tangent on both ends
does not fit both edges

Spline tangent
on both ends fits

FIGURE 7.50

Examples of the double hold line fillet

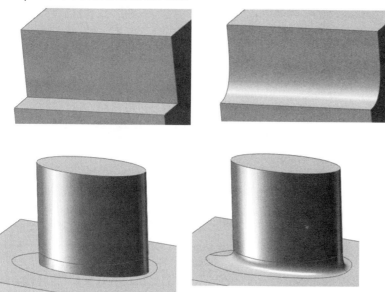

Constant width fillet

The Constant Width option of the Face Fillet PropertyManager drives a fillet by its width rather than by its radius. This is most helpful on parts where the angle of the faces between which you are filleting is changing dramatically. Figure 7.51 illustrates two situations where this is particularly useful. The setting for constant width is found in the Options panel of the Face Fillet PropertyManager. The part shown in the images is on the CD-ROM as Chapter 7 Constant Width.sldprt.

FIGURE 7.51

The constant width fillet

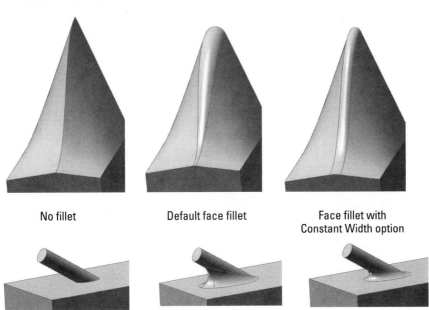

No fillet   Default face fillet   Face fillet with
                                              Constant Width option

Full round fillet

The full round fillet is very useful in many situations. In fact, it may actually work in situations where you would not expect it to. It does require quite a bit of effort to accomplish the selection, but it compensates by allowing you to avoid alternate fillet techniques.

To create a full round fillet, you have to select three sets of faces. Usually one face in each set is sufficient. The fillet is tangent to all three sets of faces, but the middle set is on the end, and the face is completely eliminated. Figure 7.52 shows several applications of the full round fillet. Notice that it is not limited to faces of a square block, but also propagates around tangent entities and can create a variable radius fillet over irregular lofted geometry.

FIGURE 7.52

A full round fillet

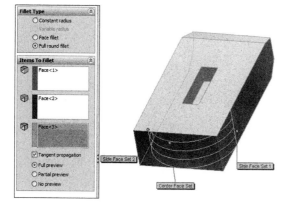

Setback fillet

The setback fillet is the most complex of the fillet options. You can use the Setback option in conjunction with constant radius, multiple radius, and variable radius fillet types. A setback fillet blends several fillets together at a single vertex, starting the blend at some "setback" distance along each filleted edge from the vertex. At least three, and often more, edges come together at the setback vertex. Figure 7.53 shows the PropertyManager interface and what a finished setback fillet looks like. The following steps demonstrate how to use the setback fillet.

Setting up a setback fillet can take some time, especially if you are just learning about this feature. You must specify values for fillet radiuses, select edges and vertices, and specify six setback distances. If you are using multiple radius fillets or variable radius fillets, then this becomes an even larger task. The steps are as follows:

FIGURE 7.53

The Setback Fillet Interface and a finished fillet

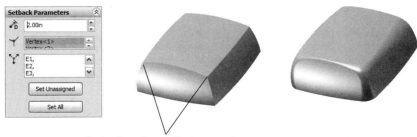

Setback vertices: all edges coming
to these vertices will be filleted

1. **Determine the type of fillet to be used:**
   - Constant radius fillet
   - Multiple radius fillet
   - Variable radius fillet

2. **Select the edges to be filleted.** Selected edges must all touch one of the setback vertices that will be selected in a later step.

3. **Assign radius values for the filleted items.** Figure 7.54 shows a sample part that illustrates this step.

FIGURE 7.54

The setback fillet setup for Steps 1 through 3

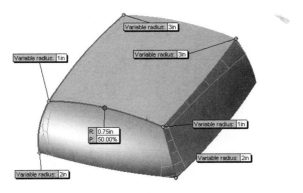

4. **Select the setback vertices.** In the Setback Parameters panel of the PropertyManager, with the second box down highlighted, select the vertices. Although this box looks like it is only big enough for a single selection, it can accept multiple selections.

5. **Enter setback values.** As shown in Figure 7.55, the setback callout flags have leaders that point from a specific value to a specific edge. The dimensions refer to distances, as shown in the image to the right in Figure 7.55. The setback distance is the distance over which the fillet will blend from the corner to the fillet.

FIGURE 7.55

Entering setback values

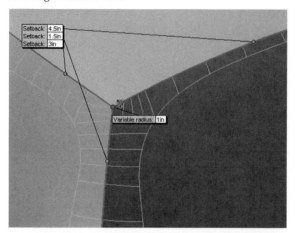

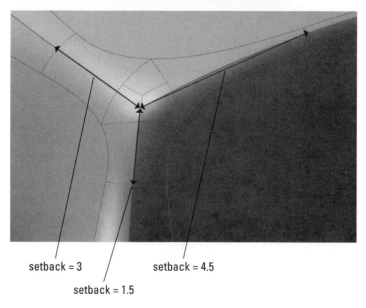

setback = 3   setback = 4.5

setback = 1.5

CAUTION When you select multiple vertices, the preview arrows that indicate which edge you are currently setting the setback value for may be incorrect. The arrows can only be shown on one vertex, and so you may want to rely on the leaders from the callouts to determine which setback distance you are currently setting.

6. **Repeat the process for all selected setback vertices.** If you are using a preview, then you may notice that the preview goes away when starting a second set of setback values. Don't worry. This is probably not because the feature is going to fail. Once you finish typing the values, the preview will return. When you have spent as much time setting up a feature as you will spend on this, seeing the preview disappear can be frustrating; however, persevere, and it will return.

Selecting a Specialty Feature

SolidWorks contains several specialty features that perform tasks that you will use less often. Although you will not use these features as frequently as others, you should still at least be aware of them and what they do, because you never know when you will need them.

Dome and Shape

The Dome and Shape features are similar in many ways. For example, they both bulge or indent a single selected face. Neither of these features really offers you much control over the actual shape; instead, the shape is controlled by the following:

- The shape of the selected face
- An internal algorithm
- Various settings
- A constraint sketch

While each of these elements influences the shape of the feature, this influence is not predictable or controllable — it is more of a random or approximate affect. When SolidWorks first released the Shape feature, they advertised it as a complex shape-creation tool. In fairness, it does create complex shapes, but they are not truly intentional, predictable, or controllable, and are certainly not anything that you would use on a consumer product. Dome and Shape are quick approximations, and rarely achieve professional-looking results.

BEST PRACTICE Dome and Shape features are best used when you are looking for a generic bulge or indentation, and are not too concerned about controlling the specific shape. Occasionally, one of these features may be exactly what you need, but when you need more precise, predictable control, then you should use the Fill, Boundary or Loft feature.

Because there are more similarities than differences between the Dome and Shape features, I've listed the differences first to distinguish them:

- The Dome feature can create multiple domes on multiple selected faces in a single feature, although it creates only a single dome for each face. Shape can shape only a single face for each command.

- Using the Elliptical Dome setting, Dome can create a feature that is tangent to the vertical. Shape is always tangent to the face that you have selected to create it.

- Shape has controls named Pressure, Bend, and Stretch, implying that you should visualize its function as an elastic membrane with positive or negative fluid pressure that causes it to bulge or collapse inward.

The similarities between the features include the following:

- Both features can use constraint sketches to limit their shape.
- Both features work on non-planar faces.
- Neither feature can establish a tangent relationship to faces bordering the selected face.
- Neither feature can span multiple faces.
- Both features display a temporary untrimmed four-sided patch that extends beyond the selected face when you use them on a non-four-sided face.
- Both features function on solids.
- Neither feature functions on surfaces.

The Dome and Shape interfaces are shown in Figure 7.56. Notice that the Shape feature is not integrated into the PropertyManager (SolidWorks features used to all use dialog boxes in the graphics window until they were moved to the PropertyManager to save space. This is still true as late as early releases of SolidWorks 2009, and is always a sign of a feature that is not used often. As is the case with a rarely used feature that is not very useful, the feature may disappear rather than be updated.

The Dome feature has two notable settings: the elliptical dome and continuous dome.

The elliptical dome is available only on flat faces where the boundary is either a complete circle or an ellipse. The cross-section of the dome is elliptical, and does not account for draft, which means that it is always tangent to the perpendicular from the selected flat face.

The continuous dome is a setting for any non-circular or elliptical face, including polygons and closed-loop splines. The setting results in a single unbroken face. If you turn the continuous dome setting off, it functions like the elliptical dome setting. Figure 7.57 shows the most useful settings for the Dome feature.

FIGURE 7.56

Dome and Shape interfaces

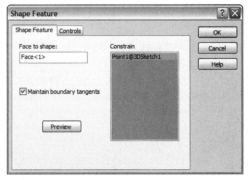
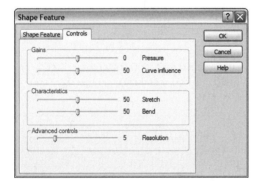

FIGURE 7.57

Settings for the Dome feature

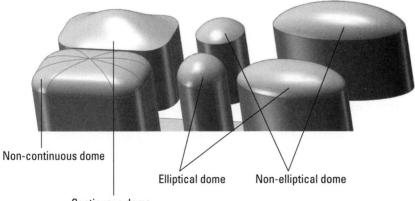

Non-continuous dome

Elliptical dome

Non-elliptical dome

Continuous dome

Wrap feature

The Wrap feature enables you to wrap 2D sketches around cylindrical and conical faces. However, trying to wrap around 360 degrees can cause some difficulties. Although all the available information on the Wrap feature says that you can wrap onto a conical surface, it fails to mention that the point of the cone must be cut off in order for it to work.

The Wrap feature works by flattening the face, relating the sketch to the flat pattern of the face, and then mapping the face boundaries and sketch back onto the 3D face. The reason why it is limited to cylindrical and conical faces is that these types of geometry are *developable*. This means that the faces can be mapped to the flat pattern through some relatively simple techniques that happen behind the scenes. Developable geometry can be flattened without stretching. You will see in a later chapter that sheet metal functions are limited in the same way and for the same reasons.

SolidWorks does not wrap onto other types of surfaces, such as spherical, toroidal, or general NURBS surfaces, because you cannot flatten these shapes without distorting or stretching the material. There is software that can flatten these shapes, but it is typically done for sheet-metal deep drawing applications, which highly deform the metal. Figure 7.58 shows the Wrap PropertyManager interface.

FIGURE 7.58

The Wrap PropertyManager interface

The Wrap feature has three main options:

- Emboss
- Deboss
- Scribe

Scribe

Scribe is the simplest of the options to explain, and understanding it can help you understand the other options. Scribe creates a split line-like edge on the face.

Several requirements must be met in order to make a wrap feature work:

- The face must be a cylindrical or conical face.
- The loop must be a closed loop or nested closed loop 2D sketch.
- The sketch must be on a plane that is either tangent to or parallel to another plane that is tangent to the face.
- Wrap supports multiple closed loops within a single feature.
- The wrap should not be self-intersecting when it wraps around the part (self-intersection will not cause the feature to fail, but on the other types, Emboss and Deboss, it may produce unexpected results).

Scribes can be created on solid or surface faces. Scribed surfaces are frequently thickened to create a boss or a cut.

Emboss

The Wrap Emboss option works much like the scribe, but it adds material inside the closed loop sketch, at the thickness that you specify in the Emboss PropertyManager. Embossing can only be done on solid geometry. If the feature self-intersects, then the intersecting area is simply not embossed, and is left at the level of the original face. One result is that creating a full wrap-around feature, such as the geometry for a barrel cam, requires a secondary feature. This is because the Wrap feature always leaves a gap, regardless of whether the sketch to be wrapped is under or over the diameter-multiplied-by-pi length.

 **To work around this problem, you can use a loft, extrude, or revolve feature to span the gap.**

When you use the Emboss option, you can set up the direction of pull and assign draft so that the feature can be injection molded. This limits the size of the emboss so that it must not wrap more than 180 degrees around the part.

Deboss

Deboss is just like emboss, except that it removes material instead of adding it.

Figure 7.59 demonstrates all these options. The part shown in the images is available on the CD-ROM with the filename `Chapter 7 Wrap.sldprt`. For each of the demonstrated cases, the original flat sketch is shown to give you some idea of how the sketch relates to the finished geometry.

FIGURE 7.59

The Wrap Feature options

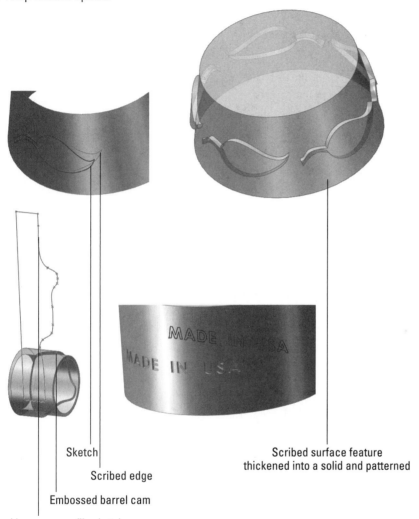

Sketch

Scribed edge

Embossed barrel cam

Closed loop cam profile sketch

Scribed surface feature
thickened into a solid and patterned

Keep in mind that this feature is not like the projected sketch. A projected sketch is not foreshortened on the curved surface, but is projected normal from the sketch plane. A sketch that is one inch long will measure one inch along the curvature of the surface and will measure less than one inch linearly from end to end.

The scribed part in the previous figure was created on a conical surface body. The surface was then thickened as a separate body and patterned.

CROSS-REF Chapter 26 covers working with multiple bodies, and Chapter 27 covers surfaces.

The embossed cam employed a workaround with a revolve feature to close the gap that is always created when wrapping all the way around a part.

The example with the debossed text employs a direction of pull and draft so that the geometry can be molded.

Flex

The Flex feature is different from most other features in SolidWorks. Most other features create new geometry, but Flex (and Deform, which follows) takes existing geometry and changes its shape. Flex can affect the entire part, or just a portion of it. Flex works on both solid and surface bodies, as well as imported and native geometry.

Figure 7.60 shows the Flex PropertyManager interface. Flex has four main options and many settings. The four main options are as follows:

- **Bending.** Establish two trim planes to denote the ends of the bent area, and specify an angle or radius for the bend.

- **Twisting.** Establish two trim planes to limit the area of the twist, and enter the number of degrees through which to twist.

- **Tapering.** Establish two trim planes to limit the area of the taper. The body will be larger toward one end and smaller toward the other end.

- **Stretching.** Establish two trim planes to limit the area to be stretched. You can stretch the entire body by moving the trim planes outside of the body.

BEST PRACTICE Flex is not the kind of feature that you should use to actually *design* parts, but it can be extremely valuable when you need to show a part in an "in use" state. A simple example would be a rubber strap that stretches over something when it is used, but that is designed and manufactured in its free state. The geometry that you can create by using the flex functions is not generally production-model quality, but it is usually adequate for a looks-like model.

Figure 7.61 shows examples of each flex option using a model of a rubber grommet. The part shown in the figure can be found on the CD-ROM with the filename `Chapter 7 Flex.sldprt`.

FIGURE 7.60

The Flex PropertyManager interface

In some cases, the triad and trim planes are slightly disoriented. The best thing to do in situations like this is to simply reorient the triad using the angle numbers in the Triad panel of the PropertyManager. This is also a solution if the planes are turned in such a way that the axis of bending is not oriented to the bend that the part requires.

The Flex feature is very conscious of separate bodies. In some cases this can be helpful, but in default situations when there is only one body in the part, it can be annoying. Remember to select the body to be affected in the very first selection box at the top of the PropertyManager.

TIP If you want to bend only one of the tabs on the grommet, then the best solution is to split the single body into two bodies, and flex only one of the bodies. The examples shown for twisting and stretching use this technique.

CROSS-REF Splitting a single body into multiple bodies is covered in Chapter 26.

You can place the trim planes by selecting a model vertex, by dragging the arrow on the plane, or by typing in a number. Be careful when dragging the plane arrows because dragging the border of the plane drags the flex value for the feature. (Dragging the plane in a bending operation is like changing the angle or radius for the bend.)

FIGURE 7.61

A rubber grommet in various flex states

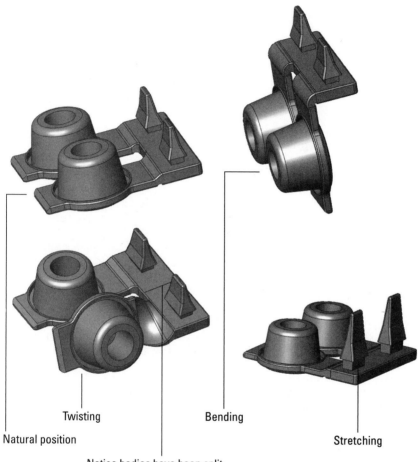

Twisting

Bending

Natural position

Stretching

Notice bodies have been split

Using the triad can be very tricky. Moving the triad in the bending option moves the axis of the bend, and so it determines whether the bend will compress or stretch the material. The position of the triad also determines which side of the bent body will move or stay stationary, or if both sides will move. Placing the triad directly on a trim plane causes the material outside the bend on that side of the trim plane to remain stationary.

I highly recommend taking a look at the models that are provided with this chapter to examine the various functions of the Flex feature more carefully. The model uses configurations, which are covered in Chapter 10.

Deform

Like the Flex feature, Deform changes the shape of the entire model without regard to parametrics, features, history, or dimensions. Some software packages call this technique *global shape modeling*. Also like Flex, Deform works on surface bodies as well as solids. Deform can also handle imported geometry as well as SolidWorks native parts. Model complexity is not an issue unless the part runs into itself during deformation.

The Deform feature is also another feature type that you may not use to actually design anything, but that you may use to show a model in a deformed state.

Also, it is a minor point, but if you use the large icons setting, notice that the toolbar icon used for Deform is the wrong one. The icon used for large icons is the Boundary Cut icon. Just be careful if you use large icons.

BEST PRACTICE Typically, if you want a model to have a certain shape, then you need to intentionally and precisely model it with that shape. The problem with using deform and flex geometry for actual design data is that they both create fairly approximate geometry, and this process yields a result that is not completely intentional. The shape that you finally achieve is the result of arbitrary uncontrolled function of the feature, not necessarily creating a shape that you had clearly envisioned beforehand.

Deform has three types:

- **Point.** This type deforms a portion of the model by pushing a point and the geometry around it.

- **Curve to Curve.** The most precise and useful deform type. Select an existing edge and force the edge to match a curve.

- **Surface Push.** This type of deform, while conceptually a very interesting function, is nearly unusable in practice. The part is deformed into a shape vaguely resembling an intermediate shape between the existing state of the part and a "tool" body.

Figure 7.62 shows the PropertyManager interface for the Deform feature. The interface is different for each of the three main types, and also changes, depending on selections within the individual types. The interface shown is for the curve to curve type because I believe this to be the most useful type.

Point Deform

The Point Deform option enables you to push a point on the model, and the model deforms as if it were rubber. Figure 7.63 shows the PropertyManager, as well as a before-and-after example of the Point Deform function. The key to using this feature is to ensure that the Deform Region option is turned off. Aside from that, you just have to use trial and error when applying the Deform option. The depth, diameter, and shape of the deformation are not very precise. Also, you cannot specify the precise location for the point to be deformed. Again, this is best used for "looks-like" models, not production data.

In the model from Figure 7.63, two Point Deform features are used, one to apply some shape to the back and one to apply some shape to the seat.

FIGURE 7.62

The PropertyManager interface for the curve to curve deform

FIGURE 7.63

The Deform Point PropertyManager and a before-and-after example

Curve to Curve Deform

Because this option uses curve (or sketch or edge) data, it is a more precise method than the other deform types. The main concept here is to transform a curve on the original model to a new curve, thus deforming the body to achieve the new geometry.

The model shown in Figure 7.64 has been created using the curve to curve deform. The part starts as a simple sweep (sweep an arc along an arc), and then a split line is created to limit the deform to a specific area of the model. The model is on the CD-ROM with the filename `Chapter 7 Deform Curve to Curve.sldprt`.

Using the curve to curve deform option

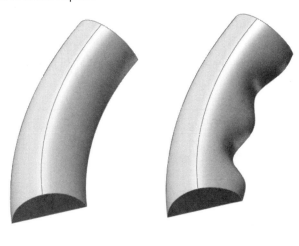

Surface Push Deform

I do not go into much detail on the Surface Push Deform type because it is not one of the more useful functions in SolidWorks. In order to use it, you must have the body of the part that you are modeling, and a tool body that you will use to shape the part that you are modeling. The finished shape does not fit the tool body directly, but looks about half-way between the model and the tool body, blended together in an abstract sort of way. It looks like the dent that would result from an object being thrown very hard at a car fender, in that neither the thrown part nor the fender is immediately recognizable from the result.

Indent

 The Indent feature is what the Surface Push Deform is trying to be, or should try to be. Indent uses the same ingredients as the Surface Push, but it produces a result that is both intelligible and useful. For example, if you are building a plastic housing around a small electric motor, then the Indent feature shapes the housing and creates a gap between the housing and the motor. Figure 7.65 shows the PropertyManager interface for the Indent feature, as well as a before-and-after shot of the indent.

Using the Indent feature

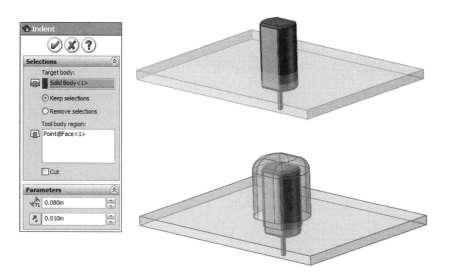

In this case, the small motor is placed where it needs to be, but there is a wall in the way. Indent is used to create an indentation in the wall using the same wall thickness, and placing a gap of .010 inches around the motor. The motor is brought into the wall part using the Insert ➪ Part command. This is a multibody technique. Multibodies are examined in detail in Chapter 26.

Tutorial: Bracket Casting

When you follow this tutorial, you are encouraged to follow the directions the first time to make sure that you understand the concepts involved, and then to go through it again, this time deviating from the instructions to see if you can expand your understanding by experimentation. To try bracket casting, follow these steps:

1. Open a new part using an inch-based template.

2. On the Right plane, draw a circle centered at the origin with a diameter of 1.50 inches, and a second circle placed 4.000 inches vertically from the first, with a diameter of 2.250 inches.

3. Exit the sketch, and make sure Instant 3D is turned on. The Instant 3D icon is on the Features toolbar, and looks like a ruler with an arrow. Click on the sketch in the graphics window, and pull the Instant 3D arrow to create a solid. Edit the feature (right- or left-click on the feature either in the graphics window or in the FeatureManager and click the Edit Feature icon, which is the yellow and green block with a hand pointing to it). Now enter numbers by hand so that you extrude the sketch 1.000 inch using a From condition of Offset by 1.000 inch, such that the offset and the extrude depth are in the same direction. Rename this feature **Bosses in the FeatureManager**. Figure 7.66 shows the results of these steps.

FIGURE 7.66

The results of Steps 1 to 3

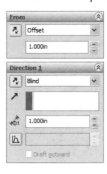
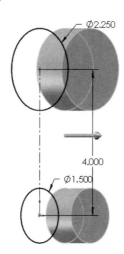

NOTE These steps produce multiple bodies that will be merged in a later step. Multiple-body parts are covered in more detail in Chapter 26. You can tell that there are multiple bodies by looking at the Solid Bodies folder near the top of the tree, and expanding the folder. The bodies are listed in the folder.

4. **On the Top plane, open a new sketch and draw a horizontal construction line across the cylinder, from the midpoint of one side to the midpoint of the other side.** To pick up the automatic relations for the midpoints more easily, it is recommended that you orient the view, normal to the sketch, or use the Top view. It does not matter if you make the relations to the top or bottom cylinder, because the midpoints of the sides are in the same place when they are projected into the sketch plane.

5. **Next, draw an ellipse (Tools ⇨ Sketch Tools ⇨ Ellipse) centered at the midpoint of the construction line and that measures .700 inches horizontally and 1.375 inches vertically.** Exit the sketch.

6. **Show the sketch for the Bosses feature (click the plus icon next to the Bosses extrude to show the sketch, and then right-click the sketch and select Show).**

7. **Create a plane parallel to the Top plane at the center of the larger circle.** You can access the Plane creation interface at Insert ⇨ Reference Geometry ⇨ Plane. If you select the Top plane from the flyout FeatureManager and the center of the larger sketch circle from the graphics window, the interface automatically selects the Parallel Plane At Point option. Click OK to create the plane. Rename this plane **Top Boss Plane.**

8. **Draw a second ellipse on the Top Boss Plane.** Do not draw a construction line as you did for the first ellipse; instead, you can just make the center point of the second ellipse directly on top of the first ellipse's center point. The dimensions should be 1.000 inch horizontal by 1.750 inches vertical. Figure 7.67 shows the results up to this point.

FIGURE 7.67

The results up to Step 8

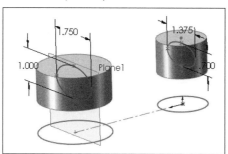

> **TIP** When you are sketching on parallel planes that are separated by some distance and trying to pick up automatic relations, it is often very helpful to be looking "normal to" the sketch, so that you can see how other entities are projected into the sketch plane.

9. **Use the Loft feature to loft between the two ellipses.** Be sure to select the ellipses in approximately the same location so that they do not twist. If the loft preview accidentally twists, then use the connectors (light-blue square dots on the sketches that are connected by a straight line) to straighten out the loft.

NOTE Notice that this feature joined together the other two disjoint bodies with the body that was created by the loft into a single body. This is a result of selecting the Merge Result option in the Options panel.

TIP If you want to experiment, expand the Start/End Constraints panel and apply end conditions for the loft. This causes the loft to change from a straight loft to a curved loft.

10. **Right-click all sketches that are showing, and select Hide.** Do the same for the Top Boss Plane. This cleans up the display to prevent it from becoming confusing. However, if you prefer to see the sketches, then you can leave them displayed.

TIP You can either hide or show different types of entities in groups by using the View menu. Hide All Types hides everything, and disables the options for individual entity types to be used.

11. **Open a sketch on the Right plane.** Sketch an ellipse such that the center is oriented 1.750 inches vertically from the Origin, and the ellipse measures .750 inches horizontally and 1.500 inches vertically.

12. **Extrude this ellipse using the Up To Next end condition.** If Up To Next does not appear in the list, then change the direction of the extrude and try it again.

13. **Show the sketch of the Bosses feature by expanding the feature (click the "+" next to it), right- or left-clicking on the sketch icon, and selecting the Hide/Show icon (eyeglasses).** Next, open a sketch on the Right plane. Sketch two circles that are concentric with the original circles, with the dimensions of .875 inches and 1.250 inches. Exit the sketch.

14. **Use Instant 3D to create an extruded cut that goes through the large circular bosses.** This feature will look like a boss extrusion at first, so when you have finished dragging its depth, a small toolbar with two icons appears. One of the icons allows you to add draft; the other allows you to turn the boss into a cut. Figure 7.68 shows the state of the model up to this step.

15. **Start a fillet feature, and select the face of the Loft feature.** Assign a radius of .200 inches.

NOTE Although this fillet is created by selecting a face, it is not a face fillet. Selecting a face for a regular constant radius fillet simply fillets any edge that is on the face.

16. **Create a mirror feature, using the Right plane as the mirror plane.** In the Mirror PropertyManager, expand the Bodies To Mirror panel, and select anywhere on the part. Make sure that the Merge Solids option is selected. Click OK to accept the mirror.

17. **Orient the view to the Front view, and then turn the view on its side (hold down Alt and press the left- or right-arrow key six times).**

18. **Open a new sketch on the Front plane.** From the View menu, make sure that Hide All Types is not on, and show Temporary Axes. Draw and dimension a horizontal construction line, as shown in Figure 7.69.

FIGURE 7.68

The results up to Step 14

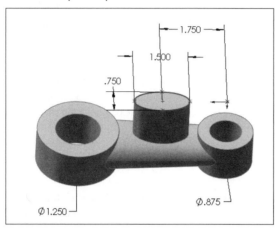

FIGURE 7.69

The results up to Step 18

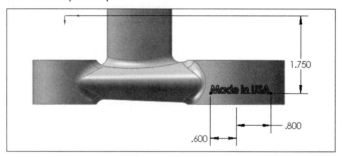

19. **With the construction line selected, start the Sketch Text command (Tools ➪ Sketch Entities ➪ Text).** Make sure that the line appears in the Curves selection box.

20. **Click in the text box, and type Made in USA (or your name or company name).** Select the text and click the Bold button. Deselect the Use Document Font option, change the font to use units, and set the height to .175 inches.

21. **Click OK to exit the Sketch Text PropertyManager, and click OK again to exit the sketch.** You can turn off the Temporary Axis display.

22. **Click Insert ➪ Features ➪ Wrap.** You should be prompted to select a plane or a sketch. Use the Flyout FeatureManager to select the sketch that you just created with the sketch text in it. Next, select the cylindrical face of the boss to see a preview of the text wrapped onto the face. If the text appears backwards, then click the Reverse Direction option in the Wrap PropertyManager.

23. **Select the Emboss option, and assign a thickness of .025 inches.** Click in the Pull Direction selection box and select the Front plane. Click OK to accept the feature.

24. **Save the part and close it.** If you would like to examine a reference part, you can find it on the CD-ROM with the filename `Chapter 7 Tutorial Bracket Casting.sld-prt`. The finished part is shown in Figure 7.70.

FIGURE 7.70

The finished part

Tutorial: Creating a Wire-Formed Part

Follow these steps to create a wire-formed part:

1. Open a new part using an inch-based template.

2. Open a sketch on the Right plane and sketch a circle that is centered on the Origin with a diameter of 1.500 inches.

3. Create a Helix, Constant Pitch, Pitch, and Revolution, where the Pitch = .250 inches, Revolutions = 5.15, and Start Angle = 0. The Helix command is found at Insert ➪ Curve ➪ Helix/Spiral.

4. Create a sketch on the Front plane, as shown in Figure 7.71. Pay careful attention when adding the construction line, as shown. This line is used in the next step to reference the end of the arc.

5. Open a sketch on the Right plane and use Figure 7.72 to add the correct relations and dimensions. Be aware that the two sketches shown are on different sketch planes, which makes it difficult to depict in 2D. You can also open the part from the CD-ROM for reference.

FIGURE 7.71

The results up to Step 4

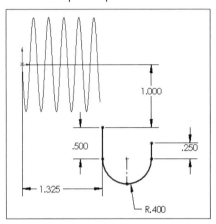

FIGURE 7.72

The sketch for Step 5

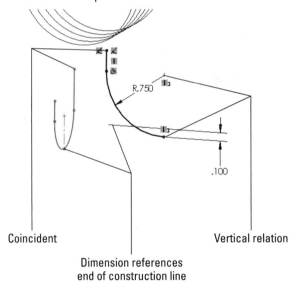

Coincident   Vertical relation

Dimension references
end of construction line

6. **Exit the sketch and create a projected curve.** The Projected Curve function is found at
   Insert ⇨ Curve ⇨ Projected Curve. Use the Sketch on Sketch option.

7. **Open a 3D sketch.** You can access a 3D sketch from the Insert menu. Select the helix and click Convert Entities on the Sketch toolbar. Then select the projected curve and click Convert Entities again. You now have two sections of a 3D sketch that are unconnected in space.

8. **Draw a two-point spline to join the ends of the 3D sketch entities that are closest to one another.** Assign tangent relations to the ends to make the transition smooth. Figure 7.73 illustrates what the model should look like at this point.

FIGURE 7.73

The results up to Step 8

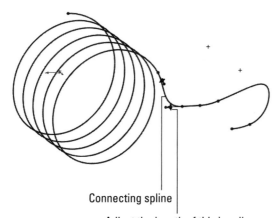

Connecting spline

Adjust the length of this handle

TIP You may have to adjust the length of one of the spline tangency length arrows to keep the spline from remaining inside the cylinder of the helix.

9. **Open a sketch on the Right plane, and draw an arc that is centered on the Origin and coincident with the end of the 3D sketch helix.** The 185-degree angle is created by activating the dimension tool and clicking first the center of the arc, and then the two endpoints of the arc. Now place the dimension. This type of dimensioning allows you to get an angle dimension without dimensioning to angled lines. Exit the sketch.

10. **Create a Composite Curve (Insert ➪ Curve ➪ Composite) consisting of the 3D sketch and the new 2D sketch.**

11. **Create a new plane using the Normal to Curve option, selecting one end of the composite curve.**

12. **On the new plane, draw a circle that is centered on the end of the curve with a diameter of .120 inches.** You need to create a Pierce relation between the center of the circle and the composite curve.

13. **Create a sweep feature using the circle as the profile and the composite curve as the path.** To create the sweep, you must first exit the sketch.

14. **Hide any curves that still display.**

15. **Click Insert ⇨ Cut ⇨ With Surface.** From the Flyout FeatureManager, select the Right plane. Make sure that the arrow is pointing to the side of the plane with the least amount of material. Click OK to accept the cut. The finished part is shown in Figure 7.74.

FIGURE 7.74

The finished part

Summary

SolidWorks has a wide range of feature types to choose from, ranging from simple extrudes and revolves to more complex lofts and sweeps. It also offers a range of specialty features that may not be useful on a day-to-day basis, but that have their place in the modeling techniques that you need to know to get the job done.

Some features, such as extrude, fillet, and flex, have so many options that it may be difficult to take them all in at once. You should browse through the models on the CD-ROM for this chapter and use the Rollback bar (described in detail in Chapter 11) to examine how the parts were built. You can then try to create a few on your own.

Chapter 8

Patterning and Mirroring

Patterning and mirroring in SolidWorks are great tools to help you improve your efficiency. The software provides many powerful pattern types that also help you accomplish design tasks. In addition to the different types of patterns, there are many more detailed options that enable functionality that you may not have considered. A solid understanding of patterning and mirroring tools is necessary to be able to build the maximum amount of parametric intelligence into your models.

Patterning in a Sketch

You can use both pattern and mirror functions in Sketch mode, although sketch patterns are not a preferred choice. The distinction between patterning and mirroring in Sketch mode is important when it comes to sketch performance.

PERFORMANCE Although there are many metrics for how software performs, in SolidWorks, the word performance means the same thing as speed. Sketch patterns have a very adverse effect on speed.

You might hear a lot of conflicting information about which features are better to use in different situations. Users coming from a 2D background often use functions such as sketch patterning because it's familiar, without questioning whether there is a better approach. When in doubt, you can perform a test to determine which features work best for a given situation.

In this test, I made a series of 20-by-20 patterns using circles, squares, and hexagons. The patterns are both sketch patterns and feature patterns, and I created them with both Verification On Rebuild and Geometry Pattern turned on and off. Verification On Rebuild is a setting that you can access through Tools ➪ Options ➪ Performance, and Geometry Pattern is a setting that is applicable only to feature patterns.

CROSS-REF For a more complete description of the Verification On Rebuild, see Appendix A.

NOTE Given that this is the second edition of this book, I thought it would be useful to run these tests again on the new versions of the software and with my original hardware. The results of the test redo are very interesting. Most of the feature rebuild times are longer, in the range of twice to three times as long. The Verification On Rebuild results are the exception. These results are faster by about 20 percent. This compares rebuild times from the 2007 (Service Pack 2) and 2009 (alpha) releases, and both tests were done without RealView.

Table 8.1 shows the rebuild times (in seconds) of solid geometry created from various types of patterns as measured by Feature Statistics (found at Tools ⇨ Feature Statistics). Sketch patterns are far slower than feature patterns, by a factor of about ten. The biggest speed reduction occurs when you use sketch patterns in conjunction with the Verification on Rebuild setting, especially as the number of sketch entities being patterned increases.

Generally, the number of faces and sketch relations being patterned has a significant effect on the speed of the pattern. The sketch pattern times are taken for the entire finished model, including the sketch pattern and a single extrude feature, using the sketch with the pattern to do an extruded cut. The sample parts are on the CD-ROM for reference. Look for the filenames beginning with "Reference1" through "Reference7."

TABLE 8.1

Pattern Rebuild Times

Pattern Type	Default	Geometry Pattern	Verification on Rebuild
20 × 20 sketch circle	3.02	n/a	11.0
20 × 20 sketch square	10.1	n/a	112
20 × 20 sketch hex	17.4	n/a	232
20 × 20 feature circle	.28	.78	.29
20 × 20 feature square	.84	1.44	.84
20 × 20 feature hex	1.28	1.86	1.28

The most shocking data here is the difference between a sketch pattern of a hex when extruded as cuts into a flat plate compared to a feature pattern of a single extruded hex with each using the Verification On Rebuild option. That is not a typo. 1.28 seconds compared to 232 seconds. Do you still like sketch patterns? Figure 8.1 shows one of the parts used for this simple test.

FIGURE 8.1

A pattern part used for the test

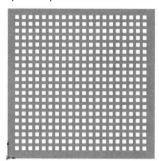

One interesting result of this test was that if a patterned extruded feature creates a situation where the end faces of the extruded features have to merge into a single face, the feature can take ten times the amount of time to rebuild as a pattern with unmerged end faces. This was an inadvertent discovery. I'm sure there are many such discoveries that you could make on your own if you were to investigate rebuild speeds for end conditions for cuts such as Through All, Up To Face, Up To Next, and so on, as well as the difference between cuts and boss features. Further, using Instant 3D can be an impediment when editing very large sketches simply due to the effects of the preview.

Further sketch myth debunking

People often say that it is best practice to fully define your sketches. I completely agree with this statement. However, I have heard people go to the extent to say that fully defined sketches solve faster, with the rationale being that SolidWorks has to figure out how to solve the underdefined sketch, but the fully defined sketch is already spelled out. Let's find out.

In this example, I created a sketch pattern of 4 × 4 rectangles, and use the Fully Define Sketch tool to add dimensions. Then I copied and pasted the sketch and removed all the dimensions and relations. Figure 8.2 shows the Feature Statistic results.

It is safe to say that fully defined sketches are best practice, but it is not due to rebuild speed. Sketch relations are costly. Patterning sketch relations are even more costly. The rebuild time does not even come close to the time that it takes the Fully Define Sketch tool to create all the dimensions and relations in the first place. This combination of geometry, software, and hardware took about 30 seconds of CPU time to add the relations and dimensions.

FIGURE 8.2

Comparing rebuild times of a fully defined sketch to a completely undefined sketch

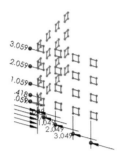

Patterning a sketch

It is best to pre-select the sketch entities that you want to pattern before using the Sketch Pattern tool. If you do not pre-select, then after the PropertyManager is open, you can only select entities to pattern one by one because the window select is not available for this function.

 **When creating a linear sketch pattern, be sure to select the Add Dimension check boxes. If these dimensions are not added, then editing the pattern becomes more difficult.**

Linear Sketch Pattern

 The Linear Pattern PropertyManager is shown in Figure 8.3.

The Direction 1 panel works predictably by establishing the direction and spacing, and then the number. The Angle setting enables you to specify a direction that does not rely on anything outside of the sketch.

The Direction 2 panel works a little differently. You must first specify how many instances you want, and then the other information becomes available.

Circular Sketch Pattern

 The Circular Sketch Pattern defaults to the sketch Origin as the center of the pattern. You can move and position this point using the numbers in the PropertyManager, but you cannot dimension it until after the pattern is created. Again, this is another feature where you need to pre-select because window selection is not available (patterned sketch entities must be selected one by one to go into the Entities to Pattern panel). Figure 8.4 shows the Circular Pattern PropertyManager.

FIGURE 8.3

The Linear Pattern PropertyManager

FIGURE 8.4

The Circular Pattern PropertyManager

Mirroring in a Sketch

Mirroring in a sketch is a completely different matter from patterning in a sketch. It offers superior performance, and the interface is better developed. Mirrored entities in a sketch are an instrumental part of establishing design intent.

Two methods of mirroring items in a sketch are discussed here, along with a method to make entities work as if they have been mirrored when in fact they were manually drawn.

Mirror Entities

Mirror Entities works by selecting the entities that you want to mirror along with a single centerline, and clicking the Mirror Entities button on the Sketch toolbar. It is a simple and effective tool that you can use on existing geometry. This method is the fastest way to use the tool but there are other methods. You can preselect or post select, using a dialog box to select the mirror line, which does not need to be a centerline.

One feature of Mirror Entities may sometimes cause unexpected results. For example, in some situations, Mirror Entities will mirror a line or an arc and merge the new element with the old one across the centerline. This happens in situations where the mirror and the original form a single line or a single arc. SolidWorks may delete certain relations and dimensions in these situations.

Dynamic Mirror

As the name suggests, Dynamic Mirror mirrors sketch entities as they are created. You can activate it by selecting a centerline and clicking the button on the Sketch toolbar. Dynamic Mirror is not on the toolbar by default; you need to select Tools ⇨ Customize ⇨ Commands to add it to the toolbar. You can also access Dynamic Mirror through the menus at Tools ⇨ Sketch Tools ⇨ Dynamic Mirror.

When you activate this function, the centerline displays with hatch marks on the ends and remains active until you turn it off or exit the sketch. Figure 8.5 shows the centerline with hatch marks.

FIGURE 8.5

The Dynamic Mirror centerline with hatch marks

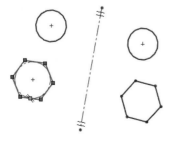

Symmetry sketch relation

I have covered the Symmetry sketch relation in previous chapters on sketching, but I mention it here because it offers you a manual way to mirror sketch entities. There are editing situations when you may not want to create new geometry, but instead use existing entities with new relations driving them. To create the Symmetry sketch relation, you must have two similar items (such as lines or endpoints) and a centerline selected.

Mirroring in 3D sketches

Chapter 31 deals with 3D sketches in more detail, but I discuss the mirror functionality here to connect it with the rest of the mirroring and patterning topics. 3D sketches can contain planes and if you are sketching on a plane in a 3D sketch, you can mirror items on it. You cannot mirror general 3D sketch entities.

Sketch patterns are also unavailable in the 3D sketch, but starting with the 2009 release, you can use the Move, Rotate, and Copy sketch tools on planes in 3D sketches. Combining one questionable functionality (3D sketches) with another (sketch patterns) does not usually improve either one.

Geometry Pattern

The SolidWorks Help file says that the Geometry Pattern option in feature patterns results in a faster pattern because it does not pattern the parametric relations. This claim is valid only when there is an end condition on the patterned feature such that the feature will actually pattern the end condition's parametric behavior. The part shown in Figure 8.6 falls into this category. The improved rebuild time goes from .30 to .11 seconds. Although a 60 percent reduction is significant, the most compelling argument for the use of the Geometry Pattern is to avoid the effect of patterning the end-condition parametrics.

Because of this speed differential, you need to be careful about using the Geometry Pattern option. SolidWorks turns this option on by default for some patterns where you may not wish to use it for rebuild time reasons.

Under some conditions, Geometry Pattern will not work. One example is any time a patterned face merges with an unpatterned face. These situations can be difficult to identify. Figure 8.7 shows a pattern that cannot be created using the Geometry Pattern option. The boss merges with the side face of the block, which generates the error message shown in the figure. The circular part shown in the image is an exception where the partial cylindrical bosses merge with the side of the cylinder, but Geometry Pattern works.

In some situations, SolidWorks error messages may send you in a loop. One message may tell you that the pattern cannot be created with the Geometry Pattern turned on, so you should try to turn it off. When you do that, you may get another message that says the pattern will not work, and that you should try to use the Geometry Pattern setting. In cases like this you may try to use a different end condition, or change the selection of features patterned along with the feature, such as fillets. You may also try to pattern bodies or even faces rather than features.

FIGURE 8.6

A geometry pattern test

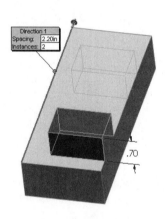

Geometry pattern off — Parametrics are patterned

Geometry pattern on — Parametrics not patterned

FIGURE 8.7

Merged faces

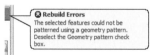

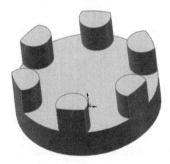

Patterning Bodies

I cover multiple bodies in depth in Chapter 26, but need to deal with it briefly here. Any discussion of patterning is not complete without a discussion of bodies because using bodies is an available option with all the pattern and mirror types.

SolidWorks parts can contain multiple *solid* or *surface* bodies. A solid body is a solid that comprises a single contiguous volume. Surface bodies are defined differently, but they can also be patterned and mirrored as bodies.

There are both advantages and disadvantages to mirroring and patterning bodies instead of features. The advantages can include the simplicity of selecting a single body for mirroring or patterning. In cases where the geometry to be patterned is complex or there is a large number of features, patterning bodies also can be much faster. However, in the example used earlier with patterning features in a 20-by-20 grid of holes, when done by patterning a single body of 1" × 1" × .5" with a .5" diameter hole, patterning bodies gives a rebuild time of about 130 seconds with or without Verification On Rebuild. It is the function that combines the resulting bodies into a single body that takes most of the time. This says that for large patterns of simple features, patterning bodies is *not* an efficient technique. Although I do not have an experiment in this chapter to prove it, I believe that creating a pattern of a smaller number of complex bodies using a large number of features in the patterned body would show a performance improvement over patterning the features.

Another disadvantage of patterning or mirroring bodies is that it does not allow you to be selective. You cannot mirror the body minus a couple of features without doing some shuffling of feature order in the FeatureManager. Another disadvantage is that if the base of the part has already been mirrored by a symmetrical sketch technique, then body mirroring is not going to help you mirror the subsequent features. Also, the Merge Bodies option within the mirror feature does not work as you would want it to. It merges only those bodies that are part of the mirror to bodies that are part of the mirror. Pattern Bodies does not even have an option to merge bodies. Both of these functions are often going to require an additional combine feature (for solid bodies) or knit (for surface bodies) to put the final results together.

Some of these details may seem obscure when you're reading about them, but when you begin to work patterning bodies and begin trying to merge them into a single body, read over this section again. The inconsistency between the Merge option existing in Mirror but not in Pattern is unexplainable, and a possible opportunity for an enhancement request.

CROSS-REF Bodies are discussed in more detail in Chapter 26. Surface modeling is covered in Chapter 27.

Patterning Faces

Most of the pattern types have an option for Pattern Faces. This option has a few restrictions, the main limitation being that all instances of the pattern must be created within the boundaries of the same face as the original. Figure 8.8 shows an example of the Pattern Faces option working with a Circular Pattern feature.

A circular pattern using the Pattern Faces option

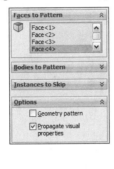

To get around this limitation, you can knit and pattern the surface body, as shown in Figure 8.9.

Patterning a surface body

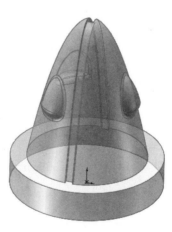

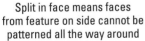

Split in face means faces
from feature on side cannot be
patterned all the way around

 **Working with surface bodies is covered in Chapter 27.**

Patterning Fillets

You may hear people argue that you cannot pattern fillets. This is partially true and partially untrue. It is true that fillets as individual features cannot be patterned. For example, if you have a symmetrical box and a fillet on one edge and want to pattern only the fillet to other edges, this does not work. However, when fillets are patterned with their parent geometry, they are a perfectly acceptable candidate for patterning. This is also true for the more complex fillet types, such as variable radius and full radius fillets. You may need to use the Geometry Pattern option, and you may need to select all the fillets affecting a feature, but it certainly does work.

Understanding Pattern Types

Up to now, I have discussed patterns in general; differentiated sketch patterns from feature patterns, face patterns, and body patterns; and looked at some other factors that affect patterning and mirroring. I will now discuss each individual type of pattern to give you an idea of what options are available.

Linear Pattern

The Linear Pattern feature has several available options:

- **Single direction or two directions.** Directions can be established by edge, sketch entity, axis, or linear dimension. If two directions are used, the directions do not need to be perpendicular to one another.

- **Spacing.** The spacing represents the center-to-center distance between pattern instances, and can be driven by an equation.

- **Number of Instances.** This number represents the total number of features in a pattern, which includes the original seed feature. It can also be driven by an equation. Equations are covered in detail in Chapter 9.

- **Direction 2.** The second direction works just like the first, with the one exception of the Pattern Seed Only option. Figure 8.10 shows the difference between a default two-direction pattern and one using the Pattern Seed Only option.

- **Instances to Skip.** This option enables you to select instances that you would like to leave out of the final pattern. Pink dots are the instances that remain, and the red dots are the ones that have been removed. Figure 8.11 shows the interface for skipping instances. You may have difficulty distinguishing the red and pink colors on the screen.

FIGURE 8.10

Using the default two-direction pattern and the Pattern Seed Only Option

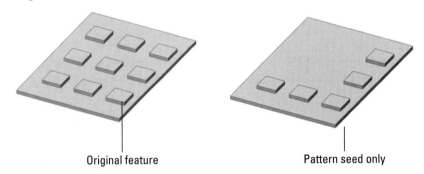

Original feature   Pattern seed only

FIGURE 8.11

Using the Instances to Skip option

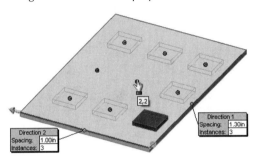

- **Propagate Visual Properties.** This option patterns the color, texture, or cosmetic thread display, along with the feature to which it is attached.

- **Vary Sketch.** This option in patterns is often overlooked and not widely used or understood. While it may have a niche application, it is a powerful option that can save you a lot of time if you ever need to use it.

Vary Sketch allows the sketch of the patterned feature to maintain its parametric relations in each instance of the pattern. It is analogous to the Geometry Pattern. Where Geometry Pattern disables the parametric end condition for a feature, Vary Sketch enables the parametric sketch relations for a pattern.

To activate the Vary Sketch option, the Linear Pattern must use a linear dimension for its Pattern Direction. The dimension must measure in the direction of the pattern, and adding the spacing for the pattern to the direction dimension must result in a valid feature.

The sketch relations must hold for the entire length of the pattern. Figure 8.12 shows the sketch relations and the resulting pattern. The preview function for this feature does not work.

FIGURE 8.12

Using the Vary Sketch option

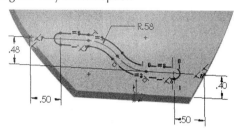 

ON the CD-ROM To better understand how this feature works, open the sample file from the CD-ROM called `Chapter 8 Vary Sketch.sldprt`, and edit Sketch2.

Edit the .40-inch dimension. Double-click it and use the scroll arrow to increase the dimension; watch the effect on the sketch. If a sketch does react to changes properly, then it cannot be used with the Vary Sketch option. In this case, the .40-inch dimension is used as the direction. The direction dimension has to be able to drive the sketch in the same way that this one does. These dimensions cannot pass through the Zero value and cannot flip directions or move into negative values.

To make the sketch react this way to changes in the dimension, the slot was created using the bi-directional offset that was demonstrated in an earlier chapter, which means that the whole operation is being driven by the construction lines and arcs at the centerline of the slot. Sketch points along the model edges are kept at a certain distance from the ends of the slots using the .50-inch dimensions. The arcs are controlled by an Equal Radius relation and a single .58-inch radius dimension. The straight lines at the ends of the slots are controlled by an Equal Length relation.

This type of dimensioning and relation creation is really what parametric design is all about. The Vary Sketch option takes what is otherwise a static linear pattern and makes it react parametrically in a way that would otherwise require a lot of setup to create individual features. If you model everything with the level of care that you need to put into a Vary Sketch pattern feature sketch, then your models will react very well to change.

Circular Pattern

The Circular Pattern feature requires a circular edge or sketch, a cylindrical face, a revolved face, a straight edge, an axis, or a temporary axis to act as the Pattern Axis of the pattern. All the other options are the same as the Linear Pattern — except that the Circular Pattern does not have a Direction 2 option, and the Equal Spacing option works differently.

Equal Spacing takes the total angle and evenly divides the number of instances into that angle. The name *equal spacing* is a bit misleading because all Circular Patterns create equal spacing between the instances, but somehow everyone knows what they mean.

Without using the Equal Spacing option, the Angle setting represents the angular spacing between instances.

The Vary Sketch option is available in Circular Pattern as well. The principles for setup are the same, but you must select an angular dimension for the direction. The part shown in Figure 8.13 was created using this technique.

FIGURE 8.13

A Circular Pattern vary sketch

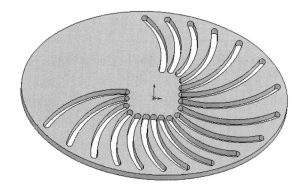

Curve Driven Pattern

A Curve Driven Pattern does just what it sounds like: it drives a pattern along a curve. The curve could be a line, an arc, or a spline. It can be an edge, a 2D or 3D sketch, or even a real curve feature. An interesting thing about the Curve Driven Pattern is that it can have a Direction 2, and Direction 2 can also be a curve. This pattern type is one of the most interesting, with many options available.

For an entire sketch to be used as a curve, the sketch must not have any sharp corners — all the entities must be tangent. This could mean using sketch fillets or a fit spline. The example shown in Figure 8.14 is created using sketch fillets. This pattern uses the Equal Spacing option, which spaces the number of instances evenly around the curve. It also uses the Offset Curve option, which maintains the patterned feature's relationship to the curve throughout the pattern, as if an offset of the curve goes through the centroids of each patterned instance. The Align to Seed option is also used, which keeps all the pattern instances aligned in the same direction.

FIGURE 8.14

The Curve Driven Pattern using sketch fillets

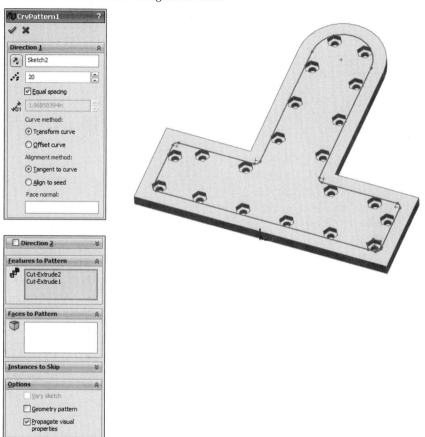

Figure 8.15 shows the same part using the Transform Curve positioning option and Tangent to Curve alignment option.

Instead of an offset of the curve going through the centroids of each patterned feature instance, in the Transform Curve, the entire curve is moved rather than offset. On this particular part, this causes a messy pattern. The Tangent to Curve option gives every patterned instance the same orientation relative to the curve as the original.

The Face Normal option is used for a 3D pattern, as shown in Figure 8.16. Although this functionality seems a little obscure, it is useful if you need a 3D curve-driven pattern on a complex surface. If you are curious about this example, it is on the CD-ROM with the filename Reference 3d Curve Driven.sldprt.

FIGURE 8.15

Using the Transform Curve and Tangent to Curve options

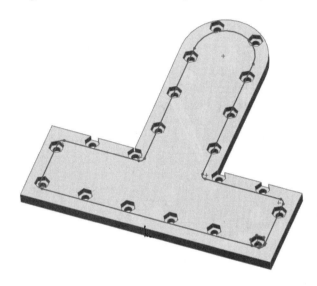

FIGURE 8.16

Using a 3D curve-driven pattern

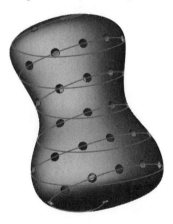

Using a Direction 2 for a curve-driven pattern creates a result similar to that in Figure 8.17. This is another situation that, although rare, is good to know about.

FIGURE 8.17

Using Direction 2 with a curve-driven pattern

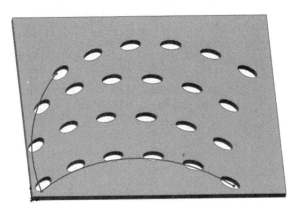

The rest of the Curve Driven Pattern works like the other pattern features that have already been demonstrated.

Sketch Driven Pattern

Sketch-driven patterns use a set of sketch points to drive the locations of features. The Hole Wizard drives the locations of multiple holes using sketch points in a similar way. However, the Sketch Driven Pattern does not create a 3D pattern in the same way that the Hole Wizard does. Figure 8.18 shows a pattern of several features that has been patterned using a sketch-driven pattern. A reference point is not necessary for the first feature.

The Centroid option in the Reference Point section is fine for symmetrical and other easily definable shapes such as circles and rectangles, where you can find the centroid just by looking at it, but on more complex shapes, you may want to use the Selected Point option. The Selected Point option is shown in Figure 8.19.

Table Driven Pattern

A table-driven pattern drives a set of feature locations, most commonly holes, from a table. The table may be imported from any source with two columns of data (X and Y) that are separated by a space, tab, or comma. Extraneous data will cause the import to fail.

The X,Y Origin for the table is determined by a Coordinate System reference geometry feature. The XY plane of the Coordinate System is the plane to which the XY data in the table refers.

You can access the Coordinate System command through the menus at Insert ➪ Reference Geometry ➪ Coordinate System. You can create the Coordinate System by selecting a combination of a vertex for the Origin and edges to align the axes. Like the Sketch Driven Pattern, this feature can use either the centroid or a selected point on the feature to act as the reference point.

FIGURE 8.18

Using a sketch-driven pattern

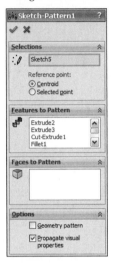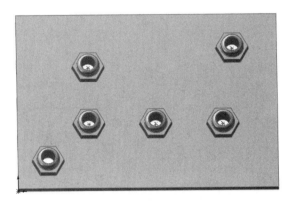

FIGURE 8.19

Using the Selected Point option in a sketch-driven pattern

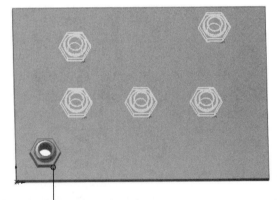

Selected point corresponds to the
sketch points in the pattern

The fact that this feature is still in a floating dialog box points to its relatively low usage and priority on the SolidWorks upgrade schedule. The interface for the feature is rather crude in comparison to some of the more high-usage features. This interface is shown in Figure 8.20.

The Table Driven Pattern dialog box

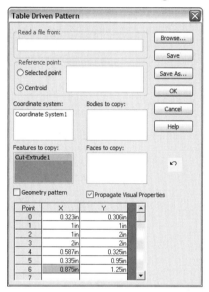

Fill Pattern

The Fill Pattern feature fills a face or area enclosed by a sketch with a pattern of a selected feature. The type of pattern used to fill the area is limited to one of four pre-set patterns that are commonly used in gratings and electronics ventilation in plastics and sheet metal. These patterns and other options for the Fill Pattern are shown in Figure 8.21.

The Pattern Layout panel enables you to control spacing and other geometrical aspects of the selected pattern layout, as well as the minimum gap from the fill boundary. This is most useful for patterns of regularly spaced features with an irregular boundary.

FIGURE 8.21

Using the Fill Pattern feature

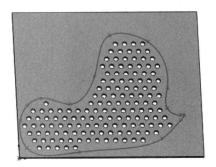

Cosmetic Patterns

Cosmetic Patterns are not patterns in the same sense as all the other pattern types in SolidWorks. Cosmetic Patterns do not actually create any geometry, just the appearance of geometry. They are applied using RealView functionality, which may or may not be available to you depending on your hardware, in particular your video card.

NOTE   **More information is available on RealView capable video cards from the SolidWorks corporate Web site, at www.solidworks.com/pages/services/ VideoCardTesting.html?lsrc=quick_links.**

Cosmetic Patterns are appropriate if your manufacturing method does not require actual geometry. For example, rapid prototyping requires explicit geometry in order to build a part, but a perforated sheet metal panel or a knurled cylindrical handle may require only a note on a drawing for the shop to set up a manufacturing process to create the geometry.

To apply a Cosmetic Pattern to a face, feature, body, or entire part, use the RealView tab from the Task Pane, and select Appearances ⇨ Miscellaneous ⇨ Pattern or ⇨ RealView Only Appearances. Drag and drop the desired pattern onto the model, and use the pop-up to apply it to a face, feature, body, or the entire part. Figure 8.22 shows the RealView tab of the Task Manager with some of the Cosmetic Pattern options.

CROSS-REF You can find more details about RealView appearances in Chapter 5.

FIGURE 8.22

Cosmetic Pattern options in the RealView tab of the Task Manager

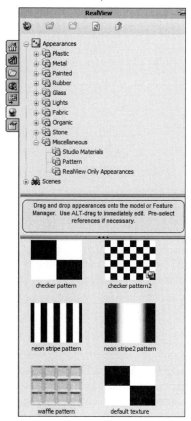

Mirroring in 3D

Because symmetry is an important aspect of modeling parts in SolidWorks, mirror functions are a commonly used feature. This is true whether you work on machine parts, sheet metal, injection-molded, cast, or forged parts. I discussed sketch-mirroring techniques earlier in this chapter, and now I will discuss 3D mirroring techniques.

Mirroring bodies

Earlier in this chapter, I discussed patterning bodies. I mentioned that the patterning and mirroring tools in SolidWorks do not have adequate functionality when it comes to body management. Neither tool allows the patterned or mirrored bodies to be merged with the main body if the main body is not being patterned or mirrored. Figure 8.23 shows the Options panels for both the Linear Pattern (on the left) and the Mirror (on the right) features. Here you can see that the pattern function has no provision whatsoever for merging bodies. The Mirror appears to have the functionality, but it applies only to bodies that are used or created by the Mirror feature.

In future versions of SolidWorks, these features will hopefully be outfitted with more complete merge and feature scope functionality, such as Extrude features.

FIGURE 8.23

Options panels from the Linear Pattern and Mirror PropertyManagers

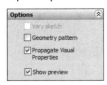 

BEST PRACTICE Mirroring bodies is the fastest and simplest method when a part has complete symmetry. However, this may not be an option if the part is not completely symmetrical. Also, the decision to mirror must often be made when you are creating the first feature. If the first feature is modeled as a sketch that is built symmetrically around the Origin, then you may need to cut the part in half to mirror it. This is an adequate modeling technique, although it is not as clean as it could be.

Mirroring features

Features can be mirrored across planes or flat faces used as the plane of symmetry. If you are mirroring many features, then it is best to mirror them all with a single mirror feature rather than to make several mirror features. You may have to do this by moving the mirror feature down the tree as you add new features. Depending on your part and what you are trying to accomplish, it may be better to mirror bodies than features, but you should not go too far out of your way or model in a contrived manner to make this happen.

Mirroring entire parts

Often when modeling, you are required to have a left- and a right-handed part. For this, you need to use a method other than body or feature mirroring. The Mirror Part command creates a brand new part, by mirroring an existing part. The new part does not inherit all the features of the original, and so any changes must be created in the original part. If you want different versions of the two parts, you need to use Configurations, which have not been covered yet in this book.

CROSS-REF   Configurations are covered in detail in Chapter 10.

You can use the Mirror Part command by pre-selecting a plane or planar face. You should be careful when choosing the plane because the new part will have a relationship to the part Origin, based on the plane on which it was mirrored.

The Mirror Part command is found in the Insert menu. When mirroring a part, you can bring several entity types from the original file to the mirrored part. These include axes, planes, cosmetic threads, and surface bodies. Sketches and features are two commonly requested items to be brought forward by the Mirror Part command, but this is not possible in the current version of the software.

Mirror Part invokes the Insert Part feature, which is covered in more detail in Chapters 26 and 28, on Multibodies and Master Model techniques, respectively.

One of the options available when you make a mirrored part is to break the link to the original part. This option brings forward all the sketches and features of the original part, and then adds a Move/Copy Body feature at the end of the tree that simply mirrors the body.

NOTE   Under normal circumstances, you cannot get the Move/Copy Body feature to mirror a body. SolidWorks has applied some magic pixie dust behind the scene to make this happen.

Tutorial: Creating a Circular Pattern

Follow these steps to get practice with creating circular pattern features:

1. **Draw a square block on the Top plane centered on the Origin, 4 inches on each side, .5-inch thick extruded Mid Plane with .5-inch chamfers on the four corners.**

2. **Pre-select the top face of the block and start the Hole Wizard.** (Pre-selection avoids a 3D placement sketch.) Select a counterbored hole for a 10-32 socket head cap screw, and place it as shown in Figure 8.24.

3. **Create an axis using the Front and Right planes.** Click Insert ⇨ Reference Geometry ⇨ Axis. Select the Two Planes option, and select Front and Right planes from the flyout FeatureManager. (Click the bar that says Axis at the top of the PropertyManager to access the flyout FeatureManager.) This creates an axis in the center of the rectangular part.

FIGURE 8.24

Start drawing a plate with holes.

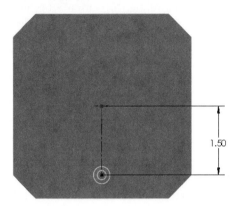

1.50

4. **Click the Circular Pattern tool on the Features toolbar.** Select the new Axis in the top Pattern Axis selection box in the Circular Pattern PropertyManager. Select the Equal Spacing option and make sure that the angle is set to 360°. Set the number of instances to 8.

5. **In the Features To Pattern panel, select the counterbored hole.** Make sure that Geometry Pattern is turned off.

6. **Click OK to finish the part, as shown in Figure 8.25.**

FIGURE 8.25

The finished circular pattern

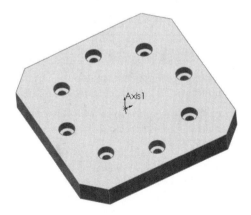

Axis1

Tutorial: Mirroring Features

Follow these steps to get some practice with creating mirror features:

1. **Open the file from the CD-ROM called** `Chapter8 Tutorial2.sldprt`.

2. **Open a sketch on the side of the part, as shown in Figure 8.26.** The straight line on top is 1.00 inch long, and the angled line ends 2.70 inches from the edge, as shown.

FIGURE 8.26

The sketch for the Rib feature

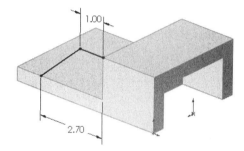

3. **Click the Rib tool on the Features toolbar or select it from the menu at Insert ⇨ Features ⇨ Rib.** Set the material arrow to go down toward the block, and the thickness setting to go to the inside by .375 inches. The PropertyManager and the preview should look like Figure 8.27.

4. **Create a linear pattern using the rib, making it go 2 inches into the part.**

5. **Create a chamfer on the same side of the part as the original rib, as shown in Figure 8.28.** The chamfer is an Angle-Distance using 60° and .5 inches.

6. **Create a round hole, sized and positioned as shown.**

7. **Mirror the hole and the chamfer about the Right plane.** The parametrics of the chamfer will have difficulty patterning, and so you need to use the Geometry Pattern option. The finished part is shown in Figure 8.29.

FIGURE 8.27

Applying the Rib feature

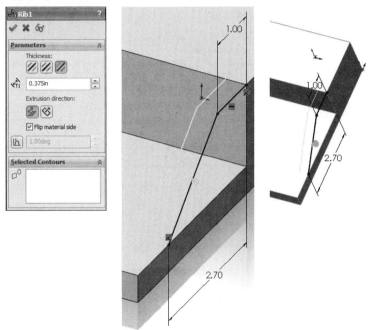

FIGURE 8.28

Additional features on the part

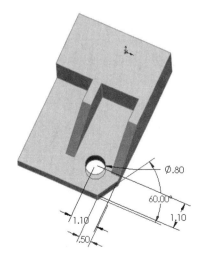

FIGURE 8.29

The finished part

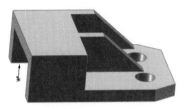

Tutorial: Applying a Cosmetic Pattern

1. **Open the file from the CD-ROM for Chapter 8 called** `Chapter 8 - tutorial - cosmetic pattern.sldprt`.

2. **Click the RealView tab in the Task Pane.** These steps will work whether or not you have RealView actually turned on.

3. **Expand the Appearances heading, then the Metal heading, then Steel, and then drag the Sandblasted Steel icon from the lower panel onto the part.** When the pop-up appears, select the Part icon, to apply the appearance to the entire part. Figure 8.30 shows the Task Pane and the pop-up.

4. **Now expand the Miscellaneous listing (under Appearances), and the Pattern heading.** drag the Waffle Pattern onto the large cylindrical face of the part, and then Alt-click the Face icon in the pop up toolbar. Using the Alt key while dragging or to select face, feature, body or part automatically activates the PropertyManager to edit the appearance. Figure 8.31 shows the Appearances PropertyManager.

5. **In the Mapping tab of the Appearances PropertyManager, select the cylindrical mapping under the Mapping Style section of the Mapping Controls panel.**

6. **Change the Rotation to 45 degrees, and choose the smallest Mapping Size.**

FIGURE 8.30

Applying an appearance to a part

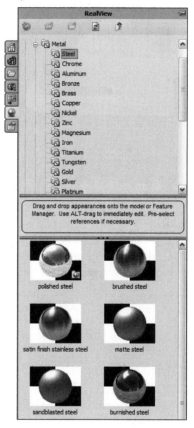

FIGURE 8.31

The Appearances PropertyManager

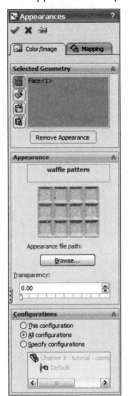

Summary

Feature patterns and mirrors are powerful tools, but they require some discipline to benefit from their usefulness. Patterns in particular are extremely flexible, with many types of functions and options available. You should avoid sketch patterns if possible, not only because of performance considerations, but also because complex sketches (sketches with a lot of entities and relations) tend to fail more often than simple sketches.

Chapter 9

Using Equations

Parametric sketch relations are not the only way to drive dimensions with intelligence. You can also use equations, link values, and global variables. Equations help you to create simple or complex mathematical relations between dimensions. Link values are essentially a quick way of making two dimensions equal. Global variables can be used in equations like other dimension names. These three techniques are all very similar and related to one another in the interface, but are used in different ways in different situations.

Equations are a very powerful extension of the set of parametric power tools that SolidWorks offers to users. Like other aspects of the software, they can cause problems if used incorrectly, and have functionality that may appear incorrect at times, but it is all for good reason.

Understanding Equations

You can find the Equations tool on the Tools toolbar or through the menus at Tools ⇨ Equations. Figure 9.1 shows the Equations main interface along with the Add Equation window. As I have noted with other areas of the interface, Equations still uses a floating dialog box. SolidWorks has put most functions in the PropertyManager, because equations tend to be more horizontal than vertical, while the PropertyManager is more vertical than horizontal.

FIGURE 9.1

The Equations interface

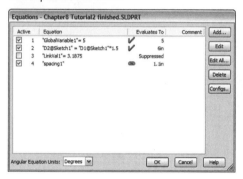
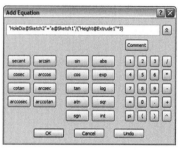

Using the Equations interface, you can turn off equations temporarily by deselecting the Active check box in front of the equation. Equations can also be deactivated by a design table. I will discuss design tables in more detail in Chapter 10, which discusses configurations.

BEST PRACTICE Although I do not cover configurations until Chapter 10, I will mention part of the relationship between equations and configurations here. Equations and configurations (particularly those that are driven by a design table) should probably not be mixed. This is not because they do not work together, but more for the sake of organization. When controlling dimensions, it can become confusing if the changes are being driven from multiple sources. Also, there is no reason not to bring your equations into Excel rather than using the comparatively limited equation functionality offered by SolidWorks. Of course, every user will have his own reasons for working one way or another, and this is really just a question of personal preference.

Creating equations

Equations are easy to create and useful for many purposes. A common situation where you would use an equation is to space a pattern of holes evenly along an edge, including the gap on both ends, where the gap at the ends is half of the regular spacing. Before you write an equation, you need to take care of a few organizational details.

Naming dimensions

It is not necessary to name every entity in every SolidWorks document, but you should get in the habit of naming important features, sketches, and even dimensions. Dimensions become particularly important when you use them in equations, configurations, and design tables. Under most circumstances, you do not use or even see dimension names, but with equations, you do.

Named dimensions make a huge difference when you want to recognize the function of an equation by simply reading it. A most obvious example would be the difference between D3@ Sketch6 and Length@WindowExtrusionSketch. The first name means nothing, but the second one is descriptive if you are familiar with the part.

To name a dimension, click the dimension and go to the PropertyManager. In the Primary Value panel shown in Figure 9.2, type the new name for the dimension in the Name text box. You cannot use the symbol @ in dimension names because it is used as a delimiter between the name of the dimension and the feature or sketch to which it applies. Also be aware that even though the software allows you to change the name of the sketch or feature in the Dimension PropertyManager, it will not accept this change.

FIGURE 9.2

Renaming a dimension

BEST PRACTICE You should keep dimension names as short as possible while still making them unique and descriptive. This is because space in the interface is often limited, and when combined with sketch or feature names (and even part names when used in an assembly), the names can become difficult to display in a readable fashion.

TIP You can show dimension names as a part of the dimension itself by accessing the setting at Tools ➪ Options ➪ General ➪ Show Dimension Names. Another useful piece of information is that the FeatureManager Filter filters dimension names. Figure 9.3 shows the filter displaying features and sketches that contain a dimension containing the filtered word "height." Other filtered words display in tool tips, but dimension names appear not to.

Building the equation

When creating an equation in SolidWorks, it is often a good idea to write it out on paper first. Examine the part shown in Figure 9.4, where the relevant dimensions have been named and displayed. The behavior to be driven by the equations is that the number of holes — called Instances here — is the driving variable. From that number, the spacing of the holes is calculated over the length of the part. There is also a gap on each end of the pattern of holes. This gap (measured between the center of the last hole and the end of the part) needs to always be half of the spacing between the holes. The sigma symbols to the left of the dimensions indicate that an equation is driving it. Dimensions driven by equations cannot be directly edited.

FIGURE 9.3

Using the FeatureManager Filter to filter dimension names

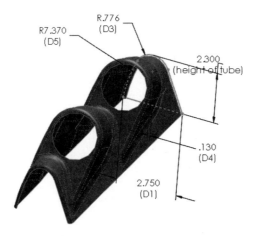

FIGURE 9.4

Variables for the hole pattern

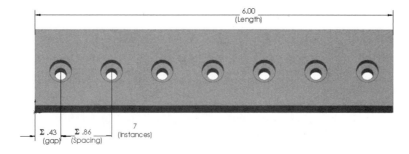

In this case, more sophistication has not been implemented to account for the diameter of the holes possibly interfering with one another when there are a large number of holes. In other words, because there are two values that need to be calculated (the spacing and the gap), you need to create two equations. Because the gap dimension is always half of the spacing, the spacing needs to be calculated first, as follows:

```
Spacing = Length / ((Instances-1)+1)
```

The *Instances* −1 term stands for the number of spacings. If you have two holes, then there is only one spacing. The +1 term stands for the two half-spacings for the two ends. The second equation is simpler and looks like this:

```
Gap = Spacing / 2
```

The order of the equations is important. SolidWorks solves the equations in the order in which they are listed in the Equations dialog box. Because the gap is dependent on the spacing, the spacing must be calculated before the gap. If it is done the other way around, you can get into a situation where it takes two rebuilds to finalize a set of equations, or even a situation where in every rebuild, all of the numbers change. This is called a circular relation, and is a common error in order or history dependent functions, not just in SolidWorks, but in many CAD applications. Figure 9.5 shows the resulting set of equations.

FIGURE 9.5

Equations for the hole pattern

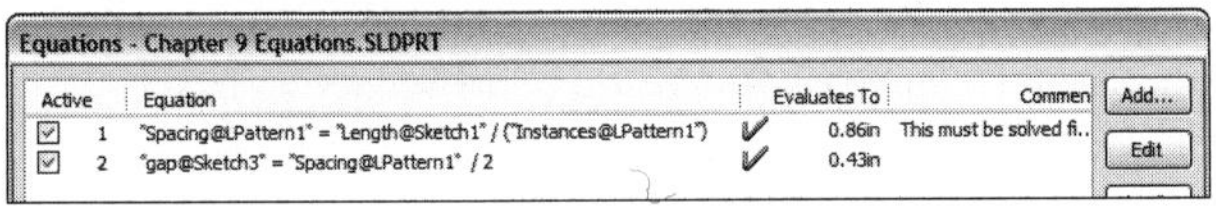

Before beginning to build the equation, you should first display the dimensions that you need to use to create the equation. You can add dimensions to the equation by clicking them from the graphics window. To do this, right-click the Annotations folder at the top of the FeatureManager, and select Show Feature Dimensions. You should also select the Display Annotations option if it is not already on. When you have done this, all of the dimensions that you need to create every feature are displayed. Also be sure to turn on Tools ⇨ Options ⇨ General ⇨ Show Dimension Names.

TIP   For models that have more than a few features, showing all of the dimensions in the entire model may overload the screen with information. In this case, you can double-click a feature from the FeatureManager to show all of the dimensions on that feature.

To build the equation, first use the Equation button on the Tools toolbar to open the Equations dialog box. Then press the Add button to display the Add Equation dialog box. To add dimensions to the equation section, just click the dimension. You can use the keypad on the dialog box or on your keyboard to add operators and syntax. All standard rules of syntax apply for the order of operations, use of parentheses, and driving versus driven sides of the equation.

Using comments

Notice the comment to the right of the first equation in Figure 9.5. Comments can be very useful for annotating equations for yourself or others. Two important reasons to annotate are to remember the significance of variables or dimensions and to add special notes about the logic of the equation.

You can make comments for equations by using a single quote after the end of the equation, or by using the Comment button in the Add Equation dialog box. In the following example,

```
"Spacing@LPattern1" = "Length@Sketch1" / ("Instances@LPattern1") 'This must be
    solved first
```

the comment, "This must be solved first," is applied to the equation using the single quote before the comment.

Adding to the earlier discussion about projected changes to the Equation interface, several standard selection functionalities do not work in the Edit Equation dialog box. These include triple-clicking to select all (although double-clicking works to select a single word) and pressing Ctrl+A to select all.

> **TIP** You can make general comments for the model in the Design Journal, a Microsoft Word document that is embedded into the SolidWorks file. The Design Journal is found in the Design Binder folder near the top of the FeatureManager.

> **ON the CD-ROM** You can find the part used in this section on the CD-ROM with the filename Chapter 9 Equations.sldprt.

Using driven dimensions

Sometimes it is more convenient to use a driven (reference) dimension in an equation. This is particularly true when using geometry is the best way to calculate a number. For example, if you are manufacturing a helical auger in 90-degree sections from flat steel stock, then you need to design the auger in 3D, but begin to manufacture it in 2D.

What is the shape of the auger when flat? The best way to figure this out (aside from lofted bends, which are discussed in Chapter 29) is to use a little high school geometry, a construction sketch, and some simple equations.

Figure 9.6 shows a 90-degree section of an auger blade. The outside diameter is 12 inches, and the blade width is 3 inches. The overall height is 4 inches. In this case, the auger is represented as a surface because the thickness is ignored. Surface features can be useful in situations like this (used as construction geometry) and are discussed in Chapter 27.

FIGURE 9.6

Representation of the auger

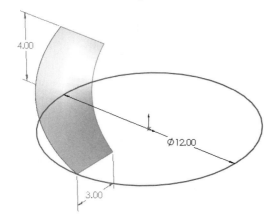

ON the CD-ROM You can find the part for Figure 9.6 on the CD-ROM with the filename `Chapter 9 Auger.sldprt`.

With this information, you can calculate the lengths of the 3D edges using a sketch and a simple equation. In Figure 9.7, the hypotenuses of the triangles represent the helical edges of the helices. By making the triangles the same height as the auger section, and by making the horizontal side of the triangle the same length as a quarter of the inside or outside diameter by using simple equations, the geometry and sketch relations calculate the flat lengths of the inside and outside edges of the auger (length of triangle side = diameter of circle × pi / 4). In this way, the triangle is used to simplify the calculation, and give it a visual result.

FIGURE 9.7

Triangles calculate the length of the helical edge.

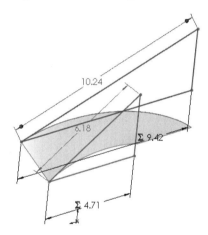

From this point, you can calculate the flat pattern again, using SolidWorks' sketch-solving capabilities as the calculator. Think of the auger as being the cardboard tube inside a roll of paper towels. If you examine one of these tubes closely, you see that it is simply a straight and flat strip of cardboard that has been wound around a cylinder. What was the flat, straight edge of the original board is wound into a helix. This method is simply reversing that process.

This example requires the little-used arc-length dimension to drive the size of the arc. The hypotenuse dimensions are shown by driven or reference dimensions, and these are used to drive the arc-length dimensions, as shown in Figure 9.8. Remember that you can create arc length dimensions by using the Smart Dimension tool to click both endpoints of the arc and then the arc itself. Arcs driven by arc length dimensions often do not react to changes predictably, given the radius and center or end point locations are not necessarily defined.

FIGURE 9.8

Figuring the flat pattern of the auger

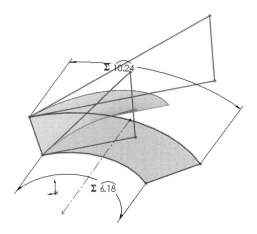

The reasoning behind this example may be a little difficult to grasp, but the equations and the sketches are certainly simple.

CAUTION Using reference dimensions on the driving (independent, or right) side of the equation can in some situations require more than one rebuild to arrive at a stable value (meaning a value that does not change with the next rebuild). SolidWorks issues a warning when it sees that you are using a reference dimension in an equation, but it does allow it.

 Equations are listed in the Equations folder in the FeatureManager. You can edit or delete them through the right-mouse button menu.

Equation tricks

Some functions that are allowed in SolidWorks equations are often viewed as parlor tricks, but they actually do have some practical applications. The two functions that fall into this category are IIF and SWITCH. If you are familiar with a programming language, you may already be familiar with these two functions. If not, I describe them next.

IIF

In words, this is how an IIF statement is used:

If some relationship is fulfilled, then the IIF function returns a value. If the relationship is not fulfilled, then it returns a different value.

A more technical description is

```
IIF(expression, value if true, value if false)
```

In practice, you could use it like this:

```
IIF(x>5, x-1, x+1)
```

which reads, "if x is greater than 5, then subtract 1 from x; if not, then add 1 to x." One of the reasons why this is considered a parlor trick is that this function causes the value of x to oscillate between two numbers (depending on the number that it starts with) with each rebuild. It may be difficult to imagine an application where this sort of behavior would be desirable, but when you combine it with a macro that simply rebuilds a model a number of times, you can use it to create a certain animation effect.

ON the CD-ROM   A simple example of the `IIF` function can be found on the CD-ROM with the filename `Chapter 9 Oscillate.sldprt`. The equation is shown in Figure 9.9.

FIGURE 9.9

An equation using `IIF`

TIP   You can find some great examples of this function at `www.mikejwilson.com`, along with many other extremely creative examples of SolidWorks modeling. The model on this site called `Ship in a Bottle.sldprt` also includes a macro that will rebuild the model a certain number of times, which is useful for animations that are created in this way.

SWITCH

The `SWITCH` function enables you to have a list of relationships with associated values. The value of the first relationship in the list that is satisfied is returned by the `SWITCH` function. For example,

```
switch (x>2, 1.5, x>1, .5 x<1, 2.5)
```

reads as follows: "if x is greater than 2, then the answer is 1.5; if x is not greater than 2 but greater than 1, then the answer is .5; if x is not greater than 1 but less than 1, then the answer is 2.5."

As you can see, this function does not cover all situations, but it does create a condition where the value cycles through three different numbers in a specific order. Is this useful? Possibly. Again, the main application for this function would be a simple animation for changing the size or shape of SolidWorks components that cannot be done in other more conventional ways.

Using Link Values

Link values are simply a way to link several dimensions together, making them equal. A link value is not exactly like an equation that sets the dimensions equal, because it does not depend on order like an equation does. All dimensions are set to the same value simultaneously.

Link values are available by right-clicking the dimension. Unfortunately, they are not available from the right-mouse button menu when the dimension tool is active. To apply a link value to a new dimension, you must place the dimension, exit the dimension tool, right-click the dimension, and select Link Value.

Link values are listed under the Equations folder in the FeatureManager. Figure 9.10 shows the link values in a listed part, and the drop-down list from which you can select them or type them. Notice again that the Link Values feature also operates from a dialog box instead of the PropertyManager.

FIGURE 9.10

Link values listed in the FeatureManager, and the Shared Values interface

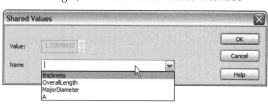

 **NOTE** Another way to access link values is through the Modify dialog box. If you click the down arrow at the right end of the dimension value box, you can select between Link Values and Equations. In fact, if you press the Down Arrow key on the keyboard, the Equation interface becomes available. There is no similar trick to get Link Values to appear.

The first link value that is assigned in a part must be manually typed in. After you add the first one, you can link other dimensions to this link value by using the scroll arrows shown in Figure 9.10. You cannot edit link values, meaning you cannot change a dimension from linking to a value called "height" to a value called "length." In order to change the value to which a dimension is linked, you must first unlink the value and then relink it. The Unlink function is available from the right-mouse button menu in the same way that you assign link values. Dimensions that have a link value have the small chain symbol displayed to the left of the dimension.

To link several dimensions to the same value at the same time, you can CTRL select multiple dimensions and then right-click one of them and select Link Value. It will link all the dimensions selected at once. (Thanks to Brian McElyea for this suggestion!)

 There is one link value name that has a special significance. If you use the name *thickness*, then a Link To Thickness option appears in all extrude dialog boxes. This is intended to reflect sheet metal functionality, but it is useful for models of various manufacturing techniques.

To take this one step further, you can save a part template with a *thickness* link value; all of your new parts will also have this functionality right from the start. To save the template with a link value, you must create at least one dimension to assign the link value, and then delete the geometry (and the dimension); however, the link value will remain.

Link values of different types are not necessarily interchangeable. You cannot use angular dimension link values on radius, diameter, or linear dimensions. You can use linear and diameter link values interchangeably, but not angle link values.

Using Global Variables

Global variables are assigned in the Equations dialog box as simply the variable name equaling the value. Figure 9.11 shows a list of equations, link values, and global variables. When you are typing in the name of the variable, you do not need to add the quotation marks; they are added automatically.

FIGURE 9.11

Equations, link values, and global variables

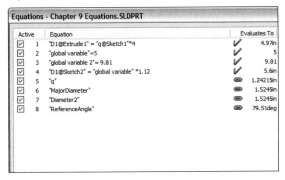

Despite the word *variable* in the name global variable, the values are not variable. They are fixed, and only changeable through the Equations dialog box. The only place where you can use global variables is in equations. You cannot directly enter them into dialog boxes for dimension values, or use them like Link Values.

You can use custom and file properties to drive equations. If you right-click your Equations folder and select Show Properties, you see that the default file properties already exist in the list:

Global Variable

 Custom Property

 Default File Property

FIGURE 9.12

Equations and properties

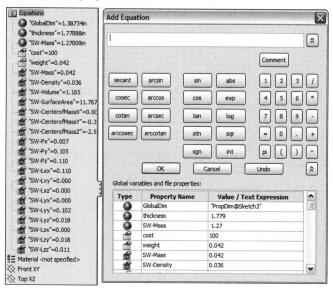

In the equation editor shown on the right in Figure 9.12, you can expand the list of global, custom and default properties for easy selection and placement into equations. Any custom properties you add that are of the type "number" are automatically added to this list, and can also be used in equations. Notice that the custom property "cost" is a property saved in my template and gets picked up for use here.

Using Expressions

Expressions, unlike all of the previous variables, values, and equations, can be entered directly into dimension dialog boxes in the Modify dialog box and PropertyManager value boxes. The expressions have to be composed of numbers and mathematical operators. An expression such as

```
2.375+(4.8/3) -1.1
```

is perfectly acceptable, as is

    1+1/2

or

    1 1/2.

In the second case in this example, the plus symbol is understood.

Other types of operations are also available, such as changing units in a dimension box. For example, if you are editing a part in inches, and enter 40mm, then SolidWorks does the conversion for you. You can even mix units in a single expression such as 4.875+3.5mm, where the inch part is assumed as the document units.

SolidWorks does not remember the expression itself, only the final value. Expressions can be entered into any place where you enter dimensions for SolidWorks features.

Tutorial: Using Equations

Follow these steps to get some practice with using equations:

1. **Start from the part on the CD-ROM with the filename** Chapter9 Tutorial Start.sldprt.

2. **Show the dimension names.** This setting is found at Tools ⇨ Options ⇨ General ⇨ Show Dimension Names.

3. **Double-click the Circular Pattern feature to display the angle and number of instances of the feet and related features.** You may have to move the angle dimension to see the pattern instance number.

4. **Click the instance number.** Change the name of the dimension to # (pound or number sign) in the Dimension PropertyManager. Make sure that Instant3D is turned off when doing this.

5. **Double-click the first feature, which is the revolve, and rename the 3.60-inch dimension to** CapRad, again by selecting it and using the PropertyManager.

6. **Write an equation that drives the number of legs by CapRad/7.**

    a. Open the Equations dialog box at Tools ⇨ Equations.

    b. Click Add to add an equation.

    c. Double-click the Circular Pattern and click the # dimension. Make sure that the name of the dimension is listed in the equation box, and type an equal sign.

    d. Double-click the Revolve feature and select the CapRad dimension; then type the characters /1.5.

    e. Add a comment to the equation to reflect which dimension is driving which dimension.

7. Click Rebuild, press Ctrl+B or Ctrl+Q to rebuild the model, and observe whether any update takes place.

8. Rename the 6.00-inch dimension for the height of the revolved feature to DomeHt.

9. Create a second equation that drives the DomeHt dimension at the current ratio of the height to the radius.

   a. Create a global variable called Ratio = 6/3.6 (1.66667) in the Equations dialog box.

   b. Create the equation. The equation will take the form of DomeHt = (Ratio) × CapRad. You can use the drop down under the calculator pad to select the Ratio variable from the list.

10. Use a link value to make the radii of Fillet1 and Fillet2 the same.

11. Double-click the revolve feature. Change the .CapRad dimension to 5 and rebuild. You should observe 3 feet. Change it again to 6, and you should see 4 feet.

12. Save and close the part with a new name, including your initials or the date.

Summary

SolidWorks equations and related dimension-management tools are powerful, but often leave you wishing for a little more flexibility and control. The interface is not up-to-date with the rest of the SolidWorks interface, and so I would look to see an updated equation interface soon that integrates dimension input, link values, and global variables.

If you want to encourage SolidWorks to revise certain features, then you can go to the SolidWorks Web site and submit an enhancement request. They do look at customer input when developing or updating functionality.

Chapter 10

Working with Part Configurations

onfigurations, also known as simply configs, are variations of a part in which dimensions are changed, features are suppressed (turned off), and other items such as color or custom properties may be controlled. Configurations enable you to have these variations within a single part file, which is both convenient and efficient.

This chapter deals only with part configurations, but you should be aware that assemblies can also have configurations. Assembly configurations can use different part configurations, among other things. This will mean more to you as you learn about part configurations.

CROSS-REF Assembly configurations are discussed in Chapter 14.

One example of the use of configurations is Toolbox. By default, Toolbox uses configurations to create many sizes of hardware within a single part file. For example, the Socket Head Cap Screw is a single part in Toolbox that contains thousands of potential sizes. You can change the size of a Toolbox part by simply varying the dimensions of the existing features. Toolbox parts also have features that you can turn off and on (suppress and unsuppress, respectively), particularly those related to thread representation (swept versus revolved versus cosmetic). Changing dimensions and suppressing or unsuppressing features are the most commonly used techniques available through configurations.

IN THIS CHAPTER

Controlling items with configurations

Using design tables

Tutorial: Working with configurations and design tables

329

Controlling Items with Configurations

With every new release of SolidWorks software, it seems that there are new items that become "configurable," that is, able to be driven by configurations. Configurable items for parts include the following:

- Feature dimensions, tolerances, driving/driven state
- Suppression of features, equations, sketch relations, and feature end conditions
- Which sketch plane is used by a sketch
- Configuration-specific custom properties
- Part, body, feature, and face colors
- Derived configurations
- The ability to assign properties such as mass and center of gravity
- Configuration of base or split parts
- Size of Hole Wizard holes

You can work with configurations in one of three ways: manually making changes to dimensions and features, using the Configure Feature/Modify Configurations table, or through an Excel based design table. I describe the manual method first, to give you a good understanding of how to intervene with configs manually when you need to. Design tables are a fantastic way to organize and manage config data and options, but they also require a bit of syntax, and so I will describe them in a separate section later in this chapter.

Finding configurations

 You can handle configurations in the ConfigurationManager. This is a tab at the top of the FeatureManager area.

TIP You can split the FeatureManager interface into two by dragging the splitter bar at the top of the panel. This is a very useful function that allows you to see the FeatureManager in the upper panel and the PropertyManager or ConfigurationManager in the lower panel. Remember also that starting with SolidWorks 2009, you can detach the PropertyManager from the left hand side panel area.

Deleting configs

Each part has a default config named "Default." There is nothing special about this config; you can rename it and even delete it. At least one config must always remain in the tree, and you cannot delete the current configuration. If you would like to remove a config, then you need to switch to another config first, and then delete it.

In relation to part configurations used in assemblies, you cannot delete a part config if it is being used in an assembly that is open and resolved. Nor can you delete a configuration referenced by an open drawing. In order to delete a config such as this, you need to either close the assembly or change the part config used in the assembly.

CROSS-REF **Chapter 14 deals with configurations of assemblies in depth. The current chapter deals only with configurations of parts. Configurations of drawings do not exist.**

If you try to delete a part configuration being used by an open assembly, SolidWorks simply gives the message "None of the selected entities could be deleted" without explanation.

If you delete a configuration of a part that is used in an assembly, but the assembly is not currently open, the next time the assembly is opened it issues the message "The following component configurations could not be found . . . . If the configuration was renamed the same configuration will be used, otherwise the last active configuration will be substituted for each instance."

As you can see, a configuration that is simply renamed is dealt with differently than a configuration that is deleted. In any case, you need to be careful when dealing with parts with configurations that are used in an assembly.

NOTE **Many users get into the habit of clicking out of any error, warning, or message box that comes up, often without reading what it has to say. It is important to read error and warning messages when they come up. Some of them, such as the configuration message shown previously, are vitally important to the integrity of your design data. They are sometimes actually useful.**

You can delete groups of configs by window select ➪ Shift+select or Ctrl+select in the ConfigurationManager. You can also use the right-mouse button menu, much like regular features in the FeatureManager. None of the configurations selected to be deleted may be active, or referenced by other open and resolved documents.

Sorting configs

In the ConfigurationManager, configs are listed alphabetically, not in the order in which they are created. This has several advantages, especially when you have a large number of configs. For example, if configs are named by size in a part that you are working with, then when you select a configuration, you can type in a number, and the selection scrolls to that place in the list of configs. This makes it easier to select the one you are looking for, much the same as it works in Windows Explorer.

Alphabetization

This alphabetized order is significant because many other sections of the SolidWorks interface are not alphabetized, which causes problems when you are searching for items in larger lists. Sections that are not alphabetized include Help/Contents, Files Of Type lists in Open and Save dialog boxes, and the Tools/Options/File Locations, Entity Color list. If you are inclined to send in an Enhancement Request, alphabetization is one topic that would benefit everyone and should be fairly easy for SolidWorks to implement.

Naming configs

In order for this sorting and alphabetization to work, you must first name the configs properly. For example, if you have a list of sizes or config names from 1 to 100, then you should use 001, 002...100 as your syntax. This makes the config names easier to browse and type in. Syntax becomes most important when you place a part with many configs into an assembly, because you must select a config from the list, and typing in the first few numbers is often faster and easier than scrolling to it.

ON the CD-ROM The CD-ROM contains a part called `Chapter 10 Config Names.sldprt`, which illustrates proper naming and alphabetization.

To understand this technique better, you can open the part called `Chapter 10 Config Names.sldprt` from the CD-ROM, split the FeatureManager area, and change one of the panes to display the ConfigurationManager. Click one of the configuration names, and type in a number between 001 and 100. The highlight scrolls to the number that you typed in. Thoughtful selection of the configuration names can save you and your coworkers a lot of time when you need to insert select configs into an assembly. Figure 10.1 shows this arrangement.

CROSS-REF The splitter bar and other portions of the FeatureManager interface appear in Chapter 2.

Activating configurations

Within a part file, to change the display from one configuration to another, you must first switch to the ConfigurationManager panel, and then either double-click the desired config or right-click it and select Show Configuration.

FIGURE 10.1

The split FeatureManager, displaying the ConfigurationManager

Alternatively, you can right-click the config in the ConfigurationManager and select Show Preview, as shown in Figure 10.2. A small preview thumbnail displays in the PropertyManager panel. However, not all configurations will have previews. For example, in a part with many configs that have been generated automatically by a design table, the configurations may not have previews because the config itself has never actually been rebuilt. Previews exist only when the configuration has been activated at least once, the image on the screen generated, and the part then saved. SolidWorks stores both the body (geometry) and the preview image of the part so that next time you access the configuration, the software does not have to rebuild everything again.

FIGURE 10.2

Showing a configuration preview

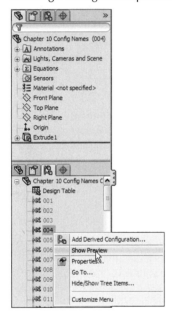

You can even select a configuration while opening a file. This allows you to save time by avoiding two model rebuilds. To take advantage of this option, you must use the File ➪ Open interface, which is shown in Figure 10.3. You can select the config from the lower-right drop-down [Configurations] list. In the 2009 software release, you cannot type the name in for selection. In 2007 software, which uses a list box instead of a drop-down box, you are able to do so. However, the Display States drop-down box is not available in the Open dialog in SolidWorks 2007.

FIGURE 10.3

Selecting a configuration from the Open dialog box

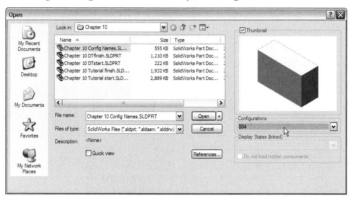

Creating configurations

You can create configs manually, using the Configure Feature/Modify Configurations table or through Excel-driven design tables. Design tables are extremely useful for situations where there are more than a few configs, or more than a few items are being controlled. You should use design tables because they keep things very organized within the spreadsheet grid.

For now, I am going to focus on creating and manipulating configs manually so that you can become familiar with them without also worrying about Excel and design table syntax.

Making a new config

To make a new config, you can right-click the top-level icon in the ConfigurationManager, which displays a part symbol and the name of the part, and select Add Configuration. If you right-click an existing configuration, SolidWorks will make a derived config, which I discuss later in this chapter. Figure 10.4 shows the right-mouse button menu and the Properties dialog box that you can use to set up the new config.

Configuration properties and options

The name of the config is important mainly for quick access and organization purposes. The configuration description is also important, because it can display in the ConfigurationManager, and even in the Assembly tree. (You can also use the FeatureManager Filter to search configuration descriptions.) This is important when the name of the config is numerical rather than descriptive, and you would like to also have a description but not include it in the name. The config description can also appear in place of the filename in the Assembly tree display. I discuss this in more detail in Chapter 12. Config descriptions can be driven manually through the Configuration Properties dialog box or through a design table if you have many configs to manage. You can display config descriptions through the right-mouse button menu, as shown in Figure 10.5.

FIGURE 10.4

Creating a new configuration

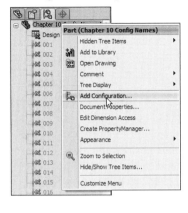 

FIGURE 10.5

Enabling configuration descriptions

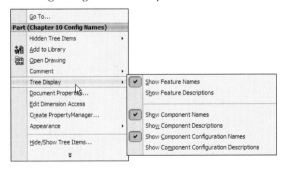

I discuss the Bill of Materials options in Chapter 24, but the option is set in the Configuration Properties to use the filename, the configuration name, or a custom name that the user specifies. You can save this setting with a template. You achieve control over configurations through the combination of the Configuration Properties and the Advanced Options, which I discuss next.

BEST PRACTICE Although you can change the preferred settings at any time, it is definitely a best practice to make a template early on when you are using SolidWorks to model parts. SolidWorks remembers the Bill of Materials options and Advanced options that you set for the Default configuration and uses them in document templates. This is true for both part and assembly templates.

Advanced options

The two advanced configuration options are found in the bottom panel of the Configuration Properties PropertyManager: Suppress features and Use configuration specific color. While the second option is self-explanatory, the first one is not, and often catches new and even experienced users off guard.

Suppress features refers to how inactive configurations should handle new features that are added to the part. For example, if you have two configs, 1 and 2, and config 1 is active and you add a new Fillet feature, what happens to that feature in config 2? If this option is turned on, the new features are suppressed in the inactive configs. If it is turned off, the new features will be unsuppressed when the inactive configs are activated. This creates a much bigger challenge for manually created configurations than for design table-driven configs because changing suppression states for several features across multiple configs is much easier in a design table than in manual config management.

The Modify dialog box

The Modify box enables you to change dimensions by just double-clicking the dimension, and changing the value. When you change a dimension using the Modify box in a part that has more than one configuration, an additional button appears on the Modify box, shown in Figure 10.6.

FIGURE 10.6
_____

The Modify dialog box

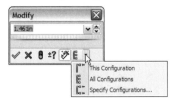

Modify has three options for configuring dimensions: This Configuration, All Configurations, and Specify Configurations. Choosing the Specify Configurations enables the Modify Configurations dialog box, which I take a look at shortly.

If you are manually managing configurations, it is important that you always use this box to configure dimensions. If you make a mistake and change a dimension for All Configurations that should have been changed for This Configuration, you could have to fix a lot of data. This is one reason why I believe manual configuration management only works for simple configurations schemes, and you should use design tables when you have more than a couple configs.

Negative dimensions

SolidWorks 2009 brings into play the use of negative dimensions. Negative dimensions can only be used within the Modify box, and cannot (or should not) be used in other places. The negative sign serves only to change the direction of the dimension, and then it is discarded.

An equation that results in a negative dimension will flip the sense of the dimension every time it is rebuilt. This may be a useful trick, but will probably serve as an annoyance for most modeling. When you put a negative dimension in a Modify dialog box, the dimension changes sense (direction) and the negative sign disappears after one rebuild. If you put a negative dimension into a Modify Configurations dialog box, it will also disappear, and change the direction of the dimension for all configurations. When you enter a negative dimension into a design table, the negative is retained (until the next time you open the design table), and the sense of the dimension is retained only for the configs to which you assigned negative dimension values.

NOTE This design table functionality is something that arouses my suspicion. I would not build a design intent scenario based on negative dimensions in design tables. The functionality seems unintentional, unstable, or otherwise subject to change.

Negative dimensions can only be assigned to sketch dimensions, not to feature dimensions. You cannot change the extrusion direction by making the blind depth negative.

Using the Modify Configurations box

The Modify Configurations box, shown in Figure 10.7, enables you to create and modify configured features and dimensions in a more organized way than by using simple manual methods described earlier, but without getting involved in an Excel-based design table, described later in this chapter. Do not confuse the Modify Configurations box with the Modify box, which is used to change dimensions.

FIGURE 10.7

Using the Modify Configurations box

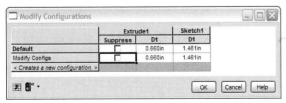

| | Extrude1 | | Sketch1 |
	Suppress	D1	D1
Default	☐	0.660in	1.461in
Modify Configs	☐	0.660in	1.461in
< Creates a new configuration. >			

With the Modify Configurations box active, double-click a dimension to add it to the configured features list. You can add configurations on the fly by typing in the appropriate box, and change values or states of features by double-clicking and entering numbers or checking the box in the appropriate column.

The Modify Configurations interface is still a relatively new part of the software. I still tend to use either the manual or Excel-based techniques. I have not yet found a use for the middle ground offered by the Modify Configurations box, but I can see where it might be valuable for people who might want to configure a couple of features without getting involved in a big spreadsheet.

Plus, I should mention that much folk-lore exists surrounding what is perceived as a problematic relationship between Excel and SolidWorks. Some users claim that Excel often causes SolidWorks to crash. Beyond that, many workplaces may not have Excel available to them, either because of the cost or g because they use a non-Microsoft solution for spreadsheet applications. These users still want the functionality of design tables even if Excel is not installed on their machines.

The Modify Configurations box does not give you control over everything. Some things that you can configure, you cannot drive from this dialog, such as part color, custom properties, and so on. Design tables are still the most powerful way to go, but Modify Configurations offers a lot of flexibility and immediacy.

You can also access the Modify Configurations box from the right-click menu selections Configure Dimension and Configure Feature.

Using Custom PropertyManagers

Starting in SolidWorks 2009, you have the ability to create custom Property tab interfaces by using the Property Tab Builder. This function is described in more detail in Appendix A. The function is an administrative function, which is why it is listed with the implementation information rather than with the user info.

Derived configurations

Derived configurations are configs that are dependent on other configs. You can create them from the right-mouse button menu on a configuration instead of on the top level in the ConfigurationManager, and they appear indented underneath the parent config. Figure 10.8 shows the right-mouse button menu and the position of the derived config in the tree.

Derived configurations maintain the same values and properties of the parent config unless you break the link to the child config by explicitly changing a value in the child config. For all other values, the child config value changes when the parent config value changes.

FIGURE 10.8

Creation and placement of the derived config

One very nice application of derived configs is to use them for simplified configurations, and set the properties so that any features that are added to the parent config are also added to the derived config. You can do this by setting the Advanced Option Suppress Features to Off. This causes the derived config to inherit *only* features that are added to the parent, and not to other configs. You can use the simplified configs for Finite Element Analysis (FEA), making drawings of models where all of the edge breaks have actually been modeled. You can also used use them for the reverse (a complex config rather than simple) to have a config that includes fillets for rendering purposes that are otherwise not there. And you can create and maintain derived configs using design tables, which are discussed in the next section.

File size considerations

A long-standing dispute has raged over the effects of file size on speed. Here are the facts: When SolidWorks creates a configuration, it stores information about the 3D geometry and a preview thumbnail of the configuration inside the part file. This makes it faster to access the configuration the next time because it has only to read the data, rather than read other data and then recalculate the new data. As a result, saving the stored data allows you to avoid having to recalculate it.

Many people assign more important to file size than I do, and use it as a criterion on which to base decisions about which features or techniques to use or not use. If I can use a single file instead of multiple files by using configurations, it is the technique I prefer. Libraries of parts can often be made more manageable by using configured parts rather than a lot of individual parts.

CROSS-REF Appendix A contains a section on Data Management that has several options for dealing with data and large file sizes.

PERFORMANCE File size has a negative effect on speed when you are sending data across the Internet or working across a network. If the data is on your hard drive, then storing data instead of calculating it offers a big benefit.

Controlling dimensions

Controlling dimensions with configurations is simple. You need only three things to start: one dimension and two configurations. Because you already know how to create these elements, you are ready to start. Configurations require that you spend some time developing "design intent" for parts. Configurations drive changes in models, and if they are improperly modeled, configurations cause feature or sketch failures.

I will start with the example of a simple block. A fully dimensioned block has three dimensions. Make sure that you have manually created at least two configurations. Double-clicking the model brings up all the dimensions, and double-clicking one of the dimensions brings up the familiar Modify dialog box. Or *almost* familiar, I should say; Figure 10.6 shows that there is a small difference in the new Modify dialog box. It now has a drop-down list where you can specify whether this change applies only to this config, to all configs, or to specified configs. If you select specified configs, then the Modify Configurations box on the top in Figure 10.7 appears, where you can select which configs this dimension change applies to.

Once you are finished, you can toggle back and forth between the configs by double-clicking each of the configs in the ConfigurationManager. Although this is simple, if you forget to change the drop-down list from the All Configurations setting to either the This Configuration or the Specify Configurations setting, then you apply the change to all of the configurations. This shows that building a configuration manually is fine for a few simple changes, but it can become unwieldy if you are changing more than a few dimensions in this way. You would then have to remember which dimensions were changed to what. As you can see, using design tables is a better method for multiple dimensions.

Controlling suppression

 Suppressing a feature is just like turning it off; the feature appears as grayed-out text in the FeatureManager. With configurations, you can suppress a feature in one config and unsuppress it in another. When dealing with manual configuration techniques, there are two methods for controlling suppression: manually suppressing features, and creating configurations with the appropriate options for the inclusion of new features that I discussed previously in this chapter.

In addition to the Suppress toolbar button, you can also use the Unsuppress and Unsuppress with Dependents functions. When you suppress a feature, any feature that is dependent on it is also suppressed. If you then use the Unsuppress feature, it unsuppresses only the feature itself. However, Unsuppress with Dependents brings back all of the dependent features, as well.

PERFORMANCE **Suppressing complex features is a great way to improve performance. Experienced users often create a configuration of a part that they use as a simplified config, where patterns, fillets, and extruded text features are suppressed. This becomes more important as you start working with assemblies. For reasons which I will discuss in the assemblies chapters, it can be a great advantage to make a configuration for each part called "simplified." You can, in fact, make a second configuration in template files so that new parts and assemblies automatically have this built into them.**

Generally, SolidWorks users employ a combination of these methods, mainly because configurations are not usually started on a complete model; they are often added when the model is still in progress, and so features are added after the users create the configurations.

On the left side of Figure 10.9, you can see a feature that is alternately unsuppressed and suppressed in the tree. The text and icon for the suppressed feature are grayed out. You can suppress features from the right-mouse button menu on the feature, from the Edit menu, or through a tool on a toolbar. The Suppress button is not on a toolbar by default, but you can find it in the Tools ➪ Customize ➪ Commands dialog box, along with the other buttons for the Features toolbar. Only the Edit menu offers the options of Unsuppress With Dependents and This Configuration/All Configurations/Specify Configurations options for each of the Suppress, Unsuppress, Unsuppress With Dependents functions.

Using Unsuppress With Dependents can save you a lot of time or the hassle of looking for all of the features dependent upon a feature which had been suppressed. Because it is not available on the right-mouse button menus, this function is less used than it might otherwise be.

FIGURE 10.9

Suppressing a feature

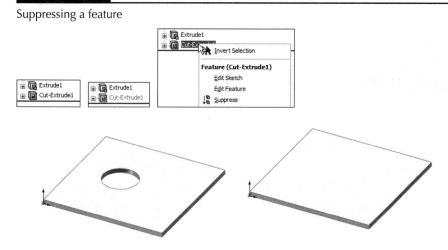

Controlling custom properties

Custom properties fall into a category of model data called *metadata*, which is text-based information. This metadata is meant for any text-based data that you would like to accompany the part, such as description, material, vendor, vendor part number, price, or even cost. Several reasons may compel you to use custom properties, including [being able to use] search criteria for a Product Data Management system, automatically filling out drawing title blocks, or adding information to the Bill of Materials.

When you are using custom properties with configurations, you must use the Configuration Specific Custom Properties interface, which enables you to have custom properties that change with each configuration. This is useful for situations such as different part numbers for configurations, and many other situations that are limited mostly by your use of configs. The Custom tab of the Summary Information dialog, shown in Figure 10.10 still applies custom properties that do not change with the configurations to the part.

The interface for managing custom properties manually is shown in Figure 10.10. You can access this dialog box through menus at File ➪ Properties. If you are using a newer version of SolidWorks, then you may notice that the interface has improved drastically in recent versions.

FIGURE 10.10

The Configuration Specific tab in the Summary Information dialog box

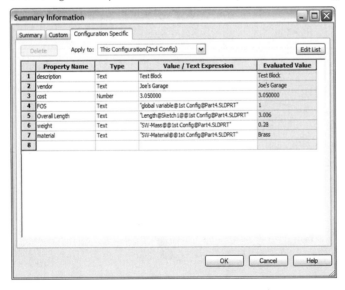

You can also link custom properties to mass properties, model dimensions, link values, and global variables by selecting from the drop-down list under the Value/Text Expression column, which appears when you select a cell in the column, as shown in Figure 10.10. To link a custom property to a model dimension, simply place the cursor in the Value/Text Expression box that you want to populate, and click a dimension in the graphics window. Again, managing this data for a single config or only a few configs is easy enough; however, it can quickly become unwieldy, which is where using design tables can make a huge difference.

Controlling colors

Face, feature, body, and part colors as well as materials are also configurable. Just switch to the configuration you want to control, and make the changes.

Controlling sketch relations

You can individually suppress or unsuppress sketch relations using configurations. Figure 10.11 shows the Display/Delete Relations PropertyManager interface, at the bottom of which is the Configurations panel. To suppress a relation, select it from the list and select the Suppressed option in the Relations section above the Delete buttons.

FIGURE 10.11

The Display/Delete Relations dialog box for configuring sketch relations

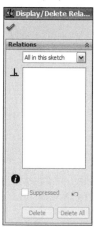

> **TIP**   This is another situation where Delete is not used as an editing option. Using this technique, you can save sketch relations, or activate different sets of relations in different configs; this technique allows a single sketch to react to changes differently.

Controlling sketch planes

You cannot configure the Offset distance in the From option for extrudes, but you *can* configure the sketch plane for the sketch that is used in the feature. The Sketch Plane PropertyManager interface expands when configurations are present, as shown in Figure 10.12.

FIGURE 10.12

The Sketch Plane PropertyManager interface for configuring a sketch plane

> **TIP**   Another way to change the sketch plane is to put the sketch on an offset plane or a plane that can otherwise be driven by a dimension (for example, using reference sketch geometry). Actually moving a sketch to another plane can cause the sketch to rotate or flip. Moving the plane it is on is a better option that does not cause the sketch to rotate or flip.

> **CAUTION**   Changing sketch planes indiscriminately can have serious consequences for your model. "Face/Plane Normals" sometimes point in different directions, and can cause a sketch to flip, rotate, or mirror when you change it from one plane to another. One strange result is that changing it back to the original location can cause the sketch to flip again, but in a different way so that it does not go back to its original location/orientation. As a result, every time you change the configuration, the sketch could appear in a new and unexpected location or orientation.

Controlling configurations of inserted parts

 Inserted parts have a long history in SolidWorks. They have had several names in the past, and some sources (including SolidWorks documentation such as training documents and even help files) still use some of these legacy names out of habit or precedence. For example, you will sometimes hear inserted parts called *derived* or *base* parts. Both of these terms are obsolete.

> **CROSS-REF** Inserted parts are discussed in detail in Chapter 28, which describes master model techniques.

Inserted parts use one part as the starting point for another part. The inserted part sits as a feature in the FeatureManager of the child part. You can insert just the body geometry itself, or you can bring forward reference geometry, sketch data and all features, and break the link to the original part if you wish to.

The role of configurations with inserted parts is that the configuration of the inserted part can be controlled from the child component. For example, you may have designed an engine block for an automobile. This engine block is a casting, and using configurations, you have both the six-cylinder and the eight-cylinder blocks in a single-part file. This model represents the "as cast" engine block. The next step is to make the block with all of the secondary machining operations, such as facing mating surfaces, boring cylinders, drilling and tapping holes for threaded connections, and so on. As a result, the as-cast part is inserted into the as-machined part, and the configuration is selected before you add the cut features. As the name suggests, you add inserted parts through the menus using Insert ⇨ Part.

The interface for assigning the configuration is shown in Figure 10.13. Simply right-click the inserted part feature and select List External References. It would seem to make more sense if the configuration could be selected when the part is first inserted, but it does not work this way; you have to select the configuration after the part is inserted.

Library features

Library features can have configurations, and they carry those configurations with them into the part in which they are placed. Unfortunately, part configs cannot reference different library feature configs.

> **CROSS-REF** Chapter 17 discusses the Hole Wizard, and Chapter 18 discusses library features.

FIGURE 10.13

Assigning the configuration of an inserted part

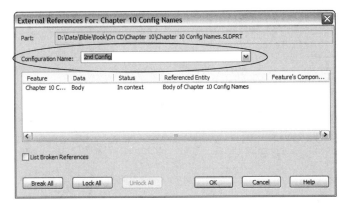

Configurations for library features are created in exactly the same ways that configurations are created for other parts. The technique for saving the configs to the library feature is discussed in Chapter 18.

Unconfigurable items

As important as it is to know what you *can* do, it is equally important to know what you *cannot* do. The following is a list of items that are not configurable. Although this list is not complete, it contains many of the more relevant items that cannot be configured:

- Library feature configs

- Blocks

- Extrude direction or From Offset dimension or direction

- Most of the values in features such as Deform, Freeform, and Flex

While Library Features can be configured, once you drop them into a part and click the OK button, the configurations are no longer accessible (unless you have selected Link To Library Part), so a part's configurations cannot select the configuration of a Library feature. A part's configurations can, however, change the dimensions of a library feature.

Using Design Tables

In addition to describing some of the basic concepts involved with configurations, the first part of this chapter has offered reasons for using design tables. For example, while manual configuration management can be haphazard, and is highly prone to mistakes, design tables lay everything out in an Excel spreadsheet. Although many new users ask whether they can use a different replacement spreadsheet program, you must use Excel for design tables.

NOTE The versions of Excel that are supported by SolidWorks for design tables are 2000, 2003, and 2007. Although Excel 97 may still work, Microsoft no longer supports that product.

Excel is a format that is easy to read and print out, and even non-SolidWorks users can understand and work with it. Although there is some special syntax that you need to use with design tables, for most uses, SolidWorks can create the syntax automatically for you, and so there is a minimum of manual data entry. If you are careful to name dimensions, features, and configurations properly, design tables should be easy to understand and manage. In Excel you can also color cells, rows, and columns in such a way that large amounts of tabulated data are easier to sort through. In addition, because design tables use Excel, they can also use all of Excel's calculation capabilities.

BEST PRACTICE When using equations and design tables, it is considered best practice to name dimensions, sketches, features, and other configured items. However, it is not recommended to mix design tables with SolidWorks equations. Besides the fact that Excel equations are far more sophisticated than those of SolidWorks, driving dimensions from too many locations can be confusing when you edit the part after you have forgotten the details of how the part was built.

It is a great idea to document design intent using comments in the features or the Design Journal. You should also add comments to design tables as needed.

What Can Be Driven by a Design Table?

Just because something can be configured does not necessarily mean that it can also be driven by a design table. Here is a small list of items that fit into this category:

- Sketch plane configuration
- Suppressed sketch relations
- Suppressed dimensions (suppressed dimensions become driven dimensions)

However, the good news is that there are many items that can be driven by a design table. Table 10.1 lists these items, along with their associated syntax.

TABLE 10.1

Items That Can Be Driven by a Design Table

Item	Syntax (Goes in Column Header)	Possible Values (Goes in Field Cell)	Default Value If Field Is Blank
Configs of Inserted Parts	$configuration@<part name>	<config name>	not evaluated
Configs of Split Parts	$configuration@<split feature name>	<config name>	not evaluated
Comment Column	$comment	comment text	blank
Configuration Description	$description	description text	<config name>
BOM (Bill of Materials) Part No.	$partnumber	$d, $document = document name $p, $parent = parent config name $c, $configuration = config name <text> = custom name	config name
Feature Suppression State	$state@<feature name>	suppressed, s unsuppressed, u	present suppression state
Dimension Value	dimension@<feature name> dimension@<sketch name>	allowed numerical values	not evaluated
Parent Config (creates a derived config)	$parent	parent config name text	not evaluated
Config Specific Custom Property	$prp@<property name>	property name text	not evaluated
Equation State	$state@<equation number>@ equations	suppressed, s unsuppressed, u	unsuppressed
Light Suppression State	$state@<light name>	suppressed, s unsuppressed, u	unsuppressed
Sketch Relation Suppression	$state@<relation name>@<sketch name>	suppressed, s unsuppressed, u	unsuppressed
User Notes (same as comment)	$user_notes	Text	blank
Part or Feature Color	$color $color@<feature name>	see SolidWorks Help, Colors, Parameters in design tables	0, black
Assigned Mass	$sw-mass	allowed numerical values	value from Mass properties

Item	Syntax (Goes in Column Header)	Possible Values (Goes in Field Cell)	Default Value If Field Is Blank
Assigned Center of Gravity X, Y, Z Coordinates	$sw-cog	allowed numerical values in the format of *x, y, z*	value from Mass properties
Dimension Tolerance	$tolerance@<*dimension name*>	see SolidWorks Help, Tolerance Keywords and Syntax in Design Tables	none

Creating a simple design table

When you prepare to create a design table, you generally need to give appropriate names to dimensions, sketches, and features. Remember that while the feature is the most visible item and the easiest to rename, most of the dimensions probably belong to the sketch, which you may also need or want to rename. Names should reflect the function or location of the item. It is a good idea to show dimension names when renaming items (remember that you can show dimension names by turning on the option at Tools ⇨ Options ⇨ General ⇨ Show Dimension Names). Figure 10.14 shows the result of renaming the feature and dimension.

FIGURE 10.14

Renamed features and dimensions

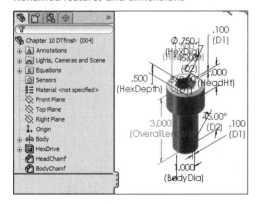

You can use one of the following three techniques to add a design table to a SolidWorks part through the menu selection Insert ⇨ Tables ⇨ Design Tables:

- **Insert Blank Design Table.** This method starts from a blank template that contains the underlying framework, but no values.

■ **Auto-create Design Table.** This method populates the new design table with any existing configurations and items that are different between the configs.

■ **From File.** This method allows you to create a design table externally and then import it.

Although I prefer the Auto-create method, it is most appropriate for when you have existing configurations. The From File method is best when a design table has been exported from another part, saved externally, and brought into the current part. For the following example, I am using the Insert Blank Design Table method.

ON the CD-ROM   **If you would like to follow along with these steps to create the design table, you can use the part from the CD-ROM with the filename `Chapter 10 DTstart.sldprt`.**

Figure 10.15 shows the results of starting with the new blank design table. You may notice that the window title bar at the top says SolidWorks, but the toolbars look a lot like the Excel interface. This is because Excel is actually running inside of SolidWorks. Clicking outside of the Excel window can cause the Excel window to close, although there are several items outside of the Excel window that you can select without the window closing, such as features in the FeatureManager and dimensions in the graphics window. You can also rotate and pan the view in the graphics window without closing the Design Table window. If you are very careful, you can also drag the thin hatched border of the Excel window to adjust its size or location.

Design Tables also can be edited in a separate window, which makes editing easier, but makes adding dimension and feature names more difficult. To edit the table in its own window, right-mouse button on the Design Table in the FeatureManager and select Edit Table In New Window.

FIGURE 10.15

The interface where you can create the design table, and the resulting blank design table

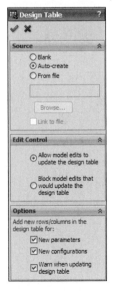
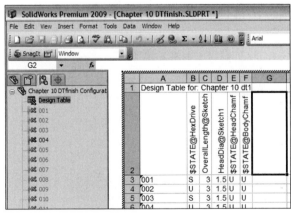

Figure 10.16 shows a fully developed design table, with some complexity. Although your first design table does not need to be this complex, this example demonstrates what you can do with this feature.

The config names go in the first column, and the feature or property names go in the second row. The first row is reserved for the name of the table. All of this is automatically set up by SolidWorks.

NOTE Because you are actually working in Excel when working with design tables, you can use Excel formatting, which is how the text in Figure 10.16 is rotated 90 degrees for the column headers. (To rotate text in a table, right-click the cell, group of cells, or row; select Format Cells; and then select the Alignment tab).

In our new design table, the next step is to type in some configuration names. Because you are working in Excel, all of the fill functionality is available. In the example shown in Figure 10.17, I have typed in the first three values of 001, 002, and 003, then window-selected the cells, and dragged the fill handle on the selection window to fill the number pattern to populate a larger area. To find more information about this technique, look for Fill or Automatically Number Rows in the Excel Help files.

FIGURE 10.16

A fully populated design table

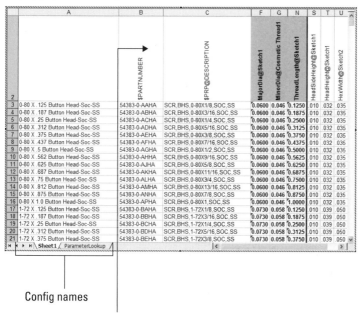

Config names

Feature or property syntax from table

FIGURE 10.17

Filling in configuration names

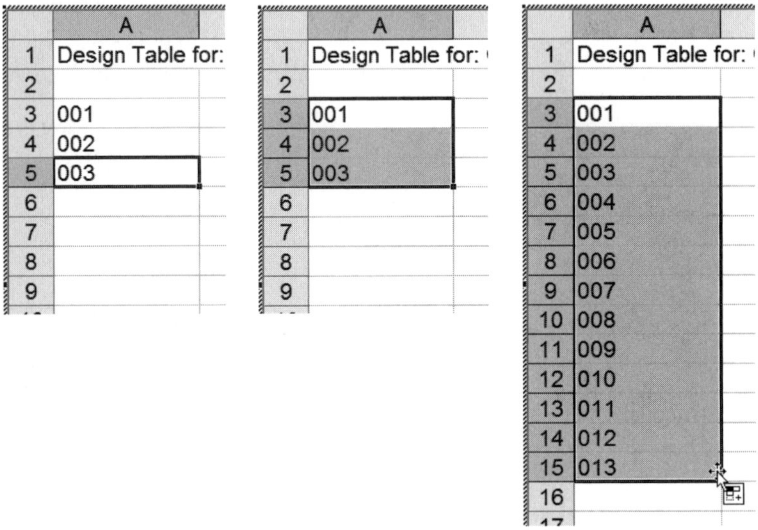

The next step is to fill in some feature and dimension names in the second row. The first thing that you do is to suppress the HexDrive feature. To make this the first feature in the list, click in cell B2, and then double-click the HexDrive feature in the FeatureManager. The name of the feature and its current suppression state are added to the design table with all of the necessary syntax and correct spelling.

To rotate the text in this row vertically, right-click row number 2, select Format Cells, click the Alignment tab, and turn the orientation to 90 degrees. The word *unsuppressed* displays in all capitals and fully spelled out, while all you need is a U or an S. Replace the word with an S, and double-click the line between the column heading letters B and C at the top of the Excel window, to condense column B as much as possible. Alternate the rest of the rows between *U*s and *S*s to either suppress or unsuppress the HexDrive feature in various configurations. Figure 10.18 shows the current state of the design table.

Close the Design Table window, and click OK on the message box that lists the new configurations created by the Design Table. Now split the FeatureManager, set the lower pane to the ConfigurationManager, and double-click some configurations. Notice that in the configs where you specified an S, the HexDrive is suppressed, and no longer appears in the model.

You can now add a dimension to the design table. To add a dimension, it is most convenient to display the dimensions on the screen at all times. To show all of the dimensions in the part, right-click the Annotations folder in the FeatureManager and select Display Annotations. If the dimensions do not display, then you may have to go back and select Show Feature Dimensions. Arrange the dimensions so that you can clearly see them all, as shown in Figure 10.19.

FIGURE 10.18

Building the design table

	A	B	C
1	Design Table for: Chapter 10		
2		$STATE@HexDrive	
3	001	s	
4	002	u	
5	003	s	
6	004	u	
7	005	s	
8	006	u	
9	007	s	
10	008	u	
11	009	s	
12	010	u	
13	011	s	
14	012	u	
15	013	s	

FIGURE 10.19

Dimension and annotation display settings

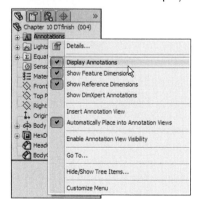
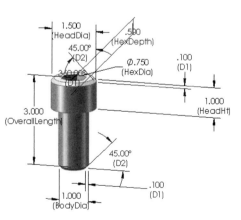

To display the design table again, locate it in the ConfigurationManager, , right-click it, and select Edit Table. Editing the feature changes the settings used for the design table. Edit Table in New Window is an option that you will use later because it simplifies many things; however, for now, the Edit Table option makes it easiest to add new items to the design table.

NOTE If a window appears with the name Add Rows and Columns, just click OK for now. This window lists parameters that have changed in its lower pane, and it is asking you if you would like to add any of the changed parameters to the design table. If you would like to add them, just select the parameter in the lower pane and click OK. If not, just click OK.

If the design table displays on top of your model, you can either move the model or move the design table. Moving the design table is a bit tricky, and involves dragging the striped-line border of the Excel window; remember not to grab it at the corners or midpoints, because this will simply resize it. If you click inside the border, nothing happens. If you click outside of the border, the Excel window closes. Moving the model may be easier. To do this, just Ctrl+drag in blank space in the graphics window; it pans the display so that you can see the part dimensions.

With cell C2 selected, or whatever the next available cell is in the second row, double-click the OverallLength dimension in the graphics window. SolidWorks adds the proper syntax to the design table, along with the current value for the first configuration in the list. Fill in values for the rest of the configurations. You can then calculate these values in Excel using any of the available techniques.

Exit the design table and toggle through the various configurations to see their different lengths. These examples should get you started on more complex configurations and design tables. Any dimensions that are controlled by the design table (and that are therefore locked) display in pink on the screen.

Design table settings

Figure 10.15 shows the PropertyManager for design tables. After you have created the table, you can edit the table settings by right-clicking the table and then selecting Edit Feature. Edit Feature enables you to edit the settings for the table only; it does not enable you to edit values within the table.

Linked design table

By selecting the From File source option, you can create a design table from an external file; you can also link the table to the external file. When you use the other two options, Blank and Auto-Create, SolidWorks stores the Excel file within the SolidWorks document. Linking to an external file may be useful if you have a non-SolidWorks user who is entering data into the design table, or if a single table controls multiple parts.

Edit control

The Edit Control panel has two options, which act as a toggle. The Allow model edits to update the design table option is self explanatory, as is its opposite, the Block model edits that would update the design table option. If the Allow model edits option is selected, and you make a manual change to the model, the next time you open the design table, SolidWorks warns you about the change and that it will update the design table. Likewise, if you try to make a manual change and the Block model edits option is selected, you receive a warning that the value cannot be changed.

Options

The Options settings determine the behavior when you are using the Allow Model Edits option and a new item has been configured. For example, the design table may already exist, and you manually add a configuration and suppress a feature.

Configurations that have been added manually are displayed somewhat differently from configs that are being managed by the design table. Figure 10.20 shows the two configurations at the bottom of the tree with square symbols, while the design table configs have Excel symbols.

FIGURE 10.20

Manually created configs versus design table–created configs

After you manually add the config and suppress the feature, the next time you open the design table, the Add Rows and Columns dialog box appears. Most users are simply annoyed by this, but that may be because they do not understand what it does or why it appears. In the example shown in Figure 10.21, a new configuration has been manually added; it appears in the Configurations box as Manually Added Config, and in the Parameters box, it looks like a feature named BodyChamf has been either suppressed or unsuppressed manually. The appearance of this dialog box means that SolidWorks is asking you if you would like to include these items in the design table. If so, then simply select the items you would like to add to the design table and click OK. If you do not want to include the items in the design table, then simply click OK or Cancel. If you click OK, then you will not be offered these choices again; if you click Cancel, then the next time you open the table, the dialog box with the same choices will reappear. If you never want to see this dialog box again, then make sure that all of the options in the Options panel shown in Figure 10.15 are turned off.

FIGURE 10.21

The Add Rows and Columns dialog box

Editing the design table

As I mentioned earlier, when you open the design table inside the SolidWorks window, it can sometimes be difficult to work with. One way to handle this problem is to only edit the design table inside SolidWorks when you want to add new features to the column headers, and when adding new configurations or editing the field values, edit the table in a separate window. This option appears on the right-mouse button menu, as Edit Table in New Window. It allows you much more flexibility in resizing the Excel window, changing zoom scale, and other operations, but it does not allow you to double-click a dimension so that it is added automatically to the column header.

CAUTION   When working on design tables, it is a good idea to avoid conflicts with other sessions of Excel by closing any other Excel windows. The combination of operating Excel spreadsheets inside both SolidWorks and Excel has been known to cause crashes, or the "Server Busy" warning message. If you are diligent about having only one session of Excel active at a time when you are working on design tables (or Excel BOMs), then there is less likelihood of a crash or conflict.

Tutorial: Working with Configurations and Design Tables

Throughout this book, parts that I use for one purpose may also be interesting for other purposes as well. For example, the part used in this tutorial uses a loft with guide curves where both guide curves are created in the same sketch. The guide curve sketch is made from symmetrical splines where I have used the spline handles to change the shape smoothly and in a controlled way. I have also used a curve-driven pattern to go around an elliptical shape.

> **TIP**   If at some point you decide that you have made mistakes from which you cannot recover, or you would simply like to start over again, you can select File ⇨ Reload. This is the same as exiting the part without saving, and then reopening the part to start from the beginning.

To start working with configurations and design tables, follow these steps:

1. **From the CD-ROM, open the part called** Chapter 10 Tutorial start.sldprt. Take a moment to become familiar with this part by using the rollback bar to see how it was made. In particular, look at the two patterns, which need to be parametrically linked. Figure 10.22 shows the part.

FIGURE 10.22

The Chapter 10 Tutorial start.sldprt file

2. **Manually create a configuration for the part called Size 1.** Remember that to create a configuration, you must show the ConfigurationManager tab in the FeatureManager area, and right-click the name of the part at the top level. It is better to do this by splitting the FeatureManager window and setting the lower pane to the ConfigurationManager.

3. **Set the Advanced option to both Suppress Features and Use Configuration Specific Color (both turned on).**

4. **Before closing the Add Configuration PropertyManager, click the Color button on the Advanced Options panel of the Configuration PropertyManager and select a different color for the Size 1 configuration.** The color does not change immediately. It will change after you close the PropertyManager.

5. **Turn on the Tools ⇨ Options setting to Show Dimension Names.** (Remember, this is the third option on the General page.)

6. **Double-click the feature CrvPattern1 in the FeatureManager.** A number 6 with a D1 under it will appear on one of the holes in the pattern. If you have changed your part to a blue color, then it may be difficult to see, because the text will also be blue.

7. **Change the name of the dimension to Hole# by clicking the dimension and using the PropertyManager.**

8. **Change the value of the number to 8, and be careful to also change the drop-down setting to This Configuration Only instead of All Configurations.** If you forget to do this, then you will have to go to the other configuration and set it back to 6.

9. **Click the Rebuild symbol (which resembles a traffic light) to show the changes before exiting the Modify dialog box.** Notice that the CrvPattern2 fails after rebuilding CrvPattern1 with eight instances. Click the green check mark icon to exit the Modify dialog box, and then make the same changes to the CrvPattern2, from changing the dimension name and the number of patterned instances to eight (remember to use the This Configuration Only setting). The part should now look like Figure 10.23.

FIGURE 10.23

The model after Step 9

10. **When you double-click to change configurations the SolidWorks interface now shows a part with a different color and a different number of holes and ribs.** After the first change between configurations, the changes should happen quickly because SolidWorks has stored the geometry.

11. **Go to File ⇨ Properties, and select the Configuration Specific tab.** Set the Apply To drop-down list to Default, and type a Property Name of **description** and a Value of **Gray Vent Cover**. Now change the Apply To drop-down setting to Size 1 and type a description for the new configuration using the name of the color that you applied to this config. Figure 10.24 shows the two states of the data.

Setting the Configuration Specific custom properties

12. **Exit the Custom Properties dialog box.** Now that you have made a few changes manually, the following steps guide you through bringing these changes into a design table and using the design table to make additional changes.

13. **From the menus, select Insert ⇨ Tables ⇨ Design Table. Use Auto-create as the Source, allow model edits, and turn on all three option in the Option panel. Click OK to create the design table.** Figure 10.25 shows the design table that you have automatically created.

14. **Use the striped border to move the window without closing it.** This may take some practice. If the window closes, just right-click the design table in the FeatureManager and select Edit Table. Move the window to a place where you can see the model clearly.

15. **If a cell in the second row of the design table is selected, select a different empty cell that is not in the second row (this prevents data from automatically populating cells until you have the correct data).** Now double-click the Extrude1 feature in the FeatureManager. Find the .500" (D1) dimension on the screen. Right-click the dimension and rename it BaseThk.

16. **Click the next open cell in the second row, and double-click the .500" dimension that you just renamed.** You may have to use the handles at the corners and side midpoints to resize the Excel window to see everything. Add another configuration row and the additional values in the cells, as shown in Figure 10.26. The color number is determined by a formula that you can find in the help section under the topic Color Parameter.

FIGURE 10.25

The automatically created design table

	A	B	C	D	E	F
1	Design Table for: Chapter 10 Tutorial start					
2	$DESCRIPTION	$COLOR		$PRP@description	Hole#@CrvPattern1	Rib#@CrvPattern2
3	Default	Default	12632256	Gray Vent Cover	6	6
4	Size 1	Size 1	255	Red Vent Cover	8	8

FIGURE 10.26

Make additions to the design table.

	A	B	C	D	E	F	G
1	Design Table for: Chapter 10 Tutorial start						
2	$DESCRIPTION	$COLOR		$PRP@description	Hole#@CrvPattern1	Rib#@CrvPattern2	BaseThk@Extrude1
3	Default	Default	12632256	Gray Vent Cover	6	6	0.5
4	Size 1	Size 1	255	Red Vent Cover	8	8	0.8
5	Size 2	Size 2	16711680	Blue Vent Cover	10	10	1
6							

17. **Remember that this part needs to have the number of ribs always equal to the number of holes.** This is simple to do in Excel. Click in the first row value for the Rib# number. This is cell F3 in Figure 10.25. Type the equal sign, and then click in the cell to the left, E3. You can also simply type **=E3** in this cell. This links the Rib# cell to the Hole# cell.

18. **Use the Window Fill feature by selecting the dot at the lower-right corner of the selected F3 cell and dragging it down to also include cells F4 and F5, as shown in Figure 10.27.**

FIGURE 10.27

Copying the equation to other cells

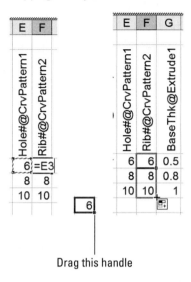

Drag this handle

19. **Click in a blank space to exit the design table.** Double-click through the configurations in the ConfigurationManager to see the results of your efforts.

Summary

Configurations are a powerful way to control variations of a design within a single part file. Many aspects of the part can be configured, while a few cannot. Manually created configurations are useful for making a small number of variations and a small number of configurations, but they become unwieldy when you need to make more than a few variations of either type.

Design tables are recommended because they allow you to more clearly see all of the changes that have been made for all of the configurations. Having the power of Excel available allows you to access many functions that are not shown here, such as using lookup tables and Concatenate functions to build descriptions or configuration names. I will briefly revisit design tables in the section on assembly configurations to expand on the information here and to incorporate the additional assembly configuration information.

Chapter 11

Editing and Evaluation

I f you work like I do, then you probably create a part once, but edit it many times. As I often say, design for change is really at the core of most of the modeling work that you will do in SolidWorks, and deletion is not an editing option.

You do the most good — or the most harm — in the initial stages of modeling, when you are setting up parametric relations between features and sketches. For this reason, editing often quickly turns into repair. Granted, some changes are simply unavoidable, but a thorough knowledge of editing — and repairing — can help you to understand the how, what, and why of modeling best practice.

This chapter starts with some very basic concepts of editing, which you may have picked up if you have been reading this book from the beginning. Because this is the last chapter in Part II, and the last that deals strictly with part modeling, it also contains a summary of part modeling best practice techniques and a set of model evaluation tools that can help you evaluate the manufacturability and aesthetic properties of parts. I have included these evaluation tools in a chapter on editing because the evaluate-edit-evaluate cycle is one of the most familiar in modeling and design practice.

Using Rollback

Rolling back a model simply means looking at the results of the design tree only up to a certain point in the model history. In SolidWorks, you can actually change history — that is, you can change the order in which operations are completed. As a result, the chronological order in which features are created is not necessarily related to the order in which these features display in the design tree, or the order in which the operations are completed.

You can use several methods to put the model in this rolled-back state:

- Dragging the Rollback bar with the cursor.

- Right-mouse button clicking and selecting one of the Rollback options.

- Editing a feature other than the last one in the design tree. (SolidWorks rolls back the model automatically.)

- Using the Tools ➪ Options setting that allows you to control the Rollback bar with the arrow keys.

- Saving the model while editing a feature or sketch, and then exiting the model. When the part is opened again, it is rolled back to the location of the sketch that was being edited.

- Pressing Esc during a long model rebuild. This method is supposed to roll you back to the last feature that was rebuilt when you pressed Esc; however, in practice, I have rarely seen it do this, and it usually just rebuilds the entire model anyway.

Using the Rollback bar

The Rollback bar, which typically appears at the bottom of the FeatureManager in SolidWorks part documents, enables you to put the part into almost any state in the model history. This is not the same as the Undo command, but is the equivalent of suppressing everything in the FeatureManager after a certain point. Figure 11.1 shows the Rollback bar in use. Notice how the cursor changes into a hand icon when you move it over the bar.

FIGURE 11.1

Using the Rollback bar

Consumed features

When you use a sketch for a feature such as a Sketch Driven Pattern, the sketch is left in the design tree, in the place where it was created. However, most other features, such as extrudes, *consume* the sketch, meaning that the sketch disappears from its normal order in the FeatureManager and appears indented under the feature that was created from it. Consumed sketches are sometimes also referred to as *absorbed* sketches.

Examining the parent-child relationship

In genealogical family tree diagrams, the parent-child relationship is represented with the parent at the top, and the children branched below the parent. In SolidWorks, parent-child relationships are tracked differently. Figure 11.2 shows the difference between a genealogical family tree and the SolidWorks design tree.

FIGURE 11.2

Different interpretations of the structure of parent-child relationships

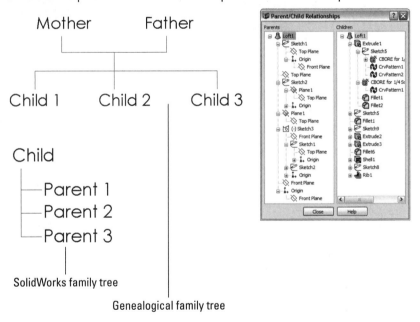

You can display the parent-child relations between SolidWorks features as shown in Figure 11.2 by opening the right-mouse button menu on any feature, and selecting Parent/Child. This helps you to determine relationships before editing or deleting, so that you can see which features will be removed or go dangling.

When SolidWorks puts the child feature at the top, it is, in effect, turning the relationship upside down, but long-time users have all somehow learned to look at this without questioning it. In the SolidWorks FeatureManager, the earlier point in history is at the top of the tree, but the children are listed earlier than the parents. Once you look at it this way, you can see that SolidWorks has chosen a very unintuitive method to display the features in the tree. The SolidWorks method stresses the importance of solid features over other types of sketch or curve features.

It appears to be even less intuitive when you think of the order in which features are created. For example, you create an extrude from a sketch, and so the sketches exist before the extrude in the FeatureManager. However, when you create the extrude, SolidWorks places the sketch underneath the extrude. In fact, this restructuring can become more apparent when a sketch (for example, Sketch1) is created early in the part history, and then not used to create a feature (for example, Extrude5) until much later. If you roll down the FeatureManager feature by feature, you arrive a point at the end of the design tree where Extrude5 appears and Sketch1 suddenly moves from its location at the top of the tree to under Extrude5 at the bottom of the tree.

This scenario may cause a situation where many sketches and other features that are created between Sketch1 and Extrude5 are dependent on Sketch1, but where Sketch1 suddenly appears after all of these other features. As this example shows, the more closely you examine how the relationships are depicted, the more counterintuitive they appear.

The only thing that you can do about this relationship structure is to realize that SolidWorks displays many relations upside down, and learn to understand it and not get confused in the process. In some ways, ignorance is bliss, because if you do not know that the relationships are shown in a confusing way, then it might not occur to you that there is anything wrong.

One way to get around difficulties in understanding the chronological order of features when compared against the relationship order of features is to roll back a model tree item by item. This can help you sort through the issues. Also remember that from SolidWorks' point of view, the solid feature is the most important item in the tree and is what the rest of the items in the tree support. SolidWorks has made the solid features easily visible and accessible in the tree.

There is a movement afoot among a group of users to try to convince SolidWorks to enable the tree to be displayed in multiple ways, one of which would be a strictly linear, chronological way. Another option would be graphically showing the hierarchical links between features, and still another would be a traditional "genealogical" tree approach. If you would like to encourage SolidWorks in one of these directions, please fill out an enhancement request.

Rolling back features with multiple parents

Take an example such as a loft with guide curves. If you create the guide curves first, and then you create the loft profiles by referencing the guide curves, the loft automatically reorders these sketches when they display under the loft feature such that the profiles are listed in the order in which they were selected. The guide curves are also shown in the order that they were selected. This is shown in Figure 11.3. This restructuring can really be confusing, especially if you want to go back and edit any of the relationships between the sketches. It becomes even more so if the sketches have been renamed so that the names do not clearly reflect the natural order of the sketches before they were all consumed by the loft feature. You can find this example on the CD-ROM with the filename `Chapter 11 Loftwgc.sldprt`.

NOTE In this example, the two guide curves were created as part of a single sketch, and the SelectionManager was used to select them as individual open curves. This is why the Guide Curves sketch is represented with the contour symbol rather than a regular sketch symbol.

Viewing consumed features in their original order

If you want to view consumed sketches in their original order — for example, the sketches in the loft feature in Figure 11.3 — you must first expand the feature so that you can see the consumed sketches, and then rollback between the feature and the first sketch. At this point, a warning message appears, stating that the sketches will be temporarily unabsorbed during editing. You can then move the Rollback bar again to show the sketches.

This maneuver can become complicated when you have two sketches absorbed by a projected curve: the projected curve absorbed by a composite curve and the composite curve absorbed by a sweep feature. To isolate the original projected sketches, you need to experiment with the placement of the Rollback bar, as shown in Figure 11.4.

FIGURE 11.3

Multiple parents and sketch reordering

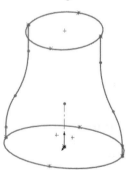

FIGURE 11.4

Rollback of nested, absorbed features

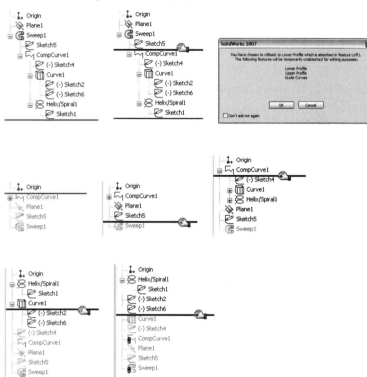

To view consumed sketches in their original order, follow these steps:

1. Expand the sweep.

2. Rollback between the sweep and the profile sketch.

3. Answer the prompt that appears.

4. Roll down so that you can see the unabsorbed sketches and curves.

5. Expand the composite curve.

6. Rollback to just after the composite curve.

7. Rollback so that you can see the contents of the composite curve.

8. Expand the projected curve.

9. Rollback to just after the projected curve.

10. Rollback so that you can see the contents of the projected curve.

Enhancement requests

This is a great time to talk about enhancement requests. The SolidWorks Web site (www.solid works.com) has a section for users to submit suggestions for adding new features or changing existing ones in the SolidWorks software. Users have been able to do tricky rollbacks such as this for the last several releases, but it seems evident that all of the possible ramifications of this technique have not been considered. Because changes are made on the basis of popularity, I recommend that if you are interested in seeing this functionality improved, you should submit an enhancement request for this particular function.

Other Rollback techniques

The Rollback feature is available through the right-mouse button menu. Just right-click a feature and select either Rollback or Roll to Previous. If you are already rolled back and you right-click below the Rollback bar, then you can access additional options to Roll Forward and Roll to End.

Editing any feature other than the last feature also serves to rollback the model while you are in Edit mode. As soon as you rebuild the feature or sketch, SolidWorks rebuilds the entire design tree.

The Tools ➪ Options ➪ View setting for Arrow Key Navigation enables you to use the up- and down-arrow keys to manipulate the Rollback bar. Under normal circumstances, the arrow keys control the view orientation, but after you have moved the Rollback bar once using the cursor, the up- and down-arrow keys control the Rollback bar. The left- and right-arrow keys have no effect on the Rollback bar.

CAUTION The one situation where this technique does not work as expected is when you are working on a part in the context of the assembly, with the design tree rolled back. The down arrow simply causes the Rollback bar to roll immediately to the end of the design tree. This bug existed at least as far back as 2007, and persists in 2009.

You can save the model while it is still rolled back. In previous versions, you had to roll to the end of the FeatureManager before saving, and then rollback to where you were and keep working. This made working in Rollback mode fairly frustrating (if you wanted to save the model) and dangerous, as crashing without saving means potentially losing a lot of data.

Reordering Features

As you already know, feature order can make a difference in the final shape of a part. For example, this order:

1. **Extrude**
2. **Cut**
3. **Fillet**
4. **Shell**

gives you a very different part from this order:

1. **Extrude**
2. **Shell**
3. **Cut**
4. **Fillet**

The results of these different orders are shown in Figure 11.5. (The part is split and partially transparent for demonstration purposes only.) You can view this part on the CD-ROM; it is filename `Chapter 11 Reorder.sldprt`.

FIGURE 11.5
_____

Parts that use a different feature order

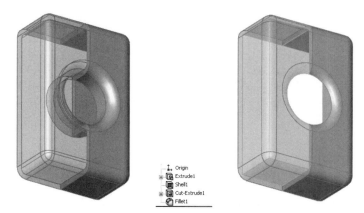

On the part in the previous example, it is fairly simple to reorder the Shell feature by dragging it up the design tree. As a result, the well created by the Cut feature is not shelled around (to create a tube) if the cut comes after the shell. Also, notice the effect of applying the fillets after the shell rather than before it. The corners inside the box are sharp, while the outside corners have been filleted. When you apply the fillet before the shell, fillets that have a radius larger than the shell thickness are transferred to the inside of the shell.

 When you are reordering the features, a symbol may appear on the reorder cursor that says that you cannot reorder the selected feature to the location you want. In this case, you may want to select the Parent/Child option from the right-mouse button menu to investigate. Sketch relationships, feature end conditions, and faces or edges selected for features such shell, patterns, and mirror can cause relationships that prevent reordering.

If two adjacent features are to swap places, it generally does not matter whether you move one feature up the design tree or you move the other one down. However, there are isolated situations that are usually created by the nested, absorbed features discussed earlier, where one feature cannot go in one direction, but the other feature can go in the opposite direction, achieving the exact same result. If you run into a situation where you cannot reorder a feature in one direction even though it appears you should be able to, try moving another feature the other direction.

Reordering Folders

There are times when, regardless of which features you choose to move and of which direction you choose to move them in, you are faced with the task of moving many features. This can be time-consuming and tedious, not to mention have the potential to introduce errors. To simplify this process, you can put all of the features to be moved into a single folder, and then reorder the folder. Keep in mind that the items in the folder need to be a continuous list (you cannot skip features), and you can only reorder the folder if each individual feature within the folder can be reordered.

BEST PRACTICE **Folders are frequently used for groups of features that go together and that may be suppressed or unsuppressed in groups. You can also use folders in assemblies. Folders are frequently used for the mass of cosmetic fillet features that are often found at the end of design trees for plastic parts or for groups of hole features.**

To create a folder, right-click a feature or a selected group of features and select Add to New Folder. Folders should be renamed to have a name that helps identify their contents. You can reorder folders in the same way as individual features. When you delete a folder, the contents are removed from the folder; they are not deleted.

You can add or remove features to or from the folders by dragging them in or out. If a folder is the last item in the FeatureManager, the next feature that is created is not put into the folder; you must place it in the folder manually. You cannot drag features out of a folder and place them immediately after it, because they will just go back into the folder. If you want to pull a feature out of a folder and place it after the folder, there must be another feature between the feature that you are moving and the folder. However, you can pull a feature out of the folder and place it just *before* the folder.

Using the Flyout FeatureManager

The Flyout FeatureManager resides at the top-left corner of the graphics window, and was introduced when SolidWorks began to consolidate floating dialog boxes into the PropertyManager window. The PropertyManager goes in the same space as the FeatureManager, and is sometimes too big to allow this area to accommodate both managers in a split window.

The Flyout FeatureManager enables you to select items from the design tree when the regular FeatureManager is not available because it is covered by the PropertyManager. It usually appears collapsed, so that you can only see the name of the part and the part symbol. To expand it, click the plus icon next to the name of the part in the Flyout FeatureManager.

You can use the Flyout FeatureManager in parts or in the assembly. However, you cannot use the Flyout FeatureManager to suppress or rollback the tree.

CROSS-REF   Other functionality and limitations of the **Flyout FeatureManager** that relate to its function in assemblies can be found in Chapters 12 to 15.

You can access the settings for the Flyout FeatureManager at Tools ➪ Options ➪ FeatureManager ➪ Use Transparent Flyout FeatureManager in Parts/Assemblies.

You may prefer not to work with the flyout FeatureManager. If this is the case, you can use the detachable PropertyManager instead. Detaching the PropertyManager removes the need for the flyout. I often dock the detachable PropertyManager where the flyout FeatureManager would go. The main advantage of using the detachable PropertyManager instead of the flyout FeatureManager is that with the detachable PropertyManager you don't have to locate features in the FeatureManager that were already in view.

Figure 11.6 shows the difference between the flyout FeatureManager on the left, and the detachable PropertyManager on the right. My preference is clearly the detachable PropertyManager. When you use this, everything is predictable, and you don't have to go hunting for features that were listed right in front of you when you do something that opens a PropertyManager. I usually decrease the overall size of the SolidWorks application window, and place the PropertyManager to the left of the SolidWorks application. This works best on a wide aspect monitor. If you use a small monitor or a normal aspect monitor, using the Auto Collapse option with the PropertyManager docked to the right of the FeatureManager (where the flyout FeatureManager would otherwise go) is also a good option.

You may correctly ask "what's the difference?" The difference is that when you do something like editing a sketch plane, the current state of the FeatureManager is covered over and replaced by the PropertyManager. You may have had the new plane you wanted to use in view. Especially with long FeatureManagers, in both parts and assemblies, when the flyout appears, you have to again scroll to find the plane that was right in view. This has been a problem since SolidWorks started employing the PropertyManager many releases ago. However you use the detachable PropertyManager, I think you will find it an improvement over the flyout.

FIGURE 11.6

Comparing the flyout FeatureManager with the detachable PropertyManager

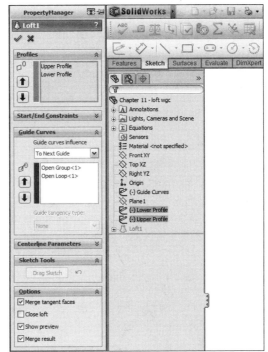

Summarizing Part Modeling Best Practice

This section is a summary of best practice suggestions for modeling parts. Best practice lists are important because they lay the groundwork for conservative usage of the software, which is helpful for new users and users who are trying to experiment with the limits of the software.

I believe that it is only after you respect the rules and understand why they are so important, that you know enough to break them. However, best practice lists should not be taken too seriously. They are not inflexible rules, but conservative starting places; they are concepts that you can default to, but that can be broken if you have good reason.

- Always use unique filenames for your parts. SolidWorks assemblies and drawings may pick up incorrect references if you use parts with identical names.

- Using Custom Properties is a great way to enter text-based information into your parts. Users can view this information from outside the file by using applications such as Windows Explorer, SolidWorks Explorer, and Product Data Management (PDM) applications.

- Learn to sketch using automatic relations.

- Use fully dimensioned sketches when possible. Splines are often impractical to fully dimension.

- Limit your use of the Fixed constraint.

- When possible, make relations to sketches or stable reference geometry, such as the Origin or standard planes, instead of edges or faces. Sketches are far more stable than faces, edges, or model vertices, which change their internal ID at the slightest change and may disappear entirely with fillets, chamfers, split lines, and so on.

- Do not dimension to edges created by fillets or other cosmetic or temporary features.

- Apply names to features, sketches, and dimensions that help to make their function clear.

- When possible, use feature fillets and feature patterns rather than sketch fillets and sketch patterns.

- Combine fillets into as few fillet features as possible; this also allows you to control fillets that need to be controlled separately, such as fillets to be removed for Finite Element Analysis (FEA), drawings, and simplified configurations; or added for rendering.

- Create a simplified configuration when building very complex parts or working with large assemblies.

- Model with symmetry in mind. Use feature patterns when possible.

- Use link values or global variables to control commonly used dimensions.

- Do not be afraid of configurations. Control them with design tables where there are more than a few configs, and document any custom programming or automated features in the spreadsheet.

- Use display states when possible instead of configurations.

- Use multi-body modeling for various techniques within parts; it is not intended as a means to create assemblies within a single part file.

- Cosmetic features — fillets, in particular — should be saved for the bottom of the design tree. It is also a good idea to put them all together into a folder.

- Use the setting at Tools ➪ Options ➪ Performance ➪ Verification on rebuild in combination with the Ctrl+Q command to check models periodically and before calling them "done." The more complex the model, or the more questionable some of the geometry or techniques might be, the more important it is to check the part.

- Always fix errors in your part as soon as you can. Errors cause rebuild time to increase, and if you wait until more errors exist, troubleshooting may become more difficult.

- Do not add unnecessary detail. For example, it is not important to actually model a knurled surface on a round steel part. This additional detail is difficult to model in SolidWorks, it slows down the rebuild speed of your part, and there is no advantage to actually having it modeled (unless you are using the model for rapid prototype or to machine a mold for a plastic part where knurling cannot be added as a secondary process). This is better accomplished by a drawing with a note. The same concept applies to thread, extruded text, very large patterns, and other features that introduce complex details.

- Do not rely heavily on niche features. For example, if you find yourself creating helices by using Flex/Twist or Wrap instead of Sweep, then you may want to rethink your approach. In fact, if you find yourself creating a lot of unnecessary helices, then you may want to rethink this approach as well, unless there is a good reason for doing so.

- File size is not necessarily a measure of inefficiency.

- Be cautious about accepting advice or information from Internet forums.

If you are the CAD Administrator for a group of users, you may want to incorporate some best practice tips into standard operating procedures for them. The more users that you have to manage, the more you need to standardize your system.

Using the Skeleton or Wide Tree Approach

SolidWorks is not the first parametric modeler to challenge the linear logic of genealogical analysis. The users of software like Pro/ENGINEER are responsible for developing many of the concepts and best practice techniques that SolidWorks users use today.

> **NOTE** The term Skeleton in Pro/ENGINEER has a different significance than the way it is being used here. SolidWorks does not have any feature or function named "skeleton." The term is just being used to refer to a set of sketches, planes, axes, and reference points used to lay out the major faces and features of a part.

The SolidWorks Help files, tutorials, and training curricula have encouraged users in some respects to take a "fast and loose" approach to modeling, which lends itself best to simple models that are not changed frequently. Little thought is given to the structure of the part; the focus is on the final shape. The main consideration seems to be the simplest way to do something, or how it *could* be done rather than how it *should* be done. This mentality fit well with the initial several releases of the SolidWorks software, which at that time was marketed as being simple and fast.

The software has progressed immensely since those days. It is now entirely plausible to create complex castings and plastic parts with many hundreds of features, weaving in and out of surface and solid techniques, multi-bodies, and external references. This is a far cry from the typical tutorial or training part, which still tend to have fewer than 15 features, half of which may be fillets. With the simpler parts, you hardly give a thought to parent/child relationships, rebuild times, or the consequences of

continued

making changes that cause a feature to fail, because the whole part can be rebuilt from scratch in ten minutes anyway. This is because the people who know the software best were doing brief sales demo vignettes and small models that could be finished before the students fell asleep.

SolidWorks users have traditionally been taught to build each feature linearly, on top of the one that came before. This is the genealogical equivalent of each generation having a single child, and then that child having a single child, and so on. The family tree, or FeatureManager, winds up looking like a long staircase, with each generation related only to the generation immediately before it. In the SolidWorks world, this creates long, linear, daisy-chained relationships between consecutive features.

It turns out that even though this has been hailed as the pinnacle of associative, parametric, history-based modeling, it is not really such a great idea, especially as the parts begin to get more complex. When each feature is dependent upon the one before it, all of the features must be solved in a particular order, and if one feature fails, so do all of the features that come after it. This also slows down the rebuilding process. Especially as we move into the age of parallel multi-threaded processing, a linear set of commands or features must be executed in order one after the other, and there is really little room for parallel processes.

The sophistication of the documentation provided with SolidWorks software has not kept pace with the sophistication of the software itself, which I suppose is why you are reading this book rather than the help files provided with the software. The documentation is still based on the simple scenarios, and the advanced user is left to figure things out on his or her own.

As the software gets more sophisticated, the models created with the software can get more sophisticated, and the methods used to build the models must also get more sophisticated. It's time to leave the linear modeling approaches behind.

Rather than using a linear daisy-chain modeling scenario, it is better practice to base features on entities that are less likely to fail or change in such a way that dependent downstream features also fail. In earlier chapters, I have already suggested that you make sketch relations to other sketches when possible instead of model edges for this very reason.

Taking that scenario one step further, what if a handful of sketch and plane features were used to centralize control of all of the rest of the features? What if every feature, to the extent possible, related back to these "skeleton" features? Features such as fillets, shell, and draft by design require selections from solid geometry, but other features, such as any feature created from sketches, could be made with only reference to those original skeleton sketches and planes. The parent/child relationship would look very different for a model made in this way. Instead of looking like a long staircase, this tree would look more like a tree that gets wide very quickly. There would be fewer "generations," but each generation would be more populated.

The first thing to notice is that errors in features at the top of the tree do not cascade down the tree as they do in the "stairstep" model. Second, it is always much easier to find how a model is constructed, because all the reference geometry used to build it is set up in the first few features. This scenario also has the potential to make better use of multi-threaded processing because the logic is less linear and more parallel.

Using Evaluation Techniques

You can use evaluation techniques to evaluate geometry errors, demonstrate the manufacturability of a given part, or to some degree to quantify aesthetic qualities of a given part, or section of a part. I discuss evaluation techniques here because the design cycle involves iterations around the combination of evaluate-edit-evaluate functions. I discuss the following techniques in this section:

- Verification on rebuild
- Check
- Zebra Stripes/RealView/Lights and specularity
- Curvature display
- Deviation analysis
- Tangent edges as phantom
- SimulationXpress

Many of these techniques apply specifically to plastic parts and complex shapes, but even if you do not become involved in these areas of design or modeling, these tools may help you to find answers on other types of products as well.

Verification on rebuild

Verification on rebuild is an option that you can access through Tools ➪ Options ➪ Performance ➪ Verification on rebuild. Under normal circumstances (with this setting turned off), SolidWorks checks each face to ensure that it does not overlap or intersect improperly with every adjacent face. Each face can have several neighbors. This option is shown in Figure 11.7.

FIGURE 11.7

The Verification on rebuild option

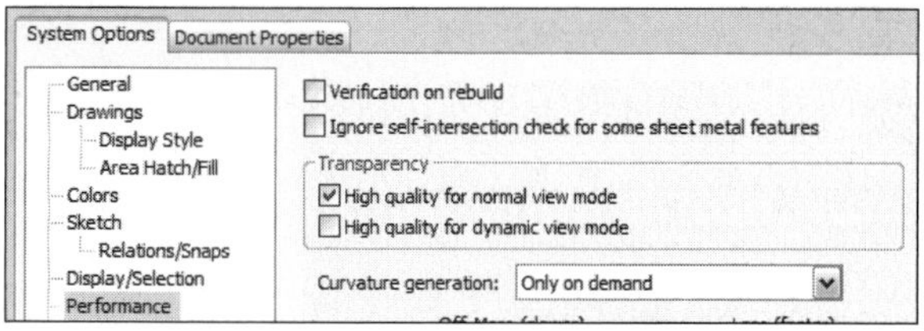

With the setting turned on, SolidWorks checks each face with every other face in the model. This represents a better check than with the setting off, and a greatly increased workload. The switch is off by default to prevent rebuild times from getting out of control. For most parts, the default setting is sufficient; however, when parts become complex, you may need to select the more advanced setting.

If you are having geometry or rebuild error problems with a part and cannot understand why, then try turning Verification on and pressing Ctrl+Q. Ctrl+Q applies the Forced Rebuild command, and rebuilds the entire design tree, whether or not SolidWorks determines that it is needed. Ctrl+B, or the Rebuild command, only rebuilds what SolidWorks determines needs to be rebuilt.

If you see additional errors in the design tree that were not there before, then the combination of Verification on rebuild and Forced Rebuild has worked. If not, then your problem may be else-where. You still need to fix any errors found this way.

PERFORMANCE For speed reasons, it is normal practice to turn Verification on rebuild off, and to use it selectively to check models with potential errors. The type of speed degrada-tion that you can see is in the 10-percent to 60-percent range. Some of the performance degrada-tion as relates to patterns is documented in Chapter 8.

Check

 Check is a tool that checks geometry for invalid faces and other similar geometry errors. It is also often used to find open edges of surface bodies, short edges, and the minimum radius on a face or entity. I usually apply the Check tool before turning on the Verification on rebuild option. The Check tool points to specific face or edge geometry (not features or sketches) that is the cause of the problem. When it finds general faults the locations that the Check tool points to may or may not have something obvious to do with a possible fix.

Much of the time, the best tool for tracking down geometry errors is the combination of experience and intuition. It is not very scientific, but you come to recognize where potential problems are likely to arise, such as attempting to intersect complex faces at complex edges. Figure 11.8 shows the Check Entity dialog box.

FIGURE 11.8

The Check Entity dialog box

Reflective techniques

Evaluating complex shapes can be difficult. Subjective evaluation is typically personal, and requires an eye for the type of work you are doing. Objective evaluation requires some sort of measurable criteria for determining a pass or fail, or it enables you to assign a score somewhere in the middle.

One way to subjectively evaluate complex surfaces, and in particular the transitions between surfaces around common edges, is to use reflective techniques. If you look at an automobile's fender, you can tell whether it has been dented or if a dent has been badly repaired by seeing how the light reflects off of the surface. The same principle applies when evaluating solid or surface models. Bad transitions appear as a crease or an unwanted bulge or indentation. The goal is to turn off the edge display and not be able to identify where the edge is between surfaces for the transition to be as smooth as if the whole area were made from a single surface.

Zebra Stripes

Zebra Stripes can be activated one of two ways, through the menus at View ➪ Display ➪ Zebra Stripes, or from a toolbar button on the View toolbar. The technique that was really made for analyzing complex shapes is Zebra Stripes. This places the part in a room that is either spherical or cubic, where the walls are painted with alternating black-and-white stripes (although you can change the colors and the spacing of the stripes). The part is made to be perfectly reflective, and the way that the stripes transition over edges tells you something about the qualities of the faces on either side of the edge. Four conditions are of particular interest:

- $c0$ = faces contact at edge
- $c1$ = faces are tangent across edge
- $c2$ = curvature of each face is equal at the edge and the transition is smooth
- $c3$ = rate of change of curvature of each face is equal at the edge

The Zebra Stripes tool can only help you identify $c0$, $c1$, and $c2$, and only subjectively. This feature is of most value between complex faces. Figure 11.9 illustrates how the Zebra Stripes tool shows the differences between these three conditions.

Notice how on the Contact-only model, the Zebra Stripe lines do not line up across the edge. On the Tangent example, the stripes line up across the edges, but the stripes themselves are not smooth. On the Curvature Continuous example, the stripes are smooth across the edges. The part shown in Figure 11.16 is a surface model, and can be found on the CD-ROM with the filename `Chapter 11 Zebra Stripes.sldprt`.

> **TIP** You should rotate the model a lot when you are using the Zebra Stripes tool. Changing the density of the lines can also help, as can increasing the image quality (Tools ➪ Options ➪ Document Properties ➪ Image Quality). Turning off the edge display may also help.

FIGURE 11.9

Contact, tangency, and curvature continuity

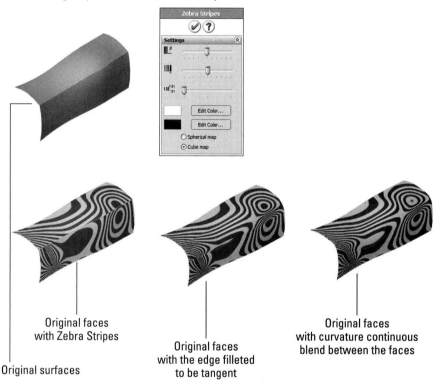

Original surfaces

Original faces
with Zebra Stripes

Original faces
with the edge filleted
to be tangent

Original faces
with curvature continuous
blend between the faces

RealView

 RealView Graphics display is only available to users with certain types of video cards. To see whether your card supports RealView, check the SolidWorks Web site.

RealView causes reflections that can be used in a way similar to the reflections in Zebra Stripes. Rotate the part slowly and watch how the reflections flow across edges.

CROSS-REF **RealView techniques and usage are covered in more depth in Chapter 5.**

Lights and specularity

If the other methods are not working for you, then you can also try to use simple lights with the specularity turned up. This does not work as nicely as the highly reflective Zebra Stripes and RealView techniques, but the bright spots created by the specularity settings for lights can give similar results for evaluating the quality of transitions between faces.

Curvature display

 Model curvature can be plotted onto the model face using colors, as shown in Figure 11.10. The accuracy of this display leaves a bit to be desired, but it does help you identify areas of very tight curvature on your part. Areas of tight curvature can cause features such as fillets and shells to fail.

FIGURE 11.10

Curvature display

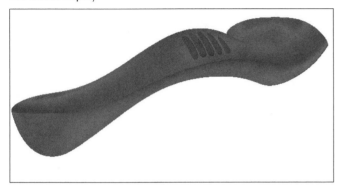

Deviation Analysis

 Deviation Analysis measures how far from tangent the surfaces on either side of a selected edge actually are. For example, the edges shown in Figure 11.11 are found to be fair, but not very good. I prefer deviations of less than 0.5 degrees. Often with some of the advanced surface types such as Fill, Loft, and Boundary, SolidWorks can achieve edges with less than 0.05-degree maximum deviation.

FIGURE 11.11

An example of Deviation Analysis

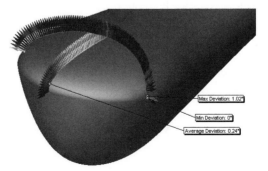

Max Deviation: 1.02°
Min Deviation: 0°
Average Deviation: 0.24°

While Deviation Analysis helps to quantitatively measure how close to tangent the faces on either side of the selected edge are, you must still run Zebra Stripes to get the complete picture of the flow between faces. Both tests have to return good results to have an acceptable face transition.

Tangent Edges as Phantom

Using the Tangent Edges as Phantom setting is an easy way to evaluate a large number of edges all at once. This feature does not do what the Zebra Stripes tool does, but it gives you a good indication of the tangency across a large number of edges.

Although this is an easy method to use, it is not completely reliable. I have not seen this function deliver false positives (edges displayed as tangent when in fact they were not), but I have seen many false negatives (edges that display as non-tangent when in fact they were). Figure 11.12 shows a situation where the edges are displayed with solid edges, but Deviation Analysis shows them to have a zero-degree maximum deviation.

FIGURE 11.12

Using the Tangent Edges as Phantom setting

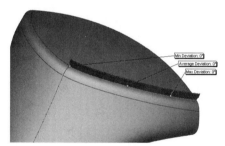

SimulationXpress

SimulationXpress (formerly COSMOSXpress) is a limited version of SolidWorks Simulation (formerly COSMOS Works) that is bundled with SolidWorks to acquaint users with FEA. The full version of SolidWorks Simulation does a wide range of analysis, from vibrations to large deformations. SimulationXpress is a very quick and easy wizard for simple stress analysis on stand-alone parts with simple constraints. It does simple linear stress analysis on a single part with a single material using only fixed constraints. You can also use SimulationXpress to do a simple stress/weight optimization based on dimensions that you select to be altered.

You can start SimulationXpress through the Tools menu. The interface guides you through a very simple wizard. If you have any familiarity with FEA applications, you will find SimulationXpress easy to understand and use.

Material

The first step in running a simple analysis is to assign a material. Once you have made your selection, click Apply. Figure 11.13 shows some of the materials selection.

FIGURE 11.13

Assigning a material in SimulationXpress

The material assigned through the SimulationXpress interface is applied as a SolidWorks material, complete with RealView, if applicable.

Restraint

You can apply restraints to the part. The restraints are limited to Fixed for the faces that are selected. Figure 11.14 shows the interface and the restraint symbols on the part.

FIGURE 11.14

Applying restraints

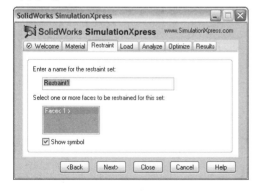

Load

You can apply loads to faces as force or pressure. You can also select multiple faces. Figure 11.15 shows loads that are applied on the sample part.

FIGURE 11.15

Applying a load

Analyze

The analysis automatically takes care of the mesh. An animation plays as the analysis runs. This is shown in Figure 11.16.

FIGURE 11.16

Analyzing the model

Results

The results that can be shown are the stress distribution, the displacement distribution, and the deformed shape of the model. A stress plot is shown in Figure 11.17. You can use a number of good ways to export the results, including as eDrawings, AVI, and HTML (Hypertext Markup Language).

A Stress plot for the analysis

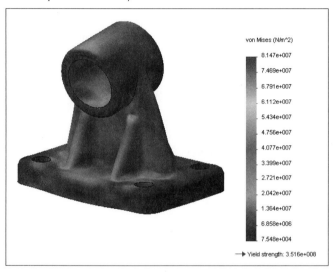

Optimization

Optimization takes a single dimension and varies it to try to achieve the best stress-to-weight ratio. As shown in Figure 11.18, the gussets have been made smaller to reduce weight and to keep the Factor Of Safety above 4.

Optimization results

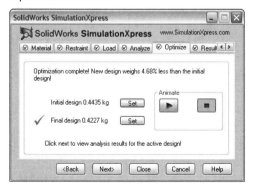

Tutorial: Making Use of Editing and Evaluation Techniques

Using this tutorial, you make some major edits to an existing part. You use some simple loft and spline commands, and work with the rollback states and feature order, as well as some evaluation techniques. Please follow these steps:

1. **Open the existing part with the filename** `Chapter 11 Tutorial Start.sldprt`. Roll the part back and step through it feature by feature to see how it was made. Edit the loft feature to see which sketches were used to create it. This can help you to understand how the part was built. Exit the loft command and move the rollback bar back to the bottom of the tree.

2. **Start the Deviation Analysis tool (Tools ⇨ Deviation Analysis).** Select the edges, as shown in Figure 11.19.

Deviation analysis of an existing part

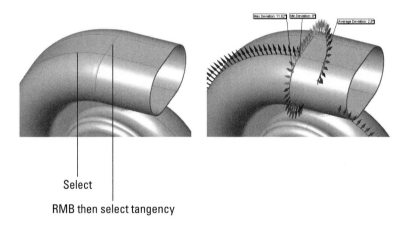

Select

RMB then select tangency

The maximum deviation is about ten degrees, which is far too much. This part needs to be smoothed out, which you can do using splines in place of lines and arcs.

3. **The first step is to make the outlet all one piece with the spiral.** You can do this with a Fit Spline. You need to create the Fit Spline before the loft profiles and after the spiral.

   Expand the loft, and rollback between the loft feature and the first sketch. Answer OK to the prompt, and then rollback to just after the spiral, as shown in Figure 11.20.

FIGURE 11.20

Rolling back to just after the spiral

4. **Right-click the spiral in the FeatureManager and show it.** Open a new sketch on the Top plane.

5. **Try to draw a horizontal line from the outer end of the spiral.** You will notice that you cannot reference the end of the spiral.

TIP Curves that are absorbed into other features are notoriously difficult to work with. Generally, you need to select them from the FeatureManager to do anything at all with them. Also, if you need to reference an end of an absorbed curve, you are better off using Convert Entities to make it into a sketch entity.

6. **Notice that you cannot select the spiral from the graphics window.** Even when selected from the FeatureManager, it appears not to be selected in the graphics window. Ensure that it is selected in the FeatureManager, and then click the Convert Entities button on the sketch toolbar.

7. **Draw a horizontal line from the outer end of the spiral and dimension it to be three inches long, as shown in Figure 11.21.**

8. **Select both the converted spiral and the line, and click Tools ⇨ Spline Tools ⇨ Fit Spline.** Set the Tolerance to .1 and make sure that only the Constrained option is selected. Click OK to accept the Fit Spline. Test to make sure that a single spline is created by moving your cursor over the sketch to see if the whole length is highlighted.

NOTE The Fit Spline feature fits a spline to a set of sketch entities within the specified tolerance. It can be a useful tool for smoothing out sketch geometry.

CAUTION Do not exit the Fit Spline by pressing the Enter key as you do with other commands, because it simply exits you out of the command without creating a spline.

9. **Exit the sketch, and create a new plane.** Click Insert ⇨ Reference Geometry ⇨ plane. Select the Parallel Plane at Point option. Select the Right plane from the Flyout FeatureManager and the outer end of the Fit Spline that you have just created. Click OK to accept the new plane. This is illustrated in Figure 11.22.

FIGURE 11.21

Preparing for the Fit Spline

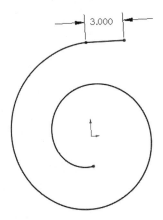

FIGURE 11.22

Creating a new plane

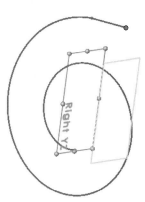

10. **Drag the Rollback bar down between Sketch3 and Loft1.** If it goes beyond Loft1, then you need to navigate back to this position again.

11. **Right-click Sketch3 and select Edit Sketch Plane.** Select the newly created Plane1 from the Flyout FeatureManager, and click OK to accept the change.

12. **Notice that the loft profile has moved to a place where it does not belong.** This is because the sketch has a Pierce constraint to the spiral, and there are multiple places where the spiral pierces the sketch plane.

    Edit Sketch3 and delete the Pierce constraint on the sketch point in the middle of the construction line. Create a Coincident relation between the sketch point and the outer end of the Fit Spline, as shown in Figure 11.23. Do not exit the sketch.

FIGURE 11.23

Sketch3 in its new location

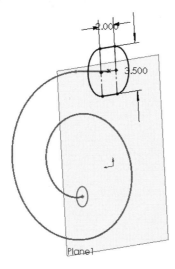

13. **One of the goals of these edits is to smooth out the part.** Remember that the Deviation Analysis told you that the edges created between the lines and arcs in Sketch3 were not very tangent. For this reason, it would be a good idea to replace the lines and arcs in Sketch3 with another Fit Spline.

    Right-click one of the solid sketch entities in Sketch3, and click Select Chain.

14. **Create another Fit Spline using the same technique as in Step 8.** Exit the sketch.

15. **Drag the Rollback bar down one feature so that it is below the Loft.** Notice that the Loft feature has failed. If you hold the cursor over the feature icon, the tooltip confirms this by displaying the message, "The Loft Feature Failed to Complete."

16. **Edit the Loft feature.** Expand the Centerline Parameters panel if it is not already expanded, and delete the Spiral from the selection box. In its place, select the Spiral Fit Spline.

17. If the loft does not preview, check to ensure that the Show Preview option is selected in the Options panel, at the bottom.

18. If it still does not preview, right-click in the graphics window and select Show All Connectors. Position the blue dots on the connector so that it looks like Figure 11.24.

19. Click OK to accept the loft. The loft should be much smoother now than it was before. In addition, the spiral feature should no longer be under the loft, and should now be the first item in the design tree.

20. Drag the Rollback bar down to just before the Shell feature. Notice that Fillet5 has failed. Move the mouse over Fillet5. The tooltip tells you that it is missing some references. Edit Fillet5 and select edges in order to create fillets, as shown in Figure 11.25.

FIGURE 11.24

Positioning the connectors

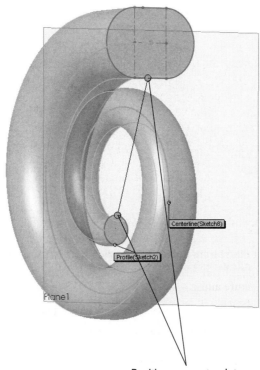

Position connector dots
in approximately corresponding
locations on the two loft profiles

FIGURE 11.25

Repairing Fillet5

Make selections to fillet edges

21. **Right-click in the design tree and select Roll To End.** This causes the FeatureManager to become unrolled all the way to the end.

22. **The outlet of the involute is now longer than it should be.** This is because the original extrude was never deleted from the end. Right-click the Extrude1 feature and select Parent/Child. The feature needs to be deleted, but you need to know what is going to be deleted with it.

23. **The Shell is listed as a child of the extrude because the end face of the extrude was chosen to be removed by the Shell.** Edit the Shell feature and remove the reference to the face. (A Shell feature with no faces to remove is still hollowed out.)

24. **If you right-click Extrude1 and select Parent/Child again, the Shell feature is no longer listed as a child.**

25. **Delete Extrude1, and when the dialog box appears, press Alt+F to select Also Delete Absorbed Features.**

26. **Edit the Shell feature and select the large end of the loft.** Exit the Shell feature. The results up to this step are shown in Figure 11.26.

27. **Drag a window in the design tree to select the four fillet features.** Then right-click and select Add to New Folder. Rename the new folder Fillet Folder.

28. **Click the Section View tool, and create a section view using the Front plane.**

29. **Reorder the Fillet folder to after the Shell feature.**

30. **At this point, you should notice that something does not look right.** This is because creating the fillets after the Shell causes the outside fillets to break through some of the inside corners. The fillets should have failed, but have not, as shown in Figure 11.27.

FIGURE 11.26

The results up to Step 26

FIGURE 11.27

Fillets that should have failed

31. Go to Tools ➪ Options ➪ Performance, and turn on Verification on rebuild. Then click OK to exit the Tools, Options, and press Ctrl+Q. The fillets should now fail.

32. Click Undo to return the feature order to the way it was.

33. Save the part.

Summary

Working effectively with feature history, even in complex models, is a requirement for working with parts that others have created. When I get a part from someone else, the first thing that I usually do is to look at the FeatureManager, and roll it back if possible to get an idea of how the part was modeled. Looking at sketches, relations, feature order, symmetry, redundancy, sketch reuse, and so on are important steps in being able to repair or edit any part. Using modeling best practice techniques helps to ensure that when edits have to be done, they are easy to accomplish, even if they are done by someone who did not build the part.

Evaluation techniques are really the heart of editing, as you should not make too many changes without a basic evaluation of the strengths and weaknesses of the current model.

Part III

Working with Assemblies

The chapters of Part III detail the tools you need to be familiar with in order to get the most from your assemblies. Of these, Chapters 12 and 16 are my favorites. These are loaded with best practice suggestions and tips for efficient workflow. Chapter 16, the in-context chapter, is particularly important for SolidWorks users from many different fields who need or want to make parametric relations between parts. A lot of erroneous information floats around the SolidWorks community on this topic, and this chapter helps you separate the helpful information.

Chapter 12

Building Efficient Assemblies

C hapter 4 provides a brief introduction to the basics of assemblies, how to put parts together, the basics of mating, and so on. The basic process for putting assemblies together remains the same for assemblies of any size, but once the assembly passes a certain point — and this point is likely different for each user or application — the assembly will benefit from some sort of organization or management techniques. This chapter introduces you to the tools and techniques that are available to help you manage performance issues as well as general-use issues, efficiency, browse-worthiness, or searchability.

Identifying the Elements of an Assembly

From Chapter 4, you know that an assembly can contain parts and mates. However, the simple tutorial in Chapter 4 does not go beyond this low level of detail. While the tutorial may have gotten you started, it does not provide enough information to make you competent with the broad range of decisions that you must make to create efficient real-word assemblies. Real-world assemblies can become very complex.

As the assembly grows in the number of parts and design requirements, you may need to add some of the following types of assembly elements. (You may already be familiar with some of these parts from having worked with part documents.) The assembly elements are listed here with brief explanations, and detailed either later in this chapter or in other chapters.

IN THIS CHAPTER

Identifying the elements of an assembly

Using SpeedPaks

Using subassemblies

Using folders

Working with tree display options Finding useful assembly tools

Tutorial: Managing the FeatureManager

- Assembly equations
- Assembly Layout feature
- Assembly layout technique
- Assembly reference geometry (plane, axis, point, coordinate system)
- Parts
- Subassemblies
- Folders for parts
- Folders for mates
- Mates
- Assembly features (cuts that are made once the parts are assembled)
- Component patterns
- In-context reference placeholders
- Smart Fasteners
- Smart Components
- Virtual components
- Envelopes
- Assembly configurations
- Assembly Design Table
- Assembly Bill of Materials (BOMs)
- Hidden/Suppressed/Lightweight/SpeedPak
- Sensors
- SpeedPak
- BOMs
- Hole Series

These elements are shown in Figure 12.1.

Standard reference geometry items

The three standard planes and the Origin are all familiar to you in the assembly FeatureManager design tree, as are the other standard items, such as the Annotations, Design Binder, Sensors, and Lights and Cameras folders. These items offer the same standard functionality of their part document counterparts.

FIGURE 12.1

Elements of an assembly

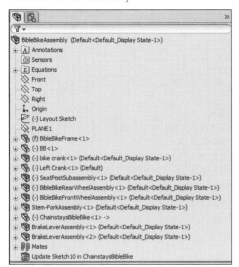

NOTE **Remember that you can use the Tools ➪ Options ➪ FeatureManager page to permanently turn on or off various folders in the header of the FeatureManager. Also be aware that some folders when set to Automatic do not automatically turn on when they should. In cases like this, you should manually go to Tools ➪ Options ➪ FeatureManager to set them to Show.**

Assembly equations

Assembly equations work mainly like part equations, but with some additional complications and considerations. For example, one of the additional features of assembly equations is the ability to drive the dimensions of one part from another part. The syntax is slightly different for this application, as shown in Figure 12.2. Overall, issues with equation order and using driven dimensions on the right side of the equation are the same between parts and assemblies.

CROSS-REF **Equations are discussed in detail in Chapter 9.**

FIGURE 12.2

An assembly equation driving one part from another

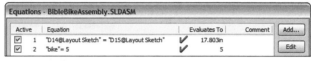

External references

Notice the "->" symbol after the Equations folder in the Assembly FeatureManager. This means that there is an external or in-context reference. An external reference means that aspect of the part is dependent upon something outside of the part. This has file management implications because you must maintain the names of the files so that they always recognize the other file involved in the external relation. In-context means that one part has a relation to another part in positions determined by an assembly. So in this case, the in-context external reference can only be solved if the original part, the referenced part, and the assembly where the relationship was created are all open at the same time.

CROSS-REF In-context references are discussed in depth in Chapter 16.

When one part drives another part in this way, the assembly must also be open to drive the relationship. If just the two parts are open individually, then changing the driving part does not update the driven part; because the relationship was created in the context of the assembly, the assembly must also be open to facilitate the change.

Link values and global variables

Link values and global variables also work in assemblies, but they do not work between parts. Local assembly sketches can use these functions, and the parts can use them when edited in the context of the assembly, but they cannot cross any document barriers (links must remain within a single document).

Renaming

Equations update with new part names regardless of how the part is renamed. Names of subassemblies also update when assembly files are renamed. This includes renaming a document using the Save As command, using SolidWorks Explorer, or using Windows Explorer. It also includes redirecting the assembly to the new part name, as well as renaming the assembly using each of these techniques. If the assembly can find the part and recognizes the part as the one that it is looking for, then the equation will work.

Some of the methods named previously for renaming parts are not recommended; for testing purposes I specifically tried to break the relationships in the equations in using them. SolidWorks Explorer and the Save As methods can be effective when used properly. References between files are a different issue altogether from an equation's references to local file names.

Recommendations

While assembly equations are certainly a valid way to control part sizes, I would recommend using assembly or part configurations, possibly with design tables, to accomplish something similar.

CROSS-REF Assembly configurations are discussed in Chapter 14. Design tables are discussed in Chapter 10.

CAUTION You may have unexpected results if a single dimension is controlled from more than one location. For example, if you have a part-level equation and an assembly-level equation, then one of the equations will be automatically set to Read Only and will not be used.

Assembly layout sketch

In SolidWorks 2008, a new assembly level feature was added to the software called a Layout. Prior to 2008, the word *layout* referred to any assembly level sketch that you used to position or size parts or features within parts. The distinction between the technique and the formal assembly feature is bound to be confusing, especially because they accomplish mostly the same things with a few differences. SolidWorks' new Layout feature only works in assemblies, but layout techniques have been used in parts as well as assemblies for many years. In this chapter I will describe the old technique, and leave the new Layout feature for Chapter 16. When you look at the two functionalities, the new feature is definitely intended to be used as an in-context tool, while the existing technique can be used most easily as a reference for controlling part position (through mating) rather than a way to directly control the sizes and shapes of the parts.

CROSS-REF The new Layout feature is described in more detail in Chapter 16, while the technique using assembly sketches to lay out an assembly is described here. The material in this chapter is written as if the Layout feature does not exist, mainly to give you a straightforward view of how it works without worrying about two different functions at the same time.

The layout sketch is a very useful tool for constructing complex assemblies or for laying out a mechanism in an assembly. Sketches in the assembly have the same characteristics as they do in the part environment. In Figure 12.3, the assembly layout sketch is indicated with a heavy, dashed line for emphasis.

When combined with in-context techniques, assembly layout sketches can help to determine the shape of parts. You can also use layout sketches to mate assembly components to far more robust and dependable mates, rather than mating part to part. The sketch shown in Figure 12.3 is used for both of these techniques. The shape of the frame and the major pivot points are established in the 2D sketch. The wheels are also mated to the sketch.

When you use an assembly layout sketch for either the in-context part building or simply part positioning, the main advantage that it offers is having a single driving sketch that enables you to change the size, shape, and position of the parts. You can use as many layout sketches as you want, and you can make them on different sketch planes. This enables you to control parts in all directions.

FIGURE 12.3

An assembly layout sketch

One of the drawbacks of this technique is that you give up dynamic assembly motion. To move the parts, you have to move the sketch. The part does not move until the sketch is updated. If you need to combine layout functionality with dynamic assembly motion, see the Layout feature in Chapter 16.

Virtual components

Virtual components are covered in more depth in Chapter 16. Virtual components are parts that are created in the context of the assembly, and are at least temporarily stored in the assembly. You can save them out so that they are external to the assembly and can be reused in other assemblies.

BEST PRACTICE Virtual components are a technique that is useful for concept work in assemblies, but you will not see them show up on any best practice list. The main limitation of this technique shows up in the form of data management and reuse.

Assembly reference geometry

Planes and axes are frequently created within assemblies to drive symmetry or placement of parts. You can use assembly layout sketches to create the reference geometry entities. When you create reference geometry within the assembly in this way, be aware that the normal history-based parent/child relationships are still followed. The familiar icons for reference geometry entities are also used in the assembly tree.

History-based and non-history-based portions of the assembly tree

Because features such as sketches and reference geometry are history-based and found in the assembly tree, at least a portion of the assembly FeatureManager is history-based. However, not all of it is. For example, the list of parts and subassemblies is not history-based.

Sketches and reference geometry may appear before or after the list of parts, subassemblies, and mates. All of the remaining entity types that can be found in the assembly FeatureManager are also history-based features, and you can reorder them in the tree. However, several situations can disrupt the process. Under normal circumstances, sketches and reference geometry at the top of the assembly FeatureManager are solved, then the parts are rebuilt if required, and then the mates are solved. This ensures that the sketches and reference geometry are in the correct locations so that if parts are mated to them, then all of the components end up being the correct size and in the right position.

Assembly-level reference geometry can be created that references component geometry instead of layout sketches. This creates a dependency that changes the usual order. For example, the planes are usually solved before the part locations, but when the plane is *dependent* on the part location, the plane has to be solved *after* the part. If a part is then mated to the plane, you are beginning to create a dependency loop, such that the plane is solved, followed by the part, then the plane again because the part has moved, and then the mate that goes to the plane has to resolve the part.

BEST PRACTICE If you are a bit confused by all of this, don't worry. You can simply follow this rule: Do not mate to anything that comes after the mates in the assembly FeatureManager tree. This includes assembly planes or sketches that are dependent on part geometry, assembly features such as cuts, in-context features, component pattern instances, Series Holes, or Smart Fasteners.

This is probably a lot of information if you are a new user, but if you remember this rule, then you can avoid creating models with circular references, where A is dependent on B, which is dependent on A — a never-ending loop that causes major problems for large assembly rebuild times.

Parts and subassemblies

Parts and subassemblies are shown with their familiar icons in the design tree. You can reorder and group them in folders, which is covered in the next section.

 Parts are sometimes shown with a feather, which indicates a lightweight part, and assemblies can have an icon that indicates a flexible subassembly.

 Special icons also exist for hidden and suppressed components.

Folders

 You can create folders to organize and group both parts and mates. I discuss this technique in detail later in this chapter.

Mates

The Mates area remains a constant, single folder, but you can organize it by reordering the mates and grouping them into folders. Each mate is shown with a symbol corresponding to the type of mate it is, but the mate folder is shown as a pair of paperclips.

Assembly features

In manufacturing, once parts are assembled, secondary machining operations are sometimes applied to them to ensure that holes line up properly, or for other purposes. For example, assembly features can be cut extrudes, cut revolves, or hole features. These features appear only in the assembly, not in the individual parts.

You should not confuse assembly features with in-context features. In-context features are created in the assembly with a reference between parts, but the sketch and feature definition are in the part itself.

Starting with SolidWorks 2009, features created in the assembly can be propagated to reside in the affected parts.

Component patterns

Component patterns can pattern either parts or assemblies by creating either a pattern defined in the assembly, or a pattern that follows a pattern feature created in a part. The pattern is listed as a feature in the assembly FeatureManager, and all the instance parts appear indented from the pattern feature in the design tree. You can hide or suppress each instance, change its configuration, and in most ways control it as if it were a regular part in the design tree.

Because the options for locally defined patterns are comparatively limited, users generally like to use part feature patterns to drive the component patterns when possible.

> **PERFORMANCE** To improve performance, it is best to pattern subassemblies if possible. If it is not possible, then patterning a group of parts is the next best option. Making multiple patterns, one for each part, is an inefficient way to accomplish the same thing.

In-context reference update holders

It is difficult to get a good picture of assemblies in general without including a discussion about in-context references, but to treat the subject properly, it also requires its own section, and in fact, this book gives in-context modeling its own chapter (Chapter 16). When you create a reference between parts in an assembly, the assembly needs to remember which parts are involved in the reference, and what the spatial relationship between them is. The parts also need to remember which assembly was used to create the relation because the parts are positioned in the assembly, and the reference has meaning only with regard to a particular relative position between the parts.

When you create the relation, a placeholder has to be left behind in the assembly to hold this information. This placeholder is called an Update Holder. The Update Holders do not display by default. To see them, you must right-click the top level in the FeatureManager and select Show Update Holders. They only exist when in-context references exist in the assembly, and there is one Update Holder for each in-context reference (one holder per sketch or feature). You cannot do very much with the Update Holders, other than query them for parent/child relations and to list the external relations, but they serve as a reminder that you have in-context references to maintain. Several years ago, they were displayed by default, but they were later hidden by default, presumably because users were confused by the presence of something that you could not do anything with. In-context modeling methods are often scorned by some users, and if you have a list of 50 or 60 Update Holders, then you may be perceived as an overzealous novice. For more information on this feature, see Chapter 16.

Popular perceptions of in-context techniques aside, in-context modeling is powerful. If you follow the best practice suggestions outlined in Chapter 16, you will soon gain confidence and master this technique rather than being frightened by it. The functionality works, and if you do not abuse it, it will serve you well.

Smart Fasteners

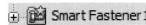 Smart Fasteners are assembly features that automatically select Toolbox parts for use in standard-sized holes, and you can use them in many different ways. The Smart Fastener feature in the assembly FeatureManager is used to edit the definition of the Smart Fastener, which can include adding items such as nuts and washers. You can also use Smart Fasteners in conjunction with the Hole Wizard to place appropriate holes and matched fasteners, all in a single step.

CROSS-REF Smart Fasteners, Toolbox, and the Hole Wizard are discussed in detail in Chapter 17.

Hole Series

The Hole Series is a Hole Wizard–type feature that you apply in an assembly. This wizard leaves the feature icon in the assembly, but also adds features directly to the individual parts. It also adds in-context Update Holders to the assembly FeatureManager, as shown in Figure 12.4. The Series Hole is designed to go through a series of parts, placing the appropriate hole type in each part, counterbore, through, threaded, and so on.

FIGURE 12.4

Adding in-context Update Holders

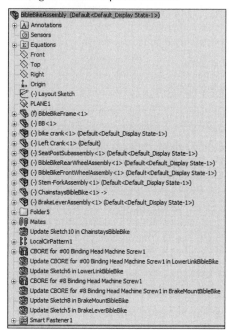

 # Using SpeedPaks

A SpeedPak is a derived configuration of an assembly that keeps only selected solid bodies and faces, but can represent the rest of the assembly with non-selectable display data. A SpeedPak can be used to replace an entire subassembly within an upper-level assembly. SpeedPaks are intended to increase performance with very large assemblies and drawings.

Figure 12.5 shows first the SpeedPak PropertyManager, which is accessed by right-clicking an active configuration, and selecting Add SpeedPak. Each configuration can have only one SpeedPak.

Figure 12.5 also shows the configuration list with the SpeedPak listed indented under the Default config, and the entire assembly. The final image shows the SpeedPak inserted into an assembly document, consisting of a single face and two solid bodies. Notice the special icon associated with SpeedPaks. You can change a part in an assembly from or to a SpeedPak in the same way that you would change a configuration, using Component Properties.

FIGURE 12.5

Managing SpeedPaks

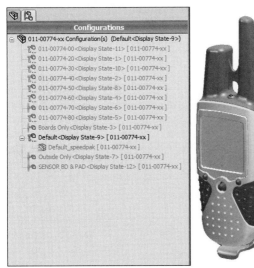

Model of Garmin assembly from the SolidWorks demo sets

Remember this is a tool for increasing assembly speed, and to increase speed, there is always something that you have to give up. If your expectations of the tool are in line with the actual functionality, you will be very satisfied with the functionality SpeedPaks offer.

Using Ghosts

You can use any faces or bodies that you select in the Include lists either manually or through the Quick Include sliders (which automatically select bodies and faces based on size) in assemblies to mate to or in drawings to dimension to. Any geometry that is not selected is included as a ghost — it displays, but cannot be selected. When the cursor gets near ghost geometry, the ghost fades away, revealing only selectable geometry. Notice at the bottom of the SpeedPak PropertyManager that you can also choose to remove the ghost data and further increase the memory savings.

Sharing Self-contained Data

The SpeedPak is self-contained. All the selected face and body geometry is saved inside the assembly. If you want to send someone a visual representation of an assembly, make a SpeedPak configuration and send only the assembly file — no parts are required. This is the equivalent of being able to put an eDrawing file into an assembly. This is one of the better performance ideas to come out of SolidWorks in some time.

Using SpeedPak with drawings

You can even use SpeedPaks with drawings. Just remember that only the faces or bodies in the Include lists can be dimensioned to. Some functionality exists for the ghost data, such as BOM inclusion and numbered balloons. Ghost data displays as gray on the drawing, while geometry in the Include list is black.

Using Subassemblies

The first tool for organizing assemblies is the subassembly. A subassembly is just a regular assembly that is used as a component in another assembly.

BEST PRACTICE The number of levels of subassemblies is not limited to a specific number, although for different sizes and types of assemblies, I encourage you to establish a best practice for your company. For example, establish a guideline that suggests that subassemblies of 100 parts or less go no deeper than three levels.

You can use several criteria to determine how subassemblies are assigned:

- Performance
- BOM
- Relative motion
- Pre-fabricated, off-the-shelf considerations
- According to assembly steps for a process drawing
- To simplify patterning

The underlying question here is based on the multiple functions of your SolidWorks assembly model. Is it primarily a design tool? A visualization tool? A documentation tool? A process tool? As a design tool, the assembly is used to determine fits, tolerances, mechanisms, complex shapes that span parts, and many other things. As a visualization tool, it simply has to look good and possibly move properly if that is part of the design. As a documentation tool, it is important how the model relates to the BOM, and the order in which subassemblies are added. As a process tool, you need to be able to show the assembly in various intermediate states of being assembled.

I have seen companies create multiple assembly models for different purposes. Sometimes the requirements between the different methods are contradictory and cannot all be met at the same time with a single set of data. Again, depending on what information you need to be able to extract from your SolidWorks models, you may want to approach assembly modeling and organization differently.

Creating subassemblies from existing parts

You can create subassemblies from parts that already exist in an assembly. To do this, select the parts that you want to add to the subassembly using shift+, Ctrl+, or box select techniques, and then select Form New Subassembly Here from the right-mouse button menu. You are then prompted to assign a name or possibly select a template for the new subassembly.

CAUTION When creating a new subassembly from existing parts or when moving parts into or out of a subassembly from the upper-level assembly, some things may be lost. For example, mates are moved from the upper level to the subassembly. If you have in-context relationships, they may be removed. Operations that create subassemblies cannot be undone easily.

Once you have created the subassembly, you can add or remove components using the drag-and-drop method. For example, Figure 12.6 shows the cursor that indicates that the part named Left Crank is being moved into the subassembly named bike crank. To move a part out of a subassembly, simply drag the part into the upper-level assembly.

FIGURE 12.6

Moving parts into a subassembly

> **NOTE**   When you are dragging a part out of an assembly and into another one, you may again see the cursor symbol that appears in Figure 12.5. If you do not want this to happen, then hold down the Alt key while dragging. The cursor symbol changes to the Reorder cursor (a reversed, L-shaped arrow), and the part is placed after the subassembly rather than within it.

Insert a new subassembly

Along with the right-mouse button menu option Form New Subassembly Here, which takes existing parts and puts them into a newly created subassembly, you can use another option called Insert New Subassembly. The names of these functions do not adequately describe the difference in what they do. Insert New Subassembly inserts a blank subassembly at the point in the design tree that you indicate by right-clicking it. You can place components into the subassembly by dragging and dropping them from the main assembly, or you can open the assembly in its own window, and insert parts by using the usual methods.

Dissolving subassemblies

If you would like to get rid of a subassembly but want to keep its parts, then you can use the Dissolve Subassembly option through the right-mouse button menu. This option has some of the same consequences of the Form New Subassembly Here option in that mates are moved from the subassembly to the upper-level assembly, and you may lose in-context relations and assembly features.

Organizing for performance

Performance in SolidWorks is a euphemism for speed. Subassemblies can contribute to speed-saving modeling techniques by segmenting the work that the software needs to do at any one time.

Solving mates

The mates that contribute to putting the pieces of an assembly together are solved at the level of the top assembly. Under normal circumstances, subassemblies are treated as static selections of parts that are welded together, and their mates are not solved at the same time that the top-level assemblies' mates are solved. This segmenting of the mates leads to improved performance by only solving one set of mates at a time.

Mates are usually solved as a single group unless there is a special situation, such as mates to in-context features, component pattern instances, or an assembly feature, all of which have already been described in this chapter. When one of these situations occurs, the mates have to be divided into separate groups or solved multiple times. This is done transparently behind the scenes so that the user does not have to worry about it.

Flexible subassemblies

When you create subassemblies, the mates for these parts are not solved in the upper-level assembly. This means that if a subassembly is a mechanism, the mechanism does not allow Dynamic Assembly Motion in the upper-level assembly. For example, in Figure 12.7, the front fork is a linkage mechanism, but it is also a subassembly. Without reassembling the parts of the fork in the upper-level assembly, you can allow the mates from the fork subassembly to be solved in the upper-level assembly by using an option in the Component Properties dialog box, which is also shown in Figure 12.7. When you select the Flexible option in the Solve As section, you enable the mates of this subassembly to be solved in the upper-level assembly.

FIGURE 12.7

Creating a flexible subassembly

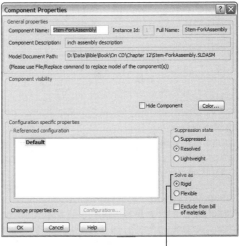

Solve as flexible or rigid

To access the Component Properties dialog box, right-click the subassembly and select Component Properties from the menu.

Flexible subassemblies are another source of great superstition in SolidWorks software, particularly with users that have used the software for several years. In releases past, flexible subassemblies required all instances to be flexible, and required a different configuration for each flexible instance. This was very inconvenient, and a lot of users remember trying to get flexible subassemblies to work with a painful expression.

In SolidWorks 2009, and in fact for a couple of releases prior, the flexible subassemblies functionality is practical and reasonably reliable.

Legacy data

If you have assemblies that were built in older versions of SolidWorks (such as SolidWorks 2001+), mates used to be split up into multiple *mate groups*, which represented the groupings that mates were solved in. This was forced by mating to the history-based features in the assembly FeatureManager. SolidWorks no longer displays mate groups, but the groups are still used in the background to solve mates. This is another change that SolidWorks has made to the software that simplifies the user's interaction with the software, but also makes it obvious that things are now happening behind the scenes that you can't control.

Organizing for the BOM

The Bill of Materials, or BOM, is a table that is placed either into a drawing of an assembly or in an assembly itself. This table shows the parts used in the assembly and includes other information, such as part numbers, descriptions, and custom property data.

CROSS-REF SolidWorks BOM functionality is discussed in depth in Chapter 24.

Businesses often represent assemblies and subassemblies in various ways by using MRP (Manufacturing Resource Planning) or ERP (Engineering Resource Planning) software. The methods that accountants and manufacturers use to organize assemblies are not always the same as those that an engineer or designer might choose, but some companies require the BOM on the drawing to match the MRP or ERP Bill of Materials.

BEST PRACTICE When forced into modeling something in an unnatural way to satisfy an outside requirement such as special BOM requirements, it might be best to detach the unnatural part and model normally. In the situation mentioned here — where MRP is forcing how the assembly is put together by requiring the BOM to match MRP — I recommend separating the BOM from the assembly structure. This ensures that the BOM becomes a manually maintained document, rather than building an assembly that makes other SolidWorks functions difficult. Alternatives to this approach would be to make configurations or entirely new assembly documents to drive the BOM.

Grouping subassemblies by relative motion

A more natural way to group subassemblies is by considering relative motion. In the bicycle example, each wheel is a separate subassembly because it moves as a unit relative to the rest of the assembly. Figure 12.8 illustrates where relative motion might be on the bicycle.

Grouping subassemblies by relative motion is great for assembly modeling, but it does not usually reflect product reality very well. Using this method, you often end up with parts in the subassembly that will have to be disassembled in order to actually put the physical parts together. However, if your only consideration is ease of modeling, then this is probably the method to use.

FIGURE 12.8

Grouping subassemblies by relative motion

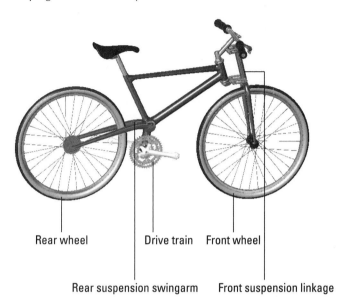

Rear wheel   Drive train   Front wheel

Rear suspension swingarm   Front suspension linkage

Organizing groups of purchased components

If you are modeling a product that is created from a shopping list of purchased components, then it may make the most sense to organize your subassemblies into groups of parts that are purchased together. In fact, purchased subassemblies are often modeled as single parts, except when relative motion is required in the purchased assembly.

For example, in the bicycle assembly, the sprockets on the rear wheel are purchased as a separate unit, and yet the part that mounts onto the wheel moves relative to the sprockets that are driven by the chain. This is an example of a purchased part that would be modeled as a subassembly to show relative motion. The bicycle chain, another purchased subassembly, has not yet been added to this assembly, and is a more complex model. The desire to show all of the individual links moving through the path may override both the complexity of assembling it and the performance considerations of exercising all of the mates.

Although the BOM method of organizing assemblies sometimes leads to unnatural solutions, you should not discard it altogether. If you can devise concessions in order to make the BOM work automatically, then you should do this.

Depicting an assembly process

Manufacturing and assembly processes need to be documented as well as individual part design. You often need to create exploded-view assembly instructions for manufacturing or service documentation at each step of a multi-step assembly process. Figure 12.9 shows a page of this type of process documentation.

Assembly process documentation

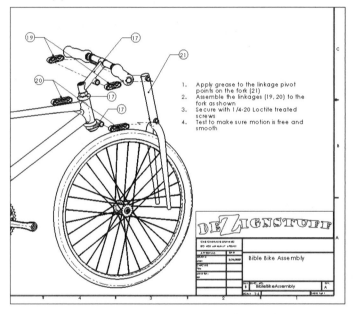

This is certainly a task that is different from the initial design or modeling of the assembly, and it may require an entirely separate model. Generally, you can perform the different steps by using a separate configuration for each process step, with exploded views for each configuration.

Item numbering

Balloons number the parts according to the item number that is used in the BOM, but of course you do not know the item numbers until the BOM is created. You can influence the item numbers by reordering the parts in the assembly (which I discuss later in this chapter), by manually editing item numbers, or by manually numbering the balloons. I cover all of this in detail in Chapter 24.

Individual steps

Each step corresponds to an assembly configuration (discussed in Chapter 14), and you can place them on a separate sheet of the drawing (discussed in Chapter 21). Each configuration can have multiple exploded views, if necessary, to show all of the steps.

Patterning considerations

The most efficient way to pattern large numbers of components in an assembly is to pattern a single subassembly with all of the components to be patterned in it. While this may not be easily combined with some of the other considerations that I mentioned previously, it is another option that you can use to organize assemblies.

Using Folders

Folders are primarily used in the assembly FeatureManager for grouping parts and mates into either special classifications for easy browsing, or groups that can be easily hidden and shown, or suppressed and unsuppressed, as appropriate. Figure 12.10 shows some examples of these folders.

FIGURE 12.10

Folders that are used to organize components and mates

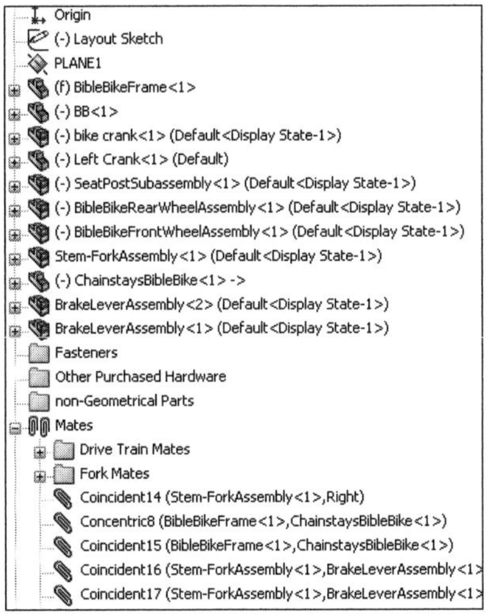

Creating folders in the FeatureManager

You can add folders to the assembly FeatureManager in one of two ways:

- Add existing components to a new folder
- Create an empty new folder

Add To New Folder

To use the Add To New Folder tool, right-click a component or mate (or selection of components or mates) and select Add To New Folder from the menu. This moves the component or mate into the folder. Folders do not affect the assembly in any functional way; they are simply for organization, to speed browsing and selection.

Create New Folder

To simply create a new folder without putting anything into it right away, right-click either the Mates area or the components list, and select Create New Folder from the menu.

Adding items to existing folders

To move an item into an existing folder, just drag the item (component or mate) onto the folder. If the folder is expanded, showing its contents, then you can also drag the item as if you were reordering a feature in the FeatureManager of a part, and drop it in the list of items where you would like it.

If you are dragging a part or assembly and trying to put it immediately after an assembly, then a cursor may appear, like the one shown in the center in Figure 12.11. This cursor means that the part is going to become part of the assembly. If this is not what you are trying to do, then hold down the Alt key while dragging; the part is placed into the folder immediately after the assembly, instead of being made a part of the assembly. The third image in Figure 12.11 shows the cursor with the Alt key pressed.

FIGURE 12.11

Moving items into folders

Reordering items in the tree

There are times when you may want to reorder items in the assembly tree. For example, you may want to place items close to one another in the tree, or you may be preparing to put items that are next to one another into a single folder. You may want to reorganize components for the BOM display.

You can reorder mates simply by dragging them. Mates display in the order in which they are created, but the order is not significant. They can be reordered however you like.

Components also display in the order in which they are added to the assembly, and you can reorder them in any way you like.

BEST PRACTICE It is often useful to have an ordering strategy that helps you work with the model. I usually try to keep the biggest parts, or the parts that everything else is mated to, or the part that is treated as "ground," as the first part in the assembly. The fasteners and other cosmetic or BOM-driving parts are put at the end of the tree, usually in a descriptive folder.

Working with Tree Display Options

Display options for items in the FeatureManager are often overlooked, but can be useful for displaying data about parts, subassemblies, mates, and features. Figure 12.12 shows the right-mouse button menu options. You must right-click the top level assembly name in the FeatureManager to access this menu.

FIGURE 12.12

Tree display options in assemblies

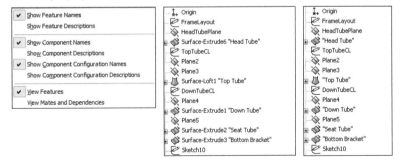

NOTE All these options are available for parts and drawings as well, except for the View Features option and the View Mates and Dependencies option, which are related to assemblies.

Show feature names and descriptions

If you are so thorough that you have added descriptions to your features, then you are doing well. This option refers to the descriptions of features in the parts. The middle image in Figure 12.12 shows a section of the FeatureManager for the bicycle frame part; some of the features have had descriptions added with both of the options for feature names and feature descriptions turned on. The image to the right in Figure 12.12 shows the result of turning off the feature name, with only the feature description option turned on. If no feature description has been created, then the feature name displays. Feature descriptions always appear in double quotes.

Show component and config names and descriptions

The image to the left in Figure 12.13 shows the default arrangement of displaying component and configuration names in the assembly FeatureManager. This example uses the rear wheel assembly from the bicycle assembly. In assemblies, you cannot turn off the component names and the component descriptions. SolidWorks issues this statement when you try to turn off both the name and the description: "You cannot hide both the component name and the file name. At least one must be visible in the tree."

FIGURE 12.13

Component name options

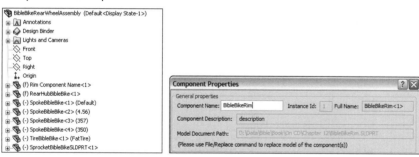

Using names other than the part filename in the assembly FeatureManager

The message in the previous paragraph distinguishes between the *filename* and the *component name* that is listed for individual parts or subassemblies in the assembly FeatureManager. You can specify the component name in the Component Properties dialog box by right-clicking the component in the assembly FeatureManager and selecting Component Properties.

However, you can assign a component name for a component that is different from the filename only if a special setting is turned off. (The setting defaults to on.) You can access this setting through Tools ⇨ Options ⇨ External References ⇨ Update Component Names When Documents Are Replaced. What the name of the setting has to do with showing a component name in the FeatureManager is not exactly clear, but these are the steps that you have to go through if you want to change how the part and subassembly names display in the assembly FeatureManager.

After going through the preceding steps, you still receive the warning message about the filename and the component name. This is apparently an "unintended feature," or bug, and should likely say that you cannot turn off both the component name and the component description at the same time.

There may be a situation where you want to show a name other than the filename in the FeatureManager. For example, your company may be using sequential part numbers for the filenames that are difficult to read, and you want something descriptive in the design tree so that you do not need a cross-reference sheet next to your computer that equates filenames to meaningful descriptions.

If you prefer, you can avoid a lot of problems by just using the part description instead of the filename or the component name. The choice is up to you.

BEST PRACTICE Because the component name options are convoluted and obscure, and will need to be set on each computer where you would like to use them, I do not recommend them. It is simpler and more reliable to use either the default component name (which is the same as the filename) or the component description.

One of the problems with using the component description is shown in Figure 12.14, where the user did not enter proper descriptions for the parts, and SolidWorks used the default description in the templates. The tire and spokes use configurations, which display in the figure.

FIGURE 12.14

An example of what can occur when you do not enter proper descriptions for parts

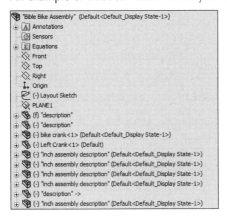

Viewing features, mates, and dependencies

The last set of options, shown in Figure 12.12, defines what displays under the name of each component. The default setting is for the part's features or the subassembly's components to display, just as if the part or subassembly were open in its own window.

The View Mates and Dependencies option can also show the features, but they are placed into a separate folder. This option makes it very easy to see the mates that are assigned to an individual component. For example, in Figure 12.15, the image to the right shows the mates directly under the BibleBikeFrame part. This often makes troubleshooting much easier because it isolates the mates for a single part. Notice also that the first folder under the part name in the image to the left in Figure 12.15 is the Mates folder. This indicates that, regardless of whether you choose to display mates or features, you always have easy access to the other type.

FIGURE 12.15

You can view features, as well as mates and dependencies.

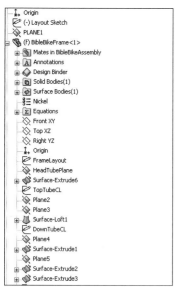
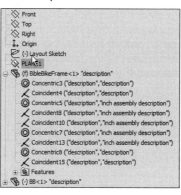

Another technique for displaying mates is to split the FeatureManager and to show the PropertyManager in one pane. As a result, any parts that are selected show their mates in the PropertyManager pane. If two selected parts have mates in common, then the common mates appear in bold type, as shown in Figure 12.16. This is an extremely useful method for looking at mates.

Showing mates in the PropertyManager pane

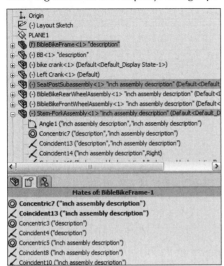

Finding Useful Assembly Tools

SolidWorks is incredibly complex software, and there are many tools to do many small tasks. As thick as this book is, I have still just hit the highlights. This is true nowhere more than it is in assemblies. Users have such wide expectations of the software in various areas, and everyone needs something different. Many tools exist to help you put together, maintain, and evaluate efficient assemblies. The tools in this section are important tools that don't fit into the other categories.

Using Sensors

Sensors provide an alert if a monitored value goes outside of a specified range. Sensors can be used in parts or in assemblies. the types of values that you can monitor with Sensors are dimensional values, mass, volume or surface area, interference detection between select components, and Simulation data (stress analysis values).

Of these, in assemblies, interference detection is of most concern.

To create a sensor in an assembly, right-click the Sensors folder in the assembly FeatureManager. If the Sensors folder is not there, go to Tools ⇨ Options ⇨ FeatureManager page and turn it on. Figure 12.17 shows the Sensor setup interface.

FIGURE 12.17

Setting up a sensor in an assembly

Using the AssemblyXpert

The AssemblyXpert is the successor of the now defunct Assembly Statistics. You can find it on the Tools menu, or use Tools ➪ Customize to place it on the Assembly toolbar. AssemblyXpert gives suggestions about things you can do to improve the performance of an assembly, such as updating files to the new version and looking at Large Assembly Mode, and highlights existing errors in the assembly mates, in-context, and supposedly circular references.

I was not able to confirm that AssemblyXpert would find a circular reference, but SolidWorks and I might be using different definitions of circular reference. My definition is if you make a list of parts referencing other parts, and the references form a loop, with one part as the start and end point. AssemblyXpert could not find this kind of reference loop. SolidWorks may be using a more explicit definition where specific geometry within a part is both driving and driven.

Figure 12.18 shows the AssemblyXpert results. Notice that the results include the information formerly included with the Assembly Statistics: part and subassembly count, along with mates, unique parts, and so on.

The information in the AssemblyXpert is certainly useful, particularly for new-ish users who may not know to look for things like this already. You can use it as both a diagnostic and a learning tool.

FIGURE 12.18

AssemblyXpert results

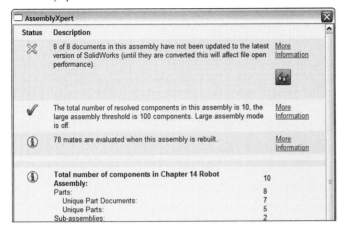

Tutorial: Managing the FeatureManager

This tutorial uses the `BibleBikeAssembly.sldasm` file found on the CD-ROM for Chapter 12. Open the file and follow these steps to learn about managing the FeatureManager:

1. **Create a new subassembly within the existing assembly using the parts BibleBikeFrame and ChainstayBibleBike.** Name this new assembly `FrameAssembly. SLDASM`.

2. **Reorder the new FrameAssembly to the top of the design tree.**

3. **Reorder the other parts and assemblies so that the bigger assemblies appear higher on the list, and the parts appear at the bottom.** (Remember that the Alt-drag option to prevent a component from being placed into a subassembly.)

4. **Drag the part called BB (for Bottom Bracket) into the BibleBikeFrame Assembly (drag without using the Alt key).** The assembly FeatureManager at this point is shown in Figure 12.19.

5. **Select both wheels and then click Add To New Folder from the right-mouse button menu.** Name the new folder **Wheels**, and move it to the bottom of the tree.

6. **Expand the Mates folder, select the first four mates, and put them in a new folder (select Add To New Folder from the right-mouse button menu).** Name the new folder **Centering Mates**.

FIGURE 12.19

The starting state and the state as of Step 4

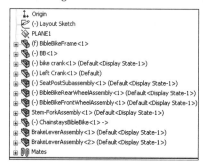
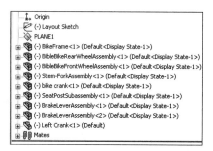

Summary

Assemblies are more than simply parts and subassemblies put together with mate relationships; several other types of features and placeholders can also exist in the assembly FeatureManager. Organizing assembly components is fairly straightforward and can offer benefits for finding parts as well as controlling suppression and display states globally.

The assembly FeatureManager contains several options for the data to display for subassemblies, parts, configurations, and features within. Remember that all of this data that you include in your SolidWorks documents can be accessed and reused later on, and so it is worth the effort. Descriptions can be very important, both at the part level and also for features and configs.

Chapter 13

Getting More from Mates

In SolidWorks assemblies, mates are the basic units that either make everything work together and function properly, or fill the tree with errors and warning symbols. When properly handled, mates enable your assembly to react predictably to changes in parts exactly the same way that sketch relations drive changes in part features. As a result, mates and sketch relations often have the same function and even the same weaknesses to watch out for.

This chapter goes one step further with mates, by not just simply putting parts together with Coincident and Concentric mates, but also mating parts when tolerances, gaps, and symmetry become issues. You will also learn about the more advanced mate types that may be useful for special situations.

One of the assumptions that I make in this chapter is that assembly mates are not just used for positioning parts, but also for motion. Making motion work takes a little more than just establishing the right spatial relationship between parts; it usually also involves analyzing the open degrees of freedom.

From time to time, I have met users who take the "AutoCAD" approach to putting parts together into assemblies, by simply placing parts at the correct X- and Y- coordinates without assigning any relationships to the parts around them. This defeats most of the purpose of creating parametric, associative assemblies in the first place. Assembly mates are an extremely powerful tool for enabling your assemblies to react predictably to change.

Applying Mates

An average assembly of 100 parts is likely to have almost 300 individual mates. If you create these parts one at a time, taking perhaps a minute for each mate, you would spend five hours just applying mates. Any time that you can save applying mates is a benefit to you — assuming you still get the correct results — because it is time that you can spend doing something else. In this section, you will learn efficient mating strategies, as well as speedy techniques.

Mating Through the Mate PropertyManager

The Mate PropertyManager is the default method for applying mates, and was used briefly in Chapter 4. The Mate PropertyManager interface is shown in Figure 13.1. You can create mates by pre-selecting entities before applying the Mate command or selecting them after you open the Mate PropertyManager. The three types of mates are Standard, Advanced and Mechanical.

FIGURE 13.1

The Mate PropertyManager interface

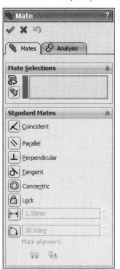

Mate workflow

If you make a lot of mates, it is important to have an efficient rhythm when working with the interface. Assuming you have the Mate PropertyManager already active, the most efficient way to use the Mate interface is as follows:

1. **Click the first entity.**

2. **Click the second entity.**

3. **Click OK on the right-mouse button cursor icon, which is shown in Figure 13.2.**

FIGURE 13.2

The OK option on the right-mouse button cursor

Or, if the automatic default mate type is not the mate that you want to apply, select it from the popup list, which is shown in Figure 13.3.

FIGURE 13.3

The Mate selection popup list

4. **Click the green check mark icon from the popup list.**

5. **Repeat Steps 1 to 4.**

6. **After the last mate, press Esc, the green check mark icon, or the red X icon from either the PropertyManager or the confirmation corner in the upper-right corner of the graphics area.**

View and model positioning

Sometimes you will have to rotate the model to achieve the correct view in order to select faces or edges. There are also times when you will want to *pre-position* so that the model snaps into the correct position automatically. You can rotate individual parts in an assembly by dragging with the right-mouse button. You rotate the view by dragging with the middle mouse button, or MMB. You can move parts by dragging them with the left mouse button, or LMB. You can pan the view by pressing Ctrl and dragging with the MMB. When you drag a part with the LMB while the Mate PropertyManager is active, SolidWorks does not add the selected entity to the Mate Selections list.

To summarize these actions:

■ To rotate an individual component in an assembly, drag with the right-mouse button.

- To move an individual component in an assembly, drag with the LMB.

- To rotate an assembly view, drag with the MMB.

- To pan an assembly view, Ctrl+drag with the MMB.

Also be aware of the view manipulation tools available by clicking the triad in the lower-left corner:

- To rotate normal to an axis, click its triad axis

- To rotate by 15° about an axis (angle can be specified at Tools ➪ Options ➪ View), Alt+click its triad axis

- To rotate by 90° about an axis, Shift+ click its triad access

- To zoom to fit, double MMB click in the graphics window (same as the F hotkey)

> **TIP** If you have a *Spaceball* or 3D motion controller, you can perform all of these actions more easily and simultaneously using one hand for view rotations and the other hand for selections. You can also use a Spaceball to move parts.

Select Other

The Select Other command enables you to select items that are hidden by other items. It is often used to select faces that are hidden behind other faces without rotating the part. You can apply the Select Other command through the right-mouse button menu. Right-click where the face would be if you could see it. A list of entities displays, and you can select the entity you want from this list or from the graphics window.

Moving your mouse over an entity in the list highlights the entity in the graphics window. Pressing Tab or scrolling the mouse wheel cycles through the entities one by one. Clicking faces with the right-mouse button hides them, which allows you to see further down into the part or assembly. Clicking with the LMB either in the graphics window or the selection list box selects the item. Figure 13.4 shows the Select Other cursor and dialog box.

FIGURE 13.4

The Select Other cursor and dialog box

The item about to be selected highlights orange in the graphics window.

Although this selection method is also used for other purposes, it is often used for selecting faces for mating.

Multiple Mate mode

Multiple Mate mode enables you to select one face in order to mate multiple faces from other parts to it. Figure 13.5 shows the interface for this mode, which you can toggle to from the Mate PropertyManager interface. Multiple Mate mode is the paperclip with the lightning bolt icon without any text on it. This function works only with the Standard Mate types, not with any of the Advanced mates, which I discuss later in this chapter.

FIGURE 13.5

The Multiple Mate mode interface

You can create a special folder for all of the multiple mates by selecting the Create multi-mate folder check box in the Mate Selections PropertyManager. You can also automatically link the values for distance and angle mates with link values by selecting the Link dimensions check box.

SmartMates

SmartMates are mates that you can create automatically by dragging one part onto the other without invoking the Mate command. There are three different methods that you can use to apply SmartMates:

- Alt+dragging the part
- Dragging the part from one window to another
- Using Mate references

Alt+dragging a SmartMate

Probably the easiest way to quickly create a SmartMate is by Alt+dragging. One, two, or even three mates can be applied at once by holding down the Alt key while dragging a face or edge from one part onto a face or edge on another part.

When you are dragging a part while pressing the Alt key, the part is made transparent to allow you to see other part faces that you may want to mate it to. A special cursor appears when a SmartMate is about to be applied. Figure 13.6 shows the cursors that appear for adding Concentric and Coincident mates.

FIGURE 13.6

Applying a SmartMate

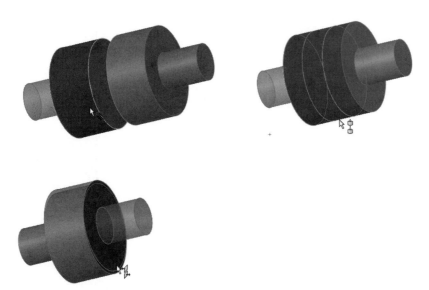

When you drop the face or edge onto the mating face or edge to complete the mate, you must use the popup Mate toolbar to accept or alter the mate. In the examples in Figure 13.6, a face is being dragged onto another face. However, you can also drag edges and vertices. Mates are limited to being either Coincident or Concentric.

The *peg-in-hole* mate is actually the combination of a Concentric mate and a Coincident mate. This is the type of mate that is created between a screw and a hole, and is the result of Alt+dragging a circular edge onto a circular edge. When the circular edges are created by the intersection of a cylindrical face and a flat face, the Concentric mate goes between the two cylindrical faces, and the Coincident mate goes between the flat faces. The peg-in-hole mate is illustrated in Figure 13.7. The top two images show the state of the parts before the SmartMate. The image in the lower left shows the SmartMate orienting the part in the wrong way so that the two parts interfere. In the image in the lower right, the part to which the SmartMate is applied has been reoriented by pressing Tab before the SmartMate is accepted by dropping the part.

TIP You can use the Tab key to flip the alignment if a SmartMate tries to put parts together in the wrong way. If you are in the process of Alt+dragging, make sure to release the Alt key before pressing Tab. The Alt+Tab combination is a Windows shortcut to show a list of open applications.

FIGURE 13.7

Using SmartMate to create the peg-in-hole mate combination

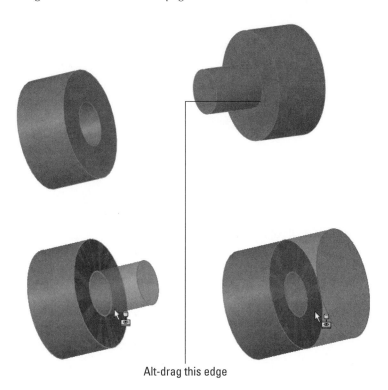

Alt-drag this edge

Drag between windows

The same is true when copying a part in the graphics window of an assembly. You can simply Ctrl+drag a face of the part to the face of the new location.

Mate references

Mate references are model faces, edges, or vertices that are pre-selected and used in a SmartMate-like fashion when dragging a part in from Windows Explorer or from a library window. Mate references are discussed in Chapter 19 in the course of discussing library parts.

Mating with macros

If all of the confirmations and extra mouse-clicks to open and close windows are not for you, and you are just applying simple mates, then you may want to use macros to mate parts. Macros are not going to give you the same flexibility, but they do improve speed. However, you have to have the parts ready to go when you press the macro button, or you will create the wrong mate.

You can find macros for Coincident, Concentric, Parallel, Perpendicular, and Tangent mates on the CD-ROM. For example, to use the concentric macro, you would need to pre-position the parts so that they are within 90 degrees of the proper alignment, have one of the parts mated in place such that that only one part will move, select the two cylindrical faces, and then run the macro. Ideally, the macro would be connected to a hotkey, so the workflow for this process would be extraordinarily fast. You would click the face, click the face, then press the hotkey, and the parts would fly together.

Like SmartMates, macros work best for the simpler mate types where you do not need to select any options. The workflow with macros can be very fast, but you have to have the parts prepositioned and be very sure of what you want. Click one face, click another face, hit a hotkey to activate the macro, and the parts fly together.

Mating for Motion

Dynamic Assembly Motion is a powerful tool for visualizing the motion of mechanisms in SolidWorks. It works best if there is a single open *degree of freedom*.

Degree-of-Freedom analysis

When working with motion in SolidWorks, you need to be comfortable with the concept of degrees of freedom. When inserted into an assembly, each model has six degrees of freedom:

- Translation in X (tX)
- Translation in Y (tY)
- Translation in Z (tZ)
- Rotation about X (rX)
- Rotation about Y (rY)
- Rotation about Z (rZ)

When applying mates, and especially when troubleshooting motion or overdefinition problems, it is important to look at how each mate translates into degrees of freedom being tied down. For example, a Coincident mate, planar face to planar face, ties down one translation degree of freedom (in the direction perpendicular to the faces), and two rotational degrees of freedom (about directions which lie in the plane of the faces). What remains are two translational degrees of freedom in the plane of the faces and one rotational degree of freedom about an axis perpendicular to the planar faces.

A point-to-point Coincident mate ties down three translational degrees of freedom, and the part can only rotate.

An edge-to-edge Coincident mate ties down two translational and two rotational degrees of freedom. As a result, a part that you mate in this way can only slide along the mated edge and rotate around the mated edge.

TIP When using face-to-face Coincident mates, it takes three mates to fully define a block type part. When using edge-to-edge Coincident mates, it only takes two mates. You should read through the section on that summarizes mate best practices before adopting this approach.

Something to be careful about is that a degree-of-freedom analysis frequently predicts an over-defined mate scenario when SolidWorks does not in fact display any errors or warnings. For example, if one block is mated to another with the simple case of three face-to-face Coincident mates, and each Coincident mate ties down one translational and two rotational degrees of freedom, then the mating scenario ties down 9 degrees of freedom, so the part is overconstrained by three rotational degrees of freedom. However, SolidWorks has a lot of forgiveness built in, so it frequently allows situations like this, where parts are severely overconstrained. When troubleshooting an overconstrained situation, you should not take this forgiveness for granted. If an assembly reports as overconstrained and the reason is not intuitively obvious, try reducing some of the degrees of freedom constrained. For example, instead of making two faces coincident, consider making them simply parallel, or mate a point to a face instead of two faces.

BEST PRACTICE This may be an overly cautious approach, but it can mean the difference between an assembly that works and one where errors are frustratingly persistent. If you are careful to approach all parts with the degree-of-freedom analysis in mind such that any newly added mate does not duplicate any of the degrees of freedom that are already tied down, then you will have fewer assembly mate errors and fewer problems with assembly motion.

This means that instead of the traditional three face-to-face Coincident mates, you would have one face-to-face Coincident mate (one translational degree of freedom, two rotational degrees of freedom), one edge-to-face Coincident mate (one translational degree of freedom, one rotational degree of freedom) and one point-to-face Coincident mate (one translational degree of freedom). This accounts for three translational and three rotational degrees of freedom without over-defining any of them.

It is true that SolidWorks internally compensates for over-defined degrees of freedom, but relying on it to do so and then tempting fate by methodically over-defining all assemblies is a risk that you do not have to take, even though it is common practice.

Best bet for motion

The best bet for creating motion in a SolidWorks assembly is to leave open a single degree of freedom. This means that there is only one way the part can move, back and forth, either translation or rotation. Computers in general do not respond well to ambiguity. Dragging an item that may move in several ways is more likely to cause jerky or hesitant motion.

A good example of this kind of problem with motion can be found in one of the sample assemblies that install with SolidWorks. I have included this example on the CD-ROM for your convenience, and it is shown in Figure 13.8. The filename for the assembly is `Plunger.sldasm`.

FIGURE 13.8

An assembly displaying best bet for motion

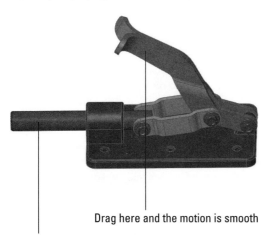

Drag here and the motion is smooth

Drag here and the motion is poor

If you drag the assembly parts from the locations shown in Figure 13.8, the performance varies. This is because when you drag the handle parts, for every position of the handle, there is only one solution for the rest of the parts. However, when dragging the plunger bar, for every position of the plunger bar, there are two possible positions for both the links and the handle (one possibility is as shown, and the other would be with the handle interfering with the base of the assembly). This kind of ambiguity causes problems in SolidWorks assemblies such as assemblies that have open degrees of freedom but will not move or move in a jerky fashion.

Another example of difficulties related to open degrees of freedom and motion is shown in Figure 13.9. The grippers at the end of the arm move when the rest of the arm moves, but the grippers cannot be independently controlled. To fix this problem, you may want to either use the Fix/Float option (available through the right-mouse button menu), or use configurations with mates suppressed or unsuppressed. Fix the part that you want to remain stationary closest to the part you want to move. Remember to Float the part when you are done. Be aware also that fixing a part may over define some mates. You can open this assembly from the CD-ROM, in the filename called `Chapter 13 Robot Assembly.sldasm`.

FIGURE 13.9

A robot arm assembly with degree-of-freedom conflicts

Working with Advanced and Mechanical Mate Types

Advanced and Mechanical mate types greatly expand the number of ways that you can put parts together into assemblies. Advanced mate types include the following:

Advanced mates:

- Symmetric
- Width
- Path Mate
- Linear Coupler
- Limit

Mechanical mates:

- Cam
- Hinge
- Gear
- Rack and Pinion
- Screw
- Universal Joint
- Belts and Chains

You can access Advanced and Mechanical mates by expanding the corresponding panels on the Mate PropertyManager shown in Figure 13.1.

 I have not spent any time explaining the standard mates. If you understand sketch relations, the mate relations fall into place easily. One exception to this is the Lock mate. Lock is different than Fix. Fix pins a part to the background. The Lock mate locks two parts to one another, so that they always maintain the same relationship to one another, regardless of how they move with respect to other parts. This section goes into some detail on all of the advanced and mechanical mates, with a brief example of each.

Symmetric mate

The Symmetric mate works a lot like the Symmetry relation in sketches, except that a plane is used as the plane of symmetry instead of a construction line. Figure 13.10 shows a Symmetric mate being applied to the gripper jaws. The Symmetric mate is listed in the Advanced Mates pane of the Mate PropertyManager.

Cam mate

The Cam mate creates a special instance of either the Coincident or Tangent mate. Four conditions exist with the Cam mate:

- **Coincident.** Vertex on the follower mated to a cam that is created from a single closed-loop face (spline, circle, ellipse).
- **Tangent.** Cylindrical or planar face mated to a cam that is created from a single closed-loop face.
- **CamMateCoincident.:** Vertex on the follower mated to a cam that is created from multiple faces. This condition enables the follower to go all the way around the cam, not stopping at the broken faces or following the extension of a single face.
- **CamMateTangent.** Cylindrical or planar face mated to a cam that is created from multiple faces. This condition enables the follower to go all the way around the cam, not stopping at the broken faces or following the extension of a single face.

FIGURE 13.10

Applying a Symmetric mate

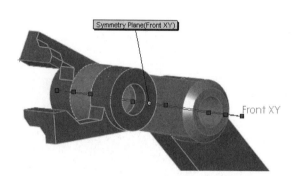

Figure 13.11 shows both single-face and multi-face cams, along with the Cam Mate interface. The two assemblies are available from the CD-ROM in the file named `Chapter 13 Cam.sldasm`.

FIGURE 13.11

Using Cam mates

If you open the assemblies and spin the cam plate, you will notice that in both cases, the flat follower does not work very well. In fact, in the single face cam assembly, it does not work at all.

NOTE Barrel (cylindrical) cams cannot use the Cam mate to create cam motion, but they do work with the Path mate.

Width mate

The Width mate is often used as a replacement for the Symmetric mate in situations where parts are modeled with some tolerance, and have a gap rather than touching face to face. The Width mate requires two pairs of faces to be selected, and works particularly well when a part has to be spaced evenly between two faces and there is no mid-plane; for example, when a square key is placed in a square keyway that is somewhat larger than the key. If a mid-plane is available, the Symmetric mate may be a better option, or at least a faster one to mate given the Symmetric mate only requires two faces and a plane. Figure 13.12 shows a good application for a Width mate as well as the PropertyManager interface for the mate.

FIGURE 13.12

Applying a Width mate

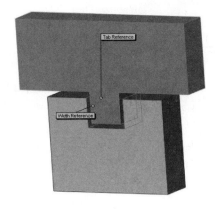

Gear mate

The Gear mate enables you to establish gear type relations between parts without making the parts physically mesh. You can also apply gear ratios and directions without physical connections, so that you can have a shaft in and a shaft out of a black-box transmission. You can open the assembly shown in Figure 13.13 from the CD-ROM. It is named Chapter 13 Gear Mate.sldasm. To see the effect of the mate, open the assembly and rotate the parts. Then edit the mate and change the ratio and direction. The selection for the Gear mate is just two cylindrical faces.

FIGURE 13.13

Applying a Gear mate

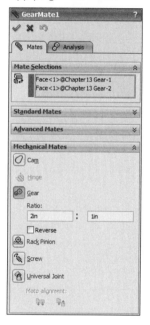

Rack and Pinion mate

The Rack and Pinion mate takes rotational motion of one part and turns it into translational motion for a second part. Again, the parts do not need to be physically connected and can be simple representations of the actual geometry that is needed to drive the motion in the real world. Figure 13.14 shows an assembly that uses the Rack and Pinion mate. You can find this assembly on the CD-ROM with the filename `Chapter 13 RackPinionMate.sldasm`.

FIGURE 13.14

Applying a Rack and Pinion mate

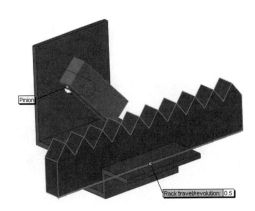

On the CD-ROM, open the assembly named Chapter 13 Robot Limit Mate.sldasm. Drag the Robot Tower part. Notice that it only rotates within a limited angle. LimitAngle2 is the mate that is driving this motion.

Limit mates

You can apply limits to distance and angle mates in order to allow the parts to move within a certain range of values. Figure 13.15 shows the PropertyManager interface for the Limit Angle mate. Limit mates accept zero and negative values that are not normally accepted for dimensions in SolidWorks. When used properly, Limit mates can be an extremely powerful tool for creating more realistic motion in assemblies.

FIGURE 13.15

The Limit Angle PropertyManager

Screw mate

The Screw mate functions just the way the name suggests. For every revolution of a part relative to another part, the part moves in a linear direction by a specified amount. This mate requires two cylindrical faces, and a pitch value, as shown in Figure 13.16.

FIGURE 13.16

Setting up a Screw mate

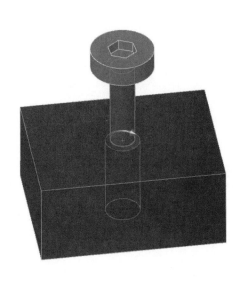

Screw mates can be handy for lead screw animations. I would probably not recommend them for general modeling, but for animations, they are a fantastic addition to the mate toolbox.

Path mate

The Path mate is the one that makes complex barrel cam motion possible, as well as other types of path driven motion. Another application for this mate type beyond barrel cams is for the motion of a camera in a fly-through animation. The Path mate requires a point or vertex on one part and a curve selection in a second part. The path selection, if it is not just a single sketch or curve entity, requires the use of the SelectionManager, which allows you to select multiple end-to-end entities to form closed or open paths. Figure 13.17 shows the setup for a Path mate.

NOTE On the barrel cam in Figure 13.17, notice that a sketch point is being driven along the path. In reality, this does not exactly reflect the motion of the follower around the cam surface. The Path mate does not take into account the tangent contact point between the surfaces; it simply drives the point along the curve. There is a slight amount of error in this scenario, such that the leading or trailing surface of the follower will interfere with the cam, depending on the angle of the cam surface.

FIGURE 13.17

Setting up a Path mate

Linear Coupler mate

The Linear Coupler mate relates the motion of one part in one direction to another part in either the same or a different direction. You can also apply a ratio between the motions. The directions do not have to be parallel or anti-parallel; they can be at right angles, or at any angle. The mate only controls motion in one direction, so other directions are free to move.

This mate can be used to simulate symmetric motion, or geared motion without modeling the rest of the detailed mechanism. Figure 13.18 shows the setup for this mate.

Chapter 4 has a tutorial that discusses the Belt/Chain functionality as it relates to sketch blocks. The functionality using solid parts as pulleys and sprockets is very similar. You can initiate the Belt/Chain function from a toolbar button on the Assembly toolbar or through the menus at Insert ➪ Assembly Feature ➪ Belt/Chain.

FIGURE 13.18

Setting up a Linear Coupler mate

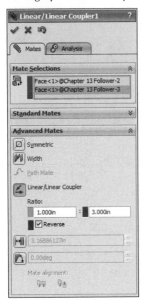

Hinge mate

The Hinge mate is just a shortcut for making a Concentric and a Coincident mate, but it does it all in a single feature, in a single interface. Figure 13.19 shows the PropertyManager interface for the Hinge mate.

Belt/Chain

The Belt/Chain assembly feature is not technically a standalone mate type, but it uses mates to accomplish its task. The Belt/Chain feature can be used in two ways: to create relationships between sketch blocks or to create relations between parts. This feature also creates a sketch and a solid part representing the belt or chain.

FIGURE 13.19

Setting up a Hinge mate

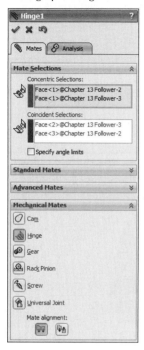

Editing and Troubleshooting

You should become proficient with editing and troubleshooting assembly mates. If you are not comfortable with repairing and modifying mates, then you may find assemblies frustrating to work with; as a result, you may avoid making changes to your assemblies. However, once you master the techniques, you will be less afraid of errors and more confident and willing to experiment with assembly changes.

Editing existing mates

If you are editing just one mate, then you can simply right-click it and select Edit Feature (or left-click and click the Edit Feature button if you are using Context Toolbars). Remember that you can find mates in places other than the Mates folder at the bottom of the assembly FeatureManager; most notably, you can find them in folders under the parts that they are mating together.

You can make several types of changes to mates, including changing the selections, the mate types, and the mate alignment. These types of changes are all shown in Figure 13.20, which displays a mate being edited. The selected faces are highlighted in the graphics window.

FIGURE 13.20

Editing a mate

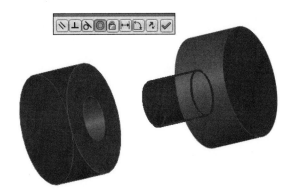

To edit multiple mates consecutively without exiting the Mate PropertyManager, it is best if you pre-select the mates. Pre-selected mates are shown in the Mates panel, as shown in Figure 13.20. You can switch from editing one mate to another by simply selecting the new mate in the Mates panel. If you select only one mate before clicking Edit Feature, but realize later that you want to edit multiple mates, you can select more mates through the FeatureManager.

When mate entities are lost, the mate displays as grayed out, as shown in Figure 13.21. Also shown is a mate that cannot be resolved; for example, a face coincident to two points separated in space. You can repair the missing reference problem by selecting the Invalid reference in the Mate Selections window and then selecting the correct item from the graphics window.

The yellow triangle is a warning symbol that shows that a mate is satisfied, but it is in conflict with another mate that is not satisfied.

FIGURE 13.21

Repairing mates with missing references

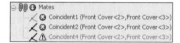 

Troubleshooting

It is best to troubleshoot an assembly mate problem as soon as it appears, and not after it has time to become complicated by other issues. Failed mates also cause performance problems because SolidWorks keeps trying to solve the mates that are in conflict with one another.

Assembly problems often appear to be far larger than they actually are. For example, the entire tree may light up with warnings and error symbols when one extra mate is applied. You can use several approaches to troubleshoot situations like this. In fact, I sometimes purposefully over-define mates just to locate a left-over mate or a mate that is not supposed to be there.

Two types of symbols may help you to distinguish the kinds of errors that are present in different mate features. The yellow triangle that contains an exclamation point is really not an *error*; it is actually more of a *warning*. It tells you that this mate is in conflict with other mates (this symbol is used for a variety of warnings), but that the mate is still satisfied. One of the other mates with which it conflicts is probably not valid, and so this type of warning is usually accompanied by an actual error symbol where the mate is not satisfied.

The red circle containing the X is a failed mate. This is a mate that is in conflict *and* is invalid. If it is also a Coincident mate, then the two Coincident entities are not coincident.

Distinguishing between the warnings and the errors

You can use the following troubleshooting techniques:

- **Last in first out.** When a mate is added that causes warning and error signs to appear throughout the design tree, you can usually correct the problem by removing this last mate.

- **Single elimination.** If you are sure that the last mate added is correct, then you may want to go backwards up the tree starting at the bottom, suppressing individual mates until you find one that causes the warning and error signs to disappear from the tree.

- **Single addition.** It may be easier to take the opposite approach, by suppressing all but the mates that you are sure of, and then gradually unsuppressing mates until the conflict reappears.

- **Suppress a part.** With all of the mates active, try suppressing an individual part to see if this makes a difference. If it does, then unsuppress the part and look at the mates for that part in the Mates folder under the part.

- **Mate Xpert.** The Mate Xpert is an automated routine that creates subsets of groups of conflicting mates. Each subset of mates has one mate that is not satisfied because of the conflict. This may help you to find the cause of the conflict. Figure 13.22 shows the Mate Xpert interface. You can access the Mate Xpert from the right-mouse button menu on mates with errors.

FIGURE 13.22

The Mate Xpert interface

 When a mated part is fixed (using the Fix option), the conflicting mates are automatically suppressed without notifying the user.

Examining Mate Options

The Options pane of the Mate PropertyManager is shown in Figure 13.23. Most of the options are self-explanatory, except for Use for positioning only. This option positions a part but does not apply a parametric mate. Some users make extensive use of this option for various applications where you need the part located precisely, but do not need or want a mate feature in the tree. Positioning parts for Animator animations where the part does not move according to a mate is one example of a use for this option.

FIGURE 13.23

The Options pane of the Mate PropertyManager

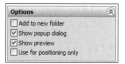

Reviewing Mate Best Practices

Sometimes best practice recommendations can contradict one another, and for each best practice recommendation that you find, there are likely several specific situations where the recommendation is invalid. As a result, you should apply the following recommendations carefully.

- Each assembly should have at least one part that is either fixed or fully mated to the standard planes of the assembly so that it cannot move relative to the assembly.

- You should use fixed parts sparingly. One part that serves as a "ground" for the assembly should be fixed. Other than that, the parts of imported assemblies are sometimes fixed to keep them from being moved accidentally.

- Do not mate to time-dependent features in the assembly tree, or to in-context features in parts. You may want to refer to Chapter 12 for a refresher on time-dependent features in the assembly tree. This can create circular references where the assembly must be rebuilt multiple times to fully resolve the positions of all parts and sketches.

- When possible, it is best to mate all parts to the "ground" part. Creating *daisy-chain* mates (where A mates to B which mates to C, and so on) forces the mates to be solved in a particular order, which may take more time to solve than otherwise. If all of the mates relate to established assembly references, the mates may be more stable. Chapter 11 describes using a skeleton in a part to make sketch and feature relations to. A similar concept can be applied in an assembly, by mating parts to an assembly sketch.

- When possible, leave part positions fully defined, especially when other geometry is dependent upon the position of parts. Some examples include in-context features, assembly features, or assembly-level reference geometry, which are dependent on part geometry.

- Constraining the rotational degree of freedom for components such as screws, washers, and nuts is usually considered excessive. At times, too many open degrees of freedom may cause problems with complex motion, such as a gripper on the end of a robotic arm. SolidWorks functions well when there is a single, well-defined path between two points, but when there are multiple options, the software may become confused.

- Do not leave errors unresolved in the tree.

- Remember to use subassemblies to break up the number of mates that are solved in the top-level assembly.

- Limit the use of flexible subassemblies.

- Do not mate to entities that may be removed later by suppressing or unsuppressing features, especially edges or faces that are created by features such as fillets. For this reason, it is usually best to wait until parts are complete before you use them to create an assembly, although this is rarely practical.

- Use a degree-of-freedom analysis to prevent mates from becoming over-defined.

Tutorial: Mating for Success

In this tutorial, you will put together a model of a robotic arm to better understand some of the mate issues discussed in this chapter. Follow these steps to mate for success:

1. **Open the part named** `Chapter 13 Robot Base.sldprt` **from the CD-ROM.**

2. **In the part document window, click the Make Assembly From Part icon, and click the cursor on the Origin of the assembly to place the part Origin at the assembly Origin.** The part is automatically fixed in place.

 3. **Click Insert ⇨ Component ⇨ Existing Part/Assembly.** Click the Browse button in the PropertyManager, and find the part called `Chapter 13 Robot Tower.sldprt`. This part contains a Mate reference to help you mount it to the base. If you bring the cursor near the big circular hole in the base, you can see the transparent preview of the tower snap into place. Click to accept this placement. Figure 13.24 shows this placement in progress. Notice that the cursor appears as a SmartMate cursor for the peg-in-hole mate. When the part is dropped, check the mate list to confirm that a Concentric and a Coincident mate have been applied by the Mate reference.

FIGURE 13.24

A Mate reference being used to SmartMate a component

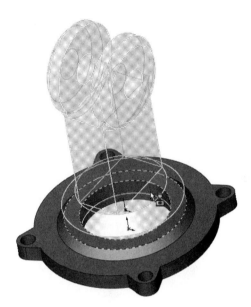

4. **Open the part with the filename** `Chapter 13 Arm.sldprt,` **the Default configuration, in its own window, and click Window⇨Tile Vertically.** The part and the assembly should be open in adjacent windows.

5. **Click the face inside the hole without the chamfer around it in the Arm part, as shown in Figure 13.25.** Then drag it into the assembly to the cylindrical face inside the hole at the top of the Robot Tower part. The concentric SmartMate symbol should appear on the cursor.

6. **Click the green check mark icon to accept the Concentric mate. Move the part to test that the mates are correct.**

7. **Click the Mate tool on the Assemblies toolbar.** Expand the Advanced Mates panel and click the Width mate.

FIGURE 13.25

Displaying a SmartMate when dragging between windows

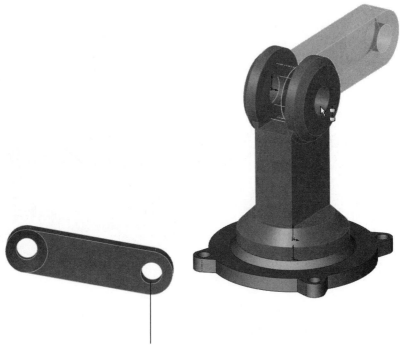

Drag the inner face of the hole

8. **In the Width Selections box, select the two inner faces of the Robot Tower part, and in the Tab selections box, select the outer faces of the Arm part.** The selection should look as shown in Figure 13.26.

9. **Open a Windows Explorer window, and select the following parts: Chapter 13 Robot Arm2 and Chapter 13 Robot Gripper.** Drag these parts into the SolidWorks assembly window, and drop them in a blank space.

10. **Select the chamfered faces of the Arm and Arm2 parts and create a Coincident mate between them.** You can make Coincident mates between conical faces as long as the cones are the same angle. This special case acts like a combination of Concentric and Coincident mates. Figure 13.27 shows the selections and the results.

11. **Create a copy of the gripper part so that there are two instances of it in the assembly.** You can do this by Ctrl+dragging the part within the assembly window, with the Mate PropertyManager closed.

FIGURE 13.26

Creating a Width mate

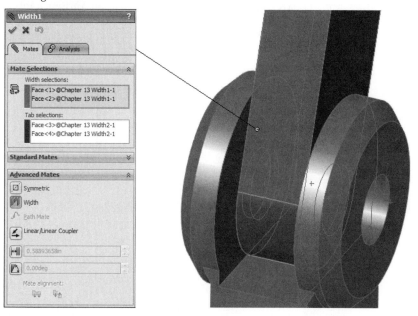

FIGURE 13.27

Making conical faces coincident

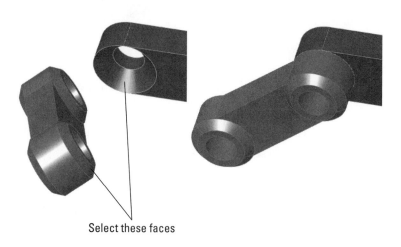

Select these faces

12. **Mate both of the grippers to the Arm2 end using the same mating technique that you used for the previous conical face Coincident part.**

13. **Once you have applied these parts, try moving the various joints of the assembly.** Notice that it is difficult, if not impossible, to isolate the motion of just a single part. This is because there are too many open degrees of freedom, and a lot of ambiguity.

14. **Fix Arm2 to allow you to move the gripper parts as you want.** Create a Symmetric mate between the indicated faces of the grippers and the Front plane of the Arm2 part, as shown in Figure 13.28.

FIGURE 13.28

Creating a Symmetric mate

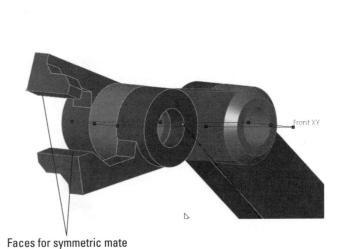

Faces for symmetric mate

15. Practice making angle mates, suppressing mates, and fixing parts to limit motion.

16. Save the assembly and exit the file.

Summary

A thorough understanding of mates, and editing and troubleshooting techniques in particular, makes the difference between a real assembly artist and a user who struggles through or avoids certain tasks. There is a lot about mates that is not simply straightforward, but with practice, you can understand and master them. You can put assemblies together quickly, with a focus on rebuild performance and Dynamic Assembly Motion.

Although best practice concepts should not dominate your designs, they are great guidelines to start from. Watch out for the pitfalls outlined in the section in this chapter that summarizes mate best practices to avoid making big mistakes.

Chapter 14

Assembly Configurations and Display States

Assembly configurations enable you to control many things, including part configurations, suppression, visibility, color, and assembly feature sizes. They also allow you to control assembly layout sketch dimensions, mate values, suppression states, and several other items. What you will learn in this chapter about assembly configurations builds on the information in Chapter 10, which discusses part configurations. In this chapter, you will also learn how design tables are used in conjunction with SolidWorks assemblies.

Display States are a better performance alternative to using configurations to control visibility of parts in assemblies. I discuss Display State options at length in this chapter.

IN THIS CHAPTER

Using Display States

Understanding assembly configurations

Creating exploded views

Tutorial: Working with assembly configurations

Using Display States

Users have always been able to show parts transparent and shaded at the same time, and a common workaround for combining Shaded and Wireframe modes has been to display the parts as Shaded with Edges, but to make some parts completely transparent. This gives the effect of some parts being shown in Wireframe mode. Because of Display States, this workaround is no longer necessary.

Display States also allow you to change between visualization modes more quickly than configurations. Configurations require a lot of data to be saved and accessed for each config, which can cause big delays when switching between configurations, but you can change between Display States almost instantaneously.

Display States and configurations

Display states are independent of configurations. Display states were introduced in 2006, and initially they were dependent upon configurations, so that states had to be copied between configs. In 2008, display states were made independent from configs so all of your display states will control the display of all configs. To control the display, you can use the Display Pane that flies out from the FeatureManager when you click the double-arrow icon in the upper-right corner of the FeatureManager. This is shown in Figure 2.1 in Chapter 2. Figure 14.1 shows the Display Pane in action, along with an assembly showing parts in different Display States.

FIGURE 14.1

The Display Pane and an assembly with parts in different Display States

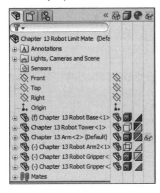

The column symbols for the Display Pane are as follows:

 ■ Hide or Show state of the part

 ■ Display Mode options for each component:

 ■ Appearances

 ■ Transparency

 ■ Default Display

■ Component/Part Color (see Note)

The difference between a component and a part in SolidWorks assemblies is that a component is a generic way of identifying any top-level item in an assembly, and may be a single part or a subassembly. It always refers to a specific instance of the part within the assembly. In the case shown in Figure 14.1, the gripper jaw part is used twice, and so there are two instances of the gripper jaw. One instance has its component color set to yellow, and the other instance uses the part color. (The component color is also referred to as an *override* of the part color). The part color is what you see when you open the part in its own window. The component color is only set in the assembly, and you can only see it in that particular assembly; it never affects how the part displays in any other assembly that the part is shown in.

When there is a difference between the part and component display properties (when an override exists), the component property appears as the upper-left triangle, in the color column of the Display Pane, and the part property appears as the lower-right triangle. You can only see these triangles in the Appearance column.

In addition to this talk of components and overrides, SolidWorks is transitioning to focusing more on what is called the Appearance, which includes RealView materials, colors, and textures, including all of the settings formerly known as Optical Properties.

Appearance overrides are discussed in Chapter 3, but I will briefly summarize it here, showing the lowest priority at the top:

- ■ Part
- ■ Body
- ■ Feature
- ■ Face
- ■ Component

If you override the appearance or display mode for a component in a subassembly, and the upper-left triangle appears in the Display Pane, you can remove the override through either the left-mouse button (LMB) or right-mouse button (RMB) menu. Figure 14.2 shows the LMB menu from a component of a subassembly with overrides.

FIGURE 14.2

You can remove overrides in the Assembly Display Pane.

When you select Clear Override, SolidWorks clears any overrides for the currently selected subassembly component. Clear All Top Level Overrides clears all overrides in all subassemblies in the entire top-level assembly. There is no intermediate option to clear all top-level overrides for a particular subassembly; if you want to distinguish between overrides at that level, you need to clear several individual overrides. The options to remove overrides do not affect top-level components.

The active Display State appears in angle brackets after the configuration name and the filename at the top of the FeatureManager, as shown in the image on the left in Figure 14.3. Display States are created and managed in the ConfigurationManager, in a panel at the bottom of the ConfigurartionManager, as shown in the image on the right in Figure 14.3. To create a new Display State, simply right-click in the Display Pane and choose Add Display State. It seems a little counterintuitive that in the place where you create Display States you cannot see the list of Display States.

FIGURE 14.3

Display States shown in the FeatureManager and the ConfigurationManager

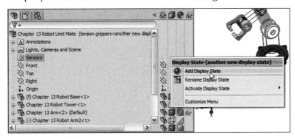

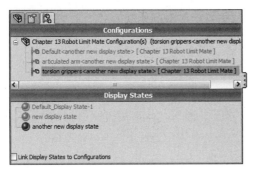

PERFORMANCE Display States offer a huge performance gain over configurations when used to control display of parts. The reason for this is that SolidWorks saves some model information for each configuration. In the past, configurations were sometimes created only for display purposes, and changing them required reading the model geometry again. When a configuration is created only for the purpose of hiding or coloring a part, this takes up a lot of additional file space and CPU time. Display States change much faster than configurations — almost instantaneously — and they add very little file size to use.

Display States and drawings

Display States can be shown on drawings, although the behavior is not perfect. If you only show or hide parts in Display States, you will escape most of the problems. It seems for Display States that change the display mode (wireframe, shaded, and so on) to work properly, you have to set the view itself to Shaded, then select the display state from the PropertyManager for the view. The big catch here is that you have to change the Display State of the parent view, changing the Display State of a projected view does nothing, even though the controls are available. Projected views cannot have a Display State that is independent from the parent view.Drawing views are discussed in depth in Chapter 21.

Understanding Assembly Configurations

Assembly configurations are used for many different purposes, including assembly performance, simplified assemblies, variations of assemblies, assemblies in different positions or states, and many others. Like part configurations, assembly configs also have a few best practice type suggestions. Configuration settings for assemblies control how the assembly appears in a Bill of Materials (BOM), what happens to parts, features, or mates that are added to other configurations, and so on. All of these are discussed in this section.

Configurations for performance

One of the best tools to make large assemblies easier to work with is assembly configurations. You can use several techniques to improve the speed of working with assemblies. Although this information is presented in a list of techniques, it is important to select a method that fits the situation.

Suppressing components and features

The most obvious use of configurations for improving assembly speed is to have a configuration or several configurations with suppressed components. One thing to watch out for when doing this is that configurations are not used in the place of subassemblies. If subassemblies are appropriate for the task, then you should use subassemblies. If not, then you should group and suppress parts using configurations.

> **TIP** Remember that you can use a folder for parts and suppress the folder. If you are just using configurations to hide parts, consider using Display States, given they are more efficient for that purpose. Also remember that Speedpak, discussed in Chapter 12, is a subset of configurations. SpeedPak is a simplified representation, allowing you to select faces and bodies to represent the entire subassembly for performance reasons.

Schemes that you may want to use for suppressing parts need to have configurations that isolate functional areas of an assembly, configs that remove the fasteners or purchased components, configs that remove complex parts, configs that only leave the parts used in in-context relations, configs that suppress patterns and assembly features, assembly configs that use simplified part configs, configs that show the assembly in different positions, or variations of the assembly using different part configurations. So many possible schemes for creating assembly configurations exist that it is pointless to try to list them all. Use your imagination, make sure that it makes sense, and give it a try.

TIP Avoid using fasteners to locate parts. The relationship should go the other way. (Fasteners should be located by the holes in parts.) You should already have in place any parts that the fastener stack will touch before the fasteners are added. If parts added after the fasteners are either mated to the fasteners or the holes are created from the fasteners using in-context techniques, then suppressing the fasteners also suppresses the mates that locate those parts, and will cause problems with any in-context features.

If you suppress the "ground" part or any part that connects groups of parts, keep in mind that this can cause other parts to float in space unattached. Obviously this is not a good situation, and you should avoid it if possible. One way to avoid it is to use an assembly layout sketch and mate the parts to the sketch instead of to the ground part.

Aside from components, other items can also be suppressed to improve performance, such as assembly features and component patterns. Do you really need to see all of those parts patterned around the assembly to work on it in a simplified representation? You may be able to suppress the parts. If you feel that you cannot suppress parts, then consider at least using Display States to hide parts that are needed to complete the parametrics but do not need to display.

PERFORMANCE The biggest killer of assembly speed is the dreaded circular reference. You can make circular references in a couple of different ways, but they are usually the result of mixing history-based functions (mates, in-context sketch relations, feature references) with non-history-based functions (parts shown in the Assembly FeatureManager). This allows you to create partial or complete loops of references, where A references B, which references A. These are a particular problem with in-context references, which are discussed in more depth in Chapter 16.

Configuring SpeedPaks

One of the nice developments in SolidWorks 2009 is the SpeedPak. SpeedPaks are described in more detail in Chapter 12. A SpeedPak is a configuration that uses only specific faces and bodies to represent an entire assembly, instead of opening all of the parts in the assembly. In fact, a SpeedPak stores the geometry in the assembly file so it doesn't have to open any part files at all.

Part of the reason I mention SpeedPak in the configuration chapter is that it is a form of configuration; another reason is that SpeedPaks are configurable. So you can have top-level assembly configurations that call on subassemblies to use their SpeedPaks. That can be of significant help with very large assembly performance.

Using part configurations for speed

I have discussed simplified part configurations in Chapter 10, and they can consist of configs with cosmetic features such as small fillets and extruded text, or other cosmetic details that are suppressed. Assembly configurations can use different part configurations, which, for example, would enable you to make an assembly config called "Simplified," and in it reference all the Simplified part configurations.

> **TIP** When opening an assembly through the Open dialog box, the Advanced option enables you to open the assembly and create a new assembly configuration that uses part configurations of a given name, if available. The default part configuration name entered in the text box is, I think, suggestive of how SolidWorks intended for this function to be used. As shown in Figure 14.4, it is "Simplified." In previous versions, the Advanced button was conspicuously placed on the front of the Open dialog, but by 2009 it has been changed to a selection cleverly hidden in the list of configurations, as shown in the image of the configuration drop-down list.

Other special operations for assembly configurations in the Open dialog box include creating a new configuration that has all the components suppressed. This allows you to see the structure of the assembly without fully resolving all of the components. Another option is to open the assembly with a new configuration, where all the components are resolved. Beyond that, the Open dialog box also allows you to select a specific configuration to open to so that you do not have to wait for the last saved config to load and then make the change.

FIGURE 14.4

The Advanced option for assemblies in the Open dialog box

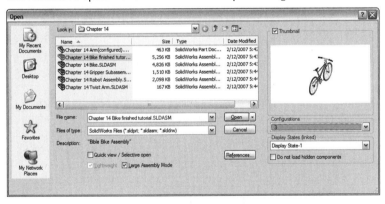

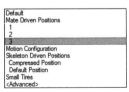

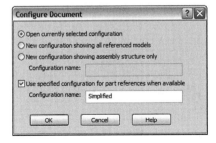

Advanced Component Selection

The Advanced Component Selection dialog box was formerly called Advanced Show/Hide Components. It is shown in Figure 14.5. You can access this dialog box by right-clicking the configuration name in the ConfigurationManager, and selecting Advance Select.

The Advanced Component Selection dialog box

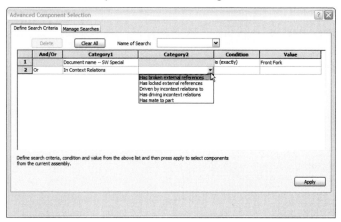

This tool enables you to establish search criteria and show or hide parts, based on the criteria. Multiple criteria can be used, stored, and retrieved. This tool is generally underused, and in my experience, users are always surprised to find it in the software. It has been there since about 1998, having undergone a face lift in the last two releases. The Category 1 options enable you to search on things like document name, in-context status, part mass, and several other standard SolidWorks info. Category 2 can be either custom property info or structured options for Category 1 such as specific in-context conditions.

Isolate

Isolate works like the inverse of the Show command. If you select multiple parts and click Isolate from the right-mouse button menu, the selected parts remain shown, and everything else becomes hidden. A little pop-up gives you the option of showing the removed components in a Wireframe or Transparent display mode, or of saving the current display as a new Display State. This is a very useful function, as shown in Figure 14.6.

FIGURE 14.6

The Isolate function

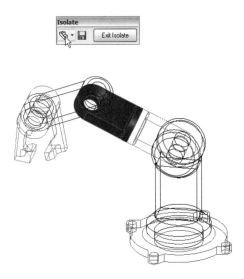

SolidWorks Utilities Simplify Assembly

If you have the SolidWorks Office bundle or higher, then you can activate the Utilities add-in. You can do this by selecting Tools ⇨ Add-ins, and then turning on Utilities. This displays a Utilities menu with the Simplify option. The Simplify Assembly tool is shown in action in Figure 14.7. This tool shows up in the Task pane (right side of the screen). It has recently been updated so if you have not seen it in a while, you may want to check it out again.

The Simplify Assembly tool can find features in the parts of the assemblies that are under a certain size or that take up less than a certain percentage of the volume of the part. You can then suppress these features in special derived configurations.

Controlling display performance

Overall, SolidWorks performance is split into two categories: CPU (central processing unit) processing and GPU (graphics processing unit) processing. This is essentially the difference between calculating the parametrics and geometry, as opposed to the graphics and display. Which of these functions your computer performs better can vary widely, depending on your hardware, drivers, and system maintenance, among other factors.

FIGURE 14.7

The Simplify Assembly tool

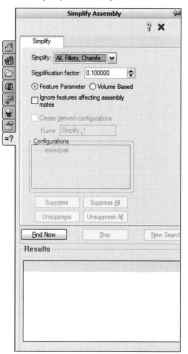

When trying to speed up the performance of an assembly, the biggest impact is obviously made if you can reduce the load on both the CPU and the GPU. You can do this by suppressing a part. When a part is suppressed, it is neither calculated nor displayed, and so the load on each processor for that part is zero.

When you hide a part, its parametric features are still calculated by the CPU; however, because the part is hidden, it creates no load on the GPU. If you have a good main processor and a questionable video card, then you will achieve a greater benefit from removing graphics load from your display.

Lightweight parts

On the other hand, if you want to still show a part but not calculate any of its parametric relations, you should use Lightweight parts. You can find Lightweight default settings in Tools ➪ Options, on both the Assemblies and Performance pages. You can make parts lightweight through the right-mouse button menu. The opposite of Lightweight is Resolved. *Resolved* means that the part is fully loaded, its parametrics are loaded and calculated by the CPU, and its graphics display data is calculated and shown by the GPU.

To summarize this section, there is a four-way relationship between the Resolved, Lightweight, Hidden, and Suppressed states, as shown in Figure 14.8.

FIGURE 14.8

The relationship between the Resolved, Lightweight, Hidden, and Suppressed states

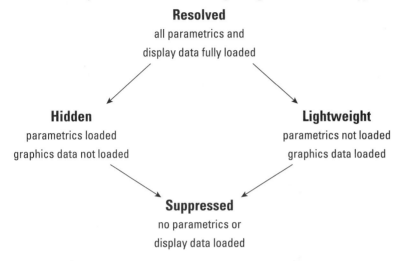

Resolved
all parametrics and
display data fully loaded

Hidden
parametrics loaded
graphics data not loaded

Lightweight
parametrics not loaded
graphics data loaded

Suppressed
no parametrics or
display data loaded

Resolved versus unsuppressed

The terminology becomes a little convoluted here because of the relationship between the four different states. In parts, the feature states are easy to remember because features can be either suppressed or unsuppressed. However, in assemblies, there are four states instead of two, and so *unsuppressed* could mean anything that is not suppressed, which still leaves three states. For this reason, *resolved* is used instead of *unsuppressed* when dealing with components in an assembly.

Configurations for positions

When you use configurations to display an assembly in various positions, you can do it a couple of ways: by changing mates or by changing a layout sketch. Mates are configurable in two ways: mates can be suppressed and unsuppressed, and angle and distance mate values are configurable in the same way that sketch dimensions are configurable. Although creating a mate scheme that enables you to reposition the assembly using mate suppression states and values is essential to this method, it may not be the best approach.

Using a skeleton or layout sketch to mate parts to may be a better approach, although this also has its drawbacks. If you mate to a layout sketch, you cannot make use of Dynamic Assembly Motion. If you use the mate scheme discussed previously, this generally means having a fully defined assembly, and this also does not allow for Dynamic Assembly Motion.

As a compromise, a good way to handle this is by using one configuration for Dynamic Assembly Motion, with one or more open degrees of freedom. You can use other configurations to fully define the mechanism and show it in particular positions using either method. Probably the best way to demonstrate this is with an example using the robot arm assembly.

Positioning with mates

First, take a look at positioning with mates. On an assembly such as this one, the goal is to position the grippers. You can do this a couple of ways, both directly and indirectly. In the assembly used for this chapter, the grippers have been rebuilt as a subassembly, which allows different types of control. Notice that the subassembly has a configuration for the closed position and one that allows Dynamic Assembly Motion. Also, the subassembly is being solved as Flexible. Figure 14.9 shows the assembly and the FeatureManager.

The assembly used for this example

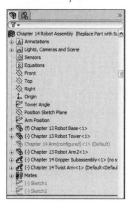 

Driving the position directly

A sketch point has been added to the subassembly to precisely identify the point on the gripper that is to be positioned. Sketch points have also been added to the main assembly to represent parts that need to be picked up by the robotic arm.

Check the derived configurations under the default config. Notice that when you switch between certain configurations, the parts seem to separate. Moving one of the links causes the parts to snap back together again. This is probably because there are so many options when moving between configurations that the software has difficulty choosing a final position. This is definitely one of the potential problems when using configured mates to show an assembly in various positions.

Notice also that although the grippers are positioned correctly, the arm is still allowed to swivel around the intended target point. You can correct this by defining an orientation for the grippers for each location. If an additional pivot were added to the assembly, then fully defining the parts would become more difficult. The arm would not be able to reach any additional points, but it would not be so limited in orienting the grippers at each point.

Driving the position indirectly

You can also use mates to drive configured positions of the assembly using a series of angle mates. This makes it more difficult because to get to a particular location, you have to do some calculations, but the angle mates appear to be more stable than simply relying on moving the parts to unconstrained positions.

If you cycle through the derived configurations under the Indirect top-level configuration, notice that mates are not suppressed and unsuppressed, rather the values are changed. This makes it somewhat more difficult to precisely position the grippers, but because it is specific about the positions of the individual parts, there is no ambiguity.

Positioning with sketches

Although this technique still uses mates to position the parts and to change the position, you change sketch dimensions rather than mate values. Sketches used to drive parts from an assembly are sometimes called *layout sketches* or *skeletons*. I also discuss them in Chapter 16 for in-context or top-down assembly techniques and Chapter 11 as a way of controlling parent/child relationships. Figure 14.10 shows the same assembly that is used for the rest of this chapter.

FIGURE 14.10

Positioning assembly components with sketches

This particular assembly is driven by two sketches on different planes to govern the position of the parts. Keep in mind that this assembly has been used for all of the other techniques as well, and so all of these techniques can exist together simultaneously, being controlled by configurations.

Examine the assembly to see how the parts are mated to the sketches. This is important. The first time you create a part such as this, you may be tempted to mate part planes to the sketch lines.

CAUTION   Mating planes to sketch lines has a very serious drawback that you must be aware of. Unlike other types of mates, which have an alignment that you can control, plane-to-sketch line mates cannot be aligned. This means that the software is as likely to align elements correctly as incorrectly on any plane-to-line mate.

BEST PRACTICE   A better way to mate part planes to sketch lines is to mate the Temporary Axes through the joints with the sketch endpoints. This solves the alignment problem.

Configurations for product variations

In this case, *product variations* means variations in size or part replacement. Some examples are a 4-foot cabinet and an 8-foot cabinet, or a two-button mouse and a three-button mouse.

As a simple example, Figure 14.11 shows the familiar robotic arm assembly, but with a variation: one of the arms has been replaced with a subassembly. The subassembly is made of the original replaced part using configurations, and there are configurations of the subassembly, which is again being used as a flexible subassembly.

FIGURE 14.11

A part that is replaced by a subassembly

Through the course of this chapter, the robot arm assembly has greatly increased in complexity, but it has retained the original information that was in the first version. Maintaining valid assembly data through manually managed configurations is difficult, and all it takes is a simple mistake to wipe out a lot of assembly configuration data. Appropriately, the next section discusses assembly design tables.

Design tables for assembly configurations

Chapter 10 dealt with part configurations and created a good framework for design tables in general. This chapter augments that information with what you need to know to use design tables effectively in assemblies.

Assembly design tables can do everything that part design tables can do, except for selecting configurations of base parts and split parts, which are not valid assembly functions. Assembly design tables can also do some things that a part design table cannot. These include:

- Suppressing the state of a part (R for Resolved or S for Suppressed)
- Assigning the component configuration for the assembly config
- Allowing you to activate the Never Expand in BOM option

If you have been using design tables for a while and are familiar with older versions, then you may have noticed that the $show parameter, which specified whether the part was shown or hidden, has become obsolete due to the new functions of Display States.

Figure 14.12 shows the design table that results from auto-creation using the robot arm assembly. Some of the columns have been hidden to make it small enough to fit on the page. If you want to see the entire table, you need to open the assembly. If you edit the design table, then you will probably want to use the Open in Separate Window option, which is easier to navigate and control.

FIGURE 14.12

An auto-created design table from the robot arm assembly

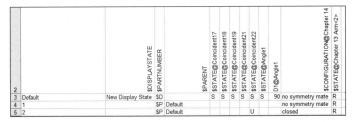

Assembly configuration dos and don'ts

Assembly configurations have some potential pitfalls that you can avoid of you pay attention to some of these dos and don'ts.

- Avoid using Delete as an editing option when working with configurations. Delete is forever and for all configs.
- Avoid the use of in-context relations to size parts when you are also using configurations to size parts. A non-configured part driven by a configured part only causes confusion.

- Avoid using configurations to represent document control type revisions. I have seen people attempt to do this, but in the end, it limits the kinds of edits you can make to your parts and assemblies, and it is far too easy to make a mistake that wipes out all of your diligence. In the end, this is not a viable technique.

- If you are working with manually created configs, then you should create a new configuration and activate it before making the changes. Otherwise, you will end up trying to set the original config back to the way it was.

- Remember to select the This Configuration Only option for changed dimensions, instead of leaving it at the default All Configurations setting.

Creating Exploded Views

Exploded views enable you to display an assembly taken apart so that you can see all of the parts. They are great for assembly documentation, assembly instructions, and for visualizing assemblies with concealed internal parts.

I have included exploded views in the assembly configurations chapter because, like Display States, exploded views are found in the ConfigurationManager under the configuration. Each config can have only a single exploded view with multiple steps, and you can copy exploded views between configurations.

When you are creating the exploded view of the top-level assembly, and a subassembly already has one, you can include the subassembly's exploded view in the top-level exploded view. While you are creating exploded views, mates are temporarily suspended.

To initiate a new exploded view, switch to the ConfigurationManager, right-mouse button click a configuration name, and select New Exploded View, as shown in Figure 14.13.

Figure 14.13 also shows the Explode PropertyManager interface. This interface includes a helpful How-To section at the top to give you a hint of where to start. You can initiate Exploded View from an assembly toolbar button or through the right-mouse button menu on a configuration.

FIGURE 14.13

Initiating a new exploded view

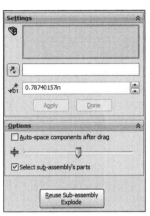

If you are creating assembly instructions or an animation from the exploded view (using SolidWorks Motion or the right-mouse button options, Animate Explode, or Animate Collapse), then you may need to be more careful about *how* the parts are exploded. You can create explode lines that show how the parts go back together.

To begin, you can explode the Base and the Tower down and back, respectively. A single part can explode in multiple directions, or multiple parts can explode in a single direction. These two parts are shown exploded in Figure 14.14. Select the base, and then drag the arrow of the Triad that moves in the direction that you want the part to move.

FIGURE 14.14

Exploding the base

The Tower part is a little more difficult because it is not lined up with the direction in which it needs to be exploded. To remedy this, highlight the Direction box in the PropertyManager and select a face that is normal to the direction that you want to drag, or an edge that is in this direction. Then drag the appropriate arrow on the triad again, as shown in Figure 14.15.

TIP SolidWorks Help says that you can drag the sphere of the triad onto a face to change the direction, rather than selecting a face in the Direction box. However, it fails to mention that you have to hold down the Alt key while dragging it in order for it to stick to an entity.

Exploding the Twist Arm subassembly provides the opportunity to show a couple of useful subassembly functions. You can explode the parts of a subassembly either together as a unit or individually. You can even reuse explode steps from the subassembly, which is what you will do here.

FIGURE 14.15

Changing the direction of the explode

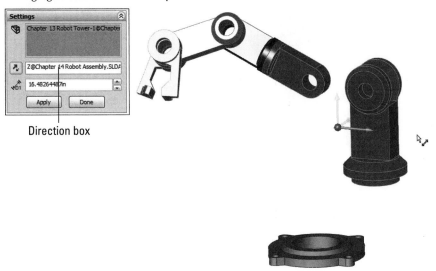

Direction box

To explode the subassembly as a single part and then reuse its explode steps from the subassembly file, ensure that the Select sub-assembly's parts option is off, as shown in Figure 14.16.

CAUTION You cannot reuse a subassembly's explode steps if the subassembly is set to Flexible. SolidWorks will tell you that there are no explode steps to reuse if you try to reuse the explode steps of a flexible subassembly. In order to work around this, you can set the subassembly to solve as Rigid, reuse the explode steps, and then set the subassembly back to Flexible. Although awkward, this is an effective workaround to this problem.

TIP While exploding the parts, you should rotate the view from time to time. Unless you are creating the explode for a particular point of view, the explode may look very different if you rotate it a little.

For the final explode step, the grippers will explode individually in opposite directions. Remember that these parts belong to another subassembly. If you create an explode step with the Select sub-assembly's parts option turned off or on, you will not be able to change it later, and so you need to pay careful attention to what you are doing.

FIGURE 14.16

Exploding a subassembly

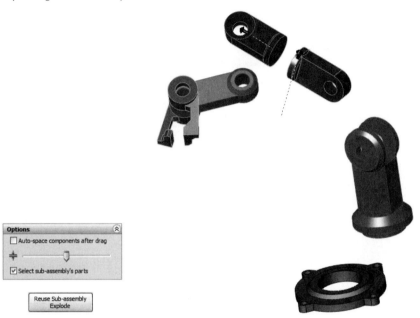

Turn on the Select sub-assembly's parts option, select one gripper, Alt+drag the triad to set the direction, and then drag the distance of the explode. If you are in the mood to submit an enhancement request to SolidWorks, then you may want to request a Symmetrical Explode function for situations such as this. Figure 14.17 shows the finished result of the explode.

You may have noticed that each explode step creates a dashed line to show where the explode came from. Unfortunately, these dashed lines cannot be turned into usable explode lines on documentation. You must create explode lines manually, using 3D sketches. Although 3D sketches can be very tricky to use, for this purpose, you can limit their function to simple straight lines. As long as you try for simple results, the Explode Lines feature should work well.

Before I begin to discuss the Explode Lines feature, I'll take a minute to look at the terminology, which can be confusing. For example, the opposite of *explode* is *collapse*. Unfortunately, the opposite of *expand* is also *collapse*, and so when the assembly is exploded and you want to collapse it, the right-mouse button menu on the Exploded View displays one entry called Collapse and another called Collapse Items. You must remember that *Collapse Items* refers to expanded ConfigurationManager lists, while *Collapse* refers to un-exploding the Exploded View.

FIGURE 14.17

The finished explode

Another example is that the PropertyManager and Tooltips call the function *Route Line* (which can be easily confused with a function of the SolidWorks Routing software), but on the toolbar and menu, it is referred to as *Explode Sketch*. Further, the tool that you use to start the Explode Sketch function is on the Explode Sketch toolbar itself, and does not seem to exist on any other toolbar. You must access it from the Insert menu, by selecting the command called Explode Line Sketch. Figure 14.18 shows some examples of the above-mentioned terminology.

FIGURE 14.18

Interface and terminology inconsistencies in the exploded view and Explode Line functions

 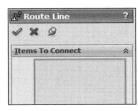 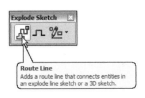

To initiate the Explode Line Sketch function, you can select Insert ➪ Explode Line Sketch. This displays the Explode Sketch toolbar and the Route Line PropertyManager interface. Creating nice

explode lines takes a little practice, but it is easiest with circular parts, or circular features on parts with other shapes. Selecting circular edges makes the line start from the center of the circle.

If after you have selected two circular edges, the explode line goes the wrong way, you can click the arrow at the start of the line. Notice in Figure 14.19 that the line seems to take an unnecessarily circuitous route. This is because the explode directions were not square to the assembly Origin. To work around this problem to some extent, you can deselect the Along XYZ option in the Route Line PropertyManager. You can move the jogs by bringing the cursor close to the line, and selecting the arrows that pop up.

FIGURE 14.19

Redirecting explode lines

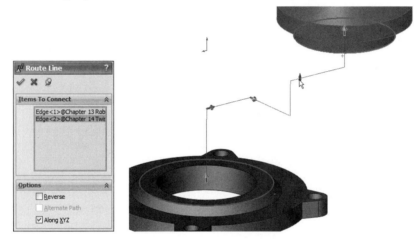

 If you need to route an explode around other lines or parts, you can use the Jog Line in the explode sketch.

Figure 14.20 shows the difference between using the Along XYZ option (image to the left) and turning it off when the explode was not square to the assembly Origin (image to the right). The completed explode lines are shown in Figure 14.21.

FIGURE 14.20

The Along XYZ option, selected and deselected

FIGURE 14.21

Completed explode lines

You can animate the explode or collapse from the right-mouse button menu. To do this, right-click the exploded view, and select Animate Explode or Animate Collapse. This method does not offer recording or Photoworks rendering like Animator software, but it is fast and easy. You cannot see explode lines during an animation.

Tutorial: Working with Assembly Configurations

To begin this tutorial, open the assembly named `Chapter 14 Bike.sldasm`. This assembly is made from the same parts as the assembly that was used in Chapter 12, but it will be used differently here. This file contains all of the aspects that you need to work with in this chapter, including subassemblies, motion, and part configurations.

To learn how to work with assembly configurations, follow these steps:

1. **Prepare to use configurations by splitting the FeatureManager window into an upper and lower pane.** Place the FeatureManager on the top and the ConfigurationManager on the bottom.

2. **Before starting to make changes to this assembly, add the top-level configurations that you will need, as follows:**

   - Small Tires
   - Motion Configuration
   - Skeleton Driven Positions
   - Mate Driven Positions

   The configurations will list alphabetically.

3. **Make sure that the Advanced options for each configuration are set to Suppress New Features And Mates and Suppress New Components.**

4. **Activate the Small Tires configuration.** Figure 14.22 shows the FeatureManager up to this point.

5. **Open the Front Wheel Assembly in its own window and switch to the ConfigurationManager.** Add a configuration called Small Tires, and change the tire to the configuration called Small Tire, which has already been created.

6. **Switch back to the main assembly window (using Ctrl+Tab), right-mouse button click the Front Wheel Assembly in the FeatureManager, and select Component Properties.** Select the Small Tire configuration for the Front Wheel assembly, as shown in Figure 14.23.

7. **Repeat Steps 4 to 6 for the Rear Wheel assembly.**

8. **Double-click another configuration from the list and watch the assembly change from small to fat tires.**

FIGURE 14.22

The FeatureManager and ConfigurationManager up to Step 4

9. **Change to the Motion configuration.** right-mouse button click the Stem-Fork assembly, select Component Properties, and set the assembly to be solved as Flexible.

10. **Exit the dialog box and check to see that the fork linkage mechanism moves by dragging the fork.** Notice that the fork works but that the front wheel does not move with it. The bike design is not yet complete, and so you do not need to worry about that at this point. Putting the front wheel in the fork assembly could be used to make the wheel move with the fork.

11. **Switch to the Skeleton Driven Positions configuration.**

12. **Display the assembly Layout Sketch at the top of the FeatureManager.**

FIGURE 14.23

Changing the tires in the Component Properties dialog box

13. Create two new derived configurations under the Skeleton Driven Positions configuration, one called Default Position and the other called Compressed Position.

14. Activate the Default Position configuration, and make a coincident mate between the Top plane of the Chainstay part and the sketch line indicated in Figure 14.24. Again, the wheel does not move at this time.

15. Activate the Compressed Position configuration and make a coincident mate between the same plane and the line that is angled up at 10 degrees.

NOTE For these configs you also need to set the Advanced options just as you set the top-level configs in Step 3. If you do not do this, you may need to manually suppress the unwanted mates in the appropriate configurations.

16. Switch to the Mate Driven Position configuration. Change the stem-fork assembly to a flexible subassembly (right click, Component Properties, Solve as Flexible).

17. Add new derived configurations called 1, 2, and 3. While creating the new configs, ensure that the Suppress new features and mates and Suppress new components options are selected. Leave the 1 configuration activated.

18. Make an angle mate between the Bike assembly Top plane and the face of the link, as shown in Figure 14.25. When you do this, do not be surprised if the fork suddenly flies off to an unexpected location. This appears to be a bug with how SolidWorks 2009 (prerelease 2) handles flexible subassemblies. If you press Ctrl+Q, the fork will go back where it belongs.

FIGURE 14.24

Positioning the rear of the bike

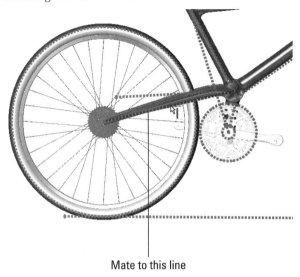

Mate to this line

FIGURE 14.25

Using angles to position the fork

19. Once the mate is complete, double-click the angle dimension (you may have to double-click the angle mate to get it to display and then zoom out to see it), and change the value to 18 degrees. Again, with the change the fork may fly to an unexpected location. Pressing Ctrl-Q brings it back.

20. Switch to the 2 configuration, unsuppress the angle mate made in Step 18 and change the value to 25 degrees. You may have to change the 2 configuration to Flexible, although it should inherit this property from the parent config.

> **NOTE** You need to set the Fork assembly to solve as Flexible for each configuration.
> You may also need to control the alignment for the angle mate manually for each
> configuration.

Summary

Display States in the assembly can save you a lot of time because they change faster than configurations and offer more options for visualization, including mixed display modes.. Assembly design tables can select Display States and drive many other parameters in assemblies.

The Exploded View functionality in SolidWorks has some unusual aspects that you need to work around; however, it is a valuable and useful function, and is worth the extra steps. Assembly configurations are a very powerful tool for product variations and performance, especially when combined with SpeedPak.

Chapter 15

Component Patterns

I n SolidWorks assemblies, the word component can refer to either parts or subassemblies at the top level of an assembly. Component patterns can therefore be patterns of parts, subassemblies, or combinations of parts and subassemblies.

RFORMANCE For best pattern performance, you should use subassemblies as the patterned unit as much as is practical. Multiple patterns of individual components are not as efficient as a single pattern of multiple components. A single pattern of a single component, where the single component is itself a subassembly, is the best choice, if available.

Another performance issue is the fact that component patterns require external references (for the direction or center of the pattern). These external references have the potential to increase rebuild times if you do not choose them carefully.

Although you can experience possible performance problems with patterns, they can also significantly decrease the number of mates in an assembly, which always improves performance.

Component patterns come in two varieties: local patterns, which include linear and circular patterns, and feature-driven patterns, which are driven by a feature pattern in a part. The local patterns are obviously somewhat limited, but because feature-driven patterns follow patterned features, they can also be driven by sketch-driven patterns. Curve-driven and fill patterns can also be used.

It is possible to focus only on the basics, to simply be able to make patterns that exist in the present moment. However, if you are interested in creating features that will adapt to future changes, then you will find this chapter useful.

Using Local Component Patterns

Local component patterns are limited to linear and circular patterns. The linear pattern directions work just like the linear pattern feature in parts, and must reference a line, axis, edge, and so on to establish the direction. In an assembly, this means that the feature uses model geometry from a part (solid or surface edges, sketches, reference geometry), an assembly sketch entity, or an assembly reference geometry entity (such as an axis). This is important to keep in mind if you are concerned about circular references.

BEST PRACTICE If you have a feature pattern in a part, you should take advantage of it and use a feature-driven pattern instead of a local pattern.

Local pattern references

If you still need to create a local pattern, it is best to use a reference that is not dependent on part geometry. Remember that when part geometry is used for this purpose, the parts must be solved first (sketches and features rebuilt), then the mates must be solved (to position the parts), then any in-context references must be solved (which may change the part geometry), and then any assembly features or component patterns must be solved. As a result, it is best practice to use as pattern direction references assembly sketches that do not reference anything else. The assembly sketches should sit at the top of the assembly FeatureManager to ensure that they are not picking up references from the history-based features in the design tree (mated components, patterns, assembly features, and so on).

When a local pattern really requires a reference from a part, you have no alternative. However, if you can avoid this by using a sketch assembly skeleton to which the parts are mated and also used for the pattern references, then you should do so. At all costs, you should avoid using in-context features, assembly reference geometry that is dependent on part geometry, and assembly features for the local pattern reference.

Figure 15.1 shows a sample organization of one way that you can set up an assembly to properly control local component patterns. The lines shown can be created in either two 2D sketches or a single 3D sketch. The lines are dimensioned from planes, which allows them to be angled for patterns that are not square to the coordinate system of the assembly, but still lie on its main planes.

In most situations the rebuild time penalty of using model geometry to establish pattern direction is fairly slight. The sketch method is probably most justifiable in large, complex assemblies, or in assemblies requiring long rebuild times. Figure 15.1 also shows the PropertyManager interface for the local pattern.

Notice where the pattern is placed in the FeatureManager. You can reorder the pattern feature in the design tree, but you cannot move it above the mates. Interestingly, you can move the sketches after the pattern, even though the pattern is dependent on one of the sketches. Obviously, SolidWorks is working with the order behind the scenes in such a way that the user cannot make mistakes.

FIGURE 15.1

The Assembly FeatureManager for local component pattern setup

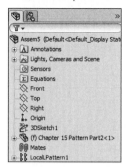

Pattern seed only

All of the aspects of the interface should be familiar, such as the direction, instances, and spacing. The Pattern seed only option is also used in feature patterns.

Patterning the seed only is designed to allow you to create a single pattern in two directions that are separated by 180 degrees, where the internal instances do not overlap one another. For example, if you take a basic two-directional pattern and change the angle between the directions so that they are anti-parallel (parallel but going in opposite directions), then all of the component instances that were between the two legs of the L created by the two directions will come to overlap one another when they are laid out in a straight line.

Figure 15.2 shows how a 5-by-4 pattern with 20 instances becomes a 1-by-8 (the seed is not counted twice) pattern. To be clear, the figure shows a two-direction pattern where the angle between the directions becomes shallower and shallower, until the two directions are parallel or anti-parallel. When this happens, the other 12 instances are overlapping the remaining ones. When you use the Pattern seed only option, you are only patterning the two legs of the L, and not the instances in between. Having parts that overlap can cause problems with Bills of Materials (BOMs) and mass properties due to having duplicate parts.

Instances to Skip

The Instances to Skip option for component patterns, shown in Figure 15.3, works just like the equivalent option for features. Click the dots in the graphics window to toggle each instance of the pattern. On the screen, the instances to keep use pink dots and the instance to skip use orange dots. The colors are almost indistinguishable at a relatively wide spacing.

When to use the Pattern seed only option

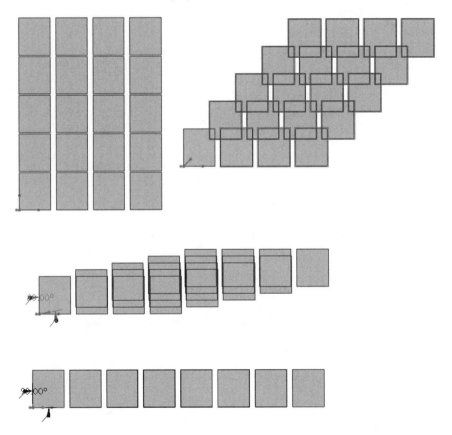

FIGURE 15.3

The Instances to Skip option

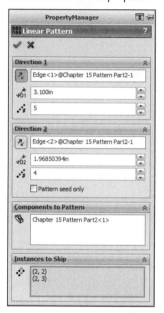
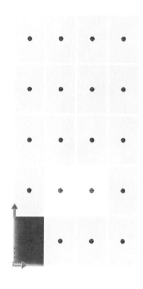

Using Feature-Driven Component Patterns

By their very nature, feature-driven component patterns break some of the best practice suggestions in this book, because the pattern is driven by part geometry, and the part must first be solved
(by solving features internal to the part) and then placed (by solving mates); only then can the feature-driven pattern be solved. Still, I recommend using feature-driven patterns over local patterns
when available because of the parametric link.

NOTE   For the feature-driven component patterns, the location of the initial component is
important. You need to match the placement of the initial component with the position of the original feature from which the pattern was created, not one of the patterned
instances. You can get around this requirement if you use the Select Seed Position option. When
you do this, the feature pattern instances all appear with dots and you can select which instance
to use as the seed. Again, the selected dot is blue and unselected dots are purple, nearly indistinguishable at the size and spacing of the dots. Figure 15.4 shows the PropertyManager interface for a feature-driven component pattern.

You can nest feature-driven component patterns such that one component pattern is patterned by
another component pattern, just like feature patterns. The second pattern can be a local pattern or
a feature-driven pattern.

The feature-driven Component Pattern interface

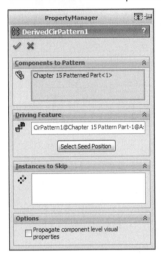
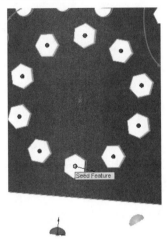

Understanding Other Pattern Options

Figure 15.5 shows the right-mouse button menu for a component pattern.

The component right-mouse button menu

Dissolve Pattern

The Dissolve Pattern option removes the component instances from the pattern feature and puts them in the main part of the assembly FeatureManager. The components just become normal components in the assembly without the intelligence of the pattern feature placing them. The components are left in the assembly without any mates, simply floating in position.

Add to New Folder

You can add patterns to folders. If you have a list of patterns at the end of an assembly, it may make sense to group them into related folders for the purpose of organization. This is the same as using folders for features, mates, or components.

Component pattern display options

You can change the appearance of individual component pattern instances individually or collectively as a pattern feature. Figure 15.6 shows the display pane where you can control these display options.

FIGURE 15.6

The display pane for controlling display options

Component patterns and configurations

Individual instances of the component pattern also enable you to control configurations. After you create the pattern, you can select individual instances and change their configs. This can be extremely useful if you have a mechanism subassembly shown in various positions; for example, patterned around an indexing dial.

Tutorial: Creating Component Patterns

To learn how to create component patterns, follow these steps:

1. **Open a new assembly.** Create a new 3D sketch and draw three lines from the Origin out at odd angles so that they do not pick up horizontal or vertical automatic relations. Draw two of the lines, then rotate the view and press the Tab key and draw the third line.

2. **Apply sketch relations such that each line lies on a plane. One line on the Front, one on the Top, and one on the Right.**

3. **Exit the sketch when you are done.**

4. **Open the part from the CD-ROM named** `Chapter 15 Pattern Part.sldprt.` This part already contains several features so that you can practice using feature-driven component patterns.

5. **Insert the part into a new assembly.** Locate the part at the assembly Origin such that the part Origin matches the assembly Origin.

6. **Open the part called** `Chapter 15 Patterned Part.sldprt,` **and place it in the assembly.**

7. **Place the small part on one of the original feature of the rectangular pattern of round holes near the origin, as shown in Figure 15.7.** All of the original features are colored red. Remember that Alt+dragging the circular edge on the flat side of the part allows you to SmartMate the part to the round holes. It cannot help you with the rectangular or hex holes. For these, it may be best to show the sketch for the holes and place the part with respect to the sketch entities.

8. **Create feature driven patterns (Insert ⇨ Component Pattern ⇨ Feature Driven).** Try to use each of the patterns from the pattern part. For each new pattern, make a copy of the patterned part and place it in one of the holes. Remember the use of the Select Seed Position option to pick a feature pattern instance instead of the original feature.

9. **Once you have created a few feature-driven patterns and have a better understanding of how it is done, right-click the top level of the assembly FeatureManager and select Collapse Items (near the bottom of the menu). The point is just to get practice placing a part and patterning it with an existing feature pattern. The assembly might look like Figure 15.8 when you are done.**

10. **Create a local pattern (Insert ⇨ Component Pattern ⇨ Linear Pattern).** Select one of the sketch lines drawn in Step 1 as a pattern direction.

FIGURE 15.7

Placing the Patterned Part

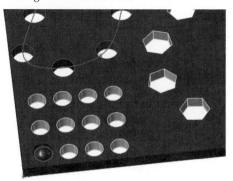

FIGURE 15.8

Several Feature-driven patterns

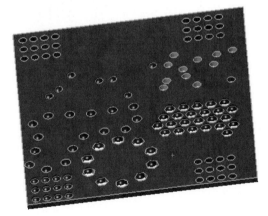

11. Highlight the Components to Pattern selection box. Select the first part in the FeatureManager and then Shift+select the last pattern feature. This patterns everything in the assembly.

12. **Make the spacing four inches with three instances.**

13. **Create a second direction using another of the sketch lines with six-inch spacing and four instances.**

14. **Notice how the preview shows 12 instances of the patterned assembly.** Click the option for Pattern seed only and see how the preview changes to seven instances. Figure 15.9 shows this difference. Click OK to accept the feature.

493

FIGURE 15.9

The difference between 2 direction patterns with and without the Pattern Seed Only option

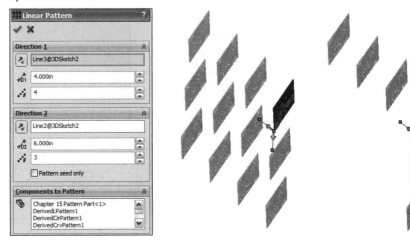

Summary

Performance and best practice are both issues that require compromise. Patterns can cause a performance reduction because of the nature of the references. However, they can also improve performance because the need for extra mates is reduced and it is easier to simplify the assembly by suppressing the pattern feature.

Feature-driven patterns are driven by feature patterns, and transgress best practice suggestions, but they also add a parametric link, which updates the component pattern automatically. They also offer many more options, being driven by the pattern options available to features in a part.

Chapter 16

Modeling in Context

The topic of in-context modeling often lends itself to questionable advice and suggestions based on an incomplete understanding of it or a superstition, even from experienced users. In this chapter, I present best practice suggestions and offer a balanced explanation with each one so that you can evaluate it for yourself. I give you enough facts so that you can decide for yourself if in-context techniques fit into your process.

If you are well disciplined in your modeling practices, and understand the functionality and potential problems of in-context modeling, then you can avoid these problems. However, if you have had one bad experience, you may be still focusing on it, and fail to see the positive side of using in-context modeling. Although dangers *do* exist, they often result from disregarding the rules.

Understanding In-Context Modeling

In-context modeling is also known as *top-down* modeling. It is a technique used to create relationships between two parts in the context of an assembly, where the geometry of one of the parts is controlled by both the other part and the mates that position them relative to one another.

In-context, or top-down, modeling may be contrasted against *bottom-up* modeling. Bottom-up modeling involves making the parts in their own individual windows and assembling the finished parts into an assembly with mates.

In its most common form, a sketch in one part in an assembly is related to another part in the assembly. The relationship is specific to that particular assembly, and is only relevant *in the context of* that assembly. For example, you may create a box and put it into an assembly. You must then create a lid that is parametrically linked to the size and shape of the box. You can create a lid part in the context of the assembly such that the lid always matches the box. Sketch relationships, dimensions, and feature end conditions from the lid can reference the box. When the box changes, the lid also changes *if the assembly is open*.

The assembly maintains a record of each in-context reference. If the box is changed with both the assembly and the top open, then the top updates, but if the box is changed without the assembly being open, then the lid will not update until the assembly is opened. The record of the reference that the assembly maintains is held in what is called an *update holder*, and in recent versions, it is all but forgotten.

CROSS-REF   Chapter 12 discusses in-context reference update holders. These are the pointers in the assembly that hold the reference information. These holders are hidden by default, and do not enable any real functionality, but they do serve as a reminder that the assembly has in-context references, and can be queried to tell you what parts the in-context relations go between.

Advantages of in-context modeling

The advantages of in-context modeling are obvious. I spent the first couple of chapters of this book discussing the strengths of parametric design, and in-context modeling is just an extension of parametric techniques to include parts in the context of an assembly. Making a change to one part and having all related parts update offers indisputable advantages.

Potential problems with in-context modeling

Some issues may arise from the technique of driving changes from a different part model. There are no problems with the *overall concept* of in-context modeling; the problems occur with the *practical application of the technique*. In particular, the biggest problems seem to arise when in-context techniques are combined with other techniques. You must be very careful about file management issues when in-context references exist in your assembly.

Dealing with the Practical Details of In-Context Modeling

Figure 16.1 shows a simple box with the sketch of a simple top for the box. Notice in the FeatureManager that two parts are listed as the Box Top and Box Bottom. The .050-inch offset is creating a sketch in the Top part that is driven by the edges of the Bottom part. This simple assembly demonstrates the in-context process in the sections that follow.

The top of the box being built in-context

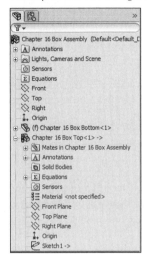

.050

The in-context process

You can perform in-context modeling using one of two basic schemes. You can build parts from the very beginning in the context of the assembly (using the Insert ➪ Component ➪ New Part menu option) or you can start them using bottom-up techniques, creating the parts in a separate part window, adding them to the assembly, and then adding additional in-context features later.

Starting out in-context

To start a new part in the context of an assembly, you will first assume that the assembly contains another part. Creating a new part in a blank assembly is not very interesting. In this case, I am using the assembly shown in Figure 16.1. To create the new part, click Insert ➪ Component ➪ New Part. This command is also available through a toolbar button that you can place on the Assembly toolbar. At this point, SolidWorks prompts you select a face or plane on which to locate the new part. The selected face or plane actually determines the Front plane of the new part, a new sketch is opened on that plane, and an InPlace mate is added to the assembly. In contrast to older versions, you no longer have to name the part immediately; you can choose to save it as an external or internal part the next time you save the assembly. More detail on virtual part functionality is available later in this chapter.

The InPlace mate

The mate that SolidWorks adds automatically when a part is created in-context is called an *InPlace* mate. This works like the Fixed option, but is actually a mate that is listed with the other mates and that may be deleted, but not edited.

The InPlace mate clamps the part down to any face or plane where it is applied. It is meant to prevent the in-context part from moving. I will explain later in this chapter why it is so important for in-context parts not to move. Although the InPlace mate clamps the part down, I have heard people report bizarre behaviors with the InPlace mate reportedly allowing parts to move unpredictably. I do not put much stock in these reports; other things could easily cause this, stemming from operator error instead of broken software. Often the cause turns out to be a user who is not paying attention to what is going on.

Alternative technique

If you are concerned about using the InPlace mate, then I would suggest an alternative technique. Instead of using the Insert ➪ Component ➪ New Part command, you should simply create a blank part and save it to the desired location. You can then insert the existing but blank part into the assembly and mate the three planes to the assembly or to the part, as appropriate. You can then edit the part in-context, the same as if you had created it in-context. The only difference between parts developed this way and parts created in-context is the InPlace mate. The InPlace mate cannot be edited and does not have relations to other geometry in the usual sense. Many people feel more secure with real mates to real geometry, which you can identify and change if necessary.

Valid relations

Sketches, vertices, edges, and faces from the other parts in the assembly can be referenced from the in-context part as if they were in the same part as the sketch. Most common relations are concentric for holes, and coincident for hole centers. Converted entities (On-Edge relations) make a line-on-edge relation between the parts, and Offset sketch relations are also often used.

Other types of valid in-context relations include in-context sketch planes, and end conditions for extrude features such as Up to Face and Up to Body. Beyond that, you can copy surfaces from one part using the Knit Surface feature, or the Offset Surface feature. I discuss surfacing in more detail in Chapter 27.

Working in-context

When you are working in-context or using in-context data, visual cues offer information about the part that you are working on. The following topics are all meant to help you understand what is going on.

Text color

When you are working in-context, the FeatureManager text of the part that you are working on turns blue. This should make it immediately obvious first that you are working in-context, and second, which part is being edited.

Part color and transparency

You can control the color and transparency behavior of parts in the assembly where a part is being edited in-context through the Tools ➪ Options ➪ Colors page. Figure 16.2 shows a detail of this page. Appendix B discusses Tools ➪ Options settings in more detail. The option at the bottom of the dialog determines whether the colors specified in the list at the top are used or ignored. If they are ignored, the parts retain the same colors as if you were not using in-context techniques.

FIGURE 16.2

Part-color settings for in-context control

Setting that control in-context editing colors

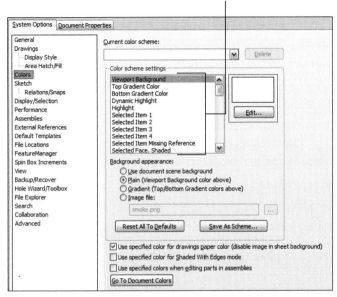

An additional setting in Tools ⇨ Options is found on the Display/Selection pane. Here, you can control the transparency of the parts not being edited. Figure 16.3 shows this setting.

FIGURE 16.3

Part transparency for in-context control

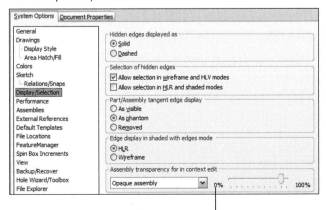

In-context part color transparency control

The options in the Assembly Transparency drop-down list are:

- **Opaque Assembly.** All parts that are not being edited when an assembly component is being edited in-context turn opaque, even if they are otherwise transparent.

- **Maintain Assembly Transparency.** Leaves all assembly components in their default transparency state.

- **Force Assembly Transparency.** Forces all the parts, except for the one being edited in the assembly, to become transparent.

These options reflect personal preference more than anything else, but it is useful to have a reminder as to whether a part is being edited in the assembly or the assembly document is being edited in its own window.

 **TIP**   **The color selected in the box shown in Figure 16.2 controls both the text color and the color of the part shown in the graphics window.**

Edit Component button

 You can use the Edit Component button in two ways. First, after you have created a part in-context, seeing the Edit Component button depressed serves as a reminder that you are editing the part rather than editing the assembly. Along with the part color and transparency displays, this is important because assembly functions such as mates, exploded views, and others are not available when you are editing the part.

Second, you can use the Edit Component button to begin or finish editing a part that is already in an assembly. When you are editing a part in the context of an assembly, the title bar of the SolidWorks window reflects the fact that you are editing a part in an assembly, the toolbar changes to a part-editing toolbar, and the lower-right corner of the taskbar displays the words *Editing Part*, as shown in Figure 16.4.

Third, a confirmation corner image exists in the upper right corner of the graphics window when you are editing a part in the context of the assembly. This makes it easier to exit Edit Component mode.

FIGURE 16.4

Indicators that you are editing a part in-context

Editing a component can also mean editing a subassembly in the context of the top-level assembly. You can create in-context assembly features and mates if necessary; however, you will do this far less frequently than editing parts in-context.

NOTE **Creating in-context relations is not the only reason to edit a part or subassembly in the context of the top-level assembly. Sometimes it is simply more convenient to do normal editing when you are in the top-level assembly, so that you can see how the part relates to other parts after making changes in the assembly without making relations between the parts.**

Editing a subassembly in the context of the upper-level assembly is often useful as well, to see how changing subassembly mates affects the top level.

Probably the most common mistake that users make around the issue of editing the part versus editing the assembly is when they add a sketch. If you intend to add a sketched feature to a part in the context of an assembly, but you fail to switch to Edit Part mode before creating the sketch, then the sketch ends up in the assembly rather than the part; you can only do limited things with a sketch in an assembly. Likewise, if you intend to make an assembly layout sketch, but you do not switch out of Edit Part mode, then you end up with a sketch in a part that cannot do what you want it to do.

Fortunately, SolidWorks has added a remedy for the first situation anyway. When you make a sketch in the assembly but need to make a feature in the part, you can choose the Propagate feature to parts option in the Feature Scope of the PropertyManager for the feature, as shown in Figure 16.5.

Notice in the image on the right that the last sketch in the part appears as derived. This means that the sketch and the feature are still driven from the assembly, but they have been propagated to the part enough to allow the feature to be edited in the part. I wouldn't go this route just because you made a mistake and it's simpler to do this than to move the sketch to the part, but it is an option that is valid in some situations.

Interestingly, this feature cannot be deleted from the part; you must delete it from the assembly.

External reference symbol

The external reference symbol appears as a dash followed by a greater-than sign. External references do not only indicate in-context features. You can also create external references by using the Split Part command as well as the Insert Part (base or derived part) or the mirrored part functions. Figure 16.6 shows the expanded FeatureManager for a part with an in-context reference in a sketch.

External references can have four states, which are also shown in Figure 16.6. These are:

- In-context
- Out-of-context
- Locked reference
- Broken reference

FIGURE 16.5

Propagating an assembly feature to the part

FIGURE 16.6

The in-context "carrot" on Extrude1

In-context

I have already discussed the in-context relationship earlier in this chapter.

Out-of-context

Out-of-context means that the document — usually but not necessarily an assembly — where the reference was created is not open at the time. It is indicated by an in-context symbol followed by a question mark. You can open the document where the reference was created through the right-mouse button (RMB) menu, using the Edit In Context option. Edit In Context opens either the parent part of an inserted part, or the assembly where the reference was created for an in-context reference. When you open the referencing document, the out-of-context symbol changes to the in-context symbol.

Locked reference

You can lock external references so that the model does not change, even if the parent document changes. The symbol for this is ->*. Other features of the part may be changed, but any external reference within the part remains the way it is until the reference is either unlocked or removed. In the Box-and-Top example I mentioned earlier, this means that if the Bottom part is changed, and the external reference on the Top is locked, then the Top will no longer fit the Bottom.

One of the best things about locked references is that you can unlock them. They are also flexible and give you control over when updates take place to parts with locked references.

Broken reference

The broken reference is another source of controversy. Some users believe that if you make in-context references, the best way to respond to them is to break them immediately. However, I would argue that using the Break References function is *never* a good thing to do. I believe that you should remove the reference by editing the feature or the sketch or change it to make it useful.

The problem with a broken reference is that it has absolutely no advantage over a locked reference. For example, while locked references can at least be unlocked, broken references cannot be repaired. The only thing that you can do with a broken reference is to use Display/Delete Relations or to manually edit features to completely remove the external reference. Perhaps it would be better for SolidWorks to replace Break References with a function called *Remove References*. Would anyone like to make an enhancement request?

BEST PRACTICE Best practice is to not put yourself in a situation where you are using either locked or broken references. Parametric relations should not change if the driving geometry does not change. Again, as is typical with CAD software, things may happen that you cannot explain, but there is always a reason for it (even if it is not immediately apparent).

You cannot selectively lock or break external relations. For example, all the external relations in the part can be locked, all the external relations can be broken, or none of them can be locked or broken. If you need to selectively disable relations, then you should consider suppressing features, sketch relations, end conditions, or sketch planes.

List External References

You can access the locked and broken references through the List External References option on the right-mouse button menu of any feature with an external reference symbol. Figure 16.7 shows the name and path of the assembly where the external reference was created, as well as the part names and entity types.

FIGURE 16.7

The External References dialog box

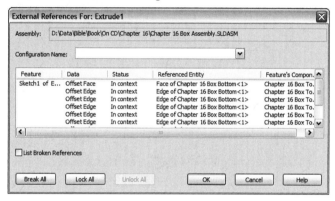

No External References

The No External References button on the Assembly toolbar is also available through Tools ➪ Options ➪ External References ➪ Do Not Create References External To The Model. As its name suggests, this setting prevents external relations from being created between parts in an assembly. When you offset in-context edges or use Convert Entities, the resulting sketch entities are created without relations of any type.

This lack of references includes the InPlace mate, which is not created when a part is created in-context. As a result, when you add the part to the assembly, if you exit and later re-enter Edit Part mode, then SolidWorks reminds you that the part is not fixed in space by displaying the warning shown in Figure 16.8.

This message should remind you that in-context features should be used only on parts that are fully positioned in the assembly.

External reference settings in Tools ➪ Options

The Tools ➪ Options ➪ External References pane of settings controls many aspects of the behavior of external references. You can find a full description of all the options in Appendix B; however, I will discuss two of these options in this section. I have discussed one of these references earlier — No External References — and I discuss the other feature, Multiple Contexts, next. This page in the Tools ➪ Options dialog box is shown in Figure 16.9.

FIGURE 16.8

The dialog box that warns you about adding in-context relations to an under-defined part

SolidWorks 2009

The part you are editing is not mated or fixed in space. Adding in-context features may produce undesirable results. It is recommended that you position the component before doing so.

OK

☐ Don't ask me again

FIGURE 16.9

The Tools ⇨ Options ⇨ External References pane

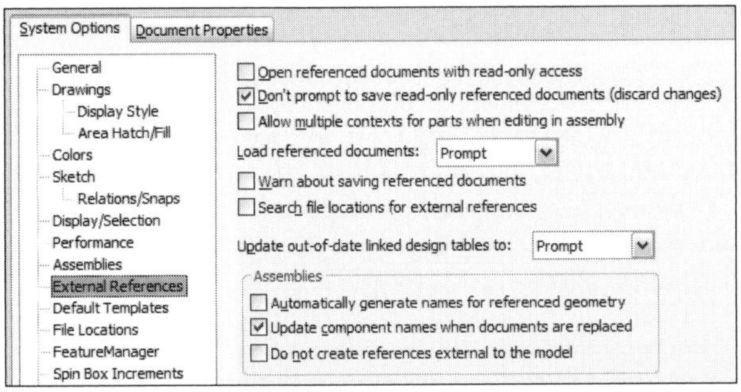

In-context best practice suggestions

In-context techniques are most frequently misused by beginning users. Many users purchase the software because of the promise of parametric relationships between parts. However, this is a technique that requires a fair amount of discipline, restraint, foresight, and judgment.

The potential problems associated with overuse or misuse of in-context techniques primarily include performance problems (speed) and lost references due to file management issues. Users may also experience problems with features or sketches that change with each rebuild. The following section contains best practice suggestions that can help you avoid these situations.

Multiple contexts

Multiple contexts occur when a part has references that are created in multiple assemblies. By default, multiple contexts are prevented from happening. If you place a part that already has external references into a different assembly, a warning appears, as shown in Figure 16.10.

Although SolidWorks displays many warnings about multiple contexts, you may still run into situations where you need to use them. For example, you may have a subassembly where a part, such as a top plate of a stand, has in-context references to locate a set of mounting holes. When you place the subassembly into the top-level assembly and mount another assembly to the top plate, another set of in-context holes is required in the top plate.

FIGURE 16.10

The warning message that appears about multiple contexts

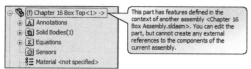

Figure 16.11, at the top, shows the first table and points out the in-context relations. At the bottom, the large bracket appears for the machine that is mounted to the table top using more in-context relations. The External References dialog boxes for the two different in-context features appear in Figure 16.12. Notice that the Assembly fields at the top of the External References dialog boxes are different. You can only achieve this by activating the Allow multiple contexts for parts when editing in assembly option shown in Figure 16.9.

NOTE The Tools ➪ Options setting for multiple contexts is a system option. This means that this option is either on or off for every document on a single machine, but when the assembly is used on another machine, the option is off. Rather than always leaving this option on for all documents on a given computer, I think it would be best if it were a document-specific option that traveled with the document, rather than sticking to the machine — another possible enhancement request.

BEST PRACTICE The best practice is to avoid creating multiple-context references. If you need to do this, then be very careful about naming files, and remember to turn off the multiple-context option when you have finished creating the reference.

If you receive a multiple-context part from someone else, the best thing to do is to determine whether you have all the files required to make it work. Right-click the external reference symbol and select Edit In Context to determine whether SolidWorks can find the right files.

Aside from doing some programming, the only way to find out whether a part was created as a multiple-context part is to examine the External References list for each in-context feature. This can be very time-consuming. Although multiple-context parts should be very rare, it is impossible to determine ahead of time whether or not a part that you have received is a multiple-context part, at least without programming.

I once worked on a part that had both some in-context and some out-of-context features. Of course, this looks strange when you realize what you are looking at because in most situations, if any references are out-of-context, all references will be out of context. After some examination, I discovered that there were multiple contexts, which were created because of poor file management. The assembly had changed names slightly and caused the original in-context relations to not be recognized. I will discuss in-context relations and file naming later in this chapter.

FIGURE 16.11

Using multiple contexts

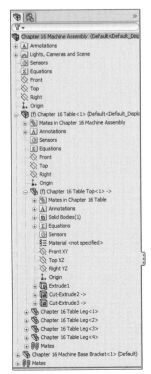

FIGURE 16.12

External References dialog boxes

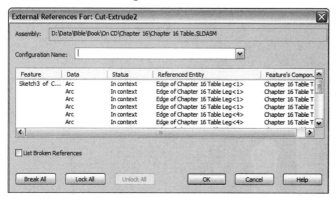

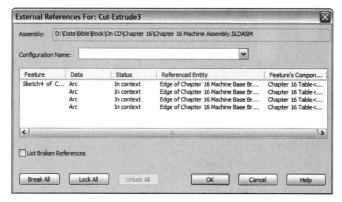

In-context with configurations

On the surface, mixing in-context references with configurations sounds like it is combining two powerful techniques that should offer you great control over models. Although this may sometimes be true, I want to caution you about some of the effects that combining these two techniques may cause. In particular, you should be careful about part configurations, particularly configurations of the *referenced* part.

If you are using in-context relations to parts with configurations, then you may want to consider a few things. First, look at the door-hinge part shown in Figure 16.13. At the top are three configurations of one of the hinge plates. The second hinge plate is built in the context of the assembly so that it will always match the first plate. At the bottom are the results of changing the first hinge-plate part configuration in the assembly. This looks like an ideal situation because the second hinge plate always changes to match the first hinge plate. What could be wrong with this?

FIGURE 16.13

Combining in-context references with configurations

The problem here is that you can only show the size of the second hinge plate that corresponds to the configuration of the first plate that is active in the assembly. If you had two instances of the hinge assembly in a top-level assembly, then you would be able to show only one size for the second plate.

A second situation where combining in-context references and configurations can cause you trouble is if you have referenced the edges of a part from another part, and a configuration of the referenced part either adds or removes fillets or chamfers, thus breaking the edges. Either of these situations can cause the in-context sketches or other features to fail. This may be a reason to reference the underlying sketches, rather than the model edges or faces themselves.

In some situations, configurations work well with in-context relations. One example of this would be when an assembly has many configurations used for positioning parts. Use one configuration for the sole purpose of creating in-context relations.

In-context with motion

You should make in-context references between parts where there is no relative motion. The parts themselves can move relative to the rest of the assembly, but they should remain stationary relative to one another. The parts should also be fully defined to ensure that they will not move; you should not simply count on avoiding dragging underdefined parts.

In some cases, such as an assembly of imported parts, it may make sense to fix parts in bulk rather than to mate them. When you are using in-context relations, you need to take extra care to ensure that the parts do not move around. When parts move around, in-context features also move.

Obviously, if the motion is around a circular hole, and the in-context feature is circular and is not affected by the rotation of the referenced part, then it makes less difference; however, if there is a keyway, that may change things. You need to pay attention when combining underdefined parts and in-context features.

BEST PRACTICE For best practice, you should avoid in-context relations between parts when relative motion is allowed between these parts.

In-context with multiple instances

Another situation that can cause problems is when multiple instances of an in-context part are being used in the assembly. In cases like this, you need to be careful and consistent, by always using the same instance to create the in-context relations. You can do this by putting parts into folders, or by giving the in-context part a special component color.

One trick used by some people is to use one instance of an in-context part for the in-context relation, and a second instance of the part to allow motion. In-context relations are tied to one specific instance of a part, regardless of how many of those parts are in the assembly. You might want to set the driving in-context part aside, by putting it in a folder, changing its color, or hiding it.

In-context and file management

Understanding what you are doing with file management is imperative when working with parts that depend on in-context features. Because the references are stored in both the part that is doing the referencing and the assembly where the reference is created, improperly changing the name of either document or even the referenced document is bound to cause problems. For example, if you rename an in-context part using Windows Explorer, then the assembly will not recognize the part, as I demonstrated in an earlier chapter. This also means that any in-context references will not update. The part will show the out-of-context symbol.

BEST PRACTICE For best practice, you should use either the SolidWorks Save As command or SolidWorks Explorer to rename parts and assemblies. This applies to all parts and assemblies, but doubly to in-context documents.

In-context and mates

I mentioned this earlier, but a section on in-context best practices would not be complete without issuing the warning against mating to in-context features. Mating parts to in-context features creates a parametric daisy chain, thus establishing an order in which assembly features and mates must be solved. This always creates performance problems in assemblies, especially large ones. The SolidWorks AssemblyXpert looks for this condition when examining assemblies.

Circular references

Circular references in assemblies are a bigger problem than most people realize. In fact, most people do not realize that circular references *are* a problem, or, for that matter, that they even exist.

A circular reference takes the form of "Part A references Part B, which references Part A." It creates a circular loop that really wrecks assembly rebuild times. Part feature design trees are not susceptible to this sort of looping because the part FeatureManager operates in a linear fashion (at least when it comes to applying relations between sketches or features).

The Assembly FeatureManager is solved in this order, or an order that is very similar:

1. **Solve reference geometry and sketches that are listed before parts in order, at the top of the design tree.**
2. **Rebuild individual parts as necessary.**
3. **Solve the mates and locate the parts.**
4. **Solve in-context features in parts.**
5. **Solve reference geometry and sketches listed after the mates.**
6. **Solve assembly features and component patterns.**
7. **Loop to Step 3 to solve mates that are connected to anything that was solved after the first round on the mates.**
8. **Continue to loop until complete.**

As you can see, even if you do not have a reference such as "Part A references Part B, which references Part A," it is still possible to get a highly convoluted, if not entirely circular, loop. Many users with smaller assemblies in the hundreds of parts complain about very poor performance. The SolidWorks AssemblyXpert claims to identify circular references, but I have never seen it actually work on circular reference assemblies I have created intentionally for the purpose of testing it.

Skeletons and layouts

When you are making in-context references, a technique that can help you avoid circular references is to always create references to parts that are higher in the design tree. You can expand on this idea until a single entity is at the top of the design tree, to which all in-context references are made. This could take the form of a layout sketch, or a skeleton. These concepts are discussed in Chapters 11, 12, and 13. I discuss the Layout feature, which is different from the layout sketch, later in this chapter as an additional in-context tool.

Remember that the layout sketch consists of a single or even multiple sketches that control the overall layout of the assembly, as well as all the relationships between parts. When you refer all the relations to a single entity that does not change with part configurations, or lose or gain filleted edges, the intra-part parametrics become much stronger and more stable.

When you are building a mold for plastic injection molding, a single sketch can control the size and position of the plates, pins, and so on. If all the 3D parts are mated to the 2D sketch, or use the 2D sketch by converted entities, then the parts will move with the sketch. This same technique is important and useful for any type of die or punch design, along with many other types of design.

In-context and libraries

Library parts should never contain in-context references, especially if the in-context references are out of context. Small library assemblies may have in-context references between the parts, but a single part should not have features created in-context. External references may be unavoidable in the form of mirrored or inserted parts, but in-context references are completely avoidable.

Removing relations

You can remove in-context sketch relations by using the Display/Delete Relations tool. You can sort the relations by selecting the Defined In Context option, as shown in Figure 16.14.

If you are considering using the Break Relations tool, then you should either reconsider and use Lock Relations instead or simply remove all the in-context relations altogether.

Other types of in-context references are not as easy to remove as sketch relations. When you see the External Reference symbol on a sketch, it could be the sketch relations, or it could be the sketch plane that was in-context. In order to remove the reference from an in-context sketch plane, you must redefine the plane locally in the part.

You should also not forget end conditions such as Up To Surface, Offset From Surface, or even From Surface. If an external reference symbol remains on a feature, you can use the Parent/Child option on the right-mouse button menu to locate it. Remember that using an edge or vertex for a plane definition can cause an in-context relation.

FIGURE 16.14

Sorting sketch relations by type

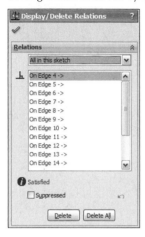

Should you use mating or in-context?

Despite all my encouragement for you to use in-context modeling, you should not become overly enthusiastic about in-context relations. This can cause you to do things such as using in-context relations to locate parts, or using in-context instead of mating parts.

In-context modeling is like chocolate: a little is a wonderful thing, but too much can be bad for you. You should only use in-context to locate or size features. In-context is initially so fast and easy to use that it can be addictive, but you need to think before you use it because of the speed and file management implications these relations will have later on in your design process.

Communicating design intent

If someone else needs to use your model after you are done with it and possibly edit it, then you should leave some clues to help this person understand how the model works, and how it is best changed. For example, you can use descriptive feature and sketch names, comments that are associated with features, the Design Binder to add documentation, and the Design Journal to write notes. You can even put HTML links in notes that display in the graphics window.

In-context design intent may not always be obvious, and an impatient user may find it more expedient to delete the in-context references and replace them with either local relations or no relations at all. The more you document your intent, the more likely others will be to follow it.

Other Types of External References

The external reference symbol (- >) indicates in-context features that have been created in the context of an assembly, but it also indicates three other types of external references:

- Inserted parts
- Split parts
- Mirrored parts

Inserted parts

I discuss inserted parts to some extent in Chapter 10, and in more detail in Chapter 28. In the past, inserted parts have also been called base parts and derived parts, and some users still use those names.

An inserted part is simply an entire part that has been inserted into another part. This is sometimes referred to as a *pull* operation because the data is pulled from the original part into the child part. The part may be inserted at any point in the history of the design tree, and it may create an additional body within the part or be added to the existing one. Additional features can also be added to the inserted part.

Items that can be brought along with the inserted part are solid bodies, surface bodies, planes, axes, sketches, cosmetic threads, and even features. You can also use a particular configuration of the inserted part in the child part. I discuss this aspect in Chapter 14, dealing with configurations, and also in Chapter 28, dealing with master models.

You can use inserted parts for many modeling applications, such as cast parts and secondary operations. You first insert the original cast part into a new blank part. Then, you add cut and hole features until the part resembles the finished part.

Another application for inserted parts is a single part that has been built from several models. For example, I once worked on a large, rather complicated plastic basket, where the basket was modeled as three individual parts, and then reassembled into a single part. Another application may be to insert a part as a body into a mold block to create a mold cavity. To insert a part into another part, you can select Insert ⇨ Part.

Split parts

I discuss split parts in detail in Chapter 28, in the section about master models. Inserted and split parts are both master model techniques, as are a few more techniques that I discuss in Chapter 28. Some people also include in-context techniques with the master model tools because this is a way of making several parts update together.

Split parts are sometimes called a *push* operation because the data is pushed from the original multi-body part to the individual child parts. The *split* function takes a single body and splits it into several bodies, optionally saving the bodies out as individual parts. This is done for various reasons, such as creating a single, smooth shape out of several different parts; for example, automobile body panels or the various covers and buttons on a computer mouse. You can use the split parts technique for other applications, as well. Sometimes a product is designed as a simple, single solid to keep the modeling simple, and because it is not known how the parts will be assembled or manufactured. When the manufacturing decisions are made, the part can be split into several models that have the engineering details added to them.

Mirror parts

You can mirror a right-handed part to create a left-handed part. To activate the Mirror Part command, you must select a plane or planar face. Then, select Insert ➪ Mirror Part to initiate the Mirror Part command.

Mirror parts can also use configurations, and so if you have one of those "mirrored exactly except for . . ." parts, you can select the configuration of the parent from the child document.

Using the Layout feature

I described the Layout feature briefly in Chapter 12, where I also described layout sketches. This is an unfortunate naming gaffe on the part of SolidWorks. Two highly useful functions do nearly the same thing, one of which is simply a technique that has existed for years, and the other, a newly added formal feature. For this reason, I will always capitalize the name of the new Layout feature and refer to it as a feature, while I'll refer to the layout sketch in lowercase and as either a sketch or a technique.

The Layout feature is simply a 3D sketch that is given special treatment within an assembly. It works best with sketch blocks. To initiate a Layout, click the Layout button on the Layout tab of the assembly CommandManager or activate it from the Insert menu. Once you are in a Layout, SolidWorks puts you into a 3D sketch with the Front (XY) plane activated, so it displays a small grid.

CROSS-REF 3D sketches are addressed in Chapter 31.

For now, you primarily treat the 3D sketch as much like a set of 2D sketches as possible. The main difference is that you can double-click on a different plane to start sketching on the new plane, and you will always see this small grid when a plane is active.

3D sketches have some limitations when you are working with Layouts, such as lacking the capabilities to use sketch patterns and Sketch Pictures.

Using the Layout workflow

Here is the general workflow for working with the Layout feature:

1. **Open a new or existing assembly.**

2. **Click the Layout toolbar button on the Layout tab of the CommandManager.**

3. **Sketch on the plane in the 3D sketch to create 2D sketches representing parts of a mechanism or other assembly.**

4. **Make selections of the sketch into blocks representing individual parts.**

5. **Insert multiple instances of the blocks to represent multiple instances of the parts.**

6. **Use sketch relations to put the blocks together like mating parts in an assembly.**

7. **Test the mechanism by dragging sketches.** (Blocks function like a single sketch entity, so you can drag them within the sketch like parts in an assembly.)

8. **Right-click the block (from inside or outside the Layout) and select Make Part From Block (also a button on the Layout toolbar). See Figure 16.15.**

NOTE The icons for Make Part From Block are slightly different between large and small icon sizes. The icon shown previously is a large icon.

Virtual components

Virtual components always exist with in-context workflows, and frequently with the Layout workflow. Virtual components are parts created in the context of an assembly that are saved within the assembly, not saved externally. You can save a virtual component externally, but you cannot make an externally saved part into a virtual component.

Virtual components are primarily intended to be used as quick, temporary, conceptual tools, rather than as a way to make parts that will be a permanent part of the assembly. Any time you use the Insert ➪ Component ➪ New Part, and select a template and a plane to put the part on, the part is placed immediately into the assembly, and you can start working without worrying about having to save the assembly and the part. This saves a lot of time initially. Later on, when you save the assembly, SolidWorks prompts you to save the parts externally as well, or you may choose to leave the parts internal to the assembly.

BEST PRACTICE It is considered best practice to save any parts that will be a permanent part of the assembly as external files. Virtual components should be limited to temporary parts or possibly non-geometry, BOM-only parts like glue or paint.

FIGURE 16.15

Tools you encounter when using Layout

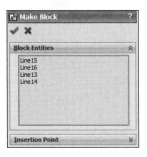

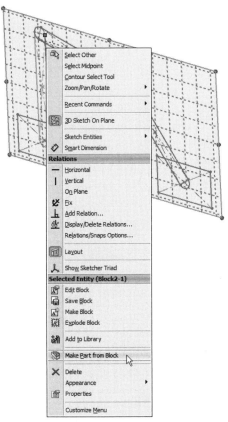

Tutorial: Working In-Context

Follow these steps to get a feel for the workflow of working with parts in the context of an assembly:

1. **Open the assembly named** `Chapter 16 Tutorial Table.sldasm`.

2. **Set the colors that are to be used during in-context editing.** Remember that two settings control this — one at Tools ➪ Options ➪ Colors, and the other at Tools ➪ Options ➪ Display/Selection, as shown in Figure 16.16.

FIGURE 16.16

Setting in-context colors

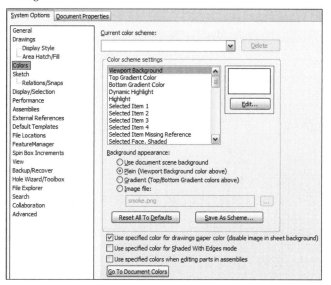

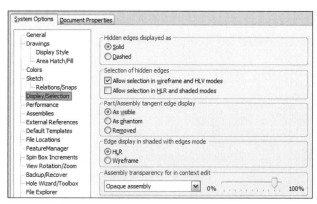

Set the Assembly, Edit Part color to a shade of blue, and the Assembly, Non-Edit Parts to a shade of gray.

Also set the Assembly Transparency for In Context Edit setting to Force Assembly Transparency, with the slider at around 90 percent.

3. **Now you are ready to begin.** Select the Table Top part, and click the Edit Component button on the Assembly toolbar. This command is also available through both the right-mouse button menu and the drop-down menu as Edit Part. (If you right-click a subassembly, the Edit Subassembly option becomes available.) Notice that the Table Top part and the FeatureManager text turn the same color.

4. **Expand the Table Top part in the Assembly FeatureManager, select the Front plane, and open a new sketch on it.** Notice that you cannot select the edges of the transparent parts through the transparency, even if the Select Through Transparency option is turned on (Tools ➪ Options ➪ Display/Selection). This setting applies only to faces, not to edges. Instead, change the display mode for the entire assembly to Wireframe.

5. **Now select the 16 hole edges on the legs.** It does not matter whether you select the top edges or the bottom, or even a combination of top and bottom. Use the Convert Entities command to project the edges into the sketch plane as circles, as shown in Figure 16.17.

FIGURE 16.17

Converting entities in-context

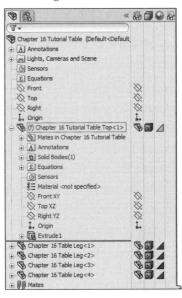
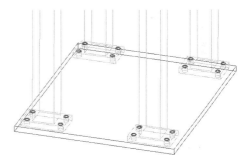

6. **Create a cut that goes Through All.** You may have to change the direction of the extrude to get it to work. Exit Edit Component mode using the confirmation corner and save the tutorial assembly.

7. **Now open the file named** `Chapter 16 Tutorial Machine Assembly.sldasm`. Notice that the Table Top part in this assembly is using the Wireframe display state, which is assigned in the Display pane.

8. **Right-click the part and select Edit Part from the list, or select the part and click the Edit Component button on the toolbar.** A warning will display that the part has features that were created in the context of another assembly. You can edit the part, but you cannot add any more external references (in-context features) to it.

9. **Toggle off the Edit Component button on the Assembly toolbar to exit Edit Part mode.**

10. **In Tools ➪ Options ➪ External References, select the Allow Multiple Contexts for Parts When Editing in Assembly option.** Now try to edit the Table Top part again in the context of the assembly. This time, no warning message displays.

11. **Make sure that you are editing the Table Top part.** It will not change colors as specified in the Tools ➪ Options ➪ Colors settings because it is using the Wireframe display mode. Ensure that the status bar in the lower-right corner displays *Editing Part* rather than *Editing Assembly*.

12. **Open a sketch on the Front plane, and convert the four edges of the holes, as shown in Figure 16.18.**

13. **Cut the holes using the Through All setting.** Again, be aware of the direction of the cuts. Toggle out of Edit Component mode and press Ctrl+S to save the assembly. Figure 16.19 shows the finished assembly.

14. **Open the Machine Base Bracket part in its own window by selecting Open Part from the right-mouse button menu.** The part is shown in Figure 16.20.

15. **Select the Front plane and select Insert ➪ Mirror Part.** This creates a new part and opens a new PropertyManager interface, as shown in Figure 16.21.

FIGURE 16.18

Creating holes in-context

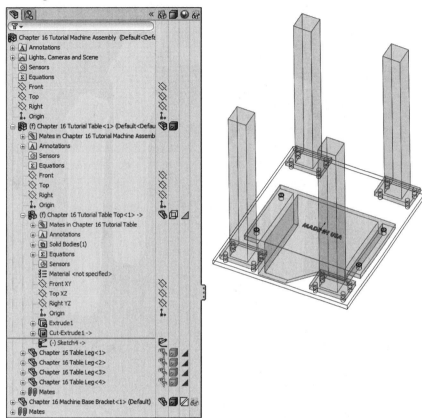

FIGURE 16.19

The assembly as of Step 13

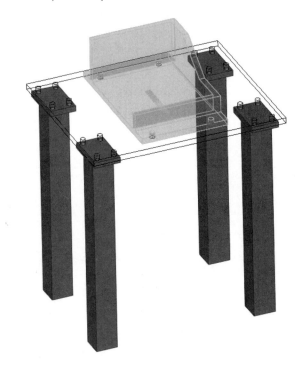

FIGURE 16.20

The Machine Base Bracket part, ready for mirroring

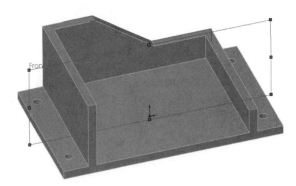

FIGURE 16.21

The Mirror Part PropertyManager

In this case, select Solid Bodies and click OK.

NOTE Notice that I used the Insert ⇨ Mirror Part command, but the PropertyManager says Insert Part. The Mirror Part functionality uses the Insert Part function, but adds a feature to mirror the body once it is inserted. Notice all the entity types you can transfer, and the fact that you can break the link to the original part. Also note that the template used for this part was chosen based on the settings at Tools ⇨ Options ⇨ Default Templates ⇨ Always Use These Default Document Templates or Prompt User To Select Document Template.

CROSS-REF I discuss the function of Mirror/Insert part in more depth in Chapter 26.

16. **Notice that the new part is indeed a mirrored copy of the original.** You can see that the "MADE IN USA" text on the bottom is backwards. Fortunately, a configuration exists specifically for this purpose. Change the configuration by selecting For Mirroring in the Configuration Name drop-down list in the External References dialog box (from the right-mouse button selection List External References), as shown in Figure 16.22. Notice that this configuration removes the extruded text from the model.

17. **Add your own "MADE IN . . ." extruded text to the bottom of the part.** Save the part.

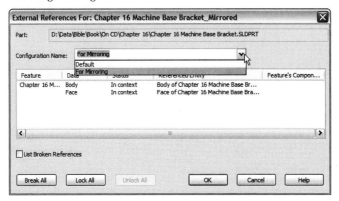

FIGURE 16.22

Selecting a configuration

Summary

Although in-context functions are powerful and seductive, you should use them sparingly. In particular, be careful about file management issues such as renaming parts and assemblies. The best approach is to use SolidWorks Explorer or the Save As command with both the parts and assemblies open.

In-context techniques including the Layout feature are the pinnacle of true parametric practice, and enable you to take the concepts of design intent and design for change to an entirely new level.

Part IV

Creating and Using Libraries

Part IV contains arguably some of the most challenging material in the entire book. The topics treated here go well beyond basic modeling and into administration of automated libraries. Libraries always take time to set up, but particularly the custom libraries can have huge design automation payoffs if done properly. Explore this part with an eye toward the possibilities rather than focusing on roadblocks.

Chapter 17

Using Hole Wizard and Toolbox

The Hole Wizard and Toolbox are two applications that go together because they both work from a single database of matching hole and fastener sizes. One of the most useful examples of combining these two applications is the ability to automatically place holes through multiple parts and put appropriately sized screws and hardware into the holes, all in one step. The hole knows which fastener or stack of fasteners needs to go together.

Many automatic aspects of Toolbox exist, and I find the concept behind the combination of Toolbox and the Hole Wizard compelling. As usual, there is often a disconnect between concept and implementation, and this situation is no different. Practical details conspire to keep Toolbox from being used quite often in SolidWorks using companies. This chapter aims to give you the information you need to decide how or if to implement and use Toolbox in your work.

IN THIS CHAPTER

Using the Hole Wizard

Understanding Toolbox

Tutorial: Gaining experience with the Hole Wizard and Toolbox

Using the Hole Wizard

The Hole Wizard enables you to place holes for many types of screws with normal, loose, or close fits. You can create Hole Wizard holes as assembly features in an assembly or as features in individual parts that are built in the context of an assembly using the Series Hole functionality. This tool is called a *wizard* because it guides you through the process step by step. The process of creating a Hole Wizard hole can be summarized as follows:

1. **Pre-select the face to put the holes on, although this is not required.** This turns out to be an important issue that is related to the type of placement sketch, and I revisit this subject later.

2. **Select the type of hole; for example, counterbored, countersunk, drilled hole, tapped hole, pipe tap, or legacy.**

3. **Set the standard to be used, such as ANSI inch, ANSI metric, or ISO.**

4. **Select the type of screw.** For example, a counterbored hole can accommodate a socket head cap screw or a hex head screw, among others.

5. **Select the size of the screw.**

6. **Select the fit of the screw into the hole, such as normal, loose, or close.**

7. **Select the end condition of the hole.**

8. **Select options for clearance and countersinks or edge breaks.**

   Alternatively, you can use or assign a Favorite. A favorite is a hole with settings that you use frequently and want to save. I discuss these later in this chapter.

   You can use Custom Sizing when you need a hole with non-standard dimensions.

9. **Locate the center of the hole or holes.** You can place multiple holes in a single Hole Wizard feature, even on different faces and curved faces. I address the specifics of this step later in this chapter.

10. **Click OK to accept the type, size, and placement of the hole.** Figure 17.1 shows the Hole Wizard PropertyManager interface.

FIGURE 17.1

The Hole Wizard PropertyManager Interface

Anatomy of a Hole Wizard hole

Hole Wizard holes are made of two sketches: a center placement sketch and a revolved cut profile. Figure 17.2 shows a simple part with an expanded Hole Wizard feature. Notice that the feature is named for the size and type of the hole.

FIGURE 17.2

A design tree containing a Hole Wizard hole

> **NOTE**   Another useful aspect of naming the hole feature is that if you change the type or size through the Hole Wizard interface, the name changes to match. If you create a Hole Wizard feature with more than one hole, there is still just a single revolved sketch. A multiple-hole Hole Wizard feature works similar to making a revolved cut and using a Sketch Driven feature pattern to create the multiple instances.

Placement sketch

The placement sketch is listed first under the Hole Wizard feature. It contains one or more sketch points marking the hole centers. It may also contain construction geometry with relations and dimensions to parametrically locate the hole centers. I discuss placement sketches in more detail in the next section.

Hole sketch

The revolve profile sketch is not on an identifiable sketch plane that you can reuse for other features, although that would be useful. You can change the sketch dimension outside of the wizard interface, and if you later use the wizard to edit it, then the changes appear in the Custom Sizing panel. Figure 17.3 shows the Custom Sizing panel with the changed counterbore diameter highlighted.

The Custom Sizing area of the Hole Specifications panel

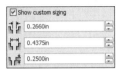

If you select any of the choices from the Options panel, the revolved sketch profile is altered to accommodate the change. For example, if you check the box for a near side countersink, the sketch changes to add a line for the countersink; a separate chamfer feature is not added.

2D versus 3D placement sketches

Possibly one of the most difficult aspects of the Hole Wizard for new users to grasp is the use of 2D and 3D sketches to place the centers of the holes. There is a condition that is not immediately obvious, which is that if you *pre-select* a flat face, then the placement sketch is 2D, and if you do not pre-select a flat face (meaning that if you just start the Hole Wizard without having selected a flat face), then the placement sketch is 3D.

The reasoning behind this is that the most general case that can handle any kind of hole placement is a 3D sketch. A 2D sketch requires that the user select the sketch plane.

Advantages and limitations of the 2D sketch

The main advantages of the 2D sketch method are the simplicity and completeness of the available tools. Everyone knows how to manage 2D sketches, sketch planes, dimensions, and construction geometry.

A limitation of the 2D sketch is that the holes that you create through this method are limited to a single planar face. Sometimes this creates a great limitation, while other times it does not matter.

Advantages and limitations of the 3D sketch

The obvious advantage of the 3D placement sketch is that it can put a set of holes on any set of solid faces, regardless of whether they are at different levels, are non-parallel, or are even non-planar. This function offers multiple holes, multiple faces, and multiple directions. In situations where that is what you need, nothing else will do.

A limitation of the 3D sketch is that it can be fairly cumbersome. Dimensions work very differently in 3D sketches compared to 2D sketches. For example, to create and place a hole in a specific position on a cylinder, you need to follow these steps:

1. Begin with a circle with a diameter of one inch, drawn on the Top plane, and extruded using the Mid-plane option one inch.

2. Start the Hole Wizard without any pre-selection, either through the Features toolbar or by selecting Insert ⇨ Features ⇨ Hole ⇨ Wizard.

3. **Set the interface to use an ANSI inch, one-quarter-inch, and counterbored hole for a socket head cap screw.** Use Through All for the End Condition, and a Normal fit, with a .100-inch head clearance (in the Options panel), and no custom sizing changes. These settings are shown in Figure 17.4.

FIGURE 17.4

The Hole Wizard settings for the socket head cap screw

4. **Click the Positions tab, which is located at the top of the PropertyManager window.** The interface automatically changes to a 3D sketch with the Point tool turned on. This means that wherever you click, you create a point.

NOTE Be careful about clicking when the Point tool is turned on. For example, if you click in a blank space, the Point tool places a point off the part. SolidWorks will try to use the point later to create a hole in empty space, which usually causes an error.

5. **Click the cylindrical surface of the part.** The surface appears orange when you move the cursor over it to indicate that an OnSurface sketch relation will be created between the sketch point and the cylindrical surface.

6. **The hole should be positioned from one end of the cylinder.** Using the SmartDimension tool, click one flat end face of the cylinder and the sketch point. Place the dimension and give it a value of .300 inches, as shown in Figure 17.5.

Locating the point angularly around the cylinder is more difficult. You can use several methods to do this, but this example shows one using construction sketch geometry.

FIGURE 17.5

Dimensioning the 3D Placement sketch point

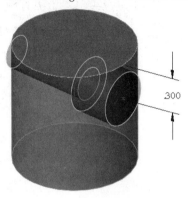

.300

> **TIP**
> To force a 3D dimension to have a certain orientation, dimension from a plane or planar face rather than from an edge, vertex, or sketch entity. A dimension from a plane is always measured in a direction perpendicular to the plane, but a dimension from a line or point is always measured by the shortest distance between the entities. Two-dimensional sketches can force dimensions to be horizontal or vertical, but 3D sketches cannot.

> **CAUTION**
> 3D sketches have the ability to make planes within the sketch, without leaving the sketch environment. Planes that are made in this way are not created using the same methods as regular planes, and do not follow documented techniques reliably. For this reason, I recommend finding other more reliable methods to do the same things rather than using the planes inside the 3D sketch.

7. **With the Line tool activated while still in the 3D sketch, Ctrl+click the flat end face that the previous dimension referenced.** This moves the red "space handle" origin to the selected face, and constrains any new sketch entities to that face. You are still in the 3D sketch, but are constrained to the selected plane, and still must play by all the 3D sketch rules. The elements of 3D sketches are described in detail in Chapter 31.

8. **Turn on the Temporary Axes view by selecting View ⇨ Temporary Axes.**

9. Place the cursor near the center of the activated end face; a small, black circle appears, indicating that the end point of the line will pick up a coincident relation to the temporary axis. Draw the line so that it picks up an AlongX sketch relation. The cursor shows the relations about to be applied, just like in a 2D sketch.

10. Draw a second line again from the center, but this time do not pick up any automatic relations. This line should also be on the flat end face.

 **NOTE** Although you can set these lines to display as construction lines if you like, this is not required for the feature to work; the lines also work as regular solid lines.

11. Put an angle dimension between the lines, and change the angle to 30 degrees. To be thorough (which is always recommended in 3D sketches, which have a tendency to handle underconstrained sketch geometry unpredictably), constrain the ends of the lines to the circular edge of the cylinder. At this point, the part looks like Figure 17.6.

FIGURE 17.6

The example part at the end of Step 11

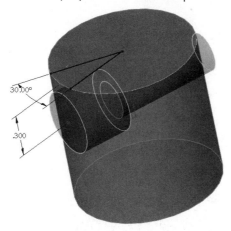

12. Create an AlongY sketch relation between the points indicated in Figure 17.7. The hole centerpoint on the cylindrical face is one of the points, as well as the endpoint of the angled line. Change the angle dimension to ensure that it is controlling the sketch point as expected.

ON the CD-ROM You can find the finished part from this example on the CD-ROM named Chapter 17 3D Hole Placement.sldprt.

FIGURE 17.7

Control the placement of the 3D sketch point around the cylinder.

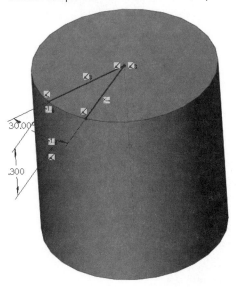

Making and using Favorites

Hole Wizard Favorites store types of holes that you use frequently so that you can simply recall a favorite, rather than manually making all the changes every time you use the same hole. Favorites are saved to a database named Default.mdb as you create them, and are immediately available from all other part documents. You can also save favorites to a special file type, with the extension `*.sldhwfvt`. Other users can then load these files and add your favorites to their Default.mdb databases. This is a convenient way to create company standards for hole features.

Shared Toolbox installations share a SWBrowser.mdb between several users, making Hole Wizard favorites available to everyone. I cover how to set up shared Toolbox installations later in this chapter.

Creating a Hole Wizard Favorite

To create a Hole Wizard Favorite, set up a Hole Wizard hole as you normally would, and then use the Add Favorite button to add it to the Favorites database. The Hole Wizard Favorite panel contains five buttons:

■ **Apply Defaults/No Favorites.** Removes favorite settings from the current interface, setting all values back to their defaults.

■ **Add or Update Favorites.** You can use this button to either add a new favorite to the database or change the name or other settings for an existing favorite.

 ■ **Delete Favorite.** Removes a favorite from the database.

 ■ **Save Favorite.** Saves a favorite to an external file with the extension `*.sldhwfvt`, which can be loaded by other users and added to their databases.

 ■ **Load Favorite.** Loads a saved favorite file.

Storing custom holes

You can use Hole Wizard Favorites to store custom holes. Create the hole with its custom sizes, and then add the favorite and give it a recognizable name. The custom hole will now be available to anyone who connects to the same database file.

Administering Hole Wizard Favorites

The database file is typically found in the `Data` subdirectory of the SolidWorks installation directory, but an option in Tools ⇨ Options ⇨ File Locations ⇨ Hole Wizard Favorites Database theoretically enables you to move the file to somewhere else.

Further, the `*.sldhwfvt` files do not have an entry in the File Locations list, but seem to always default to the `lang\english` subdirectory of the SolidWorks installation directory. Neither this location nor the `Data` directory makes sharing among multiple users very convenient, but both file types can be copied to other installations. You may want to read through Chapter 18 to learn about setting up libraries for all file types.

BEST PRACTICE It is a best practice to create a folder for library type files that you want to save and use with a future version of SolidWorks. You can specify the locations for these files through Tools ⇨ Options ⇨ File Locations. I recommend a location such as `D:\Library`. This moves the file off of the same drive as the operating system, in case you need to reformat, and it keeps it out of the Program Files area to prevent it from being lost or overwritten when SolidWorks is installed, uninstalled, upgraded, or changed in other ways. Even for files that need to remain in the SolidWorks installation directory (such as macros), it is best to also have these backed up in a library location.

Favorites quirks

Hole Wizard Favorites seem to have a couple of quirks that are possibly "sub-optimal," as they say. First, you can only see the favorites for a specific type of hole when that type of hole is activated in the interface. For example, if you have a number of favorites for countersunk holes, but you currently have the counterbored hole icon activated, you will not be able to see the countersunk favorites until you switch to the countersunk icon.

If you have a lot of favorites, this may be beneficial, but if you have only a few favorites, or you do not use favorites frequently, it may be confusing, and can create some unnecessary steps to find all your favorites.

A second quirk occurs when you allow SolidWorks to name the favorites and you have fractional values such as ¼ — which happens now and then in hole sizes — and then try to save the favorites. Each favorite is saved as a separate file, using the name that was automatically assigned to it by SolidWorks as the filename. Unfortunately, the character "/" is not allowed in a filename, and so it fails.

Using the Hole Series

The Hole Series enables you to make a series of in-context hole features in individual parts that are connected by a Hole Series assembly-level feature. It is intended for a stack of parts where, for example, the top part has a counterbored hole, the middle part has a clearance through hole, and the final part has a blind threaded hole. You can also do this by using an existing hole to align the rest of the series.

Hole Series interface

The Hole Series used to be part of the Hole Wizard, but has since been exported as a separate tool. It is now a five-step, wizard-based feature, ending with populating the new hole with a fastener using Smart Fasteners functionality. The Toolbox add-in is required to use Smart Fasteners. Figure 17.8 shows the interface for the various steps.

Basic Hole Series steps

When using the Hole Series feature, you must follow these basic steps:

1. **Have an assembly open with two or more parts in it that need to be fastened together.**

2. **Initiate the Hole Series tool by selecting Insert ➪ Assembly Features ➪ Hole ➪ Hole Series.** It is also available as a toolbar button, but it is not on the toolbar by default. The Hole Series also depends on pre-selection to decide whether it uses a 2D or 3D sketch for the placement sketch. You should always pre-select a flat face before creating a Hole Series feature.

3. **If the Hole Series is to be started from an existing hole, then select it in the Hole Position panel.** If not, then use sketch points, construction geometry, dimensions, and sketch relations to locate the hole centerpoints.

4. **Use the tabs at the top of the PropertyManager to advance from one panel to the next.**

   ■ The Start Hole Specification refers to the part where the series of holes starts.

   ■ The Middle Hole Specification is for all parts between the first part and the last part.

   ■ The End Hole Specification is the last part and is either a through clearance hole or a threaded hole.

FIGURE 17.8

The Hole Series interface

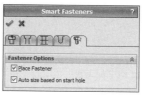

The finished feature leaves an in-context feature in each part, with the Hole Series part in the assembly, as shown in Figure 17.9.

FIGURE 17.9

The finished Hole Series

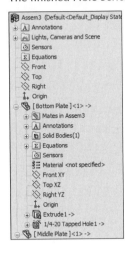

Understanding Toolbox

I recommend that you read this section through, from beginning to end. If you read a paragraph out of context, then you may not understand the point that I am making. With Toolbox, it is vital that you know what you are doing, to ensure the quality of your production data regarding fasteners and hardware.

CAUTION Improper installation, maintenance, or management of Toolbox can cause the loss of all useful information about fasteners and hardware in your assemblies.

Toolbox is an add-in that requires SolidWorks Office or higher, although you can also purchase it separately. In this book, I typically avoid talking about add-ins because the amount of material simply becomes overwhelming at a certain point; however, Toolbox is the cause of much consternation among users and CAD Administrators, and so it deserves some attention.

Toolbox creates fasteners and other hardware components on the fly or reuses existing parts when possible. Technically, it is not a library, but a *configurator*. Libraries store existing components, while configurators build them on the fly from information supplied by the user.

One advantage of configurators is that the parts start out very compact because there is only the default size, and the sizes are efficiently stored in a database, and created as needed.

The advantage of a library is that it allows you to simply plug in the parts and they work. All Toolbox really needs to do for users is provide a library of parts. Anything more than that is only beneficial if it offers some improvement over a simple library of existing parts without introducing any risks or setbacks.

How Toolbox works

Because Toolbox is not a library, and is not passive the way a library is, there is a component of it that is active. To make an analogy, no one asks how a staircase works, because it does not work, it simply exists, and people use it. An escalator, however, is a different issue. With an escalator, there is a complex installation, and then to use it, you have to know how to get on and get off, and what to do if it stops working. The end results of using the staircase and using the escalator are the same (you start at the bottom and arrive at the top), but the complex automation is supposed to save you some effort.

That is one way you can look at Toolbox. The end product is supposed to be the same as using a static library of parts, but there is some mechanism behind the scenes that has to be set up and maintained properly in order for it to work in the way you expect. Most SolidWorks books, tutorials, or training materials are going to ask you to accept what happens inside Toolbox as a "black box" and to just assume that the end results are exactly what you need and intend. Here, I supply you with information about how it works, so you can decide how useful it will be for you.

The database

Toolbox has three major components:

- Default parts of one size, with named dimensions and features
- A database containing all size information for all parts and Hole Wizard holes
- A software application with settings and an interface

When Toolbox is installed, it starts as a set of SolidWorks parts with named features and dimensions, some suppressed features (depending on settings), some dlls (executable programs), and a database. The parts have a single Default configuration, which is typically one of the size extremities, either the largest or smallest. The database starts out about 87MB, and includes all the size information for all the parts, as well as all the standards information.

If you create a *custom standard* in Toolbox, it actually replicates a section of the database. By doing this, the database file can easily double in size.

Later, you will see that a network installation of Toolbox requires the database to be on the network, and every time you create a new fastener, it has to open the database. As a result, simply placing a screw in an assembly can mean that even if your assembly is located on your local hard drive, you still have to open a very large database file across the network. The first rule about performance with SolidWorks is to work locally rather than across a network.

By default, the database is located at `C:\Solidworks Data\lang\English`. You can open this file with Microsoft Access or Excel.

> **NOTE**   When specifying network paths, it is best to specify a universal naming convention, or UNC, path rather than a mapped address. A UNC address follows the format, `\\Server\Shared Folder`. The advantage of the UNC over the mapped drive is that mapped drives can vary from one computer to another, but the UNC is always the same.

The Configurator application

If you have just installed Toolbox the way that most, if not all, new users do, then you will accept all defaults and trust the software that you just purchased to not give you bad advice. In this situation, the database is installed locally and Toolbox is set to use configurations for sizes.

When you put a Toolbox part into an assembly, you do not even notice anything other than the part going into the assembly, although it may hesitate while the large database is opened. If you check the part configurations, you may notice that there is a Default config and a new config that represents the size that you just created. Every new size that you create makes another new configuration. Figure 17.10 shows a Toolbox part with the FeatureManager and ConfigurationManager open showing several configurations that Toolbox created in this particular fastener.

FIGURE 17.10

A Toolbox part showing the FeatureManager and ConfigurationManager

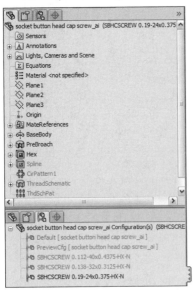

Next, you may receive an assembly from a client. Often, because Toolbox parts are located in an area where you would not necessarily look for parts, users send assemblies and parts, but do not send Toolbox parts. You may think that this is okay; after all, you have Toolbox on your system, and so it should pick up your toolbox parts. The truth is that when receiving an assembly from someone else, you are better off if one of the parties does not have Toolbox on their system.

Huge Screws

If both you and the client who sent the assembly have Toolbox, then you should be okay, right? Well, yes and no. Yes, your client's assembly will pick up your Toolbox parts, but no, it will not work properly because you do not have all of the same configurations and sizes that your client has. In cases like this, you will experience what I have come to refer to as the Huge Screws syndrome. When SolidWorks finds the right file but cannot find the right configuration, it uses another configuration, usually the Default, which is generally the biggest size. This is where the Huge Screws name came from.

Part of the really bad news is that if you save your assembly with the Huge Screws, SolidWorks has no way of knowing that the huge screws are not the correct screws, and you can only solve the problem manually by going through the assembly and reassigning sizes to the huge screws.

You can work around this by opening an assembly that has not yet been saved with the Huge Screws, by using the Advanced option in the Open dialog box (you can find this in the Configurations list), and selecting the New configuration showing assembly structure only option. With this option, all components are suppressed. You can unsuppress any non-Toolbox parts and continue working. Ask your client to send you his Toolbox parts and then unsuppress those parts in the assembly, making sure that it finds the right parts, which is best done by having the correct parts already open before you open the assembly. These options are shown in Figure 17.11.

FIGURE 17.11

Opening an assembly with all parts suppressed

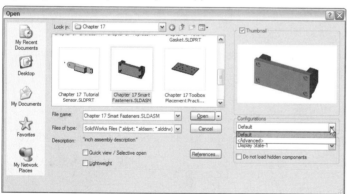

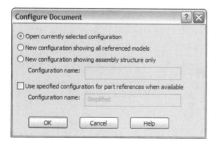

If you replace your Toolbox parts with the Toolbox parts from the client, you may experience the same problem in reverse if you had configs that your client did not. In the end, it would be great to be able to merge the two parts to combine all of the available sizes into a single file. There is a way of doing that, which I will describe later, but it is a convoluted workaround. Files that have the same names and different content are at the top of the list of things you shouldn't do in file management, and yet the SolidWorks Toolbox system frequently creates this very situation.

A slight retraction

To be fair, SolidWorks has fixed the Huge Screws problem in the 2007 version, by coming up with a clever method for figuring out which size is missing and building it on the fly when the assembly is opened. Additional information about the Toolbox parts is now stored in the assembly, which helps identify the missing parts. Unfortunately, the fix only works for assemblies that use the parts from the 2007 or later library and assemblies that have been built in SolidWorks 2007 or later. To sum up, if you have assemblies built in an older version of SolidWorks, and your Toolbox library becomes corrupted or lost, or you are sent an assembly that uses a different Toolbox library, even if you are working in a version later than SolidWorks 2007, you cannot benefit from this fix.

This is disappointing in many respects because anyone who has existing Huge Screws problems will continue to have them until they rebuild the assembly or manually repair the configurations. It is doubly disappointing because the information needed to re-create the correct configuration has always been stored in the assembly — the filename and the configuration name are enough — but SolidWorks has missed an opportunity to really fix this problem.

Before the Summary at the end of this chapter, I have some recommendations if you are still interested in using Toolbox.

Toolbox organization

Toolbox parts can be organized in a number of ways. The raw parts are organized as follows:

- Standard and Units (for example, ANSI Inch or ANSI Metric; most standards do not include multiple units, they assume metric).

- Hardware Type (such as bearings, bolts, and bushings).

- Each type is organized differently, but bolts and screws are organized by drive or head type (for example, you have socket head screws, hex head, and thumb screws).

- Filenames look like `Socket Button Head Cap Screw_AI.SLDPRT`, where the `AI` represents ANSI Inch.

Figure 17.12 shows this organization in part. Also notice the warning message in the Design Library window. It is telling you that your Toolbox is not set up optimally for sharing between users. I describe how to handle this situation later in this chapter.

FIGURE 17.12

Toolbox content organization

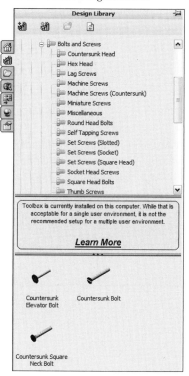

Configurations or parts?

By now you are probably unsure about the use of configurations in general. If so, that is not the impression I am trying to convey. Configurations in themselves are not the problem; the problem here is in the file management practice of having files with the same names but different content. Mixing that with the practice of trying to treat "configurator" software like a "library" exacerbates the problem.

That said, you have two options regarding how you create different sizes. The default option is that sizes are created as configurations within a single part. The other option is that sizes are created as individual files.

The best time to make this choice is before you install SolidWorks. Unfortunately, before you install SolidWorks, you probably do not have any idea that these issues exist. The reason for making this decision not just early, but immediately, is that if you start using the default setting (configurations), and make a few configurations for some parts, and then switch to using the Save Parts setting, the parts that are saved out will all have the pre-existing configurations and thus different sizes.

If you find yourself in this situation, it is better to reinstall Toolbox or simply to copy over a new default set of parts with no configurations.

You can access the option to either Create Configurations or Create Parts by selecting Toolbox ➪ Configure ➪ Define User Settings, as shown in Figure 17.13. I discuss the other settings in this dialog box later in this chapter.

Which is better?

The following list contains some pros and cons for each option.

Configurations are better for:

- Controlling data across several sizes. For example, a design table can drive custom properties that are added to all configurations. Doing this with many individual parts would be very messy.

- The interface to select configurations from a list is easier to work with than the interface to select a part from a list.

- File management organization is somewhat easier for configured parts.

FIGURE 17.13

Toolbox settings for the Create Configurations or Create Parts options

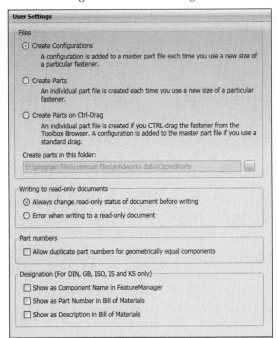

Separate parts are better for:

- Keeping the file size small.
- Replacing all of one size part with another.
- A guarantee that you will never have the Huge Screws problem.

Materials or custom part numbers in Toolbox

Maybe your company uses screws of different materials or finishes in your products. Toolbox, in its default arrangement, does not have an option to deal with this directly. If you ask a tech support person whether materials and custom part numbers can be used in SolidWorks, she will tell you "of course, simply enter in the desired quantity when making the part." The implication here is that you do them one at a time, and that whoever creates the part uses the same syntax as everyone else.

Figure 17.14 shows the interface for adding a Toolbox part to an assembly. You can access this interface by dragging a Toolbox part from the Design Library window into the assembly graphics window. The materials assignment is usually intended to be done as part of the Description. You can access this interface and the Part Number fields through the Add Favorite button in the upper-left corner of the Favorites panel.

The way that SolidWorks expects you to work with materials and custom part numbers is simply not practical unless you have one person doing all of the work, and you do not have many parts to create. SolidWorks does not provide any direct way to mass-populate data of this type.

One method to work around the lack of a mass-population tool is to first create all of the sizes for a part using configurations. Then auto-create a design table and you can use Excel techniques to build descriptions, custom part numbers, materials, and whatever custom property you want to have.

Another method to do this is to create a custom standard for materials. A custom standard essentially copies a high level in the database such as ANSI Inch. You can specify a name such as Company X Stainless Hardware, or Company X Black Oxide Hardware.

I have already mentioned that adding custom standards greatly increases the size of the database, and contributes to the delay in adding the Toolbox parts to an assembly. If this is not a handicap for you — and you should at least try it — then it may be a more viable way to incorporate materials and finishes.

Toolbox in a multi-user environment

You can make Toolbox work the way it is intended to a few ways. The most reliable way is to remove your computer from the network, and to not bring in any assemblies from external sources that were created referencing Toolbox parts. That sounds like an extreme measure, but it is necessary, as Toolbox's weaknesses come from sharing Toolbox data.

FIGURE 17.14

Adding a part number and description to a new Toolbox part

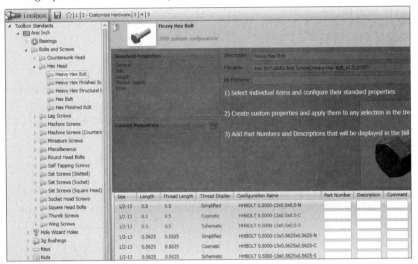

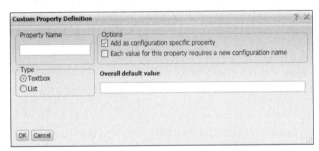

Unfortunately, most SolidWorks users do not have the luxury of being able to dictate the environment in which they work. They generally share files with other users across a network, in a PDM system, or across the Internet through FTP, e-mail, or VPN. If each user has their own Toolbox installation locally, as happens with the default installation, then you could run into the same problems as described above when receiving an outside client's files, especially if they are using configurations. As a result, you must somehow share Toolbox.

Sharing Toolbox

You can share Toolbox by redirecting the Common Files part of the SolidWorks installation to a shared network location. This part of the installation is shown in Figure 17.15.

FIGURE 17.15

Locating the Toolbox library during installation

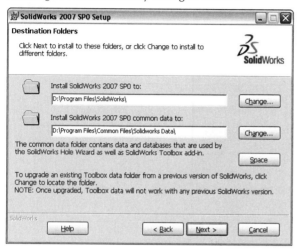

Sharing an existing Toolbox library

This is fine for the first installation, but for any installation where a version of the software already exists on your computer, the shared files also already exist. There is no installation option to accommodate this situation, and so you have to either install over the shared documents or install to a dummy location and redirect SolidWorks to the shared files manually. You have to go through this installation, even the dummy installation, because it is installing the *application* part of Toolbox. Remember that a Toolbox installation has three components: the empty default library part files, the database with all of the information in it that is used to populate the library, and the application dlls that make everything work.

It is particularly important to pay attention to this if the library has been changed. If you overwrite the database, it is not really important unless, for example, standards have been changed, or custom properties added. However, if the library has been changed (for example, by adding configurations) and a later installation overwrites it, then you can cause yourself or someone else a lot of difficulties.

For this reason, you need to know how to manually redirect Toolbox to a different location. Tools ➪ Options ➪ Hole Wizard/Toolbox is the location of this setting, as shown in Figure 17.16.

FIGURE 17.16

Locating the Toolbox database from Tools ➪ Options

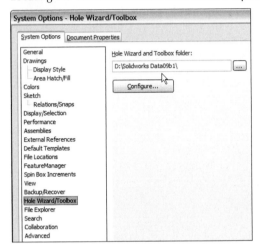

Toolbox administration

If you have only one user, you can do what you like — even use the default installation — and Toolbox should work for you. If, however, you are administering an installation with more than one user, you need to be informed of the issues involving setting up and using Toolbox mentioned previously, and a few more mentioned next.

Read-only setting

If a Toolbox is shared, is it possible that multiple people can access the same files at the same time? This is one of the most frequently asked questions about Toolbox administration. If two people need to write to a file at the same time, then that can cause problems. In order to remedy this, SolidWorks plays referee between multiple users who are accessing the same Toolbox files.

You need to apply the following settings to share Toolbox files on a network:

- Toolbox ➪ Configure ➪ Define User Settings ➪ Always Change Read-only Status of Document Before Writing; this option should be on.

- The Windows users should have full permissions to access the SolidWorks Data directory, and the SolidWorks Data\Browser directory should be set to Read-only for all users.

Upgrading SolidWorks with Toolbox

It is time to upgrade. You have your SolidWorks 2010 disks, and SolidWorks 2009 is installed. You can now go ahead and install SolidWorks 2010, but when it comes to the part in the installation shown in Figure 17.15, take notice again of what you are doing. The installation may default to the SolidWorks 2009 Toolbox location. If you overwrite this location, then you will not be able to use Toolbox with SolidWorks 2009 (because the library will be a future version). If you intend to use multiple versions, then you also need to maintain multiple Toolbox installations.

You should also consider what would happen if you make a mistake and completely overwrite the SolidWorks 2009 library that contains all of the configuration data that you have worked hard to create. When upgrading, you do not want to overwrite your existing library. The following is a set of steps to help you upgrade safely and effectively:

1. **Install the new version with Toolbox in a new location; for example, SolidWorks 2010 Data or a directory name that helps to distinguish this library from another.**

2. **Copy the old SolidWorks 2009 data (containing the correct configurations) over the top of the new SolidWorks 2010 data.**

3. **Browse to the** `Toolbox\data` **utilities subdirectory of the SolidWorks installation directory and run** `UpdateBrowserData.exe`**.** The interface for this program is shown in Figure 17.17.

FIGURE 17.17

The UpdateBrowserData.exe interface

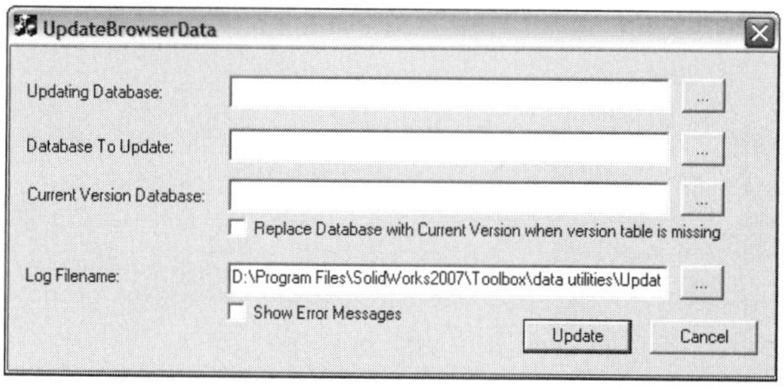

4. **Select the Updating Database field and use the ellipsis button to browse to** `Toolbox\data utilities\lang\English\updatedb.mdb` **in the SolidWorks installation directory.**

5. **Select the Database To Update field and browse to** `SWBrowser.mdb`. You can find this file by following the `ToolboxPartFolder` path in the `Toolbox.ini` file and looking in the `\lang\english` subdirectory.

6. **Click Update.**

This prevents you from overwriting your old version, while still copying the old version to the new installation and avoiding the Huge Screws syndrome.

Adding custom Toolbox parts

You can add your own parts to Toolbox by simply dragging-and-dropping them. Drag-and-drop is available in third-level folders. Levels are counted from the Standard folder, which is level 1. You will not be able to use your custom parts with Toolbox special functionality like Smart Fasteners.

Adding folders to Toolbox

You can add folders to Toolbox through the right-mouse button menu. Just right-click a first- or second-level folder, and select New Folder. You can create a new level-1 folder by right-clicking the Toolbox icon, as shown in Figure 17.18.

FIGURE 17.18

Adding a new folder

Merging Toolbox libraries

You can merge Toolbox libraries by simply copying or moving one folder in with the existing library folders. Another type of merging may be less successful. If you have two Toolbox parts from different sources and they have different sets of size configurations, you may want to merge them to get the benefits of both sets of sizes.

Unfortunately, there is no direct way of doing this in Toolbox. The best way would be to auto-create design tables in both parts, and then to copy the configurations from one design table to the other design table. This should effectively copy configurations between parts, although you may need to remove any duplicate configuration rows.

Toolbox and PDM

This topic could be a chapter on its own, but I will not delve too deeply into it here, because it goes beyond the intended scope of this book. A discussion of Toolbox requires some mention of how it may be used in conjunction with a Product Data Management (PDM) product.

Toolbox and Workgroup PDM, or any other PDM product for that matter, can be a challenge to combine. Generally, it is useful to be able to see the fasteners in PDM because of the Bill of Materials (BOM) capabilities, quantities, Where Used options, and complete searches. Some users choose not to put library parts in the vault because they are not revision-managed documents. All the same, revision management is not the only reason to put items in the vault.

Looking at it from the Toolbox point of view, Toolbox cannot work with its parts in the vault, and if changes were allowed to the parts (sizes add configurations), then you would need to check in the part every time you added a size. This is not necessarily a problem, but it does become awkward.

Some PDM products allow files to exist outside the vault, while pointers to the files exist within the vault. This is one very good option for using Toolbox with a PDM product.

Another good option is to simply use the Create Parts setting. This creates individual files that are easier to manage. It may also be important for a different reason: some PDM products, such as Workgroup PDM, do not distinguish configurations as separate controllable or separately identifiable documents.

Toolbox settings

You can find Toolbox settings in the Toolbox menu, by selecting the Configure option. The Configure Data dialog box shows a five step process:

1. **Select your hardware**
2. **Customize your hardware**
3. **Define user settings**
4. **Set permissions**
5. **Configure Smart Fasteners**

Select and Customize Hardware

The Select Hardware page shows all of the standards. If you are not using certain standards, you can turn them off by deselecting their check mark. You can do the same for folders and even specific parts within the standard. If you have added folders or custom parts in the Design Library window, they appear here.

As you expand the standard, and then the fastener type and the specific head types, you can select individual parts. The Hex Screw on the Customize Hardware page is selected in the list shown in Figure 17.19.

FIGURE 17.19

The Toolbox Customize Hardware page

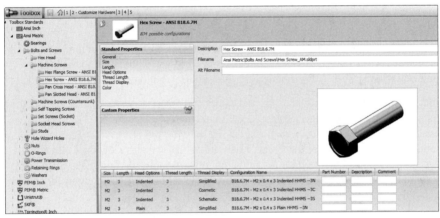

Several functions are available through this interface for Toolbox parts:

- You can offer alternate filenames.

- You can disable specific sizes.

- You can add custom property information.

- You can limit the available lengths.

- You can limit the available thread types. Available thread types are shown in Figure 17.20.

Available thread display options

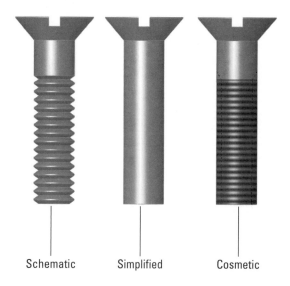

Schematic   Simplified   Cosmetic

User Settings page

The User Settings page is where you can set the config and part options. If you choose to create parts, then you also need to specify a location for the parts to be kept. If you choose a network location, it is best to use the UNC path, rather than a mapped drive because mapped drives may not reconnect on startup and may be mapped to different letters from computer to computer, but the UNC always points to the same location from any point on the network. The User Settings page is shown in Figure 17.21.

Properties tab

The Properties tab enables you to set up properties that appear in the PropertyManager. For example, you can enable fill-in or drop-down lists for values. Properties can be enabled for specific items, as shown in Figure 17.22.

Smart Fasteners tab

The Smart Fasteners tab controls Smart Fasteners, which I discuss later in this chapter. The tab is shown in Figure 17.23. As an example of the types of settings you can use here, you can control which screw types are used with which types of Hole Wizard or non-Hole Wizard holes.

FIGURE 17.21

The User Settings page

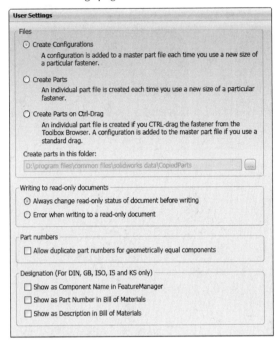

FIGURE 17.22

The Define user settings page

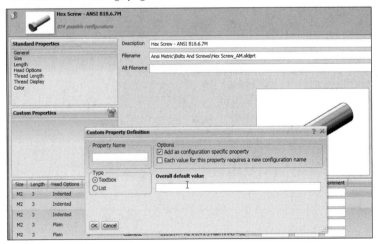

FIGURE 17.23

The Configure Smart Fasteners page

Using Toolbox

Up to now in this chapter, I have addressed Toolbox mainly from the administrative point of view; now I will show it to you from the user's point of view. Toolbox has two components: Toolbox and Toolbox Browser. In practice, the *Toolbox* component is often ignored, and the *Toolbox Browser* component is generally referred to as Toolbox.

The Toolbox Browser is the Task pane interface, and is found on the Design Library tab, as shown in the image to the left in Figure 17.24. The Toolbox component is found in the Toolbox drop-down menu. It includes structural steel shapes, grooves, cams, and beam and bearing calculators.

Turning Toolbox and the Toolbox Browser on

You can turn on Toolbox and the Toolbox Browser through the Tools ⇨ Add-Ins dialog box. The column of check boxes on the left indicates that the add-in will be active for the current session of SolidWorks only. The column of check boxes on the right indicates that the add-in will be active every time the software starts up, as shown in Figure 17.25.

FIGURE 17.24

Toolbox and the Toolbox Browser

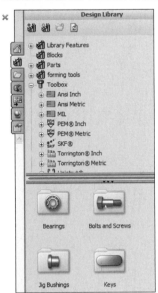

FIGURE 17.25

Turning Toolbox on in the Tools, Add-ins interface

Once the Toolbox Browser is turned on, you can use it by expanding the Task Pane at the right of the SolidWorks graphics window and clicking the Design Library, which looks like a stack of books. In this panel, you will see the Toolbox screw symbol. Expand icons until you find the fastener or other hardware that you are looking for, and then drag the part into the assembly.

Populating holes

Holes can be populated in several ways, such as dragging-and-dropping, populating multiple holes at once (Smart Fasteners), and using feature-driven component patterns. I discuss manual and patterning options here, and Smart Fasteners in the next section.

Drag-and-drop

The simplest way to bring Toolbox parts into an assembly is to drag-and-drop them. Position the part that the fastener goes into so that you can see the edge of the hole where the screw head will go. Then browse to the correct fastener, and drop the fastener onto the edge, as shown in Figure 17.26.

FIGURE 17.26

Dropping a fastener onto a hole

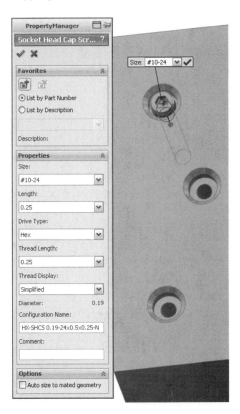

Toolbox parts will even automatically size themselves based on the hole. It is best to use Hole Wizard holes if you are going to use this function of Toolbox parts. Hole Wizard and Toolbox are meant to work together.

When you place the fastener, a PropertyManager appears that enables you to select various properties of the part, including the length, overriding the automatically selected size, the thread representation, and if you want the fastener to change in size when the hole changes. Also after placing the fastener, a handle at the end of it enables you to drag the length of the fastener, which will snap to predetermined lengths.

Populating multiple holes at once

Figure 17.27 shows the progression from a plate with holes in an assembly. In this example, you would select the edges of the holes, then select a fastener, and then choose Insert Into Assembly from the right-mouse button menu, to fully populate the part.

FIGURE 17.27

Populating multiple holes at once in an assembly

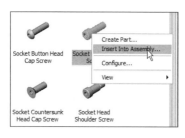

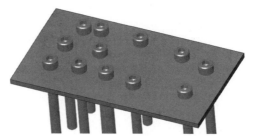

Feature Driven component patterns

Chapter 15 discussed Feature Driven component patterns (also known as derived patterns), where a pattern of parts in an assembly is driven by a feature pattern in a part. You can find this assembly feature in the assembly menus under Insert ⇨ Component Patterns ⇨ Feature Driven.

Smart Fasteners

Smart Fasteners are Toolbox parts that know what holes they go into automatically. The database that holds all the information for Toolbox part types and sizes also holds the information for the sizes of the holes. It is only natural that SolidWorks try to combine this information and use it to its best advantage. You can use Smart Fasteners in two ways: asking SolidWorks to automatically place fasteners in existing holes or placing hole series holes and fasteners simultaneously in the context of the assembly.

Smart Fasteners with Hole Series

One way to use Smart Fasteners is in conjunction with Hole Wizard Hole Series. Hole Series creates the holes through multiple parts at once, creating the appropriate type of hole through each part, and then Smart Fasteners automatically places fasteners in the holes, even including nuts and washers. To do this, you can select the option on the last panel of the Hole Series PropertyManager interface, as shown in Figure 17.28. If you are planning on using Smart Fasteners, using them in conjunction with the Hole Series holes is your best bet.

FIGURE 17.28

The Place Fastener option

The Smart Fasteners with Hole Series is a function that you should be careful with. It is very effective, but it may cost you some performance (speed). The Hole Series is an Assembly Feature (sketch) that drives several in-context features (holes), and then parts are mated to those in-context features (fasteners).

Smart Fasteners Populate All

Smart Fasteners functionality has an even more automatic component. Once an assembly has parts mated into place, you can place fasteners into parts with appropriate holes by face, by part, or for the entire assembly at once.

CAUTION You may not want to spend a lot of time trying to use this type of the Smart Fasteners functionality. I have tried to find examples where Smart Fasteners works well and predictably, but with limited success. I have searched through training examples, through tutorial files from SolidWorks, and have even made some of my own example files. I have looked for presentations from user groups and SolidWorks World that use Smart Fasteners, but no one appears to be talking about this functionality. Although in theory, it offers interesting functionality, in reality, it receives very little attention — definitely a warning sign.

The one assembly that I did find where Smart Fasteners worked surprisingly well (in fact, almost perfectly) was from the sample files that installed with SolidWorks. Upon closer examination, the reason this worked well was because it used assembly features for the holes, and so the holes did not appear in the individual parts. If that is the price that you have to pay just to get fasteners to populate automatically, then I would rather put them all in manually.

The limitations of Smart Fasteners

Smart Fasteners have some documented limitations where you should not expect them to work:

- Holes in single parts
- Holes created by extruding a nested loop
- A mirrored hole or cut features
- Holes in mirrored, imported, or derived parts
- Misaligned holes
- Holes with a large difference in diameter
- Holes with large gaps between them (a large gap in the axial direction)
- Holes made using different techniques (such as sketch pattern versus feature pattern)

If you would like to try out Smart Fasteners, then you can use the assembly included on the CD-ROM called Chapter 17 Smart Fasteners.sldasm. In this assembly, half of the holes are done correctly, and the other half are not: the screws are put in either backwards or head-first. The documented method for flipping the fasteners is to expand the Smart Fastener, right-click the series, and select Flip. In this case, my attempts resulted in success about half of time, which was somewhat higher than my attempts with other assemblies. In some cases, screws were put in the ends of shafts without holes, on filleted edges, and unfortunately missed most of the places that I *did* want the screws to go.

Organizing Toolbox parts in an assembly

Assembly FeatureManagers are hard enough to manage when they become full of parts; they become even more unmanageable when they also need to include the many types of fastener parts. As a result, I recommend that fasteners, as well as any other type of part that is found in large quantity in the assembly, be organized into folders, as shown in Figure 17.29. You should also group parts of the same size or function together.

FIGURE 17.29

Organizing Toolbox parts into folders

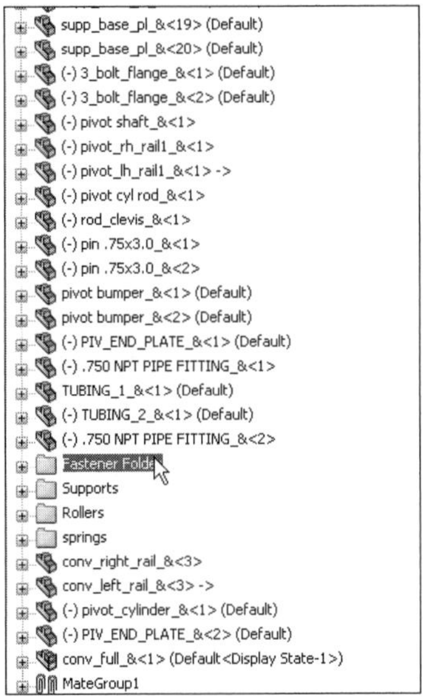

Recommendations

After spending almost an entire chapter saying what you *should not* do, it is finally time to say what you *should* do. Toolbox can be downright dangerous if you install and use it improperly; however, the following recommendations work in most situations.

Just to be clear about this, the most serious file management problems with Toolbox show up when you use configurations, which just happens to be the default option. Still, I'm a big fan of using configurations in general, and especially with library parts, but a Toolbox implementation with configurations is challenging.

The simplest setup that works

If you are a single user who does not share files over a network with other users, then installing SolidWorks and Toolbox with the default settings should work for you. This appears to be the arrangement that the developers had in mind when they programmed the tool, because it is the only scenario in which it works as expected.

Be careful if you ever receive an assembly from another Toolbox user, because this is the one situation that can cause immediate trouble. If the user also sends his Toolbox parts, then I recommend that you open all of his Toolbox parts before you open his assembly, so that the assembly is certain to access his Toolbox parts instead of yours.

If you need to include materials and mass-populate custom properties, then I recommend that you go through the exercise of building all of the configurations of all of the parts, and then use an auto-created design table to drive the properties. If you have more than one user, then this technique will not work for you, unless both users work independently from one another.

A complete setup that works

If you have multiple users that share assemblies, then you need to also share the Toolbox library. If you share assemblies only among yourselves, meaning only with other users who are also sharing Toolbox, then sharing Toolbox should be good enough. However, if you share assemblies with Toolbox users who do not share your Toolbox library, then you should probably go through the exercise of populating all of your parts with all of the available configurations. If you do not receive assemblies from outside of your group with Toolbox parts in the assembly and you have network performance problems, it may be a good idea to install Toolbox locally, but to set it to use the Create Parts setting, where the parts are on a shared network location.

If you use a PDM system, then I would definitely install Toolbox locally, and use the Create Parts setting. The sharing occurs through the PDM system. Library parts should be non-revision managed parts, but you may want to have a representation of the fasteners so you can do where-used searches and BOMs.

The least problematic technique is to turn Toolbox off altogether and either buy or make your own library of static parts. You can then distribute these files internally in your organization, as well as to any other people upstream or downstream from you who also share files with you. You can build this type of library by using Toolbox's config population tool; materials or other custom properties are then dealt with the way you want, probably using auto-created design tables.

Of course, there is a downside to that too, and that is that you lose all of the nice automation features available with Toolbox. The best option if you want to keep Toolbox is to use the Copy Parts option, install locally, use a PDM system, and if you get assemblies from Toolbox users who aren't part of your network, insist that they either use your parts or send you their parts.

Tutorial: Gaining Experience with the Hole Wizard and Toolbox

Figure 17.30 shows a section view of the assembly used for this tutorial. Notice that there is a gasket under the Sensor part.

A section view of the tutorial assembly

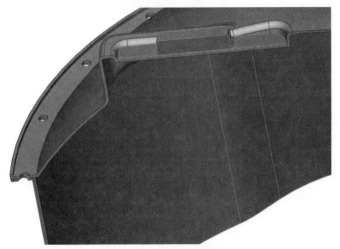

This tutorial assumes that you have a working copy of Toolbox running on your computer. If you do not have Toolbox, then you can proceed to the next chapter. This tutorial also assumes that your Toolbox is using the default Create Configurations setting, although it can also work with the Create Parts setting. To get some experience using this tool, follow these steps:

1. **Open the assembly from the CD-ROM called** `Chapter 17 Tutorialstart.sldasm`.

2. **Make sure that the Toolbox Browser is turned on by selecting Tools ⇨ Add-Ins ⇨ Toolbox ⇨ Toolbox Browser.**

3. **Expand the Task pane, found on the right side of the graphics window, and display the Design Library panel, which contains the Toolbox icon.** Expand the ANSI Inch standard, and the Bolts and Screws folder, and finally click the Hex Head bolt, as shown in Figure 17.31 on the left. Drag-and-drop the Hex Head bolt into the indicated hole. It snaps into place because of the Mate Reference that is used on the Toolbox part. Use the settings shown in the PropertyManager to size the bolt.

FIGURE 17.31

Select and place a fastener.

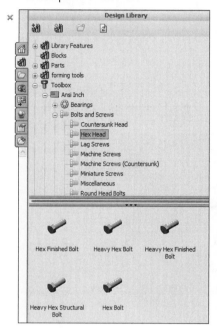

4. **Add a flat washer and nut to the bolt, as shown in Figure 17.32.** The washer is Plain Washer Type A, Preferred - Wide Flat Washer. The nut used is Hex Nut, Heavy Hex Nut.

5. **Right-click the bolt, either in the graphics window or in the FeatureManager, and select Edit Toolbox Definition, toward the bottom of the menu. Change the length of the fastener to 1.625 inches.** Notice that the bolt is too short, as shown in Figure 17.33.

 If you try to apply Smart Fasteners to the hole, you will notice that the fastener is placed incorrectly.

6. **Create a Feature Driven component pattern (Insert ⇨ Component Pattern ⇨ Feature Driven) using the circular pattern of holes on either the Top or Base parts.** Pattern the bolt, washer, and nut all in the same component pattern.

7. **Zoom in on the sensor on the top of the assembly.** There is a gray gasket between the orange sensor and the blue top parts. Click one of the flat ends of the sensor part and then click the Hole Series toolbar button, or select Insert ⇨ Assembly Feature ⇨ Hole ⇨ Hole Series.

FIGURE 17.32

Specifying the washer and nut

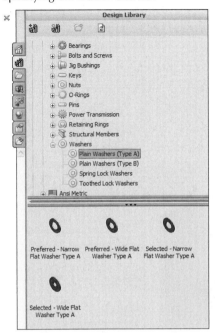

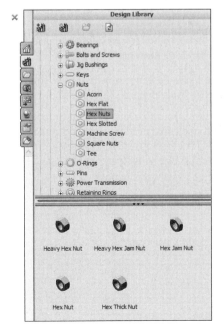

FIGURE 17.33

The bolt is too short.

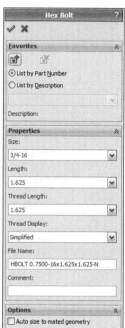

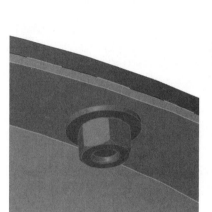

TIP   Remember that the pre-selection of a flat face is important so that you can use a 2D placement sketch, rather than a 3D placement sketch.

8. **Make sure that you select the Place Fastener option on the final tab when you get there, as well as the Create New Hole option. This workflow is different from previous versions.**

9. **Make three sketch points and use construction geometry and dimensions to locate the holes, as shown in Figure 17.34.** The size and types of holes are determined in a later step. (This is the reverse of the normal Hole Wizard, where you first determine the type and size of hole, and then you establish the positions.)

10. **Click the Next button (the blue arrow pointing right) to move to the First Part hole specification.** Set it to a counterbored hole, for a #10 binding head screw, with a head clearance of .025 inches, as shown in Figure 17.35, in the image to the left. Click the Next button to advance to the Middle Parts hole sizing.

FIGURE 17.34

The positions of holes in Step 9

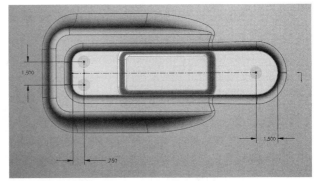

FIGURE 17.35

Sizing the holes

11. **In the Middle Parts PropertyManager, make sure that the Auto size based on start hole option is on, as shown in Figure 17.35, in the middle image.** This creates a normal fit clearance hole for the gasket part. Click Next to advance to the hole definition for the Last Part.

12. **In the End Hole Specification panel, make sure that you select the Hole rather than the Tap option, as well as the Auto size based on start hole option.** This is shown to the right in Figure 17.36.

13. **Proceed to the Smart Fasteners tab.** Make sure the Place Fastener option is selected, along with the Auto size option.

FIGURE 17.36

The Smart Fastener PropertyManager

14. **Add a washer and a nut to the bottom stack of the binding head screws.** Using the Stack Components panel of the final tab of the Hole Series / Smart Fastener interface, add a washer and a nut to the bottom stack.

15. **A dialog box appears, enabling you to add a washer and a nut, as shown in Figure 17.37.** You may want to roll the model over so that you can see the components being added to the underside of the screw. You can add other properties to the parts using the Properties button. Notice that the screw has been lengthened to accommodate the added components.

 If you add a washer to the top stack, the hole does not automatically become larger, and it may cause an interference. Be careful about your choice of top-stack washers.

FIGURE 17.37

Adding washers and nuts

> **NOTE** You may have noticed that this time, Smart Fasteners worked almost flawlessly and certainly saved you some time. Although this tool is not applicable to other purposes, when used with the Hole Series, it is quite useful.

16. You may want to group the fasteners and even the fasteners' mates into folders, as shown in Figure 17.38.

FIGURE 17.38

The finished Assembly FeatureManager interface

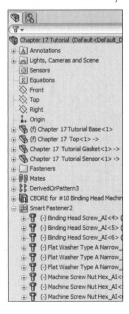

CAUTION The final version of the assembly on the CD-ROM may open up on your computer with Huge Screws if you open it before completing the tutorial. This is because the configurations used in the assembly are on *my* computer. Although you have the same parts, before doing this tutorial, you may not have the same configurations, and so they cannot be found and come in Huge instead. This was intentional; it is a practical reminder of this problem and how easily it can happen to you.

Summary

The Hole Wizard can make holes based on 2D or 3D sketches. The type of hole that you create depends on whether or not you have pre-selected a flat face before clicking the Hole Wizard tool. Two-dimensional sketches are far easier to use than 3D sketches.

I have met people who claim to have had good success with Toolbox even in a shared environment, but given that the problems with the tool are so easy to demonstrate, these people are either extremely disciplined or extremely lucky. For all users except those who work alone and do not share files with other Toolbox users, Toolbox can cause a number of major problems. You can develop techniques to prevent you from experiencing Huge Screws; for example, either not sharing assemblies with other Toolbox users or pre-populating all of your configurable parts with all possible configurations. Further, Smart Fasteners that you use in conjunction with Hole Series violate any best practice guidelines that you could name when it comes to assembly performance and circular references; however, if you can work with that, then it is a really sophisticated technique.

Chapter 18

Working with Library Features

L ibrary features are features that you create once and re-use many times. They are intended to be parametrically flexible to fit into many types of geometry, but they can also be of a fixed size and shape. You will use all the information that you have learned in previous chapters about designing for change, and design intent in this chapter, as well as learn how to create, use, and store library features.

Using Library Features

Library features reside in the Design Library, which is located in the Task Pane to the right of the graphics window.

> **TIP** You can actually detach the Task pane from its docking location and move it wherever you want, leave it undocked, or even move it to a second monitor.

If you are a long-time SolidWorks user, then you may still know the Design Library as the Feature Palette. Another change to the old library features and palette features is that they have been combined, thus removing some of the limitations of the old palette features.

You can use library features for snap rings, grooves for o-rings, custom holes, mounting bosses for plastics, mounting hole patterns, electrical connector holes, and so on.

One very useful aspect of library features is that they can be driven by configurations and design tables. Once the feature is in the part, the configurations are still available, and so you can change the config of an applied library feature at any time.

You can also link a library feature to an external file. This enables you to change a feature or set of features in several parts at once, if they are all externally linked to the file.

Getting started with library features

Library features are simple to use, and only slightly less simple to set up. For that reason, in this chapter, I discuss using them first, so that you know what kind of behavior you are trying to create when you go to make your own features. As a result, setting them up should make a little more sense.

To use a library feature, you just drag-and-drop it onto the appropriate geometry. You are then prompted to select references in the new part that match the base geometry that the library feature is attached to. You can be fairly creative with references, but one of the goals is to make the library feature work with as few references as possible, in order to make it easy, fast, and reliable to use.

SolidWorks software installs with several sample library features in the Design Library. The following demonstration uses some of these standard library features. Later, you can add library features from the CD-ROM to your Design Library.

The Library Feature interface

Library features work best if they go from a certain type of geometry to a similar type of geometry; for example, from rectangular to rectangular, or from circular to circular. This is because the relations or dimensions that link the feature to the rest of the part tend to be dimensions from straight edges or concentric sketch relations. Of course, there are other ways of applying library features, but these are the most prevalent. Library features can be applied unconstrained and then constrained, or moved later, but the process is cleanest when it all just falls together correctly the first time.

Task pane

You do not have to save the part or do anything special before applying a library feature. All you need to do is find the Task pane. The Task pane is the window that flies out from the right when you open SolidWorks. You may have turned it off and forgotten about it, in which case you can turn it back on by selecting View ⇨ Task pane.

The Task pane automatically closes when you click outside of it unless you pin it open using the pushpin icon in the upper-right corner of the window. When you do this, any toolbars that appeared on the right side of the Task pane control tabs are moved out and positioned between the graphics window and the Task pane, which now remains open by default.

You can also detach the Task pane by dragging the bar at the top of the pane. Figure 18.1 shows the Task pane docked to the right side of the SolidWorks window.

FIGURE 18.1

The Task pane docked to right side of the SolidWorks window

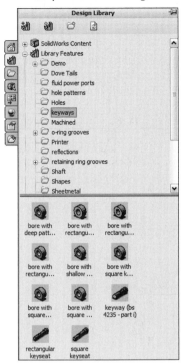

> **TIP** If you are using dual monitors, you can drag the detached Task Pane onto the second monitor, which allows you to use the Task Pane and at the same time gives you more room in the graphics area. You must do this for each session; the Task Pane does not remember positions on a second monitor.

Design Library

The Design Library tab displays an image of a stack of books. It is the overall library area for all sorts of elements in SolidWorks, which I discuss later in this chapter. The only part of the Design Library of concern right now is the Features folder. If you expand this folder, you can see that it is populated with some sample features.

Open a new part and create a cylinder using any method you want (for example, extrude, revolve). Make the diameter three inches and the length a little more than one inch.

In the Inch features folder, click the folder called o-ring grooves. The first feature in the list is called *face static – gas*. Drag-and-drop this feature onto the end flat face of the cylinder. As shown in the image to the left in Figure 18.2, the PropertyManager displays a yellow information panel explaining the process.

The next step is to select the configuration, as shown in the image to the right in Figure 18.2. Not all library features have multiple size configurations, but these ones do. The configs in this case are driven by design tables. Select configuration 330.

FIGURE 18.2

Placing the feature and selecting the configuration

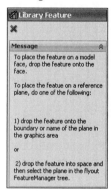

When you select the configuration, the interface changes. In this case, only a sketch relation locates the feature; it is not located by dimensions. Notice that in the References panel shown in Figure 18.3, there is an Edge entry with a question mark, which turns to a check mark after you select the edge. This means that the library feature needs a circular edge to locate it. Notice that a small window appears, displaying the library feature. You may not be able to distinguish it in Figure 18.3, but the circular edge around the face that the library feature is on is highlighted in green. This indicates that you need to select an edge that has the same relation to the library feature as the highlighted edge. Pick the circular edge of the part on the end of the cylinder where you want to place the library feature.

Next, use a rectangular part where the library feature is located by using dimensions rather than sketch relations. Create a rectangle 1.5 inches by 2 inches, and extrude it to about 2 inches in depth.

FIGURE 18.3

Locating the library feature

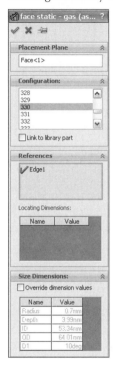

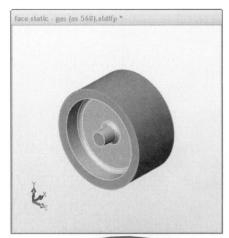

Next, in the Design Library, browse to features, then inch, and then the fluid power ports folder, and drag the sae j1926-1 feature onto the end of the extruded rectangle. Select the 38-24 size from the configurations list. A window appears, prompting you for reference selections, as shown in Figure 18.4.

TIP It is often helpful to orient the part that is receiving the library feature in the same way as the part shown in the preview window. This helps you to visualize which edges to select.

Placing a library feature with dimensions

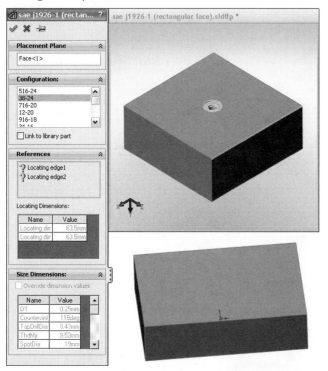

After the locating edges have been identified, the Locating Dimensions box becomes active, and you can change the values of the dimensions to locate the feature. Further, in the Size Dimensions pane at the bottom of the PropertyManager, clicking the Override dimension values option allows you to change dimensions of the feature itself.

When you use a library feature with a design table, the design table is not brought into the part with the library feature. If the part already had a design table, this would cause multiple tables, which is not currently possible in SolidWorks. The configurations in the design table are brought forward, however.

If you override the feature dimensions using the Override Dimension Values option in the Size Dimensions panel of the Library Feature Property Manager when feature configurations already exist, then a new configuration is created in the list of feature configurations called Custom Configuration. It appears that multiple custom configurations are not allowed, and so if you have to make changes, then you must ensure that they are right before you use the library feature in a part.

Other Design Library functions

The Design Library has other functions besides library features. For example, you can use it as a repository for other items that you use frequently.

Annotations

You can store commonly used annotations in the Design Library. If you look at the Annotations folder with the default sample annotations, you see a combination of symbols and blocks. You can use symbols and notes in 3D models, but you can only use blocks in sketches or 2D drawings. Keep in mind that not all annotation types can be used in all places.

Annotations can be stored in the library as favorites or blocks. Many file extensions are used for different types of favorites, but they typically begin with `*.sld` and end with `fvt`, as in `*.sldweldfvt`. Figure 18.5 shows the default location of the Design Library, and the Thumbnail view of the favorites and blocks in the Annotations folder.

FIGURE 18.5

The Annotations folder in Windows Explorer

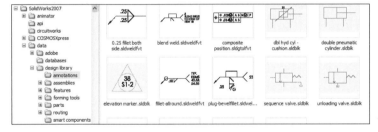

Location of the Design Library folder

If you frequently work with different types of annotations, then you should organize the library into subfolders to separate symbols, annotations, and blocks, and move these folders to a different location. By default, the Design Library folders are found at C:\Documents and Settings\All Users\ Application Data\SolidWorks\SolidWorks 2009\Design Library\. You should store them in another location, not in the SolidWorks installation directory, but in an area that you have selected to maintain SolidWorks data between releases. For example, I have a folder at `D:\Library` that contains folders for macros, templates, library features, library parts, favorites, and so on. You can easily back up or copy these files from one computer to another, although you must quit SolidWorks before making these changes.

After moving the library, you have to point SolidWorks to the new location. To do this, select Tools ➪ Options ➪ File Locations ➪ Design Library. Delete the old location and browse to the new location. You should move other items in this list and redirect any items that you use, such as the templates and any other items you use frequently. Once you have specified the settings, they should be retained when you install service pack upgrades or future versions.

Library parts

The Design Library can also store commonly used library parts. One of the advantages of using the library for parts is that on placement into the assembly, if configurations are available in a part, then a window pops up, enabling you to select which configuration to place into the assembly.

NOTE In many cases, using the Design Library for library parts is thought to be an acceptable replacement for the automated function of Toolbox. If you use Toolbox to make the parts and populate them with configurations, and then save the parts out of Toolbox and into the Design Library, many options, including naming conventions, and more flexible use of custom properties become available that are not available through Toolbox.

Figure 18.6 shows the configuration selection window. Note that this is alphabetically listed, and you can type in the box to go to the configuration that you want.

FIGURE 18.6

Inserting library parts with configurations

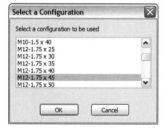

Parts inserted from the library parts folder can also take advantage of the Mate References functionality in the same way as Toolbox, by allowing parts to snap into place.

Sheet metal forming tools

I only mention sheet metal forming tools here as a part of the library. They work much like other library features, but they do so within the specialized functions of sheet metal parts in SolidWorks. I discuss sheet metal forming tools in Chapters 29 and 30. Forming tools folders have special properties. If you want to use the parts in a folder as forming tools, you must right-click-the folder in the Design Library, and select Forming Tool Folder. The only other library type that needs special folders is library assemblies.

Assemblies

You can use library assemblies in SolidWorks in the same ways that you use library parts, because they are inserted into the top-level assembly as a subassembly. For subassemblies that require motion, such as universal joint subassemblies, you can set the subassembly to solve as flexible.

 When saving assemblies to the library, it is recommended that you put the parts in a separate folder to segregate the parts of different assemblies.

Routing

Routing is a separately purchased add-in that is included with SolidWorks Office Premium. It includes piping, tubing (rigid and flexible), and wiring. Routing makes extensive use of libraries and automation, but is not part of the scope of this book. Look for another Wiley title to be published on this topic.

Smart Components

Smart Components are components that resize by automatically selecting configurations, depending on the size of the geometry onto which they are being dropped. For example, a clamp with many sizes driven by configurations would select the correct config when dropped onto different sizes of cylinders. This is a very useful tool. Smart Components are discussed in Chapter 19.

Creating Library Features

When you save library features to the library, they use the file extension `*.sldlfp` (library feature part). They must contain some base geometry, which simulates the part onto which the feature will be dropped. The base geometry is not transferred to the new part; only features that are marked with the "L" in the FeatureManager (for Library) are transferred to the new part. Figure 18.7 shows the FeatureManager of a library feature part.

Creating a library feature

When creating a library feature, the first problem that you need to solve is how the feature will be located on a new part. Does it need to be placed on cylindrical parts, rectangular parts, other types of shapes, or does this matter at all? Will the feature be located by using dimensions or sketch relations, or will it just be placed underdefined and later fully defined manually rather than automatically?

You may have noticed in one of the earlier examples that the sample fluid power ports had two versions of the same feature. One version is intended for the feature to be placed on the flat end of a cylinder, and the other version is intended to be placed on a rectangular face.

FIGURE 18.7

The FeatureManager of a library feature part

A few limitations

Library features can contain multiple features of different types. They may add and remove material, even within a single library feature. However, a few limitations exist. For example, they require a base feature, and multibody features and external references are not allowed, nor are surfaces, sheet metal, weldments, or molds related features. In addition, you cannot add a scale feature (a feature that affects the entire body) to the library, nor can you apply library features to an assembly.

Creating a new library feature

To start a new feature, the first decision that you need to make is what shape to make the base. Is the feature a type that is usually going to go onto a single shape or multiple shapes? Regardless of your decision, you or whoever ends up using the feature will have the flexibility to change, or simply not use, the relations when you place the feature.

For this example, I use a rectangular base. The library feature that I want to create consists of two boss extrudes, a cut extrude, and several fillets. Here is how it works:

First, you need to create a rectangular extrusion. The size should be bigger than the feature that goes on it, and representative of the face of the end part onto which this feature will typically be placed.

Next, in beginning to create the features that you want to reuse, it is very important that you pay attention to any references outside of the sketch; these include absolutely *anything* outside the active sketch, such as the sketch plane, references to edges, the Origin, other planes, other sketches, and axes. Although these references are allowed, each reference to anything that is not already part of the library feature must be reconnected when you place the feature on a new part.

The ideal situation is obviously a single drag-and-drop, but generally speaking, at least one other step is usually needed. The initial drag-and-drop determines the face for the feature to start from, and from there, you usually need to locate features, either by using relations or dimensions. A concentric relation locates the feature in a single reference selection of a circular edge (although it may also need to be rotated), and dimensions typically require a dimension in the X dimension, and another one in the Y dimension.

Figure 18.8 shows the base feature and the first feature of the library feature. The only relations between the sketch of the library feature and the base feature are the sketch plane and the two dimensions.

FIGURE 18.8

Creating a library feature

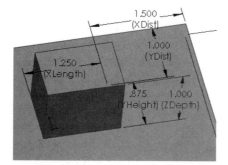

NOTE Notice that names have been assigned to all the dimensions, sketches, and features. This is because the dimension names all display in the interface. If you look back to Figure 18.4, in the Size Dimensions pane, dimension names make it easy to know which dimension to change, whereas the D1 dimension leaves you guessing as to what it applies to.

You should ensure that subsequent features after the first one reference only the first feature of the library feature (which is the second feature in the part). This is not a mandatory requirement, but a helpful guideline. You can make additional references, but they should be limited to the same items that were already referenced, if possible. Users who model carelessly or do not pay attention to what they are doing, typically have trouble making library features that function and are easy to use.

Now you can add the second extruded feature, being careful to reference only geometry that is going to move with the library feature. Figure 18.9 shows the newly added feature. If you would like to follow along with the building of this feature, you can open the part from the CD-ROM under the filename `Chapter 18 First Library Feature.sldlfp`.

FIGURE 18.9

Adding the next feature to the library feature

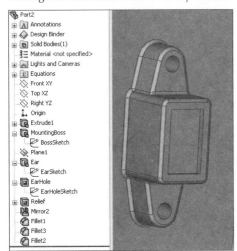

Notice that a plane has been added. The plane is made to only reference geometry that is internal to the library feature; it is perpendicular to an edge at the midpoint, which simultaneously locates and orients the plane correctly to enable it to be used to mirror the Ear feature.

Also notice that the EarSketch uses the same face reference from the base feature. This will appear in the Reference list as a single reference.

NOTE   **SolidWorks has made some changes that affect library features in two ways that may not be immediately obvious. First, before SolidWorks allowed multi-body parts, the first feature of the part was always called the *base feature*. This terminology remains, even though the concept of a base feature is obsolete. (The first feature in a part may be reordered so that a different feature becomes first.)**

Second, SolidWorks used to distinguish between palette features and library features. Palette features were limited to a single reference, and library features were a bit less user-friendly but more powerful. They have been combined and improved to what we have today.

Saving the library feature

You can use two methods to save a library feature. You can either drag-and-drop into a Design Library folder, or use the Save As method. Because Save As is a little more common, I describe it first.

The first step in saving the library feature is to select all the features in the FeatureManager that are intended to be a part of the library feature. Collapse the features first so that the sketches belonging to features are not selected. If the sketches are selected, you may get a warning message saying that all the selected features cannot be used in the library feature. Do not worry; the sketches still will be included.

> **TIP** Remember that you can Ctrl+select individual features, Shift+select a range, or click-and-drag a box in the FeatureManager to select multiple features. Also keep in mind that if you do not select a feature (other than the base feature), then it will not be placed into the part when you insert the library feature. If there were any relations to the omitted feature, they may display as errors or warnings when you place the feature.

With the features selected, click File, click Save As, and under Files of Type drop-down list, select the *.sldlfp file type. Browse to the Design Library folder, and save the part. Figure 18.10 shows the FeatureManager of the finished library feature.

FIGURE 18.10

The finished library feature part

Display of the Library Feature icon

During the Save As process, a new folder was added to the Design Library named Bosses, as shown in Figure 18.10. Notice the new icon for the library feature in the lower window. You may notice that some of the default library features saved in the Design Library have a bluish background. This occurs because of the SolidWorks viewport background color, which you can set in Tools ⇨ Options ⇨ Colors. Even if you never see that color because you are using a gradient background or a scene, SolidWorks still uses the color specified by that setting as the background when saving thumbnails and previews. I always set this color to white for this reason, so that document backgrounds in previews do not have the blue color.

You may want to orient and zoom the library feature before saving it, so that it displays clearly in the panel. One of the techniques that I like to use is to make the base feature a different color than the library feature itself; this helps you to more easily determine what is the geometry that will be transferred and what is just dummy material.

Figure 18.11 shows various settings for displaying the icons in the Design Library. Which one you select will depend on your screen resolution, the number of icons that you want to display, and the quality of the preview images.

The real test for a library feature comes when you actually use it. This feature is re-created perfectly on the new part, but I have noticed one problem. When the feature was placed, it was 90 degrees away from the orientation that I wanted it to be in. It seems that the only way to make the feature rotatable is to create it with parallel and perpendicular relations rather than horizontal and vertical ones, so that one of the references can act as a rotation reference.

Figure 18.12 shows the completed library feature placed on a part.

FIGURE 18.11

Display modes for the Design Library

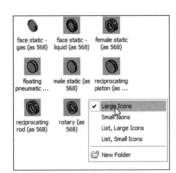

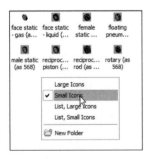

FIGURE 18.12

The completed library feature placed on a part

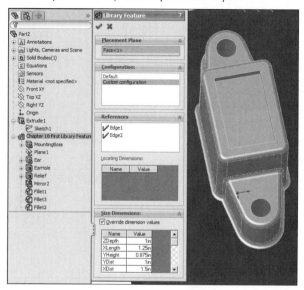

Once you place a library feature on a part, it can be edited, unless you select the Link to library part option in the Configuration pane, in which case the feature is driven externally from the `*.sldlfp` file. Link to library part is only available when the feature is first placed; it is not available when you edit an existing library feature in a part.

One of the available right-mouse button menu options is to dissolve the library feature so that all the constituent features become regular features in the main part. Doing this on a configured library feature will destroy the configurations.

Creating a library feature from an existing part

When creating a library feature from an existing part, you use essentially the same process, but it is actually somewhat more difficult to achieve the correct results. It is best to remove all the features that do not either form the base feature or go into the library feature itself. This can cause a lot of broken references. It may be better to use a different technique such as creating a new part with only the base feature. You can then Ctrl+drag the desired features from the existing part to the new part, set up the rest of the library feature, and save it with a `*.sldlfp` extension.

You can also create a library feature by dragging and dropping, although there are some limitations with this technique that seem to override the convenience. However, there is a workaround for the biggest limitation. If you select faces from features and drag them into the lower Design Library window, then an Add to Library PropertyManager interface appears to enable you to start creating a library feature. The Add to Library PropertyManager interface is shown in Figure 18.13. You must select the features from the flyout FeatureManager. This is the source of one of the limitations. In the example, the plane cannot be selected by this method. The workaround for this is to complete the feature without the plane, right-click the icon in the Design Library window, and then select Open. With the library feature open in its own window, right-click the plane feature and select Add to Library; that individual feature is then added.

Adding folders to the library

You can add folders to the library in two ways, either by right-clicking in the Design Library window and selecting New Folder, or by using the Windows Explorer interface. Another right-mouse button menu option is Add Existing Folder, which enables you to add a folder from another location to the library. The folder is not moved or copied, but a shortcut is added to the Design Library, and the contents appear in the lower pane.

FIGURE 18.13

The Add to Library PropertyManager interface

TIP After a library feature has been edited, or folders or documents have been added to the library using Windows Explorer, you can press F5 in either the lower or the upper window to update the display for that window, or use the Refresh icon located at the top of the Task Pane.

Locating and Internal dimensions

When you create a library feature, SolidWorks adds two folders to the FeatureManager, the References folder and the Dimensions folder. In turn, the Dimensions folder has two more folders, Locating Dimensions and Internal Dimensions. All of this is shown in Figure 18.14.

The References folder shows the entities you used to reference the library feature. These are the features you are prompted to select on placing the library feature in a new part. No additional work on your part is required with this folder.

The Dimensions folder lists all of the dimensions in the library feature. Some of these dimensions are used to locate the feature to the dummy block, and some of the dimensions are meant to size the feature itself. When you make a library feature, it is recommended that you separate the locating features from internal features by dragging the dimensions into the separate folders. The Locating Dimensions can be changed while placing the library feature, but the Internal Dimensions cannot be accessed. You might want to limit user access to some dimensions if you have standard tooling for the library feature that you are creating.

FIGURE 18.14

References, Locating and Internal dimensions in a library feature

Understanding Dissection

Dissection is a process that SolidWorks goes through by which it examines all the parts on your computer and makes Design Clipart of the sketches and features. People who might get some use from this function are those who have not modeled a lot of parts, and will tend to reuse the same features over and over again. The types of data it will try to recycle for you are extrudes and cuts, sketches, blocks, and tables from drawings.

The first interaction most people have with this function is learning how to turn it off. In early versions of SolidWorks 2008, Dissection began automatically at 11 p.m. by default on every machine the software was installed on. This is characterized by your computer starting to run small SolidWorks windows in the background. You can find the setting to turn Dissection on or off at Tools ⇨ Options ⇨ Search. Dissection is connected to SolidWorks Search, another function many users prefer to turn off.

Tutorial: Working with Library Features

This tutorial guides you through customizing a Hole Wizard hole to use as a specialty library feature, then storing it in the library, editing it, and placing it in a part. Follow these steps:

1. **Open a new part, and create a rectangular base feature, about three inches high by three inches wide, and three inches deep.**

2. **Pre-select a flat face and start the Hole Wizard.**

3. **Create a counterbored hole for a Heavy Hex Bolt, ½-inch, Normal Fit, Blind, 1.2 inches deep.** Locate the hole with dimensions from two perpendicular edges, as shown in Figure 18.14. Click the green check mark icon twice to accept the hole settings.

4. **Select Tools ⇨ Options ⇨ General, and turn on Show Dimension Names.**

5. **Double-click the counterbored hole feature in the FeatureManager to show the dimensions.** Make sure Instant3D is turned off for the next step.

6. **Left click one of the dimensions that you created to locate the center of the hole, and rename the dimension in the Dimension PropertyManager using names that it will have meaning when you place the dimension, such as XDir, or YDir.** Do this for both dimensions.

7. **Edit the second sketch of the hole.** Figure 18.16 shows what the sketch should look like before and after the edit.

CAUTION   **Do not delete any of the named dimensions in a normal or revised Hole Wizard hole. SolidWorks has a checking mechanism that looks for these names, and it will display an error if the named dimension is not there. If there is no use for the dimension, it still has to be there, although it does not need to be used for its original use. You could rename another dimension with the name or simply dimension the centerline or an otherwise unused construction line. It does not matter about the function of the dimension, as long as there is a dimension with that name in the sketch.**

FIGURE 18.15

Placing a hole

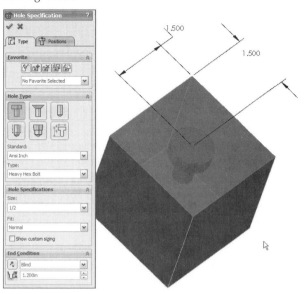

TIP You should also name any new dimensions that you may want to change. These dimensions will have more meaning when you are placing the feature if they have names. Be aware that the two angled lines are parallel and equal length. This will allow you to get a fully defined sketch.

FIGURE 18.16

Reconfiguring the hole

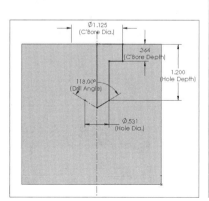
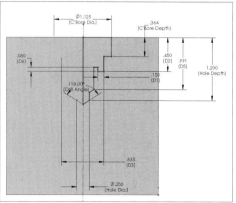

TIP
Remember that to get the diameter dimensions shown in Figure 18.15 (instead of radius dimensions), you must use the dimension tool to select the centerline (construction line) and the line or endpoint on one side, and then move the cursor to the other side of the centerline to place the dimension (the order of selection does not matter). When the cursor crosses the centerline, the dimension will display as a diameter instead of a radius.

8. When you are done editing the sketch and renaming dimensions, exit the sketch.

9. Click the CBORE feature twice, or click it once and press F2, to rename it as SpecialHole.

10. Pre-select the same flat face that the first hole feature was placed on, and start the Hole Wizard again.

11. Place a #8-32 tapped hole, accept the default depth, and specify a center-to-center distance of .75 inches between it and the SpecialHole in the Horizontal or Vertical direction. Rename the radial dimension as **MountRad**.

12. Using a cylindrical face of the SpecialHole, make a circular pattern of the new tapped hole, creating a total of four instances of the tapped hole. Make the SpecialHole Feature red and the tapped hole and pattern yellow.

13. Split the FeatureManager window into two by using the splitter bar at the top. Change the lower panel to the ConfigurationManager.

14. Rename the Default configuration to Size1.

15. Create a new configuration called Size2. Double-click the SpecialHole feature and change the dimension named C'Bore Dia to 1.5 inches. Be sure to change to This Configuration Only, using the drop-down menu.

16. Make a dimension change for the MountRad dimension to 1 inch. The results to this point are shown in Figure 18.17.

FIGURE 18.17

The results after Step 16

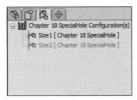

17. **Auto-create a design table by selecting Insert ⇨ Design Table, and then selecting the Auto-Create option.** Edit the design table to look like Figure 18.18. Hide or delete extra columns that don't match the data shown.

FIGURE 18.18

The design table for the SpecialHole feature

	A	B	C C'Bore Dia.@Sketch2	D MountRad@Sketch5	E	F	G
2		$DESCRIPTION					
3	Size1	Size1	1.125	0.81			
4	Size2	Size2	1.5	1			
5	Size3	Size3	1.625	1.06			
6	Size4	Size4	1.75	1.13			
7	Size5	Size5	1.875	1.19			
8							
9							
10							
11							

Sheet1

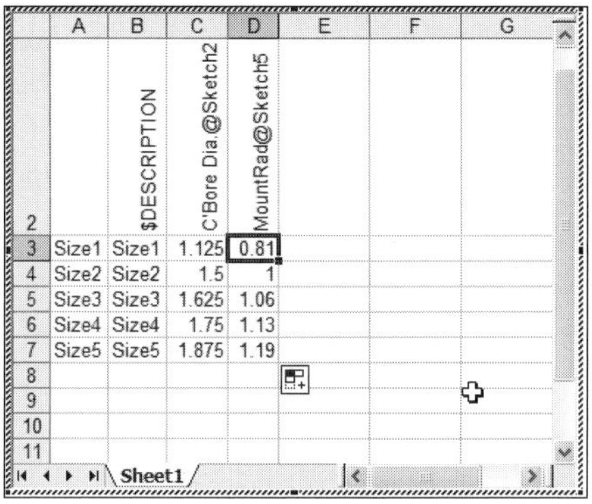

TIP Remember that to fill the first two columns up to Size5, you can make the two-by-two selection of the Size1 and Size2 entries in the first two columns, and pull down the handle in the lower-right corner of the selection box until the appropriate boxes are filled.

18. **Manually fill in the C'Bore Dia values, but in cell D3, type the equation =C3/2+.25.** Then use the same Fill technique to populate cells D3 to D7. Click outside of the Design Table to close it.

19. **Test the configurations to make sure that they all work.**

20. **In the Design Library, browse to a folder where you would like to put this library feature.** (Make sure that it is not used by assemblies or sheet metal forming tools.) Click a face created by the SpecialHole feature, and drag the feature into the lower pane of the Design Library. The Add to Library PropertyManager should appear on the left.

21. **Although you selected a feature and dragged it into the library, the Items to Add field appears blank.** Select the SpecialHole, tapped hole, and circular pattern features using Ctrl select for multiple selections, either through the detachable PropertyManager, the split FeatureManager or the flyout FeatureManager. Selecting the features from the graphics window does not work.

22. **Position and zoom the view of the part so that when it is saved, you see a good preview of the library feature.** Also, if you have not changed your background color from blue to white, this would be a good time to do so.

23. **In the Save To pane, make sure that you select the correct folder, then fill in a file-name, and click OK.** Figure 18.19 shows the completed PropertyManager interface for this function.

 **You may notice that there are two library entries in the window. This is because an additional path has been added in Tools ⇨ Options ⇨ File Locations ⇨ Design Library.**

24. **If the new library feature does not appear in the Design Library, then click in the Design Library and press F5.** If you do not like the way that it displays, then right-click in a blank space inside the lower library window and select one of the other three options.

25. **To edit the preview image of the feature, right click the feature in the Design Library window, select Open, reposition or zoom the view, and save it.** Click in the Design Library and press F5 again.

FIGURE 18.19

Saving the library feature

> **TIP**   It is recommended that when placing a library feature, you should close the original library feature window. The workflow proceeds much more smoothly if the part is closed before you use it.

26. **Open the part from the CD-ROM called** `Chapter 18 Tutorial Blank.sldprt`. If you would like to examine the version of the SpecialHole part that I created, it is stored with this data as well.

27. **Drag the SpecialHole library feature from the Design Library onto the face of the blank part.** Place the feature near the squared-off end. Select a configuration from the list in the PropertyManager.

> **TIP**   Although there is no prompt, when the Library Feature interface hesitates and there are configurations in the library feature, it is waiting for you to select a configuration. A prompt actually does exist, but it appears in the lower-left corner of the screen on the status bar in a tiny font, and most users probably do not notice it.

28. **Try to orient the part in the same way that it appears in the preview window, as shown in Figure 18.20.**

FIGURE 18.20

Orienting the part and selecting references

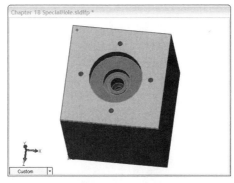

29. **Select edges on the Blank part that correspond to the preview window.** Click OK to accept the placement of the feature.

30. **Double-click the SpecialHole feature and change the X and Y placement dimensions to place it one inch from the edges in both directions.**

> **NOTE**   You may remember from Chapter 10 that library feature configurations cannot be controlled by part configurations. In order to show different library feature configurations in different part configurations, you need to suppress one library feature and insert another. This is the best available workaround. It may be time to visit that enhancement request site again.

31. **Place another library feature onto the blank part.** Select a configuration, and click the green check mark icon, without selecting edges for the references.

32. **Notice that the feature in the FeatureManager appears with an exclamation mark.** If you investigate the cause of this, then you can see that the two dimensions that should be attached to edges are dangling because you did not select the references while placing the library feature. This was done on purpose to show a different technique.

33. **Expand the library feature and the SpecialHole feature, and edit the first sketch in the Special Hole.** This is the placement sketch. Delete the two dimensions that appear in dangling colors.

34. **Add a concentric sketch relation between the placement point and the arc edge of the Blank part. Exit the sketch.** The error message should now be gone and the hole should now be placed in the center of the arc.

35. **Right-click the second library feature and select Dissolve Library Feature.** Figure 18.21 shows the finished part and FeatureManager. Good job!

> **NOTE**   When you dissolve a library feature, you lose any access to any configurations. Some users insist on dissolving every library feature, so that they can see regular features in the FeatureManager. This technique may also be useful if you would like to reorder some of the individual features within the library feature.

FIGURE 18.21

The finished part

Summary

Library features are very useful in automating frequent design tasks. They are easy to create, easy to store, easy to apply, and easy to automate. Setting up the features for the most flexibility often takes careful planning and attention to the detail of the references that you use. The more data you reuse, the more time you will save by automating and centralizing your libraries.

Chapter 19

Using Smart Components

IN THIS CHAPTER

Understanding Smart Components

Using Smart Components

Making Smart Components

Tutorial: Working with Smart Components

Smart Components are one of the more effective design automation tools to come from SolidWorks in the last several releases. This is functionality that can save you a lot of time; the more standard parts or assemblies with associated part-level features that you insert into your assemblies, the more time it can save you.

Smart Components are parts or assemblies that you can place into an upper-level assembly and that carry with them mounting features and hardware (cut-outs, mounting holes, and even fasteners). Smart Components are configurable, and can automatically size themselves on cylindrical parts.

Understanding Smart Components

A Smart Component can comprise several elements:

- A single part or an assembly that may use size configurations
- A configurable library feature that usually serves as mounting holes or a viewing window for the Smart Component
- Associated hardware that may also be driven by size configurations
- A training assembly that is used to define the Smart Component

Some minor limitations exist, as you might expect:

- A Smart Component part cannot have references that are external to the Smart Component group of which it is a member

597

- When placed in the assembly, the associated library feature can only affect one component
- The associated library feature is limited to one of several feature types:
  - Extruded or revolved cuts or bosses
  - Hole Wizard holes
  - Simple hole features

The setup time for Smart Components can be significant for the first one or two that you create, especially if you choose to make use of the auto-size option. The complexity of setup depends mainly on the number of configurations and configured parts that you use. The auto-sizing function takes the most time to set up because it requires matching configurations, and the auto-size table takes a while to manage, especially for multiple parts. Still, if you end up placing a given part with associated features and other components many times manually, or you have others in your group that do it, this technique can save you and your team a lot of time.

Using Smart Components

Figure 19.1 shows a simple assembly. It took approximately 20 minutes to model all the parts, set up the Smart Component, and test it in an assembly. This example does not use auto-sizing, but it does use a library part, an in-context feature, and two instances of a single hardware piece. This is an excellent example of Smart Component functionality because it is fast to create and fast to apply and saves you some time whenever you use it.

FIGURE 19.1

A simple Smart Component

Getting started with a simple Smart Component

In this assembly, you first place the electrical connector part in the assembly, mate it in place, and then apply Smart Components. You can apply Smart Components by clicking the Smart Component icon that appears on the part in the graphics window when you select it. SolidWorks then prompts you to select the inside and outside faces of the sheet metal part (the hardware references the outside and the cut-out feature references the inside). SolidWorks then creates the cut-out as an in-context feature that it places in the sheet metal part.

When you create the Smart Component, a new folder is added to the FeatureManager of the component. This folder contains all the required information about the other elements, such as the in-context feature, any other parts that go with the Smart Component, the "training assembly" location, and the face references to locate everything. Figure 19.2 in the image to the left shows this folder in the connector part that is used in this example. The image to the right shows what is added to the assembly FeatureManager when you add a Smart Component. The only thing that existed in the design tree shown in Figure 19.2 before the Smart Component was the Test Box sheet metal part.

FIGURE 19.2

The Smart Component folder in the connector part

Feature tree
of Smart Component

Feature tree of assembly where a
Smart Component has been used

A star appears on the part symbol at the top of the FeatureManager, indicating that the part is a Smart Component. You can place this Smart Component by following these steps:

1. **Create an assembly, and add the target part to it.** The target part is the one that the Smart Component will be mated to, and the one that will have the in-context cut-out inserted into it.

> **CAUTION**   It is a good idea to save the assembly *before* you add the Smart Component to it. If the Smart Component is placed before the assembly is saved, the assembly has a tendency to forget that it has not been saved, and bumps the in-context feature to out-of-context when the name is changed from whatever the default name is (for example, `Assem1.sldasm`) to the name that you assign to it.

2. **Put the Smart Component into the assembly.** You can do this in the same way that you would add any normal part, including from the Design Library. If you use a part frequently enough to make it into a Smart Component, then you are probably going to want to have it in the Design Library for quick access. In fact, you can add a Smart Component to an assembly without using any of the Smart Component options.

3. **Mate the Smart Component in the assembly.** In this case, it was done with a face-to-face coincident mate and a pair of distance mates.

4. **Next, apply Smart Components by clicking the Smart Component symbol on the part.** If this symbol does not appear, then select the part in the FeatureManager. Figure 19.3 shows the Smart Component symbol on the part. If you have inserted many instances of a Smart Component, then each instance has the option to apply the Smart Component features and associated components.

FIGURE 19.3

The Smart Component symbol on a part

5. **At this point, an interface similar to that of the Library Feature interface appears, with the small prompt window and a box for selecting references, as shown in Figure 19.4.** After you select the references, and click the green check mark icon, the Smart Component, as well as the Smart Feature (in-context feature) and associated hardware components, are placed, and the job is done. You can rotate the part in the small preview window to get a better look at the part.

FIGURE 19.4

The interface for adding the Smart Feature and additional components of the Smart Component

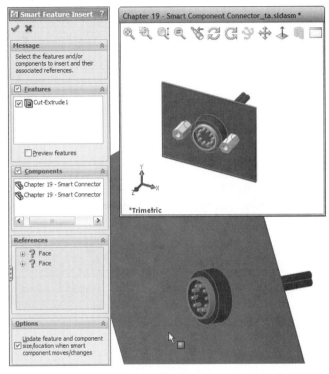

Auto-sizing Smart Components

Auto-sizing is the ability of a Smart Component to automatically select a size from a list of configurations, based on the size of geometry onto which it is being dropped. At this time, the only shape that can be auto-sized is the cylindrical shape.

Figure 19.5 shows the effects of auto-sizing. Notice the two shaft holders. These are two instances of the same part, using different size configurations. When you drag the Smart Component over the small end of the stepped shaft, the configuration corresponding to that shaft size appears. As you drag the part along the shaft and the shaft diameter increases, the next-larger Smart Component configuration appears. This is part of the functionality of Smart Components. Each configuration of the Smart Component is set up to fit onto a range of shaft diameters. If the diameter of the shaft is outside of the range or between sizes, then the Smart Component is not applied.

FIGURE 19.5

A Smart Component with auto-sizing

Sizes are governed by a configurator table, which looks similar to a design table, but works somewhat differently. The configurator table relates the configurations of the Smart Component to configurations of the individual parts, which may also change size with the Smart Component. This serves as a subset of the function of a design table in an assembly, assigning part configurations to assembly configurations. Figure 19.6 shows a sample configurator table made for the assembly shown in Figure 19.5.

FIGURE 19.6

A configurator table

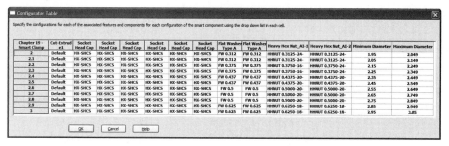

When you look at this table, you begin to understand why creating auto-sizing Smart Components is much more involved than in the first example in this chapter. The configurations of the Smart Component are listed to the left, and the individual part configs can be selected in each cell from a drop-down list of all available configs for that part. There is no way to set configs for multiple components at once, nor is there a copy-and-paste function. These shortcomings combine to make this format somewhat less user-friendly than an Excel-based design table.

Most notable are the Minimum and Maximum Diameter columns to the right. These columns supply the parameters that make the auto-size function work. While the range of sizes used here is too large for real-world design (+/− .050 inches), it serves to convey the idea. More important, SolidWorks understands that mating sizes are not always exactly equal, and the ability to use a range rather than exact values accommodates this very nicely, although it can be tedious to set up.

Another aspect of the setup shown here is that it uses Toolbox parts. If you want to use the auto-size functionality, then you need to be using configurations for Toolbox parts. You should pre-build all the needed configurations, and ensure that they are always available.

Making Smart Components

The most important point to remember about Smart Component setup is that you need to do it only once for each Smart Component. The second most important point is that the first setup is the most difficult. After that, subsequent setups become much easier to create. Adding components to the Smart Component is not so time-consuming unless the additional components are also configured and also auto-sized.

Smart Components must contain at least one associated component and one in-context feature, or have the configurator table filled out and functional. If you try to create a Smart Component from a standalone part, then nothing happens; the Smart Component interface simply closes because there is nothing for it to do. You may combine all three elements (associated component, in-context feature, and auto-size), but you must have at least one element.

Getting started with a simple Smart Component

Because the electrical connector shown in Figure 19.1 has already been used to demonstrate the insertion of a Smart Component, it is used here to demonstrate how to create one.

All that you need to make a Smart Component with an associated Smart Feature (in this case, a cut-out and mounting holes) and mounting hardware (in this case, two stand-off screws) is the part itself. The part can even be an imported part (a Smart Component made from dumb geometry).

From the CD-ROM for Chapter 19, open the file named `Chapter 19 - Connector Start. sldprt`. This part is shown in Figure 19.7.

FIGURE 19.7

An electrical connector part

There is nothing special about this part. I modeled it in SolidWorks using standard features, and there are no configurations or special features. It could have been downloaded from 3D Content Central. It represents an electrical connector that may be mounted in a sheet metal electrical enclosure.

The first step in setting it up is to create a mock assembly with a dummy part representing the sheet metal box. The part does not need to be complex or even sheet metal for that matter; it just needs to be close to the thickness that you would expect the Smart Component to be mounted to. The assembly is called a *training* assembly, not because you are learning how to make a Smart Component, but because you are training the Smart Component to be *smart*.

1. **Make a simple rectangular part, approximately 4 inches square and about .06 inches thick.** Save the part to your hard drive. Give a name to the part so that it is clear that it belongs to this training assembly.

2. **Place the rectangular dummy part into a new assembly, with a name that is both unique and identifiable.**

3. **Put the connector into the assembly.** Mate the part so that the flange is flush with the rectangular piece. Also use distance mates to locate the connector planes from the edges of the part, similar to Figure 19.8 in the image to the left.

FIGURE 19.8

Placing the connector on the dummy part

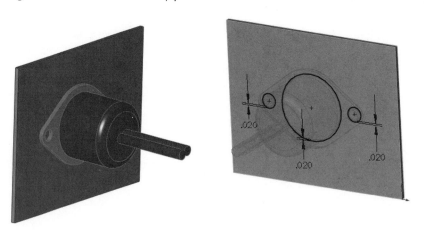

4. **Next, edit the dummy part in context (right-click the dummy part in the assembly and select Edit Part), and offset edges of the connector part to extrude a cut, as shown in Figure 19.8 in the image to the right.** Offset the two mounting holes and the area around where the connector will stick through the sheet metal by about .02 inches.

5. **Exit Edit Component mode and add two instances of the part named** `Chapter 19 –` `Smart Connector Hardware.sldprt` **to the assembly.** Mate the hardware part to the in-context hole, making sure that it goes to the outside thickness of the dummy sheet metal part.

 I have spent a fair amount of time trying to convince you that it is a best practice to *avoid* mating parts to in-context features, and yet here I tell you to do exactly that. Another thing I have tried to stress is that best practice suggestions are more like guidelines. If you are having performance problems with an assembly, then this may not be a great technique to use. However, sometimes there is a price to pay for sophisticated functionality, and if you think that your design can afford the price and will benefit from this functionality, then you should use it.

6. **Now that everything is in place, click the Make Smart Component tool on the assembly toolbar.** If the button is not there, you can add it to the assembly toolbar by selecting Tools ➪ Customize menu, or by selecting Tools ➪ Make Smart Component. The resulting interface is shown in Figure 19.9.

FIGURE 19.9

The Smart Component PropertyManager interface

7. In the Smart Component selection box, select the connector part.

8. In the Components selection box, select the two hardware components.

9. In the Features selection box, select the in-context feature from the dummy part.

10. **You are now finished setting up the Smart Component.** Click the green check mark icon to accept the changes and exit out of the PropertyManager, and save the file.

Creating an auto-sizing Smart Component

The simple Smart Component took about 20 minutes to model and set up. That is not too bad for a feature that you might use a lot. The benefits are somewhat modest, placing three components and a feature.

However, when it comes to the auto-sizing example that is shown next, the benefits are more extensive. A total of seven individual parts are placed (including Toolbox parts) — three of which are automatically sized, depending on the geometry into which the Smart Component is dropped — and an in-context feature is added.

To begin, open the part from the CD-ROM named Chapter 19 – Clamp Start.sldprt. Notice that this is a multibody part. There is no special knowledge that you need to have about multibody parts to complete this task. Multiple bodies are discussed in detail in Chapter 26.

1. **With the Clamp Start part open, notice that several configurations already exist.** If you click through the configurations or examine the design table in the part, you can see that various dimensions change. The primary dimension that changes is the diameter of the hole, and this change drives the diameter of, and distance between, the mounting holes.

NOTE You can only drive auto-sizing by cylindrical geometry.

2. **Part of the Smart Component definition includes applying a Mate Reference to the part, so that the big hole automatically snaps to cylindrical geometry.** Another aspect is that it adds in-context holes that match the mounting holes to the plate. Figure 19.10 shows the assembly that this part is meant to go into. The clamp snaps onto the stepped shaft and adds holes to the plate.

3. **Open the file named** Chapter 19 Autosize Training Assembly.sldasm. This has been prepared to help you get started with the Smart Component training.

NOTE The shaft is not necessary in the training assembly. The training assembly is intended to create the in-context Smart Feature and to create the configurator table. The shaft part has been added here for visualization only.

4. **Insert the clamp part into the assembly, and mate it concentric to the shaft and coincident to the blue plate.** It does not matter where the clamp sits along the shaft, but it should be fully mated into the location so that it does not slide back and forth. A distance mate from a plane or planar face would be a good choice.

FIGURE 19.10

The assembly where the Smart Component will be used

5. Edit the plate in the context of the assembly, and convert entities from the mounting holes in the clamp to create holes in the plate that align with the holes in the clamp.

6. Exit the Edit Component mode.

7. Activate Toolbox, select the four holes, as shown in Figure 19.11, and insert Socket Head Cap Screws, ⅜ by 24 by ⅜ inches. If you do not have Toolbox or choose not to use it, then a part with the correct name and sized configurations is provided on the CD-ROM.

8. Use the same fastener to place in the mounting holes, using the correct size for the hole. The length will be set later. Use a default length of 2.25 inches for both mounting holes.

FIGURE 19.11

Inserting four screws at once using Toolbox

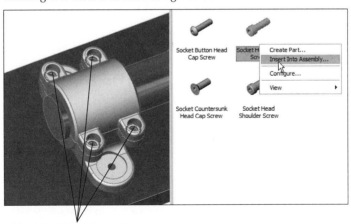

Pre-select these four edges

> **NOTE**   Working with the length of the fasteners is not a clean operation in Smart
> Components. The length is dependent on the thickness of the plate, which is not
> controlled by the Smart Fastener, nor can the Smart Fastener account for it, except through
> mates. (Remember that auto-sizing is driven only by a diameter.) Later in this chapter, you will
> see how the washers and nuts are put in place on the underside of the plate, but the screw
> length cannot be automatically calculated (unless the screw itself had an in-context relation to
> the nut).

9. Place washers and nuts on the screws on the backside of the plate.

10. **This is where the process becomes a little convoluted.** When the shaft diameter
    changes, the hole in the clamp changes to match (within the ranges that will be estab-
    lished). As the clamp becomes bigger, bigger screws are needed to secure the clamp and
    the holes grow further apart. Bigger screws mean additional configurations for the screw,
    washer, and nut parts. Remember that the configurations do not necessarily exist. I
    would not count on a Smart Component working if this meant that Toolbox had to create
    new configurations.

    To create this example, I have pre-populated the Toolbox parts with all the configura-
    tions needed for the range of sizes involved with this Smart Component. When you make
    your own Smart Components, you will have to do the same thing if you intend to use
    auto-sizing with Toolbox parts. The difficulty here is that the configurations include the
    diameter size of the screw as well as the length, which is unknown until you place the
    part.

    All you have to worry about in this step is to make sure that the configurations are avail-
    able and that the screws are placed properly.

11. **Up to this step, you have just assembled the parts as if this were the only time you
    were going to do it.** The automation of the process comes next. Figure 19.12 shows the
    training assembly to this point. The shaft and plate are shown in wireframe because they
    are external to the Smart Component.

12. **This is the point in the previous example where the Make Smart Component com-
    mand was used, and it is no different here.** Click the Make Smart Component tool on
    the assembly toolbar.

13. **Figure 19.13 shows the filled in Smart Component PropertyManager.** Activate the
    Smart Component selection box and pick the clamp part.

    In the Components selection box, select the six screw instances, the two washers, and the
    two nuts.

    In the Features selection box, select the in-context feature or features that are associated
    with the Smart Component.

> **NOTE**   Although the in-context feature can affect only a single part, this does not mean that
> you are limited to a single in-context feature. In most cases, only one feature is
> needed, but I am sure that there are situations where more than one would be useful. Also,
> remember that the in-context features are limited to extruded and revolved bosses and cuts,
> Hole Wizard holes, and simple hole features.

FIGURE 19.12

The training assembly up to Step 11

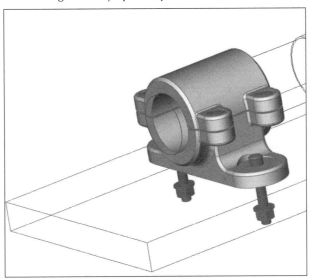

14. **The configurator table is simply a table that enables you to select which component configurations are to be used with which Smart Component configuration.** It looks and works very much like an assembly design table, but it is not Excel-based, and every cell must be set explicitly rather than using techniques for mass population or assigning properties to a range of configs, such as you can do with a real design table.

   Each cell has a drop-down list of all the available configurations for that component. If you have four instances of a single component, then you have to set each instance of each component. Figure 19.14 shows the configurator table for this example.

NOTE If the configurator table were to ever be as easy to use as, for example, an Excel design table, then Smart Component complexity could increase significantly. The configurator table could even ideally be created *from* an assembly design table. Instead of a single component with its associated hardware and mounting features, think of larger-scale sub-assembly attachments. This sort of work is possible now, but with configurator tables as cumbersome as they are, it is difficult to do more than a handful of parts.

15. **Click OK.** You are now done creating the auto-sizing Smart Component!

FIGURE 19.13

The Smart Component Property Manager

FIGURE 19.14

The configurator table for the Clamp Smart component

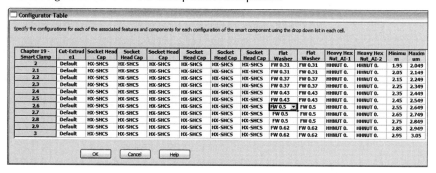

Chapter 19 - Smart Clamp	Cut-Extrude1	Socket Head Cap	Socket Head Cap	Socket Head Cap	Socket Head Cap	Socket Head Cap	Socket Head Cap	Flat Washer	Flat Washer	Heavy Hex Nut_AI-1	Heavy Hex Nut_AI-2	Minimum	Maximum
2	Default	HX-SHCS	HX-SHCS	HX-SHCS	HX-SHCS	HX-SHCS	HX-SHCS	FW 0.31	FW 0.31	HHNUT 0.	HHNUT 0.	1.95	2.049
2.1	Default	HX-SHCS	HX-SHCS	HX-SHCS	HX-SHCS	HX-SHCS	HX-SHCS	FW 0.31	FW 0.31	HHNUT 0.	HHNUT 0.	2.05	2.149
2.2	Default	HX-SHCS	HX-SHCS	HX-SHCS	HX-SHCS	HX-SHCS	HX-SHCS	FW 0.37	FW 0.37	HHNUT 0.	HHNUT 0.	2.15	2.249
2.3	Default	HX-SHCS	HX-SHCS	HX-SHCS	HX-SHCS	HX-SHCS	HX-SHCS	FW 0.37	FW 0.37	HHNUT 0.	HHNUT 0.	2.25	2.349
2.4	Default	HX-SHCS	HX-SHCS	HX-SHCS	HX-SHCS	HX-SHCS	HX-SHCS	FW 0.43	FW 0.43	HHNUT 0.	HHNUT 0.	2.35	2.449
2.5	Default	HX-SHCS	HX-SHCS	HX-SHCS	HX-SHCS	HX-SHCS	HX-SHCS	FW 0.43	FW 0.43	HHNUT 0.	HHNUT 0.	2.45	2.549
2.6	Default	HX-SHCS	HX-SHCS	HX-SHCS	HX-SHCS	HX-SHCS	HX-SHCS	FW 0.5	FW 0.5	HHNUT 0.	HHNUT 0.	2.55	2.649
2.7	Default	HX-SHCS	HX-SHCS	HX-SHCS	HX-SHCS	HX-SHCS	HX-SHCS	FW 0.5	FW 0.5	HHNUT 0.	HHNUT 0.	2.65	2.749
2.8	Default	HX-SHCS	HX-SHCS	HX-SHCS	HX-SHCS	HX-SHCS	HX-SHCS	FW 0.5	FW 0.5	HHNUT 0.	HHNUT 0.	2.75	2.849
2.9	Default	HX-SHCS	HX-SHCS	HX-SHCS	HX-SHCS	HX-SHCS	HX-SHCS	FW 0.62	FW 0.62	HHNUT 0.	HHNUT 0.	2.85	2.949
3	Default	HX-SHCS	HX-SHCS	HX-SHCS	HX-SHCS	HX-SHCS	HX-SHCS	FW 0.62	FW 0.62	HHNUT 0.	HHNUT 0.	2.95	3.05

File management with Smart Components

You may expect that with the training assembly, there is an extra burden of file management with Smart Components. This may seem counterintuitive, but in fact, the only file that you need to worry about is the Smart Component itself.

This is not explained very well (or at all) in any of the documentation, but the Help and every reseller demonstration that I have seen on the topic all recommend that you simply *delete* the training assembly once you are done with it because it is not needed any more. This seems like saying that you should delete all the mates in an assembly or the sketch relations in a part. How do you edit the Smart Component if you delete the assembly in which it is created?

It turns out that all of the information to re-create the training assembly is stored in the Smart Component itself. This includes the in-context feature (which is stored as a library feature), and the locations of any associated components, as well as the configurator table. Figure 19.15 shows a part of the FeatureManager of a Smart Component. As you can see, the in-context feature, the associated components, and the face references are all listed there.

FIGURE 19.15

Part of the FeatureManager of a Smart Component

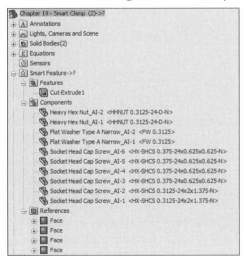

I was skeptical of this originally and had to test it thoroughly to ensure that deleting the training assembly would not cause any data to be lost, and so I can assure you that it works. Go ahead and delete the assembly.

Editing Smart Components

Expanding somewhat on the discussion about whether or not to keep the training assembly file, here is a little exercise that you can try. Make a Smart Component by going through the preceding steps, by using the following tutorial, or by creating one of your own. Just make a simple one with perhaps one associated component and an in-context feature. Then go ahead and delete the training assembly.

With the defining assembly gone, there appears to be no way to edit the setup of the Smart Component. Right-mouse button click the Smart Feature folder in the FeatureManager of the Smart Component, and select Edit in Defining Assembly, as shown in Figure 19.16. What happens next is that SolidWorks re-creates the defining assembly from the data that is stored in the Smart Component. This assembly is saved in a system temp folder using the name <Smart Component name>_ta.sldasm. If the Smart Component uses an in-context feature, it is saved to the temp directory as a library feature file using the name of the dummy part, and appending _lf to the filename; for example, Dummy_lf.sldlfp.

FIGURE 19.16

Selecting the Edit in Defining Assembly command

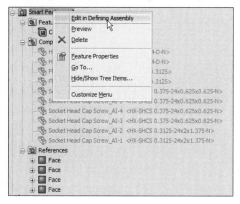

The Edit Definition button appears in the upper-right corner of the graphics window. The Edit Definition button is shown to the right in Figure 19.16. If you click this button, the Smart Component PropertyManager interface appears again, enabling you to change the selection of associated components and in-context features, to change the auto-size setting, or to edit the configurator table.

Thus, all the settings are preserved, and the training assembly exists only as a phantom in a temp directory. Although this appears to be counter-intuitive, it works.

Tutorial: Working with Smart Components

This tutorial guides you through creating a Smart Component that only uses the auto-sizing feature. This enables you to manually create parts that snap to size like Toolbox parts, but without using Toolbox functionality. Follow these steps:

1. **Open the part from the CD-ROM that has the filename** `Chapter 19 – Tutorial Start.sldprt`. This part originally came from Toolbox, and already contains a few configurations.

2. **Make an assembly that contains** *only* **this part.**

3. **Make the part into a Smart Component, and turn on the option to auto-size.**

4. **Select the small diameter of the part as the concentric mate reference.** Figure 19.17 shows the selection.

FIGURE 19.17

Selecting the concentric mate reference face

5. **Click the Configurator Table button, and fill the table in so that it looks like Figure 19.18.** Some configurations are blank. This is because only the rows that have minimum and maximum values are used by the auto-size function. The rest are overlooked.

6. Close the configurator table, and save the assembly.

Filling in the configurator table

Chapter 19 Tutor	Minimum Diameter	Maximum Diameter
Default		
HX-SHCS 0.138-3		
HX-SHCS 0.19-32		
HX-SHCS 0.19-32		
HX-SHCS 0.19-32	0.1	0.199
HX-SHCS 0.25-20		
HX-SHCS 0.25-20		
HX-SHCS 0.25-28	0.2	0.249
HX-SHCS 0.3125-		
HX-SHCS 0.3125-		
HX-SHCS 0.3125-		
HX-SHCS 0.3125-		
HX-SHCS 0.375-2		
HX-SHCS 0.375-2		
HX-SHCS 0.375-2		
HX-SHCS 0.375-2		
HX-SHCS 0.375-2	0.25	0.449
HX-SHCS 0.4375-	0.45	0.469
HX-SHCS 0.4375-	0.47	0.479
HX-SHCS 0.4375-	0.48	0.499
HX-SHCS 0.5-20x	0.5	0.529
HX-SHCS 0.5-20x	0.53	0.549
HX-SHCS 0.5-20x	0.55	0.579
HX-SHCS 0.5-20x	0.58	0.599
HX-SHCS 0.625-1	0.6	0.629
HX-SHCS 0.625-1	0.63	0.659
HX-SHCS 0.625-1	0.66	0.699
HX-SHCS 0.75-16	0.7	0.8
HX-SHCS 0.875-1	0.801	1.109
HX-SHCS 1.25-12	1.11	2
PreviewCfg	0.801	1

7. **Exit the assembly and, in the part file, save it to a folder in your Design Library.** If you do not know where your Design Library is located, then select Tools ⇨ Options ⇨ File Locations ⇨ Design Library.

8. **Display the part in the Design Library panel of the Task pane.**

9. **Open the part from the CD-ROM with the filename** Chapter 19 Tutorial Plate. sldprt. Place this part into a new assembly.

10. **Drag the Tutorial Start (Smart Component) from the Design Library into the assembly, and move the part over the holes in the plate.** As you drag the part up and down the row of holes, the part changes sizes to match each hole. Figure 19.19 shows all the holes that are populated with the matching Smart Component sizes, as driven by the configurator table.

11. **To edit the configurator table, open the Smart Component part in its own window.** Then right-click the Smart Feature folder and select Open In Defining Assembly.

12. **An assembly opens that was created from the data stored in the part.** Click the Edit Definition button that appears in the upper-right corner of the graphics window.

13. **Reassign the minimum and maximum diameter values for the ³⁄₁₆-inch and ¹⁄₄-inch configurations to the shortest lengths.** For example, the chart shows the ³⁄₁₆-32x.75-inch configuration to be assigned to a minimum of .1 and a maximum of .199. Move the .1 and .199 values up two cells to the ³⁄₁₆-32x ¹⁄₄-inch configuration. Do something similar for the ¹⁄₄-28x1-inch configuration. The edited part of the chart now looks like Figure 19.20.

FIGURE 19.19

Smart Component parts match holes in the part.

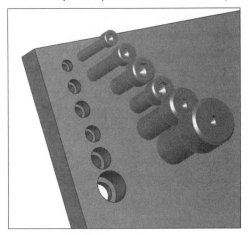

FIGURE 19.20

The edited configurator table

Chapter 19 Tutor	Minimum Diameter	Maximum Diameter
Default		
HX-SHCS 0.138-32x0.5x0.5-N	0.1	.199
HX-SHCS 0.19-32x0.25x0.25-N		
HX-SHCS 0.19-32x0.4375x0.4375-N		
HX-SHCS 0.19-32x0.75x0.75-N		
HX-SHCS 0.25-20x0.625x0.625-N	.2	.249
HX-SHCS 0.25-20x1.375x1.375-N		
HX-SHCS		

> **TIP** You may have difficulty expanding the width of the column that contains the configuration names, thus making it difficult or impossible to read the ends of the long config names. However, like Excel, you can expand the height of the rows, which causes the config names to wrap, as shown in Figure 19.20.

Summary

Smart Components can automate the placement of a main component, as well as associated mounting features and components. It can also offer automatic resizing options, depending on the geometry to which it is mated. The setup for Smart Components varies from simple to complex, with auto-sizing causing most of the complexity.

Part V

Creating Drawings

Part V, Creating Drawings, walks you through the tools you need to make drawings work for you. The main focus is on task automation where possible, and where it supports the end goal. Sometimes automation is not the answer and manual processes are better, so be prepared for answers that you may not expect.

Chapter 20

Automating Drawings: The Basics

Engineering drawings include a lot of repetitious information from one drawing to the next. The information is not always exactly the same, but it is usually in the same format and of the same type. For example, part drawings always include information about who made the drawing, when the person made it, what the material and surface finish of the part are, and some basic notes that depend on the use of the drawing (manufacturing, assembly, or inspection).

All of this information needs to appear consistently on each drawing, every time. However, humans are not always good at following dull routines, which is why we have computers to help with these boring or difficult tasks.

The Difference Between Templates and Formats

Simply put, *templates* are collections of document-specific settings and default views, saved in the *.prtdot (part template), *.asmdot (assembly template), and *.drwdot (drawing template) file types.

Formats, more formally called "sheet formats," are exclusive to drawing documents, and contain the sheet size, the drawing border-line geometry, and the text/custom property definitions that go with the text in the drawing border. Formats can also include company logo images.

You can save formats in drawing templates; in fact, this is the method that I both use and recommend. Using SolidWorks' default settings, you specify the size and the format when creating a new drawing from a blank template;

however, when the format is already in the template, the size is taken care of ahead of time, and so the templates end up being saved as sizes. Of course, you can change formats later if you need to use a larger drawing sheet.

Can templates be changed on existing documents?

Can you change templates on existing documents? No. This is one of the most common questions from new users. Perhaps if SolidWorks received enough enhancement requests on this topic, they would be willing to change the software to enable the user to transfer the settings from an existing template to one or more existing documents.

Currently, once you create any kind of document from whatever kind of template, you cannot change the underlying template. However, you can change all of the settings, which is for the most part equivalent.

SolidWorks 2009 offers custom drafting standards, which fulfills much of the function that the ability to swap templates would achieve. You can take a drafting standard such as ISO or ANSI, make adjustments to it, and save the standard out to a file which you can distribute to other users. You can change the standard at Tools ➪ Options ➪ Document Properties ➪ Drafting Standard. You can load and save standards from the same location. More detailed on what can actually be changed within the drafting standard is in Appendix B, and additional detail comes later in this chapter.

While *templates* cannot be reloaded, *formats* can be. You might want to reload a format (drawing border and associated annotations) if you have made changes to the information or line geometry.

Why have different templates or formats?

Different formats must be maintained for different sheet sizes. If you do contract design or detailing work, then you may need to maintain separate formats for different customers. Some people also choose to have different formats for the first sheet of a drawing and a simplified format for the remaining sheets.

Why you should maintain different templates is an easier answer. First, if you put formats on the templates, then you are making separate templates for various size drawings. Also, separate templates are frequently created for different units or standards, because templates contain document-specific settings. I also keep a blank drawing template with no format on it just to do conceptual scribbles or to make an informal, scalable, and printable drawing without the baggage that typically accompanies formal drawings.

CAUTION   **SolidWorks can install with default document templates that use different standards. Be careful of the difference between drawings with ANSI (American National Standards Institute) and ISO (International Organization for Standardization) standards, or more importantly, the use of third-angle projection versus first-angle projection. Figure 20.1 shows the difference between a third- and first-angle projection. Third angle is part of the ANSI standard used in the United States, while first angle is part of the ISO standard used in Europe.**

FIGURE 20.1

FIGURE 20.1

Third-angle versus first-angle projection

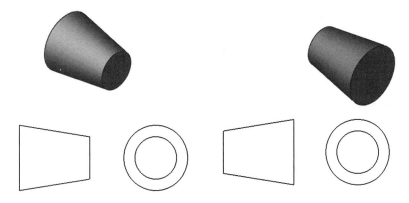

If you work for a company that does a lot of international work, then you may have to deal this issue more frequently. The setting that controls the projection angle is not in Tools ⇨ Options (where you might expect it to be), but in the Sheet Properties, which you can access by right-mouse button clicking anywhere on the blank drawing sheet and selecting Properties.

Custom drafting standards

In my experience, in companies that work in the real world, no one follows any of the single drafting standards perfectly. Each company seems to have its own interpretation or exceptions to the standards. SolidWorks is coming to grips with this in a practical way. Starting with SolidWorks 2009, you can create your own custom drafting standards, equivalent to the established ISO and ANSI standards. These standards can allow you to save all of the settings found in Tools ⇨ Options ⇨ Document Properties to a single standard that you can then transfer to other users.

To make your own custom standard, make changes to the various settings for annotations, symbols, dimensions, and so forth, and then go back to the Drafting Standard page of the Document Properties tab, rename the Overall Drafting Standard, and save the standard to a file. I have created a new standard, which is shown in Figure 20.2.

FIGURE 20.2

Creating a new customized drafting standard

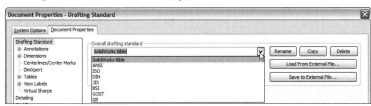

The drafting standard file type has the extension of *.sldstd. If someone else has sent you a standard file, you can read it in to your drawing, assign it, and your drawing will assume all of the customized properties.

ON the CD-ROM I have saved a custom standard file and put it on the CD-ROM for Chapter 20. You can load this file into an open drawing using the interface at Tools ➪ Options ➪ Document Properties ➪ Drafting Standard.

Creating Drawing Formats

Drawing formats can be either simple or difficult; the good news is that you can choose which one you want to use.

Customizing an existing format

The simple solution is to customize an existing format for your own use. This generally works well, and you can usually finish the task in a few minutes, depending on your requirements. The easiest option is to take the existing SolidWorks sample formats and add a few things such as a company name, logo, and tolerance block to them. You can also use formats from other drawings, editing and saving them out as your own.

Sample formats

The sample formats that installed with SolidWorks are located in C:\Documents and Settings\All Users\Application Data\SolidWorks\SolidWorks 2009\. They include ANSI sizes A to E, and ISO sizes A0 to A4. You can probably find enough space on the formats to place a company logo and some standard notes.

You cannot open a format directly — it must be on a drawing — and, so, to get a closer look at the format, you must make a new drawing using the format.

NOTE Templates that have been saved with a format already on them skip the step of prompting you to select a format. This allows you to create new drawings more quickly. If you select one of the default SolidWorks templates, these do not have formats on them, so you are prompted to select a format immediately. Figure 20.3 shows the interface for selecting a format that displays after you have selected the template for a drawing.

Editing a format

In the drawing, you are either editing the sheet or editing the format. You can think of the sheet as being a piece of transparent Mylar over the top of the drawing border format. In order to get to the format, you have to peel back the Mylar layer. Drawing views go onto the sheet, and so when you edit the format, any drawing views that may be there disappear.

FIGURE 20.3

Selecting a format

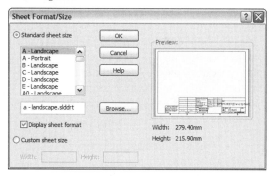

To peel back the sheet and gain access to the format, right-click a blank area of the sheet and select Edit Sheet Format. This right-mouse button menu is shown in Figure 20.4. Be careful of the terms here, which include Sheet and Sheet Format. The sketch lines of the format light up like a sketch becoming active, and at the lower right-hand corner, on the status bar, a message appears, saying Editing Sheet Format.

FIGURE 20.4

Selecting the edit sheet format

The lines in the format border are regular SolidWorks sketch entities, but they display a little differently. Also, sketch relations are sometimes not used in formats because solving the relations causes the software to be a bit sluggish. Typically, Trim, Extend, and Stretch functions are the best sketch tools for editing lines.

Using Insert ⇨ Picture in the drawing, you can use most common image types to insert logo or other image data onto your drawing or format. Not all compression styles are supported, however. I have had difficulty with compressed TIFF images. Be aware of the file size of the image when you put it into the format, as images can be large, and all of that extra information will travel around with each drawing that you create from the format. Figure 20.5 shows a bitmap placed in the format.

You can resize the image by dragging the handles in the corners and move it by simply dragging it. The bottom image in Figure 20.5 shows the Print Preview window. I included it here to show that the outline around the image that displays while you are working in SolidWorks does not print out.

FIGURE 20.5

Placing an image

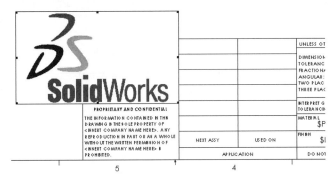

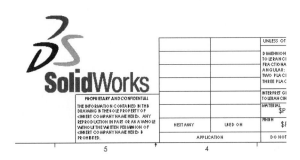

Managing text

SolidWorks allows you to make a text box of a specific size that causes text to wrap. This is particularly useful in drawings. The upper image in Figure 20.6 shows a new annotation being added. The lower image shows the same text box after the corner has been dragged.

Adding an annotation and wrapping the text

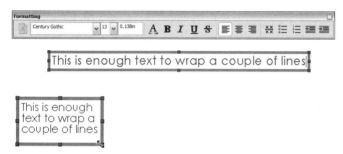

> **TIP** When dragging the text box, it may seem intuitive to drag the middle handle on the end, thinking that shortening the box will cause it to wrap. However, that only works if the box has some space on the bottom to wrap to; SolidWorks does not automatically expand the text box down the way PowerPoint does. You are better off dragging a corner to get the wrap to work.

Custom properties

The most important part of the drawing format is the custom properties. While the rest of the format is just for display, custom properties use automation to fill out the title block using matching custom properties in either the model or the drawing document. Custom properties can pull items such as filenames, descriptions, materials, and other properties from the model associated with the sheet, or they can pull data from the drawing itself, such as the sheet scale, filename, sheet number, and total sheets. If you are seriously looking to automate drawings, you cannot overlook custom properties.

Custom property data entry

Custom property data entry happens at the part or assembly level. This information is then reused in the drawing format and in tables such as BOMs and revision tables, as well as searches using the FeatureManager filter and all PDM (Product Data Management) systems make use of SolidWorks custom properties. You can enter the data several ways, but the two most prominent ways are through the Summary Information dialog and through the Custom Properties Tab in the Task Pane.

Summary Information

Figure 20.7 shows the Summary Information dialog. This functionality has existed in SolidWorks for several releases. You access this dialog through the menus at File ➪ Properties. You can select Property Names from a drop-down list or type in your own, assign types of data, and enter in a specific value for the property. The Value/Text Expression column also has a drop-down list from which you can select several pre-set variables, such as mass, density, and even link values used in the part.

The Summary Information dialog

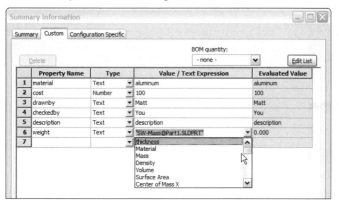

This is a perfectly functional way of entering data, but the fact that it is somewhat out of the way, hidden in the menus, means that it does not get used as much as it should. So SolidWorks came up with another way of entering data.

The Custom Properties Tab

The Custom Properties Tab of the Task Pane enables you to quickly and easily access and assign custom properties within a document. Figure 20.8 shows the process of building your own Custom Properties Tab. You can start the Custom Property Tab Builder by either using the Create button on the Custom Properties Tab or through the Start menu, at Programs ➪ SolidWorks ➪ SolidWorks Tools ➪ Property Tab Builder.

FIGURE 20.8

Using the Custom Properties Builder and Custom Properties Tab

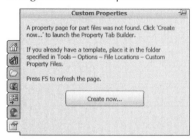

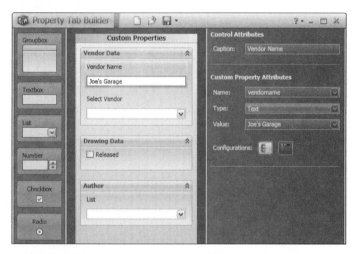

The interface enables you to add drop-down lists, toggles, and text entry boxes. This offers a lot of flexibility in the entry of custom property data, and is a very nice addition to the software.

Property link display

Figure 20.9 shows the existing custom property formatting in the default format being used for this example.

Custom property formatting in the title block

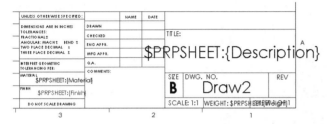

The syntax $PRP or $PRPSHEET indicates that the property that follows the syntax is to be pulled from either the current document (drawing) or from the model specified in the Sheet Properties, respectively. This is an important distinction to make. Most of the time, custom properties are typed in at the part or assembly level so that the data can be reused by drawing properties, BOM, or even design tables.

Notice that all of the notes in the format that are showing raw syntax are pulling data from the model. "Draw2," and the Scale notes are driven by the drawing. When no value exists for the property to display, you have an option of what to show. The top portion of Figure 20.10 shows the settings in the View menu that control the display of syntax of the custom property links. In general, it is common to turn off the error display, and to show the link variables.

Link variable display options and effects

Errors and link variables

The errors in Figure 20.10 are caused by links to the local document for which there is no corresponding property. For example, the "ERROR!: COMPANYNAME" message is linked to "$PRP: COMPANYNAME," but the local custom property COMPANYNAME does not exist. If it existed but had a null or space value, the error would disappear.

Likewise, with the option to display link variables turned on, the syntax that calls model custom properties displays until there is some value for it to pull from. If a part is put onto the drawing, then some of the properties are filled in because properties and values exist to pull from, and the rest of the properties simply disappear to make space. Notice in Figure 20.11 that the Material property has been filled in, but the Finish property has not. This is because there is either no Finish property in the part on the drawing or a null value in the Finish property.

FIGURE 20.11

Custom properties filled in by a part

UNLESS OTHERWISE SPECIFIED:		NAME	DATE	Dezignstuff	
DIMENSIONS ARE IN INCHES TOLERANCES: FRACTIONAL± ANGULAR: MACH± BEND ± TWO PLACE DECIMAL ± THREE PLACE DECIMAL ±	DRAWN	Matt	1/8/2007	TITLE:	A
	CHECKED	You	1/10/2007		
	ENG APPR.	None	1/12/2007	Cast Clamp	
	MFG APPR.	Prelim	1/12/2007		
INTERPRET GEOMETRIC TOLERANCING PER:	Q.A.	None	1/13/2007		
	COMMENTS:				
MATERIAL Cast Iron				SIZE **B**	DWG. NO. Chapter 19 - Smart Clamp	REV **B**
FINISH ERROR!:Finish					
DO NOT SCALE DRAWING				SCALE: 1:1	WEIGHT: 0.814	SHEET 1 OF 1
3		2		1	

TIP When initially setting up the format, it can be useful to have a dummy model already on the drawing. The dummy model should have all of the custom properties in it that you intend to use in your drawings. This prevents the blank fields or error messages from appearing during setup.

NOTE If you drag-and-drop a part onto a drawing while editing in the Sheet Format, the views may appear for a split second and then disappear again. This is because you cannot display drawing views while editing the Sheet Format. Once you exit the Sheet Format and go back to editing the sheet, the views can display once more.

Creating linked properties

It is easy to create annotations that are linked to properties. Begin as if you are creating a note:

1. **Click the Note toolbar button on the Annotations toolbar, or click Insert ⇨ Annotations ⇨ Note.**

2. **Place the note on the drawing.** The Formatting toolbar appears.

3. **Click the Link To Property button in the Text Format pane of the Note PropertyManager.** This displays the Link to Property dialog box, as shown in Figure 20.12, which gives you the option of linking to a custom property in the current (drawing) document or in the model (part or assembly) that is on the drawing.

FIGURE 20.12

The Link to Property dialog box

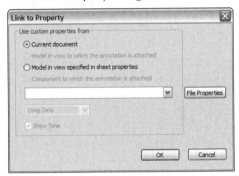

4. **If the desired custom property is not in the drop-down list shown to the right, then you can type it into the text box or click the File Properties button to edit the properties.** This button is not available for the model if there is no model on the drawing, in which case you must type in the name of the property manually.

Using the Title Block function

The Title Block function was added in the 2009 version of the software. Title Block enables the person who sets up the sheet format to specify an area that contains notes that are easy to access without editing the format. You can even cycle through these notes in a specific order by pressing Enter or Tab. Figure 20.13 shows the resizable black border of the Title Block, the Title Block PropertyManager, and where the Title Block sits in the drawing FeatureManager.

FIGURE 20.13

Using the Title Block function

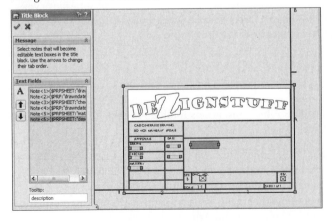

You can access the Title Block to edit or define it by right-clicking in the Sheet Format (while editing the Sheet Format, not the sheet) and selecting either Define Title Block or Edit Title Block, as the situation requires.

The Title Block can be any size you like, but it must remain rectangular, and you can only create one Title Block area. The area bounded by the Title Block box is used to zoom the display to make it easier to fill in the text boxes. If you want to include areas in different corners of the drawing in the Title Block area, you will need to make the Title Block box as big as the entire sheet, and the user will have to manually zoom to each corner.

Select each Note item to add it to the list in the PropertyManager selection box. Use the arrows to the left of the box to assign the order in which the user cycles through the boxes. The idea is that the user clicks in a box within the Title Block area, fills it in, then presses Enter or Tab to get to the next box. The order will loop if the user does not start on the first box listed in the PropertyManager.

ON the CD-ROM You will find a sample template with a format with a Title Block definition added to it on the CD-ROM. The file is called `title block.drwdot`. Add it to your template library folder and try it out.

Creating a format from a blank screen

There is no graceful way to say this, and so I'll just say it: SolidWorks is not really good at manipulating a lot of 2D sketch-line data such as what you find in drawing title blocks. I have gone through the process of making my own formats, as well as the process of importing DWG data from which to create them. By the time you have everything centered, in the right color, on layers if you are using them, and the text aligned, you have used up more than a couple of hours. If you choose to custom build one size and then use it to create the rest of the sizes, you need to be patient. SolidWorks typically turns off the most useful parametric sketch functions when working with a format (what SolidWorks considers a large sketch) because of speed problems. If you would like to turn these settings back on, they are located at Tools ➪ Sketch Settings.

SolidWorks is not the best program for making a nice-looking drawing border. If you insist on creating your own, set aside some time for it, and have an idea of what you are trying to achieve, maybe sketched out by hand or in a printout of a title block that you would like to replicate. You can also use the DWG Editor, which is much better suited to this kind of work.

The Modify Sketch tool may be useful in moving entities around the screen, and even scaling them. You can also access a useful hidden command by right-clicking the name of the drawing in the FeatureManager and selecting Move from the menu, as shown in Figure 20.14. A small dialog box appears that enables you to move the entire format by a specified distance.

TIP If you need to use construction geometry to help you size or locate objects or text while manually creating your Sheet Format, then you do not need to delete the geometry when you are done. You can put all of the construction geometry on a specially created drawing layer and turn the layer off.

FIGURE 20.14

The Move Drawing dialog box

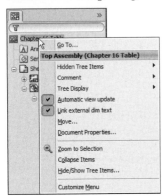

Creating a format from an imported DWG/DXF file

If you want to create your format from an imported DWG or DXF file, then locate the file that you would like to import, and open it from the File ⇨ Open dialog box. The DXF/DWG Import screen appears, as shown in Figure 20.15.

FIGURE 20.15

The DXF/DWG Import screen

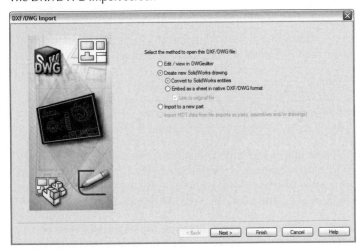

The sample files used for this example can be found on the CD-ROM for Chapter 20 if you are interested in following along. You will find five *.DWG format files. You can use any of them to create a format, but I suggest either the A or B size. To make a drawing format, you can select the Create New SolidWorks drawing and Convert to SolidWorks entities options. Although one of the other options contains the word *format*, it is not being used in the same sense, so do not be misled. When this selection is complete, click Next. Figure 20.16 shows the next screen.

FIGURE 20.16

The Drawing Layer Mapping screen

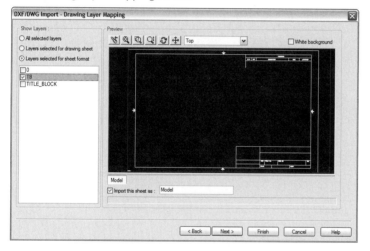

Select the Layers selected for sheet format option. Select the TB layer, leaving the other layers off. Every imported file will be different in this respect, because layers used by title blocks vary widely. Click Next when you have made these selections. Figure 20.17 shows the Document Settings screen.

The important features in the Document Settings screen are the Document template selection and the Geometry positioning options.

Document template selection is only important if you plan to save the format with a template. Be sure to select a template that does not already have a format saved in it. In the Geometry positioning section, if you can get the software to center the title block for you, definitely take advantage of this functionality and use the Center in sheet option. Once you are happy with these settings, click Finish. The resulting format is shown in Figure 20.18.

FIGURE 20.17

The Document Settings screen

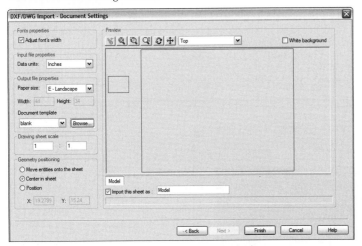

FIGURE 20.18

The finished imported format

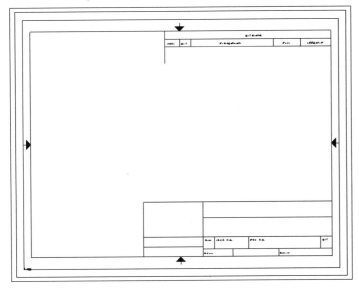

From here, you can add the links to custom properties as described earlier, as well as logo images, loading favorites, and blocks. You can now save the format as described in the next section.

NOTE Using the Color Display Mode button on the Line Format toolbar toggles the display from using the layer color to using the SolidWorks sketch colors. Another setting that affects sketch display in drawings is found at Tools ➪ Options ➪ System Options ➪ Drawings ➪ Display Sketch Entity Points, which shows endpoints and arc center points in the same way that they are shown in feature sketches.

Saving the format

You can save drawing formats in two ways, either with the template, or separate from the template. You cannot edit formats separate from a template, but they do have their own file type, *.slddrt.

NOTE If you are wondering how the extension *.slddrt relates to a sheet format, what is now known as *sheet format* used to be called a *drawing template* (thus, the *drt* of slddrt). What is now called a template did not exist in 1997. The shift in architecture and, more importantly for users, the shift in terminology has left many people a bit confused.

Saving templates is covered in the next section. To save a format, select File ➪ Save Sheet Format. You can do this with or without the format being active. Save the format into a location with other formats, and give it a descriptive but unique name. If you have not yet done so, this is a good opportunity to create a separate folder, outside of your SolidWorks installation folder, that contains your most frequently used files. Remember also to tell SolidWorks where this library location is through Tools ➪ Options ➪ System Options ➪ File Locations ➪ Sheet Formats.

Even if you have saved a format with a template, it is a good idea to also save the format on its own. This is because you might want to use that format on an existing drawing that has a different format on it, or use it on a second sheet.

Second sheet formats

When you have multi-sheet drawings, it is often important to have a simplified or specialized format for the second sheet. Figure 20.19 shows sample page-one and page-two formats side by side.

Adding new sheets

You can add sheets to a drawing by using the Add Sheets icon to the right of the sheet tabs at the bottom of the SolidWorks window, or through the right-mouse button menu of the sheet tab at the lower-left corner of the drawing window. If you right-click the first sheet tab, the sheet that is added gets the format that is used on the first sheet. If you right-click the second sheet tab, the added sheet gets the second sheet format.

First and second sheet formats

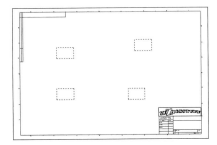

Reloading formats

If a format has been changed, and you would like to update a drawing to the new format, this option is available in the Sheet Properties, as shown in Figure 20.20.

Updating a format through the Sheet Properties

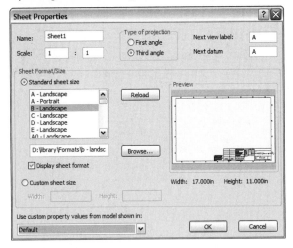

Creating Drawing Templates

Document-specific settings are an important part of the template, and it is probably best to get one size drawing completely set up the way you want it, and then create the other sizes from this drawing. This helps to ensure that the settings, such as bent leader length, font, and line weight, are the same for all of the templates. Uniform settings on drawings give them a consistent look, and make them easier to read. An in-depth discussion of document-specific settings at Tools ⇨ Options ⇨ Document Properties can be found in Appendix B. Drafting standards are also controlled by drawing templates.

Using Predefined views in drawing templates

When I use drawing templates, one of my favorite techniques to get to a multi-view drawing quickly is to put one Predefined view on the template along with appropriate views projected from the Predefined view. A Predefined view establishes an orientation and location on the drawing sheet. You can add multiple Predefined views and align them with one another on the drawing sheet so that a drawing is automatically populated by the model, but this is not recommended because if you decide to change the orientation of the drawing, you have to change each Predefined view independently. If you set up a single Predefined view and make the rest of the views with projected views, changing the orientation of the Predefined view causes all of the projected views to update associatively. You cannot directly change the orientation of a projected view. Predefined views and views projected from Predefined views appear blank until they are populated with model geometry. The *predefined* part of a Predefined view is the orientation and placement of the view.

Figure 20.21 shows a template using Predefined and projected views. You can access Predefined views on the Drawings toolbar; although it is not there by default, you can place it on the toolbar through the Tools ⇨ Customize ⇨ Commands interface. You can also access Predefined views through Insert ⇨ Drawing Views ⇨ Predefined. Projected views are also accessed from the Drawings toolbar.

Once a Predefined view has been placed, you can select an orientation for it from the PropertyManager. Figure 20.22 shows the Drawing View PropertyManager. The orientation for a view is set in the top Orientation panel. In addition to orthogonal views, you can also create isometric and other custom views as Predefined views.

FIGURE 20.21

Predefined views on a template

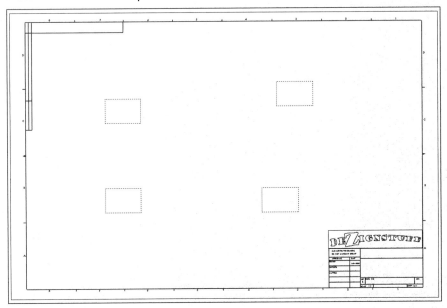

FIGURE 20.22

The Drawing View PropertyManager

After the view has been oriented, you may want to create more views on the drawing that also become populated by model geometry. This is where the projected views are used. Make sure that the drawing properties are set to the correct projection angle.

Because the rest of the views have been created relative to the Front view, none of the views needs to be rotated as it would if, for example, the Top view were placed above the Back or Right views.

Although it is not on this drawing, many drawing templates include a third-angle projection symbol as a part of the Title Block, which is in the format. Figure 20.23 shows first- and third-angle projection symbols. These are included as blocks with the sample data in the SolidWorks installation. Blocks are discussed in more detail in Chapter 22.

FIGURE 20.23

Projection angle symbol blocks

 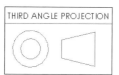

Aligning Predefined views

You can align views to one another through a view's right-mouse button menu, as shown in Figure 20.24. Projected views are aligned to one another automatically, but if you chose to use a Predefined view rather than a projected view to one side of the original Predefined view, you can use the Align Vertical by Origin or the Align Horizontal by Origin command. This ensures that the parts in each view are aligned. Aligning by center should not be used for projected views on an engineering drawing, because it is not guaranteed to line up edges in adjacent views.

Populating a drawing with Predefined views

Four methods exist to populate a drawing with Predefined views:

- **Drag-and-drop.** Drag a part or assembly from the FeatureManager and drop it in the drawing window. All Predefined views are automatically populated.

- **Insert Model.** Right-click a view and select Insert Model. From the interface, browse for the model to be displayed in all of the related (projected) views.

- **PropertyManager.** Select a predefined view, and from the PropertyManager, select Browse in the Insert Model panel.

- **Make Drawing from Part/Assembly.** Click the Make Drawing From Part/Assembly button in the Standard toolbar and select a template that uses Predefined views.

FIGURE 20.24

Alignment options

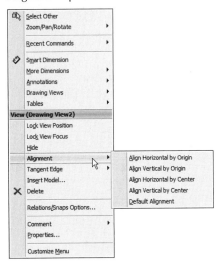

Predefined views and sheet scale

When Predefined views are created, they are set to follow the sheet scale by default; however, you can manually set them to have a custom scale. If you are using the automatic scaling option (found at Tools ➪ Options ➪ System Options ➪ Drawings ➪ Automatically Scale New Drawing Views), the sheet scale is automatically changed when the drawing views are populated to make a nice fit of the model geometry on the drawing. The scales used by the automatic feature are all standard multiples of two, so you do not have to worry about odd scale factors on your drawings.

Predefined view limitations

The function and expectations of Predefined views are fairly straightforward, although there are a few things that could be improved. For example, SolidWorks does not allow you to create predefined section or detail views. Also, the View Palette does not preview the populated Predefined views.

Using styles and blocks in templates

Starting in SolidWorks 2009, the functionality formerly known as *favorites* is now known as *styles*. In SolidWorks, styles function like styles and formatting in Microsoft Word, or other word-processing software, by adding underlines, bold formatting, and even items such as tolerances and symbols. Hole Wizard Styles are described in Chapter 17, and work similarly to Dimension and Note Styles (described in Chapter 22). This chapter is concerned with the fact that styles can be saved to files, and loaded to documents. In particular, they can be loaded to documents that can be saved as templates, thus maintaining the loaded styles. Several types of styles can be loaded into and saved with drawing templates, including dimension, note, GD&T, weld, and surface finish symbols.

When a style is loaded into a template, any document that you create from that template can use any of the loaded styles. The many file types for styles exist mainly to transfer styles from one document to another, but they are not needed once the style is loaded. As a result, before saving a template, you should gather together your styles into your library folder and load them into the template.

You can load styles by going to the interface for the type of favorite, for example, dimensions or notes. Figure 20.25 shows the top of the Note PropertyManager interface, which contains the Styles panel.

FIGURE 20.25

The Styles panel for the Note PropertyManager

The buttons in the Styles panel of the Note PropertyManager interface have the following functions:

 ■ Apply the default attributes to the selected notes

 ■ Add or update a style

 ■ Delete a style

 ■ Save a style

 ■ Load a style

This section is concerned with the last function, Load a style. After clicking this button, you can load multiple styles at once by Shift-selecting them through the Open dialog box that appears.

Even symbol types that can be applied by dragging-and-dropping from the Design Library can also be loaded as styles. However, I prefer dragging from the Design Library because you get a preview of the symbol; with the styles, you just see a text tag.

Blocks can also be loaded into a template or used from the Design Library as drag-and-drop items.

Custom properties in templates

Part of the usefulness of templates is that you can do work once, and have it replicated many times. This is an excellent example of process automation. One of the ways that you can take advantage of this feature is by putting default custom properties in your templates. In many cases, simply having a default value for something is better than no value, and a default value may even prompt you to put a value with real significance in the property. For example, the Description of a document is extremely important, especially if you are using sequential part numbers for your file-names. A custom property named Description can be added to your template, and the default value is used unless it is changed when the template is used in a document.

You have already seen how custom properties used in parts can be instrumental in filling out a title block on a drawing. Custom properties in part and assembly documents work exactly the same as they do in drawings. The custom properties interface is shown in Figure 20.26.

FIGURE 20.26

The custom properties Interface

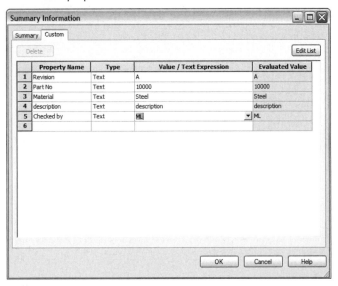

Saving a template

Drawing templates are saved through the Save As menu, by selecting Drawing Templates in the Files of Type drop-down list. This automatically takes you to the folder for the templates, as specified in Tools ⇨ Options ⇨ File Locations ⇨ Templates.

In the case where a template and format have been saved together and are being saved together, but the format also needs to be saved to its own file, saving the template with the changed format only changes the format for documents that are made from that point forward with that template.

You may also save out the format to its own file from the edited template. Formats are needed in their own file (in addition to existing within a template) for situations when you have an existing drawing and want to change the size of the sheet, and then need a format to put on the sheet. Another situation is when a drawing may come in to your organization from an outside contractor, and they have not used your format; in this case, you can simply replace their format with yours, or you can send them your format (and template, for that matter), from which the contractor can create all drawings for you.

Separate formats are important for when you have multi-sheet drawings. When adding a sheet, you also need to add a format. You can save multi-sheet drawing templates in which the first and second sheets have different formats on them.

Creating Blocks

Blocks are an important aspect of automating drawing creation. They enable you to combine text and sketch geometry and to annotate common features on drawings. Blocks are discussed in Chapter 4 (sketch blocks) and also in Chapter 22 (creation, editing, and placement). Blocks can be used for many purposes, including the following:

- Tolerance blocks on drawings that might change with the process (if you do not have separate formats that already contain this information)

- Electrical or pneumatic schematic symbols that can be snapped together

- Flowchart type symbols

- Fluid flow-direction arrows

- Special markers calling attention to a specific detail

- Sheet formats that can be created as a block, enabling you to move it around as a single entity much more easily

You can create blocks by selecting a group of sketch entities, annotations, or symbols and then clicking Tools ⇨ Block ⇨ Make.

CROSS-REF For more information on the creation, editing, management, and placement of blocks, see Chapter 22.

Summary

Getting your templates and formats correct creates an excellent opportunity to save some time with drawings by automating many of the common tasks through the use of templates, Predefined views, multiple formats, blocks, favorites, and linked custom properties. Setup becomes more important when you are administering a larger installation, but is also important if it is just for yourself. One of the most important things that you can do is to establish a file library and direct your Tools ⇨ Options ⇨ File Locations paths to the files. There is nothing quite as productive as having something that works right the first time, and every time.

Chapter 21

Working with Drawing Views

Twelve years ago, when I first moved from AutoCAD to SolidWorks, one of the most difficult concepts to understand was that in SolidWorks you do not create lines in the drawing view, and in fact, you cannot move any of the lines in the view at all. The drawing view was in effect a snapshot of the 3D model from a particular point of view. The snapshot could be updated, but it could not be manipulated manually.

At first, this seemed a little bit confining. However, once I understood it, the concept became liberating rather than confining. It meant that I did not have to worry about the drawing views being inconsistent or incorrect. All I had to worry about was the 3D model being correct.

If you are a new user, then you should feel confident that SolidWorks properly maintains the views better than you could do it manually. Any type of view from any point of view of even the most complex model or assembly geometry can be updated perfectly.

To be fair, there are some things that SolidWorks has difficulties with, but knowing this now means that you will be ready for these issues and know how to deal with them when or if they occur. One issue arises from assemblies that contain parts that interfere. HLR (hidden lines removed) display of interfering parts can show extra lines or hide lines that should be shown. At other times, you may have issues with lightweight parts. When possible, it is best to work with model geometry that is fully resolved as well as high-quality drawing views.

Creating Common View Types

The previous chapter discussed Predefined views in templates. Predefined views make it faster to automatically create drawings with consistently placed, simple views. However, sometimes you may need to create views on templates that do not have Predefined views, or you may need a special arrangement of views. SolidWorks has a good assortment of view types to make practically any type of view that you may need.

NOTE   When creating or changing either the geometry or the settings that control how a view is displayed, the view may become cross-hatched, indicating that the model needs to be rebuilt. To resolve this problem, press Ctrl+B to rebuild the drawing.

Using the View palette

The View palette is shown in Figure 21.1. It is activated automatically if you use the Make Drawing From Part tool, unless the drawing template that you select has Predefined views on it. In this case, the Predefined views are populated, and the View palette is not activated.

FIGURE 21.1

The View palette

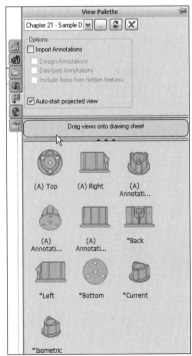

The View palette contains all of the standard named views, the current view of the model, custom named views, and any annotation views (views that the model was in when annotations were added to it). You can drag-and-drop these views on the drawing.

If multiple parts are available, they are listed in the pull-down menu at the top of the panel. You can also browse, refresh, or cancel out of the view from this same area.

To activate the View palette without using the Make Drawing From Part tool, simply create a new drawing document, ensure that the Task Pane is available, and click the View Palette tab in the Task Pane. Then use the ellipse button (. . .) to browse to a part. After you select a part, the palette window is populated with views of the model. This method has the advantage of enabling you to see the views before you put them down. It does not link views in the same way that the Predefined and projected views are linked, however. I find this interface somewhat difficult to use, and prefer to set up the Predefined views in templates or to use the Multiple Views option in the Model Views PropertyManager, which is shown later in this chapter.

Model

Model views are one of the few types of views that are not dependent on another view. Everything has to start from somewhere, and most drawings have to start with either a named or Predefined view.

You can place named views by using the Model View button on the Drawings toolbar or by clicking Insert ⇨ Drawing View ⇨ Model. Using the Model View PropertyManager is a two-step process, and is shown in Figure 21.2. In the first step, you select the model, and in the second step, you set the options for the view. Views dragged from the View Palette are also Model views.

Open documents

The large selection box in the Part/Assembly to Insert panel displays any models that are open in SolidWorks at the moment. If the model that you are looking for is not in the list, then you can use the Browse button to look for it.

I find this part of the interface to be clumsy because an extra step is involved that was not there before. It used to be that when you chose to place a named view, you would open the Browse dialog box directly, but now there is an intermediate step. For this reason, I try to use a workflow that avoids this PropertyManager. I typically use the Create Drawing From This Part/Assembly if the part is open, and if not, I drag-and-drop the part onto a new drawing created from a template with Predefined and projected views on it. This combination saves a lot of extra steps.

One of the annoying quirks of this interface occurs in the first step when you are using the PropertyManager (the image to the left in Figure 21.2). If you click in the drawing window for some reason (for example, if you are expecting it to simply place a view), then a prompt appears, stating that you have selected a drawing document, and that only parts and assemblies can be inserted into drawings.

FIGURE 21.2

The Model View PropertyManager

Thumbnail Preview

This is a nice option that shows the part that you selected in the Open Documents window. It is a useful feature, but, because it is collapsed by default, it is easy to miss. After it is used the first time, it retains the setting.

Start Command When Creating New Drawing Option

The Start Command When Creating New Drawing option causes this PropertyManager to open up immediately when a new drawing is created. If you click in the drawing window, then the prompt appears, telling you that you are not paying attention.

Cosmetic Thread Display

Many people see the High and Draft quality options and assume that the option refers to the quality of the view, while in fact it refers to the quality of the cosmetic thread display. Cosmetic threads can display in either high or draft quality. The distinction is made for performance reasons. The difference in terms of display is that in high-quality mode, hidden cosmetic threads (cosmetic threads that are behind a face) do not display in shaded mode.

Number of Views and Orientation

This is the one function that almost redeems the Model View PropertyManager for me. In Single View mode, you select the view that you want to place from the Orientation panel, place the view, and then move on. In Multiple Views mode, you select all views that you want to be displayed, including choices such as Current Model View and any named or annotation views that are created in the model interface. These views are indicated on the drawing as boxes (representing view borders), as shown in Figure 21.3.

FIGURE 21.3

Placing multiple views

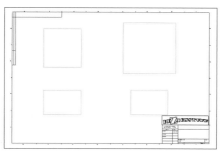

This is really useful functionality. It makes view selection and placement very easy and is visually clear. Unfortunately, the Single View setting is the default setting, and the PropertyManager does not remember the last setting that was used. Still, the combination of Multiple Views and Orientation is far better, in my opinion, than the View Palette, which I find visually confusing and non-intuitive.

Auto-Start Projected View Option

The one option in the Options panel is Auto-Start Projected View, which, on the placement of a view, automatically enables you to place more views. This option only works when you have selected the Single View option in the Number of Views panel.

Display Style

You can set the default display style in Tools ⇨ Options ⇨ System Options ⇨ Drawings ⇨ Display Style. This panel provides an override for views being placed. This panel also allows you to control High or Draft Quality views, which are described later in this chapter.

Scale

SolidWorks drawings always default to showing views at the overall sheet scale, unless the System Option on the Drawings page called Automatically Scale New Drawing Views is turned on. If this setting is on, the sheet scale saved with the drawing template is overridden. For example, a 1:1 sheet scale can be changed automatically to 1:4 by the setting.

You can change the sheet scale through the sheet properties, which were discussed in Chapter 20. Controlling views with the sheet scale makes it much easier to change the size of a drawing and to scale all of the views together. Individual views can be displayed at the view scale, and detail views are typically created at a different scale automatically. The scale setting is found at Tools ⇨ Options ⇨ System Options ⇨ Drawings ⇨ Detail View Scaling. Detail views, covered later in this chapter, automatically get a note showing the custom scale for the view. You can create a note that functions in the same way as the automatically created "Scale" text manually from a note and a link to a custom property for views where the link to the sheet scale has been broken manually.

 **TIP** A note that automatically links to the scale of a drawing view is something you could consider creating a note style or block for.

Dimension Type

Even in non-orthogonal (isometric) views, true dimensions should be used for most drawing views. Projected dimensions depend on the angle of the edge to the view plane.

Cosmetic Thread Display

If something is worth having, it is worth having twice. This panel appears in both steps, just in case you missed it in the first step.

Projected view

 The Projected view type simply makes a view that is projected in the direction that you dragged the cursor from the selected view. Be aware that first-angle and third-angle projections result in views that are opposite from one another. For example, if you drag at a 45-degree angle, the result is an isometric view. When placing an isometric view that you have created in this way, SolidWorks constrains the new view to a 45-degree-angle line through the Origins of the two views. To place the view somewhere other than along this line, press the Ctrl key while placing the view to break the alignment. The PropertyManager for the Projected View is shown in Figure 21.4.

FIGURE 21.4

The Projected View PropertyManager

When you use the pushpin on the Projected View PropertyManager, you can place multiple projected views from the originally selected view, or select a new view to project views from. Display properties and scale of the projected views are taken from the parent view.

Standard 3 view

 The Standard 3 View tool on the Drawings toolbar can also be accessed at Insert ⇨ Drawing View ⇨ Standard 3 View. This places a Front view, and projects Top and Right views for third-angle projection drawings.

Detail view

 The Detail view is activated from the Drawings toolbar or at Insert ⇨ Drawing View ⇨ Detail. Either way, you can use the function in two different ways: one that is fast and easy and the other that gives you more control but is not quite as fast.

Pre-drawn detail circle

The detail "circle" can be drawn before you initiate the Detail View command. When you pre-draw a detail circle, you must ensure that you are sketching in the view and not on the sheet. To draw in the view, the view must be activated. You can activate a view by clicking in the view or by bringing a sketch cursor inside the boundary of the view. When you activate a view, the status bar in the lower-right corner of the SolidWorks window displays the message, Editing Drawing View, as shown in Figure 21.5.

The dotted border in the image to the left shows that the view is selected, and the status bar shows that it is activated. The image to the right with the solid corners indicates that the view has Locked Focus. You can lock focus on a drawing view by double-clicking it or by right-clicking and selecting Lock View Focus from the menu.

Activated drawing views

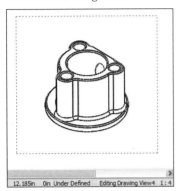 

If a view is not activated or the focus is not locked on the view, then any sketch elements that you draw will be placed on the drawing sheet. While sketching in a drawing view, it is a good practice to watch the status bar.

The point of all of this is to sketch a closed loop in the view so that it can be used for a Detail view. The closed loop can be a circle, ellipse, spline, series of lines, or any other shape, as long as it is a closed loop. The closed loop is called a *circle* for the purposes of the Detail view in SolidWorks terminology.

A setting controls how the circle displays, in particular whether it displays as drawn or as an actual circle. This setting is found at Tools ➪ Options ➪ System Options ➪ Drawings ➪ Display New Detail Circles as Circles. This setting appears to be obsolete. It no longer works correctly in SolidWorks 2009. It appears to be overridden by settings in the Detail Circle PropertyManager. The different results are shown in Figure 21.6.

FIGURE 21.6

Drawing a closed loop with the Display Detail Circles as Circles option both on and off

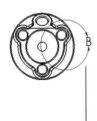 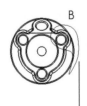 

Display Detail Circles
as Circles turned on

Display Detail Circles
as Circles turned off

Once you create the loop, you can click the Detail View toolbar button and place the view. The view is automatically scaled by the factor set at Tools ➪ Options ➪ Drawings ➪ Detail View Scaling. By default, this scale is set to twice the parent view scale, but you can reset the default to whatever you like.

Detail circle drawn in-line

A faster way to complete the Detail view is to simply click the Detail View toolbar button without pre-selecting or pre-drawing the loop. This activates the Circle sketch tool immediately, which activates the view as soon as you bring the cursor over the view, so that when you draw the circle, it is sure to be in the view rather than on the sheet.

Alternatively, you could swap the circle tool for an ellipse or spline; this works just as well, but offers more flexibility. Regardless of the sketch tool, when you close the loop, SolidWorks prompts you to place the view. The workflow for this in-line method is better than the old-school pre-drawn loop technique.

Editing a Detail view

You can edit a Detail view by dragging the circumference of the detail circle to a new diameter, dragging the center of the detail circle to a new location, or by selecting Edit Sketch from the detail circle right-mouse button menu. This method enables you to edit sketch relations or otherwise edit the sketch that you used for the detail. When you are done with the sketch, you can use the Confirmation Corner to click OK.

You can delete Detail views by selecting and deleting the detail circle. Deleting the detail circle gives you the option to delete the resulting view as well as the original sketch. Also, deleting the detail view gives you the option to delete the detail circle and the original sketch.

Section view

Section views in SolidWorks offer many options such as Default Section view, Partial Section view, Aligned Section view, and Editing a Section view.

Default Section view

The Default Section view has the same in-line and pre-drawn optional techniques as the Detail view, as well as the same advantages and disadvantages.

Section views may have a straight line that may go through the center of a cylindrical feature. Even though you are in a drawing and not in a model sketch, you may still benefit from model sketching techniques. For example, to draw a straight vertical line through the model shown in Figure 21.7, in the images on the left, you can hover the cursor over a circular edge to wake up the center, and then pick up the inference lines to the center. Another technique is to show the temporary axes (using the View menu), just sketch the line, and then assign a sketch relation in the same way that you would in a feature sketch. This technique is shown in the images on the right.

Aligning a line in a Section view sketch

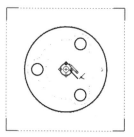
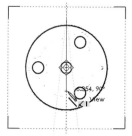
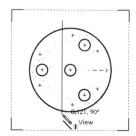

You can also use jogged section lines with the default section tool. Similar sketch relation tech-niques are more common in jogged sections because there are more sketched lines. The results are shown in Figure 21.8.

Partial Section view

A Partial Section view is created when the section line does not cut all the way across the model. In Figure 21.9, the line that is drawn to create the Partial Section view was the vertical section line. The prompt that appears enables you to confirm that you intended to create a partial section cut. If you answer No to the prompt, the result is an error, with the new view displayed in the dangling color.

FIGURE 21.8

Default and jogged Section views

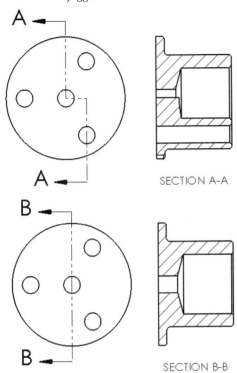

SECTION A-A

SECTION B-B

FIGURE 21.9

A Partial Section view

SECTION C-C

Sketched line

You can use another technique to create a section that looks like a partial section, but is not considered a partial section by SolidWorks. You can create it by drawing perpendicular lines, and selecting the line to be used as the projection direction for the section before clicking the Section View tool. This differs from a true partial section in that it shows half of the model unsectioned. It is also similar to the Aligned Section view, but it does not unfold the second sectioned side. When the prompt shown in Figure 21.9 displays, clicking Yes causes the resulting view to look like the view on the left in Figure 21.9. Clicking No causes the view shown in Figure 21.10 to appear. Creating the view shown in Figure 21.9 requires only a single sketched line, while Figure 21.10 requires perpendicular sketched lines.

FIGURE 21.10

Another Section view

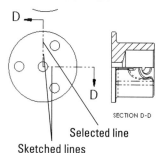

Sketched lines
Selected line
SECTION D-D

Aligned Section view

The Aligned Section view takes two separate sections at right angles to one another and lays them out flat on the page. It is essentially two partial sections that display side by side. The section lines look identical to those shown in Figure 21.10, but the resulting view is different, as shown in Figure 21.11. The finished view aligns with the selected sketch element.

FIGURE 21.11

The Aligned Section view

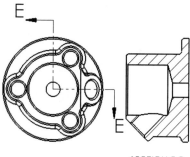

SECTION E-E

Editing a Section view

Section views are edited in the same way as detail views. You can edit the section lines directly by dragging, or the section line sketch through the right-mouse button menu. You can use the Edit Sketch command through the section line right-mouse button menu to edit sketch relations, or to add or remove sketch elements to the sketch.

Section views are also deleted in the same way as detail views, with the option to also delete the underlying sketch for the section. When you delete one segment of the section line, the resulting view, as well as the underlying sketch, is also deleted.

Creating Other View Types

SolidWorks is able to create any type of view that you need. If you can define what the view should look like, then SolidWorks can create it. The only limit is your creativity.

Crop view

The Crop view is simply a view that looks like a Detail view without requiring a parent view. This feature allows you to reduce the number of views on a sheet, and save some room. However, a cropped view may be confusing if it is not clear which area is being detailed in the cropped view.

Unlike Detail views, in Crop views, the closed loop must be sketched in the view before you invoke the command. To make the Crop view, draw the closed loop as shown in Figure 21.12 in the image to the left, and then click the Crop View button on the drawing toolbar or access the command at Insert ⇨ Drawing View ⇨ Crop.

FIGURE 21.12

A sketch loop and a Crop view

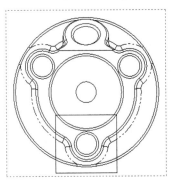

To edit a Crop view, right-click the view, expand the arrow next to Crop View, and select either Edit Crop or Remove Crop. Removing the crop does not delete the sketch that the crop was created from.

Broken-out Section view

The Broken-out Section view is another view type that alters an existing view rather than creating a new view. It also requires a closed loop sketch. The Broken-out Section view is very useful in assembly views where parts are obscured by other parts, in particular when a set of parts are inside a housing and you want to show the inside parts without hiding the housing. Of course, you can also use Broken-out Section views on parts with internal detail.

Broken-out Section views act like a cut that is created from the drawing view. Any faces created by the cut are hatched. Figure 21.13 shows a simple assembly view using a Broken-out Section view. On the left is the view with the driving sketch (in this case, a closed loop spline), and on the right is the finished view. You cannot create Broken-out Section views using existing detail, section, or alternate position views.

A Broken-out Section view

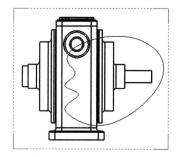 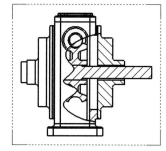

Drawing the closed loop

Broken-out Section views are initiated from an existing view either with or without a pre-drawn closed loop. If the loop is pre-drawn, then you must select it before clicking the Broken-out Section toolbar button on the Drawings toolbar or accessing the command at Insert ⇨ Drawing View ⇨ Broken-out Section.

If the view has no pre-drawn, pre-selected loop, then initiating the function activates the spline sketch tool. It is not necessary to use a spline as the closed loop for this view type, but Broken-out Section views are traditionally created with a freehand sort of boundary, even when drawn manually.

If the loop is closed in an uninterrupted workflow, then after the last spline point is drawn, joining the spline back to itself, the Section Scope dialog box appears. This enables you to select any parts that are not to be sectioned. It is customary to avoid sectioning shafts, screws, or other cylindrical components. Using the Section Scope, the image on the right in Figure 21.13 would be altered to look like the image on the right in Figure 21.14.

The recommended workflow is to initiate the function from the toolbar, use the spline to create the closed loop, and to not pre-draw a loop. This makes everything flow more smoothly, and you create the view surprisingly quickly. If you must use a sketch tool other than the spline, then you must pre-draw it. Even if you simply change sketch tools when the Broken-out Section view automatically activates the spline, because the workflow has been broken, creating the closed loop does not automatically display the Section Scope interface.

FIGURE 21.14

Using the Section Scope

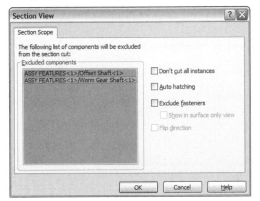

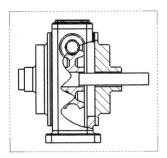

Selecting the depth

After you make the Section Scope selections, the next step is to set the depth of the cut. You can do this in one of several ways. Broken-out Section views are usually applied to the center of a hole if available, or in other ways that show the view as cleanly as possible. If you know the depth of the cut that you want to make, then you can type it in as a distance value. Of course, that raises the question "Distance from *what*?" to which the answer seems to be "from the geometry in the view that would come the farthest out of the screen toward the user." Users most often choose the distance when it does not matter *exactly* how deep the cut goes or exactly *where* it cuts, but to give a relative position.

In situations when you want to cut to the center of a particular feature or up to an edge, it is far easier and less bothersome to simply select the geometry from a drawing view. For example, Figure 21.15 shows the PropertyManager interface where the depth of the cut is set. In this example, the edge of the shaft in the view to the right has been selected. This tells SolidWorks that the cut should go to the center of the shaft. Another possibility is to show the temporary axes, as shown in Figure 21.15, and to select an axis through the center of the shaft.

FIGURE 21.15

Setting the depth of the Broken-out Section view

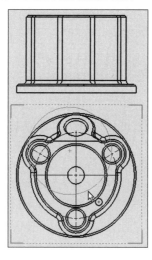
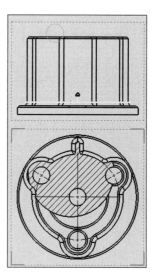

Editing the view

At this point the view is finished. Now you may choose to edit the view in some way, such as by changing the sketch, the depth, the section scope, and so on. Figure 21.16 shows how the

Broken-out Section view is positioned in the Drawing FeatureManager. It is listed as a modification to an existing drawing view. The Broken-out Section right-mouse button menu is also shown. Selecting Edit Definition displays the PropertyManager, shown in Figure 21.15. Selecting Edit Sketch enables you to change the section spline shape. Selecting Properties displays the dialog box shown to the right in Figure 21.16. This contains options for the underlying original view as well as the Broken-out section modification to the original view. Only the Section Scope tab is added by the Broken-out Section view. The rest of the options are for normal view properties.

FIGURE 21.16

Editing the Broken-out Section view

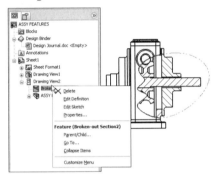

Break view

Break views are typically used to display parts that are very long in one dimension on a drawing in such a way that you can see both ends or other important features. You can break views more than once in the same direction, or even in opposite directions. Figure 21.17 shows the full view of a part and a view that was broken twice. Notice that the dimensions are correct, and any dimension that includes a broken length has a special dimension line.

The PropertyManager in Figure 21.17 shows a bit of a discrepancy in terminology. Using "Break" as the name of the view seems a little awkward, and I much prefer it as it is shown here in the PropertyManager as "Broken View." It is inconsistent, but you get the idea anyway.

To create a Break view, click the Break toolbar button on the Drawings toolbar, or select it at Insert ➪ Drawing View ➪ Break. You need to place break lines in pairs, and you can choose from one of four break symbol styles, as shown in Figure 21.18. You can change the style from the right-mouse button menu or from the PropertyManager.

FIGURE 21.17

Dimensions on a Break view

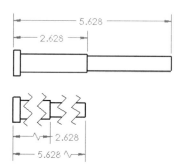

FIGURE 21.18

Selecting the break symbol

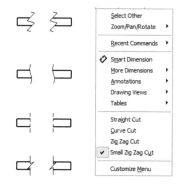

The Broken View PropertyManager also enables you to set the gap size and the style of the break. The gap refers to the gap between the break lines in the finished broken view. The setting here overrides the default for this view only. The default setting is a template setting found in Tools ➪ Options ➪ Document Properties ➪ Detailing. Other options that you can set in this location are the break line extension (the distance the lines extend past the model edges) and the break line font (on the Line Font page of the Document Properties tab). The setting that enables the broken symbol on a dimension is found on the Dimensions page, and is named Show Dimensions As Broken In Broken Views.

You can remove individual breaks in a broken view by selecting one of the break lines and pressing Delete. You can add breaks by applying the Break command and adding more breaks to a view. You can alter breaks by simply dragging the break lines. In past versions, it was possible to get the view very confused by dragging one set of breaks to interfere with another set of breaks. That problem has been fixed by not allowing break lines to be dragged past one another.

Starting with SolidWorks 2009, broken views now allow you to dimension the break lines themselves so that when the model changes, you can control the location of the break lines relative to part geometry.

Consider using the Unbreak option from the right-mouse button menu to temporarily unbreak a view to make dimensioning more convenient.

Auxiliary view

An Auxiliary view is a view that is projected from a non-orthogonal edge. This type of view is often necessary to view features (such as holes drilled at an angle) square on, so that they appear circular in the view rather than foreshortened and elliptical. An auxiliary view is shown in Figure 21.19 in the image to the left. If the edge that the view was created from is updated, then the auxiliary view will reorient itself. The image to the right shows an auxiliary view projected from an arbitrarily drawn sketch line. The line or edge used to project an auxiliary view cannot be reselected; however, if a sketch is used to project the view, then the Edit Sketch option is available through the view arrow right-mouse button menu.

FIGURE 21.19

Two Auxiliary views

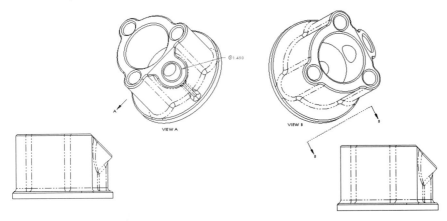

Alternate Position view

The Alternate Position view is only available for views of an assembly and shows the assembly in two different positions (not from different viewpoints; this requires an assembly that moves). This is another view type that does not create a new view, but alters an existing view. Figure 21.20 shows the PropertyManager interface for this view type, a sample view that it creates, and the way that it is represented in the drawing FeatureManager.

FIGURE 21.20

The Alternate Position view

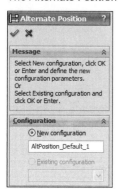
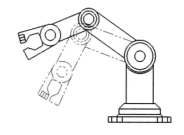

To create an Alternate Position view, ensure that you have an assembly on the active drawing that can have multiple positions, and click the Alternate Position View button from the Drawings toolbar, or select the same tool at Insert ➪ Drawing View ➪ Alternate Position.

Next, click in the drawing view to which you want to add the alternate position. The PropertyManager shown in Figure 21.20 prompts you to select an existing configuration for the alternate position or to create a new configuration. If you choose to create a new config, then the model window appears, a new config is created, and you are required to reposition the assembly. The alternate position is shown in a different line font on the same view, from the same orientation as the original.

TIP The best way to create this view is to either create two configurations used exclusively for the Alternate Position view or to have two configurations where you know that parts will not be moved, suppressed, or hidden. The main idea is that you need to ensure that these configurations remain in the same position or are changed intentionally, knowing that it will alter this drawing view.

To delete an Alternate Position view, select it in the drawing FeatureManager, and press Delete.

Predefined view

Predefined views are discussed in depth in Chapter 20, and are primarily used as views on drawing templates.

Empty view

Empty views are just that — empty. The reasons for creating an Empty view can include making a view from a sketch, or a schematic from blocks, or combining several elements — such as blocks, sketches, imported drawing geometry, annotations, and symbols — into an entity that can be moved as a group on a drawing.

Custom view

You can create Custom views by orienting the view in the model document, and saving the view. Remember that views can be saved in the View Orientation window, which you can access by pressing the spacebar. Custom views are placed on the drawing using the Named View functionality.

While not appropriate for showing dimensions, views using perspective are most useful for pictorial or illustrative views. The only way to get a perspective view on a drawing is to save a custom view in the model with perspective turned on. You can access the Perspective option at View ➪ Display ➪ Perspective, and you can edit the amount of perspective at View ➪ Modify ➪ Perspective.

Relative view

The Relative view enables you to create a view that does not necessarily correspond to any of the standard orthogonal views or named views. This type of view is very similar to using the Normal To tool. First select the face that is to be presented square to the view, and then select the face that represents the top of the view. When this view type is initiated, SolidWorks opens the 3D model window to allow you to select the faces needed to define the view.

This type of view is particularly useful when a part has a face that is at an odd angle to the standard planes of the part. It is in some ways similar to the Auxiliary view, except that in the Auxiliary view you cannot select which face is the top.

The Relative view has a special function that is important for drawings of multibody parts. If both faces used to establish the view are from the same body, then all of the rest of the bodies in the part can be hidden with an option in the Relative View PropertyManager, which is shown in Figure 21.21. This functionality is particularly useful in Weldments and is covered in more detail in Chapter 31. Multibody modeling is covered in Chapter 26.

FIGURE 21.21

The Relative View PropertyManager

3D Drawing View Mode

3D Drawing View Mode is not technically a drawing view type. It is a mode that enables you to select faces or edges of the model that may need to be selected for some purpose, but cannot be seen from the orientation of the drawing view. You can invoke the 3D Drawing View Mode from the 3D Drawing View toolbar button, which is on the View toolbar and can be accessed via the menus at View ➪ Modify ➪ 3D Drawing View.

Ironically, this mode does not work for the Relative view, which would be a perfect application for it. Relative view instead makes you go to the model window. 3D Drawing View Mode is intended for views such as the Broken-out Section view where a depth must be selected for the cut.

In Figure 21.22, notice the small toolbar above the drawing view. This toolbar is available while the 3D Drawing View Mode is turned on. Clicking OK on the small toolbar turns off the mode and returns the view to its previous state.

FIGURE 21.22

3D Drawing View Mode

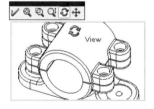

View orientation and alignment

Although you may have selected the Top view, and it displays the correct geometry, you may want to spin the view in the plane of the paper, or orient it in a particular way. You can do this using two methods. The easiest way to reorient the view is to use the Rotate View tool on the View toolbar. This rotates the view in the plane of the paper much like it rotates the model in 3D.

Another option is to select an edge in the view and assign the edge to be either a horizontal or vertical edge. Figure 21.23 shows how a view can be re-oriented using this tool, which is located at Tools ➪ Align Drawing View ➪ Horizontal or Vertical Edge.

Another option for view alignment is to align it relative to another view; this involves stacking one view on top of another or placing them side by side. You can do this by selecting the second pair of options in the menu shown in Figure 21.23, Horizontal to Another View and Vertical to Another View.

Situations may arise where a view is locked into a particular relationship to another view, and you need to disassociate the views. The Break Alignment option, which is grayed out in the menu in Figure 21.23, serves that purpose.

FIGURE 21.23

Rotating a drawing view to align an edge

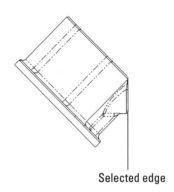

Selected edge

Using Display Options in Views

Some important display options and settings are not listed in Tools ⇨ Options, and are only available through the menus. You can find more information about the display options and settings that are available through Tools ⇨ Options in Appendix B.

Display States

Display States can be used in drawing views, but (unless you are only hiding and showing parts with the Display States) they only have an effect when a drawing view is set to Shaded Display mode. You can control Display States for drawing views in the View PropertyManager. The Drawing View Properties dialog box appears, as shown in Figure 21.24.

One of the limitations of the Display States functionality in drawing views is that when wireframe display is used, the drawing edges appear black rather than using the color settings to show wireframe in the same color as shaded. The necessary color settings are found in two places, and both settings need to be set. The System Options setting is on the Colors page and is called Use Specified color for shaded with edges mode. The second setting is in the part Document Properties (not assembly), again on the Colors page, called Apply Same Color To Wireframe, HLR, and Shaded.

FIGURE 21.24

The View PropertyManager

Display modes

With even the 2D drawing world becoming less and less black-and-white, SolidWorks drawings have the ability to apply shaded views to drawings. This is probably most useful in isometric, perspective, or pictorial views on the drawings. The shading and color may be distracting for dimensioned and detailed views, but it can also be indispensable when you need to show what a part actually looks like in 3D. Not everyone can read engineering prints, and even for those who can, nothing communicates quite like a couple of shaded isometric views.

The more standard 2D drawing display modes are Wireframe, HLR (hidden lines removed), and HLV (hidden lines visible), which work in the same way as they do in the model environment. Unless you override it on a per part basis, the Display mode is set for all of the components in the view.

Component Line Font

Individual components within an assembly can be shown in different fonts, similar to the display in the Alternate Position view. You can access this function through the component right-mouse button menu, by selecting Component Line Font. Figure 21.25 shows the Component Line Font dialog box, along with a drawing view in which a couple of part line fonts have been changed. The part can only be changed in the view where it was selected, or it can be changed across the board in all views in the active drawing where it appears. This is useful if you want to emphasize or de-emphasize certain parts in the assembly view.

FIGURE 21.25

The Component Line Font dialog box

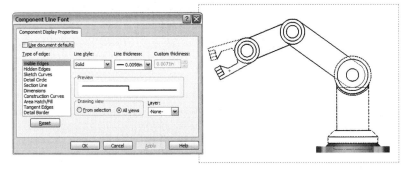

Layers

Yes, SolidWorks drawings *can* use layers. No one likes to admit this, but it is nonetheless true. You can place individual parts onto layers, and the layers can have different colors and line fonts. Most entities can be put into layers, including edges, annotations, and sketch items. Hidden layers are often used for reference information or construction entities on a drawing.

Edge display options

SolidWorks drawings and models offer some options for displaying tangent edges. Many users find it distracting when tangent edges (which in a physical part are not edges at all) are given as much visible weight as the sharp edges of, say, a chamfer. These settings are found at View➪Display, as shown in Figure 21.26. The Tangent Edges Removed option may be appropriate for parts with few fillets, but it causes a part to look oversimplified and makes details of the shape difficult to distinguish.

FIGURE 21.26

Edge display options

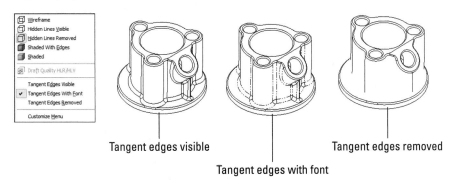

Tangent edges visible

Tangent edges with font

Tangent edges removed

View quality settings

View quality is one of those issues that keep users confused because it has changed so many times in recent releases. If you look for view quality settings, then you may be looking for some time. Are the settings with the view, the sheet, the system options, the document properties? Where are they?

You have the choice between two options for drawing view quality: High Quality and Draft Quality. The quality that you choose influences the performance of the software. Draft Quality views are noticeably rough when viewed closely, but from a distance, they are at least recognizable. However, Draft Quality is becoming less accessible, and so I would not recommend relying on this option. Although new Draft Quality views can be created, once they are set to High Quality, they cannot be set back to Draft Quality.

All views are created as High Quality unless the view quality setting is overridden. This setting is found at Tools ⇨ Options ⇨ System Options ⇨ Drawings ⇨ Display Style ⇨ Display Quality For New Views. The only other way that you can create Draft Quality views is if you open a drawing from an older version of SolidWorks that used Draft Quality views.

In Figure 21.2 earlier in the chapter, the image to the right shows the Display Style pane. This PropertyManager has been taken from a High Quality view. A Draft Quality view enables you to toggle between Draft and High quality, as shown in Figure 21.27. This means that you can switch a view from Draft to High, but not from High to Draft. Also notice in Figure 21.27 that the cursor over a Draft Quality view displays a lightning bolt symbol, indicating draft quality.

FIGURE 21.27

The Draft Quality options and cursor

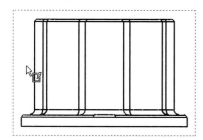

You can access the Cosmetic Thread Display setting in both the Step 1 PropertyManager and the Step 2 PropertyManager. However, you need to be careful not to misread the interface, by thinking that either of these interfaces controls the View Quality. The best advice for using the view quality settings is to forget about them. It looks like this function is being phased out or at least discouraged.

Distinguishing Views from Sheets

It is sometimes difficult for new users to understand the difference between being *in* a sketch and being *out of* a sketch, or the difference between editing the *sheet* as opposed to the *sheet format*. In the same way, confusion frequently surrounds the difference between sketching in a view and sketching on a sheet. The easiest way to determine if a sketch will be associated with a view or with the drawing sheet is to look at the prompt in the lower-right corner of the SolidWorks window, on the status bar, which displays the message, Editing Sheet, Editing Sheet Format, or Editing View.

This issue becomes especially important when you want to do something with a sketch entity, but it is grayed out and unavailable. This means that whatever entity is active is *not* the one that the sketch entity is on. Drawing views expand to contain all of the sketch entities that are associated with the view, and so if you see a view that is extended on one side, larger than it should be, then it could be extended to contain the grayed-out sketch entity. Activate the sheet and the suspected views; when the sketch entity turns from gray to black, you have found the place where it resides.

Tutorial: Working with View Types, Settings, and Options

This tutorial is intended to familiarize you with many of the view types, settings, and options that are involved in creating views. To begin, follow these steps:

1. **From the CD-ROM, open the part called** Chapter 21 – Tutorial Part.sldprt.

2. **Move the drawing template named** Inch B Bible Template.drwdot, **also found on the CD-ROM, to your templates folder.** If you do not know where your templates are located, go to Tools ➪ Options ➪ System Options ➪ File Locations ➪ Document Templates.

3. **From the window with the open part, click the Make Drawing from Part button from the toolbar.** The drawing becomes populated with three standard views and an isometric view, as shown in Figure 21.28.

4. **In the drawing document, turn on the display of the Origins.** This will help you to align a section view. Origins can be displayed through the menus at View ➪ Origin.

5. **Click the Section View tool on the Drawings toolbar.** This activates the Line sketch tool.

6. **In the Top view (in the upper-left section of the drawing), draw a vertical line that picks up the inference from the Origin.** You may have to run the cursor over the Origin to activate the inference lines. Make sure that the line goes all the way through the model geometry in the view, as shown in Figure 21.29. When you finish the line, the section view is ready to be placed. Place it to the right of the parent view.

FIGURE 21.28

Using a template with Predefined views

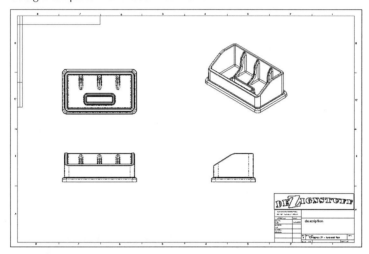

FIGURE 21.29

Creating a section view

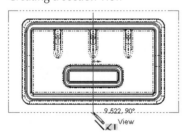

When sketching, remember to make sure that you are sketching in the view rather than on the sheet. A section view cannot be created from a sketch entity if it is not in a view. A glance at the status bar in the lower-right corner of the window lets you know if you are in Editing View or Editing Sheet.

To change the letter label on the drawing, click the section line and change the label in the top panel of the Section View PropertyManager.

 7. Bring the cursor over the sharp bend in the section line until the cursor looks like the image to the left. Double-click the cursor; the section arrows flip to the other direction, and the drawing view becomes cross-hatched. The cross-hatching indicates that the view needs to be updated.

8. **Press Ctrl+Q; the view updates, removing the cross-hatching.**

9. **Click the section line and press Delete.** Answer Yes to the prompt.

10. **Create a new section view using a jogged section line, as shown in Figure 21.30. In** order to do this, you must pre-draw the jogged section line, and press the Section View button with the part of the line that you want to use to project the new view.

FIGURE 21.30

Creating a jogged section view

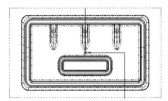
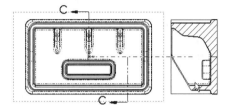

11. **Next, click the Detail View button on the Drawings toolbar.** This activates the Circle sketch tool.

12. **Sketch a circle in the Front view, located in the lower-left section of the drawing.** Try not to pick up any automatic relations to the center of the circle. One way to prevent this is to hold down the Ctrl key when creating the sketch.

13. **Place the view when the circle is complete.** Note that the view was created at a scale of 1:2. The sheet scale is 1:4, and so the detail is two times the sheet scale. The Detail view is shown in Figure 21.31.

FIGURE 21.31

Creating a Detail view

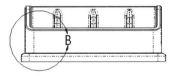
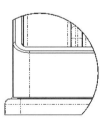

DETAIL B
SCALE 1 : 2

14. **Drag the circumference of the circle and watch the view dynamically resize.**

15. **Leave the Detail circle selected so that the center of the circle is highlighted.** Drag the center of the circle around the view. The effect is like moving a magnifying glass over the part. If you drag the center with the Ctrl key pressed, then you will not pick up any automatic sketch relations when you drop it somewhere.

16. **Click the Broken-out Section View tool on the Drawings toolbar.** Draw a spline similar to the one shown in the image to the left in Figure 21.32. Splines take a little practice.

FIGURE 21.32

Creating a Broken-out Section view

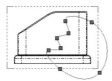 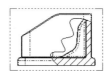

17. **Click inside the view border but outside of the part in the Top view (in the upper-left section of the drawing).** Press Ctrl+C.

18. **Click the Add Sheet icon to the right of the sheet tab in the lower-left corner of the drawing that says Sheet1, and select Add New Sheet.** If you used the template that I provided, a message may appear, saying that SolidWorks cannot find the format. This is because I only supplied you with the template file, not the format as a separate file. In any case, switch to the B size format and accept.

19. **Click any spot inside the sheet and press Ctrl+V.** SolidWorks pastes the copied view from the other sheet. Delete the section line.

20. **Click the Projected View tool from the Drawings toolbar, and then click the pasted view.** Practice making a couple of projected views, including dragging one off at a 45-degree angle to make an isometric. Make sure that one of the views is a side view showing the angled edge, as shown in Figure 21.33. Once you create the views, click model edges in the views and drag them around to a better location.

21. **Select the angled edge from one of the side views and click the Auxiliary View toolbar button.** While placing the view, press and hold the Ctrl key to break the alignment. You can resize the view arrow by selecting the corners and dragging. If you drag the line itself, then you can move it between the views. Alternatively, with the view arrow selected and the PropertyManager displayed, you can deselect the green check mark icon in the Arrow panel at the top of the window to turn off the arrow.

22. **Create a new drawing from the New dialog box.** If the automatic Model View interface appears in the PropertyManager, click the red X icon to cancel out of it.

FIGURE 21.33

Projecting views

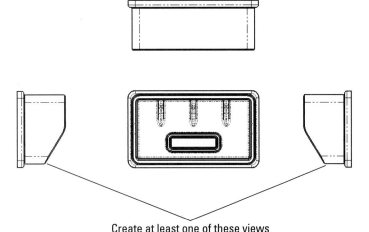

Create at least one of these views

23. **Expand the Task pane and activate the View palette (the tab that looks like a drawing icon).** Click the ellipse button (. . .) and browse for the assembly named `Chapter 21. SF casting assembly.sldasm`. This is shown in Figure 21.34.

24. **Drag the Back view onto the drawing.** Notice that when you use this technique, the views do not resize automatically, regardless of the setting at Tools ⇨ Options ⇨ Drawings ⇨ Automatically Scale New Drawing Views.

25. **Delete any view that you have created using this method.** Open Windows Explorer, browse to the assembly, and drag it into the drawing. The views that you create using this method are equivalent to the Standard 3 View tool. This time, the views auto-size.

26. **Select the Front view and change it to the Back view.** Notice that the rest of the views change to reflect the new parent view. You will get a warning about this change.

27. **Zoom in on the Back view.** Change the view to show Tangent Edges With Font through View ⇨ Display. You can also change this from the view right-mouse button menu.

28. **Click the Alternate Position view toolbar button.** Type a name in the PropertyManager for a new configuration and click the green check mark icon. SolidWorks opens the assembly model window.

29. **Rotate the handle 90 degrees and click the green check mark icon.** SolidWorks returns to the drawing and shows the new position in a dashed font, as shown in Figure 21.35.

30. **Place an isometric view on the drawing.** Change the Display Mode to make it a shaded view.

31. **Right-click inside the view but away from the parts, and select Properties.** The dialog box appears, as shown in Figure 21.36. Make sure that the view is set to use the Default configuration, and also select the Show in Exploded State option.

FIGURE 21.34

The View palette

FIGURE 21.35

Creating an Alternate Position view

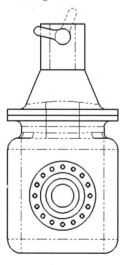

FIGURE 21.36

The Drawing View Properties dialog box

Summary

SolidWorks has the capacity to make many different types of views of parts and assemblies. In addition to the tools for projecting views, custom views saved in the model document can be saved and used on the drawing. The associative nature of the drawing to the model helps ensure that drawing views, regardless of how unusual the section angle or view orientation, are displayed in the correct size, location, and geometry.

It is sometimes better to create some of the views that require sketches by pre-sketching. Make use of workflow enhancements when possible; for example, the Broken-out Section automated workflow works well, but forcing it to be a manual process makes it awkward to use.

Chapter 22

Using Annotations and Symbols

nnotations and symbols are a major component of communicating a design through a drawing. SolidWorks has several options available to help you manage these entities to make engineering drawings look good and communicate effectively.

Using Notes

Notes are the workhorse of SolidWorks annotations. You can use notes in many different configurations and mix them with links to custom properties, hyperlinks, and text wrapping boxes. You can also use them with styles, leaders, symbols, and balloons; and you can even embed balloons into notes.

The workflow for placing notes

Sometimes users have difficulty working through some of the interfaces in SolidWorks. This is not necessarily the fault of the software, but is often because users may not fully understand how the workflow of a particular feature is supposed to function. The Model View interface from the last chapter is one that can be confusing until you have been through it a few times and gain a more intuitive feel for how it works.

Understanding the workflow is paramount to being able to use the software efficiently. I sometimes find myself using the Annotations clumsily, and sometimes wind up with blank notes, double notes, or extra lines at the ends of notes. After using the tool a few times, I get back in the groove.

For these reasons, I have added some step-by-step suggestions here to help you create an efficient workflow with annotations.

Follow these steps to create a note:

1. **Click the Note toolbar button on the Annotations toolbar.**

2. **Click in the graphics window where you want to create the note *or* click an entity that you want the note leader to point to, and *then* click where you want the note.**

3. **Type the note.** Press Enter at the end of a line, or, if you intend to force the note to wrap later, just allow the line of text to be as long as it wants to be. While you create the note, the text box expands to the right until you press Enter, and it expands down every time a line is added.

   At the end of the last line of the note, *do not* press Enter again (this creates extra lines), but you may press Esc. Esc gets you out of the note and ready to place a new note. When you press Esc twice, you get out of the note you were typing, and then get out of the Note command altogether.

4. **Another way to finish the note is to click the mouse outside of the text box.** After that, if you are done, press Esc. If you want to continue with another note, click again to place it, and start typing. If you want to place the same note as the first one again, the text is already there, so click a second time.

   SolidWorks seems to frequently change the way text aligns or inferences other entities, and in the 2009 release they have done it again. Four snap points exist, one in the middle of each side of the text box.

Fonts

SolidWorks can make use of any TrueType fonts that Windows will accept. This includes symbol, non-English, and Wingding fonts. SolidWorks does not use true monofonts like AutoCAD, because they do not have width information. Some AutoCAD monofont look-alike fonts are installed with SolidWorks that do have a very narrow width, and are shaped like some of the monofonts.

If you are a long-time SolidWorks user, you will be pleased to know that in recent versions of the software, different pieces of text within a single note can be formatted with multiple fonts, multiple sizes, bold, italics, underline, and so on. It seems like a simple thing, but it was a long time coming.

In Tools ➪ Customize, the Fonts toolbar displays as the Formatting toolbar. The Formatting toolbar also appears in the graphics area immediately over your text every time you either insert a new note or edit an existing note, unless the toolbar is already docked somewhere. The Formatting toolbar is shown in Figure 22.1.

FIGURE 22.1

The Formatting toolbar

Text boxes and wrapping

Text boxes are a more recent addition that enables the user to limit the size, particularly the width, that a note can occupy. This enables notes to wrap in tight spaces on title or revision blocks, as well as other places.

You can size text boxes immediately after placement, even while they are blank; the text then wraps as you type it. The text box expands downward automatically. Blank text boxes can be left on the drawing to provide a placeholder for future text. The blank text box has a rectangular border that contains an X, both of which are removed when you add text. If spaces are added to a text box, the text box becomes invisible, although you can select it if you know where it is. When you move the cursor over the text box, the cursor displays the note symbol.

While typing a note, it is not possible to make the note box smaller using the middle handle on the right end of the box; you can only stretch it larger. Using any corner handle, as shown in Figure 22.2, you can make the box taller, wider, or narrower. The note box will not resize smaller if the text string it contains does not contain spaces.

FIGURE 22.2

Resizing a text box using the lower-right corner handle

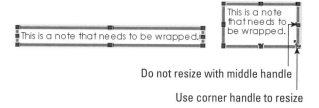

Do not resize with middle handle

Use corner handle to resize

If a custom property value is used to populate a note, and you have the View ➪ Annotation Link Variables option turned on, when you activate the text box to resize it, the text value will go away and the link variable will be displayed. This makes it difficult to dynamically resize the box to fit the note, so it might be best to turn off the Annotation Link Variable option before placing and sizing notes.

Notes and leaders

When you start to place a note, a preview shows the text box with or without a leader depending on the position of the cursor. If the cursor is over a blank section of the drawing, the note is placed without any leader. If the cursor is over a face, edge, or vertex, then a leader is added using the arrow controlled by the settings at Tools ➪ Options ➪ Document Properties ➪ Arrows ➪ Attachments. By default, a leader attached to a face uses a dot as an arrow, and a leader attached to an edge, sketch entity, or nothing at all uses a regular arrow. You can change these defaults at the options location mentioned previously, and you can change individual note leaders in the PropertyManager that becomes available when you select a note. These settings can also become part of a custom drafting standard.

Figure 22.3 shows the preview that is displayed by the cursor when you place a note over a face, over an edge, and over blank space on the drawing.

FIGURE 22.3

Placing a note with a leader

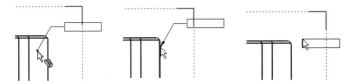

You can also change settings for bent leaders in the Tools ➪ Options ➪ Document Properties area. It is recommended that you use the same bent leader lengths for all annotations, and save them in the templates that you use. Starting with SolidWorks 2009, you can drag bent leaders manually to adjust individual annotations.

Some minor but basic functionality appears to be missing from notes in SolidWorks. Single-clicking inside an active text box places the cursor between letters, as expected. Double-clicking inside an active text box selects the entire word that you click, again as expected. Triple-clicking in Microsoft applications such as Word and PowerPoint generally selects the whole paragraph or the contents of the text box. However, the triple-click option is not available in SolidWorks notes. Ctrl+A does work to select all of the text inside a text box. If you double-click an existing note to activate it, the entire contents are highlighted immediately. You also cannot drag-and-drop selected text to move it within a text box. However, you can Ctrl+C, Ctrl+X, and Ctrl+V the text.

To format the entire note, do not activate the text box; instead, only select the note, and apply the setting to the entire note rather than to selected text within the note.

Adding a leader to a note

To add a leader to a note that was created without a leader, click the note and select the leader options in the Leader panel of the PropertyManager, as shown in Figure 22.4. After you add the leader, you can reposition the handle at the end of the leader to attach it to an entity on the drawing.

FIGURE 22.4

FIGURE 22.4

Adding a leader to a note

Multiple leaders

You can also attach multiple leaders to notes. To create a new note with multiple leaders, preselect the entities that the leaders are to be attached to, and then click the Note toolbar button.

To add a leader to an existing note, first click the note, and then Ctrl-drag the handle or small dot on the end of a leader to the second location. A note with multiple leaders is shown in Figure 22.5. To remove one of multiple leaders from a note, click the handle at the end of the arrow and press Delete.

FIGURE 22.5

A note with multiple leaders

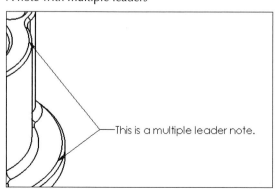

Jogged leaders

Jogged leaders have come a long way since their introduction many releases ago. You can switch a regular leader to a jogged leader by selecting an option in the PropertyManager. In Figure 22.4, the middle icon in the top row is the Jogged Leader icon. The icon to the left simply turns on the default leader, and the icon to the right turns off leaders altogether.

Once you activate the jogged leader option, you can add a jog from the leader RMB (right mouse button) menu. Notice in Figure 22.6 that two options give you control over the jogged leader – Insert New Branch and Add Jog Point.

FIGURE 22.6

Jogging a leader

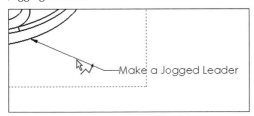

Add Jog Point

Selecting the Add Jog Point command adds a new handle to the leader that you can move around. You can add multiple jog points to the leader.

Insert New Branch

The Insert New Branch command enables you to create a new jogged leader that ends in another arrow from the selected point. This arrangement with multiple branches in a jogged leader is shown in Figure 22.7.

FIGURE 22.7

The results of adding a new branch to a jogged leader

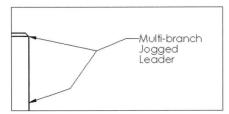

Styles

For notes, a style can apply a font, an underline or bold formatting, or any other setting from the Formatting (Fonts) toolbar to a note.

To create a note that uses the style setting from another existing note, pre-select the existing note with the style to be copied before starting the Note command; SolidWorks applies the style to the new note.

CAUTION Sometimes adding a style to a note can make other changes that you may not expect, such as turning off the leaders if a note has multiple leaders. In particular, if the style is made from a note with a jogged leader, then it turns off leaders for regular multiple leaders. Styles that are created from regular leader notes do not turn off jogged leaders.

Making a change to the leader of a note after you apply the style removes the style from the note, although the formatting remains. This does not apply to adding multiple leaders, only to changing the type of leader.

Applying a style may also remove the ability of the text to wrap, as well as any changes to the text box shape. You cannot move the corner of a text box of a note to which you have applied a style.

Styles exist only in the document in which they were created, but they can be shared to other documents by saving the style out as a separate file. Note styles use the extension, *.sldnotestl. Once you save the style, you can load it into other documents. The Styles panel of the Note PropertyManager interface is shown in Figure 22.8.

Annotation types that can use styles are:

- Note
- Dimension
- Weld Symbol
- Surface Finish
- Datum Feature
- Datum Target
- Balloon
- Auto Balloon
- Stacked Balloon
- Center Mark

It might be good to provide a list of annotation types that can be used with styles. You can find this list on page 95 of the What's New manual. There are a few types that are new to SolidWorks 2009.

FIGURE 22.8

The Styles panel of the Note PropertyManager interface

NOTE Styles before the 2009 release were called Favorites. The file type for note favorites was *.sldnotefvt. If you run across any of these legacy file types, you will at least know what they are. When loading styles, the Open dialog will see and use both the new file type and the legacy file type.

The Styles panel contains the following buttons:

- **Apply Defaults/No Styles.** Removes style settings from the current interface, setting all values back to the defaults.

- **Add or Update Styles.** This can be used to either add a new style to the database or to change the name or other settings for an existing style.

- **Delete Style.** Removes a style from the database.

- **Save Style.** Saves a style to an external file (*.sldhwfvt), which can be loaded by other users and added to their databases.

- **Load Style.** Loads a saved style file.

Styles can be loaded into document templates so that for every document created from the template, those Styles will be available.

Linking notes to custom properties

You can link notes to custom properties. The custom properties can be from the drawing, or from the model that is referenced by the drawing. I mention this kind of link briefly in Chapter 20, but discuss it more thoroughly here.

Figure 22.9 shows a note on a drawing with custom property links pulling data from the model shown on the drawing. To add these links, driven by the syntax $PRPSHEET:"material", click the icon indicated in the image to the right in Figure 22.9.

In this case, text has been combined with custom properties, but custom properties can also appear alone. The Custom Properties interface is found at Tools ➪ Properties.

When you activate the note, you may want to see the syntax, or you may want to see the actual text value of the custom property. You can find the setting that controls which one is displayed at View ➪ Annotation Link Variable.

FIGURE 22.9

Linking notes to custom properties

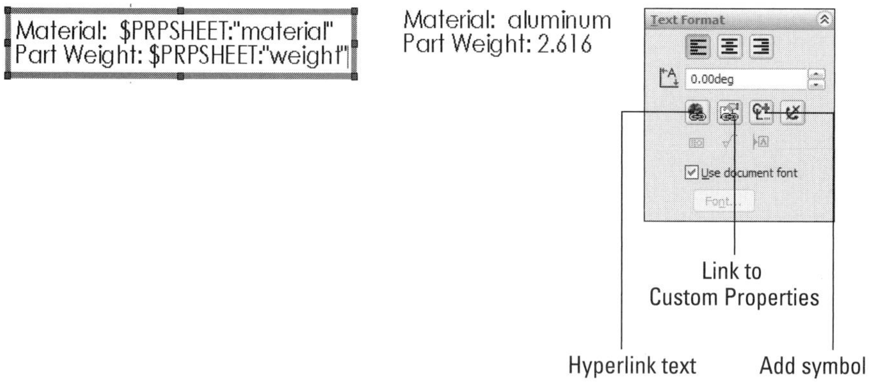

Hyperlinking text

Hyperlinking text is sometimes useful on drawings to provide a link to reference documentation, specification, test results, and so on. The first button in the third row of the Text Format panel of the Note PropertyManager enables you to add a hyperlink to text in the note. Figure 22.9 shows this panel. Either copy the URL to the hyperlink dialog box that appears, or browse to it from the dialog box.

Notes and symbols

Notes and symbols are regularly combined in SolidWorks. Symbols are discussed more fully later in this chapter, but are mentioned here because of the frequency with which they are used with notes. The image to the right in Figure 22.9 shows the Text Format panel, which contains a button to the interface where you can add symbols.

Using Blocks in Drawings

Blocks in SolidWorks can contain sketch elements and notes. When used in drawings, blocks have several common uses, including the following:

- Standard note blocks for tolerances, disclaimers, or default requirements.
- You can put together a mechanism in 2D where each block represents a part.
- Flow direction for fluid systems.

- Drawing stamps such as "Not For Release," "Preliminary," "Obsolete," and so on.

- Symbols for schematics that can be snapped together.

- You can save drawing formats as blocks to make them easier to place as a single entity.

Like styles, blocks reside in the document in which they are created, but you can save them out to a *.sldblk file, load them into other documents, and save them as a part of a document template.

Inserting blocks

You can apply blocks in several ways, including by dragging from Windows Explorer and by using the menus at Insert ➪ Annotations ➪ Block. However, the most efficient way is to access them from the Design Library. Library folders can be established specifically for blocks. Check the settings at Tools ➪ Options ➪ File Locations ➪ Blocks, and redirect this setting to a library area outside of the SolidWorks installation directory. Figure 22.10 shows the Design Library with a folder containing blocks that are selected. The blocks do not show previews in the window, but the tooltip displays large previews. You can drag blocks from the Design Library onto the drawing sheet.

FIGURE 22.10

Blocks in the Design Library

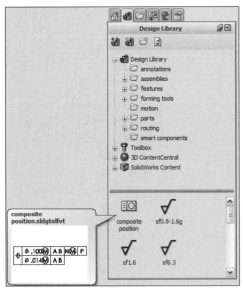

Each block has an insertion point, which snaps to any sketch entity point, even if it is in another block. This makes schematics easy to snap together. If the default insertion point is not the point that you need to snap to the other geometry, then you can place the block anywhere on the drawing and drag the point that needs to snap.

Once blocks are snapped together, to detach them from one another, you can click the point at which they touch; a Coincident sketch relation displays in the PropertyManager. Deleting the sketch relation enables you to drag the block away from the other geometry.

When blocks are inserted, you can control several options in the PropertyManager. This function may be somewhat hidden because it does not appear automatically when you place the block. After you place the block, SolidWorks wants you to place another copy of the block. If you press Esc to cancel out of placing additional blocks, then the first placed block is not selected, and so the PropertyManager does not display. Figure 22.11 shows the Block PropertyManager.

FIGURE 22.11

The Block PropertyManager

Existing Relations

This panel lists the sketch relations that are linked to the block. These may cause the block to not move properly when you drag it. This feature is most helpful when the block is being used as a representation of a part in a simulated 2D mechanism.

Add Relations

This panel enables you to quickly select sketch relations to apply when placing blocks.

Definition

Blocks can be linked to an external file, which enables all linked instances of a block to be updated at once, even if they are being used in other drawing documents. The path box for the Link to File option only displays if you select the check box.

The Edit button refers to editing the block. A toolbar button also exists for editing blocks. The Leader & Insertion Points button enables you to edit both of the controls. You can use the For Construction option to change the entire block to construction entities.

Parameters

The top field with the two circles to the left controls the scale of the block. This number affects the entire block, including the text. You also have the option to scale dimensions, so that the dimension text size (not the dimension value) increases with the overall block scale.

The Lock Angle option refers to the rotation of the block. If the Lock Angle option is not selected, then you can rotate the block if one point on it is coincident to a stationary object, such as a vertex in a drawing view.

Leader

You will recognize these options from the Notes leaders. The leader is attached to the block where the angled black handle was placed when you created the block. The leader connection and insertion points can be edited by using the Leader & Insertion Points button on the Definition panel.

Text/Dimension Display

The Display Dimensions option controls whether or not any notes and dimensions in the block are displayed or hidden.

Layer

You can assign most entities on drawings to layers, which in turn have controls for items, such as line type, color, and visibility.

Creating blocks

CROSS-REF Sketch Blocks have been covered in some detail in Chapter 3. The current chapter is limited to a discussion of blocks that may be found on drawings rather than those used in model sketches or Layouts.

You can create blocks by selecting the sketch and annotation elements and clicking the Make Block toolbar button from the Blocks toolbar, or by accessing the command through the menus at Tools ⇨ Block ⇨ Make.

By default, when you create a block, the Insertion Point panel of the PropertyManager does not expand. If you expand this panel, the blue Origin symbol represents the insertion point that is attached to the cursor during block insertion, as shown in Figure 22.12. The angled line hanging off of the left side of the block is the leader attachment point for the block. You can also drag this line around the block and snap it to sketch geometry. By default, this block does not use a leader, but if one is required, then you can turn it on when you place the block.

FIGURE 22.12

Creating a block

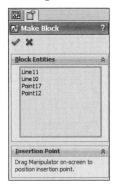
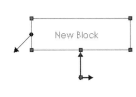

Editing blocks

Although you do not have many options when creating blocks, many more options become available when you edit them. You can access editing options for a block from four locations:

- The Edit Block toolbar button on the Blocks toolbar
- The Edit button in the Block PropertyManager
- Through the menus at Tools, Block, Edit
- From the RMB menu of the block in the Blocks folder in the drawing FeatureManager

The standard edit function gives you access to the sketch and note elements that make up the block.

Add/Remove Entities

While you are editing the block, the Add/Remove Entities button on the Blocks toolbar becomes available. This enables you to add or remove sketch or note entities from the block definition.

Rebuild

When you are finished editing the block, and you need to leave Edit mode, toggle off the Edit Block icon.

Explode

This is not technically an edit option, but it certainly does change things. Explode is available when you are not editing the block, but when it is selected. Explode returns the contents of that particular instance of the block to the drawing, removing them from the block. This removes any leaders that are attached to the block, as well as sketch relations.

Using Symbols

SolidWorks symbols are different from symbols that are a part of a font family. SolidWorks symbols fall into several categories, including weld, surface finish, hole, modifying symbols, GD&T (geometric dimensioning and tolerancing), and several flag symbols. You can also construct custom symbols.

Where can you use symbols?

You can use symbols in notes and dimensions. They also are an intrinsic part of weld symbols and surface finish symbols. Hole Callouts use symbols extensively, as do GD&T frames.

Figure 22.13 shows the Text Format panel from the Note PropertyManager and the Dimension Text panel from the Dimension PropertyManager. Both of these interfaces give you access to the symbol library.

FIGURE 22.13

Accessing symbols and the symbol library

Custom symbols

You can create custom symbols in SolidWorks, but creating them may not be as simple as you expect. In the `lang\english` subfolder of the SolidWorks installation directory is a file called `Gtol.sym`. This file stores the representations of all of the SolidWorks symbols. It is also where you can create symbols of your own. You can edit the file in Notepad.

As a warning, unless you enjoy writing scripts for the command line, or you are a fan of DOS 5.0, then you may not want to create custom symbol projects. The format for creating symbols is simple enough, but it is what you might call somewhat arcane. It is effective at creating line-art symbols that can be used with text and can even be used to contain text. If you are a little inventive with this, then you can create interesting shapes that integrate with your notes and dimensions.

Keep in mind that this topic does not appear in the Help files, but all of the instructions you need are inside the file itself. You may have to experiment a little to discover what the rules are in terms of making shapes outside of the limits of the 1X1 matrix. It is probably easier to create the geometry using Blocks functionality, but blocks cannot be inserted into text notes as easily as symbols.

Using Center Marks and Centerlines

You can apply center marks either manually or automatically to edges that project as circular in the drawing view. The settings to control automatic insertion are found at Tools ➪ Options ➪ Document Properties ➪ Drafting Standard ➪ Centerlines/Center Marks. The size of the mark at the center and the use of lines extending to the actual circular edge are also controlled on this tab, in the Center Marks section.

Figure 22.14 shows some of the options available for center marks.

FIGURE 22.14

Options available for center marks

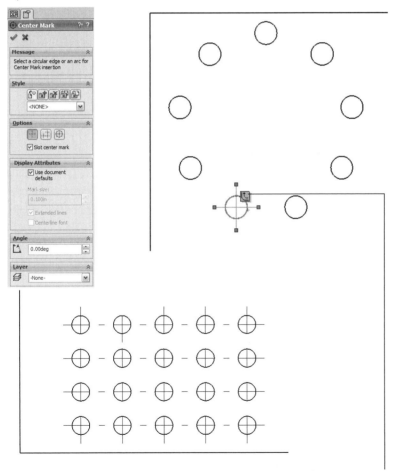

Select symbol to propagate
center mark to pattern

Center marks propagate well to patterns, and you can dimension to them individually. You can rotate center marks in views where they need to be referenced from an edge that is not horizontal. You can also place center marks into layers.

You can apply centerlines to any geometry that has a temporary axis that is perpendicular to the view. Centerlines can also be placed automatically when you place the part into the drawing. You can create centerlines by selecting a face or a pair of parallel lines or concentric arcs. Centerlines may be displayed improperly on parts that are created by mirroring, as shown in Figure 22.15. This bug was originally printed here in the 2007 version and is still active for 2009.

FIGURE 22.15

Centerlines can display improperly on a mirrored part.

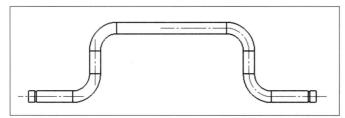

Tutorial: Using Annotations

This tutorial shows you how to use some of the tools that were discussed in this chapter. It does not cover every feature, so you should explore a little on your own and not necessarily follow the instructions exactly. Start here:

1. **From the CD-ROM, open the file named** Chapter 22 – Tutorial.slddrw. This is a drawing file with views of the part from Chapter 21, but it does not contain dimensions or annotations.

2. **Click the Center Mark tool on the Annotations toolbar.** (If the button is not there, then use Tools ⇨ Customize ⇨ Commands to place it on the toolbar, along with the Centerline tool.) Click one of the holes in the pattern of three, and click the Propagate symbol to propagate the center marks to all three holes in the pattern. The view should look like Figure 22.16 when you are done.

3. **Activate the Centerline tool to add two centerlines to the right view, in the lower-left area.** Select the cylindrical faces for each feature to place the centerlines. Click the vertical centerline and drag the ends past the edges of the part.

4. **Select the edge that is indicated in Figure 22.17, and initiate a note from the Annotations toolbar.** Type the text shown, all in one line. You can place the degree and diameter symbols from the symbol library, which you can access using the indicated button in the PropertyManager. Both symbols are in the Modifying Symbols library, also shown in Figure 22.17. Drag the lower-right corner of the text box to make the text wrap as shown.

FIGURE 22.16

Center marks and centerlines on a part

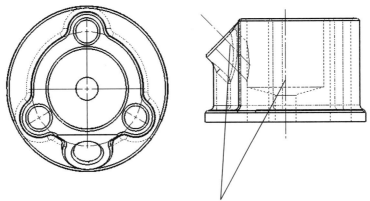

Add centerlines by clicking cylindrical faces

FIGURE 22.17

Placing symbols in an annotation

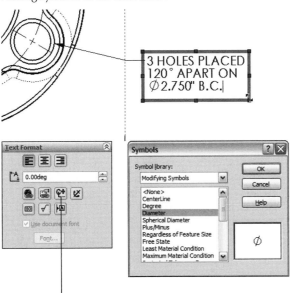

Access the symbol library

5. **Draw an arrow with a text note inside it, as shown in Figure 22.18.** Make the sketch and text into a block by window-selecting all of it and clicking Make Block from the Blocks toolbar, or by selecting Tools ➪ Block ➪ Make. Make sure that the end of the arrow

is its insertion point. You have to expand the Insertion Point panel in the PropertyManager to access this option. When the block is set up, accept it by clicking the green check mark icon. When the block is created, delete it from the drawing.

Creating a block

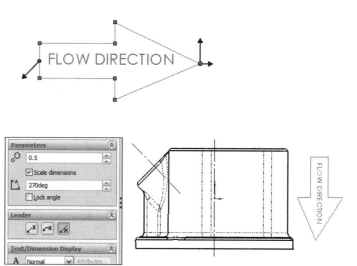

6. **Place the block using the Insert Block function, so that the block is to the right of the right view.** Once you place it, press Esc to cancel the placement of more blocks. Then select the block to activate the PropertyManager. Deselect the Lock Angle option, and set the angle to 270 degrees.

Summary

Annotations and symbols in SolidWorks have many options for connection, creation, and display. Recent releases have brought major improvements to text box–driven annotations. Custom properties and hyperlinks allow the user to populate drawing annotations with content and links to content. Sharing styles in templates is a great idea for readily available note styles.

Blocks have several flexible uses and can be updated from external files across many documents. Their use for simulating mechanisms, piecing together schematics, and annotating drawings, in addition to the Belts and Chains functionality discussed in Chapter 13, make blocks one of the most flexible functions available.

Chapter 23

Dimensioning and Tolerancing

I n years past, dimensioning and tolerancing was an art form and a science. People did, and still do, become very passionate when discussing the right way of performing these tasks. In truth, the techniques are probably not so black and white, but are highly dependent on the industry, the means of manufacture, and the purpose of the drawing. For example, drawings might be used for quotes, manufacturing, inspection, assembly, testing, and so on; and the drawings, as well as the dimensioning and tolerancing used, for each purpose could be somewhat different.

While it is important to follow standards and use manufacturing drawing conventions properly, this is not an argument that I want to reignite here. In this chapter, I will focus on how to apply the available tools in SolidWorks. You will need to decide for yourself how to apply the tools.

Putting Dimensions on Drawings

Drawings are typically not one of the hotter topics that SolidWorks users become excited about, but a few issues still ignite heated discussions. How to put dimensions onto drawings is one of these topics. This is much like the "tastes great/less filling" debate. Each side of the issue has valid points, and the question is not likely to be resolved any time soon.

At the center of this debate is whether you should place the dimensions that you use to create the model directly on the drawing, or whether you should use reference dimensions created on the drawing. In the following sections, I examine each method for its benefits and drawbacks.

Insert Model Items

Insert Model Items takes all of the dimensions, symbols, annotations, and other elements that are used to create the model, and puts them onto the drawing. Because these dimensions come directly from the sketches and features of the model, they are *driving* dimensions. This means that you can double-click and change them from the drawing the same way you can change sketch and feature dimensions, and with the same effect. As a result, changing these dimensions even from the drawing causes the parts and assemblies in which they are used to be changed.

You can insert the model items on a per-feature basis, either only bringing the items that are appropriate into the current view, or bringing items into all views. Insertion can be further broken down by type of item, and it can become as specific as pattern counts, Hole Wizard items, specific symbol types, and reference geometry types. You can select Insert ➪ Model Items, or you can access this command from the Annotations toolbar. The Model Items PropertyManager interface is shown in Figure 23.1.

FIGURE 23.1

The Model Items PropertyManager interface

Usually, the dimensions need to be rearranged, although SolidWorks does try to arrange them so that they do not overlap. Figure 23.2 shows the result of bringing dimensions into all views for the part. The part is on the CD-ROM in the Chapter 21 materials.

Figure 23.2 contains duplicate dimensions, overlapping dimensions, unnecessarily long leaders, radius dimensions pointing to the wrong side of the arc, and a lot of awkward placement. This is what you can expect from using the automatic functions. At best, these dimensions require rearranging, and at worst, they probably require that you delete and replace some of them or move them to new views where they make more sense.

FIGURE 23.2

The default placement of dimensions into all views

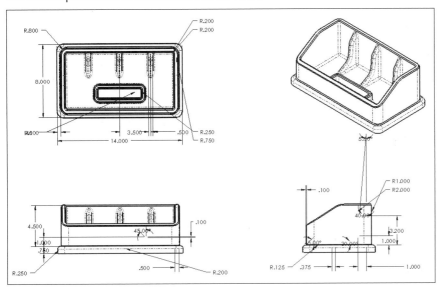

To move a dimension to another view, you can Shift-drag it from one view to the other (make sure that the dimension is appropriate in the destination view). To copy a dimension, you can Ctrl-drag it. If you cannot place the dimension in the view that you have dragged it to, then the cursor will indicate this with a special cursor symbol.

If you approach this task by placing dimensions on a per-feature or per-view basis, it does not change the number of dimensions that you will have to move; it just means that they have to be inserted more often. Keep in mind that if you choose this method, there is a significant amount of cleanup and checking that you must do. The convenience of having the dimensions put into the views for you, and the ability to actually change the model from the drawing are quite useful, but you may not save very much time or effort by doing things this way.

Using reference dimensions

One alternative to automatically inserting all model dimensions is to manually place reference dimensions. At first, this appears to be simply re-creating work that has already been done, and this is somewhat true, but there is more to the story.

However, in several important ways, these dimensions are not merely duplicates of the model items. In fact, the reference dimensions that you manually place on the drawing are quite different from the dimensions that are used in the model, unless either the dimensioning scheme of the model or the drawing is changed in some extreme way. The dimensions serve completely different purposes in the two settings, and could only be the same through some odd coincidence.

When modeling, I tend to dimension symmetrically, but only on one side, which would not be shown on a manufacturing or inspection drawing. I frequently use workarounds to avoid some special problem that forces a different modeling-dimensioning scheme than I would prefer to use. Often, a feature is located from the midpoint of an edge, which involves no dimensions whatsoever. Sketch entities may have Equal relations, which also leave sketch elements undimensioned. Dimensions may lead to faces or edges that are not in the final model or to faces that are later changed by draft or fillets. Beyond that, when draft is involved, as is the case with plastic or cast parts, the dimensions of the sketch that you used to create the feature often have little to do with the geometry that is dimensioned on a print for inspection or mold building. Dimension schemes in models reflect the need for the model to react to change, while dimension schemes in drawings reflect the manufacturing or inspection methods, in order to minimize tolerance stack-up, and to reflect the usage of the actual part.

Although there are strictly technical reasons for dimensioning drawings independently from the way the model was dimensioned, there are other factors such as time, and the neat and orderly placement of dimensions. Time is an issue because by the time you finish rearranging dimensions that were inserted automatically from the model — checking and eliminating duplicates and then manually adding dimensions that were left out or that had to be eliminated because they were inappropriate for some reason, as well as ensuring that all of the necessary dimensions are on the drawing. — it would have been much quicker to manually dimension the drawing correctly the first time using reference dimensions. Inevitably, manually inserting dimensions leads to a different scheme than would be imposed on you by using the Insert Model Items method.

In most cases, inserting model dimensions into the drawing is impractical for manufacturing or inspection drawings, unless you have simple plates with machined holes. This is because of the amount of time required to rearrange and check the dimensions, the need to ensure that you have placed the necessary dimensions and taken geometric tolerancing into account, and the simple fact that the dimensioning and sketch relations needed for efficient modeling are usually very different from the dimensioning needed for manufacturing or inspection.

I recommend that you use the manual dimension placement option, which works much in the same way as when dimensions are added to sketches. Dimensions that you place in the drawing in this way are called *driven* or *reference* dimensions. In drafting lingo, reference dimensions are "extra" dimensions that you place to ease calculations, and you usually create these dimensions with parentheses around them; in SolidWorks lingo, reference dimensions are simply driven rather than driving dimensions. You can find the setting that controls the parentheses around reference dimensions at Tools ➪ Options ➪ Document Properties ➪ Dimensions ➪ Add Parentheses By Default.

Reference dimensions and the DimXpert

You can apply reference dimensions to the 3D model or to the drawing. In this chapter, I talk mainly about adding them to the 2D drawing, but I do want to take a moment to talk about how reference dimensions in the model relate to the DimXpert functionality, which you will find later in this chapter.

Reference dimensions on the solid model

By default, when you go to add new reference dimensions to a solid model, you may see some error messages you aren't accustomed to seeing and some odd toolbars, especially for users who are used to older versions of the software. In SolidWorks 2008, the DimXpert was introduced. I discuss this later in this chapter in more detail, but if you are not expecting it, the DimXpert can interfere with reference dimension functionality.

When you activate the Smart Dimension tool, a PropertyManager appears, giving you the option to use dimensions to drive the DimXpert (the new default) or use it to place reference dimensions. Figure 23.3 shows this Smart Dimension PropertyManager for parts on the left and for drawings on the right.

FIGURE 23.3

Dimension PropertyManager for choosing DimXpert or Reference dimensions

Reference dimensions on the drawing

I've already made the case for why I think it is better to use reference dimensions on the drawing than model dimensions. This is opinion, of course, and I realize that for many simple parts, you actually *can* model them the way you would detail them, so the model items make more sense.

Reference dimensions on the drawing are simply driven dimensions, and they update when the model updates.

Using the DimXpert

The DimXpert is a tool to apply reference (driven) dimensions with tolerances to models and drawings. DimXpert employs feature and topology recognition so it can work on either native data or imported data. Use the DimXpert tab at the top of the part Feature manager, and click the Autodimension Scheme button (the first button on the left) to apply dimensions to the entire model based on selected datums.

When you use the dimensions and tolerances created with the DimXpert in conjunction with the TolAnalyst, you are able to do simple stack-up analysis. TolAnalyst is outside the scope of this book, because it is part of the Premium package and I am limiting this book to basic SolidWorks. A limitation of this system is that you can only apply location or size dimensions; you cannot apply non-dimensional geometric form tolerancing such as parallelism, cylindricity, or flatness. All controls must drive size or location, and have associated dimensions.

When you use the DimXpert on a drawing, it starts by placing a datum at a vertex or centerpoint. After that, it automatically dimensions the entire feature in the view that is the parent of the edge you select. Figure 23.4 shows the Dimension PropertyManager when DimXpert is activated. The image on the right shows a few dimensions applied by the DimXpert, along with the datum used for the dimensions in the view.

FIGURE 23.4

Dimension PropertyManager for DimXpert in drawing

  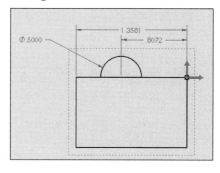

You can place the DimXpert dimensions on the drawing when placing the views either through the second page of the Model View PropertyManager, on the Import Options panel (which is closed by default). No, it's not your imagination, this is about as obscure as they could possibly make this functionality. Apparently they didn't really expect anyone to use it. Both pages of the Model View (Insert ➪ Drawing View ➪ Model, or click Model View from the View Layout tab on the Command Manager) are shown in Figure 23.5. The Import Options panel is shown at the bottom of the second page, although I have cut the second page off about half way down.

You can find this functionality in one other place: when you are dragging views from the View Palette in the Task Pane. This interface appears in the image on the right in Figure 23.5.

FIGURE 23.5

The setting to import DimXpert annotations is buried well.

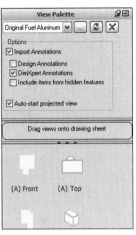

Consensus on this functionality is that it is a work in progress, and while it may offer some interesting functionality, you may not find that it is ready to save you a lot of time when you are dimensioning and tolerancing parts on a drawing. It seems that it has particular difficulty with molded or cast parts, which typically don't have parallel faces.

Annotation views

Annotation views are views in the model in which annotations have been added. Annotation views are accessed from the Annotations folder in the model FeatureManager. They are created automatically when dimensions or notes are added to the part. The annotation view can be used in the model to show the note or dimension in the view in which it was created or on the drawing to help parse the dimensions into views where they are easily read.

Annotation views can be inserted manually or automatically. You can access the settings for annotation views through the right-mouse button menu of the Annotations folder of the model, shown in Figure 23.6. The image on the right shows part of the PropertyManager you get when inserting a named view on a drawing. It shows that the Front and Top views of the model have annotations associated with them (indicated by the A on the view symbol).

FIGURE 23.6

The Annotations folder right-mouse button menu and the Model View Orientation panel

Driven dimension color

Driven dimensions on the drawing display in gray, and this can be a problem when the drawing is printed out. There are two methods that you can use to deal with this printing problem. The first method is to set the Page Properties of the drawing to force it to print in black and white. You can find the Page Properties at File ➪ Page Setup. The Page Setup dialog box is shown in Figure 23.7.

FIGURE 23.7

The Page Setup dialog box

The second method is to set the color for driven dimensions to black rather than gray. This color setting is found at Tools ⇨ Options ⇨ Color ⇨ Dimensions Non-Imported (Driven).

Ordinate and baseline dimensions

Ordinate and baseline dimensions are appropriate for collections of linear dimensions when you have a number of items that can all be dimensioned from the same reference. Flat patterns of sheet metal parts often fall into this category. When you apply ordinate dimensions, a zero location is selected first, followed by each entity for which you want a dimension. When dimensions become too tightly packed, SolidWorks automatically jogs the witness lines to space out the dimensions adequately. You can create jogs manually by using the right-mouse button menu. Once you create a set of ordinate dimensions, you can add to the set by selecting Add To Ordinate from the right-mouse button menu.

Baseline dimensions are normal linear dimensions that all come from the same reference, and are stacked together at a defined spacing. The default settings for baseline dimensions are found at Tools ⇨ Options ⇨ Dimensions ⇨ Offset Distances.

TIP Baseline dimensions work best either when they are horizontal or when the dimension text is aligned with the dimension line (as is the default situation with ISO standard dimensioning). Vertical dimensions where the text is horizontal do not usually stack as neatly because the dimension text runs over the dimension line of the adjacent dimensions. Figure 23.8 shows ordinate and baseline dimensions in the same view.

FIGURE 23.8

Ordinate and baseline dimensions in the same view

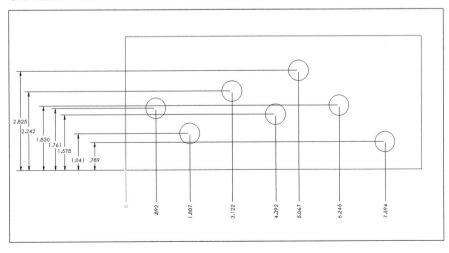

You can access ordinate and baseline dimensions from the Dimensions/Relations toolbar or by right-clicking in a blank space, selecting More Dimensions, and then selecting the type of dimension that you want to use.

Autodimensioning

If the Insert Model Items feature is not likely to produce dimensions that are usable in a manufacturing drawing, then the Autodimension feature is even less likely to do so. However, if you use autodimensioning in a controlled way, in the right situations, it can be a valid way to create selected dimensions. The Autodimension PropertyManager is shown in Figure 23.9. Autodimension is only available in the drawing environment. In the part environment, similar functionality is part of the Fully Define Sketch tool. To access Autodimension, click the Smart Dimension toolbar icon and change to the Autodimension tab in the PropertyManager. Formerly, this function had its own icon, and earlier than that, it was available in the model sketching environment.

FIGURE 23.9

The Autodimension PropertyManager interface

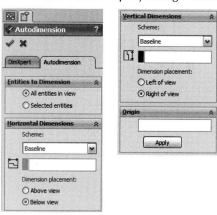

The Autodimension function can fully dimension the geometry in a drawing view. This is best for ordinate or baseline dimensioning where many dimensions are derived from a common reference, as is often the case with sheet metal parts or a plate with many holes drilled in it. You should limit the use of this option to cases where that type of dimensioning is what you would choose, having the choice of all available types of dimensions — do not allow the software to dictate the dimensioning scheme for your drawing.

NOTE   The Autodimension function is different from the Fully Define Sketch function. Autodimension works in the drawing, only adding dimensions. Fully Define Sketch works in the model sketch mode, adding dimensions and sketch relations. In previous versions, these functions were consolidated in a single function called Autodimension.

Reference sketches

For some types of dimensions, you may need to create additional reference sketch entities. For example, with angle dimensions, it may be desirable to add construction lines to help define the angle. You can add centerlines as separate axis-like entities, as discussed in Chapter 22, but you can also sketch in centerlines manually if needed. This type of sketch is most often attached to the view rather than the drawing sheet.

TIP Remember that, if necessary, you can create angle dimensions by selecting three points (vertex of the angle first) instead of two lines. When you do this, sketch lines are typically drawn to indicate the vertex of the angle.

Dimension Options

The Dimension PropertyManager contains settings, default overrides, tolerances, styles, and several other important settings for use with dimensions. The PropertyManager for driven dimensions is shown in Figure 23.10. I cover styles and tolerances specifically later in this chapter; the other panels of the Dimension PropertyManager are as follows.

Dimension Text

The Dimension Text panel enables you to add text to the dimension. You can add lines of text both above and below the dimension value itself, and you can also add text before and after the DIM value on the same line. The DIM field is what places the actual value; if this syntax is somehow deleted, you can type it back in and the dimension will still work.

The Dimension Text panel includes some formatting tools, such as justification settings and a setting for the position of the dimension line. The last two rows of buttons include the more commonly used symbols, with access to the complete library, such as any custom symbols that you may have made for the library.

Primary Value Override

The most famous of bad habit former AutoCAD users make is the override of dimension values. Apparently due to popular demand, the Primary Value Override is now available in SolidWorks, in the Dimension PropertyManager, as shown in Figure 23.10. This option was added to the software mainly to enable the creation of dimensions with words instead of numbers, as shown in Figure 23.11.

Display Options

You can control the default setting for parentheses around driven, or reference, dimensions in Tools ➪ Options ➪ Document Properties ➪ Dimensions ➪ Add Parentheses By Default.

Although you can also control dual dimension defaults in Tools ➪ Options, you can turn them on and off from this interface for individual dimensions. When you enable the Dual Dimension option, SolidWorks uses the settings from Tools ➪ Options.

FIGURE 23.10

The Dimension PropertyManager interface

> **NOTE** The Display Options have been moved to the right-mouse button menu. The options shown in Figure 23.10 are different depending on what type of dimension is selected. For the images provided, a diameter dimension was used.

The foreshortened radius is only valid for individual radial dimensions. A foreshortened radius is shown in Figure 23.12. Foreshortened radius dimensions are typically used for large radii when dimensions to the center point are not important. The Foreshortened radius function does not work on diameter dimensions. The inspection dimension is shown in Figure 23.12 with an oval around the dimension.

FIGURE 23.11

Using the Override Dimension value

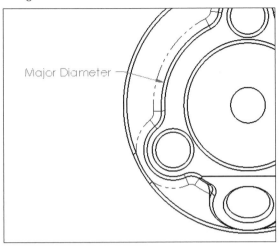

FIGURE 23.12

A foreshortened radius

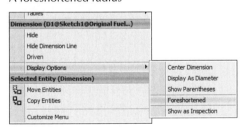

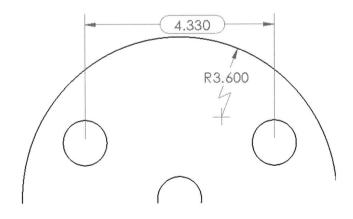

Witness/Leader Display

This panel enables you to set the arrows and dimension lines to be placed inside the witness lines. You can perform this function more easily by using the handles on the arrowheads. From this panel, you can also change the display type of individual arrowheads.

Break Lines

When you select the Use document gap option in this panel, the witness, or extension, lines of the selected dimension are broken by other crossing dimension lines, witness lines, or arrows. This is shown in Figure 23.13.

FIGURE 23.13

Broken witness lines

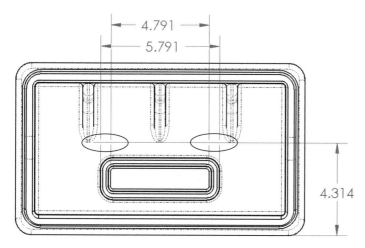

CROSS-REF Layers are discussed in detail in Chapter 25.

Adding Tolerances

You can add dimension tolerances in the Dimension PropertyManager, which you can activate by selecting the dimension that you want to modify. Available tolerance types include:

- Basic
- Bilateral
- Limit

- Symmetric
- MIN
- MAX
- Fit
- Fit with tolerance
- Fit (tolerance only)

NOTE You can also add tolerances to dimensions in models; the tolerance is brought in with the dimension if you use the Insert Model Items feature.

The Tolerance/Precision panel is shown in Figure 23.10. The appropriate number entry fields are activated when you assign the corresponding tolerance type to the dimension. The tolerance types that are available in SolidWorks are shown in Figure 23.14.

FIGURE 23.14

The available tolerance types in SolidWorks

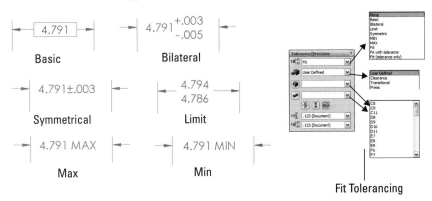

Precision

In SolidWorks, *precision* means the number of decimal places with which dimensions are displayed. Typically, SolidWorks works to eight places with meters as the default units. You can create templates that use up to that number of places as the default setting, and then change the number of places for individual dimensions as necessary. The first of the two boxes under Precision is used for the dimension precision, and the second is used for tolerance precision.

You can change Precision values for individual dimensions in the PropertyManager for the dimension, and for the entire document at Tools ➪ Options ➪ Document Properties ➪ Units.

Geometric Tolerancing

The full range of Geometric Tolerancing symbols is available for control frames, datums, datum targets, and so on. You can use the Geometric Tolerance dialog box to build control frames. This dialog box is shown in Figure 23.15. For commonly used Geometric Tolerance symbols, you may want to create and use styles.

FIGURE 23.15

The Geometric Tolerance settings

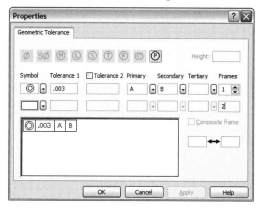

Using Dimension Styles

You can use dimension styles to apply many items to dimensions. Unlike notes, this is not limited to fonts and formatting. Some of the most common uses of dimension styles are:

- To add standard tolerances to dimensions
- To set precision values for dimensions
- To add text, such as TYP, to a dimension
- To add a commonly used GD&T (geometric dimensioning and tolerancing) reference

You can save styles from one document and load them into another document, even between document types. For example, you can load part dimension styles into a drawing.

When a style is updated from an external file, any document that it is linked to also updates. In addition, you can break links to external styles (with the appropriate button on the Styles panel). Otherwise, dimension styles have very similar functions to the other types of styles; the functions of all of the buttons on the Styles panel are the same.

Tutorial: Working with Dimensions and Tolerances

In this tutorial, you can use a single part in several different ways to demonstrate different dimensioning and tolerance functions. Follow these steps to learn more about these topics:

1. **Open the part from the CD-ROM called** Chapter 23 Tutorial.sldprt.

2. **Open the drawing from the CD-ROM called** Chapter 23 Drawing.slddrw.

3. **Tile the windows using Window ⇨ Tile Vertically, and drag the part from the top level of the FeatureManager into the drawing window.** This automatically populates the four drawing views.

4. **Delete the Top view, leaving the views as shown in Figure 23.16.**

FIGURE 23.16

The drawing after Step 4

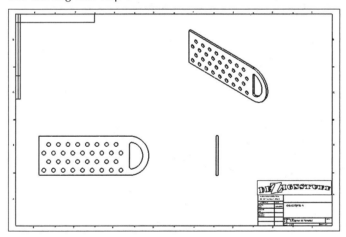

5. **Click Insert ⇨ Model Items, and ensure that the Select All option is selected for Annotations and the Marked for drawing option is selected for Dimensions.** Also make sure that the Source/Destination drop-down menu is set to Entire Model. Click the green check mark icon and watch the drawing populate.

6. **The resulting drawing is quite cluttered.** Delete and move dimensions so that the drawing looks like Figure 23.17.

FIGURE 23.17

The drawing after dimensions have been deleted and moved

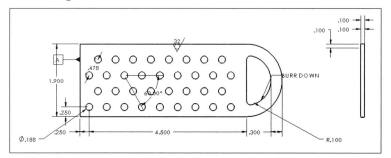

7. **Shift-drag the surface finish symbol to the Right view, and do the same with the 1.900-inch dimension.** You may have to first Shift-drag it into the other view, and then drag it again to correctly attach or position it.

8. **Create a set of horizontal ordinate dimensions from the left end of the part, and dimension the X position of each column of holes.** Do the same for rows of holes, using the bottom edge of the Front view as the zero reference. Remember that you can create ordinate dimensions by starting a normal Smart Dimension, then right-clicking to display the More Dimensions list, and then selecting your choice.

9. **If necessary, add center marks and centerlines to the view for clarity.**

10. **Select the .188 diameter dimension, and in the Dimension Text box, type TYP after the <DIM> text, and add a bilateral tolerance of +.003, -.005.** Save this as a style by clicking the Add Style icon.

11. **Apply the newly created dimension style to the R.100 dimension.** The results up to this step are shown in Figure 23.18.

12. **Make one of the dimension leaders for either the .188 or the R.100 dimensions cross the extension lines of the 4.500 dimension.** Then select the 4.500 dimension and in its PropertyManager, select the Use Document Gap option in the Break Lines panel.

13. **Place a B datum marker on the circumference of the smaller arc on the left end of the part.** Create a Geometric Tolerance control frame, as shown in Figure 23.19.

FIGURE 23.18

Dimensions and tolerances after Step 11

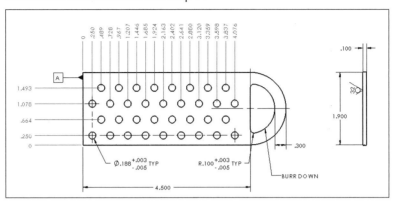

FIGURE 23.19

Creating a Geometric Tolerance control frame

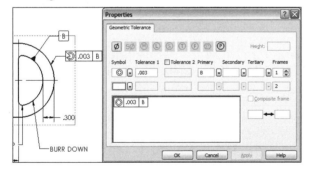

Summary

The argument about how to set up and use dimensions on drawings is as old as the process of creating geometrical plans from which objects are built. It is often difficult to separate fact and best practice from opinion. Although I leave it up to you to decide these issues for yourself, this chapter is intended to help you understand how to create the type of drawing that you want.

The biggest conflict in this subject arises over whether to place live model dimensions on the drawing or to allow the requirements of the drawing to specify which dimensions are placed where. I am by no means impartial when it comes to this question, but again, you must make the choice for yourself.

Chapter 24

Working with Tables and Drawings

S olidWorks enables you to create several types of tables on drawings, such as the Bill of Materials, or BOM. Design Tables that are used in parts and assemblies can also be shown on the drawing to create a tabulated type drawing. Hole Tables enable you to chart the center locations and sizes of holes for easy access to manufacturing data. Revision Tables can work with Workgroup PDM (Product Data Management) or by themselves to help you document the revision history of a drawing. General Tables are also available for any specialized items that are not covered by the other table types.

Driving the Bill of Materials

The Bill of Materials, or BOM, is one of the most frequently used types of tables that are available in SolidWorks. BOMs are intended for use with assemblies, but can also be used with individual parts for specialized applications. The types of information that you can expect to see on a BOM are item number, filename, quantity used, description, and any other custom property that you would like to add to it. A typical BOM is shown in Figure 24.1.

FIGURE 24.1

A sample BOM

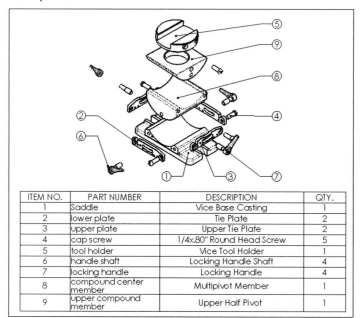

ITEM NO.	PART NUMBER	DESCRIPTION	QTY.
1	Saddle	Vice Base Casting	1
2	lower plate	Tie Plate	2
3	upper plate	Upper Tie Plate	2
4	cap screw	1/4x.80" Round Head Screw	5
5	tool holder	Vice Tool Holder	1
6	handle shaft	Locking Handle Shaft	4
7	locking handle	Locking Handle	4
8	compound center member	Multipivot Member	1
9	upper compound member	Upper Half Pivot	1

BOMs are made in one of two ways. The default BOM is made from a special SolidWorks table, while an Excel-based BOM is driven by Excel. While Excel has advantages and disadvantages, many users appear to prefer the default BOM. The reason is that little is perceived to be given up, except for the stability (crash-worthiness) compared to Excel and the options to keep manual edits.

If you plan to use anything other than the standard SolidWorks BOM templates, then you need to make your own BOM templates. If you plan to create either Excel or SolidWorks table-based templates, then you must choose one of them.

 **BOMs can also be placed directly in the assembly and even in multi-body part files starting in SolidWorks 2009.**

SolidWorks table-based BOM

The BOM shown in Figure 24.1 is a default SolidWorks table-based BOM. The differences between the displays of the two types of BOM are mainly cosmetic; the bigger differences lie in the functionality. The PropertyManager interface for the SolidWorks Bill of Materials is shown in Figure 24.2.

The PropertyManager for a table-driven BOM

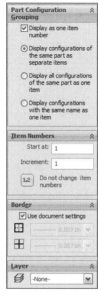

Table-based BOM templates

Like other types of data, the SolidWorks table-driven BOM starts from a template. The BOM in Figure 24.1 was created from the default BOM template. When a BOM is initiated, you can select the template in the Table Template panel at the top of the PropertyManager, as shown in Figure 24.2.

Table-based BOM templates are created in much the same way that other templates are created:

1. Specify the settings
2. Delete the document-specific data
3. Save the template

To save the template, right-click the BOM and select Save As. In the Files of Type drop-down list, select Template (*.sldbomtbt, which stands for "SolidWorks Bill of Materials Table Template"). Any of the settings, additional columns, links to properties, and so on are saved to the template, and reused when you create a new template from it.

BEST PRACTICE Put the BOM template in your library area outside of the SolidWorks installation folder. Then identify the path in the Tools ⇨ Options ⇨ File Locations area.

Table Anchor

A table anchor locks a corner of the table to a selected point on the format. If no point is selected in the format, then the table is placed at a corner of the sheet. To specify a point in the format to act as the anchor, you must be editing the format. Right-mouse button click the sheet and select Edit Sheet Format). Then right-click a sketch endpoint in the format, select Set As Anchor, and specify which type of table the anchor is for. You can set different anchor locations for different types of tables. Figure 24.3 shows the selection and menus for this option.

FIGURE 24.3

Setting a BOM table anchor

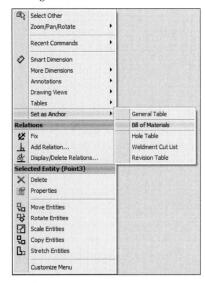

> **TIP** You should save the format and drawing template with these table anchors specified so that you do not need to re-specify them for each new document. If you want to check a Sheet Format to see what anchors exist, you can expand the Sheet.

BOM Type

As the name suggests, the Top Level Only BOM only shows components on the top level. It treats subassemblies as a single entry. As a result, if the top-level assembly shown on the drawing is made up of five subassemblies and two individual parts, and you select the Top Level Only option, then only seven items are shown in the BOM.

The Parts Only BOM ignores subassembly structure, and only displays parts in an unindented list.

The Indented Assemblies BOM shows the parts of subassemblies in an indented list under the name of the subassembly. This is the most complete list of SolidWorks documents used because it includes all parts and assemblies.

The Show Numbering option for indented assemblies is only activated after the Indented Assemblies option is checked, and you have placed the table. When you use this option, it causes subassembly parts to be numbered with an X.Y number system. For example, if item number 4 is a subassembly, and it has three parts, then those parts receive the item numbers 4.1, 4.2, and 4.3.

Configurations

The Configurations panel of the BOM PropertyManager displays slightly differently for Top Level Only BOMs compared to the other types. The Top Level Only BOM type enables the option to show multiple assembly configs and display the quantities for top-level components in separate columns, as shown in Figure 24.4. This figure shows that the configuration named "D" has some suppressed parts, including some parts that are now not used in the "D" configuration, and that therefore have a zero quantity. Notice the available options for dealing with zero-quantity parts.

FIGURE 24.4

Configuration options with the BOM

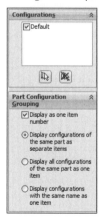

ITEM NO.	PART NUMBER	DESCRIPTION	Default/QTY.	d/QTY.
1	Saddle	Vice Base Casting	1	1
2	lower plate	Tie Plate	2	2
3	upper plate	Upper Tie Plate	2	2
4	cap screw	1/4x.80" Round Head Screw	4	4
5	Assem1	inch assembly description	1	1
6	handle shaft	Locking Handle Shaft	4	2
7	locking handle	Locking Handle	4	2
8	compound center member	Multipivot Member	1	-

Keep Missing Items

When you are making changes to a model, parts are often either suppressed or deleted altogether. Some company documentation standards require that parts that are removed from a BOM remain on the bill, and display with strikethrough formatting, although this may be a relic from days gone by when it was more difficult to remove items from hand drawings.

Keep Missing Items & Zero Quantity Display have both been moved to Tools ⇨ Options ⇨ Document Properties ⇨ Detailing ⇨ Tables screen.

Zero Quantity Display

The Zero Quantity Display settings are only used for configurations where some components are not used in some configurations. The three options that are available are:

- **Quantity Of Dash.** Substitutes a dash for the quantity value
- **Quantity Of Zero.** Uses a zero for the quantity value
- **Blank.** Quantity value is blank

Item Numbers

Item numbers for components listed in the BOM can start at a specific number and be given a particular interval. The Do Not Change Item Numbers option means that even when rows are reordered, item numbers stay with their original components.

The Follow Assembly Order option, which is also available through the right-mouse button menu, means that the order of the components in the BOM follows the order of the components in the Assembly FeatureManager. If the order is changed in the assembly, it also updates in the drawing.

BOM Contents

The BOM Contents are handled by functionality available right on the BOM or through the right-mouse button menu. Figure 24.5 shows a simple BOM with the right-mouse button menu. For example, you can drag the row numbers to reorder BOM items, and right-click to hide them. Row numbers are only displayed after you select the BOM table.

You can add columns or rows to the BOM for additional properties or manually added parts (such as items you wouldn't model like paint or glue. To change the property displayed in a column, double-click in the column header. In previous releases, many of the settings and options now found on the right-mouse button menu were found in a more complex Bill of Materials Properties window. The newer arrangement is more intuitive. Most SolidWorks users know that if they select something, and don't get the option they are looking for in the PropertyManager, they will try the right-mouse button menu.

FIGURE 24.5

The BOM Contents interface

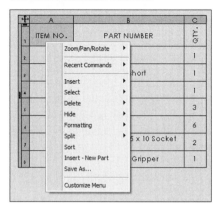

Controlling the appearance of the Table-based BOM

If you are already familiar with formatting an Excel-based BOM, then it should not take much getting used to formatting the SolidWorks table-based BOM. Figure 24.6 shows the table unselected on the left and selected on the right. While it's selected, you have access to a full range of appearance and organization options through the right-mouse button menu.

FIGURE 24.6

Selecting a column, row, cell, and table

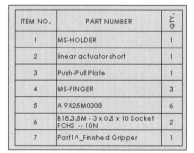

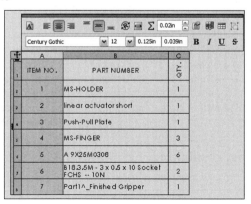

To move the table, click outside the upper-left corner and drag the table to a new location. When the table is selected, a border appears around it that is not normally visible, and is not printed with the drawing. You can change the properties of a row or a column by selecting just outside of the row or column to the top or the left.

You can establish spacing and width of rows or columns by dragging the border on the left side of the column with the split cursor or by accessing the column width setting through Formatting in the right-mouse button menu.

While it is activated, you can also expand a panel to the left and another to the top by clicking the three small arrows in the selected BOM border. Figure 24.7 shows the left panel, called the Assembly Structure panel, expanded with the cursor pointing to the three small arrows. In addition to showing the assembly structure, this panel can also show which parts are ballooned on the drawing.

FIGURE 24.7

An expanded BOM border

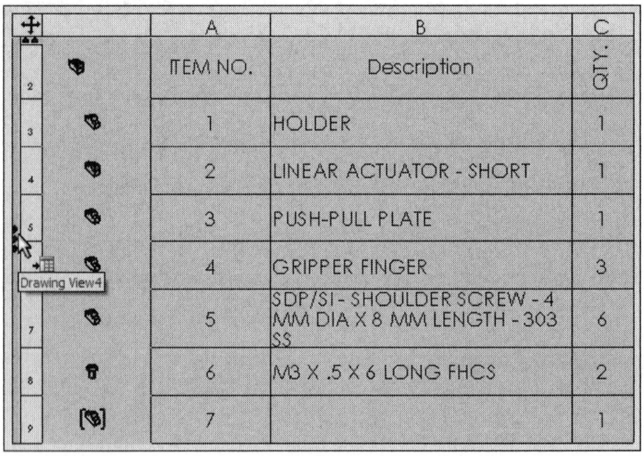

A	B	C
ITEM NO.	Description	QTY.
1	HOLDER	1
2	LINEAR ACTUATOR - SHORT	1
3	PUSH-PULL PLATE	1
4	GRIPPER FINGER	3
5	SDP/SI - SHOULDER SCREW - 4 MM DIA X 8 MM LENGTH - 303 SS	6
6	M3 X .5 X 6 LONG FHCS	2
7		1

Notice item 7 on the BOM. It has a different symbol and no name. This is a virtual component, a component created in context but not saved to its own document file; it exists only within the assembly.

Dissolving, combining, numbering, and restructuring for indented BOMS

You can dissolve an assembly in the BOM. To do this, the BOM has to show an indented list, then access Dissolve from the right-mouse button menu on the assembly icon. Any restructuring done to the BOM can be deleted by right-mouse button on the assembly icon with red arrows and selecting "Restore restructured components."

If the BOM shows several parts that are identical, and you would like to combine them, again, access the option from the right-mouse button menu.

Item numbers in indented BOMs can be flat like 1, 2, 3 or they can be detailed like 1.1, 1.2, 1.3, 2, 2.1, 2.2 to reflect parts as members of subassemblies. This option is available in the BOM PropertyManager, in the BOM Type panel, under the Indented option.

Adding rows or columns

To add a column, right-click near where you want to add the column, and select Insert ➪ Column Right or Column Left. Inserting rows is exactly the same, except for the obvious. The next thing you will want to do with a column is to assign what kind of data goes into it. You can use a custom property such as Part Weight or Vendor, as shown in Figure 24.8. Access this interface by double clicking a column header and selecting Custom Property from the drop down list.

FIGURE 24.8

Establishing the property driving the column content

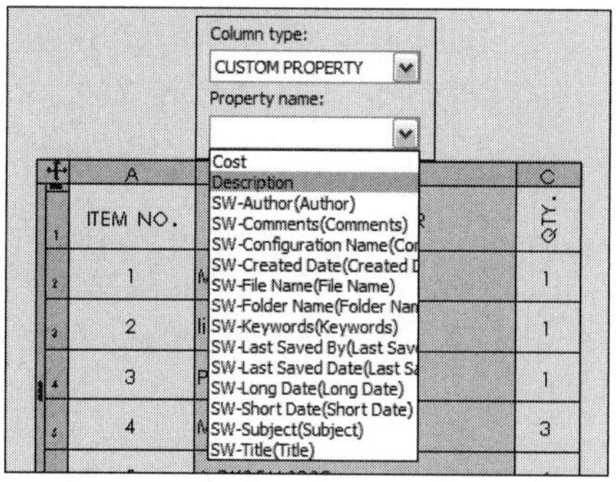

One of the really beautiful aspects of custom property management in the BOM is that if you just type text in a column set up to be driven by a part property, SolidWorks automatically updates the part with the property. If the property didn't exist in the part previously, SolidWorks also creates the property. This is another very nice addition to the software that they might have thought of years ago.

NOTE If you create a BOM with the columns and properties that you like, then you can save it to a template as described earlier in this chapter.

Excel-based BOM

In previous releases, the Excel-based BOM was the only way to add a BOM to a drawing. This feature has been replaced in most respects by the table-driven BOM, but many people still use the Excel-based BOM either out of habit or to comply with legacy standards. Figure 24.9 shows the interface for the Excel-based BOM.

The interface for Excel-based BOMs

BEST PRACTICE Unless you have a compelling reason to do otherwise, I recommend that you use the SolidWorks table-based BOM, as it is the function that will be best supported in future versions of SolidWorks software.

Using Design Tables

Design Tables that are used to drive configurations of parts and assemblies can be shown on the drawing. This is often called a *tabulated* drawing and is typical of parts that have a basic shape that is common among several sizes or versions of the part. The sizes are shown by a symbol on the drawing, with a column headed by that symbol showing the available dimensions and the corresponding size (configuration) names.

You can insert a Design Table into a drawing by selecting Insert ➪ Tables ➪ Design Table or through the Design Table button on the Tables toolbar. In either case, you must pre-select a drawing view of a part or assembly that contains a Design Table before the menu selection or toolbar button become activated.

Design Tables that are displayed in this way are often formatted visually to some extent. It is necessary to hide columns and rows unless you want the dimension or feature name syntax to display on the drawing as well as the values. Extra columns and rows are often added to make the design table readable. The image to the left in Figure 24.10 shows a design table that is formatted to be placed on a drawing. The image to the right shows the same design table with all of the information visible. The first column and the first row are hidden to make the table more readable on the drawing, and the second column and second row use the $user_notes header to format the names.

Figure 24.11 shows the drawing with the table inserted. To display the table properly, you have to edit the table in the window of the parent document and adjust the border of the table to be exactly how you want it to appear on the drawing. The adjusted table is shown in Figure 24.11.

The labeled dimensions were created by simply making reference dimensions and overwriting the <DIM> value in the Dimension Text panel of the Dimension PropertyManager. If you would like to examine this data more closely, the drawing and part are included on the CD-ROM. The drawing is named `Chapter 24 - DT.slddrw`.

FIGURE 24.10

A design table prepared to be placed on a drawing

	B	C	D	E	F	G	H	I
3		Pipe Thickness	Length	Flange Thickness	Inside Diameter	Flange Diameter	Bolt Circle Diameter	Hole Diameter
4	Size1	0.25	3	0.275	0.8	3.6	2.7	0.25
5	Size2	0.25	3.5	0.275	0.9	3.7	2.8	0.25
6	Size3	0.25	4	0.275	1	3.8	2.9	0.25
7	Size4	0.3	4	0.3	1.1	3.9	3	0.25
8	Size5	0.3	4.5	0.3	1.2	4	3.1	0.25
9	Size6	0.3	5	0.3	1.2	4.1	3.2	0.25
10	Size7	0.35	5	0.35	1.3	4.1	3.2	0.38
11	Size8	0.35	5.5	0.35	1.4	4.2	3.3	0.38
12	Size9	0.35	6	0.35	1.5	4.3	3.4	0.38

Sheet1

Worksheet in Chapter 24 - DT Part.SLDPRT

	A	B	C	D	E	F	G	H	I	J
1	Design Table for: Chapter 24 - DT Part									
2		$user_notes	PipeThickness@Sketch1	Length@Sketch1	FlangeThickness@Sketch1	ID@Sketch1	FlangeDia@Sketch1	BoltCircle@Sketch2	HoleDia@Sketch2	
3	$user_notes		Pipe Thickness	Length	Flange Thickness	Inside Diameter	Flange Diameter	Bolt Circle Diameter	Hole Diameter	
4	Size1	Size1	0.25	3	0.275	0.8	3.6	2.7	0.25	
5	Size2	Size2	0.25	3.5	0.275	0.9	3.7	2.8	0.25	
6	Size3	Size3	0.25	4	0.275	1	3.8	2.9	0.25	
7	Size4	Size4	0.3	4	0.3	1.1	3.9	3	0.25	
8	Size5	Size5	0.3	4.5	0.3	1.2	4	3.1	0.25	
9	Size6	Size6	0.3	5	0.3	1.2	4.1	3.2	0.25	
10	Size7	Size7	0.35	5	0.35	1.3	4.1	3.2	0.38	
11	Size8	Size8	0.35	5.5	0.35	1.4	4.2	3.3	0.38	
12	Size9	Size9	0.35	6	0.35	1.5	4.3	3.4	0.38	
13										
14										
15										
16										
17										

Sheet1

FIGURE 24.11

A drawing with the Design Table inserted

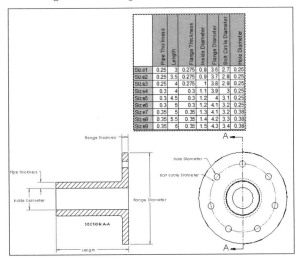

This drawing uses a part Design Table, but you can also place assembly Design Tables onto the drawing. This type of drawing is often called a tabulated drawing.

If you need to place something on your drawing such as a Design Table, but it does not appear that the Design Table is going to meet your needs, you may want to simply copy the data out of the Design Table and re-create it in a static Excel spreadsheet. The Design Table that you place on the drawing updates if it is changed in the part or assembly, just like the drawing geometry, but you must manually update an Excel spreadsheet that is from copied data. Again, you must answer the question about whether the automatic functions make up for the cost of setting them up to work for you. In many cases they do, but in other cases they require more work than they save.

Using Hole Tables

You can place Hole Tables on drawings to include information such as the size, position, and number of holes or slots of a given size on a drawing. Only circular holes and through slots are recognized. You do not have to use the Hole Wizard or simple hole features to make the holes. The Hole Table will not recognize counterbored slots or even slots with a chamfer edgebreak. The position is given relative to a selected reference position, and the holes are labeled. I do not recommend using a hole table for slots unless you first test to make sure that you are getting correct data.

Like other table types, Hole Tables can use templates. As with other templates, you should locate Hole Table templates in a library area outside of your local SolidWorks installation folder. You can then direct SolidWorks to this location using the path settings at Tools ➪ Options ➪ File Locations.

Hole Tables use anchors in exactly the same way as BOMs. For more information, see the section on table anchors earlier in this chapter.

You can find the options for Hole Tables at Tools ⇨ Options ⇨ Document Properties ⇨ Drafting Standard ⇨ Tables ⇨ Hole. These settings are discussed in detail in Appendix B.

Figure 24.12 shows the PropertyManager for a Hole Table. The image on the left is the PropertyManager you get when you create the table, and the one on the right is the one you get when you edit the table. Figure 24.13 shows the resulting Hole Table on a drawing with a part that contains holes. The table incorporates holes from multiple views, using a different zero reference for each view.

FIGURE 24.12

The PropertyManager for the Hole Table

FIGURE 24.13

A Hole Table combining holes in different views

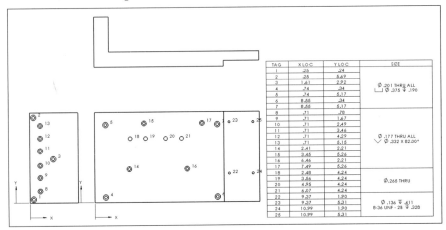

TAG	X LOC	Y LOC	SIZE
1	.25	.24	
2	.25	5.69	
3	1.61	2.92	
4	.74	.34	⌀ .201 THRU ALL
5	.74	5.17	⌴ ⌀ .375 ▼ .190
6	8.55	.34	
7	8.55	5.17	
8	.71	.78	
9	.71	1.67	
10	.71	2.49	
11	.71	3.46	
12	.71	4.29	⌀ .177 THRU ALL
13	.71	5.15	⋁ ⌀ .332 X 82.00°
14	2.41	2.21	
15	3.45	5.26	
16	6.46	2.21	
17	7.49	5.26	
18	2.48	4.24	
19	3.56	4.24	⌀.265 THRU
20	4.95	4.24	
21	6.07	4.24	
22	9.37	1.90	
23	9.37	5.31	⌀ .136 ▼ .411
24	10.99	1.90	8-36 UNF - 2B ▼ .328
25	10.99	5.31	

To initiate the Hole Table function, you must first select a view. You can access the Hole Table function through Insert ⇨ Table ⇨ Hole Table.

To specify the datum, either select an edge in each direction to serve as the zero mark for the X and Y directions, or select a vertex or point to serve as the Origin in both directions.

To select the holes to be included in the table, activate the Holes panel selection box, and either select the hole edges directly, or select the faces on which the holes are located. Once you place the table, you can add holes or change the datum information. To do this, use the right-mouse button menu of the Hole Table entry in the Drawing FeatureManager, and select Edit Feature. The right-mouse button menu is shown in the middle image of Figure 24.12. If you simply select a Hole Table that has already been created, the Properties interface displays, as shown in the top-right image. You can resize columns and rows in the same way as for BOM tables.

In the table in Figure 24.13, the Combine Same Sizes option is used, which causes several of the cells of the table to merge. If you use the Combine Same Tags option, then the hole locations are not displayed — only the hole callout description and the quantity appear. Figure 24.14 shows this arrangement.

You can control the hole callout description used in Figure 24.14 by using the file named `calloutformat.txt`, which is found in the `lang\english` subdirectory of the SolidWorks installation directory. Again, if you customize this file, then you should keep it in a library external to the installation directory and list it in the Tools ⇨ Options ⇨ File Locations area. This text file enables you to specify how hole callouts are specified for different types of holes.

The Combine Same Tags option used with a Hole Table that includes a slot

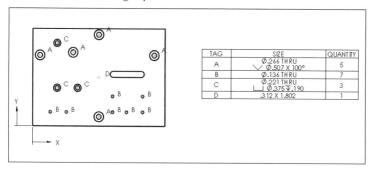

TAG	SIZE	QUANTITY
A	Ø.266 THRU ∨ Ø.507 X 100°	5
B	Ø.136 THRU	7
C	Ø.221 THRU ⌴ Ø.375 ▼.190	3
D	.312 X 1.802	1

Using Revision Tables

Revision Tables in SolidWorks can be used in conjunction with SolidWorks Workgroup PDM, but this integration goes beyond the scope of this book. The Revision Table uses a table anchor, which is used in exactly the same way as the BOM table. Revision Tables also use templates in the same way as the other table types, and it is recommended to move customized templates to a library location and specify the location in Tools ➪ Options ➪ File Locations.

Figure 24.15 shows the Revision Table PropertyManager interface where you can create and control the settings for the table. You can find the default settings for Revision Tables at Tools ➪ Options ➪ Document Properties ➪ Drafting Standard ➪ Tables ➪ Revision. These settings are described in more detail in Appendix B.

The settings that are now contained in a single PropertyManager; a toolbar and a right-mouse button menu were formerly contained in five PropertyManager pages. The new arrangement appears more manageable to me.

The image in the upper left of Figure 24.15 is the PropertyManager interface that displays when you initially create the Revision Table. The upper-right image is the right-mouse button menu for the Revision Table, and the bottom toolbar is the formatting toolbar that displays when you select the Revision Table.

You can initiate the Revision Table function through the menus or the Tables toolbar. However, this function simply creates the table; it does not populate it. You must set the table anchor in the format in order for the Table Anchor to work. Additional columns may be added or formatted to accept other data. Once you have created the columns or formatting, you can save the changes to a template, which is also available through the right-mouse button menu.

FIGURE 24.15

The Revision Table PropertyManager interface

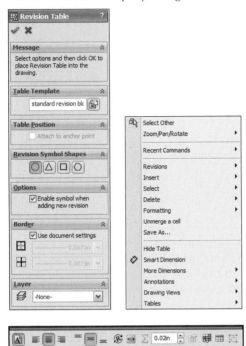

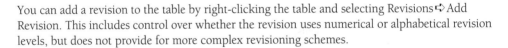

You can add a revision to the table by right-clicking the table and selecting Revisions ⇨ Add Revision. This includes control over whether the revision uses numerical or alphabetical revision levels, but does not provide for more complex revisioning schemes.

Immediately after you have created the revision, if the option is enabled, you are prompted to place a balloon that contains the revision level to identify what has been changed. To finish placing symbols, you can press Esc. When you are finished placing the balloons, you can fill in the description of the revision by double-clicking in the Description cell where you want to add text. Figure 24.16 shows a Revision Table with balloon symbols placed on the drawing.

Revision Tables work by creating a Revision custom property in the drawing document, and by incrementing this revision each time a revision is added to the table. Additional columns linked to custom properties can be added to Revision Tables and Revision Table templates.

CROSS-REF Gauge Tables and Bend Tables are specific to sheet metal parts and are covered in detail in Chapters 29 and 30.

CROSS-REF Weldment Cut Lists are a special type of table that closely resembles a BOM table in many ways. These are discussed in Chapter 31, which covers Weldments.

FIGURE 24.16

A Revision Table with balloon symbols

		REVISIONS			
ZONE	REV.	DESCRIPTION	DATE	APPROVED	
	A	ADDED CHAMFER AROUND ANGLED PORT	8/6/2005		
	B	ADDED THROUGH HOLE	11/19/2006		

Using General Tables

General Tables can be used for any type of tabulated data. Column headers can be filled with either text labels or custom property links. Regular Excel OLE objects can also be used for the same purpose, and depending on the application, you may prefer this.

The General Table uses the filename extension *.sldtbt. It can be created without a template, as a simple block of four empty cells, or you can use a template that has a set of pre-created headers.

Tutorials: Using Tables

Rather than having tutorials for every table type, this chapter has tutorials only for the BOM, Hole Table, and Revision Table. You can transfer the skills you use with these types to the other types.

Using BOMs

This tutorial guides you through the steps that are necessary to prepare an assembly for the drawing and BOM. Configurations and custom properties are used in this example. Remember that if a drawing view is cross-hatched and you cannot see the geometry, then you may have to press Ctrl+Q to rebuild it. Follow these steps:

1. **Begin this tutorial with SolidWorks closed and Windows Explorer open.**

2. **If you have not already done so, create a folder for a library that is not in your SolidWorks installation folder.** Call it `D:\Library\` or something similar. Make a folder inside this folder called Drawing Templates. Copy the file from the CD-ROM named `inch B.drwdot` to this new folder.

3. **Launch SolidWorks and go to Tools ⇨ Options ⇨ File Locations ⇨ Document Template.** Click the Add button and add the new library path to the list. Shut down SolidWorks and restart it.

4. **Open the assembly** `Chapter 24 – BOM Assy.sldasm` **from the CD-ROM.**

5. **Using the Make Drawing From Part/Assembly button, make a new drawing of the assembly from the drawing template** in the folder created in step 2 & 3.

6. **Delete the isometric view, and in its place make a new drawing view using the named model view "exploded." If prompted to use true dimensions in an isometric view, accept.**

7. **Edit the sheet format.** Right-click the sketch point at the location indicated in Figure 24.17. In the pop-up menu that appears, select Set As Anchor and then select Bill of Materials.

FIGURE 24.17

Setting the Table Anchor

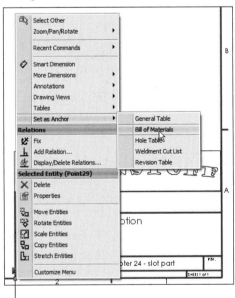

RMB on this point

8. **Exit Edit Sheet Format mode by selecting Edit Sheet from the right-mouse button menu.**

9. **Select the new view and** show it in the view in the exploded state. Then **click Insert ⇨ Table ⇨ Bill of Materials, or click the Bill of Materials button from the Tables toolbar.** Use the default selections, except in the panels shown in Figure 24.18.

FIGURE 24.18

Creating the Bill of Materials

ITEM NO.	PART NUMBER	DESCRIPTION	Angle 1/QTY.	Angle 2/QTY.
1	Bracket Angle 1	description	1	-
2	Chapter 24 - Pin Block	description	1	1
3	Clevis Male	description	1	1
4	Long	Long Pin	1	1
5	Clevis Female	description	1	1
6	Short	Short Pin	2	2
7	Bracket Angle 2	description	-	1

10. **Click inside the exploded view, but off of any part geometry, and then select the Autoballoon tool from the Annotations toolbar.** Toggle through the available options to see whether any of the possible autoballoon configurations meets your needs. If not, use the standard Balloon tool to select the part and place the balloon. This gives you more control over the attachment points and placement of the balloons.

11. **Change the balloon for the short pin to be a circular split-line balloon (do this by clicking the balloon and then switching the style in the PropertyManager).** Notice that the quantity appears in the bottom of the balloon. The drawing view and the BOM should now look like Figure 24.19.

FIGURE 24.19

The drawing view and the BOM after Step 11

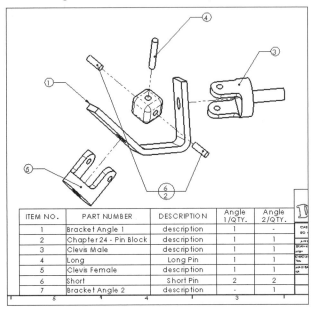

ITEM NO.	PART NUMBER	DESCRIPTION	Angle 1/QTY.	Angle 2/QTY.
1	Bracket Angle 1	description	1	-
2	Chapter 24 - Pin Block	description	1	1
3	Clevis Male	description	1	1
4	Long	Long Pin	1	1
5	Clevis Female	description	1	1
6	Short	Short Pin	2	2
7	Bracket Angle 2	description	-	1

12. **Notice that several of the parts use a default description of "description."** Edit each of these parts by right-clicking the part's row in the BOM table and selecting Open *<filename>* from the menu. Change the custom property called Description in each part. Keep in mind that this may be handled differently for configured parts.

13. **The Bracket part is listed twice using the configuration name because of the way the configurations are set up for the parts.** To list the bracket only once using the filename, open the bracket, right-mouse button click one of the configuration names in the ConfigurationManager, and select Properties. In the Bill of Materials Options panel, select Document Name from the drop-down list. Do this for the other configuration, as well.

    Notice also that the Description field holds the configuration-specific custom property for Description, which is used in the BOM.

14. **Toggle back to the drawing (using Ctrl+Tab), select anywhere on the BOM table, and then select Table Properties from the PropertyManager.** Expand the Part Configuration Grouping panel, and select the Display All Configurations Of The Same Part As One Item option. This changes how the bracket displays, as well as the pins.

15. **In this step, you will add a column to the BOM that calls on an existing custom property that is already in all of the parts.** Place the cursor over the last column on the right and right-mouse button click it. Select Insert ➪ Column Right. This places a new column to the right of the last one and displays a popup that enables you to set the column to be driven by a custom property , as shown in Figure 24.20.

16. **In the first drop-down selection box, select the Weight custom property.** Click the green check mark icon to accept the changes. If the pop up disappears and you need to get it back, double click the column header, and it will reappear.

FIGURE 24.20

Adding a column to the BOM

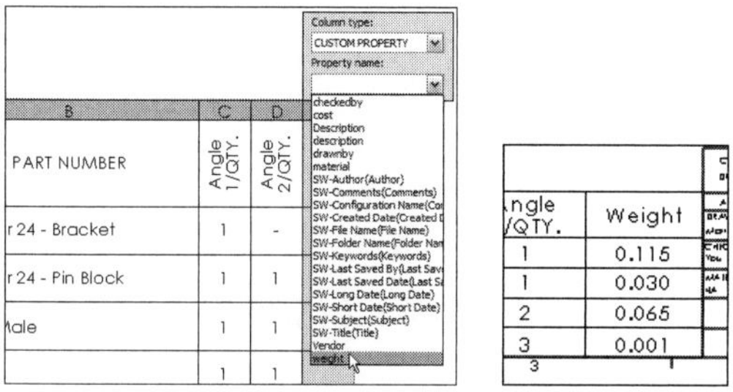

17. **The BOM with the additional column can be saved as a BOM template by right-clicking anywhere in the BOM and selecting Save As.** You can then set the type to a BOM template and the directory to the library location for BOM templates.

If you would like to compare your results against mine, the finished drawing is called `Chapter 24 – BOM Tutorial Finished.slddrw`.

Using Hole Tables

This tutorial guides you through the creation and setting changes that are common in SolidWorks Hole Tables. The part for this tutorial is the part from which the figures for the section on Hole Tables were made. Follow these steps:

1. **Create a new drawing from the template that was used for the BOM tutorial.** If you have not done the BOM tutorial, then move the drawing template named `inchB.drw-dot` from the Chapter 24 materials on the CD-ROM to your library location for drawing templates. Then create the drawing from the template.

2. **Click the Model View button on the Drawings toolbar, and browse to the part named** `Chapter 24 – Hole Table Part.sldprt`.

3. **Place a Front view and project a Left view and an isometric view.** Then press Esc to quit the command. Finally, delete the four predefined views.

4. **There is not an anchor in this template for a Hole Table.** If you would like to create one, this would be a good time to do so. Follow the steps in the BOM tutorial for specifying the anchor point.

5. **From the Tables toolbar, click the Hole Table button.** Figure 24.21 shows a section of the Hole Table PropertyManager with the selections that you need to make for this Hole Table.

FIGURE 24.21

The Hole Table PropertyManager and selections

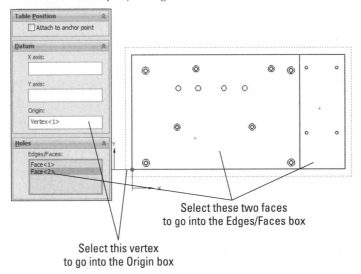

Select this vertex
to go into the Origin box

Select these two faces
to go into the Edges/Faces box

6. **Once you have completed the selections, click the Next View button at the bottom of the PropertyManager, and make similar selections in the Left view.** The holes for both views are added to a single Hole Table.

7. **The table is created using the default settings established in Tools ⇨ Options ⇨ Document Properties ⇨ Tables, but you can change them here for this specific table.** Click anywhere in the table, and then select Table Properties at the bottom of the PropertyManager. Changing from numerical to alphabetical assigns a letter to each hole type and a number to each instance of the type. Make this change and update the table. Figure 24.22 shows the table before and after the changes.

8. **Change the number of decimal places used in the Hole Table from two places to three.** You can do this in the PropertyManager.

9. **Deselect the Hide Hole Centers option in the Visibility panel.**

10. **Enable the Combine same sizes option in the PropertyManager.** This demonstrates a much cleaner table and would be a good thing to have in the tutorial.

FIGURE 24.22

Using numerical and alphabetical hole tag identification

TAG	X LOC	Y LOC	SIZE
1	.25	.24	
2	.25	5.69	
3	1.61	2.92	
4	.74	.34	⌀ .201 THRU ALL ⌴ ⌀ .375 ⩛ .190
5	.74	5.17	
6	8.55	.34	
7	8.55	5.17	
8	.71	.78	
9	.71	1.67	
10	.71	2.49	
11	.71	3.46	
12	.71	4.29	⌀ .177 THRU ALL ⌵ ⌀ .332 X 82.00°
13	.71	5.15	
14	2.41	2.21	
15	3.45	5.26	
16	6.46	2.21	
17	7.49	5.26	
18	2.48	4.24	
19	3.56	4.24	⌀.265 THRU
20	4.95	4.24	
21	6.07	4.24	
22	9.37	1.90	
23	9.37	5.31	⌀ .136 ⩛ .411 8-36 UNF - 2B ⩛ .328
24	10.99	1.90	
25	10.99	5.31	

TAG	X LOC	Y LOC	SIZE
A1	.25	.24	
A2	.25	5.69	
A3	1.61	2.92	
A4	.74	.34	⌀ .201 THRU ALL ⌴ ⌀ .375 ⩛ .190
A5	.74	5.17	
A6	8.55	.34	
A7	8.55	5.17	
B1	.71	.78	
B2	.71	1.67	
B3	.71	2.49	
B4	.71	3.46	
B5	.71	4.29	⌀ .177 THRU ALL ⌵ ⌀ .332 X 82.00°
B6	.71	5.15	
B7	2.41	2.21	
B8	3.45	5.26	
B9	6.46	2.21	
B10	7.49	5.26	
C1	2.48	4.24	
C2	3.56	4.24	⌀.265 THRU
C3	4.95	4.24	
C4	6.07	4.24	
D1	9.37	1.90	
D2	9.37	5.31	⌀ .136 ⩛ .411 8-36 UNF - 2B ⩛ .328
D3	10.99	1.90	
D4	10.99	5.31	

Using Revision Tables

In this tutorial, you create a basic Revision Table, and make a template. Follow these steps:

1. **Using a drawing that you completed in one of the previous tutorials, make sure that a Revision Table Anchor has been placed in the upper-right corner of the Sheet Format.** You must edit the Sheet Format to do this by right-mouse button clicking the point that you want to use for the anchor. Remember to select Edit Sheet from the right-mouse button menu to exit Edit Sheet Format mode.

 Ideally, the anchors for all table types should be set in templates and formats, but here it is set up to ensure that you get some practice with creating the anchors.

2. **Click the Revision Table button on the Tables toolbar.** Select the Attach to Anchor option in the PropertyManager. Click the green check mark icon to accept the table. Figure 24.23 shows the initial stub of the Revision Table.

FIGURE 24.23

The initial stub of the Revision Table

		3		2		1	
			REVISIONS				
ZONE	REV.		DESCRIPTION		DATE	APPROVED	

TIP Drawing templates can be saved with the Revision Table stub if it also has a format. The revision table is not saved with the format because it has to go on the drawing sheet.

3. **To initiate a new revision level in the Revision Table, right-mouse button click the table and select Revisions ⇨ Add Revision.**

4. **Depending on the default settings in Tools ⇨ Options ⇨ Document Properties ⇨ Drafting Standard ⇨ Tables ⇨ Revision, the first revision will be either A or 1.** If you are using PDMWorks Workgroup, then you may have other options.

5. **Depending on your options settings, you may immediately be prompted to place a balloon that contains the new revision level.** You can place balloons with or without leaders. The balloons are meant to indicate areas of the drawing that are affected by the revision. Press Esc when you are finished placing the balloons.

NOTE   Be careful when using balloons on assembly drawings or other drawings that already have balloons on them for other purposes. It may be a good idea to use a distinctively shaped balloon for Revision Tables.

6. **To add text to the Description field, simply double-click in the field and start typing.** The text automatically wraps to fit the box.

7. **Practice by adding a couple of revisions, balloons, and descriptions.**

8. **After you have added a couple of revisions, check the custom properties by going to File ⇨ Properties ⇨ Custom.** Notice that a revision property has been added, and the latest revision is represented by the value of the custom property.

NOTE   The number of revisions kept in the Revision Table is no longer an option as it was in previous releases, but in its place you can now control how Revision Tables interact with multiple sheets. For more information, see Appendix B.

9. **You can add columns in the same way that they were added to the BOM.** You can merge and unmerge cells, and link properties to cells. With the cursor over the last column (Approved), right-mouse button click and select Insert ⇨ Column Left. In the Column Properties, select Custom, and from the Properties drop-down menu, select DrawnBy. Accept the changes by clicking the green check mark icon.

10. **Save the template by right-clicking anywhere in the Revision Table and selecting Save As ⇨ Rev Table Templates.** Then save it to the appropriate location outside of the SolidWorks installation directory.

Summary

SolidWorks enables you to work with both tables that are highly specialized for particular uses, and General Tabled, which are available for any type of tabulated data. The most frequently used types are BOMs, Hole Tables, and Revision Tables. Design tables that drive part and assembly configurations can also be placed on a 2D drawing, but in these cases, some formatting is usually necessary to make the Design Table presentable and the information on it easy to read.

Other types of tables, such as Gauge Tables and Bend Tables and Weldment Cut Lists, are specialized for sheet metal and weldment parts, respectively, and are discussed in chapters that cover those topics.

Chapter 25

Using Layers, Line Fonts, and Colors

Regardless of what you think of the AutoCAD software, or the 2D world in general, AutoCAD has left its mark on CAD users of all kinds in the form of certain default expectations that people have about CAD software. A few common preconceptions are that layers, the Command Line, paper space/model space, and printing should be really difficult.

When former AutoCAD users make the switch to SolidWorks, the questions start: Where is the Command Line, How do I put parts on layers, How do I change the background color to black, and my personal favorite, Where is the zero-radius trim?

This chapter addresses AutoCAD-like functions in the SolidWorks drawing environment. The goal is not to make the functions look or work or compare in any way to AutoCAD, but to simply to make them useful in the context of the SolidWorks software. It is never productive to try to use SolidWorks as if it were AutoCAD. It is probably also counter productive to wish SolidWorks worked like AutoCAD. If you are making the transition, you will be much further ahead if you just embrace SolidWorks for what it is, and accept that it does not work like AutoCAD. You will be even further ahead if you do not assume that AutoCAD functionality is universal.

Controlling Layers

Layers are arguably one of the most visible differences between AutoCAD and SolidWorks. Layers are not available in SolidWorks 3D modeling at all — only in the 2D drawing environment — and even there, they do not see a lot of use. However, this is not to say that there is no need for them.

Layers in imported 2D data

When you import data through DXF or DWG format files, the layers that exist in the original data are brought forward into SolidWorks, and you can use them in a similar way to the original AutoCAD usage. For example, you can turn layers on or off (visible or hidden), and you can change layer names, descriptions, color, line thickness, and line style.

The way you intend to use the imported data determines how you should open the file. If you only intend to view and print the drawing, then I would suggest using DWG Editor, which is installed with SolidWorks and enables you to do almost anything you can do with basic AutoCAD. It also has the advantage of having a familiar interface for the AutoCAD user (it even has a black background!). DWG Editor is available from the Start menu, by selecting Programs ➪ SolidWorks ➪ D WGeditor.

If you need to integrate data from the imported document into a native SolidWorks drawing, you can open the DWG file from the normal Open dialog box in SolidWorks.

TIP   **If you want to make a 3D part from the 2D data in the DWG file, you may want to import the drawing into the part sketch environment. This usually leads to some speed issues. If you prefer, sketch entities can also be copied from the drawing to the model sketch. You can even copy entities from DWG Editor to the SolidWorks part sketch. The sketch needs to be open in order to paste the sketch entities. In the case where imported 2D data is brought into the model sketch, you lose all of the layer information, because part and assembly documents do not allow layers.**

The colors assigned to layers are often based on a black background, and so they can be difficult to see on a white background. The two ways of dealing with this are to change the SolidWorks drawing sheet color to something dark or to change the individual layer colors to something dark. Either method is easy, although if you have to send the 2D data back to its source, it may be best to temporarily change the drawing sheet color.

Figure 25.1 shows the layer interface with an imported drawing in the background. The colors have been changed here to improve visibility. The Layers dialog box is activated by the Layer Properties toolbar button, which is found on both the Layer and Line Format toolbars.

Be aware that many items in an imported drawing may come into SolidWorks as blocks. These items may need to be exploded before you can work with them. This is often the case with the drawing border, title block, or format.

The Layers dialog box and the Layer toolbar

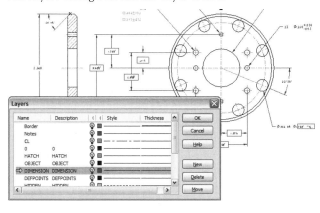

Layers on the sheet format

One of the most obvious uses of layers is on the sheet format. The sketch lines used to create the border often have a heavier line weight and a different color that easily distinguishes them from model geometry.

You can assign layers in one of three ways:

- Select existing items, and then select a layer from the drop-down list on the Layer toolbar.

- Set the active layer and create new items.

- While creating items such as sketch entities and annotations, select the layer for the new entity directly from the PropertyManager.

To set a layer to the active layer, double-click it from the Layers dialog box, as shown in Figure 25.1, or change it from the drop-down list on the Layer toolbar. When you assign an active layer, other newly created entities are also placed on the layer, not just sketch entities. Symbols, annotations, blocks, and other elements can also be put onto layers. If you are not particular about the layering scheme on a drawing, then it may be advisable to set the active layer to None, which is a valid option in the Layer toolbar drop-down list.

When you create a new layer in SolidWorks, the new layer becomes the active layer, and any new items that are added are automatically placed on that layer.

Another option when building a sheet format, or any other drawing function that requires sketching, is to use a special layer for construction geometry. This enables you to hide the layer when it is not being used, but it still maintains its relations. Hidden layers can be used in several other ways (for example, as standard notes on the drawing) and they can be easily turned on or off.

Dimensions and notes on layers

SolidWorks drawings have a tendency to be drab black-and-white drawings, in contrast to AutoCAD drawings, which often seem to take on a plethora of contrasting colors. Still, drawings do seem a little easier to comprehend when different types of items are colored differently, but in order for this to work, you must apply the coloring scheme consistently. Dimensions and annotations can also be placed on layers in the three ways described in the previous section (active layer, from the PropertyManager during creation, and through the drop-down list on the Layer toolbar). However, the line styles do not affect dimensions and notes, only the color and visibility settings.

Components on layers

Assembly drawings probably suffer the most from the monochromatic nature of most SolidWorks drawings because individual components can be difficult to identify when everything is the same color. This is why SolidWorks users typically color parts in the shaded model assembly window. It only makes sense that as users, we would want to do the same thing on the drawing.

An intuitive and easy workaround for this problem would seem to be to simply turn the drawing view to a wireframe mode in the same way that changing a drawing view to a shaded mode shows the parts in color. Unfortunately, wireframe on drawings always defaults to black edges. Even if you set a Display State using some wireframe parts where the wireframe displays in the same color as the shaded part in the assembly window, this still appears in black and white on the drawing.

Your only option to display the components of an assembly in different colors while using a wireframe display mode is to set the Component Line Font options. (Line Fonts are covered in the next section.) The Component Line Font dialog box contains a Layer setting, which you can use to put a part on a layer. If the layer is set up with a color, then the part displays with that color in all views of the drawing, or in just the current view, depending on your settings. While it does take a little time to set up the individual layers for each part and then to set the parts to the layers, it is better than the alternative, which is to do nothing.

You can access the Component Line Font dialog box by right-clicking a component in a drawing view. The Component Line Font dialog box is shown in Figure 25.2.

In normal use, the Use Document Defaults option is selected and all of the settings in the dialog box are grayed out. To gain access to these settings, you must deselect the Use Document Defaults option, as shown in Figure 25.2.

FIGURE 25.2

The Component Line Font dialog box

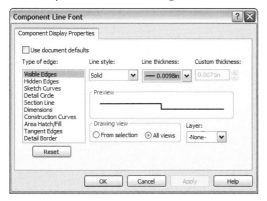

Controlling Line Format

The Line Format toolbar contains the Layer tool and four additional tools that control lines, Line Color, Line Thickness, Line Style, and Color Display Mode. These settings can be controlled separately from layers, and so they can be used in model sketches as well as on drawings. In the model, the line font can only be displayed for inactive sketches. Any sketch that is both closed and shown can be displayed with the Line Format settings.

CROSS-REF For more information on using line styles in the model, see Chapter 6.

Figure 25.3 shows the Line Format toolbar along with the interfaces for Line Color, Line Thickness, and Line Style.

FIGURE 25.3

The Line Format toolbar and related interface options

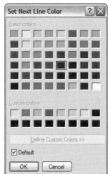

> **NOTE** The term *line font* refers to a combination of style, end cap, and thickness. Line fonts are set in the document-specific settings at Tools ➪ Options ➪ Document Properties ➪ Line Font. These settings are described in detail in Appendix B.

Using the Line Format settings

You can specify the Line Format settings using two different methods. In the first method, you can set them with nothing selected, in which case they function like System Options (the new setting takes effect for all documents that are opened on the current computer). In the second method, if they are set with sketch entities or edges selected, then the settings apply only to the selected entities.

> **CAUTION** If you change these settings with nothing selected, then the Line Format settings for color, thickness, and style function as system options.

End Cap Style

Another option for the Line Font settings is the End Cap Style. This offers an important option, especially for thick lines. The three options are flat, round, and square. Of these, the square style is usually most appropriate. In the past, flat was the default style. You can find this setting at Tools ➪ Options ➪ Document Properties ➪ Line Font. You may want to change this setting and update your drawing template files.

Figure 25.4 shows the difference between the three options of End Cap Style.

FIGURE 25.4

The End Cap Style setting options

Line Thickness settings

The Line Thickness settings are Default, Custom, and eight width settings. Interestingly, the different thicknesses are named in the interface where you set the actual thicknesses, but not in the interface where you set lines to thicknesses. Figure 25.5 shows the Tools ➪ Options ➪ Document Properties ➪ Line Thickness page.

The way the line thickness is shown in the drawing does not have anything to do with the numerical width that is assigned to it. For example, in Figure 25.5, notice that Thick(2) is set to 0.1 inch, which is much wider than Thick(3). Changing the numbers only affects printed line thickness; it does not affect the display at all.

FIGURE 25.5

The Line Weights settings in Tools ⇨ Options

System Options	Document Properties

Drafting Standard
- Annotations
- Dimensions
- Centerlines/Center Marks
- DimXpert
- Tables
- View Labels
- Virtual Sharps
- Detailing
- Grid/Snap
- Units
- Line Font
- Line Style
- **Line Thickness**
- Image Quality
- Sheet Metal

Line thickness print settings

Edit the default thickness of printed lines for each size. Modifying these values will not change the displayed line thickness.

Thin:		0.0071in
Normal:		0.0098in
Thick:		0.0138in
Thick(2):		0.1in
Thick(3):		0.0276in
Thick(4):		0.0394in
Thick(5):		0.0551in
Thick(6):		0.0787in

Reset

CAUTION The Line Weights settings are document options, not system options. As a result, two drawings with the same line type assignments may have different numerical widths; thus, the two drawings would print differently on the same computer.

Line Style setting

You can create custom line styles using the syntax shown on the Tools ⇨ Options ⇨ Document Properties ⇨ Line Style page. This is a document-specific setting, and so if you make a custom line style and want to use it in another document, then you have to save it out (as a `*.sldlin` file) and load it into the other document. Also, if you save your templates with this line style loaded, then you will not have to load the styles for any document made from that template. For more information about line styles, see Appendix B.

Color Display mode

Color Display mode toggles between the display of assigned colors and standard sketch state colors. This is primarily used in drawings when you are making sketches where sketch relations are important.

Hiding and Showing Edges

Sometimes, for illustrative purposes, it is desirable to hide certain edges in drawing views. The Hide Edge and Show Edge toolbar buttons are associated with the Line Format toolbar, although they may not be on the toolbar by default. You can use Tools ⇨ Customize to put them on a toolbar.

To use the Hide Edge tool, simply select the edges that you would like to hide, and click the Hide Edge toolbar button. To show the edges, click the Show Edge toolbar button; the cursor will now be able to select the hidden edges.

Be aware that if your view is in Draft Mode, edges that you hide will still be shown, until the view is made into a High Quality view.

Tutorial: Using Drawing Display Tools

Some of the functions described in this chapter are difficult to understand until you actually use them. This tutorial guides you through the functions step by step so that you can see them in action. Start here:

1. **From the CD-ROM, open the drawing called** Chapter 25 – Tutorial.slddrw. Make sure that the Layer and Line Format toolbars are active and that the Hide Edge and Show Edge buttons are available on the Line Format toolbar.

2. **Right-click a blank space and select Edit Sheet Format from the menu.**

3. **Window-select everything on the format and use the drop-down list on the Layers toolbar to assign the selection to the Border layer.** Notice that this changes the color and the thickness of the sketch lines.

4. **Right-click a blank space and select Edit Sheet.**

5. **Click the Layer Properties button on either the Layer or Line Format toolbar.** Add new layers for each of the part groups, bracket, clevis, pins, and blocks, assigning different colors to each layer. Figure 25.6 shows the Layers dialog box with these layers created.

FIGURE 25.6

The Layers dialog box

Be aware that creating new layers leaves the last layer that you created active, as indicated by the yellow arrow in Figure 25.6. There is no way to set the active layer to None from the Layers dialog box; you have to do this using the drop-down list in the Layer toolbar.

6. **Set the active layer to None in the Layer toolbar drop-down list.**

7. **Right-click the Bracket part in one of the views and select Component Line Font.** Deselect the Use Document Defaults option, and select the Bracket layer from the drop-down list in the lower-right corner of the dialog box, as shown in Figure 25.7. Make sure that the Drawing View option is set to All Views.

FIGURE 25.7

The Component Line Font dialog box

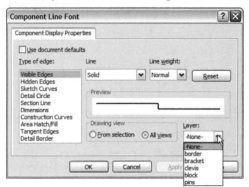

8. **Repeat Step 7 for all of the components, assigning each component to its own layer.** Notice how this makes the parts easier to identify.

NOTE   Alternatively, you could simply change the line style and weight (thickness — note the terminology inconsistencies here) for each component. This saves you creating the layers, but you lose the color settings.

9. **Open the Component Line Font dialog box for the Bracket part again.** This time, set the Line Weight to Thick (6), and click OK. You may have to rebuild the drawing to show the change (Ctrl+B or Ctrl+Q). Figure 25.8 shows a detail of the corners that are created by the thick lines. Notice the notches created at the corners.

10. **These notches are supposed to be fixed using the End Cap setting in.** In the menus, go to Tools ⇨ Options ⇨ Document Properties ⇨ Line Font, and set the End Cap Style to Square. Click OK to exit the Document Properties. In the drawing, select inside the view where you are working, and make sure that it is set to High Quality. (The setting is found in the PropertyManager for the view in the Display Style panel. If it is already set to High Quality, then there will be no other view option; if it is not, then there will be an option that is set to Draft Quality.)

    The image to the left in Figure 25.8 is the old setting with the draft quality view, and the image to the right is the new setting with the high quality view.

FIGURE 25.8

Applying thick edges

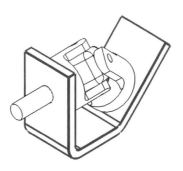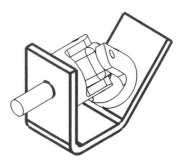

11. In the Component Line Font dialog box, set the Line Weight setting back to Default for the Bracket part, but keep it on the Bracket layer.

12. **In the isometric view, Ctrl+click all of the tangent edges on the Bracket part, as shown in Figure 25.9.** Click the Hide Edge toolbar button on the Line Format toolbar.

FIGURE 25.9

Hiding edges

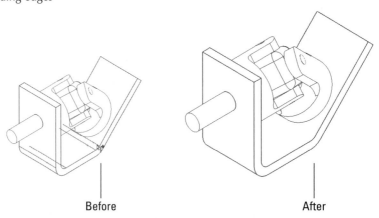

Before   After

13. **Click the Show Edge toolbar button.** The PropertyManager message changes to indicate that you can now select hidden edges, and the hidden edges are shown. Ctrl+select the hidden edges and right-click when you are done.

Summary

While SolidWorks is not primarily built around the strength of its 2D drawing functionality, it offers more capabilities than most users take advantage of. Layers in SolidWorks offer adequate functionality, but could be improved by some automation to put parts on layers automatically; this would enable SolidWorks to show the parts in wireframe with the same colors assigned to the solid.

Other line and edge display functionality is sometimes difficult to find or access, or may have obscure functions. Creating drawings that use color to make them easier to read should be easier in SolidWorks than it is in AutoCAD.

Part VI

Using Advanced Techniques

The techniques on display in Part VI certainly fall into the advanced category. Not everyone needs these tools, but for those who do, advice on them can be difficult to find from other sources. I encourage you to explore the tools available here. All three chapters really go together, so it is most beneficial to read them all in order.

Chapter 26

Modeling Multi-bodies

I f you only ever work with solids in SolidWorks, you could work in such a way that you would never need to use multiple bodies inside a single part. Almost everything that normal users normally do can be done with a single solid body and without any knowledge of multi-body functionality whatsoever.

However, to access some more powerful functionality, and options that offer more flexibility, multi-body modeling is necessary. In fact, if you want to move on to surface modeling, multi-body knowledge is mandatory because in surface modeling, multi-body is the default.

Multi-body modeling is the gateway from the basic, traditional type of solid modeling mainly described in the book up until now, into the more advanced functionality that follows. The gateway can lead two directions: it can lead to more power, more flexibility, more options, more advanced functionality, or it can lead to sloppy, bad habits that could get you or those who work with your data into some modeling hot water down the road. This chapter will help you tell the difference, and help you avoid the pitfalls.

Using Powerful Tools Responsibly

I find myself giving the same responsible-modeling speeches when discussing multi-bodies as I tend to give for in-context modeling. This is because multi-bodies present some of the same issues as in-context modeling. The first similarity is that on the surface, both techniques appear to be all-day-every-day types of design tools. The second similarity is that neither tool is what it appears to be on the surface.

The responsibility part arises when you are thinking about other users who will use the multi-body parts once they are created, including yourself. It is not always easy to remember how you executed a particular project six months and 100 models ago. Other users may have to edit your work, and if errors happen, then you have to be able to navigate the design intent without destroying the relationships in the FeatureManager or completely rebuilding it. This is the reason for trying to standardize best-practice issues, particularly with advanced functionality and particularly in larger organizations where more users may work with the data.

If you are an independent contractor and do not share your models with other SolidWorks users, then you have more flexibility to model how you like. As long as you can come back to the model and change it when you need to, more power to you.

Multi-body modeling is not assembly modeling

This concept is important, and so I will repeat it: Multi-body modeling is not assembly modeling. Many times when new users are introduced to the capabilities of multi-body modeling, the first thought that comes to mind is, "This is far easier than making assemblies." However, multi-body modeling should not be treated as a replacement for assembly modeling.

Several assembly type functions are missing or difficult to obtain from multi-bodies. They include the following:

- Interference detection
- Dynamic assembly motion
- Exploded views
- Configs for separate parts
- Display States
- Center-of-gravity calculations for individual parts
- Mass property calculations for individual parts

To say that these functions are missing from multi-bodies does not imply that they should or will be there someday. In fact, I believe that the distinction between multi-body and assembly design techniques should be kept as clear as possible. Simply because a technique is easier does not make it *better*. Above all, remember that modeling multi-body parts puts *all* of the data for *all* of the bodies in a *single* part file, in a *single* FeatureManager; there is no easy way to separate the parametric features out into individual parts later on, regardless of how complex the part becomes.

Further, creating drawings of individual bodies of a multi-body part is *far* more difficult than creating drawings of individual parts. Also, editing the features of individual bodies is not as easy as if the individual body were an individual part. When you create several bodies in a single part, you constantly have to carry the feature and design intent overhead of *all* of the features used to create *all* of the bodies to edit any individual body.

Appropriate multi-body uses

Obviously, I am trying to alarm you a little. You need to have a healthy respect for the problems that you can create for yourself and others by using multi-body modeling in inefficient or inappropriate ways. Still, appropriate uses for multi-body modeling do exist. You may hear people recommend that at the end of the FeatureManager, only a single solid body should remain, with the rest of them either absorbed or deleted. For others, anything goes. I recommend that if you decide to use multi-bodies, then you should be at least able to articulate *why* you have chosen to do so in a way that does not sound like you are making excuses for careless work.

Appropriate uses for multi-body modeling include (but are not limited to):

- As an intermediate step on the way to a single-body solid.

- As multiple or inserted bodies for reference (reference bodies may be deleted at the bottom of the FeatureManager).

- As over-molded parts.

- As parts that need to be assembled into a single, smooth shape, such as a computer mouse or an automobile body where the shape is impossible (or at least far more difficult) if done in-context.

- When the end shape of the finished product is known, but the part breaks due to manufacturing methods, and materials have not been decided yet, multi-body techniques can save a lot of time compared to modeling an assembly.

- As captive fasteners and purchased inseparable subassemblies.

- When SolidWorks weldments result in a single multi-body part.

- When features require tool bodies, such as the Indent feature.

- When the Mold tools result in a single multi-body part representing the plastic part and the major mold components.

If you are administering a SolidWorks installation of multiple users, then you may be looking for a "bright line" test to clearly define for users which types of multi-body modeling are allowable and which are not. So many possibilities exist that it is difficult to say definitively what really *should not* be done, but here is a short list that you can modify for your needs:

- Do not use multi-body modeling simply to avoid making an assembly — you must be able to cite a specific reason for using the technique.

- Do not leave a part in a multi-body state that should be joined together into a single body.

- Hiding a body is sometimes appropriate, and deleting a body is sometimes appropriate — understand the difference.

Okay, the lecture is over. The message that you should take from all of that is not to use multi-body techniques just because you can; you must have a reason for it. I do not say this because I am the *design police*; I say this because it is the criterion that I use for my own modeling, what I would like to see in models that I inherit from other SolidWorks users, and a philosophy that will serve you well if you are conscientious about it.

Understanding Multi-body Techniques

To complicate the issue somewhat, nearly all surface modeling is also multi-body modeling. In this chapter, I am referring to solids, unless I specifically state otherwise. Surface bodies are discussed in Chapter 27.

Multi-body techniques cover a wide range of functionality, and as soon as someone creates a list of what you can do with them, someone else will come up with a new technique. Still, here is a short list of techniques where multi-body functionality makes things either easier or simply possible:

- Complex shapes across multiple parts
- Tool bodies/Boolean operations
- Local operations
- Patterning
- Simplifying very complex parts
- As a bridge between solids
- Undetermined manufacturing methods
- Manipulating imported geometry

In the remainder of this chapter, I illustrate each technique using an example model, and discuss the positives and negatives of each technique.

Complex shapes across bodies

When creating a part such as a computer mouse, you encounter complex shapes that span several parts. It makes the most sense to model the entire shape as a single part, and then to break it up into separate bodies, making parts from the bodies, adding detail to individual piece parts, and then bringing the parts back together as an assembly.

CROSS-REF This method also uses the Master Model techniques discussed in Chapter 28.

A part that uses this technique is shown in Figure 26.1. This part seems to contradict what I said earlier about not being able to use exploded views with multi-body parts, but this part uses the Move/Copy Bodies feature to move bodies within the part. This function remains in the part as a history-based feature in the FeatureManager and is much more labor-intensive to create than an assembly exploded view because each body is moved by a separate feature.

FIGURE 26.1

A multi-body part with a complex shape across bodies

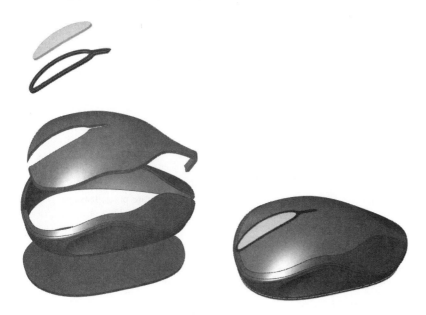

The part shown in Figure 26.1 is not complete, but the starting point for each part has been formed. This part was created from surface features that are discussed in detail in Chapter 27. The part is named `Chapter 26 – Mouse Base Part.SLDPRT` and is located on the CD-ROM. You may find it interesting to open the part to see how it has been modeled.

From here, each body is saved out to individual parts to complete the detailing, and then the parts are brought back together to create an assembly. The separate bodies in this case were created using the Split feature, which enables you to use surfaces or sketches to split a single body into multiple bodies. This is described in more detail later in this chapter.

The entire process for creating a finished assembly of finished parts is detailed in Figure 26.2. This flow chart shows conceptually how the overall shape created as a single part has moved from a single part/single body to a single part/multiple body to individual parts to an assembly of individual parts.

The image to the left in Figure 26.3 depicts how this part was modeled. The first step was to create the shape as a single body within the part. As shown in the FeatureManager, this is all contained inside the Overall Shape Features folder. This folder is presented here as a *black box* because surface features were used to create the part, and these features are not discussed until Chapter 27.

FIGURE 26.2

Master Model workflow

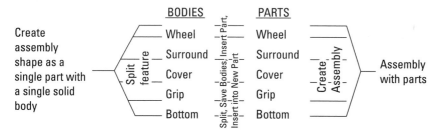

The image to the right in Figure 26.3 shows transparent surface bodies that were used to split the model into separate bodies using the Split features shown in the tree. Using this technique, you can create the overall shape as a single piece and then split it into separate parts. It is also possible to apply this technique in the context of an assembly, but this method is far more direct.

FIGURE 26.3

Splitting the part into bodies

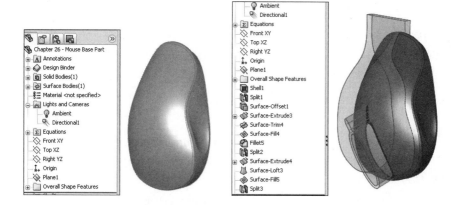

To go from the multi-body part created here to a set of separate parts uses a Master Model function, which is described in Chapter 28.

Tool bodies and Boolean operations

Some features require multiple bodies within a part, such as the Indent and Combine features, among others. Using one body to create a shape in another is a common use for bodies within a part.

Indent feature

The Indent feature was covered briefly in Chapter 7 before multi-bodies were introduced, and so it is fitting that I revisit it here so that the multi-body aspect of its use is better understood. The Indent feature *indents* the *target* body with the *tool* body. It can also use another part in the context of an assembly as the tool. The indentation can exactly fit the form of the tool, or there can be a gap around the tool. You can also control the thickness of the material around the indent. A further option is to simply cut the target with the tool instead of indenting.

Figure 26.4 shows the target part as transparent, and the tool as opaque, before and after the Indent feature has been applied. The Indent PropertyManager is also shown.

ON the CD-ROM To take a closer look at this part and the Indent feature, look at the part on the CD-ROM named `Chapter 26 - Indent Part.SLDPRT`.

FIGURE 26.4

The Indent feature using a tool body

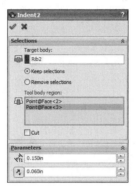

The Indent feature can be problematic if it breaks into multiple areas as it does in this part, due to the ribbing on the underside of the target body. Notice that in the PropertyManager in Figure 26.4, two selections were made in the Tool Body Region selection box. The tool body is selected on either side of the rib that bisects the tool. This concept is not very intuitive, and you may have to play with the part and the options to understand what it is doing.

The Keep Selections and Remove Selections options are equally unintuitive, but they determine which side of the target body is indented. For example, if the part of the tool body that is outside of the target body (flat side) were selected instead of the two inside regions, then the resulting part would look as it does in Figure 26.5, where the tool body has been hidden. You can achieve the same result by toggling the Keep selections and Remove selections options. These options exist because sometimes it is difficult or impossible to select the correct areas of a body that is embedded in another body.

FIGURE 26.5

Using the Keep and Remove selections options

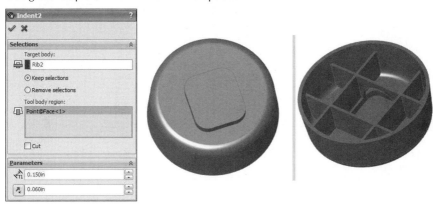

> **TIP** Also notice that toggling the Keep and Remove selections options means that only one region of the tool body would need to be selected to create the original result shown in Figure 26.4.

Move/Copy Bodies and Combine features

 The Move/Copy Bodies and Combine features can be demonstrated using the same part. The body that was used in the previous example to indent the main body is moved and then added to the main body in this example.

 Figure 26.6 shows the starting and ending points of the process, as well as the PropertyManagers of the two features used to get from one point to the other. Keep in mind that both the Move/Copy Bodies and the Combine features are history-based features listed in the FeatureManager.

FIGURE 26.6

Using the Move/Copy Bodies and Combine features

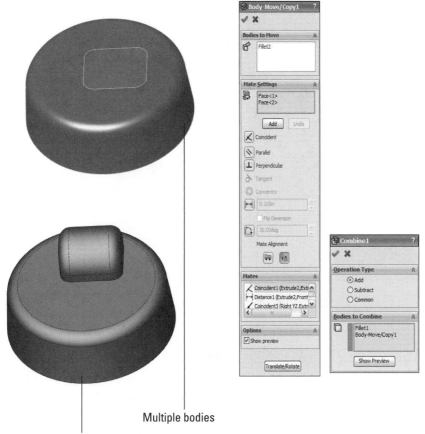

Multiple bodies

Repositioned and combined into a single body

In this case, the Move/Copy Bodies feature uses mates. These mates enable you to locate bodies in a way similar to the way they are used in assemblies. One important difference is that with bodies, you must use the actual body geometry of the body that is moving; you cannot use reference geometry such as planes. By clicking the Translate/Rotate button at the bottom of the PropertyManager, you can also position bodies using distances and angles.

By looking at the Combine PropertyManager, you will notice that common Boolean operations, such as union (add), difference (subtract), and intersection (common), are available through this interface.

> **TIP** You can use an interesting technique in this part. The features creating the smaller tool body and the Move/Copy Bodies and Combine features can be put together into a folder, and the folder itself reordered before the Shell feature. This means that the combined body is also shelled out, and the rib goes down inside of it. This produces an odd error message and unexpectedly places several features into the folder, but it does work.

You may want to open this part in SolidWorks to see exactly how all of this was done instead of relying on the figure illustrations. The part used for Figure 26.7 is on the CD-ROM and is named `Chapter 26 - Move Body.sldprt`.

FIGURE 26.7

Reordering features

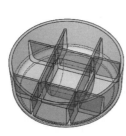

Local operations

If you have ever had a modeling situation where you needed to shell out a portion of a part but not the entire part, or you had a fillet that would work if only certain geometry were not there, then you may have been able to benefit from multi-body techniques to accomplish these tasks.

Flex feature

The part shown in Figure 26.8 first appears in Chapter 7, where I demonstrate the Flex feature. This is a rubber plug for an electronic device. In order to make one side of the part flex without flexing the other side, multiple bodies were used. The part was split into two bodies using the Split feature and a plane. One side of the part was then twisted, and the two bodies were combined back together. The Features folder contains the features that were used to build the original part geometry, which could just as easily have been either native or imported.

FIGURE 26.8

Splitting a part to perform a local operation

Shell feature

The Shell feature hollows out one solid body in a part at a time. If there are multiple solid bodies, then you must select one to be shelled. Any face of the solid that you select will be removed during the shelling. You can select a body without selecting a face by using the small Solid Body selection box under the larger Faces To Remove selection box in the PropertyManager. If you do not select any faces to be removed, then the body will be hollowed out with no external indication that the part is hollow, unless you view it in section view, transparency view, or wireframe view. Single or multiple faces can be removed. This feature works by offsetting the faces of the outside of the model, and the feature may fail if this causes problems with the internal geometry.

The Multithickness Shell option enables you to select faces that will have a different thickness from the overall shell thickness. This is one method that you can sometimes use to limit the scope of the Shell feature to a certain area of a body, but it is somewhat limited. Faces with different thicknesses cannot be tangent to one another.

I could say a lot more about creating and troubleshooting the Shell feature, but I am discussing it here mainly to show another local operation that can be handled using multi-body parts.

Because the Shell feature only works on one body at a time, splitting a part into multiple bodies can be an effective way to limit the scope of the feature. The part shown in Figure 26.9 has been split in half, and one-half has been made transparent for visualization purposes; as a result, you can see that the part is shelled on the bottom on one end and on the top on the other end. The Shell feature has no option for doing this with existing geometry. The only ways that you can do this are either through feature order or by using multi-bodies. You can find the part shown in Figure 26.9 on the CD-ROM with the name Chapter 26 – LocalOps Shell.sldprt.

FIGURE 26.9

Shelling locally

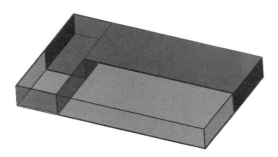

To shell the part this way with feature order, you create one block and shell it, and then create the other block and shell that. In order for this technique to work, the second shell needs to be as big as, or bigger than, the first shell. If it is smaller, then it will (or may) hollow out areas that are not intended to be hollow.

To shell the part with multi-bodies, you can use two methods. One method is to build the first block, and then build the second block, but to turn off the Merge option. This creates bodies that are side by side. You then shell one block on the bottom and the other on the top. To avoid a double-thickness wall between them, the end face can be removed along with either the top or bottom face. If you edit the part, then you may notice that one of the Shell features has two faces removed.

The second method is to build a single block, then split it using a sketch line, a plane, or a surface, and then proceed in the same way as the first method.

Patterning

Patterns of bodies are fast, powerful, and commonly used alternatives to patterning features. Chapter 8 discusses feature patterns and mirroring, and examines, at least in part, how different types of patterns affect model rebuild speeds. When appropriate, patterning bodies can also be a big rebuild time saver. When patterning a body, none of the parametrics or intelligence is patterned with it, but you must pattern the entire body. Another odd thing about patterning bodies in SolidWorks is that there is no option to join the bodies either to one another or to a main body. This requires an extra step that involves adding a Combine feature. Mirroring is the same, except that it does have an option to merge bodies, but it only merges the original body to the mirrored body. It will not merge either the original or the mirrored body to a central main body.

In this example, an imported part has a "feature" that needs to be reused around the part. The technique used here is to split away the feature as a separate body and then pattern the body around the part and join it all back together. This function can be used with native geometry as well as imported. This process is shown in Figure 26.10. This function does use a simple planar surface. A plane could have been used to split off the body to be patterned, but the plane would have also split off a part of the globe at the top, so a planar surface (which can be limited in extent where a plane can not) was used.

The image on the left in Figure 26.10 is the raw imported part. The middle image shows a planar surface created on the face of the part, where the planar surface has been used with the Split feature to cut the leg off of the part. The image on the right shows the split leg patterned around an axis that was created from the intersection of two planes.

FIGURE 26.10

Splitting away a body and patterning it

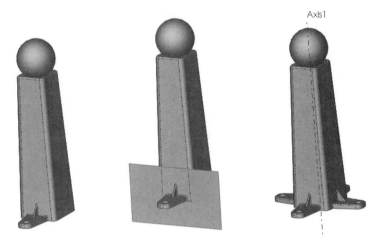

If you would like to practice with this part, it is on the CD-ROM for Chapter 26; the imported Parasolid file is named Chapter 26 - Pattern import.x_t.

PERFORMANCE In some situations, patterning bodies is a performance advantage, and in some situations it is not. You get an advantage from patterning bodies when the geometry used to create the pattern seed is complex, uses many features, or does not work or does not work well for a feature pattern.

On the other hand, if you repeat the experiments from Chapter 8 using a small body with a hole in it instead of patterning a hole feature, you find that the body pattern is far slower than the feature patterning.

Simplifying very complex parts

Certain types of parts lend themselves very well to being built in sections. For very complex parts with a lot of features, this sometimes makes sense from the point of view of segmenting the rebuild times for parts with hundreds of features. The example used to demonstrate this technique is a large plastic part built entirely from ribs, and making use of literally hundreds of solid bodies, and is shown in Figure 26.11 and Figure 26.12.

This part is molded using tooling pulls in five directions. Two of these directions are symmetrical, and the core block pulls in a single direction; as a result, in the end, the modeling has to account for three directions.

The rebuild time for a model like this can easily reach several minutes, depending on your hardware. To minimize the rebuild time, a different workflow was established for this part. First, the major inside and outside faces were created with surfaces. Next, the surfaces were saved into several other parts (using Master Model techniques that are discussed in Chapter 28). Each of these parts represents the part geometry that will pull in a particular direction from the mold. Enough information exists in the Master Model to align the features in each part.

The ribs on this part were created by making a single extrusion (the Rib feature could not be used because there was no geometry to serve as a boundary for the ribs), and then the extrusion was patterned and the pattern was mirrored. After all of the ribs were created, they had to be shaped, and so the surfaces from the Master Model were used to cut the ribs to shape.

The ribs could not be extruded with a draft or with fillets because the outer and inner surfaces were non-planar. The draft had to be built as a Parting Line draft for the same reason, and the fillets had to be applied after the draft. Further, draft and fillets can only be applied to a single body at a time; as a result, a separate draft feature and a separate fillet feature had to be applied to each body, and each rib was a separate body. Once the draft and fillets were applied, the bodies were joined into a single body.

I recognize that this description of how I made the part is a lot to follow. The point is not to show in detail how the parts were built, but to demonstrate how you can get to a part with 1200 features or more. It is precisely on parts with this level of complexity that you need to think about modeling the part in this modular fashion — build each part separately and bring each separate section of the part together as individual bodies.

Figure 26.11 shows two of the separate pull direction parts being separated from one another in the same way that the mouse part was shown exploded in the previous example. Here the frame is also modeled as a separate part, again because it was not so intimately related to the other parts, and was easily separated out.

Once this was complete for each direction, the separate parts were put together as bodies into a single part and again joined together using the Combine feature. Having all of those features in separate parts enables you to segment the rebuild time. This is the opposite of building all of the parts of an assembly in a single part, where you are simply compounding your rebuild time. Figure 26.12 shows bodies joined together as a single body.

FIGURE 26.11

A complex model created as separate parts and brought together as bodies in a single part

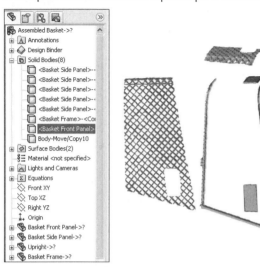

FIGURE 26.12

Bodies all joined together as a single body

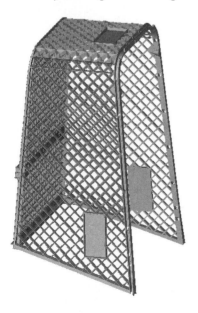

This is probably a technique that you will not use very often, but when you do, it can save you a lot of rebuild time. I use it whenever I have a model that takes more than 20 to 30 seconds to rebuild and I know that I am going to be working on it a lot; it must also lend itself to segmenting in the way that this one did.

Bridge between solids

Often when modeling, you "build what you know" and "fill in as you go." An example of this would be modeling a duct between end connections that are well defined. The duct in between is defined only by the ends, which must exist first. Another example is a connecting rod where you know the diameter of each end and the distance between the ends, and the connection between them is of secondary importance.

Figure 26.13 shows a connecting rod made in this way. In this case, the bearing seat at one end was created, and the other end was created by copying the body of the first one. From there, the link between bearing seats was created, which joined the separate bodies together into a single solid body.

FIGURE 26.13

Connecting disjoint bodies

This part contains some interesting features. First is the Thin Feature extrude that is used to make the first bearing seat, which is combined with a Mid-plane extrude to make it symmetrical at the same time. Then comes the Move/Copy Bodies feature, which copies the body in the same way that the feature in previous examples has moved bodies. Next is the use of the Extrude From option, which extrudes from a face, and then the end condition Up To Next ends the feature neatly. The part also incorporates fillets that use faces and features to form the selection.

If you are not familiar with these options, then I recommend that you open up the part from the CD-ROM and have a look at it. It is a simple part that takes advantage of nice but simple productivity-enhancing options that have been available for some time in the SolidWorks software. The part filename is `Chapter 26 - Bridge.sldprt`.

By default, Solid features have the Merge option turned on, and they automatically combine with any bodies that they touch. At the same time, they do not display errors if the Merge option is on but the new body does not touch any existing bodies.

Undetermined manufacturing methods

Sometimes you must start a design before you know exactly how the product will be manufactured. This is an example of where the geometry of the finished product exists first and is then broken up into manufacturable parts. The initial model, shown in the image at the top in Figure 26.14, is created as a single part as a result of input from marketing, but when it comes time for manufacturing input, the part count and processes keep changing. Where the parts break from one another keeps changing as well. When that kind of change is happening, having the parts created as individual parts is a big liability because it is difficult to change. Changing which bodies are merged together is much easier.

FIGURE 26.14

A towel rack, modeled as a single part, and broken into individual parts in an assembly

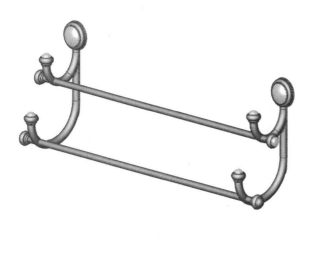

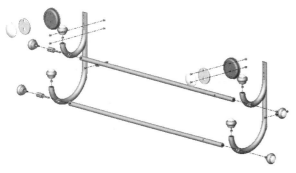

It is worth mentioning two potential difficulties that you may run into with methods like this. The first is that if you have people making drawings from parts that have been derived from bodies in a single part, then they are forced into the Reference Dimension scheme of dimensioning parts because the feature dimensions do not survive being moved from the multi-body part. This may or may not be an issue, depending on how the people doing the drawings are accustomed to working.

The second potential issue is what you do in situations where there are multiple instances of a part that has been modeled this way. If you notice the towel rack in Figure 26.14, there are several finials, spacers, rails, and other parts that are duplicated. This requires some manual assembly modeling. You can make the assembly directly from the multi-body part, but if you need to make multiple instances of particular parts, then you need to do this manually rather than automatically.

Creating Multi-bodies

In the first section in this chapter, I raised the questions of *if* or *when* multi-bodies should be used, and in the second section, I raised the question of *why* multi-bodies should be used. In this section, I simply ask, or rather answer, *how* they should be used.

Disjoint sketches

The easiest way to create multiple bodies is to simply create what SolidWorks classifies as multiple disjoint closed contours. What that means is simply two circles or rectangles that do not touch or overlap. If these are created in the same sketch, then when extruded, they will create as many bodies as there are closed loops in the sketch.

If the part has an existing solid, then creating a sketch that does not touch the solid can also create a separate body. You cannot make Multiple Thin features in a single sketch. This is presumably because the interface has no way to identify different thickness directions for different open profiles. This holds true whether or not the Multiple Thin features create multiple bodies.

If a solid feature other than a mirror or pattern touches a solid body, then the new and the old bodies will be merged into a single body.

Merge Result option

You can prevent a feature from automatically combining with other bodies by turning off the Merge Result option. This holds true between features, but not across all bodies in a part. For example, if an extrude feature uses the Merge Result option, all of the bodies that it touches become merged together, but if the original extrude feature does not touch a body, it will not be merged. This option is shown in Figure 26.15 and is found on all features that create new solid bodies except for the Patterns, Rib, and Move/Copy Bodies features.

FIGURE 26.15

The Merge Result option

Feature Scope

The Feature Scope used for multi-bodies is not the same as the Feature Scope used for assembly features, but it does function in a similar way. In assemblies, the Feature Scope identifies which parts are affected by the current assembly feature. In parts, it only applies to bodies, and can be used for features that add material as well as features that remove material (assembly features can only remove material).

The Feature Scope is a way to make the Merge Result option more selective. The Merge Result option by default does not discriminate; it causes the feature to merge with any other solid body that it touches. However, the Feature Scope enables the user to select which bodies to either merge with or otherwise affect. Feature Scope also applies to additional feature types such as cuts. The Feature Scope becomes available in the PropertyManager whenever there are multiple bodies in the part and an eligible feature is used. The Feature Scope panel is shown in Figure 26.16.

FIGURE 26.16

The Feature Scope panel

The default setting for the Feature Scope is to use the Selected Bodies option with the Auto-select option. The All Bodies option is essentially the same as using the Merge Result option. When the Selected Bodies option is on and Auto-select is off, as is shown in Figure 26.16, you must select bodies for the current feature to affect them. New bodies that are added to the model are not automatically added to the list; you need to manually edit the feature and add additional bodies to the list as appropriate.

Rib feature

The Rib feature is hypersensitive to the presence of multiple bodies; more precisely, it is sensitive to the *change* in the number of bodies. A rib only automatically merges with a body if it is the only body in the part. If a rib is created in a single body part and then the model is rolled back and an additional body is created before the rib, then the Rib feature will fail when the tree is unrolled. The error that this causes reads, "The rib is not bounded properly. The extension of the rib does not intersect the part model." Technically speaking, this is true, but like other SolidWorks error messages, that does not make it helpful. The cause of the error is that suddenly the body that the rib is supposed to merge with is no longer identified. The Rib feature has no Auto-select option. You can fix this problem by going to the Feature Scope in the Rib PropertyManager to select a body for it to merge with. The Rib feature does not use the normal Feature Scope, because the Feature Scope is intended to select multiple bodies, and the Rib feature requires a single body. There is a simple Selected Body box in the Rib PropertyManager.

After you have selected the target body, deleting the new bodies that caused the problem in the first place, thankfully, does not make the problem reoccur. However, if the body that the rib is merged with is split using the Split feature, then that *does* cause a problem. As a result, the two things that cause the Rib feature problem are rolling back and either adding bodies or splitting the body to be ribbed.

Delete Body feature

If you have created many ribs in a casting or plastic part, then it may be tedious to go through and repair them all every time the body count changes. This sort of thing happens even if the other body is just a reference body or an unused leftover.

In cases like this, you can use the Delete Body feature. Delete Body removes the body from the body folder (discussed in the Body Folders section). This is a *history-based delete*, which means that before the Delete Body feature in the tree, the body exists, and after the Delete Body feature in the tree, the body does not exist. This feature has no effect on file size, because the data for the body must still exist, and it has little, if any, effect on rebuild time. What is happening is that the body is still there; you just cannot see it and have no access to it.

Delete Body is often used for other purposes as well, primarily to clean up a model at the end of the tree. The reasoning is that multiple bodies in a part confuse people. My view on this is that if multiple bodies confuse people, then just think what a *feature* called *Delete Bodies* does for them. In either case, they have a bit to learn. My recommendation here is to remove bodies if they are getting in the way, either for a hyper-sensitive feature like the Rib feature or if they are causing visualization problems.

Cut feature

A Cut feature may create multi-bodies, either intentionally or unintentionally. When it does happen, the Bodies to Keep dialog box appears to enable you to select which bodies you intend to keep. The Bodies to Keep dialog box is shown in Figure 26.17. This dialog box was formerly called Resolve Ambiguity, which was not as descriptive as Bodies to Keep.

FIGURE 26.17

The Bodies to Keep dialog box

Notice that the Bodies to Keep settings are also configurable, and so different bodies can be kept in different configurations, which is very useful.

Split feature

The Split feature has essentially three functions:

- To split a single solid body into multiple solid bodies using planes, sketches, or surface bodies

- To save individual solid bodies out to individual part files

- To reassemble individual part files that are saved out into an assembly where the parts are all positioned in the same relative position as their corresponding bodies

The last two functions of the Split feature are addressed in Chapter 28. The part of the Split feature that concerns this chapter is the first function mentioned, which is splitting a single solid body into multiple bodies using a sketch, a plane, or a surface body.

The Split feature can not be used to split surface bodies. In fact, nothing in SolidWorks can split surface bodies. Only solid bodies can be split. This seems like a functionality oversight, and would make a great enhancement request if you have ever come across the need for this functionality.

Splitting with a sketch

When using a sketch to split a single solid body into multiple bodies, the Split process works like this:

1. **Create a sketch with an open or closed loop; even a mixture of open and closed profiles will work.** If it is open, then the endpoints have to either be on an exterior edge or hanging off into space; they cannot actually be inside the boundaries of the solid.

2. **Initiate the Split feature from the Features toolbar or from the menus at Insert ➪ Features ➪ Split.** You can do this with the sketch active, with the sketch inactive but selected, or with nothing selected at all.

3. **Click the Cut Part button.** This does not actually cut anything; it only previews the split. When this is done, the resulting bodies appear in the window below, and callout flags are placed on the part in the graphics window. These flags are often useless because they tend to point to the borders between two different bodies in such a way that it is completely ambiguous as to which body they are indicating. However, in the example shown in Figure 26.18, the result is very clear.

Check marks next to the body in the list indicate that the body will be split out. The lack of a check mark does not necessarily mean anything. For example, in Figure 26.18, notice that two boxes are checked, but this will result in a total of four bodies. If only Body 1 were selected, then the result would be only two bodies.

The callout flags and the bodies list where <None> is shown are looking for a path and filename to save the body out to a file. Again, this functionality is covered in Chapter 28 with the Master Model information.

The Save All Bodies button simply puts check marks in all of the boxes. If the Resulting Bodies box contains more than ten bodies, then the interface changes slightly, as shown in the image to the right in Figure 26.18. The Consume cut bodies option removes, or consumes, any of the bodies that have a check mark.

Splitting with a plane

Splitting with a plane gives the same type of results and uses the same options as splitting with a sketch. However, you never have to worry about the plane being extended far enough, because the cut is made from the infinite planar extension of the plane. The only thing you have to worry about with a plane is whether it intersects the part.

FIGURE 26.18

Using the Split feature

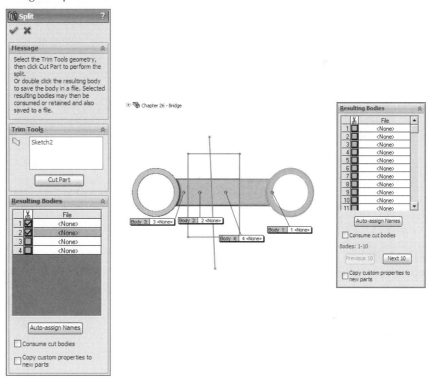

Splitting with a surface body

Surface bodies are used to split solid bodies for a couple of reasons. In the part shown in Figure 26.10, a surface body was used to make the split instead of a sketch or a plane, because both of those entities split everything in an infinite distance either normal to the sketch plane or in the selected plane. A surface body only splits to the extents of the splitting surface body. If you look closely at the part, you will notice that a plane or sketch would lop off one side of the sphere on top of the object, but the small planar surface is limited enough in size to only split what is necessary.

Another advantage to using a surface body is that it is not limited to a two-dimensional cut. The surface itself can be any type of surface, such as planar, extruded, revolved, lofted, or imported. Taking this a step further, the surface is not limited to being a single face, or a body resulting from a single feature; it could be made from several features that are put together as long as it is a single body and all of the outer edges of the surface body are outside the solid body. If you examine the mouse part shown in Figure 26.1, you will notice that it has splits made from multi-feature surface bodies.

I mention splitting with surface bodies here because this is where I discuss the Split function, even though I haven't covered the surfacing functions yet. It may be useful to read parts of this book out of order; because of the interrelatedness of all of the topics, it is impossible to order the topics in such a way that nothing ever refers to a topic that has not yet been covered.

 For more information about surface bodies, see Chapter 27.

Insert Part feature

 The Insert Part button can be found on the Features toolbar, or you can access this feature through the menus at Insert ⇨ Part.

Insert Part enables you to insert one part into another part. When inserting the part, you have the option to insert solid bodies, axes, planes, cosmetic threads, surface bodies and several other types of entities including sketches and features. The PropertyManager interface for the Insert Part feature is shown in Figure 26.19.

FIGURE 26.19

The Insert Part PropertyManager

This feature has two major functions: inserting a body as the starting point for a new part, and inserting a body to be used as a tool to modify an existing part. Notice that the basket part shown in Figure 26.11 and Figure 26.12 also uses Insert Part to put together bodies to form a finished part.

When you use Insert Part, there is no Insert Part feature that becomes part of the tree. Instead, a part icon is shown with the name of the part being inserted as a feature.

Also notice in Figure 26.19 that the Launch move dialog option appears at the bottom, and is on by default. This option launches the Move dialog box after you insert the part. This Move feature is the same as the Move/Copy Bodies feature, with the same options (translate or rotate by distance or angles, or use assembly-like mates to position bodies).

Insert Part is used in many situations, some of which are covered in Chapters 11 and 28 in the sections on Skeleton techniques and Master Model.

Secondary operations

One commonly used technique has to do with secondary operations. For example, you may have designed a casting that needs several machining operations after it comes from the foundry. The foundry needs a drawing to produce the raw casting, and the machine shop needs a different drawing to ream and tap holes, spot face areas, and so on.

Although you can use configurations to do this, using Insert Part is another way. This has nothing to do with multiple body techniques, but this is the only place where Insert Part is covered in much detail. One of the advantages of using Insert Part is that you no longer carry around the overhead of all of the features in the parent part. It is as if the inserted part were imported. The configurations method forces you to carry around much more feature overhead. Of course, the downside is that now there is an additional file to manage, but this can be an advantage because many companies assign different part numbers to parts before and after secondary operations.

Starting point

Looking back to the mouse shown in Figure 26.1, the main part has been split into several bodies. You can use Insert Part to insert the whole mouse into a new part where all of the bodies except one are deleted, and then the remaining body serves as the starting point for a new part. Many additional features are needed on all of the bodies that make up the mouse, such as assembly features, cosmetic features, functional features, and manufacturing features.

Managing Bodies

Managing bodies in SolidWorks is not as clean a task as managing parts in an assembly. As you work with bodies, you will discover some real surprises in how bodies are managed. Hopefully in this section, I can prepare you for some of the more problematic surprises.

Body folders

The top of the FeatureManager includes a pair of folders, one called Solid Bodies, and the other called Surface Bodies. These folders are only there if you have solids or surfaces in the model, and they reflect the state of the model at the current position of the Rollback bar. As a result, the folders can change and even disappear as you roll the tree back and forth in history. Figure 26.20 shows the top of a FeatureManager that has both solid and surface body folders. Notice that the number in parentheses after the name of the folder shows how many bodies are in that particular folder.

FIGURE 26.20

Body folders in the FeatureManager

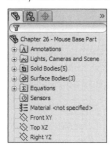

An odd fact about these folders is that you are allowed to rename the folders, but the name changes never remain. If you go back to rename the folder again, the name that you assigned is displayed; you cannot name another feature with the name that you assigned, but it is never displayed as the name of the folder.

Another problem that you may encounter with the display of FeatureManager header items in general is that when they are set to Automatic display (display only when they contain something). This does not guarantee that the folder is going to display when it should. A more direct way of saying this is that the Automatic setting works incorrectly from time to time. For this reason, I suggest using the Show option for the display of important folders. Figure 26.21 shows the page of Tools ⇨ Options that controls the visibility of folders.

By right-clicking either of the bodies folders, you can select the Show Feature History option, which shows the features that have combined to create the bodies in an indented list under the body name. This view of the FeatureManager is shown in Figure 26.22. This option is very useful when you are editing or troubleshooting bodies.

Figure 26.22 also shows the other options in the right-mouse button menu. All of the bodies in the folder can be alternately shown or hidden from this menu, as well as deleted. While the Hide or Show state of a body does not create a history-based feature in the tree, the Delete feature does, as discussed previously.

FIGURE 26.21

FIGURE 26.21

Control the visibility of FeatureManager items

FIGURE 26.22

Using the Show Feature History option

The Insert into New Part feature and the Save Bodies feature seen in this menu are discussed in Chapter 28.

You can expand the Display pane in parts, in order to show display information for bodies. In Figure 26.23, the Display pane shows the colors assigned to the solid bodies, as well as the fact that several surface bodies exist but are hidden.

FIGURE 26.23

The Display pane showing information about solid and surface bodies

The folders also make bodies easier to identify, especially when combined with the setting found at Tools ➪ Options ➪ Display/Selection ➪ Dynamic Highlight From Graphics View. This setting quickly turns the body outline red if you move the mouse over the body in the body folder.

Hide or show bodies

You can hide or show bodies in one of several ways. I have already described the method of using the bodies folders to hide or show all of the bodies at once, but you can also right-click individual bodies in the folders to hide or show from there as well. Remember that with the Context bars, you have the option to use context bars with the right-mouse button menu or not, and also context bars with left click selections. I include all context bar options in the right-mouse button menu generically.

if you can see a body in the graphics area, then you can right-click the body and select Hide under the Body heading. This works for both solids and surfaces. The Display Pane, shown to the right of the FeatureManager in Figure 26.23, can also be used to hide or show bodies, change body transparency and appearance, as well as change the display mode of bodies. Display Pane is a handy tool for visualization options.

When you are hiding or showing bodies from the FeatureManager, and not using the bodies folders, but rather using the features themselves, things get a little complicated. If you want to hide or show a solid body, then you can use any feature that is a parent of the body to hide or show the body. For example, you can use the Shell feature in the mouse model to hide or show all of the bodies of which it is a parent.

Other facts that you need to know about bodies and their hide or show states are that the Hide or Show feature is both configurable and dependent on the rollback state. As a result, if you hide a body, and then roll back, it may appear again, and you will have to hide it. Then, if you roll forward, the state changes again. Also, a body can be hidden in one configuration, and then when you switch configurations, it remains hidden. This makes it rather frustrating to work with bodies. To me, it would be nice if bodies had simple on/off toggles that were neither intelligent nor tricky.

CAUTION Some features exclude bodies if the bodies are hidden when you edit the feature. Be careful of this, and be sure to show all of the bodies that are used in a particular function before you edit it. For example, if a body is hidden, and you create a new extrude that touches the hidden body, then the new body does not merge with the hidden one *even if the Merge option is on*. If the hidden body is then shown and you edit the second body, then the bodies will merge upon the closing of the second body.

Deleting bodies

I have already mentioned that you can delete bodies using the Delete Bodies feature, and that this feature sits in the tree at a specific point in the history of the part.

Delete Bodies does not affect file size or rebuild speed. In fact, I find it difficult to come up with examples of when you should use it, other than the situation already mentioned with the Rib feature, or if a throwaway body somehow remains in the part. Some people use this feature to clean up the organization of the tree, which could be useful if there are many bodies in the part. Other users insist on keeping the tree free of extraneous bodies, and so they immediately delete bodies that have been used. To me, this technique replaces one kind of clutter with another, and means that tools that should be available to you (solid or surface bodies) are not available unless you reorder the Delete Body feature down the tree and/or roll back. In any case, this is really a matter of personal working style and not of any great importance.

Renaming bodies

Notice that the bodies that you see in the folders have been named for the last feature that touched a given body. That naming scheme is as good as any, except that it means that the body keeps changing names. If you deliberately rename a body, it will retain the name through future changes. You should follow the same rules of thumb for naming bodies as you do for naming features.

Tutorials: Working with Multi-bodies

This tutorial contains various short examples of multi-body techniques in order from easy to more difficult.

Merging and local operations

This tutorial gives you some experience using the Merge Result option and using features on individual bodies to demonstrate the local operations functionality of multi-body modeling. Try these steps:

1. **Start a new part, and sketch a rectangle centered on the origin on the Top plane.** Size is not important for this exercise.

2. **Extrude the rectangle to roughly one-third of its smaller dimension.**

3. **Open a second sketch on the Top plane.** Hide the first solid body by right-clicking it in either the FeatureManager or the graphics window.

4. **Show the sketch for the first feature, and draw a second rectangle on the far side of the rectangle from the Origin.** Make sure that the second rectangle gets two coincident relations to the first sketch, at two corners so that the rectangles are the same width. When the sketch is complete, hide the sketch that was shown.

5. **Extrude the second rectangle to about two-thirds of the depth of the first rectangle.**

> **NOTE**   Notice that the Merge option was not changed from the default setting of On for the second extrude, but because the first extrude was hidden, the second extrude did not merge with it. Be careful of subsequent edits to either of the features if the first body is shown, because this may cause the bodies to merge unexpectedly. In this tutorial, the bodies are later merged intentionally. Ideally, what you should do is deselect the Merge option of the second extrude.

6. **Shell out the second extrusion by removing two adjacent sides, as shown in Figure 26.24.** One of the sides is the top and the other is the shared side with the hidden body. The body that should be hidden at this point is shown as transparent in the image for reference only. The body was made transparent to make it easier to select the face of the second body.

FIGURE 26.24

Shelling two sides of a block

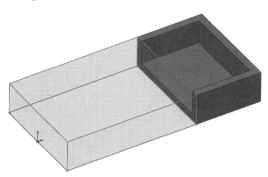

7. **Show the first body either from the Solid Bodies folder at the top of the tree or from the right-mouse button menu of the first solid feature in the tree.**

8. **Shell the bottom side of the first body, so that the cavities in the two bodies are on opposite sides.**

9. **Combine the two bodies using the Combine tool found at Insert ⇨ Features ⇨ Combine.** This feature is also available via right-mouse button in the solid body folder. Select the Add option and select the two bodies. Click OK to finish the feature. Figure 26.25 shows the finished part.

FIGURE 26.25

The finished part

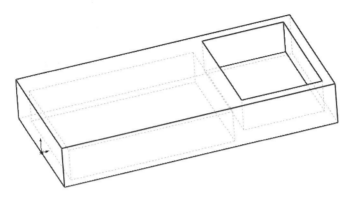

Splitting and patterning bodies

This tutorial guides you through the steps to delete a pattern of *features* from an imported body, separate one of the features, and then pattern it with a different number of features. This introduces some simple surface functions, in preparation for Chapter 27. Follow these steps:

1. **Open the Parasolid file from the CD-ROM called** Chapter 26 – Bonita Tutorial.x_t.

2. **Using the Selection Filter set to filter Face selection (the default hotkey for this is X), select all of the faces of the leg.** You can use window selection techniques to avoid clicking each face.

3. **Click the Delete Face button on the Surfaces toolbar, or access the command through the menus at Insert ⇨ Face ⇨ Delete.** Make sure that the Delete and Patch option is selected. The selected faces and the Delete Face PropertyManager should look like Figure 26.26. Click OK to accept the feature.

4. **Repeat the process for a second leg, leaving the third leg to be separated from the rest of the part and patterned.**

5. **After the two legs have been removed, click the outer main spherical surface, and then from the menus, select Insert ⇨ Surface ⇨ Offset. Set the offset distance to zero.** Notice that a Surface Bodies folder is now added to the tree, near the top.

 A zero distance offset surface is frequently used to copy faces.

6. **Hide the solid body.** You can do this from the Solid Bodies folder, from the FeatureManager, or from the graphics window.

FIGURE 26.26

The Delete Face PropertyManager

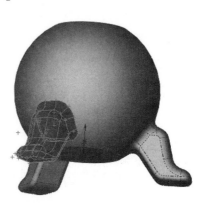

7. **Hiding the solid leaves the offset surface, and there should be three holes in it.** Select one of the edges of the hole indicated in Figure 26.27 and press the Delete key. The Choose Option dialog box appears. Select the Delete Hole option rather than the Delete Feature option. The Delete Hole operation becomes a history-based feature in the model tree. Before moving on to the next step, remember that you may need to turn off the Selection Filter for faces.

FIGURE 26.27

Using the Delete Hole option

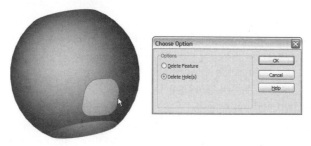

NOTE Delete Hole is really a surface feature called Untrim. Untrim is discussed more in Chapter 27, but you can use it to restore original boundaries to a surface.

8. **Once you delete the hole from the surface body, change the color of the surface body the same way you changed the colors of parts, faces, and features.**

9. **Click the surface body in the Surface Bodies folder and either press the Delete key, or select Delete Body from the right-mouse button menu. Then click OK to accept the feature. This places a Delete Body feature in the tree.** It keeps the body from getting in the way when it is not needed. This is not a necessary step, but many people choose to use it.

 **If you delete a body in this way and then need it later down the tree, you can delete, suppress, or reorder the Delete Body feature later in the tree.**

10. **Now show the solid body.** You will notice the color of the surface conflicting with the color of the solid. This mottled appearance is due to the small approximations made by the rendering and display algorithms.

11. **Initiate the Split feature through the menus at Insert ⇨ Features ⇨ Split, or on the Features toolbar.** Use the surface body to split the solid body. Click the Cut Part button, and select the check boxes in front of both bodies in the list. Click OK to accept the feature. Notice now that the Solid Bodies folder indicates that there are two solid bodies.

12. **From the View menu, turn on the display of Temporary Axes.** Initiate a Circular Pattern feature, selecting the temporary axis as the axis, and the split-off leg in the Bodies to Pattern selection box. Set it to four instances, as shown in Figure 26.28.

FIGURE 26.28

Patterning a body

13. **Use the Combine feature to add together all five bodies.** You can access this feature through the menus at Insert ⇨ Features ⇨ Combine.

Summary

Beginning to understand how to work with multiple bodies in SolidWorks opens a gateway to a new world of design possibilities. However, like anything else, not everything is perfect. Like in-context design, multi-body modeling is definitely something that you have to go into with your eyes open. You will experience difficulties when using this technique, but you will also find new possibilities that were not available with other techniques. The key to success with multi-bodies techniques is discipline and circumspection.

When using a model with the multi-body approach, make sure that you can identify a reason for doing it this way rather than using a more conventional approach. Also keep in mind the list of applications or uses for multi-body modeling mentioned in this chapter.

Chapter 27

Working with Surfaces

With Surface modeling you build a shape face by face. Faces made by surface features can be knit together to enclose a volume, which can become a solid. With solid modeling, you build all the faces to make the volume at the same time. In fact, solid modeling is really just highly automated surface modeling. Obviously there is more detail to it than that, but that definition will get you started.

You can drive a car without knowing how the engine works, but you cannot get the most power possible out of the car by only pressing harder on the gas pedal; you have to get under the hood and make adjustments. In a way, that is what working with surfaces is really all about – getting under the hood and tinkering with the underlying functionality.

The goal of most surface modeling is to finish with a solid. Some surface features make faces that will become faces of the solid, and some surface features only act as reference geometry. Surface modeling is inherently multi-body modeling, because most surface features do not merge bodies automatically.

Why Do You Need Surfaces?

In the end, you may never really *need* surfaces. It is possible to perform workarounds using solids to do most of the things that most users need to do. However, many of these workarounds are inefficient, cumbersome, and raise as many difficulties as they solve. Although you may not view some of the typical things you now do as inefficient and cumbersome, once you see the alternatives, you may change your mind. The goal for this chapter is to introduce surfacing functions to people who do not typically use surfaces, and to people who do everyday modeling. I am not trying to show how surfaces are used in the context of creating complex shapes, although you can use the same techniques, regardless of the complexity of the shape.

The word *surfacing* has often been used (and confused) synonymously with the creation of complex shapes. Not all surface work is done to create complex shapes, and many complex shapes can be made directly from solids. Many users think that because they do not make complex shapes, they never need to use surface features. This chapter shows mainly examples that are not complex shapes, in situations where surfaces make it easier, more efficient, or simply possible to do the necessary tasks.

While some of the uses of surfaces may not be immediately obvious, by the end of this chapter, you should have enough information and applications that you can start experimenting to increase your confidence.

Understanding Surfacing Terminology

When dealing with surfaces, you may hear different terminology than the terminology typically used with solid modeling. It is important to understand the terminology, which makes the techniques easier to understand. This special terminology also often exists for surfaces because of important conceptual differences between how solids and surfaces are handled.

These terms are fairly universal among all surfacing software. The underlying surface and solid construction concepts are generally uniform between the major software packages. What varies from software to software is how the user interacts with the geometry through the software interface. You may never see some of these terms in the SolidWorks menus, Help files, training books, or elsewhere, but it becomes obvious as you use the software that the concepts are relevant.

Knit

 Knit is analogous to the solid feature Combine in that it joins multiple surface bodies into a single surface body. Unlike Combine, Knit does not perform the subtract or intersect Boolean operations. It also has an option to create a solid if the resulting surface body meets the requirements (a fully enclosed volume without gaps or overlaps). However, unlike the solid bodies in Combine, which may overlap volumetrically, surface bodies must intersect edge to edge, more like sketch entities.

Knit is also sometimes used in the same way that the zero-distance offset is used, to copy a set of solid faces to become a new surface body.

One nice option that enables you to quickly see where the boundaries of a surface body lie is found at Tools ⇨ Options ⇨ Display/Selection ⇨ Show Open Edges Of Surfaces In Different Color. By default, this color is a medium blue, and you can change it at Tools ⇨ Options ⇨ Colors ⇨ Surfaces ⇨ Open Edges.

Trim

The Trim function in SolidWorks is analogous to the solid Cut. Trim simply creates an additional boundary for the surface. The underlying surface is defined by a two-dimensional mesh, and for this reason, it is usually four-sided, but may be other shapes. When the underlying surface is trimmed, the software still remembers the underlying shape, but combines it with the new boundary, which is typically how face shapes (especially non-four-sided shapes) are created.

Untrim

Untrim is predictably the opposite of Trim. All it does is remove the boundary from a surface. It can remove the boundary selectively (one edge at a time, interior edges only, and so on) or remove all the edges at once. Untrim even works on imported geometry, as described in the tutorial in Chapter 26. Figure 27.1 shows how Untrim works.

FIGURE 27.1

Untrimming a surface

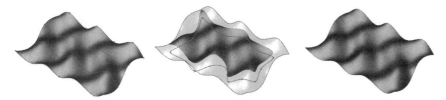

Untrim works on native and imported geometry. It is not truly like feature history in imported geometry, but it does help to uncover the underlying original shape of the face.

Hybrid modeling

Modeling software has long divided itself along Solid/Surface lines with products such as Rhino (strictly surface modeling) and early versions of SolidWorks (strictly solid modeling). However, in the last several years, modelers are increasingly enabling both methods and allowing them to interact. This hybrid modeling is a combination of solid and surface modeling. These days, it is much more common to mix methods than it was even five years ago. Surface modeling is slow because you model each face individually, and then manually trim and knit. Cutting a hole in a surface model is much more involved than cutting a hole in a solid. Solid modeling is faster because it is essentially highly automated surface modeling; however, as any software user knows, automation almost always comes at the expense of flexibility, and this situation is no different. Surface modeling puts the compromised power back into your hands.

Solid modeling tends to limit you to a type of parts with square ends or a flat bottom because solids are creating all sides of an object at once. For example, think about an extrusion: regardless of the shape of the rest of the feature, you have two flat ends. Even lofts and sweeps typically end up with one or two flat ends because the section sketches are often planar. Surfaces enable you to create one side at a time. Another way of looking at it is that using surfaces *requires* you to create one side at a time.

You will find times when, even with prismatic modeling, surfacing functions are extremely useful, if not completely indispensable. I do not propose that you dive into pure surface modeling just to benefit from a few of the advantages, but I do recommend that you consider using surface techniques to help define your solids. This hybrid approach is sensible and opens up a whole new world of capabilities. I have heard people say after taking a SolidWorks surfacing class that they would never look at the software in the same way again.

NURBS

NURBS stands for Non Uniform Rational B Spline. NURBS is the technology that most modern mechanical design modelers use to create face geometry. NURBS surfaces are defined by curves in perpendicular directions, referred to as U and V directions, which form a mesh. The fact that perpendicular directions are used means that the surfaces have a tendency to be four-sided. Of course exceptions exist, such as three-sided or even two-sided patches. Geometry of this kind is referred to as *degenerate*, because one or more of the sides has been reduced to zero length. Degenerate geometry is often, but not always, the source of geometrical errors in SolidWorks and other CAD packages.

Figure 27.2 shows some surfaces with the mesh displayed on them. You can create the mesh with the Face Curves sketch tool.

FIGURE 27.2

Meshes created with the Face Curves sketch tool

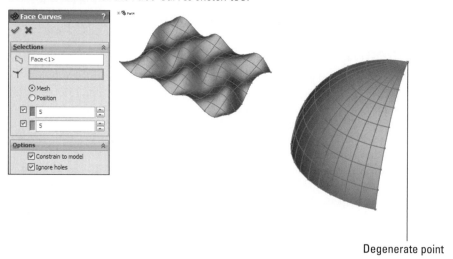

Degenerate point

An example of a competitive system to NURBS surface modeling is point mesh data. This comes from systems such as 3DSMax, which create a set of points that are joined together in triangular facets, and can be represented in SolidWorks as an STL (stereolithography) or VRML (virtual reality markup language) file. When displayed in SolidWorks, this data looks very facetted or tessellated into small, flat triangles, but when viewed in software that is meant to work with these kinds of meshes, it looks smooth. Many advantages come with this type of data, especially when it comes to applying colors and motion. However, the main disadvantage is that the geometrical accuracy is not very good. Point mesh data is typically used by 3D graphic artists, animators, and game developers.

By using a SolidWorks add-in such as ScanTo3D, it is possible to take point mesh data and create a NURBS mesh over it. This feature is not a push-button solution, but it offers capabilities where none previously existed. ScanTo3D is beyond the scope of this book, but you should find it useful if you are interested enough to read about NURBS and point meshes.

Developable surface

Developable surfaces are surfaces that can be flattened without stretching the material. They are also surfaces that you can extend easily in one or both directions. These include planar, cylindrical, and conical shapes. It is not a coincidence that these are the types of shapes that can be flattened by the Sheet Metal tools.

Ruled surface

Developable surfaces are a special type of a broader range of surface called ruled surfaces. SolidWorks has a special tool for the creation of ruled surfaces that is described in detail in the next section. Ruled surfaces are defined as surfaces on which a straight line can be drawn at every point. A corollary to this is that ruled surfaces may have curvature in only one direction. Ruled surfaces are far less limited than developable surfaces, but are not as easily flattened.

Gaussian curvature

Gaussian curvature is not referred to directly in SolidWorks software, but you may hear the term used in more general CAD or engineering discussions. It can be defined simply as curvature in two directions. As a result, a sphere would have Gaussian curvature, but a cylinder would not.

What Surface Tools Are Available?

Surface feature equivalents are available for most solid features such as extrude, revolve, sweep, loft, fillet, and so on. Some solid features do not have an equivalent, such as the Hole Wizard, shell, and others. Several surface functions do not have solid equivalents, such as trim, Untrim, Extend, Thicken, Offset, Radiate, Ruled, and Fill.

This is not a comprehensive guide to complex shape modeling, but it should serve as an introduction to each feature type and some of the details about how it operates.

Extruded Surface

The Extruded Surface works exactly like an extruded solid, except that the ends of the surface are not capped. It includes all the same end conditions, draft, contour selection, sketch rules, and so on that you are already familiar with. Figure 27.3 shows the PropertyManager for Extruded Surface.

FIGURE 27.3

The Extruded Surface PropertyManager

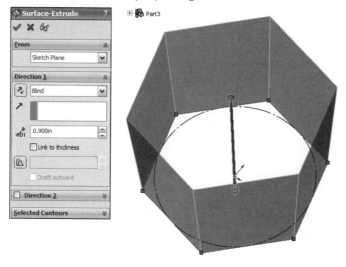

You can also create extruded surfaces from open sketches, and, in fact, that is probably a more common situation than creating a surface with a closed sketch.

When two non-parallel sketch lines are joined end to end, the result of extruding the sketch is a single surface body that is made of two faces with a hard edge between them. If the sketch lines were disjoint, then the extrude would result in disjoint surface bodies. If the sketch lines were again made end to end, but done in separate sketches, then the resulting surface bodies would be separate bodies; the second body would not be automatically knit to the first one as happens with solid features. This is an important quality of surfaces to keep in mind. If you create surfaces in different features and want them knitted into a single body, then you will have to do that manually.

Revolved Surface

The Revolved Surface functions like its solid counterpart, right down to the rules for how it handles entities that are touching the axis of revolution; nothing can cross the axis. A single sketch entity is allowed to touch it at a single point, but multiple sketch entities cannot touch it at the same point.

Swept Surface

Swept surfaces work much like their solid counterpart, and the sketch rules and available entities are the same. The main difference here is going to be that swept surfaces usually use an open contour for the profile, while swept solids use closed contours.

Lofted Surface

The main difference between lofted surfaces and lofted solids is that the surfaces can use edges and curve features to loft, rather than simply sketches and faces.

Boundary Surface

The Boundary Surface was created as a higher quality replacement for the Loft feature, but certain limitations mean that Loft has not been removed from the feature list. Boundary surface most resembles a loft, but has elements of the fill surface, and at times can also function like a sweep. It requires you to select edges or sketch elements in two different directions, directly relating to the NURBS scheme I discussed earlier in this chapter. This feature can work with only one set of edges selected.

If several edge or sketch segments combine to form one side of a direction, then you must use the SelectionManager to form the edge segments into a group. SelectionManager enables you to select portions of a single sketch or to combine elements such as sketch, edge, and curve into a single selection for use as a profile or guide curve for Boundary or Loft features.

The interface for the Boundary Surface is shown in Figure 27.4.

The types of models where you end up using the Boundary Surface are highly curvy models that are modeled mainly with surface features, and require a four-sided patch.

The main advantage of Boundary Surface over Loft is that Boundary Surface can apply a Curvature boundary condition all the way around, while Loft cannot apply curvature on the guide curves. Fill surfaces also can apply a Curvature boundary condition all the way around.

Boundary Surface can be a rather nuanced feature, but when working on the type of model that suits it well, I default to Boundary surfaces when possible. Boundary solid features are now also available, and I expect these will also take a little bit of a learning curve to understand where they are best applied.

FIGURE 27.4

The Boundary Surface PropertyManager

  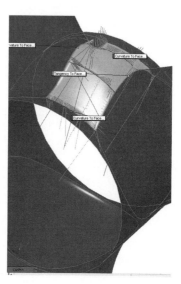

For a more detailed look at the primary shape creation tools (sweep, loft, boundary, and fill) and surface modeling in general, please refer to the *SolidWorks Surfacing and Complex Shape Modeling Bible* (Wiley, 2008).

Offset Surface

 The Offset Surface has no solid feature counterpart, but it does in 3D what the Offset Sketch function does in 2D; it may also fail for the same reasons. For example, if you offset a .25-inch radius arc by .3 inches to the inside, it fails because it cannot be offset up to or past a zero radius. The same is true of offsetting surfaces. Complex surfaces do not have a constant curvature, but are more like a spline in having a constantly changing curvature. If the offset is going in the direction of decreasing radius, and is more than the minimum radius on the face or faces being offset, then the Offset Surface feature will fail.

One of the ways to troubleshoot a failing Offset Surface is to use the Check tool to check for minimum radius. Remember that minimum radius is only a problem if the curvature is in the same direction as the offset. If a small radius will increase when it is offset, then that small radius is not the problem. The problem comes from the other direction where you are offsetting to the inside of a small radius.

Unlike the Sketch Offset function — and as was shown in Chapter 26 — you can offset surfaces by a zero distance. This is usually done to copy either solid or surface faces to make a new surface body. Zero-distance offset and Knit are sometimes used interchangeably, although Knit causes a problem if you are selecting a surface body that is composed of a single face. Knit assumes that you are trying to knit one body to another, and so, by default, it selects the body, and then fails with the message that you cannot knit a body to itself. Because Knit has this limitation, and Offset does not, I prefer the Offset tool when copying faces to make a new surface body. You may also notice that when you enter a zero for the offset distance, the Offset PropertyManager name changes automatically to Copy Surface.

Knit does have two functions that Sketch Offset does not. One of these is the option to create a solid from the knit body if it forms a closed body. The second option is somewhat more obscure, offering the ability to select all faces on one side of a Radiate surface. I discuss this option in more depth later in this chapter in the Knit Surface section.

When talking about copying surface bodies, you must also consider the Move/Copy Bodies feature, which is described in Chapter 26. When simply copying a body without also moving it, this feature issues a warning that asks whether you really intend to copy the body without moving it. This is an annoying and pointless message. Also, the Move/Copy Bodies feature does not enable you to copy only a part of a body (selected faces) or to merge multiple bodies into one like the Knit and Offset Surface features.

All things considered, I recommend using the zero-distance Surface Offset feature to copy bodies or parts of bodies unless your goal is to immediately make a solid out of it (in which case you should use the Knit feature) or when using a Radiated surface (typically in a mold-building application).

Radiate Surface

 The Radiate Surface is not one of the more commonly used surface features. It has been largely superseded by the Ruled Surface. This is because Ruled Surface does the same sort of thing that Radiate Surface does, as well as a lot more, and is also more reliable. Radiate works from an edge selection, a reference plane, and a distance. The newly created surface is perpendicular to the selected edge, parallel to the selected plane, and the set distance wide. It is probably most commonly used in creating molds or other net shape tooling such as dies for stamping and forging, blanks for thermoforming, and so on.

Figure 27.5 shows the PropertyManager and selection for creating a Radiate Surface.

> **TIP** The Radiate Surface feature does not give you a preview of the finished surface, only the small arrows that indicate the direction in which the surface will radiate. At times, you may need to switch the arrows to the other side, which you can do by using the arrow button next to the plane selection.

> **CAUTION** When creating a Radiate Surface, the use of a loop in the edge selection always results in an incorrect result, because the feature only uses the initial edge that was selected for the loop. As long as individual edges are listed in the selection box, you should be okay.

FIGURE 27.5

The Radiate Surface PropertyManager

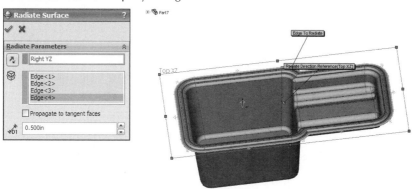

The one application where the Radiate Surface has a very interesting usage is when you combine it with the Knit function, as mentioned earlier. Figure 27.6 shows a part surrounded by a Radiate Surface in which the Knit feature is being used to select all the faces to one side of the radiated surface. The second smaller selection box in the PropertyManager that contains Face<1> is called a *seed face* and causes the Knit to automatically select all the faces on the same side of the model as the selected seed face. The requirement here is that the Radiate goes completely around the model and separates the faces into faces on one side of the Radiate and faces on the other side of the Radiate. The use of the Radiate with the Seed Face selection is extremely useful for mold creation.

FIGURE 27.6

Using Radiate Surface with Knit

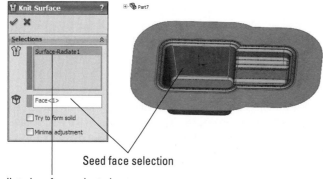

Knit Surface

The Knit Surface functionality has been discussed in the terminology section and also in the Radiate Surface section.

The one function that remains is the Try to form solid option. If the knit operation results in a watertight volume, this option turns the volume into a solid. You can also make a solid from a surface using two other functions. The Fill Surface has an option to merge the fill with a solid or to knit it into a surface body; if the knit surface body is closed, then it gives you the option to make it a solid. This is very nice, complete interface design, with options that save you many steps. The Fill Surface feature is described in more detail later in this chapter.

The other function that also creates a solid from a surface is the Thicken feature. If a surface body that encloses a volume is selected, then an option Create solid from enclosed volume appears on the Thicken PropertyManager, as shown in Figure 27.7. You can access the Thicken feature from the menus at Insert ⇨ Boss/Base ⇨ Thicken.

FIGURE 27.7

The Thicken PropertyManager

Planar Surface

Planar surfaces can be created quickly and are useful in many situations, not just for surfacing work. Because they are by definition *planar*, you can use them to sketch on and for other purposes that you may use a plane for, such as mirroring. Further, you can create a planar surface in a way that many users have long wanted to use for creating a plane, by selecting two co-planar edges or sketch lines.

However, more commonly, planar surfaces are created from a closed sketch such as a rectangle. You can create multiple planar surfaces at once, and the surfaces do not need to all be on the same plane or even parallel. This is commonly done to close up holes in a surface model, such as at the bottom of cylindrical bosses on a plastic part, using a planar circular edge. A good example of this is the bike frame part in the material for Chapter 27 on the CD-ROM, named Chapter 27 – bike frame.SLDPRT.

Remember that a planar surface was used in Chapter 26 with the Split feature to split the leg off of an imported part. This was more effective than a sketch or a plane because the split was limited to the bounds of the planar surface, not infinite like the sketch or the plane.

The planar surface does not knit itself into the rest of the surface bodies around it automatically; you have to use the Knit feature to do this.

Extend Surface

The Extend Surface feature functions much in the same way that the Extend function works in sketches. Figure 27.8 shows the PropertyManager interface and an example of the feature at work.

FIGURE 27.8

The Extend Surface PropertyManager

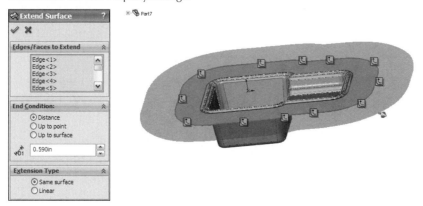

The only item here that requires explanation is the Extension Type panel. The Same surface option means that the extended surface will simply be extrapolated in the selected direction. A planar surface is the easiest to extend because it can go on indefinitely without running into problems. A cylindrical surface can only be extended until it runs into itself. Complex lofted or swept surfaces are often difficult to extend. Extrapolating a complex surface is not easy to do and often results in self-intersecting faces, which cause the feature to fail.

When the Same Surface setting works, it creates a nice result because it does not create an edge where the extension begins; it smoothly extends the existing face.

The Linear option is more reliable than the Same Surface option because it starts tangent to the existing surface and keeps going in that direction, working much like a Ruled surface, which is covered later in this chapter. It does not rely on extending the existing surface. This option creates an edge at the starting point of the new geometry.

Trim Surface

The Trim Surface feature is described briefly earlier in this chapter, but it warrants a more complete description here. Surfaces can be trimmed by three different types of entities:

- Sketches
- Planes
- Other surfaces

When you use surface bodies to trim one another, you must select one of two options: Standard or Mutual Trim. The Standard option causes one surface to act as the Trim tool and the other surface to be trimmed by the Trim tool. When you select the Mutual Trim option, both surfaces act as the Trim tool, and both surfaces are trimmed.

For an example of trimmed surfaces, open the mouse example from Chapter 26 and step through the tree. This shows examples of a couple of types of trimmed surfaces, as well as extended surfaces and others.

Many people overlook the ability to trim a surface with a plane, which can be very handy sometimes. Planes are infinite, which means you have less to worry about when it comes to changes that affect features rebuilding correctly.

Finally, trimming with 2D sketches is well known, but trimming with 3D sketches is less known. There is a 3D sketch tool called Spline on Surface that enables you to draw a spline directly on any surface body. An option exists in the Trim Surface PropertyManager to trim a surface with this type of sketch. This is very useful in many situations if you can remember that it is available.

Fill Surface

The Fill Surface is one of my favorite tools in SolidWorks. I often refer to it as the "magic wand" because it is sometimes amazing what it can do. It is alternately referred to by the SolidWorks interface and documentation as either Fill or Filled, depending on where the reference is made. You will find it listed as both in the SolidWorks interface.

The Fill Surface is intended to fill in gaps in surface bodies. It can do this either smoothly or by leaving sharp corners. You can use constraint curves to drive the shape of the fill between the existing boundaries. It can even knit a surface body together into a solid, all in one step. Beyond this, you can use the Fill Surface directly on solid models and integrate it directly into the solid automatically (much like the Replace Face function which is described later in this chapter).

Several rather complex examples of the Fill Surface are found in the bike frame example that was originally shown in Chapter 12. One of these fills is shown in Figure 27.9.

FIGURE 27.9

The Fill Surface PropertyManager and the results of applying it

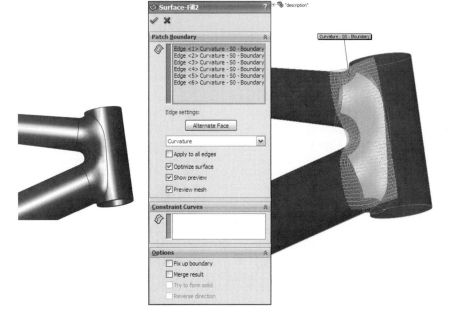

The first thing you should notice about the Fill Surface is that it is creating an oversized, four-sided patch and trimming it to fit into the available space. This is one of the reasons why I consider this to be such a magical tool. The four-sided patch I referred to earlier in the section on NURBS is shown very clearly in this feature preview. Also, the trimmed surface concept is illustrated nicely by this feature. Not surprising, if you Untrim the fill surface, then you return to the surface that is previewed here. In this one function, SolidWorks gives you some useful insight about what is going on behind the scenes.

When using the Fill Surface, it is best to have a patch completely bounded by other surfaces, as shown in Figure 27.9. Fill Surface can work with a boundary that is not enclosed, but it works better with a closed boundary.

You can set boundary conditions as Contact, Tangent, or Curvature. Contact simply means that the faces touch at an edge. Tangent means that the slopes of the faces on either side of the edge match at all points along the edge. Curvature means curvature continuous (or C2), where the fill surface matches not only tangency, but also the curvature of the face on the other side of the boundary edge. This results in a smoother transition than a transition that is simply tangent.

When you select the Optimize Surface option, SolidWorks tries to fit the four-sided patch into the boundary. Notice that on this part, even though the Optimize Surface option is on, it is clearly being ignored because the boundary is a six-sided gap, and cannot be patched smoothly with a four-sided patch. It is not necessarily an improvement to make a fill surface optimized, even when it works.

Constraint curves can influence the shape of the fill surface. An example of this is shown in Figure 27.10. The construction splines shown on the faces of the part were created by the Intersection Curve tool and enabled the spline used for the constraint curve to be made tangent to the surface.

FIGURE 27.10

The Fill Surface feature with constraint curves

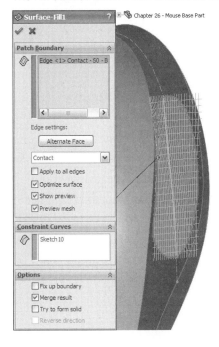

MidSurface

The MidSurface feature is not used very often. It was probably originally intended to be used in conjunction with analysis tools to create plate elements for thin walled structures. It works on parallel faces of a solid, creating a surface midway between the faces. If the faces have opposing draft (such that a wall is wider at the bottom than at the top), then the MidSurface will not work. It works on linear walls and cylindrical walls, but not on elliptical or spline-based shapes. The PropertyManager for the Mid-surface is shown in Figure 27.11.

Similar to the Planar Surface, you can also use the Mid-surface to create a surface that can be used like a plane. No plane type can create a symmetrical plane, but using a Mid-Surface, you can create a symmetrical planar surface between parallel walls.

FIGURE 27.11

The Mid-surface PropertyManager

Replace Face

The Replace Face feature does not create new surface geometry, but it does integrate existing surface geometry into the solid. It replaces selected faces of a solid or surface body with a selected surface body. Replace Face is one of the few tools that can add and remove material at the same time with a single feature.

If you were to manually perform the functions that are done by Replace Face, then you would start by deleting several faces of the solid, then extending faces, and then trimming surface bodies, and finish by knitting all the trimmed and extended faces back into a single solid body.

This is a very powerful and useful tool, although it is sometimes difficult to tell which situations it will work in. Figure 27.12 shows a part before and after a Replace Face feature has been added. The surface used to replace the flat face of the solid has been turned transparent. The first selection box is for the original face or faces, and the second selection box is for the surface body with the new faces. The tool tips for each of the boxes are Target Faces For Replacement and Replacement Surface(s), which seem a little ambiguous. I like to think of them as Old (top) and New (bottom).

Untrim Surface

The Untrim Surface is discussed in the terminology section of this chapter. You can use it either selectively on edges or on the entire surface body.

FIGURE 27.12

Using Replace Face

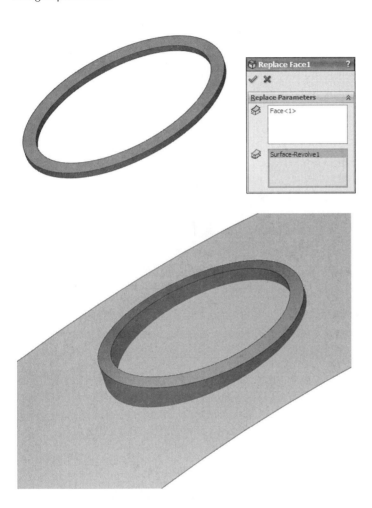

Parting Surface

 The Parting Surface is part of the SolidWorks Mold Tools. The Mold Tools are beyond the scope of this book.

Ruled Surface

Ruled surfaces are discussed in general in the section on terminology. Here I discuss the topic in more detail, and specifically with regard to the SolidWorks interface for creating Ruled surfaces.

The Ruled Surface feature in SolidWorks is one of those features that you may never have missed until you see it in action. It is extremely useful for constructing faces with draft, extending faces tangent to a direction, making Radiate surface types, building molds, and many other applications.

Figure 27.13 shows the PropertyManager interface for the Ruled Surface.

FIGURE 27.13

The Ruled Surface PropertyManager interface

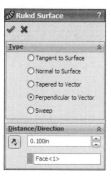

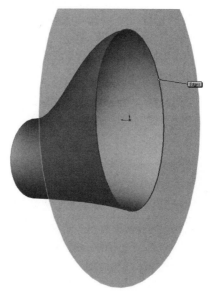

The Ruled Surface works from the edge of a solid or surface body. The feature has five basic types of operation that it can perform:

- Tangent to Surface
- Normal to Surface
- Tapered to Vector
- Perpendicular to Vector
- Sweep

The Tangent to Surface setting is self-explanatory. The Alternate Face option would be available if the base shape had been a solid, with a face filling the big elliptical hole. This would make the ruled surface tangent to the bottom face instead of the side.

Using the Normal to Surface setting, because the surface is lofted with a five-degree draft angle at the big end, making a Ruled surface that is normal to the surface means that it tilts up five degrees from the horizontal. Be careful of using this setting because it looks close to what you may be hoping that it is, but it is slightly off. One of the other options may be a better choice, depending on what you are looking for.

The Tapered to Vector setting needs a plane or axis selection to establish a direction, and then the Ruled surface is created from that reference at the angle that you set. With a combination of the Alternate Side button and the arrow direction toggle button next to the plane selection, you can adjust the cone created by this setting. The interface to make the changes is not exactly clear unless you use this function often, but it does work.

The Perpendicular to Vector setting is a better option than the Normal to Surface setting when the surface has been created with some sort of built-in draft angle. This is also the setting that looks most like the Radiate Surface feature, although it works much better than Radiate Surface.

The Sweep setting makes a face that is perpendicular to the surface created by Perpendicular to Vector. It is as if a straight line were swept around the edge. This is actually a great way to offset an edge or 3D sketch, by using the edge of the surface as the offset of the original.

Using Surfacing Techniques

I am not pretending that this section can even begin to do justice to the topic of surfacing techniques. I can give you a few basic ideas, but you will find as many surfacing techniques as you will find surfacing designers. The topic for this section could be the topic for an entire book on its own. In fact, it is the topic of an entire book covering the topic in far greater detail. You may want to use the *SolidWorks Surfacing and Complex Shape Modeling Bible* (Wiley, 2008) to continue your SolidWorks education in far greater detail and depth.

Up to Surface/Up to Body

Some situations seem to require elaborate workarounds until you think of doing them with a combination of solid and surface features, such as the part shown in Figure 27.14. This geometry could be made completely with solids, but it would be more difficult. In this case, a surface is revolved, representing the shape at the bottom of the hole, and the cut is extruded up to it. You can follow along with the part from the CD-ROM at Chapter 27 - square hole.sldprt.

CROSS-REF Chapter 7 contains more information on end conditions such as Up To Surface and Up To Body.

FIGURE 27.14

Using the Up to Body setting

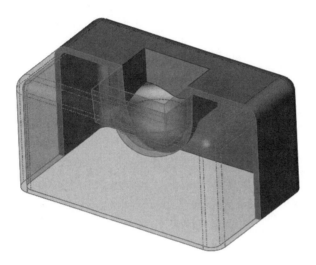

Another familiar situation is when you have a feature to place and you want to use an Offset from Surface end condition, but the feature spans two faces. In that situation, you can knit the necessary faces together (or use offset), and then extrude offset from that surface body.

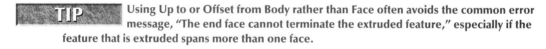 Using Up to or Offset from Body rather than Face often avoids the common error message, "The end face cannot terminate the extruded feature," especially if the feature that is extruded spans more than one face.

Figure 27.15 shows a part using an offset surface to extrude text up to where the text spans more than a single surface. This is a very common application, even if it is not text that is being extruded. The part that was used in Figure 27.15 is on the CD-ROM in the materials for Chapter 26, and is called Chapter 26 – Up To Body.SLDPRT.

Cut With Surface

 Sometimes you may need to make a cut that is more complex than what a simple extrude can do. For example, the cut may need to have shape in multiple directions. You could make the cut with multiple cut features, or even with a surface. Figure 27.16 shows a part that is cut with a surface.

When cutting with a surface, the edges of the surface must be outside of the body that is being cut. With sketches, it is advisable to have more sketch than you need so that you are not trying to cut line-on-line. The same applies to cutting with a surface, where it is advisable to have more surface than you need to make the cut.

FIGURE 27.15

Extruding text

FIGURE 27.16

Using the Cut With Surface feature on a part

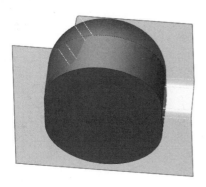 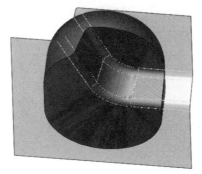

Replace Face

 The Replace Face feature can be used on imported or native geometry. You can use it to add or remove material from a part. When it adds material, it must be able to extend faces adjacent to those that are being replaced, which can be a limitation. A face or faces do not need to be replaced with the same kind or same number of faces, but the entire face that is being replaced must be removed. If you only want to replace a part of a face, then you can use a Split line to scribe the face, and then replace the part you want.

Figure 27.17 shows that the multiple faces of the letter U on this part have been replaced with a surface from an inserted part. Replace Face is a fantastic tool that you can use in a number of situations, although it is a little particular sometimes and you cannot always predict when it will or will not work.

FIGURE 27.17

Using Replace Face

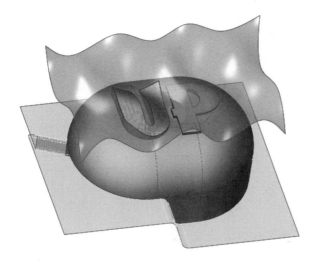

Fill Surface in action

The Fill Surface is my favorite piece of functionality in the SolidWorks software. It can get you out of modeling binds easily, and is often used to cover over nasty modeling mistakes or areas you just can't get right by any other method. In addition to duty in the complex shapes department, it can also be used as a fast way to create a planar surface in some situations. If you do much surface modeling, the Fill feature will become a staple of your diet.

NOTE   The Fill Surface is an advanced surfacing function. Sometimes, when talking about advanced surfacing functions, or indeed any software function, users have a tendency to sound a little cynical. This is because the tool is often expected to work on very complex geometry. It is not always the software's fault when it cannot perform a particular task, or does not do what you imagine you want it to do. Sometimes, the tool is simply not meant to perform certain tasks, there may be an unseen flaw in the geometry that prevents it from working, or the user does not understand the settings completely. The more complex the work, the more frequently you need to find workarounds to get something done. Avoiding problems does not make them go away, and it does not help you as a user to know how to handle them when they happen. In this book, I have chosen to take a realistic look at most of the features, and if there are problems, then I tell you.

Figure 27.18 shows the Fill Surface blending an intersection between tubes. The image to the left shows the before condition with the tubes coming together at an edge. The center image shows the edge trimmed out using the Trim feature, and the right image shows the hole blended over by the Fill Surface feature.

FIGURE 27.18

Blending with the Fill Surface

In Figure 27.19, a solid starts with a Split line on the surface. A sketch is then added, and a fill surface is created using the sketch as a constraint and the Split line as the boundary. The Merge Result option in the Fill PropertyManager has a different significance than it does in a solid feature PropertyManager, but the end result is the same. Remember that this is a surface function, and if it does not merge, then it is left as a surface feature.

If you had to go through these steps manually, then you would use the Replace Face feature to integrate the surface into the solid. The key to integrating the Fill surface directly into the solid without any additional features is the Merge Result option in the Fill PropertyManager.

Memory surface

A *memory surface* is not another new type of feature that you can select from the menu or a toolbar; it is just the name that I gave to a technique that I use from time to time. A memory surface is just a Knit or Offset surface that is made at one point in the feature tree when a particular face is whole, and reused later when the face has been broken up, but you still need to reference the entire original face. An example of this technique is shown in Figure 27.20. In this case, extra material is created around the opening, and a surface that was created in a Rollback state is used to remove it.

FIGURE 27.19

The Fill PropertyManager for merging a fill surface directly into a solid

FIGURE 27.20

Using the memory surfaces technique to cut away unwanted geometry

Tutorial: Working with Surfaces

This is another chapter that contains many important ideas, and yet there is only so much space for tutorials. The best way to learn is to experiment. I recommend that you closely follow the tutorial steps once, and then, when you understand the concepts involved, that you can go back and experiment.

Using Cut With Surface

Follow these steps to gain some experience with the Cut With Surface feature:

1. **Start by creating a new part and drawing a rectangle on the Top plane, centered on the Origin, about 4 inches by 6 inches, with the 4 inch dimension in the vertical direction.**

2. **Extrude the rectangle Mid-plane, by 2 inches.**

3. **From the Surface toolbar, select Lofted Surface, and select one 4-inch edge as a loft profile.** Then select a second 4-inch edge diagonal from the first one. This is shown in Figure 27.21.

FIGURE 27.21

Lofting a surface from the edges of a solid

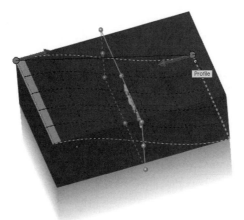

4. **Expand the Start/End Constraints panel, and set both ends to use the Direction Vector setting, selecting the plane that is in the middle of the long direction in each case.** In the part shown, the Right plane is used. Click OK to accept the feature. This is shown in Figure 27.21.

5. **From the menus, click Insert ➪ Cut ➪ With Surface.** Select the surface from the flyout FeatureManager, and toggle the arrow direction so that the top is cut off. (The arrow points to the side that is cut off.)

Using Offset Surface

Follow these steps to gain some experience with the Offset Surface:

1. **Open the part from the CD-ROM called** `Chapter 27 - Offset Tutorial.SLDPRT`.

2. **Right-click a curved face of the part and click Select Tangency in the menu.**

3. **With the faces still selected, from the Surfaces toolbar, click Offset Surface, and set the surface to offset to the outside of the part by .060 inches.** You can tell when the surface is offsetting to the outside when the transparent preview appears. If you do not see the transparent preview, then toggle the Flip Offset Direction arrow button. Click OK to accept the feature when you are satisfied.

4. **Look in the Surface Bodies folder at the top of the FeatureManager tree, expand the folder, and select the offset surface.** Then use the Appearances toolbar button to change the transparency of the surface body to about .75. You can also do this through the Display Pane, by clicking in the column following the surface body in the bodies folder that is farthest to the right, as shown in Figure 27.22. This is done so that you can see the part underneath the surface, without mistaking the surface for the actual part.

FIGURE 27.22

Using the Display Pane to change transparency

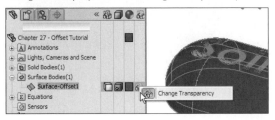

TIP It is a common practice to change surface colors to something that contrasts with the part color. I usually use a color like yellow, which suggests temporary status or construction. Some users take this a step further, and set the template colors for surface types at Tools ➪ Options ➪ Document Properties ➪ Colors. These settings do not always work; in some cases, they turn surface features to a different color, and in other situations, they do not.

5. **Select Sketch2, and select Extruded Boss/Base from the Features toolbar.** Do not mistake the extruded surface for an extruded solid. Set the end condition to Up To Body, activate the body selection box, and select the offset surface body from the Surface Bodies folder. The result is shown in Figure 27.23.

FIGURE 27.23

Extruding with the Up To Body setting

> **TIP** It is preferable to select the surface from the Surface Bodies folder, rather than the feature list or the graphics window. In this case, you want to extrude up to a body. If you make the selection from the feature list, then you are likely to select a feature (which is okay in this situation, but not in all situations). If you make the selection from the graphics window, then the selection is likely to be interpreted as a face. It is best to be as explicit as possible when making selections because SolidWorks may interpret your selection literally.
>
> In this case, it is probably a better idea to use Up To Body for the end condition than Up To Surface, because the goal is really to use the surface body as the end of the feature.

6. **To invert the lettering so that it sits below the surface rather than above the surface, you can make a few simple changes.** First, edit the offset surface feature and flip the direction of the offset so that the surface is now inside the solid rather than outside the solid. You will not be able to see it unless the solid is either transparent or in wireframe mode.

7. **Next, delete the extrude that you created to extrude the text.** There is no way to change an extrude into a cut in this context.

8. **Re-create the extrude as an extruded cut.** Use the From settings at the top of the PropertyManager window. The settings and results are shown in Figure 27.24.

   Another way to accomplish this would be to use the Move Face tool, select the faces of the letters, and move them .120 of an inch into the solid.

FIGURE 27.24

An extruded cut

Using Fill Surface blend

Sometimes fillets do not meet your needs. Blends, such as those shown in the bike frame example, are smoother and can blend just about anything. However, the technique is not exactly straightforward. Follow these steps to gain familiarity with this technique:

1. **Open the part from the CD-ROM for Chapter 27 called** `Chapter 27 - Blend.` `SLDPRT`. **Box select all of the features from the DeleteFace1 to the Shell, and suppress them.**

2. **On the Top plane, draw a square 2 inches on a side, and centered on the Origin.**

3. **Use the Split Entities tool found on the Sketch toolbar or through the menus at Tools ⇨ Sketch Tools ⇨ Split Entities.** Divide each line of the rectangle into three pieces, with the two outer pieces of each line being .6 inches (use an Equal sketch relation). The sketch should be fully defined when you are done. This arrangement is shown in Figure 27.25. This is done because the edges of the tubes need to be broken into sections.

4. **Use Delete Face to delete the ends of the four tubes.** Set the option to Delete, not the default option of Delete And Patch. This converts the solid into a surface body.

5. **Use the sketch with the split entities to trim out the center section of the tubes, keeping the outer section, and leaving four surface bodies.** This leaves each tube end, where they have been trimmed, divided into four segments, as shown in Figure 27.26.

FIGURE 27.25

Using split entities to split lines

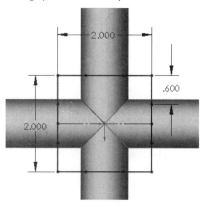

FIGURE 27.26

Split ends after trimming

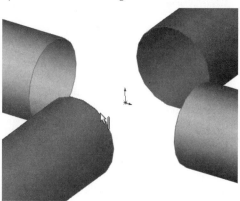

6. **Initiate the Lofted Surface feature, and select the nearest edge segments from adjacent tubes.** If the loft preview twists, then use the light-blue handles to straighten it out, or deselect and reselect one of the edges in approximately the same location as the other edge was selected. Expand the End Conditions panel and set each edge to use the Curvature setting. You may adjust the End Tangent Length option if you want, but keep in mind that this may make the part asymmetrical.

As a note, you may choose to use Boundary surface in the place of the loft. For this function, the two are similar enough.

7. **Create lofted surfaces all the way around the part, linking all the tubes.** Figure 27.27 shows the part with three of the lofts already completed and the last one in progress.

FIGURE 27.27

Adding lofted surfaces

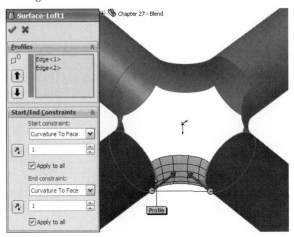

8. **Start a Planar Surface feature, and select the open ends of each tube where the faces were deleted in Step 4.**

NOTE Not all features allow you to operate from multiple bodies, but the Loft and Planar Surface features do. Features such as Fillet and Draft restrict you to creating features that are associated with one body at a time.

9. **Start a Knit Surface feature, and Shift-select all the bodies in the Surface Bodies folder (select the first body in the list and Shift-select the last body).** When you click OK to accept the feature, notice that the number of surface bodies changes to one. Selecting bodies in this way is much faster for large numbers of bodies than selecting them one at a time from the graphics window.

NOTE Notice that the open edges of the surface body are shown in a different color. At this point, there are two open edges around the holes at the intersection of the tubes.

10. **This is a situation that the Fill Surface is really meant for.** In fact, this technique was created specifically to take advantage of the Fill Surface capabilities. Right-click any of the open edges and click Select Open Loop. Initiate the Fill Surface. Change the Edge Setting option to Tangent, and make sure that the Apply to all edges option is on. Turn the Merge result option on, but leave the Try to form solid option off. The model at this point is shown in Figure 27.28, along with the PropertyManager settings that are used.

FIGURE 27.28

Creating a fill surface patch

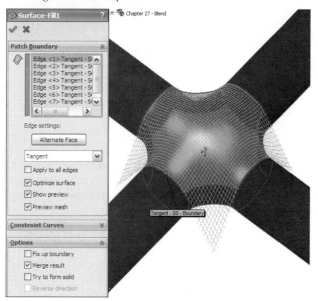

NOTE   The Optimize Surface option is ignored for this part because the opening is eight-sided rather than four-sided. Also note that you may have to change the resolution control slider to get the surface to remain convex instead of going concave in the center.

11. Click OK to accept the feature.

12. **Start another fill surface, turning the part over to use the same selection on the back and the same settings as the first fill.** However, on this one, also use the Try To Form Solid option. Click OK when the selections and settings are complete.

13. **For the last feature, apply a Shell feature, selecting the flat ends of the tubes, and shelling to .100 inches.** The final state of the model is shown in Figure 27.29.

The finished model

Summary

Surface functions have a wide range of uses other than for complex shape parts, but thinking about your models in terms of surface features requires a slightly different approach. Becoming comfortable with the terminology, and the similarities and differences between solids and surfaces, is the first step toward embracing surfacing tools for everyday work.

Of course, I would be remiss if I did not mention some of the complex tools, of which Loft and Fill are certainly the most useful.

Chapter 28

Master Model Techniques

I n this book, the term master model is used to refer to a technique where an entire assembly is laid out or has its major faces constructed in a single part, and that part is then placed into other files from which the individual parts are created. Master model techniques are usually used in situations that in-context design cannot deal with, or where in-context design is cumbersome.

Master model techniques are a product of four separate features or functions that have some similarities and some differences, and rely heavily on the knowledge of parent/child concepts, multiple bodies, and surface functions. The four features are Split, Save Bodies, Insert Part, and Insert Into New Part. In turn, these four features can be categorized into Push and Pull type functions.

As an example of a master model technique, consider the mouse model shown in Figure 28.1, which should be familiar by now. The overall shape is modeled as a single part, and is split into several bodies using multibody methods. Then, using these master model techniques, the individual bodies are used to create individual part files where detail features are added.

It may initially be a little confusing to understand that SolidWorks has four distinct features or functions that do essentially the same thing with subtle but important differences. The functionality of the four tools overlaps significantly, but none is an exact copy of another.

FIGURE 28.1

A mouse master model

Understanding the concepts of *parent* and *child* documents is key to understanding the concepts behind master model techniques. A parent document is always the driving document, so changes to the parent propagate down to the child. The child document is always dependent upon the parent. In these master model schemes, it is not always possible to find the child document from the parent, but you can always find the parent from the child.

The concepts of *Push* and *Pull* type functions are ones that I developed when working on advanced part training materials for SolidWorks Corp. Push simply means that data from the parent document is pushed out to the child. The relationship is defined in the parent document. Pull means that the child document pulls data from the parent, and the relationship is defined in the child document.

Here is a quick summary of the four tools that this chapter covers as master model tools:

- **Split.** Enables you to split a single solid body into multiple solid bodies and save (push) each body out to a separate part file. Available as a toolbar icon and a menu entry in the Insert ➪ Features menu. Creates a feature in the FeatureManager of the originating (parent) part file.

- **Save Bodies.** Enables you to save (push) all the solid bodies from a part out to separate part files. Available only via the right-mouse button menu on the solid bodies folder. Does not create a feature in the FeatureManager of the parent part.

- **Insert Part.** Enables you to pull all the solid and surface bodies, sketches, and even features from an existing part into the current part. Available as a toolbar icon and from the Insert menu.

- **Insert Into New Part.** Enables you to insert a selection of solid and surface bodies from the current part into a brand new part. Even though it is initiated from the parent document, it is classified as a Pull function because it doesn't leave a feature in the parent, but does leave one in the child.

The one common weakness of all of these tools is the file management side, or more precisely, the body management side. It boils down to a question of what happens to the child document if you rearrange the bodies in the parent document. There are a number of ways body management issues can come up. The Insert Part feature is the one that has received the most attention from SolidWorks when it comes to the robustness of file and body management issues, but Insert Part still does not cover all of the functionality (you cannot insert selective bodies, you must insert all solids or all surface bodies).

Using Pull Functions

Pull functions are initiated from the child document and pull data from the master model (parent document) into the child document. These functions insert a feature into the child that points to the parent, but do not insert a feature into the parent that points to the child.

The features that fall into this category are Insert Part and Insert Into New Part.

Insert Part

 Insert Part is initiated from the child document, through the menus at Insert ⇨ Part or from the Features toolbar using the Insert Part button (which may not be on your toolbar by default). As the name suggests, this feature pulls one part into another. Insert Part gives you the option to bring forward all solid and surface bodies, planes, axes, and sketches in addition to other options. You can even break the link between the inserted part and the parent data. This simply copies all of the sketch and feature data into the current part. The Mirror Part feature also uses this same PropertyManager with the same options. The Insert Part PropertyManager interface is shown in Figure 28.2.

FIGURE 28.2

The Insert Part PropertyManager

Figure 28.3 shows the FeatureManager of a part where the only feature is an Insert Part feature. All of the solid bodies are listed both under the normal Solid Bodies folder, and also under a second Solid Bodies folder under the inserted part icon. Other inserted items, such as surface bodies, planes, sketches, and axes, are also listed in folders under the inserted part icon.

You cannot be selective about which bodies are pulled forward, but you can delete unwanted bodies once they have all been brought in. If you are trying to handle data efficiently, this may not be the best option for you. Because you have to first bring forward all of the bodies and then delete those you don't want, the body data is still stored inside the part. Remember that the Delete Bodies feature does not actually delete anything. It simply makes it inaccessible after a certain point in the part history. If you are inserting a part with many complex bodies, you may want to use a more selective method such as Insert Into New Part or Save Bodies, each of which I describe in more detail later in this chapter.

FIGURE 28.3

The FeatureManager showing items inserted with an inserted part

For the inserted part, you can set configurations of the parent document in the External References dialog box, which is available through the right-mouse button menu of the feature that is inserted into the child document FeatureManager. The External References dialog box is shown in Figure 28.4. If the overhead of bringing many bodies forward only to be deleted is an issue for you, then you can use parent part configurations to delete the bodies first; then, from the child using List External References, you can select which configuration to insert.

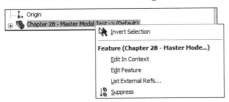

FIGURE 28.4

The External References dialog box

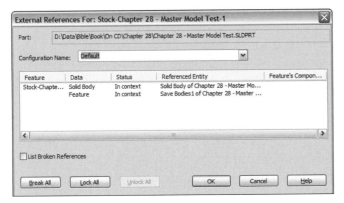

As the original inserted bodies are modified by additional features in the child document, the names change, and they are removed from the folder under the inserted part and only appear in the body folders under the top level.

File management is a real issue with all of these master model functions; in fact, it may not be an exaggeration to say that it is the *biggest* problem that arises with them, although you could say the same thing about overall body management. It is safe to say that you should be careful and follow file management best practice recommendations when performing name changes for documents with external references, especially if they use any of these features.

Insert Into New Part

Insert Into New Part qualifies as a Pull function because it does not create a feature in the FeatureManager of the parent file, even though it is actually initiated from the parent rather than from the child. This function does not have a drop-down menu location, nor does it have a toolbar button. You can initiate it from the right-mouse button menu from either the Solid or Surface Bodies folders or from the individual bodies within the folders.

This gives Insert Into New Part both advantages and disadvantages when compared to Insert Part. The advantages are that it can *selectively* insert *either* solid or surface bodies, *or even selections of both types*. You can Ctrl+select multiple bodies (solid and/or surface) to bring only the bodies forward that you need. However, it cannot bring forward planes or axes, or change the selection of what is brought forward after the feature is created. It also cannot be used to add a body to an existing part file; it can only be used to create *new* documents. This is definitely a good news/bad news situation, but with this information, you can make a more informed decision about which function to use.

When Insert Into New Part is used to place bodies into a part, the bodies are not shown in the same way that the Insert Part function shows them. Figure 28.5 shows that the Stock feature symbols are used rather than the Inserted Part symbol given individual bodies are being placed rather than entire parts.

FIGURE 28.5

Bodies placed in a part using Insert Into New Part

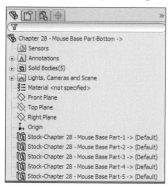

One note about this feature is that if it loses its referenced bodies, they cannot be reattached. An implication is that you cannot intentionally replace a body. Neither situation (lost references or the need to replace bodies) should come up frequently if at all for most users.

Using Push Functions

Push functions are initiated from the master model (parent document) and push data from the parent part out to a child part.. A feature in the tree of the parent identifies the point at which the model is pushed out to the child, and the child file can be found from the parent.

The first feature in the child part is a Stock feature, and contains a reference back to the parent, so that the parent can be found from the child. The features that fall into this category are Split and Save Bodies. The bidirectional identification of the source and target of the feature holds a distinct advantage over the Pull functions, which do not allow you to identify the child from the parent document.

Split feature

 I have already mentioned that the Split feature has three functions, two of which are plainly visible and one that is hidden. The Split PropertyManager is shown in Figure 28.6.

FIGURE 28.6

The Split PropertyManager

Split

The primary function of the Split feature is to split a single solid body into multiple bodies. You do this with sketches, planes, or surface bodies, and I discuss it in depth in Chapter 26. The Split feature can save both the pre-existing bodies and any bodies that result from the split as individual part files, using the Stock feature as the initial feature in the part.

Auto-assign Names

The ability to save solid bodies out to part files directly from the lower half of the Split PropertyManager has caused some serious file management problems in versions previous to SolidWorks 2009. The 2009 version of the software has fixed most of these problems. In previous versions, if you add features to a part created by saving a body out from the Split feature, making changes to the Split feature could wind up overwriting the file with the additional features. Also changing the number of bodies going into the Split feature usually had bad effects on downstream data. Still in 2009, some changes to the number of bodies (such as reducing the number of bodies, and then increasing it by manually, undoing the original change) can still result in unpredictable behavior.

Create Assembly

After you create the Split feature and you save bodies out of the Split feature, the right-mouse button menu displays an option, Create Assembly, which puts all of the parts from the bodies in the original part back together in the correct positions. Parts within the assemblies created this way are fixed in space with the same relationship to the assembly origin that they originally had as bodies to the part origin.

Save Bodies

The Save Bodies feature is accessed either from the right-mouse button menu from the bodies folders or the Insert ⇨ Features menu. Save Bodies works similarly by giving path and filename information in the Resulting Bodies selection box of the Split PropertyManager. However, Save Bodies enables you to create an assembly right in the PropertyManager for the feature, rather than as a hidden feature with no record of the assembly name created by the feature. The PropertyManager for Save Bodies is shown in Figure 28.7.

FIGURE 28.7

The Save Bodies PropertyManager

Tutorial: Working with Master Model Techniques

Some of the concepts presented in this chapter may not make much sense until you see them applied to a specific situation. The goal of this tutorial is to demonstrate the strengths and weaknesses of the various functions, as well as to give you some practical experience with the file management issues that you will encounter. The mouse multi-body part is used by each of the four tools so that you can become familiar with the differences in functionality by using the same starting point for each. To get some experience with these techniques, follow these steps:

Insert Part

To work with the Insert Part function, follow these steps:

1. **Make sure that you have access to the material from the CD-ROM for Chapter 28.** Create a new part, and insert the part named Chapter 28 - Mouse Base Part. SLDPRT. You can access Insert Part through the menus at Insert ➪ Part. After issuing the command, SolidWorks attaches the part to your cursor and prompts you to specify a location for the inserted part in the PropertyManager. Drop the part at the Origin of the child part, or simply use the green check to accept the part. There is no need to use the Move dialog box; if it appears, then turn off the option that enables it, and accept the feature. For this part, do not transfer any of the optional items, only the solid bodies.

2. **Once the feature is accepted and in the tree, right-click it and select List External Refs from the menu.** The External References dialog box is shown in Figure 28.8, with the list of configurations displayed.

FIGURE 28.8

The External References dialog box

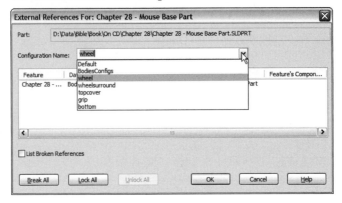

---

3. Select the Wheel configuration from the list.

4. Save and name the part file in such a way that it has the name of the technique used to create it (Insert Part) and the name of the body that it represents (such as Wheel).

NOTE A little bit of preparation work has been done on your behalf to make this tutorial flow more smoothly. If you ever choose to do modeling in this way, then you will need to know what this preparation work entails. In the mouse master model, a separate configuration was made for each body, and in that configuration, a Delete Body feature was created that deleted all of the bodies except one. The alternative to this approach is to bring all of the bodies into each new part, and use a Delete Body feature in each child part that deletes all but the one body that is needed. The advantage to using configurations is that bringing in a single body theoretically decreases the overhead for the individual part files.

5. Repeat Steps 1 through 4 for each of the five bodies in the master model.

6. If the mouse master model (Chapter 28 – Mouse Base Part.SLDPRT) is open, then close it. In any of the child parts, the inserted part feature shown in the tree should have the Out Of Context symbol on it (- >?). right-click the inserted part feature and select Edit In Context, which opens the master model.

   Notice that from the master model, you have no way of knowing where the child parts are or even *if* any child parts exist. Notice also that there is no easy way to create an assembly.

7. Create a new assembly document.

8. Drop all of the individually created parts into the assembly by selecting them in Windows Explorer and dragging them onto the assembly Origin. This is probably the easiest way to create an assembly using the Insert Part feature.

NOTE There is no link from the parent to the child, and so if the child part is renamed, the parent will not lose track of it. However, there is a link from the child to the parent, and so if the parent is renamed without the child being open at the same time, the child loses track of the parent. If the parent is changed, the child does not update unless the symbol is showing In-Context (->). If it is out of context, broken, or locked, the child does not update with the parent. Both documents need to be open at the same time to make the update happen (although they do not both need to be open when the original edit happens to the parent master model).

9. Save and close all of the parts and assemblies.

Insert Into New Part

To work with the Insert Into New Part function, follow these steps:

1. For this feature, start from the master model. Open the part Chapter 28 – Mouse Base Part.SLDPRT. Make sure that the part is set to the Default configuration. If it is set to a different configuration, the insertion of bodies will not go as smoothly as it could.

2. Expand the Solid Bodies folder in the FeatureManager. Right-click the first body in the list (Wheel), and select Insert Into New Part from the menu.

NOTE You could select multiple bodies and even combine solid and surface bodies to insert using this technique.

3. **When prompted, name the new part using the same convention used in the previous tutorial, which was to use the name of the technique (Insert Into New Part) and the name of the body.** In this part, leave the configuration setting in the External References dialog box to the Default configuration.

4. **Repeat Steps 1 through 3 for each of the bodies.**

5. **Right-click the Stock feature in the tree, and select Edit In Context.** SolidWorks opens the master model part.

NOTE Once again, there is no way back to the child document from the master model using the Insert Into New Part feature.

6. **Create a new assembly document and use the same technique from the previous tutorial to put all the parts in the assembly located from the Origin.** Again, no automated assembly creation tool exists for this method.

7. **Save all documents and close them.**

Split

To work with the Split function, follow these steps:

1. **This time, start from a copy of the master model part.** The Split feature makes additions to the model, and because you have already created assemblies based on the original, any additional features should be created using a copy of the part rather than the original. Copy it using the Copy and Paste feature in Windows Explorer, and rename the copy as Chapter 28 – Split Tutorial.

NOTE It is best to copy and rename this document before continuing with the rest of the tutorial. Otherwise, you may encounter problems with the file references, from which it is difficult to recover.

2. **With the newly copied and renamed document open, initiate the Split feature from Insert ⇨ Features ⇨ Split.**

3. **Because the bodies already exist, there is no need for the Trim tools or Cut Part functions in the Split feature, only for the resulting bodies.** To save the bodies to individual files, you must give each one a unique name. You can click the Auto-assign Names button to automatically name them with the existing names of the bodies. It might be difficult to discern where the callout flags are pointing. Once the names are all satisfactory, click OK to accept the feature.

NOTE The Consume Cut Bodies option deletes the bodies of any bodies involved in the Split feature. For most purposes, you should turn this option off. Turning the option off makes sure that the bodies are still available after the Split feature. If what you are really looking for is to eliminate the bodies once they are saved out, then you should turn on the Consume Cut Bodies option.

4. **To automatically create an assembly with all of the components located in the proper location, right-click the Split feature in the Master Model FeatureManager, and select Create Assembly.** Multiple Split features can be included in this command if bodies have been created by multiple Split features. Use the Browse button to locate and name the new assembly. Click OK when you are done. Completing this step opens the assembly that you just named and located. When you create the assembly, the parts will show up visually but may not be displayed in the FeatureManager until the assembly file is saved and reopened. You should still have access to the data through the right-mouse button menu from the graphics window.

5. **right-click one of the parts in the assembly to open it.** Notice that a Stock feature is used in the tree, and so it is possible to access the parent part and to change the parent part configuration used in the current part. Right-click the Stock feature and select Edit In Context.

6. **With the master model open, right-click the Split feature and select Edit Feature.** From here, it is possible to see where each of the child parts is located.

7. **If you rename any of the documents, then you should do this either by using SolidWorks Explorer or the Save As command with the other documents open as well.** If you want to rename the parent part (master model), then make sure that all of the child parts are open as well. (You can easily do this by opening the assembly; although the assembly was created from the master model, there is no direct link between the Split feature and the assembly.)

8. **Save and close all of the files before proceeding.**

Save Bodies

To work with the Save Bodies function, follow these steps:

1. **As before, create a copy of the original master model part and rename the copy** `Chapter 28 - Save Bodies Tutorial`.

2. **Open the renamed copy, and right-click the Solid Bodies folder.** Select Save Bodies from the menu. (Save Bodies does have its own icon that looks like the Split icon and is used to denote the placeholder feature in the FeatureManager.)

3. **The Save Bodies PropertyManager is nearly identical to the lower section of the Split PropertyManager. Use it to save the solid bodies out to separate files.** The major addition in the Save Bodies dialog box is that of the Create Assembly function directly within the PropertyManager. The primary benefit of this addition is that it retains the name and path of the assembly in this interface so you can look it up later if necessary, remedying one of the weaknesses in the Split feature.

NOTE In both the Split/Create Assembly and Save Bodies features, when an assembly is created, SolidWorks may rebuild the tree of the part as many times as you have bodies to save out. This may take some time for a complex model with a lot of bodies.

4. **After finishing Step 3, you are left in the reconstructed assembly.** Right-click one of the parts and select Open Part to open it in its own window. Notice that the Stock feature has again been used to push a single body into the part.

5. **Right-click the Stock feature, and select Edit In Context, which takes you back to the master model.**

6. **Save and close all of the files.**

Summary

Each of these four functions has strengths and weaknesses. Because of this, there is no one feature that is clearly superior to the others in all respects. Most of the weaknesses have to do with the types of data that they can work with, the ease of creating an assembly, and access to children from the parents. Unfortunately, I cannot offer a single solution that addresses all of the problems and retains each of the strengths.

The most important strengths, in my view, are the Insert Part and Insert Into New Part abilities to deal with both solids and surfaces. If you are working with surface bodies, you are forced into using one of these two functions. In particular, the Insert Into New Part function enables you to be selective about which bodies to pull into the child document. The other most important strength belongs to the Save Bodies feature, which makes the child accessible from the parent, and identifies the assembly in the parent.

Why the various strengths of these tools cannot be consolidated into one or at most two different features or even how it's gotten to the point where there are so many different functions that do approximately the same thing, is a mystery to me.

Part VII

Working with Specialized Functionality

Specialized functionality in SolidWorks makes certain tasks easier by grouping tools and making tools that only apply to a limited range of techniques. Sheet metal and Weldments are highly useful techniques in SolidWorks due to the specialized tools developed around the design styles.

Chapters 32 and 33 are new to this edition, and contain some new tools. Chapter 33 in particular deals with functionality which may be challenging to get useful results from. The animation tools do not seem to be on par with the rest of the functionality in the software, but for some types of work, they do work well.

Chapter 29

Using the Base Flange Method for Sheet Metal Parts

Many releases ago, SolidWorks changed the way that the software dealt with sheet metal parts. In the old way, the sheet metal part was created through normal modeling features, mainly centered on thin feature extrudes, but also including shell features. It did not matter how you got the geometry, as long as it had a consistent thickness and the edge faces were sheared perpendicular to the material.

The new way uses a functional feature approach, which greatly simplified the feature order requirements, and at the same time added some powerful and easy-to-use feature types. This new way is what is now called the Base Flange method, and is the main tool for sheet metal creation that most sheet metal designers use today.

The Insert Bends (old) method is still viable, but it is typically relegated to being used with imported parts and special uses such as creating rolled conical sheet metal parts or building a sheet metal part from a solid model.

Understanding the Big Picture

If you are only interested in seeing how Base Flange sheet metal parts are made, skip to the tutorial at the end of this chapter. The bulk of this chapter describes first the concepts involved, and then the detailed options in each Base Flange method feature.

The basic concept with the Base Flange method is that when you insert a Base Flange feature, SolidWorks identifies that part as a sheet metal part. The Base Flange feature is not *required* to be the first feature in the tree, but it is difficult to imagine why it would not be. You can create multi-body sheet metal parts, but you can only insert one Base Flange for each part document, and so only one body can be sheet metal. If you try to create a second Base Flange feature, then SolidWorks interprets it as an attempt to add a tab, which is the alternate function of the Base Flange tool.

When you add the Base Flange feature, a Sheet Metal placeholder feature is also automatically added before the Base Flange feature. The Sheet Metal placeholder is described later in this chapter.

Another feature is added automatically when you add the Base Flange. This one is called the Flat Pattern feature. Sheet Metal is added before the Base Flange and Flat Pattern are added at the bottom of the tree. This feature has a couple of special properties that are not found with other features. The first property is that it *remains* at the bottom of the tree when you add other sheet metal features, and the second property is that it is added as a *suppressed* feature. The Flat Pattern feature is discussed in more detail later in this chapter.

Bends may be flattened individually, or the whole part may be flattened at once. Configurations are often created with various bends flattened to show the part in various stages of the manufacturing process.

Bend Allowances can be specified by Bend Table, K-Factor, Bend Allowance, or Bend Deduction. These items are all listed in the Sheet Metal feature that is inserted as the first feature with a Base Flange.

Auto Relief has three options, which you can also set in the Sheet Metal feature. These three options are Rectangular, Tear, and Obround. Auto Relief and Bend Allowance settings are described in detail later in this chapter.

One of the general ideas about SolidWorks sheet metal is that some of the functions must create visual approximations of what the parts are going to look like, especially in the formed part. This is because the area where two bends run into one another is difficult to model. For this reason, the flat pattern may be easier to depict than the formed geometry. Many users become annoyed when the software simplifies the 3D model, but this is how the software works, and the very fine detail is probably not really needed anyway.

I find that when users' expectations of the software are reasonable, users tend to be more successful and satisfied with the results. I do not mean to make excuses for the software; I am very impressed with the functionality in the sheet metal features in SolidWorks, but it does not do *everything*, and users still need to use some imagination.

Using the Base Flange Features

The features used in the Base Flange method are easy to grasp conceptually, although they have many individual controls that may be confusing at first glance. Many of the tools can be changed by pulling handles, by using spin arrows, or by typing in specific numbers or dimensions. Maybe best of all, SolidWorks knows to change the thickness for the entire part at once.

The Sheet Metal features are all available from the Sheet Metal toolbar or through the menus at Insert ⇨ Sheet Metal, and by selecting the appropriate tool.

Base Flange /Tab feature

The Base Flange and Tab tool has three functions:

- By drawing an open contour in the first feature, the Base Flange creates a feature-like extrusion that includes the rounded corners of the bends.

- By drawing a closed contour in the first feature, the Base Flange creates a flat sheet that is shaped like your sketch for you to start from.

- When used at any time other than the first feature, it functions as a tab.

Figure 29.1 shows these three functions of the Base Flange/Tab feature.

FIGURE 29.1

The three functions of the Base Flange and Tab feature

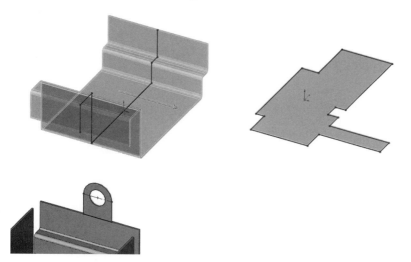

Notice that the sketch of the part at the upper left of Figure 29.1 shown in preview has all sharp corners, and that the bend radius is automatically added to each corner by the software. SolidWorks automatically adjusts when bend directions are combined to make sure that the inside radius is always the same, regardless of bend direction.

The bends are shown as BaseBend features in the FeatureManager. You can change individual bend radii from the default setting by editing the BaseBend feature, as well as by assigning custom bend allowances on a per-bend basis. You cannot change the bend angle for these particular bends because the angle is controlled through the sketch. However, for other types of bends (such as those created by Edge Flanges), you can adjust the bend angle through the feature PropertyManager.

If you need to, you can reorder all of the bends from a list that you can access from the right-mouse button menu selection, Reorder Bends on the Flat Pattern. This dialog box is shown in Figure 29.2.

FIGURE 29.2

The Reorder Bends dialog box

The BaseBend features can be suppressed, but the only effect that this has is to prevent the associated bend from flattening when the Flat Pattern feature is unsuppressed.

Sheet Metal feature

The FeatureManager is shown for the Base Flange with all of the bends below in Figure 29.3. The Sheet-Metal1 feature is automatically added to sheet metal parts as a placeholder for default sheet metal settings such as material thickness, default bend allowance settings, and Auto Relief options, as well as the default inside bend radius.

The Bend Order setting shown does not appear to have any effect when you are using the Base Flange method. In the Insert Bends method, a warning appears if the part intersects itself during bend operations, as determined by the bend order. This function may have been removed from more recent versions of the software, but the Bend Order options remain.

FIGURE 29.3

The FeatureManager after the Base Flange is added

Gauge Table

Gauge Tables are a legacy table type, which is simply an Excel spreadsheet. In SolidWorks 2009 the data from gauge tables has been consolidated with data from bend tables. However, you can still use the legacy gauge tables. The point of consolidating gauge and bend tables is so that you don't need a separate gauge table for each K-factor (or bend allowance or bend deduction).

CROSS-REF   Bend tables are described in more detail later in this chapter.

Gauge tables enable you to assign a thickness and available inside-bend radii, which limits the choices that the user has for those settings in the table. Each K-Factor has a separate table, and the choices listed in the table appear in the drop-down lists in the Sheet Metal PropertyManager. Figure 29.4 shows the top few lines of a sample Gauge Table and a Sheet Metal PropertyManager when a Gauge Table is used.

FIGURE 29.4

A sample Gauge Table and Sheet Metal PropertyManager

Type:	Steel Gauge Table					
Process	Steel Air Bending					
Bend Type:	Bend Allowance					
Unit:	inches					
Material:	Steel					
Gauge No.	Gauge 5					
Thickness:	0.2092					
					Radius	
Angle		0.25		0.50	0.75	1.00
	15	0.40		0.41	0.42	0.43
	30	0.40		0.41	0.42	0.43
	45	0.40		0.41	0.42	0.43
	60	0.40		0.41	0.42	0.43
	75	0.40		0.41	0.42	0.43
	90	0.40		0.41	0.42	0.43

If necessary, you can override the values that are used in the Gauge Table by using the override options in the thickness, bend radius, and K-Factor fields.

The Bend Allowance options (Allowance, Deduction, and K-Factor) are explained in more detail later in this chapter.

ON the CD-ROM Several sample tables with both gauge and bend data are provided on the CD-ROM that accompanies this book.

Bend Radius

This option specifies the default inside bend radius for all bends in the part. You can override values for individual bends or individual features.

Thickness

The part thickness is grayed out in the Sheet Metal PropertyManager. You can change the value by double-clicking any face of the model. The thickness displays as a blue dimension rather than a black dimension. It is easier to identify if you have dimension names turned on, because it is assigned the link value name Thickness.

All features in sheet metal parts that use the thickness value use a link value to link all the feature thicknesses. This makes it easy to globally change the thickness of every feature in the entire sheet metal part.

To save these settings to a template file, you can create a Sheet Metal feature, specify the settings, delete the Sheet Metal features, and then save the file to a template with a special name that represents the settings that you used.

TIP When a link value is named Thickness, the Extrude dialog box always shows a Link To Thickness option to link the depth of an extrusion to the Thickness link value. If you save a template where Thickness has been created as a link value, then the option is always available to you, regardless of whether or not you are making sheet metal parts.

Bend Allowance

You can control the Bend Allowance by using one of four options:

- Bend Table
- K-Factor
- Bend Allowance
- Bend Deduction

Bend Table

Two general types of Bend Tables are available, text-based and Excel-based. The first few rows of each type of table are shown in Figure 29.5. Each table can use K-Factor, Bend Allowance, or Bend Deduction.

FIGURE 29.5

Sample text- and Excel-based Bend Tables

```
Bend Allowance Tables
---------------------
# Available types are Bend Allowance/Bend Deduction/K-Factor
# Keywords (Type:, Unit:, ...) must start at the beginning of the line.
Type: Bend Allowance
Material: Steel
Unit:   meters


Thickness: 0.0005
Bend Radius (read across)    0.0000  0.0005  0.0010  0.0015  0.0020  0.0025  0.0030  0.0040  0.0050
Opening Angle (read down)
                       5     0.0002  0.0002  0.0002  0.0002  0.0002  0.0002  0.0002  0.0002  0.0002
                      10     0.0002  0.0002  0.0002  0.0002  0.0002  0.0002  0.0002  0.0002  0.0002
                      20     0.0002  0.0002  0.0002  0.0002  0.0002  0.0002  0.0002  0.0002  0.0002
```

Unit:	Inches												
Type:	Bend Allowance												
Material:	**Soft Copper and Soft Brass**												
Comment:	Values specified are for 90-degree bends												

Radius	Thickness												
	1/64	1/32	3/64	1/16	5/64	3/32	1/8	5/32	3/16	7/32	1/4	9/32	5/16
1/32	0.058	0.066	0.075	0.083	0.092	0.101	0.118	0.135	0.152	0.169	0.187	0.204	0.221
3/64	0.083	0.091	0.1	0.108	0.117	0.126	0.143	0.16	0.177	0.194	0.212	0.229	0.246
1/16	0.107	0.115	0.124	0.132	0.141	0.15	0.167	0.184	0.201	0.218	0.236	0.253	0.27
3/32	0.155	0.164	0.173	0.181	0.19	0.199	0.215	0.233	0.25	0.267	0.285	0.302	0.319

Sample Bend Tables can be found in the `lang\english\Sheetmetal Bend Tables` subdirectory of the SolidWorks installation directory. While the values may not be what you need, the syntax and organization is correct. You may want to contact your sheet metal fabrication shop to see what they are using for a table or equations.

 In the SolidWorks 2009 release, the data from gauge tables and bend tables have been consolidated, but both legacy types can still be read.

K-Factor

When sheet metal is formed from a flat sheet, bending the metal causes it to stretch slightly on the outside part of the bend, and to compress slightly on the inside part of the bend. Somewhere across the thickness of the sheet is the Neutral Plane, where there is no stretching or compression. This Neutral Plane can be at various places across the thickness, depending on the material, tooling, and process. The ratio of the distance from the inside bend surface, to the Neutral Plane, to the thickness is identified as the K-Factor, where .5 means halfway, 0 means on the inside face, and 1 means on the outside face. Typically, you can expect values between .5 and .3.

Bend Allowance and Bend Deduction

Bend Allowance and Bend Deduction are specific length values, not a ratio like the K-Factor. The Bend Allowance is essentially the arclength of the Neutral Plane through the bend region. The Bend Deduction is the length difference between a sharp corner and the radius corner, as expressed by the formula in Figure 29.6.

FIGURE 29.6

Calculating the Bend Deduction from the Bend Allowance and K-Factor

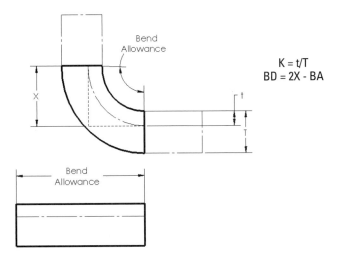

$$K = t/T$$
$$BD = 2X - BA$$

The three values are related, as shown in Figure 29.6. The dark rectangle represents the bend area. Material outside of the bend area really does not matter, although it is usually shown and used in the generally accepted formulas about bend calculations for sheet metal.

The ratio t/T (the K-Factor) is usually used from a published table or by asking your sheet metal vendor what values they typically use. The values from the tables have been developed experimentally by bending a piece of metal of known length, and then measuring the arclength of the inside of the bend and the arclength of the outside of the bend. By comparing these numbers to the original linear length of the bent area, you can find the *t* value and thus the *K* value. From the *K* value, the *BA* (Bend Allowance) value can be calculated and from that, the *BD* (Bend Deduction) value is easy to find.

The specific formulas for finding these numbers are not as important as an intuitive grasp of what the numbers mean, and how they are used, at least in relation to using SolidWorks to model sheet metal parts. The numbers used to fill out Bend Tables using K, BA, or BD values are typically taken from experimentally developed tables.

Auto Relief

Auto reliefs were formerly called Bend reliefs. You can specify three different Auto relief options to be applied automatically to bends that end in the middle of material. These options are illustrated in Figure 29.7.

FIGURE 29.7

The three Auto relief configurations: Rectangular, Tear, and Obround

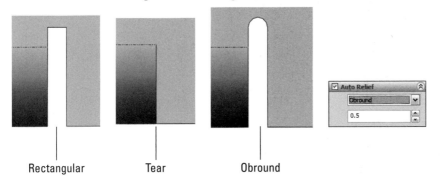

Rectangular   Tear   Obround

For the Rectangular and Obround types, you can control the width and the distance past the tangent line of the bend through the Relief Ratio selection box, which is immediately below the type selection box in the Sheet Metal PropertyManager. This ratio is the width of the relief divided by the part thickness. For the Rectangular relief, a ratio of .5 and a thickness of .050 inches means that the relief is .025 inches wide and that it goes .025 inches deeper into the part beyond the tangent line of the bend. The Obround relief goes slightly deeper because it has a full radius after the distance past the tangent line of the bend, and so it essentially goes a total of one full material thickness past the tangent line.

The Tear relief is simply a face-to-face shear of the material with no gap.

Flat Pattern feature

The Flat Pattern feature is added automatically to the end of the tree when the Base Flange feature is added. This feature is used to flatten the sheet metal part when the feature is unsuppressed. The Flatten toolbar button acts as a toggle to unsuppress or suppress the Flat Pattern feature in the tree. As mentioned earlier, the Flat Pattern has a couple of special properties that are not seen in other features. The first is that it remains at the *bottom* of the FeatureManager when other Sheet Metal features are added.

The second property of the Flat Pattern feature is that it is added in the *suppressed* state. When it is unsuppressed, it flattens out the sheet metal bends.

By editing the Flat Pattern feature, you can set a few options. The Flat Pattern PropertyManager is shown in Figure 29.8.

FIGURE 29.8

The Flat Pattern PropertyManager

The Fixed face parameter determines which face remains stationary when the part is flattened out. Generally, the largest face available is selected automatically, but if you want to specify a different face to remain stationary, you can do that here.

When the Merge faces option is on, it causes the flat pattern to form a single face, rather than being broken up by the tangent lines around the bends. This does a few things. First, selecting the face of the flattened part and clicking Convert Entities (found on the Sketch toolbar) makes an outline of the entire flattened part, which is easier to use for certain programming applications. Second, the edges around the outside are not broken up. Third, the tangent edges around the bends are not shown. The differences between flat patterns with this option on and off are shown in Figure 29.9.

FIGURE 29.9

The Merge Faces option, on and off

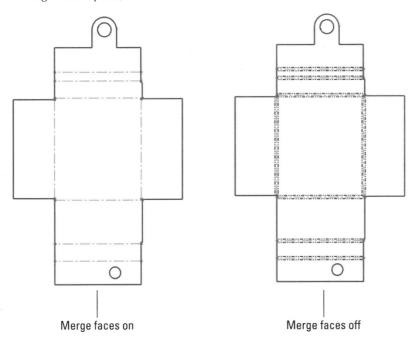

Merge faces on   Merge faces off

Bend lines are shown in both examples in Figure 29.9.

When you turn on the Simplify Bends option, it simplifies curved edges that are caused by flattening bends to straight lines from arcs or splines. When the option is off, the complex edges remain complex. Simple edges can be cut by standard punches, and do not require CNC-controlled lasers or abrasive water jets.

The Corner Treatment option controls whether or not a corner treatment is applied to the flat pattern of a part. The corner treatment is illustrated in Figure 29.10. The model used to create this corner used a Miter Flange around the edges of a rectangular sheet.

NOTE   **You can export a `*.dxf` file of the flat pattern directly from the model without creating a drawing.**

FIGURE 29.10

Using the Corner Treatment setting in the Flat Pattern PropertyManager

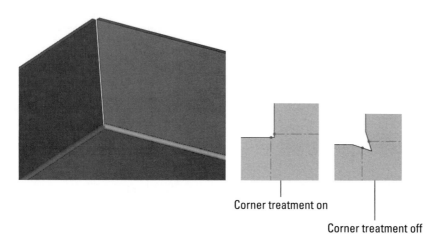

Corner treatment on

Corner treatment off

Edge Flange feature

 The Edge Flange feature is very flexible and can be changed in several ways. If you have not kept up with the changes to Edge Flange for the last couple of releases, then you may find some surprises.

Edge Flange is intended to turn a 90-degree flange from a selected straight edge in the direction and distance specified using the default thickness for the part. The default process for this feature is that you select the tool, select the edge, and then drag the distance, click a distance reference such as a vertex at the end of another flange of equal length, or type a distance value manually. You can select multiple edges, from a part which do not necessarily need to touch one another. That is all there is to a simple default flange, although several options give you some additional options for angle, length, and so on. Figure 29.11 shows the Edge Flange PropertyManager, as well as a simple flange.

Edit Flange Profile

The Edit Flange Profile button in the Edge Flange PropertyManager enables you to edit a sketch to shape the flange in some way other than rectangular, or to otherwise edit the shape of the flange. Notice in Figure 29.11 that both of the flanges made by a singe flange feature have been edited. You can do this by selecting the flange for which you want to edit the profile before clicking the Edit Flange Profile button.

FIGURE 29.11

The Edge Flange PropertyManager and a simple flange

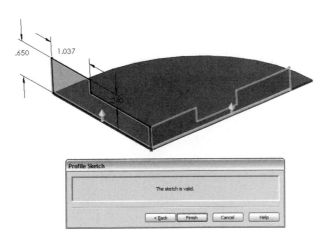

NOTE If you have added dimensions to the sketch, as shown in Figure 29.11, then you will no longer be able to use the arrow to drag the length of the flange. To edit the length, you will need to edit the sketch or double-click the feature, and then double-click the dimensions that you want to change.

You can add holes to the flange profile as nested loops. This allows you to avoid creating additional hole features, but does not allow you to control suppression state independently from the flange feature.

You can make flanges go only part of the way along an edge by pulling one of the end lines back from the edge. This works even though the end lines appear black and fully defined. A situation where the sketch has been edited this way is shown in the image to the right in Figure 29.11.

Use default radius

This option enables you to override the default inside bend radius that is set for the entire part for this feature. The bend radii for individual bends within an edge flange that has multiple flanges cannot be set; the only override is at the feature level. If you need individual bends to have different bend radii, then you need to do this using multiple Edge Flange features.

Gap distance

The gap distance is illustrated in Figure 29.12. The Gap Distance selection box is only active when you have selected multiple edges in the main selection box for this feature. The gap refers to the space between the inside corners of the perpendicular flanges.

FIGURE 29.12

Specifying the gap distance

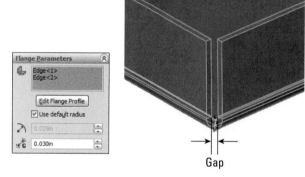

Gap

Angle

Because the Edge Flange is not dependent on a sketch for its angle like the Base Flange is, you can set the angle in the Angle panel of the PropertyManager. The values that this selection box can accept range from any value larger than zero to any value smaller than 180. Of course, each flange has practical limits. In the flange shown in Figure 29.13, the limitation is reached when the bend radius runs into the rectangular notch in the middle of the flange to the right, at about 158 degrees. The angle affects all of the flanges that are made with the feature. To create a situation where different flanges have different angles, you need to create separate flange features.

Flange Length

As mentioned earlier, if you have edited the Flange Profile sketch and a flange length dimension is applied in the sketch, then the flange length is taken from that sketch dimension. If this dimension has not been added to the profile sketch, then the options for this setting in the PropertyManager Flange Length panel are Blind and Up To Vertex. Using Up To Vertex is a nice way to link the lengths of several flanges.

FIGURE 29.13

Establishing the limit of the flange angle

Flange Position

The small icons for Flange Position should be fairly self-explanatory, with the dotted lines indicating the existing end of the material. The names for these options, in order from left to right, are:

- Material Inside
- Material Outside
- Bend Outside
- Bend From Virtual Sharp (for use when an angle is involved)

Trim Side Bends

In situations where a new flange is created next to an existing flange, and a relief must be made in the existing flange to accommodate the new flange, you can turn the Trim side bends option on to trim back the existing flange. Leaving this option off simply creates a relief cut, as shown in Figure 29.14. This is functionality that requires some imagination from the user. A real sheet metal part manufactured like this would have an area at the corner where the deformation from the bends in different directions overlaps. This overlapping bend geometry is too complex for SolidWorks to create automatically, so it offers you a couple of options for how you would like to visually represent the corner. The flat pattern is correct, but the formed model requires some imagination.

Curved edges

Edge Flanges can be created on curved edges, but the curved edge must be on a planar face. For example, if the part were the top of a mailbox, then an Edge Flange could not be put on the curve on the top of the mailbox. The flange would have to be made as a part of the flat end of the mailbox, instead.

Figure 29.15 shows Edge Flanges used on a part. Notice that reliefs are added to the ends of the bends, although they are not really needed.

FIGURE 29.14

Using the Trim side bends option

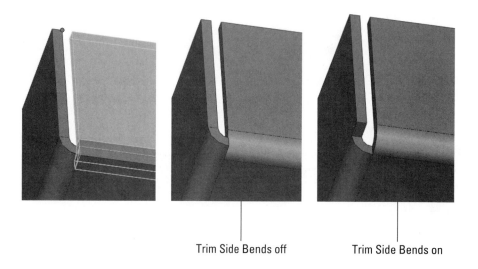

Trim Side Bends off   Trim Side Bends on

FIGURE 29.15

Curved Edge Flanges on a part

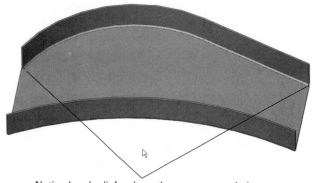

Notice bend reliefs where they are not needed

All of the edges that you select to be used with a curved Edge Flange must be tangent. This means that in Figure 29.15, neither of the Edge Flanges could have been extended around the ends of the part. You would need to create separate Edge Flange features for those edges.

Because these Edge Flanges are made in such a way that they are developable surfaces, they can be (and are) flattened in such a way that they do not stretch the material of the flange when the flat is compared to the formed shape. Doubtless there is some deformation in between the two states in the actual forming of this flange, and so its manufacturing accuracy may not be completely reliable.

Miter Flange feature

The Miter Flange feature can create picture frame–like miters around corners of parts, and correctly recognizes the difference between mitered inside corners and mitered outside corners. The PropertyManager and a sample Miter Flange are shown in Figure 29.16.

FIGURE 29.16

The Miter Flange PropertyManager and a sample part

A Miter Flange feature starts off with a sketch that is perpendicular to the starting edge of the Miter Flange feature.

TIP A quick way to start a sketch for a Miter Flange that is on a plane perpendicular to a selected edge is to select the edge, and then click a sketch tool. This automatically creates a plane perpendicular to the edge at the nearest endpoint.

Miter Flange sketches can have single lines or multiple lines. They can even have arcs. Still, remember that just because you can make it in SolidWorks does not mean that the manufacturer can make it. It is often a good idea to check with the manufacturer to ensure that the part can be made. Also, you usually learn something from the experience.

When selecting edges for the Miter Flange to go on, be sure to remain consistent in your selection. If you start by selecting an edge on the top of the part, then you should continue selecting edges on the top of the part. If you do not, then SolidWorks prompts you with a warning message in a tooltip that says that the edge is on the wrong face.

Some of the controls in the Miter Flange PropertyManager should be familiar by now, such as Use default radius, Flange Position, Trim side bends, and Gap Distance. You have seen these controls before in the Edge Flange PropertyManager.

The Start/End Offset panel enables you to pull a Miter Flange back from an edge without using a cut. If you need an intermittent flange, then you may need to use cuts or multiple Miter Flange features, as shown in Figure 29.17.

FIGURE 29.17

The Start/End Offset settings for a Miter Flange

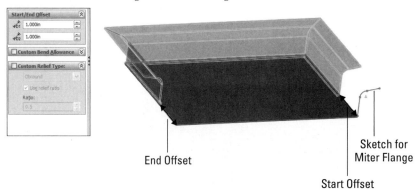

End Offset

Start Offset

Sketch for
Miter Flange

Hem feature

The Hem feature is used to roll over the edge of a sheet metal part. This feature is often used to smooth over a sharp edge or to add strength to the edge. You can also use it for other purposes, such as to capture a pin for a hinge. SolidWorks offers four different hem styles — Closed, Open, Tear Drop, and Rolled — which are shown as icons on the Hem PropertyManager. The PropertyManager for the Hem feature is shown in Figure 29.18.

One of the limitations to keep in mind with regard to hems is that SolidWorks cannot fold over a part so that the faces touch perfectly line on line. Doing this would cause the two sections of the part to merge into a larger piece, thus removing the coincident faces. SolidWorks, computers, and mathematics in general do not always handle the number zero very well. In reality, you can often see light through these hems, and so a perfectly flush hem may not be as accurate as it seems.

FIGURE 29.18

The Hem PropertyManager and a sample hem

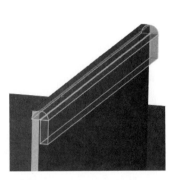

Jog feature

The Jog feature puts a pair of opposing bends on a flange so that the end of the flange is parallel to, but offset from, the face where the jog started. The Jog PropertyManager and a sample jog are shown in Figure 29.19.

FIGURE 29.19

The Jog PropertyManager and a sample jog

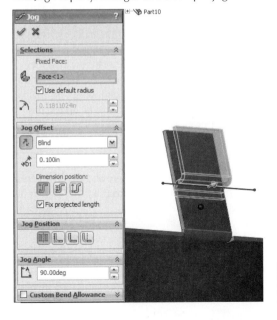

The Jog feature is created from a single sketch line on the face of a sheet metal part. The geometry to be jogged should not have any side bends; it should be a simple tab-like flange, as shown in Figure 29.19. The line to create the jog can be drawn at an angle, causing the jog to also be angled.

The three icons on the Jog Offset panel illustrate what dimension is being controlled by that setting.

Fixed Face

Like most sheet metal features, the Jog feature bends faces on the part, and when it does so, although it may be obvious to you as the user, it is not obvious to the software which face should remain stationary and which faces should be moved by the bend. The Fixed Face selection box enables you to select a face, or in this case, a part of a face, that you want to remain stationary as the rest of the faces move. The black dot on the face identifies it as stationary.

> **TIP** Problems can sometimes arise when using configurations that change sizes, because these markers for fixed faces can be pushed onto other faces. This can cause problems with assemblies and drawings, and in general makes visualization difficult. In cases like this, it may be advisable to select a larger face or one that has fewer changes, if possible, to be used as the fixed face.

Jog Offset

You can control the direction of the jog by using the arrow button to the left of the end condition selection box.

You can control the jog distance by selecting the end conditions, Up To Surface, Up To Vertex, or Offset From Surface. The default setting is Blind, in which you simply enter a distance for the offset, in exactly the same way that end conditions are controlled for features such as extrudes.

Fix projected length

One setting that may not be obvious is the Fix projected length. This refers to the length of the flange that the jog is altering. In Figure 29.19, you can see that the height of the jogged feature is the same as the height of the original feature. The jog obviously requires more material than the original, but the Fix projected length option is turned on, and so the height is maintained. If you turned this option off, then the finished height of the flange after the jog is added would be shorter, because the material is used by the jog, and additional material would not be added. For comparison, the image to the right in Figure 29.19 shows this situation.

Jog Position

The Jog Position selection establishes the relationship between the sketched line and the first bend tangent line. The Jog Position icons have tooltips with the following names, from left to right: Bend Centerline, Material Inside, Material Outside, and Bend Outside.

Jog Angle

The Jog Angle enables you to change the angle of the short perpendicular section of the jog. You can angle it to smooth out the jog (angles of less than 90 degrees) or to curl back on itself (angles of more than 90 degrees). Again, be careful to check with your manufacturer's capabilities.

Sketched Bend feature

Sketched Bend works in some respects like half of a jog. It requires the sketch line, and the Fixed Face selection. You define a bend position with the same set of icons that you used in the jog, and you assign a bend angle in the same way.

TIP You can use the Sketched Bend feature to "dog ear" corners. You do this by drawing a line across the corner at an angle and setting the angle to 180 degrees and then overriding the default radius with a much smaller one, such as .001 inches.

Unlike Jog, the Sketched Bend feature does not show you a preview. The Sketched Bend PropertyManager is shown in Figure 29.20.

FIGURE 29.20

The Sketched Bend PropertyManager

Closed Corner feature

The Closed Corner feature extends flanges on the sides to meet with other flanges. It is typically used when corners leave big open gaps, in order to create a corner that is more easily welded shut (although welds cannot be created in sheet metal parts in SolidWorks). The image to the left in Figure 29.21 shows a part where angled flanges have been applied. This creates big gaps in the corners. Although a Miter Flange may have been better, these were created using regular Edge Flanges. The image to the right shows the Closed Corner PropertyManager, as well as a preview of the corner being closed.

FIGURE 29.21

Applying the Closed Corner feature

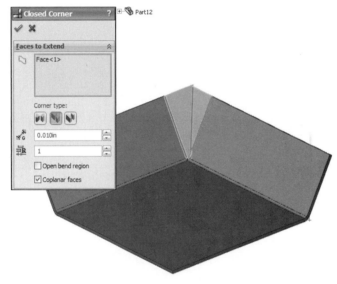

Faces to Extend

You must select the thickness face of one of the flanges in order to extend it. Selecting one face automatically selects the matching face from the other flange that you also want to extend. The Corner Type selection icons depict the selected face as red, and the three icons display tooltips: Butt, Overlap, and Underlap.

Gap

The Gap setting enables you to specify how close you want the closed corner to be. Keep in mind that you cannot use the number zero in this field. If you do, then SolidWorks reminds you to "Please enter a number greater than or equal to 0.00003937 and less than or equal to 0.86388126." It is good to know your limits.

Overlap/Underlap ratio

The Overlap/Underlap ratio setting controls how far across the overlapped face the overlapping flange reaches. Full overlap is a ratio of 1, and a Butt condition is (roughly) a ratio of zero. This ratio is only available when you have specified Overlap or Underlap for the corner type.

Open bend region

The Open bend region option affects how the finished corner looks in the bend area. If Open bend region is turned on, then a small gap is created at the end of the bend. If the option is turned off, then SolidWorks fills this area with geometry. Figure 29.22 shows the finished model with this option on and off, as well as the resulting flat patterns for each setting.

FIGURE 29.22

The Open bend region option, both on and off, and the resulting flat patterns

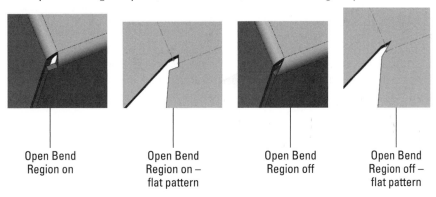

Open Bend
Region on

Open Bend
Region on –
flat pattern

Open Bend
Region off

Open Bend
Region off –
flat pattern

Corner Trim and Break Corner features

 The Corner Trim feature is available only when the sheet metal part is in its flattened state. The Corner Trim PropertyManager also has the Break Corner [Options] interface built right into it. However, the Break Corner feature is only available when the sheet metal part is in its folded state. Figure 29.23 shows the combined interface. Both functions are included here, and SolidWorks treats them as if they are part of a single function.

FIGURE 29.23

The Corner Trim PropertyManager, including the Break Corner [Options] panel

When finished, the Corner Trim feature places itself after the Flat Pattern feature in the FeatureManager. It similarly follows the suppress/unsuppress state of the Flat Pattern feature. When the Break Corner feature is used on its own, it is placed before the Flat Pattern feature. With this in mind, it seems best to use Break Corner as a separate feature unless it is being used specifically to alter the flat pattern in a way that cannot be done from the folded state.

Break Corner on its own is primarily used to remove sharp corners using either a chamfer or a rounded corner. This tool is set up to filter edges on the thickness of sheet metal parts, which is useful, because these edges are otherwise difficult to select without a lot of zooming. Break Corner can also break interior corners.

One of the main functions of the Corner Trim feature is to apply bend relief geometry to the flat pattern. The three available options are Circular, Square, and Bend Waist. These options are shown in Figure 29.24.

FIGURE 29.24

Applying the Corner Trim Relief options

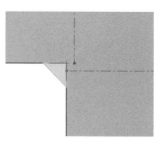

Forming Tool feature

Forming tools in SolidWorks enable you to place features that are not formed on a brake press. These are features that are not straight-line bends, but rather punched, drawn, formed, lanced, sheared, or otherwise deformed material.

One of the important things to understand about forming tools is that they do not stretch the material in the SolidWorks part in the same way that happens in a real-life forming operation. In real life, material is thinned when it is punched, stamped, or drawn. In SolidWorks, the thickness of a sheet metal part remains the same, regardless of what happens to it. For this reason, you need to be careful when using mass properties of sheet metal parts or doing stress analysis of parts that have formed features. You might consider taking your part weight from the flat pattern rather than from the formed sheet metal.

SolidWorks installs with a library of fairly simple forming tools that you can use as a starting point for your own personal customized library. You can also examine some of these tools to see how they create particular effects. The library is found in your Design Library in the Task pane. Some of the more interesting forming tools are the lances and louvers.

Creating forming tools

Forming tools are essentially a part that is used as a tool to form another part. One flat face of the forming tool part is designated as a Stopping Face, which is placed flush with the top face of the sheet metal part. You can move and rotate the tool with the Modify Sketch tool, and you can use dimensions or sketch relations to locate it.

Creating forming tools is far easier than it used to be. This section of the chapter gives you the information that you need to effectively create useful forming tools, addresses the limitations and unintended uses of forming tools, and provides a couple of hints for more complex forming tool creation.

To create a forming tool, you can use the Forming Tool button on the Sheet Metal toolbar. Figure 29.25 shows the PropertyManager interface for this tool.

FIGURE 29.25

The Form Tool PropertyManager and a sample tool

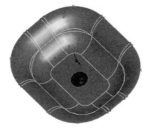

The Stopping Face turns a special color, and so do any faces that are selected in the Faces to Remove selection box. Faces to Remove means that those faces will be cutouts in the sheet metal part.

Another aspect of the forming tool is the orientation sketch. The orientation sketch is created automatically by using Convert Entities on the Stopping Face. If you have used this function in any of its previous versions, then you know that this latest iteration is far easier to create than before. However, to me, it looks like the orientation sketch has taken a step backwards. The orientation sketch cannot be manually edited, and so for forming tools where *footprints* are symmetrical, but other features in the tool are not, you cannot tell from the sketch which direction the forming tool should face. Orientation could be managed more easily in earlier versions of forming tools because the placement sketch was just a manually created sketch.

When creating a forming tool, you must remember to build in generous draft and fillets, and not to build undercuts into the tool. Also keep in mind that when you have a concave fillet face on the tool, the radius becomes smaller by the thickness of the sheet metal; as a result, you must be careful about minimum radius values on forming tools. If there is a concave face on the tool that has a .060-inch radius and the tool is applied to a part with a .060-inch thickness, then the tool will cause an error because it forms a zero radius fillet, which is not allowed. Errors in applied forming tool features cannot be edited or repaired, except by changing forming tool dimensions.

Once the forming tool is created, special colors are used for every face on the part. For example, the Stopping Face is a light blue color, Faces to Remove are red, and all of the other faces are yellow. Figure 29.26 shows the small addition that is made to the FeatureManager when you make a part into a forming tool. This feature did not exist in older versions of the tool.

FIGURE 29.26

The FeatureManager of a forming tool part

Forming Tool Library

The folder that the forming tools are placed into in the Design Library must be designated as a Forming Tool folder. To do this, right-click the folder that contains the forming tools and select Forming Tool Folder (a check mark appears next to this option).

Placing a forming tool

To place a forming tool on a sheet metal part (forming tools are only allowed to be used on parts with sheet metal features), you can drag the tool from the library and drop it on the face of the sheet metal part. Forming tools are limited to being used on flat faces.

From there, you can use the Modify Sketch tool or horizontal and vertical sketch relations to move and rotate the forming tool. It may be difficult to orient it properly without first placing it, seeing what orientation it ends up in, and then reorienting it if necessary because of the limitation mentioned earlier with not being able to edit the orientation sketch to give it some sort of direction identifier.

Configurations cannot be used with forming tools like they can with library features, although you can change dimensions by double-clicking the Forming Tool icon in the sheet metal part FeatureManager.

Forming tools are suppressed when the part is flattened.

Special techniques with forming tools

One application of forming tools that is asked for frequently is the cross break to stiffen a large, flat sheet metal face. SolidWorks has a cosmetic cross break which I discuss next. Cross breaks are clearly not something that SolidWorks can do using straight bends, but a forming tool can do it.

You can create the forming tool by lofting a rectangle to a sketch point on a plane slightly offset from the plane of the rectangle. This creates a shallow pyramid shape. Open the part from the material on the CD-ROM for Chapter 29 called `Chapter 29 - Cross Break.SLDPRT` to examine how this part was made. Figure 29.27 shows the Cross Break tool applied to a sheet metal part.

FIGURE 29.27

The Cross Break tool applied to a part

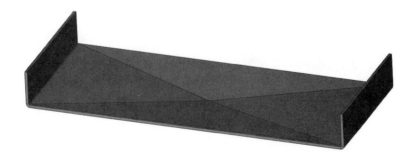

Cross Breaks

Using a forming tool to create a cross break is overkill. You may need to do it if you need to actually show the indented geometry. In SolidWorks 2009 a cosmetic cross break feature has been added. This feature enables you to specify the radius, angle, and direction used to create the cross break. It does not actually change the part geometry at all, but it does add two curve-like display entities.

When you place a Cross Break feature, you have the option to edit the sketch profile that creates the cross. This sketch has two intersecting lines. You cannot add more lines; the feature will fail if you have more than two lines in the sketch. (For example, if you wanted to put three breaks across a hexagonal face, the software will not allow this.) The lines do not have to end at a corner, but they do have to end at an edge. If the lines extend past or fall short of an edge, the feature will display a red X error icon, but it still creates the break lines where the sketch lines are.

Figure 29.28 shows the Cross Break PropertyManager and a part to which a Cross Break was applied. Notice that you can see the break lines through the solid, much like curves or cosmetic threads.

The Cross Break feature shows up in the FeatureManager just like any other feature, not like a cosmetic thread, which is the only other entity in the software that the Cross Break much resembles.

FIGURE 29.28

Creating a Cross Break

Form across bends

A second special technique is a gusset or a form that goes across bends. This can be adapted in many ways, but it is shown here going across two bends. I cannot confirm the practicality of actually manufacturing something like this, but I have seen it done.

The technique used here is to call the single long flat face of the forming tool the Stopping Face. The vertical faces on the ends and the fillet faces must be selected in the Faces to Remove selection box. The fillets of the outside of the forming tool also have to match the bends of the sheet metal part exactly. You may need to edit this part each time you use it, unless it is applied to parts with bends of the same size and separated by the same distance.

When you place the tool on the sheet metal part, you must place it accurately from side to side to get everything to work out properly.

This part is in the same location as the Cross Break file, and is called `Chapter 29 - Form Across Bends.SLDPRT`. Figure 29.29 shows the tool and a part to which it has been applied.

FIGURE 29.29

Forming across bends

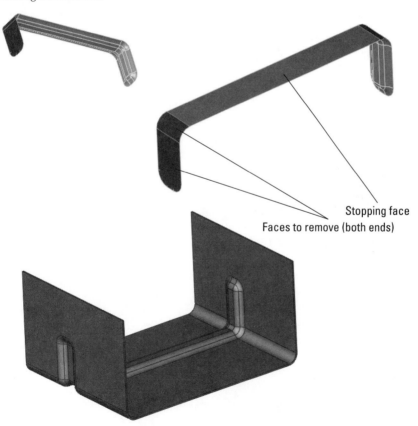

Stopping face
Faces to remove (both ends)

Lofted Bends feature

The Lofted Bends feature enables you to create transitions between two profiles. The range of functionality available through the Loft feature is not available with Lofted Bends; it is limited to two profiles with no end conditions or guide curves. Both profiles also need to be open contours, in order to allow the sheet metal to unfold.

Lofted Bends is not part of the Base Flange method, but it is part of the newer set of sheet metal tools available in SolidWorks.

Figure 29.30 shows what is probably the most common application of this feature. The bend lines shown must be established in the PropertyManager when you create or edit the feature. Bend Lines are only an option if both profiles have the same number of straight lines. For example, if one of the profiles is a circle instead of a rectangle with very large fillets, then the Bend Lines options are not available in the PropertyManager.

FIGURE 29.30

The Lofted Bends PropertyManager, a sample, and a flat pattern with bend lines

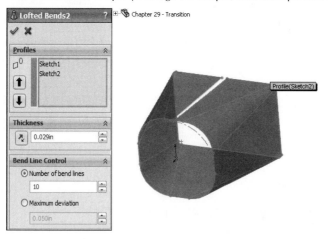

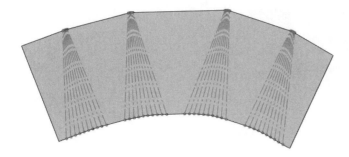

Like the forming tools, you can also use Lofted Bends in situations for which they were probably not intended. Figure 29.31 shows how lofting between 3D curves can also create shapes that can be flattened in SolidWorks. In this case, a couple of intermediate steps were required to get to the 3D curves, which involve surface features.

FIGURE 29.31

Using 3D curves with Lofted Bends to create flattenable complex shapes

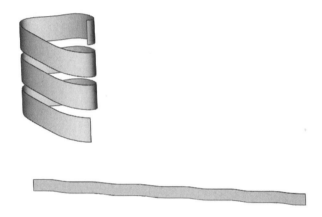

 This part is included on the CD-ROM with the name `Chapter 29 - wrap.sldprt`.

Unfold and Fold features

 Unfold is a feature that unfolds selected bends temporarily. It is typically used in conjunction with a Fold feature to re-fold the bends. This combination is used to apply a feature that must be applied to the flat pattern; for example, a hole that spans across a bend. Figure 29.32 shows the FeatureManager of a part where this combination has been applied, as well as the part itself, showing the bend across a hole, and the PropertyManager, which is the same for both features.

Both the Unfold and Fold features make it easy to select the bends without zooming in, even for small bends. A filter is placed on the cursor when the command is active, which allows only bends to be selected. The Collect All Bends option also becomes available. This feature also requires that you select a stationary face to hold still while the rest of the model moves during the unfolding and folding process.

FIGURE 29.32

Applying the Unfold and Fold features

Flatten command

The Flatten command is different from the Unfold feature in a few important ways. First, Flatten is not a feature; it is just a command that unsuppresses the normally suppressed Flat Pattern feature. The Flat Pattern feature keeps track of the bend lines for a part. The individual bends are listed under the Flat Pattern feature, and when the feature is unsuppressed, the individual bends can be suppressed. This enables you to establish configurations that can show bend processing order on the drawing or in an assembly. You can duplicate the Flatten command by manually suppressing or unsuppressing the Flat Pattern feature.

Tutorial: Using the Base Flange Sheet Metal Method

SolidWorks Base Flange method sheet metal is fun and easy to use as you will see in this tutorial:

1. **Open a new part using a special sheet metal template if one is available.**

2. **On the Top plane, draw a rectangle centered on the Origin, 14 inches in X by 12 inches in Y (or Z).**

3. **Initiate the Base Flange tool, accept the default thickness of .029 inches, and change the K-Factor to .43.** Notice that the default inside bend radius is not shown. This setting is made in the Sheet Metal feature that is placed before the Base Flange feature in the FeatureManager.

4. **After the Base Flange has been created, edit the Sheet Metal feature, and change the default bend radius to .050 inches.**

5. **Click one of the 14-inch edges and then select the Line tool from the Sketch toolbar.** This is a shortcut to creating a plane perpendicular to the end of the edge and opening a new sketch on the plane. This is useful in other situations in addition to working with sheet metal. Draw a sketch similar to that shown in Figure 29.33. The arc overrides the default inside bend radius setting, and directly controls that particular bend.

FIGURE 29.33

The sketch to start a Miter Flange

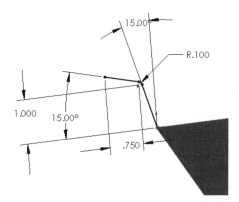

6. **With the sketch still active, press the Miter Flange button on the Sheet Metal toolbar.** Use the settings shown in the image to the right in Figure 29.34. Select three edges as shown. Remember to select the edges on the same side of the Base Flange. In particular, notice the Start/End Offset settings. Click OK when you are satisfied with the settings.

7. **Select the remaining edge that is not touched by the Miter Flange, and click the Edge Flange tool on the Sheet Metal toolbar.** Click the top point of one end of the Miter Flange to establish the flange length, using the Up To Vertex end condition.

8. **Press the Edit Flange Profile button in the PropertyManager, and manually pull the sketch back from the ends of the flange.** Add dimensions to make the flange 3 inches from the corner on the left side, and 5 inches from the corner on the right side, as shown in Figure 29.35; otherwise, use the default settings for the flange. Click OK to accept the feature when you are satisfied with the settings.

FIGURE 29.34

Specifying the Miter Flange settings

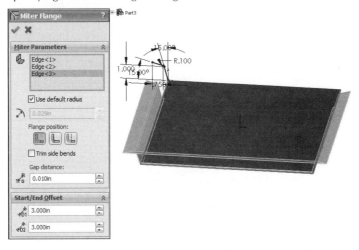

FIGURE 29.35

Creating an Edge Flange

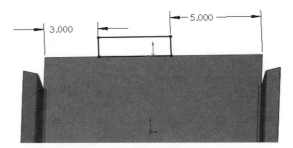

9. **Select the inside edge of the top of the Edge Flange that you have just created, and initiate a Hem feature.** Use the settings Material Inside, Closed Hem, with a length of .25 inches, and make the material go toward the inside of the box. The settings and preview of the feature are shown in Figure 29.36.

10. **Create a second Edge Flange the same height as the first, just to the right of the first flange, as seen from the point of view used in Figure 29.35.** Edit the flange profile and pull the new flange away from the existing flange. Add a dimension to make the new flange 2 inches wide. Click OK when you are satisfied with the settings.

FIGURE 29.36

Creating a hem

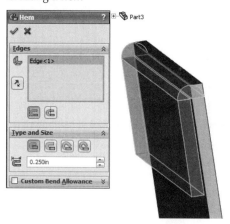

11. **Open a sketch on the inside face of the new Edge Flange and draw a line across the flange .75 inches from the end.**

12. **Create a Jog feature with the settings shown in Figure 29.37.** Make sure to set a custom bend radius by deselecting the Use Default Radius option and entering **.025 inches**. If you do not set the custom radius, then you may get a warning that the jog distance is less than a minimum jog value. Be careful when selecting the fixed face to select the side of the line with the largest area, or the face you want to remain where it is while the rest of the part bends and moves around it.

13. **From the CD-ROM, in the folder for Chapter 29, find the part named Chapter 29 – Cross Break.SLDPRT.** Copy this file to a folder in the library that you have established outside of your SolidWorks installation folder, called Forming Tools.

14. **Make sure that this folder appears in the Design Library.** You may have to press F5 or the Refresh button at the top of the Task pane. When the folder appears, right-click the folder and activate the check mark next to Forming Tools Folder.

15. **When the file has been copied and the folder has been assigned as a Forming Tool folder, drag the Chapter 29 – Cross Break part from the folder and onto the big flat face of the sheet metal part.** You will be put into a sketch that looks like Figure 29.38.

16. **Once you have dropped the feature into the sketch, drag the Origin of the sketch onto the Origin of the part, and then click Finish.** Notice that the cross break is in the middle of the part, but is too small.

FIGURE 29.37

Creating a jog

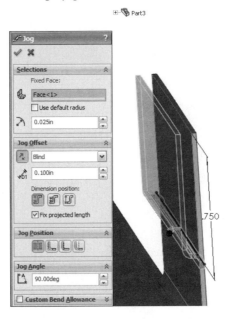

FIGURE 29.38

Placing a forming tool

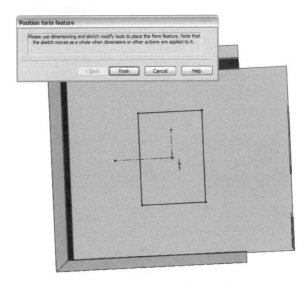

17. Double-click the new feature in the FeatureManager; a set of dimensions appear on the screen. Change the 4-inch dimension to 13.9 inches, and the 6-inch dimension to 11.9 inches. The cross break should now look like Figure 29.39.

FIGURE 29.39

Resizing the cross break to 13.9 inches

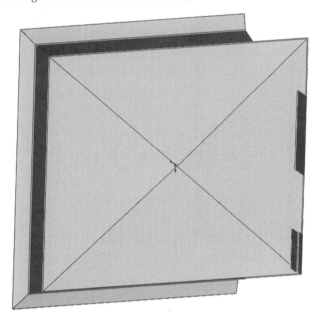

18. Create a new configuration named Flat. In this configuration, suppress the forming tool that you just placed, and unsuppress the Flat Pattern feature at the bottom of the tree.

Summary

The newer set of sheet metal tools that are available in SolidWorks is known as the Base Flange method. These tools are extremely powerful, and in most cases are very easy to use and understand. The setup of defaults is kept in the initial Sheet Metal feature, and all of the bends and bend lines are contained in the final Flat Pattern feature

Chapter 30

Using the Insert Bends Method for Sheet Metal Parts

I n Chapter 29 on the Base Flange method, I explained the coexistence of two conceptual models for the creation of sheet metal parts in SolidWorks. The Base Flange method is the newer and more powerful of these two functions. However, some functionality is available only through the Insert Bends method, and the two methods may be combined to some extent. The older method is by no means obsolete.

One of the reasons for creating a new method was that the old method was very convoluted, and required certain types of features to be put into specific locations in the FeatureManager order; this meant that the user was frequently working in Rollback mode. In the days before being able to save in Rollback mode, this was not only tedious but dangerous. This is because without the ability to save while the model was rolled back, users were more likely to lose their work.

One of the advantages of the old method was that you were able to use the features that you were accustomed to using for regular modeling, and then make it a sheet metal part when you were done. Of course, this same advantage frequently turned out to be a disadvantage, because the standard features do not have any specialized sheet metal functionality.

Today, the Insert Bends method is used for specific situations. For example, it is used for parts that have been created as generic SolidWorks models and that need to be flattened, imported parts that need to be flattened, and conical rolled sheet metal parts.

Architecture of Insert Bends

In Chapter 29, I showed that a part created with the Base Flange method had as its first feature a Sheet Metal feature, which was a placeholder for sheet metal defaults for the current part. The Base Flange feature came next, followed by additional Sheet Metal features, and the list of specialized features was completed with a suppressed Flat Pattern feature.

The structure of parts created with the Insert Bends feature is somewhat different. Figure 30.1 shows a comparison of the two methods' FeatureManagers for simple parts.

FIGURE 30.1

A comparison between default features for Base Flange and Insert Bends

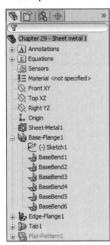

The most notable difference is that the Insert Bends part starts off with non-sheet metal features. The Rip feature also stands out, but the Rip feature is not exclusive to sheet metal. Although you can use Rip on any model, it is found only on the Sheet Metal toolbar.

The Sheet Metal feature is found in both the Base Flange and Insert Bends methods, and has the same PropertyManager function in both methods.

The new features in the Insert Bends method are the Flatten Bends and Process Bends features. The way the Insert Bends method works is that the model that is built with the sharp-cornered non-sheet metal feature is flattened by the Flatten Bends feature. The model is then reconstructed with bends by the Process Bends feature.

Making Sheet Metal from a Generic Model

The main rule that SolidWorks enforces on sheet metal models regardless of how they came to be sheet metal is that the parts should have a consistent wall thickness. When all of the geometry is made from the beginning as a sheet metal part (using the Base Flange method), there is never a problem with this. However, when the part is modeled from thin features, cuts, shells, and so on, there is no telling what may happen to the model.

If you perform an Insert Bends operation on a model that does not have a consistent wall thickness, then the Flatten and Process Bends features fail. If a thickness face is not perpendicular to the main face of the part, then the software simply forces the situation, making the face perpendicular to the main face.

Normal Cut

If a Cut feature is placed before the Sheet Metal feature, then as far as SolidWorks is concerned, the part is not a sheet metal part. However, if the cut feature is created after the Sheet Metal feature, then the model has to follow a different set of rules. The "normal shear" mentioned previously is one of those rules. In Figure 30.2, the sketch for a cut is on a plane that is not perpendicular to the face that the cut is going into. Under a normal modeling situation, the cut just goes through the part at an angle. However, in SolidWorks sheet metal, a new option is added to the PropertyManager for the cut. This is the Normal Cut option, and it is turned on by default. You could be modeling and never even notice this option, but it is important because it affects the geometrical results of the feature.

As shown in Figure 30.2, when the Normal Cut option is on, the thickness faces of the cut are turned perpendicular (or *normal*) to the face of the sheet metal. This is also important because if the angle between the angled face and the sketch changes, the geometry of the cutout can also change. This setting becomes more important as the material becomes thicker and as the angle between the sketch and the sheet metal face becomes shallower.

Starting with the 2009 release of the software, SolidWorks allows you to have angled faces on side edges, and will maintain the angle when it flattens the part. In previous versions, angles on side faces cause the Flat Pattern feature to fail. Even a cut that does not use the Normal Cut option and creates faces that are not perpendicular to the main face of the part will not cause the Flat Pattern to fail.

Rip feature

When building a sheet metal part from a generic model, a common technique used to achieve consistent wall thicknesses is to build the outer shape as a solid and then shell the part. The only problem with this method is that it leaves corners joined in a way that cannot be flattened. You can solve this problem by using the Rip feature. Rip breaks out the corner in one or both directions in such a way that it can be unfolded. Bend reliefs are later added automatically by the Process Bends feature.

Figure 30.3 shows the Rip PropertyManager and the results of using this feature. The model was created to look like a Miter Flange part.

FIGURE 30.2

Using the Normal Cut option

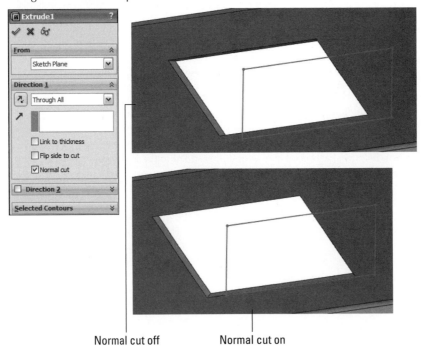

Normal cut off   Normal cut on

FIGURE 30.3

Using the Rip feature

Notice also in Figure 30.3 that after the Rip, the edges of the material are still sheared at an angle. Because the top of the part was shelled, the thickness of the part is not normal to the main face of the sheet metal. You can fix this by using the Flatten Bends feature, which lays the entire part out flat, calculates the bend areas, and corrects any discrepancies at the edges of the part.

 NOTE Rip functionality is included in the Insert Bends Sheet Metal PropertyManager when it is first initiated, although it is no longer there when you edit the part later. If you use it, the Rip data becomes a feature of its own and is placed before the Sheet Metal feature in the FeatureManager. Be aware that there are slight differences between using the Rip function as an independent feature and using it as a part of the Insert Bends feature. You may want to check this on a part you are working with to verify which method best suits your needs.

Sheet Metal feature

The Sheet Metal feature used in the Insert Bends method is very similar to the one used in the Base Flange method. However, two main differences exist: Insert Bends Sheet Metal requires the user to select a Fixed Face, and Base Flange Sheet Metal allows the use of Gauge Tables. Both features function as placeholders and otherwise contain the same information, use the same name and icon, and are inserted automatically when a different feature is created.

Flatten Bends feature

The Flatten Bends feature is added automatically by the Insert Bends tool. As mentioned earlier, it takes the model with sharp corners and lays it flat, adjusting the material in the bend area and normalizing the thickness faces around the flat pattern. A Merge Faces option is not available in the Insert Bends method except in the Flat Pattern feature, and so the flat pattern created by the Flatten Bends feature always has edges created by the tangent lines of the bends.

Notice in Figure 30.4 that the Flatten Bends feature has a sketch and several Sharp Bend features under it. The Sharp Sketch is simply an account of the bend lines, and you cannot edit it manually. The Sharp Bend features can be suppressed, in which case they are not re-formed in the Process Bends feature. You can also edit Sharp Bend features to change the default radius, bend allowance, and relief type.

FIGURE 30.4

Using the Flatten Bends feature

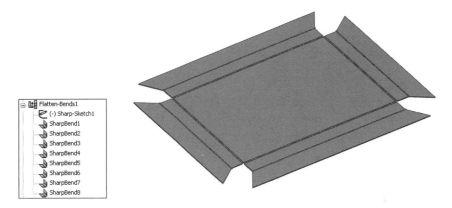

Process Bends feature

The Process Bends feature takes all the flat pattern information, the bend information, and entities in the Flat Sketch, and rebuilds the model with the formed bends. The Flat Sketch under the Process Bends feature is the Insert Bends method version of a sketched bend. You can add sketch lines here to bend panels of the part. After you add lines to this sketch, exiting the sketch causes the part to be created with a default 90-degree bend corresponding to the line. Of course, all of the Sketched Bend rules exist, such as that the line has to extend at least up to the edges of the part, the lines cannot extend across multiple faces, and construction lines are ignored.

For every bend created by a sketch line in the Process Bends Flat Sketch, a Flat Bend feature is added to the list under Process Bends. You can control the angle and radius of each of these Flat Bends by editing the Flat Bend feature. This is all illustrated in Figure 30.5.

No Bends

The No Bends tool on the Sheet Metal toolbar is simply used to roll back the model before the Flatten Bends feature in the tree with a single button click. This is primarily to add new geometry that is turned into bends through the Flatten and Process Bends features.

Flat Pattern

The Insert Bends method uses the Flat Pattern feature as well as the Base Flange method. However, it was not part of the original scheme, being added at some point after the new tools had proved their value. This enables you to make use of the new features as well, as discussed later in this chapter in the section Mixing Methods.

FIGURE 30.5

Using the Process Bends feature

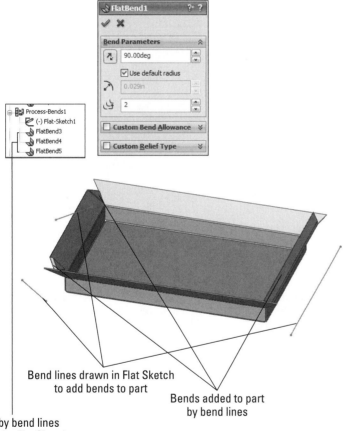

Bend lines drawn in Flat Sketch
to add bends to part

Bends added to part
by bend lines

Added by bend lines
added to the Flat Sketch

Convert to Sheet Metal

The Convert to Sheet Metal feature can use either SolidWorks native or imported data. It can also use solids as well as surfaces. The model can be shelled or not shelled, and have filleted edges or not. This feature enables you to identify which edges will become bends and automatically identifies the edges to rip.

FIGURE 30.6

Using Convert to Sheet Metal

  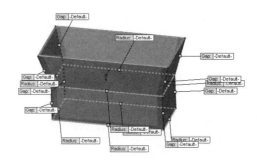

This tool is very useful for imported geometry and for parts with tricky shapes. Although the PropertyManager interface looks busy, it is fairly straight forward to use. Your first selection in the top Fixed Entity box should be a stable face, preferably an outer face on the bottom or the top. Inner faces generally do not work.

Note that you can reverse the thickness of the sheet metal, so that the solid that you start with can be treated as the volume inside the sheet metal enclosure, or the outer faces of the initial solid turn out to be the inner faces of the sheet metal part. Use the Reverse Thickness option to accomplish this.

Selecting Bend Edges is the next step, with the implication that any edge that is not a bend will be ripped. Also note that three bend edges cannot intersect at a point or one bend edge cannot intersect at the middle of another edge.

Setting default bend radius, thickness, and Auto Relief options are the same as in other sheet metal functions.

Working with Imported Geometry

Working with imported geometry starts at the point where you use the Rip feature. While imported geometry can be geometrically manipulated to some extent in SolidWorks, that is beyond the scope of this chapter. The need for a model with walls of constant thickness still exists, even if the imported model has filleted edges showing bend geometry already in the model.

FeatureWorks may be used to recognize sheet metal features or to fully or partially deconstruct the model by removing bend faces as fillets. While FeatureWorks is not covered in this book, the technique may be useful when editing imported parts with overall prismatic geometry that is common to sheet metal parts.

When a sheet metal part is imported, whether it meets the requirements immediately or must be edited in one way or another, to make a sheet metal part of it, you can simply use the Insert Bends feature or even the Convert to Sheet Metal feature.

Making Rolled Conical Parts

One of the reasons for maintaining the legacy Insert Bends method is to have a way of creating rolled conical parts. You can create cylindrical sheet metal parts by drawing an arc that almost closes to an entire circle, and creating a Base Flange from it. However, no equivalent technique for creating tapered cones exists with the Base Flange method.

With the Insert Bends method, a revolved thin feature does the job nicely. You simply revolve a straight line at an angle to the centerline, so that the straight line does not touch or cross the centerline; the revolve cannot go around the full 360 degrees, as there must be a gap. Sheet metal parts are not created by stretching the material (except for Forming Tools).

When creating a rolled sheet metal part, a flat face cannot be selected to remain fixed when the part is flattened. Instead, you can use a straight edge along the revolve gap, as shown in Figure 30.7.

> **NOTE** When a conical sheet metal part is created, it does not receive the Flat Pattern feature at the end of the FeatureManager. This is because none of the new Base Flange method features are allowed on this type of part.

FIGURE 30.7

Selecting a straight edge for a conical part

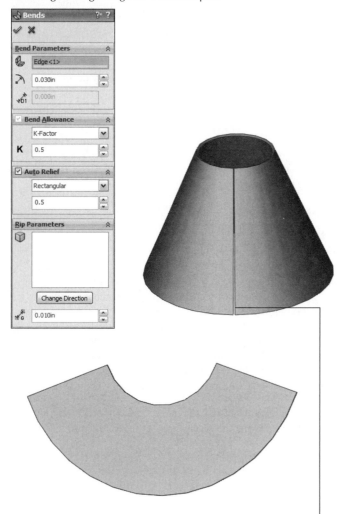

Select one of these edges in the
Fixed Face/edge selection box

Mixing Methods

If you use the Insert Bend tool on a part, you can still use the more advanced tools available through the Base Flange method, unless it is a cylindrical or conical part. A Flat Pattern feature is added to the bottom of most feature trees, and the presence of this feature is what signifies that the current part has now become a sheet metal part to the Base Flange features.

However, it is recommended that you avoid mixing the different techniques to flatten parts; for example, suppressing bends under Flatten and Process Bends, as well as using the Flat Pattern.

Tutorial: Working with the Insert Bends Method for Sheet Metal Parts

The Insert Bends method has been relegated mainly to duty for specialty functions. Gain an understanding of how this method works by following these steps:

1. Create a new blank part.

2. On the Top plane, open a sketch and sketch a rectangle centered on the Origin 12 inches in the Horizontal direction and 8 inches in the Vertical direction.

3. **Extrude the rectangle 1 inch with 45 degrees of draft, Draft Outward, in Direction 1, and in Direction 2 extrude 1 inch with no draft.** The two directions should be opposite from one another.

4. **Shell out the part to .050 inches, selecting the large face on the side where the draft has been applied.** The part should now look like Figure 30.8.

FIGURE 30.8

The part as of Step 4

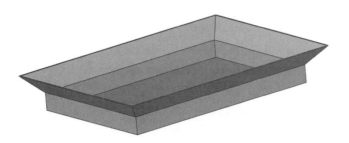

5. **Use the Rip feature to rip out the four corners.** Allow the Rip to rip all corners in both directions. The part should now look like Figure 30.9.

FIGURE 30.9

Ripping the corners

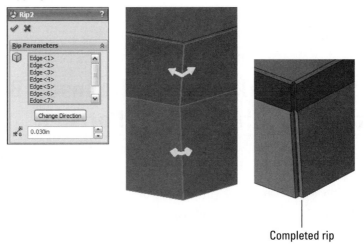

Completed rip

6. **Create an Insert Bends feature, accepting the default values,** and picking in the middle of the base of the part for the fixed face.

7. **Draw a rectangle on one of the vertical faces of the part, as shown in Figure 30.10.**

FIGURE 30.10

Adding a sketch for the cut

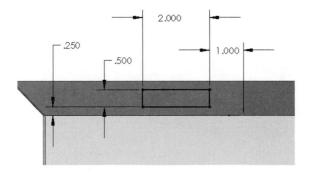

8. **Use the sketch to create a Through All cut in one direction.** Notice that the Normal cut option is on by default. Examine the finished cut closely; notice that it is different from the default type of cut because it is not made in a direction normal to the sketch, but rather in a direction normal to the face of the part. Details of this are shown in Figure 30.11.

FIGURE 30.11

Using the Normal Cut option

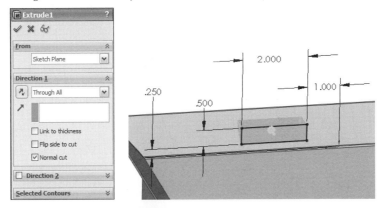

9. **Click the Flatten button on the Sheet Metal toolbar.** Notice that the Flat Pattern feature becomes unsuppressed and that the Bend Lines sketch under it is shown. This works just like it did in the Base Flange method. The finished part is shown in Figure 30.12.

FIGURE 30.12

The finished part with the Flat Pattern feature unsuppressed

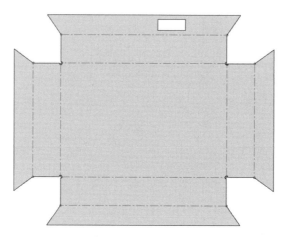

Summary

The Insert Bends method was a convoluted and complex way to create sheet metal parts, requiring a lot of jumping around between rollback states, and reordering to place features in the proper order so that everything appears on the flat pattern where it belongs. The newer Base Flange tools are far easier to use, but do not replace all of the functionality of the old technique, so you still need to know both methods to fully master sheet metal tools in SolidWorks.

Chapter 31

Using Weldments

Weldments in SolidWorks are built on driving structural profiles along sketch entities in a multi-body part environment. Weldment members can be curved, you can make them using standard or custom profiles, and you can build them from both 2D and 3D sketches. A Cut List within the part keeps track of how much of each profile is needed to fabricate the weldment. Weldments are specialized parts that are similar in some ways to sheet metal parts.

You can use weldments for round or rectangular tubular structures, structures made from channels, flanged sections, standard or custom shapes, gussets, and end caps, and they can also represent weld beads in the part. You can also use weldments to create structures that are bolted together, structural aluminum extrusion frames, vinyl window frames, and wooden frames and structures, and you can put them into assemblies with other parts such as castings, sheet metal, and fabricated plate.

Sketching in 3D

The 3D sketch is an important tool for creating weldments (and many other features) in SolidWorks. Structural frames are a large part of the work that is typically done using weldment functionality in SolidWorks, and frames are often represented as 3D wireframes. You can do this with a combination of 2D sketches on different planes, with a single 3D sketch, or with a combination of 2D and 3D sketches. If you have confidence in your ability to use 3D sketches, then that is the best way to go. Three-dimensional sketches can be challenging, but they are certainly manageable if you know what to expect from them.

Earlier chapters discuss the tools that are available for 3D sketches; this chapter covers techniques for 3D sketching.

Navigating in space

When drawing a line in a 3D sketch, the cursor and Origin initially look like those shown in Figure 31.1. The large red Origin is called the *space handle*, with the red legs indicating the active sketching plane. Any sketch entities that you draw lie on this plane. The cursor also indicates the plane to which the active sketching plane is parallel. The XY graphic shown in Figure 31.1 does not mean that the sketch is going to be *on* the XY plane, just parallel to it.

FIGURE 31.1

The space handle and the 3D sketch cursor

Pressing the Tab key causes the active sketching plane to toggle between XY, YZ, and ZX. The active sketching plane indication does not create any sketch relations; it just lets you know the orientation of the sketch entities that are being placed. If you want to create a skew line that is not parallel to any standard plane, you can do this by sketching to available endpoints, vertices, Origins, and so on. If there are not any entities to snap to, then you need to accept the planar placement, turn off the sketch tool, rotate the view, and move one end of the sketch entity.

An excellent tool to help you visualize what is happening in a 3D sketch is the Four Viewport view. This divides the screen into four quadrants, displaying the Front, Top, and Right views in addition to the trimetric or isometric view. You can sketch in any of the viewports, and the sketch updates live in all of the viewports simultaneously. This arrangement is shown in Figure 31.2. You can easily access the divided viewport screen by using buttons on the Standard Views toolbar. You can also manually split the screen by using the splitter bars at the lower-left and upper-right ends of the scroll bar areas around the graphics window. These window elements are also described in Chapter 2.

When unconstrained entities in a 3D sketch are moved, they move in the plane of the screen. This can lead to unexpected results when viewing something at an angle, moving it, and then rotating the view, which shows that it has shot off into deep interplanetary space. This is another reason for using the Four Viewport view, which enables you to see what is going on from all points of view at once.

FIGURE 31.2

The Four Viewport view

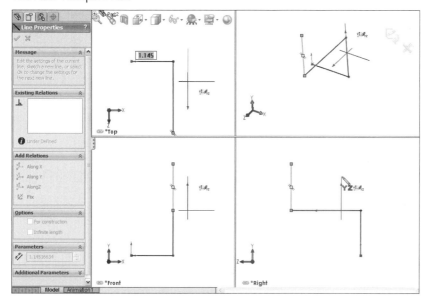

Sketch relations in 3D sketches

Sketch relations in 3D sketches are not the same as in 2D sketches. Improvements have been made in the past several versions. Pierce is not applicable in a 3D sketch, and is replaced by Coincident, because in 3D sketches, there is no difference between Pierce and Coincident. Relations are not projected into a plane in a 3D sketch the way they are in 2D.

On the other hand, several other relations are available in 3D sketches that are not found in 2D sketches, such as AlongX, AlongY, AlongZ, and OnSurface.

As mentioned earlier, relations in 3D sketches are not projected like they are in 2D sketches. For example, an entity in a 2D sketch can be made coincident to an entity that is out of plane. This is because to make the relation, the out-of-plane entity is projected into the sketch plane, and the relation is made to the projection. In a 3D sketch, Coincident means Coincident, with no projection.

As a general caution, keep in mind that solving sketches in 3D is more difficult than it is in 2D. You will see more situations where sketch relations fail, or flip in the wrong direction. Angle dimensions in particular are notorious in 3D sketches for flipping direction if they change and go across the 180-degree mark. When possible, it is advisable to work with fully defined sketches, and also to be careful (and conservative) with sketch relations.

For example, the sketch shown in Figure 31.3 cannot be fully defined without also overdefining the sketch. The main difficulty is that the combination of the tangent arc and the symmetric legs of the end brace cannot be located rotationally, even using the questionable reliability of 3D planes that are discussed next. The only workable answer to this is to create a separate 2D sketch on a real 2D sketch plane, where the plane is defined by the elements of the 3D sketch.

FIGURE 31.3

Three-dimensional sketches may be difficult to fully define.

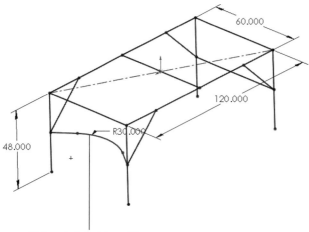

This set of sketch entities
cannot be located rotationally
within the 3D sketch

Planes in space

It is possible to create planes directly in 3D sketches. These planes function in some respects like sketch entities, by following sketch relations. Sketches can be created on these planes, and move with the planes. Having planes in the sketch also enables planar sketch entities such as arcs and circles in 3D sketches.

Unfortunately, there is a lot to watch out for with 3D planes, as they are called. The first thing to watch out for is that they do not follow their original definition like normal Reference Geometry type planes. Figure 31.4 shows the PropertyManager interface for creating 3D planes; however, keep in mind that the plane does not maintain the original relation to these initial references. The parent-and-child relations that SolidWorks users are used to are suspended for this one function, or work in the reverse from what you normally expect.

FIGURE 31.4

The three-dimensional planes PropertyManager

Three-dimensional planes cannot be fully defined unless there is some sketch geometry on the plane that is in turn related to something else. Limited types of sketch relations can be applied directly to the plane itself,. Horizontal and Vertical relations cannot be applied directly to the plane to orient it. Horizontal and Vertical relations of entities on the plane are relative only to the plane and not to the rest of the part, and so making a line horizontal on the plane does not mean anything when the plane rotates (which it is free to do until it is somehow constrained to prevent this).

Beyond this, when a plane violates a sketch relation, the relation is not reported, which severely limits the amount of confidence that you can place in planes that are created in this way. The biggest danger is in the plane rotating, because that is the direction in which it is most difficult to fully lock down. The best recommendation I can make here is reference sketch lines given some relations to something stable, preferably outside of the 3D sketch.

I am not saying it is impossible to use 3D sketches properly, just that they are very likely to misbehave if they are not tied down, and they are notoriously difficult to tie down.

The basic recommendation on this tool is to either use it at your own risk, having been warned, or simply to leave it alone. The preference is to use reference planes that are created in the familiar and reliable way. Although this requires that the planes be made beforehand, it guarantees that the planes will stay where you put them, or move in controllable ways. You can still activate regular reference geometry planes inside a 3D sketch.

If you choose to use these planes, to activate the plane for sketching, you can double-click the plane with the cursor. The plane is activated when it displays a grid. You can double-click an empty space to return to regular 3D Sketch mode. The main thing that you give up with abandoning 3D sketch planes is the ability to use the dynamic drag options when all loft or boundary sketches are made in a single 3D sketch, which I have never used except to demonstrate the idea once.

Planar path segments

Some path segments that are allowed in 3D sketches can only be used if they are sketched on a plane. These entities include circles and arcs, and can include splines, although splines are not required to be on a plane. It has already been mentioned that to sketch on a 3D Plane (a plane created within the 3D sketch), you can simply double-click the plane.

To sketch on a standard plane or reference geometry plane, you can Ctrl+click the border of the plane with the sketch entity icon active or double-click the plane. The space handle moves, indicating that newly created sketch entities will lie in the selected plane.

Dimensions

Dimensions in 2D sketches can represent the distance between two points, or they can represent the horizontal or vertical distance between objects. In 3D sketches, dimensions between points are *always* the straight-line distance. If you want to get a dimension that is horizontal or vertical, you should create the dimension between a plane and a point (the dimension is always measured normal to the plane) or between a line and a point (the dimension is always measured perpendicular to the line). For this reason, reference sketch geometry is often used freely in 3D sketches, in part to support dimensioning.

Using the Weldment Tools

Like the Sheet Metal tools, the Weldment tools in SolidWorks are specialized to enable you to create weldment-specific features in a specialized environment. Everything starts from a sketch or set of sketches representing the wireframe of the welded structural members.

Weldment

The Weldment button on the Weldment toolbar simply places a Weldment placeholder in the FeatureManager. This placeholder tells SolidWorks that this part is a special weldment part, much in the way that the Sheet Metal feature in sheet metal parts is a placeholder, and denotes a special part type. The Weldment feature moves to the top of the tree, regardless of when it is created in the part history. If you do not create a Weldment feature manually, then one is automatically created for you and placed at the top of the tree when the first Structural Member feature is created. Structural Members are discussed next in this chapter.

This feature does not offer any special default settings, except for the ability to set custom properties that transfer to all Cut list items that are created in the current part, and the fact that the Merge Result option is turned off by default in Weldment parts. The former is important when multiple weldments go together to make an assembly. You can access the custom properties interface, shown in Figure 31.5, through the Properties option on the Weldment feature right-mouse button menu.

FIGURE 31.5

The Weldment Properties interface

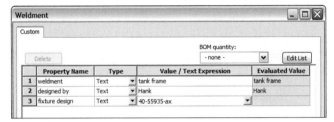

Structural Member

A Structural Member is the basic building unit of weldments in SolidWorks. You can create a Structural Member by extruding a profile along one or more path segments, and it may result in a single body or multiple bodies. The path segments may be in the form of 2D or 3D sketches.

> **NOTE** A single Structural Member feature may create multiple bodies, with each body corresponding to a single cut length of stock. In other words, the feature name "Structural Member" does not necessarily refer to a single piece of the weldment, although it may.

One limitation of the use of sketches in Structural Member features is that only two selected sketch entities may intersect at any one location. For example, at each corner of a cube, three path segments intersect, and so you can only select two of those elements at one time to create a Structural Member feature. Because each of the path segments requires a piece of metal, the leftover path segments may be used by a second Structural Member feature.

When creating the sketch for the weldment, it is important to decide what the sketch represents. For example, does it represent the centerline of the structural elements, or does it represent the closest that the elements can be to one another or to something else? You can orient and position structural shape profiles relative to the frame sketch in several ways, with positioning at the shape centroid being probably the most intuitive for closed shapes and a corner being most intuitive for angle channels.

Figure 31.6 shows a single 3D sketch of a simple frame and a Structural Member feature in the process of creation. You must select the standard first, then the type, and finally the size. A limited number of profiles come with the software, and although it is very likely that you will need to create some custom profiles, fortunately they are very easy to create.

To access a large number of weldment profiles in various standards, open the Design Library and select the SolidWorks Content icon. Under that, the Weldments folder has several zip files containing weldment profiles. Ctrl+click an icon to down load the file, and then extract the contents of the zip file to the library location you have established for your weldment profiles.

FIGURE 31.6

A 3D sketch of a frame

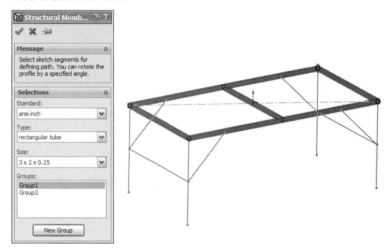

Groups

SolidWorks 2009 adds the groups functionality to weldments. The concept is simple, you can group selected path segments within a structural member feature into two kinds of groups: Parallel or Contiguous. A single structural member may have multiple groups.

Parallel groups contain parallel path segments that do not touch. Parallel groups also have the curious requirement that you have to select the structural profile before you can select more than one path segment.

Contiguous groups contain path segments that touch end to end, two segments at a time. A contiguous group cannot have one path segment intersect in the middle of another or more than two path segments intersecting at a corner.

Each group can only have a single orientation of the structural profile. If for example, each frame leg needed to have the profile rotated to a different orientation, you would need to do the legs in four separate groups instead of all in a single group.

Given those requirements, if the frame shown in Figure 31.6 were to be created entirely from the same structural profile, say ANSI inch, square tube, 3 x 3 x .025, it would require a minimum of five groups, as Figure 31.7 shows, in exploded form. The file used to create this image is included on the CD-ROM under the name Chapter 31 – Weldment groups.sldprt.

Using groups to create the welded frame

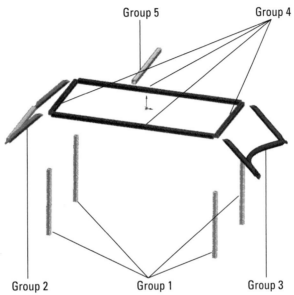

The main advantage of the new groups functionality is that each member within the group is automatically trimmed to other members of the group, and the control of gaps within or between groups. The only trimming you need to take care of separately is the trimming between members of different groups.

Locating and orienting the profile

When you apply a profile to a path segment in a Structural Member feature, the profile must have some relationship to the path segment. The default point where the path "pierces" the profile is at the sketch Origin. To change the pierce point, you can click the Locate Profile button at the bottom of the Structural Member PropertyManager, which zooms the view to present the profile sketch so that you can select another sketch point to use as the pierce point. You can select any sketch point on the profile, including endpoints, sketch points, and virtual sharp points if they are present in the sketch.

Profile sketches are generally surrounded by several sketch points, which may seem unnecessary until you consider that you can use any of the points to position the profile. The Settings panel at the bottom of the Structural Member PropertyManager is shown in Figure 31.8 and displays a profile sketch with the interface.

FIGURE 31.8

Locating the profile

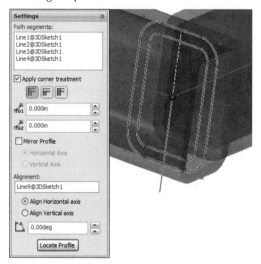

In addition to locating the profile sketch, you can also rotate the profile using the Angle field in the Settings panel. This rotates all of the bodies that are created by the Structural Member feature at the same time. In the example of the four-legged frame, if the legs are rectangular or circular, they can all be created in the same Structural Member feature because they are all rotated in the same way. However, if the legs were made from an asymmetrical shape such as an angle, then each leg would need to be made using a separate Structural Member feature, with each leg rotated differently.

Disjoint sketch segments

You can select disjoint sketch segments in a single Structural Member feature if they are parallel to the first segment and use the same profile height location and orientation. For example, in Figure 31.6, notice the four angled supports in the corners attaching to the legs. Because they are parallel in pairs, all four of these supports could not be made in a single group. Later in this section, when those path segments are actually used to place Structural Members, the additional requirement of using an angle profile means that the profiles each need to be rotated differently from one another, and thus cannot be used in a single group.

Custom profiles

Most of the custom profiles that you will need may be simply new sizes of existing profiles. You can easily create a custom profile by opening an existing profile, editing it, and saving it under a different name using the Save As command. It is important to note that when creating a weldment profile, a sketch must be selected prior to initiating the Save As command. Weldment profiles are Library Features, and use a `*.sldlfp` filename extension. Each size must be saved as a separate library feature in order to appear in the selection list. While library features are configurable, the configurations are not selectable for weldment profiles.

Other sources for custom profiles include 3D Content Central, which has a large number of erector-set aluminum extrusion profiles and the accessory hardware for those systems. Toolbox also has a Structural Steel sketch generator, shown in Figure 31.9, which allows you to generate most standard shapes. If you have Toolbox installed on your system, then you can find this tool in the Toolbox menu.

FIGURE 31.9

The Structural Steel sketch generator interface

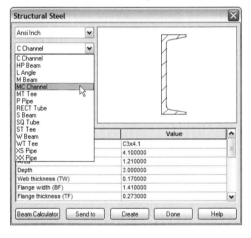

As I have said throughout this book, weldment profiles are a great candidate for storing in your special library folder, separate from the SolidWorks installation directory. To establish this library location, you can go to Tools ⇨ Options ⇨ File Locations ⇨ Weldment Profiles. Also keep in mind that if you share design duties with other users, then the library location should either be shared among users on a network, or the libraries should be copied to each user's local library. You can also share library data through a Product Data Management, or PDM, program.

If you are creating completely new custom profiles, then remember that when locating the profile relative to the path segments, you can use any sketch point. As a result, you should provide ample selections for pierce points. Virtual sharps function well around filleted corners, as well as sketch points at the centroid of a shape.

In addition to sketch geometry, the library part files should also contain custom property information about the structural shape, such as part number, supplier, material, and so on. This information propagates to the Cut list.

Corner treatments

Any intersection of sketch lines at mutual endpoints within a single group, except as noted in this section, creates a situation that requires that the corners be cut to match. Figure 31.10 shows an example of the options that are available when lines meet at right angles. Notice that within a group, you have the option to set a weld gap at the intersections.

FIGURE 31.10

Corner treatment options

To access the toolbar with the Corner Treatment options, you can click the pink dot at the intersection of the path segments. Default corner treatment settings are made in the Structural Member PropertyManager, but they may need to be adjusted individually.

Two situations do not require corner treatments. The first situation is when a line intersects another line at some location *other* than an endpoint in the same Structural Member feature; for example, a support meeting the main member in the middle. In this situation, the member that ends in the middle of the other member is trimmed to a butt joint. The second situation is when an intersecting member is created by a later Structural Member feature. You deal with this situation by using the Trim/Extend function, which I describe later in this chapter.

NOTE   You may encounter a situation where it seems like a good idea to create collinear sketch segments. In a typical extrusion, the faces created from collinear lines are simply merged together as one. However, in a weldment, this does not work when it is done in a single feature. In order to create Structural Members on collinear sketch lines, you must either extend one line to encompass the length of both lines or do the work in two separate Structural Member features.

Arc segments

When arc sketch segments are part of the selection for a Structural Member, a Merge Arc Segment Bodies option displays after the selection box in the Selections panel. This means that any *tangent* arc segment will be joined to the entities to which it is tangent, but any non-tangent entities will create separate bodies.

A tangent arc is illustrated in the curved leg brace shown in Figure 31.11, along with the Merge Arc Segment Bodies option in the PropertyManager.

FIGURE 31.11

A tangent arc segment used in a Structural Member feature

If the Merge arc segment bodies option is not selected, then a separate body is created for arc segments. The Merge arc segment bodies option applies to the whole feature, and cannot be set selectively for individual arc segments within the selected sketch entities; it is either on for all or off for all. If some arc segment bodies should be merged and others should not, then you should create separate Structural Member features.

It is also a curious limitation that only one arc may be selected if the selected path segments are disjoint. For example, the two arcs for two J shapes that do not touch could not be selected in the same Structural Member feature. The obvious workaround is to create two separate groups.

Patterning and symmetry

Bodies created by the Structural Member feature can be patterned and mirrored. Remember that there is a difference between patterning *features* and patterning *bodies*. The Move/Copy Bodies feature is also appropriate for creating bodies to be used in the weldment, although the Structural Member feature does not create them directly.

I mention this to emphasize the point that sketching with symmetry is still important, although it is more difficult with 3D sketches than with conventional 2D sketches. Symmetry in a 3D sketch can only be used when a plane is activated, and you can activate regular reference geometry planes, not just 3D sketch planes. I also mention this because in larger weldments (or when using slower computers), performance may be an issue, and mirroring or patterning bodies is certainly a performance enhancement over building parametric features.

Configurations

When you start creating a weldment, SolidWorks automatically creates a derived configuration. Both configurations are named Default, but they have different descriptions. The parent configuration description is As Machined, and the derived, or indented, configuration description is As Welded.

This arrangement holds true for any additional top-level configurations that you create in the part; they will all get the description As Machined and inherit an identically named derived configuration with the description As Welded. These configurations are meant to help you create drawings where the raw weldment is distinguished from the weldment after it has been machined, ground, and drilled.

Trim/Extend

In situations where you must create multiple Structural Member features, thus creating intersecting bodies, the interferences must be dealt with using the Trim/Extend feature. An example of this is shown in Figure 31.12. The legs and braces shown are all being trimmed by a single face on the bottom side of the rectangular section of the frame, where the small arrow appears.

Bodies may be trimmed by planar faces or other bodies. Bodies may also be trimmed before they are mirrored or patterned. Although trimming with faces gives better speed results, it may not give the same geometrical results.

The Extend option enables either trimming or extending, as appropriate. If the Extend option is not selected, then trimming is the only action available.

Using the Trim/Extend feature

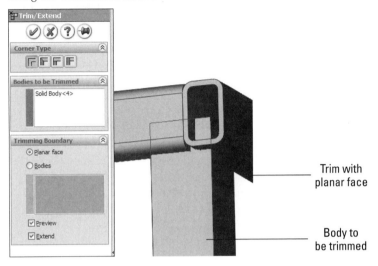

Trim with
planar face

Body to
be trimmed

End Cap

The End Cap feature closes off an open-ended Structural Member. You can add multiple end caps in a single End Cap feature. The PropertyManager and the end product are shown in Figure 31.13.

FIGURE 31.13

Using the End Cap feature

The end cap using the Outward option sits on the outside face of the member, and overlaps the thickness of the member by the inverse of the Thickness Ratio that is applied in the Offset panel. If the Use thickness ratio option is turned off, then it functions as an offset from the outer faces of the member from which it is created. When this option is turned on, the thickness ratio can range from zero to one. For a value of zero, it is flush with the outer faces of the member, and for a value of one it is flush with the inner faces of the member. Using the Inward option, the cap fits inside the hole in the member.

Gusset

The Gusset feature creates a three-, four- or five-sided gusset in a corner between Structural Members, as shown in Figure 31.14. You can place the gusset at specific locations along the edge in the corner, or offset it by a specific dimension in a specific direction by using the settings in the Parameters panel. You can control the size and thickness of the gusset in the Profile panel. There is no sketch for this feature type; it is simply created from the parameters that you enter in the PropertyManager interface. Again, if you need to make multiple Gusset features in succession, you can use the pushpin icon to keep the interface displayed until you close it by clicking the red X icon.

FIGURE 31.14

Using the Gusset feature

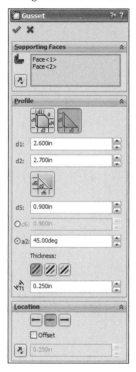

Fillet Bead

The Fillet Bead feature is somewhat limited in its ability to make realistic weld beads on a weldment part. To start with, it is limited to fillet welds, and does not weld around commonly found situations such as that shown in Figure 31.15. It works best where flat faces butt up against one another cleanly, with enough space all the way around them for the weld bead. It is often suggested that for drawings, you are better to leave the Fillet Bead feature off of the model and simply to use weld symbols or caterpillars to represent the weld bead.

FIGURE 31.15

Using the Fillet Bead interface

Using Non-Structural Components

Non-structural components are frequently needed in weldments, and include items such as feet, plates, brackets, mounting pads, castings, and other items. Simpler items that can be easily modeled in place can be placed directly into the weldment part. You can also insert parts into the weldment using the Insert Part feature, and move them into place by using dimensions or mates. In general, if any item is actually welded into the weldment, then you are recommended to place it in the weldment part; however, items that are bolted on should probably be placed into an assembly. Of course, this probably depends more on your company's documentation standards, part-numbering standards, and assembly processes than on software capabilities.

When adding a plate such as the footplate shown in Figure 31.16, the geometry is added using the standard Extrude feature, except that the Merge option is turned off by default. This ensures that non-structural components that are manually modeled, such as this part, are created as separate bodies, and not merged together with the existing structural items.

FIGURE 31.16

A foot plate added to the weldment

Using Sub-Weldments

From a modeling point of view, sub-weldments are generally used for either organizational or performance reasons to group together elements of a weldment or to break a larger weldment into more manageable pieces. This is in much the same way that subassemblies are created for the same purposes within larger assemblies. From a fabrication point of view, sub-weldments are also used to break a large weldment into pieces that can be transported or handled.

To create a sub-weldment, you can select several bodies from the Cut list, and then select Create Sub-Weldment from the right-mouse button menu. (You can also select the bodies from the graphics window if you use the Select Bodies selection filter.) This creates a separate folder for the sub-weldment bodies. You can then right-click the sub-weldment folder and select Insert Into New Part.

Using Cut Lists

The Cut list that is maintained in the model FeatureManager is simply a replacement for the Solid Bodies folder. It has most of the same functionality as the Solid Bodies folder, as well as a few additional items. The Cut Lists folder symbol in the FeatureManager can show the folder symbol in one of two potential states. These symbols are shown at the top left of this paragraph. When the cut list requires an update the top image is shown, and after the update has been performed, the bottom image is shown. Cut lists are updated automatically when a drawing that uses the Cut list is accessed, but can also be updated manually through a right-mouse button option or by the forced rebuild, Ctrl-Q.

You can access the Update command from the right-mouse button menu of the Cut List folder. Figure 31.17 shows the result of the update. The weldment solid bodies are broken down further into subfolders that reflect quantities of identical bodies. Notice that the weld beads at the bottom of the list are not in a folder.

FIGURE 31.17

The Cut list in the model FeatureManager

Custom properties

Custom properties that come from profile library features, and the Weldment feature in a part, contribute to the information that can appear in a Cut list on a drawing. You can access custom properties for individual Cut list items from the Cut List Item's right-mouse button menu, as shown in Figure 31.18.

FIGURE 31.18

The Cut List Custom Properties interface

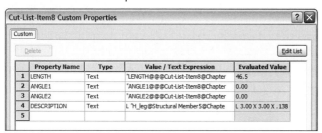

Make Weld Bead

To exclude a feature in the FeatureManager from the Cut list, you can select Make Weld Bead from the feature's right-mouse button menu. The next time the Cut list is updated, the members that were created by that feature will be listed at the bottom of the Cut List folder with the weld beads. You can set back a feature to be included in the Cut list by selecting Make Non-Weld Bead from the feature's right-mouse button menu and updating the Cut list again.

Creating Weldment Drawings

Weldment drawings have a couple of special features that distinguish them from normal part drawings. The first is obviously the Cut list. Like a BOM (Bill of Materials) in an assembly, you can place the weldment Cut list on a drawing by selecting Insert ⇨ Table ⇨ Weldment Cut List. Figure 31.19 shows a sample Cut list on a drawing. In this case, the blank rows represent non-structural components, being the foot plates and the gusset. You can manually add data for these parts either directly into the table or by adding it to the properties of the corresponding folder in the Cut list in the model document.

FIGURE 31.19

A Cut list on a drawing

ITEM NO.	QTY.	DESCRIPTION	LENGTH
1	2	L 3.00 X 3.00 X .138	32.929
2	2	L 3.00 X 3.00 X .138	32.929
3	1	TUBE, RECTANGULAR 3.00 X 2.00 X .25	68.793
4	1	TUBE, RECTANGULAR 3.00 X 2.00 X .25	60
5	4	L 3.00 X 3.00 X .138	46.5
6	1		
7	4		
8	2	TUBE, RECTANGULAR 3.00 X 2.00 X .25	118
9	2	TUBE, RECTANGULAR 3.00 X 2.00 X .25	62
10	1	TUBE, RECTANGULAR 3.00 X 2.00 X .25	58

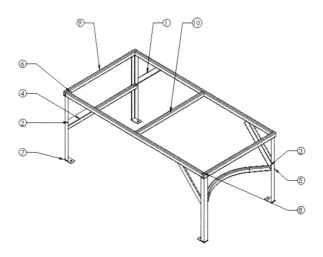

Also shown in Figure 31.18 is an auto-ballooned isometric view of the entire weldment. This works the same way that assembly auto-ballooning works, and it also corresponds to the Cut list in the same way as the assembly corresponds to the BOM.

Weldment drawings can also include views of individual bodies. You can do this by making a Relative view, selecting both faces from the same body, and then using the PropertyManager of the Relative view in the window of the solid model to control whether the view shows the entire part or just selected bodies. The Relative View PropertyManager is shown in Figure 31.20.

FIGURE 31.20

The Relative View PropertyManager

To access the Relative View PropertyManager interface, follow these steps:

1. **Click the Relative View button on the Drawings toolbar or select Insert ➪ Drawing View ➪ Relative To Model.**

2. **Right-click a blank space on the drawing sheet and select Insert From File.** Browse to the part file.

3. **Identify the faces to be shown in the particular orientations, and specify whether the entire part or the selected bodies should be shown in the view.**

Tutorial: Working with Weldments

This tutorial guides you through building a section of a tubular truss support. You can create many different types of weldments, from simple small gauge frames to large architectural designs such as this one. This tutorial also helps you to navigate successfully through some 3D sketch functionality for creating fully defined sketches.

Follow these steps to learn about working with weldments:

1. **Open a new part.** If you have Toolbox, then activate it by selecting Tools ➪ Add-Ins ➪ SolidWorks Toolbox. If you do not have Toolbox, then simply draw two concentric circles on the Front plane of a new part. The circles should have diameters of 10.02 inches and 10.75 inches. Alternatively, you can copy the library feature from the CD-ROM for Chapter 31 to the location specified at the end of Step 5.

2. **If you have Toolbox, then select Toolbox ➪ Structural Steel.**

3. **Select ANSI Inch, P Pipe, P10.** This profile has an inside diameter of 10.02 inches and an outside diameter of 10.75 inches. Click the Create button, and then click Done.

4. **Use Custom Properties to add any properties that you would like to have automatically added to the Cut list.**

5. **Remembering the technique from Chapter 18 on library features, first close any open sketches, then select the sketch from the FeatureManager, and then save the part as a Library Feature Part file to a path such as** D:\Library\Weldment Profiles\Custom\Pipe\P-Pipe10in.SLDLFP.

> **NOTE** The Custom folder (located in the first level under the Weldment Profiles) will be recognized as the Standard, similar to ANSI or ISO. The next folder down, Pipe, will be recognized as the Type, and the name of the file will be recognized as the Size, in the same way as shown in Figure 31.6.

6. **Go to Tools ➪ Options ➪ File Locations ➪ Weldment Profiles, and add your non-installation directory location to the list of folders.** Alternatively, you can remove the Program Files location from the list, and copy the files from that location to your own library location.

7. **Open another new part, and open a new 3D sketch in the part. Activate the Center Rectangle sketch entity.** Press the Tab key until the space handle (large red Origin) indicates the ZX or Top plane.

8. **Draw a rectangle around the Origin.** The sketch should now look like Figure 31.21. Apply an Equal relation to two adjacent sides of the rectangle, and dimension any of the lines as 120 inches.

FIGURE 31.21

A centered rectangle in a 3D sketch

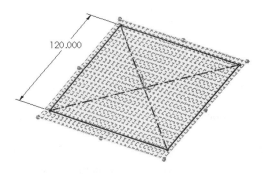

120.000

9. Select one of the lines of the rectangle, Ctrl+select the Top plane, and assign an OnPlane sketch relation.

10. Activate the Line sketch tool and press Tab until the cursor indicates the XY plane.

11. Draw a line from one corner of the square down, trying to avoid any automatic relations such as coincident relations to other points and any AlongX, Y, or Z relations. Connect the other three corners of the square with the free endpoint of the new line, as shown in Figure 31.22.

FIGURE 31.22

Adding lines

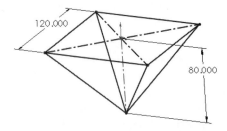

120.000

80.000

12. **Rotate the view slightly.** Notice that the first line that you drew in Step 10 and one other line are on a plane. Drag a right to left selection box around the point where the four lines converge, and assign an Equal relation to all of the lines. This makes the shape into an upside-down pyramid shape.

13. **Drag the point.** Notice that it moves up and down, although it seems a little erratic. Place a dimension between the point and the part Origin. Notice that the sketch becomes overdefined and turns red and yellow. Theoretically, this combination should work, but for some reason SolidWorks does not accept it.

14. **Using the Display/Delete Relations tool, delete all of the Equal relations that you just added to the part (it may be faster to use Undo or Ctrl+Z).**

15. **Draw a vertical construction line from the part Origin to the point where the four lines meet, and assign this line an AlongY relation.** Notice that the point drags much more smoothly. This is a good reason for using simpler relation schemes when possible. The four equal relations in this case that had to be solved simultaneously are now replaced by a single relation that is easier to solve when you drag the sketch. Apply a dimension of 80 inches to the new construction line.

16. **Draw a new line from the point where the four lines come together AlongX in the positive X direction.** Dimension this new line as 120 inches. The sketch should now look like Figure 31.23.

FIGURE 31.23

The sketch after Step 16

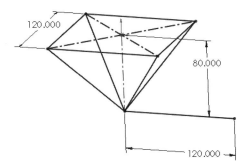

17. **Exit the sketch.** Click the Structural Member toolbar button on the Weldments toolbar. In the Standard drop-down list in the Structural Member PropertyManager, select Custom. In the Type drop-down list, select Pipe. In the Size drop-down list, select P-Pipe10in. This is the name that corresponds to the way the library feature part was saved in Step 5.

18. **In the Path Segments selection box, select the original four sides of the rectangle.** In the Settings panel, make sure that the Apply Corner Treatment option is turned on and that the End Miter icon is selected. This is shown in Figure 31.24. Accept the command when you are done.

FIGURE 31.24

The Structural Member PropertyManager and the sketch after Step 18

19. **Expand the Structural Member feature.** Notice that the four bodies are listed under it. Expand the Cut List folder. The bodies should also be listed there.

20. **Open the 10-inch pipe library feature that you created at the beginning of this tutorial.** Edit the two dimensions to subtract 2 inches from each dimension, and add a custom property description called "Support Leg." Use the Save As command to save the library feature to the same location as the original, but with the filename `P-Pipe8in. SLDLFP`.

21. **Initiate another Structural Member feature, this time selecting the 8-inch size of pipe from the Custom folder.** In the Path Segments selection box, select two of the angled lines that go to opposite corners. Keep the feature open for the next step.

NOTE   Remember that three intersecting Structural Members cannot be created with a single group. To create material on all four lines, you need two separate groups within the Structural Member feature.

22. **Make a second group with the other pair of angled lines.** Accept the feature when you are satisfied. The model should now look like Figure 31.25.

The model after Step 22

 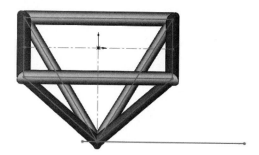

23. **Apply another Structural Member feature to the 10-foot (120-inch) section, again using the 10-inch-diameter pipe.** Notice that this member is not long enough to cut through the peak of the pyramid.

24. **Edit the 3D sketch and draw a 12-inch extension to the original line past the peak of the pyramid.** Use an additional line rather than extending the existing one. Exit the sketch.

25. **Edit the Structural Member feature to add the new line.**

NOTE You will have to turn off the Apply corner treatment option to get this technique to work. If this option is on, then SolidWorks tries to miter or otherwise create a corner treatment between the bodies, which fails when the parts are parallel.

26. **Trim the four angled members on both ends because they extend to the ends of the sketch entities rather than stopping at intersecting members.** Initiate the Trim/Extend feature. Select the four angled members in the Bodies to be Trimmed selection box. Select the four members created by the original rectangle as the Trimming Boundary, and make sure that the option is set to Bodies (as opposed to Planar Face), as shown in Figure 31.26. Accept the feature when you are done.

27. **Create another Trim/Extend feature.** This time, trim off the point end of the four angled members, using the 10-inch horizontal pipe and the small segment as the trimming boundary.

FIGURE 31.26

The model after Step 26

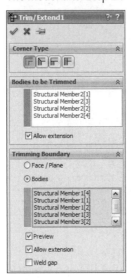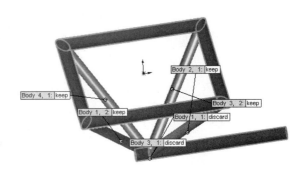

28. **Half of the support structure has been modeled to this point.** You can create the rest of it by mirroring the existing bodies. Create a Mirror feature, using the free end of the 10-foot-long member as the mirror plane, and selecting all of the bodies in the Bodies to Mirror selection box. Do not use the Merge Solids option, as you will need to do this manually. Click OK to accept the feature when it is set up properly. The PropertyManager for the Mirror feature is shown in Figure 31.27.

> **NOTE** An easy way to select all of the bodies is to use the flyout FeatureManager, select the first body in the list, and Shift-select the last body.

29. **Start the Combine feature (Insert ➪ Feature ➪ Combine), and set it to Add.** Select the two 10-foot sections and the two smaller 1-foot sections to combine them into a single continuous body. Click OK to accept the feature. Also hide the 3D sketch.

30. **Right-click the Cut List folder, and select Update.** Figure 31.28 shows before and after images of the Cut List folder.

31. **Right-click the folder for the large diameter cross member and select Properties.** Change the Description field to read Support Pod Members.

32. **Use the Create Drawing From Part/Assembly button on the Standard toolbar to make a drawing.** Place Front, Bottom, and isometric views, and then press the Esc key to quit placing views.

FIGURE 31.27

The PropertyManager for the Mirror feature in Step 28

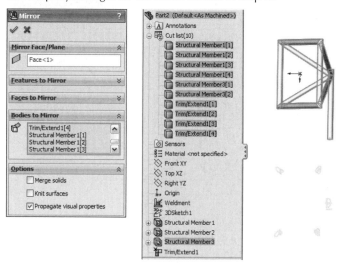

FIGURE 31.28

The Cut List folder in Step 30

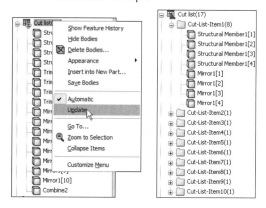

33. **Select one of the views and then select Insert ⇨ Table ⇨ Weldment Cut List.** When the PropertyManager displays, select the options that you want and click OK. Then place the table.

34. Click inside the Bottom view, and from the Annotations toolbar, click Auto-Balloon. The finished drawing looks like Figure 31.29.

FIGURE 31.29

The finished drawing

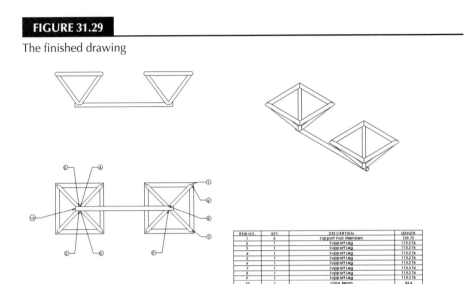

ITEM NO.	QTY.	DESCRIPTION	LENGTH
1	8	Support Pod Members	130.75
2	1	Support Leg	110.374
3	1	Support Leg	110.374
4	1	Support Leg	110.374
5	1	Support Leg	110.374
6	1	Support Leg	110.374
7	1	Support Leg	110.374
8	1	Support Leg	110.374
9	1	Support Leg	110.374
10	1	Cross Beam	264

NOTE Relative views are difficult to create with round pipe rather than rectangular tube, although starting with 2007, planes can be used as references for relative views.

Summary

Weldments are based on either a single 3D frame sketch or a set of 2D sketches, usually denoting the centerlines or edges of the various structural elements. This creates a special type of part in the same way that the Sheet Metal commands create a special type of part. Structural profiles are placed on the frame sketch to propagate and create individual bodies for the separate pieces of the weldment. Custom profiles are easily created as library features, and you can add custom properties to the library features, and the custom properties then propagate to the Cut lists.

Chapter 32

Using Plastic Features and Mold Tools

SolidWorks has several tools that are specific to modeling and evaluating plastic parts. These tools can help simplify and standardize some of the complex repetitive tasks involved with plastic part design. Another set of task-specific tools exist for automating mold cavity/core modeling tasks. So whether you are a plastic part designer or an injection mold designer, SolidWorks offers tools tailored to your needs.

Plastic parts represent a significant number of manufactured parts. You can manually do all the work that these tools automate, and sometimes you need to be able to do the work manually when the automated tools do not provide the needed options or flexibility.

Also because of the specific needs of plastic part modeling and mold design, SolidWorks has a set of powerful evaluation tools that help you query your models to check the amount of draft, thickness, and location of undercuts. Finding design-related manufacturability problems in manufacturing is expensive. Finding them in the design office is far less expensive in both money and time. A good grasp of the evaluation tools is an important component of good plastic part and mold modeling.

This chapter is written for the user who is already experienced in plastics practice and terminology, but needs to understand the SolidWorks tools used with the plastic and mold features. I assume that the reader already has a grasp of the basic plastics and mold design.

IN THIS CHAPTER

Using plastic features

Using plastic evaluation tools

Working with the Mold Tools process

Intervening manually with Mold Tools

Tutorial: Working with plastic features

Using Plastic Features

The plastic features available in SolidWorks are the Mounting Boss, Snap Hook, Snap Groove, Vent, and Lip/Groove. These features offer standardized but flexible geometry to help you make more consistent models more quickly, and with less tiresome repetition. In this chapter I also consider the various functions of the Draft feature in SolidWorks.

Other features such as Shell and Indent are frequently used in plastic parts, but I cover them elsewhere in this book. You can find all of the features in this section on the Fastening Features toolbar.

Some of these features have applications beyond just injection molded plastic parts. Many molding, casting, or "net shape" processes exist in plastic materials, as well as metals, ceramics, and composites.

Using the Mounting Boss

The Mounting Boss feature enables you to place a boss with fins and either a hole or a pin on the end. It does not enable you to place a counterbored hole or a through hole to facilitate screw bosses. It is aimed primarily at press pins.

Figure 32.1 shows the Mounting Boss PropertyManager along with the preview of the boss in progress. The part used in this figure is on the CD-ROM in the data for Chapter 32, and is called `Chapter 32 – right frame.sldprt`.

1. **Select a spot on the part that represents where the boss will attach to the part.** This can be either a flat or curved face. In the example above, because I selected a curved face, it is necessary to also supply a direction of pull. If you select a flat face, the direction selection box in the next step is not available.

2. **Select a plane, planar face, edge, or axis to establish the axis of the boss.** This is usually the direction of draw. Notice in the part shown in Figure 32.1 that an axis established early in the part is named as the Direction of Draw. In early 2009 releases, the Change Direction arrows do nothing. This step is optional. The default is the direction normal to the face selected in Step 1.

3. **Select an existing circular edge to align the boss.** The new boss will be concentric with the circular edge. This step is also optional. You can choose to use dimensions to locate the boss *after the feature is created*. If you use dimensions, you cannot locate the boss while the PropertyManager is active.

4. **The Boss panel of the Mounting Boss PropertyManager is used to establish the height and other dimensions of the central boss.** Diameter and draft dimensions are obvious. You can establish height by a dimension or by an "up to" face using the Select Mating Face option. There is no option for an "offset from face" end condition.

FIGURE 32.1

A Mounting Boss in progress

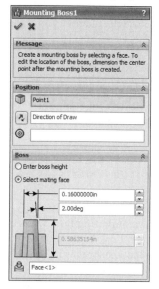

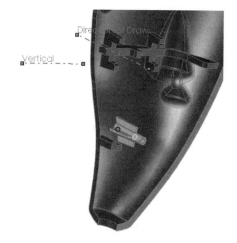

The workflow for the Mounting Boss feature is as follows:

5. **The Fins panel of the Mounting Boss PropertyManager is used to control the alignment, draft, height, width, and patterning of the ribs around the boss.** The first box is for a direction vector such as a plane, edge, [or] axis to establish the rotational orientation of the ribs. You cannot use a sketch for this. The significance of the dimensional values is obvious. The fin pattern function is also obvious except for the Equally Spaced option, which is only available when the number selected is 2. Then you must select a vector to establish the orientation of the fins, which form a right angle for a corner.

6. **The Mounting Hole/Pin panel enables you to specify a pin or hole boss and the associated sizes.** It is interesting to me that it doesn't enable through holes or counterbore holes from the outside of the part, along with associated screw sizes for clearance.

7. **SolidWorks has renamed Favorites in the rest of the software to Styles, but in the Mounting Boss and the Lip/Groove, it is still called Favorites, and saves settings like other Favorites/Styles functionality.**

8. **After you have successfully accepted the creation of the boss, if you did not use a circular edge to locate the boss (Step 3), you can expand the Mounting Boss feature in the FeatureManager and edit the 3D sketch under the boss.** Inside this sketch is a point, which you can dimension to locate precisely. Remember that dimensions in 3D sketches follow some special rules. To get orthogonal dimensions parallel to X, Y or Z axes, you will need to dimension from planes. 3D sketch dimensions do not snap to horizontal or vertical orientations like 2D sketches.

   If you have selected a flat face for the initial position of the boss, you get a 2D sketch instead of a 3D sketch.

The features created by this tool are not manually editable. They are not made of extrudes and rib features that are accessible behind the Mounting Boss interface. You have to go through the Mounting Boss PropertyManager to edit the features, and cannot edit sketches used to make the features.

SolidWorks intends this feature primarily as a means to create pin-and-hole press pin bosses. These are certainly needed, but also needed are screw bosses. You will have to size your own screw holes either for threaded inserts or for thread cutting screws. You will also need to manually create some of your own features if you want to make a counterbored clearance hole for a screw, as shown in the cross section in Figure 32.2.

An effective way to pattern a single Mounting Boss feature around a part is to use the Sketch Driven Pattern. This feature uses a sketch with a set of points where each point represents the center of a patterned instance. Refer to the model on the CD-ROM and examine the sketch driven pattern at the bottom of the FeatureManager. Use the Chapter 32 – right frame.sldprt, and change to the "nonmirror" configuration if it is not already there.

Manually making a Mounting Boss into a typical screw boss

Using the Snap Hook and Snap Hook Groove

Unlike the Lip/Groove feature, which is treated next, the Snap Hook and Snap Hook Groove features are two separate features. Lip/Groove combines both functions into a single PropertyManager to help you get results that work together more easily. Figure 32.3 shows the PropertyManager for the Snap Hook feature, along with a completed hook.

The workflow for the Snap Hook feature goes like this:

1. **Select a spot on the model that will correspond to the center of the undercut edge where the hook intersects the part.** It looks like you can select a face or an edge when you first create the feature, but the software always converts the selection to a point when the feature is accepted.

2. **Select a vector (face, edge, axis, not a sketch) to set the vertical orientation of the hook, or the "top."**

3. **Select another vector to define the "front" of the hook (the undercut side).**

4. **Choose to select a mating face or enter a number to define the height of the hook.**

The Snap Hook PropertyManager with a completed hook feature

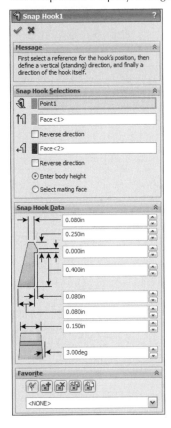

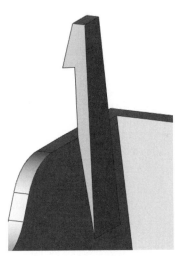

This feature uses a 3D sketch point where you made the selection in Step 1. You cannot dimension this point while setting up the feature, only by creating the feature and then going back and editing the 3D sketch absorbed under the feature. This is also the arrangement with the Lip/Groove. Remember that you cannot dimension 3D sketches the same way that you dimension 2D sketches. You may need to dimension to planes rather than edges or points to get the dimensions you really intend.

The Snap Hook Groove PropertyManager interface is shown in Figure 32.4, along with a cross section of a finished Snap Hook and a Snap Hook Groove. To use the Snap Hook Groove feature, you must have already created a Snap Hook feature. The interface seems to imply that it requires the body the groove goes into to be in the same part as the body of the hook feature, but this is not the case. You can create this feature in-context between a part with a hook and the part to receive the groove.

FIGURE 32.4

The Snap Hook Groove PropertyManager with a completed hook and groove

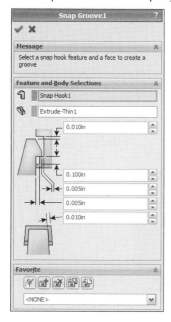

NOTE Before designing extensive undercuts into a plastic part, it is advisable to talk to the mold builder if possible. They may have either limited or special capabilities that could impact on the practicality of one approach as opposed to another. I find it is frequently beneficial to work closely with a mold designer or builder on plastic part projects.

When I model plastic parts, rarely do situations call for a generic snap feature. Usually situations require more inventiveness due to space restrictions or curvature or material thickness considerations. The Snap Hook and Snap Hook Groove features are reasonably easy to use, but may not have the flexibility for application in all situations.

Using Lip/Groove

The Lip/Groove feature is new to SolidWorks 2009, and enables you to create a matching lip and groove in either a pair of parts in an assembly or a pair of bodies within a single part. Figure 32.5 shows the Lip/Groove PropertyManager creating a groove in a part. The same interface also creates the lip feature.

FIGURE 32.5

Using the Lip/Groove feature

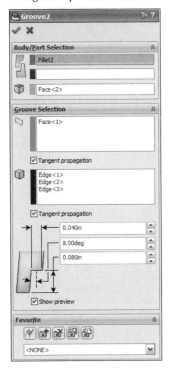

The workflow for this feature goes like this:

1. Select the part or body to receive the groove.

2. Select the part or body to receive the lip.

3. Select a plane, planar face, straight edge, or axis to establish the direction of pull.

4. Select faces that represent the parting surface along the area to get the lip/groove.

5. Select edges that the lip/groove will affect.

6. Set dimensions for both lip and groove features.

The Lip/Groove feature is useful in limited controlled circumstances that fit a narrow range of conditions. The primary limitations are that nothing can intersect the edges used for the feature, and the lip/groove must either follow a complete loop or the ends of the lip/groove must not have material next to them. If the groove would cut faces on more than two sides, it will not work.

Another limitation is that it cannot create multiple disjoint lip/groove features in a single application of the tool. So if the path is interrupted, you must use additional Lip/Groove features for each continuous path.

Because the Lip/Groove is still a new feature in the 2009 release, you might want to revisit it in a release or two to see if SolidWorks has broadened the functionality and removed some of the limitations. At this point in time, it will work in simple situations where ribs or bosses do not come all the way to the parting line.

You can employ one of several manual workarounds to make lips and grooves. Several techniques exist.

- On a planar parting line, you can use sketches offset from the edges and then extrude either a boss or a cut.

- Using a thin feature extrude (boss or cut) can also be effective on planar parting lines.

- Using trimmed and thickened (again, boss or cut) surfaces can be effective but may also be more difficult.

- One of my favorite methods, especially for non-planar parting lines, is to combine a thin feature with an extrude up to an offset surface body.

- Using a sweep to cut or add material can be effective on either planar or non-planar parting lines.

Each of these is really a work-around technique and not a specific plastic modeling tool, I will not go into depth on these techniques here. On the CD-ROM, you will find example parts that demonstrate each technique.

Using the Rib feature

The Rib feature is a flexible tool for creating ribs in a number of different situations. Ribs can be drawn in one of two different orientations, which the SolidWorks interface calls Parallel To Sketch and Normal To Sketch. The names appear only on tooltips when hovering over the icons. To be more precise, what they really mean is that the rib will be created either parallel or normal to the sketch *plane*. If the sketch is a single line, it can be very difficult to tell the difference between parallel and normal.

To me these names are not very descriptive. I call the two orientations *plan view* (view from the top, looking in the direction of draw, normal to the sketch plane) and *skyline* (looking from the side, perpendicular to the direction of draw, rib is parallel to the sketch plane). To me, these names are more intuitively descriptive.

Ribs can incorporate draft, extend, or trim the feature beyond the sketch automatically, and break normal sketch rules (plan view ribs only).

Ribs do have some limitations or opportunities for improvement, which I will discuss briefly later in this section. It is as important to understand what features *can't* do as it is to understand what they *can* do.

Figure 32.6 shows a plan view rib that violates normal sketch rules. Also shown is the Rib PropertyManager. Several models on the CD-ROM show examples of various rib techniques.

FIGURE 32.6

Rib feature

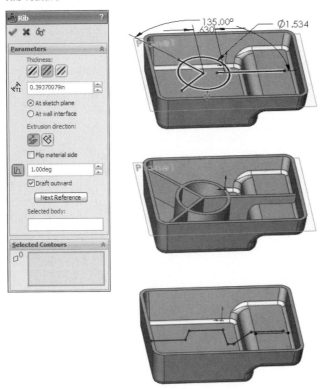

Rib feature workflow should be self-explanatory:

1. **Draw the sketch, either the plan view or skyline.** The sketch represents the top of the Rib. Material can only be added between the sketch and the rest of the part.

2. **Initiate the feature, and set the type of rib and the direction.** Use the Flip Material Side toggle to change the direction of the gray arrow, which should point from the top of the rib toward the part.

3. **Set the thickness and draft amount and direction.**

Using Draft in the Rib feature

When you create ribs, you almost always apply draft to them. You can apply draft as a separate feature, or you can apply draft as a part of the Rib feature. It is often easier to just do it as part of the Rib feature, but some people like to make all of their draft as separate Draft features to keep the part faces orthogonal for as long as possible, or they just like to organize all of the Draft features into a folder at the end of the FeatureManager so that there is never any question about which feature controls the draft.

By default, when you apply draft as a part of the Rib feature, the draft is applied from the sketch end of the rib. This can cause rib thickness problems if you have created a skyline rib where the rib may have various heights. In this case, the top of the rib will vary in thickness, and it may cause the base of the rib to be too thick. When you work this way, sometimes you have to experiment with the proper thickness at the top of the rib in order to get a thickness at the bottom of the rib that will not cause sink marks on the outside face of the part.

A solution to this is to control the thickness of the rib at the base, and then draft away from that. This process is more in line with standard plastics processes anyway, which generally give dimensions at maximum material condition, and then the draft always removes material. Thinking of draft as always removing material helps plastic part modelers and mold designers to remain "steel safe." It is always easier to remove steel from a mold (which adds material to the plastic) than it is to add steel to the mold.

Starting in the SolidWorks 2009 release, you can now specify the thickness and draft such that the base of the rib maintains a specified thickness, and the draft is applied from the base of the rib. The option to do this does not appear until you turn on the draft for the feature.

Ribs and multi-bodies

With all of the other functions around plastic parts that require or at least work with multi-body parts, I should mention some facts about the Rib tool pertaining to that issue. The Rib feature is possibly uniquely sensitive to changes in the number of bodies. For example, if you build a part and put a Rib feature in it and it only has one body, then roll back before the rib and do something that makes two bodies when you unroll the FeatureManager, the Rib feature will fail. The way to fix this error is to edit the rib and use the Feature Scope at the bottom of the PropertyManager to select which body the rib is meant to intersect. The Feature Scope box does not appear unless the part has multiple bodies.

Using Intersection Curves as reference

Ribs are features that typically go inside hollowed out parts. For that reason, ribs are often difficult to visualize, especially when they are on a plane that is deep down inside a part. When I model ribs, I often need some sort of a reference that shows where the current sketch plane intersects the wall of the part. For this I typically use Intersection Curves.

The Intersection Curve is on the Sketch toolbar. While in a 2D sketch, activate the tool, and then select faces that intersect the current sketch plane. Deactivate the tool when you are done. You may want to select all of the lines selected by the Intersection Curve tool and turn them into construction geometry. This provides a good reference for the rib sketch.

Figure 32.7 shows an example of using an Intersection Curve as a reference for setting up a rib sketch. The construction lines at the ends and below the right end of the skyline rib sketch are Intersection Curves.

FIGURE 32.7

Using Intersection Curves as reference

.133

At the ends of the shell, the intersection curves serve to give the sketch a reference point to be fully defined. Under the right end of the rib sketch, the intersection curve gives you a reference to dimension the height of the rib in the shallower section of the part. The part shown in Figure 32.7 is on the CD-ROM as Chapter 32 – skyline.sldprt.

Terminating ribs

The Rib feature automatically extends and trims ribs based on your rib sketch. This is a great ease-of-use function, but it tends to lead to sloppy sketching for Rib features. If you sketch a rib, and the sketch does not lead all the way to the wall of the part, SolidWorks extends it. If your sketch line goes past the wall, SolidWorks trims the rib so that it only goes up to the wall of the part.

Figure 32.8 shows how the two straight ribs are extended from the existing sketches on a pair of plan view ribs.

FIGURE 32.8

Extending ribs

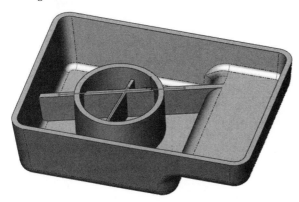

Sometimes you do not want a rib extended to the wall of the part. You may want to terminate a rib at a specific location in the middle of the part. The way to do this is to use a skyline rib and end the skyline sketch with a vertical (plus or minus draft) line that points to the base of the part. Figure 32.9 shows how to accomplish this. Notice that on the left end of the rib, it is extended straight down to the bottom of the part, and on the right side of the rib, it is extended up to the next wall.

FIGURE 32.9

Terminating a skyline rib

A final termination situation that I want to mention is one that can sometimes happen at curved edges. If the extension of the rib can not be contained by the model, the rib will fail. This is not always as obvious a situation as you might think. When a non-horizontal rib intersects a curved edge, it usually forces you to fake something a little. Figure 32.10 shows an example of why this is.

Part wall does not terminate the rib.

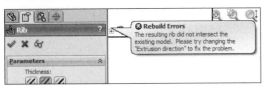

The reason for the error shown in Figure 32.10 is that even though the rib sketch intersects the edge of the part, the width of the top of the rib would go past the edge and not intersect anything. One way to deal with this is to make the sketch intersect the part a little closer to the center of the part from the edge. Another way would be to put a short vertical line at the end of the rib.

Using thin features

Thin feature extrusions are sometimes used in place of ribs. Thin features do not have all of the specialized options available with the Rib feature, but they do offer simplicity as the main attraction. Thin features can substitute for Rib features when the rib is a stand-alone rib that doesn't touch the side walls of the part. They can be used to sketch and extrude from the bottom of the rib or from the top. When extruding a thin feature with draft, the end faces get drafted as well, which might cause a problem if you are trying to attach the rib to a wall. Extruding a thin feature down from the top of the rib can replace a plan view rib, but it will not enable you to break those pesky sketch rules that the Rib feature simply dispenses with.

I personally prefer to use Rib features, except for free standing ribs where you do not want the sides extended up to the next wall.

Using Draft

 SolidWorks Draft is surprisingly powerful for as simple as it is. All of the aspects of working with Draft could take up an entire chapter all on its own. I will try to hit the most important points in this brief synopsis. The Draft feature creates three types of draft:

- **Neutral Plane draft.** Drafts faces from a plane or planar face.
- **Parting Line draft.** Drafts faces from selected edges.
- **Step draft.** Drafts faces from parting line edges, and can create a step at the parting line.

Figure 32.11 shows the PropertyManager of the draft feature, including the Draft Xpert, which is discussed later in this section.

FIGURE 32.11

Draft and Draft Xpert PropertyManagers

Neutral Plane draft

The workflow for Neutral Plane draft is as follows:

1. **Select Neutral Plane — plane or planar face at which the intersection of the drafted face does not move.** The direction of pull is always normal to the Neutral Plane.

2. **Set the draft angle — how many degrees from the direction of pull vector selected faces should be tilted.** This is *not* a cumulative angle, so applying 3 degrees of draft to a face that is already drafted 5 degrees results in 3 degrees rather than 8 degrees.

3. **Select the Direction — one side or the other side of the Neutral Plane.** The arrow points in the direction of decreasing material. If you are drafting a surface body, the "decreasing material" concept does not apply, so you just have to experiment to see which direction is the one you intend. The Draft feature does not have a preview option.

4. **Select faces to draft — use face propagation options.** Inner/Outer faces refer to inside or outside loops around the Neutral Plane face. All means all faces that have an edge on the Neutral Plane face.

Parting Line draft

The workflow for Parting Line draft is as follows:

1. **Select a direction of pull — this can be an edge, axis, sketch line, plane, or planar face.** You also have to set the direction to positive or negative along the selected direction.

2. **Select the parting lines — these are edges of the faces you want to draft.** The parting line edges remain stationary while the rest of the face tilts. Along with the parting line selection, you may also need to use the Other Face option. Every edge is adjacent to two different faces. The Draft feature automatically selects the face it thinks you want to draft, but it does not always get it right. Other Face enables you to intervene when the automatic selection is incorrect.

3. **Set the draft angle — remember that you can use the Allow Reduced Angle option if you need to.**

Step draft

The most complex of the types of draft that SolidWorks creates is the Step draft option. Step draft is used on non-planar parting lines when Parting Line draft would cause the drafted faces to be split into multiple faces.

The word "step" can be said to refer to two different aspects of this feature. First, the parting line can said to be a "stepped" parting line, because it is non-planar and at two different levels. Second, the draft actually steps out the drafted face at one level of the parting line. Step draft keeps the face intact and introduces an intentional mismatch ledge (step) at the parting line.

Figure 32.12 shows the difference between Parting Line draft and Step draft on a simplified part. The image on the left is the Parting Line draft. The middle image is Step draft where a ledge is only created on one side of the parting line. The image to the right is essentially double Step draft, where the total step size is minimized by distributing it across both sides of the stepped parting line.

FIGURE 32.12

Comparing Parting Line draft to Step draft

The draft in these images is slightly exaggerated to make it easier to see.

I was actually involved in getting this draft option introduced into the SolidWorks software. I was working for a reseller who had Fisher-Price as a customer. Fisher-Price used Pro/ENGINEER to engineer their plastic parts, and used the Pivot Draft option in that software. Their designers wanted the capabilities in their CAD tool as well, and SolidWorks agreed to add it.

The workflow for Step draft is as follows:

1. **Start with a part that has a stepped split line, where the angled line makes angles of more than 90 degrees rather than less than 90 degrees.**

2. **Create a plane that defines the direction of pull, and is located at the level of one of the split lines (for single step draft) or at the midpoint of the angled line (for double step draft).** The location of the plane will determine the "pivot" point for the drafted faces. Essentially the line of intersection between this plane and the drafted face will remain stationary and the rest of face will pivot around it.

3. **Initiate the Draft feature, and set the option to Step draft.** Consult your tooling people about whether to use tapered or perpendicular steps. Perpendicular are probably easiest to tool.

4. **Select the edges of the parting line.** Make sure that the yellow arrows indicate which faces you want to apply draft to.

The draft for the other face can be accomplished in a number of ways, but it does not require another Step draft feature. You can use a Neutral Plane feature, using the plane created in Step 2 as the Neutral Plane. It will maintain the steps created by the Step draft feature.

Some draft limitations

SolidWorks draft is powerful, but it is not omnipotent. There are things it cannot do. The main limitation of draft in SolidWorks that irritates me is that it cannot draft faces in both directions in the same feature. For example, if you have a parting line on a part, you must first draft the faces on one side of the parting line, then the faces on the other side of the parting line. This results in two separate features rather than a single feature. Is this a serious limitation? No, it is simply an inconvenience.

Further, you can only draft faces from a single body at a time. Again, this is an understandable limitation, but there are times when it is annoying and inconvenient.

However, its biggest limitation is that you can't draft a face if it has a fillet on one of its edges that runs perpendicular to the direction of pull. To get around this, you usually have to tinker with the feature order. On imported parts you might have to use FeatureWorks to remove the fillet or Delete Face to re-introduce the sharp corner.

What to do when draft fails

Draft is certainly one of those functions that require you to understand a little bit about the actual capabilities of CAD. Part of the key to success with the Draft feature is that you have your expectations aligned with the actual capabilities of the software. If you recognize a situation where the draft can not work, you may be able to correct the situation by changing feature order, combining draft features into a single feature, breaking the draft into multiple features, or changing the geometry to be more "draft friendly."

Sometimes the Allow Reduced Angle option can be used for Parting Line draft. If you use this, follow it up with a draft analysis to make sure that you have sufficient draft in all areas of the model. This option allows the software to cheat somewhat in order to make the draft feature work. The SolidWorks Help documentation actually has a more detailed explanation of when to use this option. I tend to just turn it on if a draft fails, particularly if the parting line used becomes parallel or nearly parallel to the direction of pull.

Draft can fail for a number of reasons, including tangent faces, small sliver faces, complex adjacent faces that cannot be extended, or faces with geometry errors. When modeling, it is best to minimize the number of breaks between faces. This is especially true if the faces will be drafted later. Generally, the faces you apply draft to are either flat faces or faces with single direction curvature. You can't just expect SolidWorks to draft any old junk you throw at it; you have to at least give it a fighting chance by making good clean geometry.

When draft does fail for a reason that doesn't seem obvious to you, you should use the Check utility (Tools menu) and also try a forced rebuild (Ctrl+Q) with Verification on Rebuild turned on.

Draft Xpert

Draft Xpert is a tool used to create multiple Neutral Plane draft features quickly. You can also use it to edit multiple drafted faces without regard for which features go to which faces.

Using Plastic Evaluation Tools

The plastic evaluation tools in SolidWorks enable you to automatically check the model for manufacturability issues such as draft, undercuts, thickness, and curvature. The tools used to do this are the Draft Analysis, Undercut Checker, Thickness Analysis, and Curvature tools.

Draft Analysis

The SolidWorks Draft Analysis tool is a must when working with plastic parts. The part shown in Figure 32.13 has many of the situations that you are going to encounter in analyzing plastic parts. The Draft Analysis tool has four major modes of display:

- Basic
- Gradual Transition
- Face Classification
- Find Steep Faces

Starting in the 2009 release, the Draft Analysis is found in the View ⇨ Display menu (instead of in Tools), and is either on or off, like the Section View tool. This is a benefit because it updates face colors dynamically as you model.

Basic draft analysis

The Basic draft analysis (with no options selected) simply colors faces red, green, or yellow. Colors may display transitioning if the draft shifts between two classifications. This transition type is shown in Figure 32.13 in the image to the right. For a clearer view of this method, you can find the part, `Chapter 32 Draft Analysis.sldprt`, on the CD-ROM.

You can perform all types of draft analysis in SolidWorks by selecting a reference flat face or plane, and setting a minimum allowable angle. In Figure 32.13, all walls have at least a one-degree draft, except for the rounded edge shown in the image to the right and the dome. Both of these shapes transition from an angle less than one degree to an angle greater than one degree.

This basic analysis is good for visualizing changes in draft angle, but it also has some less desirable properties, which will become apparent as you study the other types of draft.

FIGURE 32.13

Basic draft analysis results

Gradual Transition

Although the Basic draft analysis is able to show a transitioning draft, the Gradual Transition draft analysis takes it a step further. With the Gradual Transition, you can specify the colors. It is also useful because it can distinguish drafts of different amounts by color. It may be difficult to tell in the grayscale image in Figure 32.14, but the ribs, which were created at one degree, have a slightly different color than the floor of the part, and the walls also have a different color. Notice that cavity and core directions have different colors, as well. You may want to open this part in SolidWorks, re-create the settings, and run the analysis so that you can see the actual colors.

Some problems arise when you use this display mode, the first being the flat, non-OpenGL face shading that is used to achieve the transitioning colors. This often makes it difficult to distinguish curved faces, and faces that face different directions. The second problem is that you cannot tell that the boss on top of the dome has absolutely no draft. In fact, there is no way to distinguish between faces that lean slightly toward the cavity and faces that lean slightly toward the core. The third problem is the strange effect that appears on the filleted corners. The corners were filleted after you applied the draft and before the shell, and so the filleted corners should have exactly the same draft as the sides; however, from the color plot, it looks to be a few degrees more.

 Software can sometimes interpret things differently from the way that a person does. As a result, any computer analysis must be interpreted with common sense.

Due to this and some of the other problems that I mentioned earlier, I would use the Gradual Transition draft analysis in conjunction with one of the other tests. Gradual Transition gives an interesting effect, but it is not a reliable tool for determining on its own whether or not a part can be manufactured.

FIGURE 32.14

The Gradual Transition draft analysis

Face Classification

Face Classification draft analysis groups the faces into classifications using solid, non-transitioning colors. You will notice a big difference between the coloration of the Face Classification draft analysis faces and of the Basic or Gradual Transition faces. Face Classification uses OpenGL face shading, which is the same as that used by SolidWorks by default. This allows for better shading and differentiation between faces that face different directions. The Basic Analysis coloration looks like all of the faces are painted the same flat hue, regardless of which direction they are facing, which makes shapes more difficult to identify. The non-Open GL alternate shading method makes it possible to display a transition in color. SolidWorks OpenGL shading cannot do this.

Another advantage of using the OpenGL shading is that the face colors can remain on the part after you have closed the Draft Analysis PropertyManager.

Face Classification draft analysis also adds a classification that is not used by the Basic draft analysis. *Straddle faces* refer to faces that straddle the parting line, or faces that, due to their curvature, pull from both halves of the mold. These are faces that need to be split. On this part, a straddle face is shown in Figure 32.15.

FIGURE 32.15

Face Classification draft analysis and a straddle face

Straddle face

The light bulb icons to the left of the color swatches enable you to hide faces by classification. This is useful when you are trying to isolate certain faces, or visualize a group of faces in a certain way. This can be an extremely useful feature, especially when you have a very complex part with a large number of faces, some of which may be small and easily lost in the mix with other larger faces.

The face counts that appear in the color swatches are a very helpful feature that is absent from the Basic draft analysis.

BEST PRACTICE I prefer Face Classification draft analysis because it is the clearest. If I need additional detail regarding other types of faces, then I may run a Steep Face draft analysis as a supplement. The best practice here is not that you follow my favorite type of draft analysis, but that you understand what you need to know and then use the appropriate tools to find this information. This may include running multiple analyses to collect all of the necessary information.

Find steep faces

A *steep* face is defined as a face that transitions from less than the minimum angle to more than the minimum angle. Steep faces are different from straddle faces in that straddle faces are actually positive *and* negative, while steep faces are either entirely positive or entirely negative. On this part, the dome inside the part is classified as a steep face, as shown in Figure 32.16.

A steep face

Thickness Analysis

Thickness Analysis is part of the SolidWorks Utilities, which are part of SolidWorks Office or higher. After you have activated the Utilities add-in (Tools ⇨ Add-ins ⇨ SolidWorks Utilities), Thickness Analysis appears under the Utilities menu.

You can run Thickness Analysis in two modes: Show Thin Regions and Show Thick Regions. Of these, Show Thick Regions is the most versatile.

Show Thin Regions

The Show Thin Regions option, or the "Thinness" Analysis, requires you to input a minimum acceptable thickness. Every face with a thickness above this value is turned a neutral gray, and every face with a thickness below this value is displayed on a graduated scale.

Figure 32.17 shows the PropertyManager for this analysis and its result on the same part used for the draft work in the previous sections.

FIGURE 32.17

Results of the Thinness Analysis

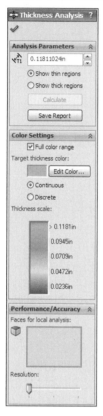

One of the things to watch out for here is that some anomalies occur when you apply this analysis to filleted faces. The faces shown as colored were created by the Shell feature and should be exactly .100 inches thick. However, it does correctly represent the undercut on the end of the part and the thickness of the ribs. A nice addition to this tool would be the identification of minimum thickness faces. Perhaps you can submit another enhancement request.

Show Thick Regions

The Show Thick Regions option works a little differently from Show Thin Regions. You need to specify an upper thickness limit value, beyond which everything is identified as too thick. In these examples, the nominal wall thickness of the part is shown as .100 inches, and the thick region limit is set to .120 inches. For this type of analysis, the color gradient represents the thicknesses between .100 inches and .120 inches, while in the Thinness Analysis, the color gradient represents the values between .100 inches and 0 inches.

Figure 32.18 shows how this analysis produces some anomalous results, especially at the corners, and also in the middle. Again, this is a useful tool, if not completely accurate. You can use it to find problem areas that you may not have considered, but you should certainly examine the results critically.

FIGURE 32.18

Results of the Thickness Analysis

The Treat corners as zero thickness option should always be on. I have never seen a situation where turning it off improved the results; in fact, I have found that turning it off has always made corners and fillets behave worse.

This feature can generate a report, which to some extent answers questions about how or why it classifies faces in the way it does. To get a complete picture of the situation, it may be useful to look at the report when you are using the results to make design or manufacturing decisions. A sample of the report is shown in Figure 32.19.

FIGURE 32.19

A sample of a Thickness Analysis report

Summary

Total surface area analyzed	70.019in^2
Critical surface area(% of analyzed area)	3.102in^2 (4.43%)
Maximum deviation from target thickness	0.02in
Average weighted thickness on critical area	0.104in
Average weighted thickness on analyzed area	0.098in
Number of critical faces	27 Face(s)
Number of critical features	9
Minimum thickness on analyzed area	0.007in
Maximum thickness on analyzed area	0.197in

Analysis Details

Thickness range	Number of faces	Surface area	% of analyzed area
0.1in to 0.105in	16	2.253in^2	3.22%
0.105in to 0.11in	5	0.353in^2	0.50%
0.11in to 0.115in	2	0.288in^2	0.41%
0.115in to 0.12in	4	0.208in^2	0.30%

Undercut Detection

The Undercut Detection tool is found under the View menu, relocated from the Tools menu. It is also an on or off display tool, which changes dynamically as you change the model. Undercut Detection is conceptually flawed in that it gives incorrect results every time. However, if you think of the labels as being changed slightly, the results become partially usable.

Even if you and your mold builder know that a part has absolutely *no* undercuts, the Undercut Detection tool will nonetheless always identify *all* of the faces to be undercut. In fact, the only faces that this tool will identify as *not* undercut are faces that have no draft on them. The only time it correctly identifies an undercut is when it classifies the undercut as Occluded Undercut. Faces that have no draft and are occluded undercut are improperly identified as simply No Undercut.

You may want to avoid this tool because too much interpretation of incorrect results is necessary; however, if you still want to use it, then here is a translation guide that may help:

- **Direction 1 Undercut** — should read Pull from Direction 2
- **Direction 2 Undercut** — should read Pull from Direction 1
- **Straddle Undercut** — should read Straddle faces

- **No Undercut** — should read No draft in the primary draft direction, but may be occluded undercut faces

- **Occluded Undercut** — should read Occluded Undercut faces that have draft in the completely irrelevant primary draft directions; does not include occluded undercut faces that have no draft in the primary direction

Figure 32.20 shows the PropertyManager for this function and the results. If you would like to test it for yourself, the part is on the CD-ROM with the filename `Chapter 32 Draft Analysis. sldprt`.

FIGURE 32.20

The results of the Undercut Detection tool

 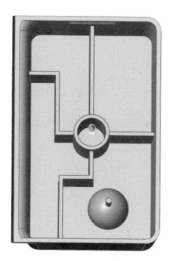

Working with the Mold Tools Process

The SolidWorks Mold Tools are intended to help you create cavity and core blocks for injection molds. They do not provide libraries or functionality for building the entire mold or mold components. Mold Tools entail a semi-automatic process to follow, with the tools in order on the toolbar. Mold Tools rely heavily on surfacing tools, and require a fair amount of manual intervention for certain types of parts. The next section deals with the manual intervention techniques. This section deals with the idealized semi-automatic process.

In order to fully understand the formalized Mold Tools process, it might be helpful to understand SolidWorks capabilities with mold geometry in general. First, understand that to create cavity and core geometry in SolidWorks, you are not required to use the Mold Tools. You can manually model surfaces or solid features to accomplish the same tasks. Surface features are widely used for mold modeling because they allow you far more control than solid features.

You can also make mold geometry using an assembly of in-context parts or multi-body techniques. The formal Mold Tools functionality uses the multi-body approach. This has benefits and drawbacks.

With the formal SolidWorks process, you start in part file with just the final plastic part in it, and then build both the cavity and core blocks around the plastic part. You also build any side actions or core pins within the part file, which seems a bit clumsy. To me, mold creation is better suited to assembly techniques, but that is not how SolidWorks built their functionality.

Figure 32.21 shows the part of the Mold Tools toolbar that identifies the process. From the left to the right, the icons are:

- Split Line
- Draft
- Move Face
- Scale
- Insert Mold Folders
- Parting Lines
- Shut-off surfaces
- Parting Surfaces
- Tooling Split
- Core

FIGURE 32.21

The Mold Tools

Mold Tools are really meant for tooling engineers, but part designers often use the first part of the process to apply draft to parts. Tooling engineers often need to add or correct draft to plastic parts they receive from part designers without draft or not designed with any process in mind whatsoever.

CROSS-REF The Split Line feature was covered in Chapter 7, and is not covered again here. Draft was covered earlier in this chapter.

The general workflow for using Mold Tools to create cavity and core blocks for an injection mold is as follows:

1. **Create split lines to add draft where needed.**

2. **Create draft as needed (Move Face can be used to angle faces much like the Draft feature).**

3. **Scale the part up to compensate for shrinkage during molding.**

4. **Identify the parting lines that separate cavity faces from core faces.**

5. **Create Shut-off faces, which are surfaces that close any through holes (windows or pass-throughs) in the part, and represent places where the steel from the cavity side of the mold directly touches steel from the core side of the mold.** These openings in the part are capped by surface features.

6. **Create Parting surfaces.** These are the faces outside the part where the steel from opposite sides of the mold touch.

7. **Create the Tooling Split.** Tooling Split uses the faces of the Shut-offs, Parting Surfaces, and the faces of either the Cavity or the Core side to split a block into two sides.

8. **Create any Core features.** Core is an unfortunately named feature in SolidWorks. Even in mold lingo, the word has several meanings, and it doesn't become any clearer when translated into SolidWorks terminology. In this case, the word "core" refers to the material used to make core pins, side action, slide, lifter, or pull in a mold.

If you were to create a mold with manual modeling functions, you might go through roughly the same steps in the same order. The SolidWorks process often breaks down in the automated surface modeling areas, such as shut-offs and parting surfaces. You may need to manually intervene in the process for these steps. Fortunately, the SolidWorks process is flexible enough to allow for manual modeling as needed.

Each one of these process steps may have several steps of their own. Cavity and core creation is far from a push-button operation, but when you understand the overall process, the detailed steps become clearer.

Using the Scale feature

 The Scale feature is used to make the plastic part slightly larger to compensate for plastic shrinkage during molding. Scale is driven by a multiplier value, so a part that is twice as big gets a scale factor of 2, half as big gets a scale factor of .5. Plastic materials have a shrink rate that is usually measured in thousandths of an inch per inch of part. Five thousands inch per inch is equal to a 0.5 percent rate. If the part is four inches long, the mold cavity to produce it must be 4.020 inches with that material. The 0.5 percent rate is equal to a scale factor of 1.005.

Some materials have *anisotropic* shrink rates, meaning they shrink different amounts in different directions. SolidWorks has a means to compensate for this, although it may not always be practical.

Usually the shrink directions are identified as "in the direction of flow" and "across the direction of flow," and the direction of flow of molten plastic inside a mold cavity is not always a straight line. Any anisotropic shrink applied to a part in SolidWorks is an approximation at best. If you turn off the Uniform Scaling option in the Scale feature, SolidWorks enables you to set different scale factors for X, Y, and Z directions. The Scale PropertyManager is shown in Figure 32.22.

FIGURE 32.22

The Scale PropertyManager

Insert Mold Folders

Mold Folders are folders that the Mold Tools add underneath the Surface body folders. You can add these folders manually using the Insert Mold Folders button on the Mold Tools toolbar. They are used to organize the different groups of faces used in separating the cavity and core solid bodies. The folders that are added are:

- Cavity surface folder
- Core surface folder
- Parting surface folder

Parting Lines

The Parting Lines feature identifies (automatically or manually) the edges that separate the cavity faces from the core faces. Figure 32.23 shows the PropertyManager as well as the preview for this feature. The edge selections for this feature were mostly manual. SolidWorks intends for you to use the red arrow shown after you select an edge to propagate the selection around the part by pressing Y for yes if the red arrow indicates the correct next edge of the Parting Line or N for no if it does not.

In this case SolidWorks gives me a message that says that the parting line is a complete loop around the part, but the part has some through holes, so it requires shut-off surfaces to close the holes.

FIGURE 32.23

FIGURE 32.23

The Parting Lines interface

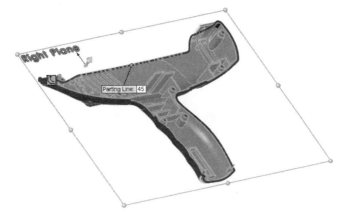

The Parting Lines feature can also split faces if need be. You might need to split a face that straddles the parting line. For example, a filleted face might bridge across the parting line and need to be split.

Shut-off Surfaces

The screw holes that go through this housing require shut-off faces in order to create the mold cavity and core. You can't just seal off one end of the holes; you have to pay attention to which end of the hole is where the draft in opposite directions meet. In this case, the counterbored holes from the outside have to be drafted from the outside, so they must be sealed or shut off from the inside.

When you initiate the Shut-off Surfaces feature, SolidWorks identifies some of the necessary shut-offs for you. Figure 32.24 shows this.

FIGURE 32.24

Creating Shut-offs

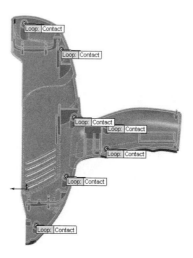

When all appropriate edges around all of the holes and slots are selected, the Shut-off Surfaces PropertyManager message window turns green and says "The mold is separable into core and cavity."

The tags on the loops in the graphics window will say either "No Fill," "Contact," or "Tangent." No Fill means that you do not want SolidWorks to create the shut-off surfaces. You will do these manually. Sometimes shut-off surfaces require complex or multi-feature shut-offs, which you have to do manually. The Contact condition means that the shut-off surface just needs to touch the edges, usually at a right angle. Tangent should be obvious.

Sometimes you need a combination of conditions in a single shut-off, in which case you will need to finish the feature manually. When the parting line and shut-off surfaces are complete, SolidWorks will automatically knit together all the surfaces in each Cavity and Core folder into a single surface body.

Parting Surface

The Parting Surface in SolidWorks works best on planar parting lines that are convex all the way around. That is to say that it will work okay on a part with a parting line that looks like an "O" from the direction of pull, but may not work optimally on a part that looks like a "C." In fact, it might be safe to say that the Parting Surface is in many cases unusable for any but the simplest parts. The part that I have been using as an example for this section is too much for the Parting Surface feature for two reasons: it is non-planar and the parting line has two concave areas (corners where handle intersects the housing).

There are not enough options with this feature to make it work in most situations in which it doesn't work by default, so I don't think it is worth going into in any further detail here. What this boils down to is that for 70 percent or more of your Parting Surfaces, you will need to create your own manually, which I show you how to do in the next section.

Just to show an example that does work, I have created a very simple part and brought it to this point using the Mold Tools process. When the process works as it should, and even when you have to create surfaces manually, you will wind up with one complete surface body in each of the Mold Tools Folders — Cavity, Core, and Parting surfaces. From this you can see that the Parting Surface and Cavity Surface define the top side of the Cavity block. Likewise, the Parting Surface and the Core Surface define the top side of the Core block.

In Figure 32.25, the Parting Surface is transparent so you can see both the Cavity and Core surface bodies. The grayscale image may not show this distinctly, but if you open the part from the CD-ROM, it will become obvious.

FIGURE 32.25

A completed Parting Surface

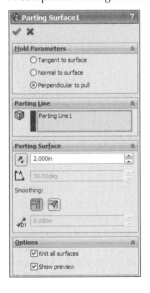

Tooling Split

Assuming you have completed the Parting Surface either manually or through the SolidWorks Mold Tools, the next step is the Tooling Split. If you complete the Parting surface manually, make sure it is knit together as a single surface body, and then in the Surface Bodies folder, drag the knit surface into the Parting Surface folder. Tooling Split will not work unless all of the surface bodies are in their correct folders.

Figure 32.26 shows the PropertyManager for the Tooling Split feature, along with a preview of the feature. The feature will produce two solid bodies, representing the cavity and core blocks of the mold. This model is included on the CD-ROM, under the name `Chapter 32 - frame mold tools.sldprt`.

FIGURE 32.26

The Tooling Split PropertyManager and finished product

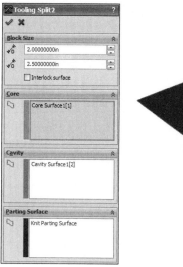
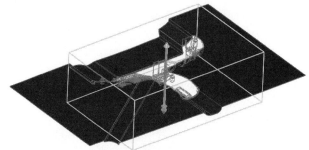

A tooling engineer would probably change a few things about the layout of this split, but for the purposes of learning how the tools work, this is sufficient. The Parting Line of the front part of the device should probably face forward instead of up to prevent as much vertical steel in the mold as possible.

To send the cavity and core blocks to a shop for mold building, you will probably want to separate the multi-body part into individual part files. Use the techniques from Chapter 26 for this (Save Bodies, Insert Into Part, Insert Into New Part).

NOTE To check the cavity and core blocks to make sure that they make the shape desired, make a new block that is larger than the original part, making sure to turn off the Merge Result option. Then use the Combine tool to subtract the mold parts from the new block. Then use the inverse scale to shrink it back down to the original scale factor.

Also note the Interlock surface option in Figure 32.26. Most if not all of the examples of molds that you see created with SolidWorks mold tools are going to employ parting line interlocks. This is not because most molds are built that way, but because it is the main way that SolidWorks gets around the limitations in the Parting Line functionality.

Core

In this case, I will use the Core feature to create a set of core pins. All of the standing steel that creates the counterbores for the screw bosses is made from separate replaceable pins. You can use many techniques to locate pins rotationally. This is not a lesson in mold design, but only in mold modeling techniques.

You can either pre-create a sketch or just make a sketch when the Core feature asks you for it. The Core feature is looking for a sketch that will cut out the block of mold material that you want to make a core of. Again, you can use this for side cores or core pins. In this case, I want to make several core pins.

To start, activate the Core feature; then sketch circles centered on each of the screw boss cores in the Cavity body. When I exit the sketch using the Confirmation Corner, SolidWorks prompts me for an extrusion depth for the sketch to create the feature. The Core PropertyManager and the feature preview are shown in Figure 32.27.

FIGURE 32.27

The Core feature

Again, you can save out these core pins as individual part files. You can use similar techniques to create side cores or lifters or other types of side actions.

Intervening Manually with Mold Tools

You have already seen that any sort of mold modeling resembling even a moderately complex part requires some level of manual intervention to get the Mold Tools to deliver usable results. You can do the entire mold modeling process manually, without using any of the semi-automated tools from Mold Tools. You may even come across situations where you do not need to use surface modeling at all. These situations will tend to be parts with a planar parting line, with no shut offs or cores.

I know several experienced mold designers, and they all tend to use different techniques, from cutting away chunks with solids, to using all manual surfacing methods, to using about 80 percent Mold Tools techniques and the rest manual surfacing. To me, it makes most sense to use the Mold Tools for the things they are good at, because they do speed up some tasks such as planar shut-offs, and separating out the cavity and core faces.

I want to run through two examples of manually intervening in the Mold Tools process. The first will be to create a passing shut-off (shut-off with a stepped parting line), and the second will be how I created the Parting Surface shown in Figure 32.25.

Passing Shut-off

Snap features are often achieved in molds by using passing shut-offs rather than some sort of a lifter or horn pin slide. Eliminating actions from a mold can be economical, as long as the passing shut-off does not introduce wear or alignment problems. When creating parts that require this sort of feature in the mold, it is a good idea to consult your mold builder.

Passing shut-offs can be difficult to visualize, even for seasoned professionals. It might be a good idea to open up the part on its own and see the geometry for yourself. The filename on the CD-ROM is `Chapter 32 – passing shut off start.sldprt`. This is a clip that holds a CD in place in a plastic case. The draft analysis colors have been left on it to help you see which faces belong to which side of the mold. There are no undercuts on this part, as shown in Figure 32.28.

In this part I have actually modeled two pair of passing shut offs.

Using the rollback bar is probably the best way to see what is going on with this part. The surfacing involved here may be confusing to you if you are not well versed with surfacing, but looking at the part and understanding the steps will help you learn. The basic steps to create the surface body called Shut-off 1 are as follows:

1. Create Ruled surface for the planar edges.

2. Loft surfaces between the parting line edges and the Ruled surface.

3. Extrude a flat shut-off face at the parting line of the snap feature.

4. Use the Cavity or Core knitted body to trim the extruded surface.

5. Use the extruded surface to trim the ruled and lofted surfaces.

6. Knit the surface bodies together.

FIGURE 32.28

A part that requires passing shut-offs.

The hardest part of creating this passing shut off is visualizing what the interface between the steel from opposite sides is going to look like. It is best to keep it as simple as possible. Tool builders request a wide range of angles for the passing shut off (mold steel touching at steeply angled faces). I have heard them say that the minimum draft they can possibly stand is anywhere from 5 to 15 degrees of draft. I try to give at least 8 degrees, more if I can. The tool builder will also look for a minimum land on the top of the shut-off boss, generally not less than 1 mm, or approx 0.050 inches, to work with round numbers.

Don't be discouraged if you don't completely understand this the first time around. The concept itself is difficult, and visualizing the geometry is extremely difficult.

Non-planar Parting Surfaces

Frankly, the method SolidWorks uses to create the Parting Surface is insufficient for most tasks. It will work well if you are molding a range of Frisbees or dinner plates, but it will not work well for hand-held medical devices. Figure 32.29 shows the part on the CD-ROM named `Chapter 32 – frame parting surface.sldprt`. The result is entirely unacceptable for several obvious reasons.

An automatically created Parting Surface for the hand-held medical device

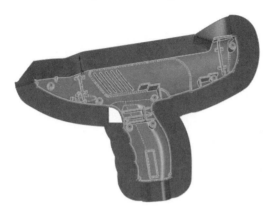

From this you can learn that the SolidWorks Mold Tools are not reliable for concave parting lines or non-planar parting lines. Flat parting line disks and boxes work well. Beyond that, expect to need to do some manual surface modeling.

NOTE   If you want software that will do automatic parting surfaces for you, consider MoldWorks and SplitWorks from R&B software. This software also includes highly automated mold libraries and aids to help you model and document every aspect of mold hardware.

To manually create the parting surfaces for this part, I tackled the hard part first, which turns out to be easy once you know a couple of tricks. The first thing I did was to create a sketch and use it to lay out directions that I could pull off the non-planar sections of the parting line. Figure 32.30 shows three lines that identify the non-planar top, base of grip, and trigger areas. The sketch lines lead in directions that those edges could be projected without running into other geometry.

Then the edges of each non-planar portion of the parting line were converted into sketch entities in a 3D sketch, and extruded as a surface along each of these three directions. From there, it was simple to create planar surfaces between the non-planar sections. This technique may not work for all non-planar parting lines, but it does work for this one.

FIGURE 32.30

Projecting non-planar sections

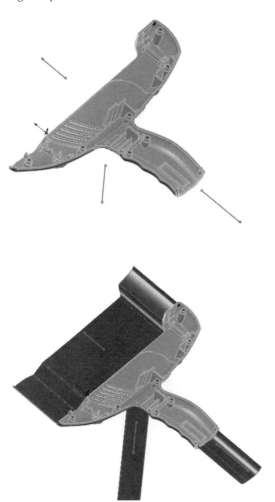

Tutorial: Working with plastic features

This is a tutorial that walks you through adding several plastics features to a simple part, running some plastics evaluations on it, and then making the cavity and core blocks for the mold using a couple of different techniques. The goal of the tutorial is to make you familiar with the workflow of the tools rather than to teach every available option.

1. To create a simple plastic part, start by opening a new SolidWorks part file.

2. Draw a Centerpoint Rectangle on the Top XZ plane centered on the Origin, 4 inches (vertical) by 6 inches (horizontal).

3. Extrude 1 inch with 2 degrees of draft, using the Draft Outward option.

4. Apply fillets to the vertical edges with 0.5 inch radius.

5. Apply a fillet to the face nearest the origin with a 0.25 inch radius.

6. Draw a circle on the Top plane centered on the Origin with a 0.75 inch diameter, and extrude it through the part as a cut, using 2 degrees draft, without the Draft Outward option.

7. Shell the part with a 0.10 inch thickness, removing the top face (large end of the extrusion).

8. Draw a rectangle on the Front plane 0.25 inch deep by 0.5 inch wide where the top of the rectangle is coincident with the top edge of the part. Cut through one side of the shelled block. To do this without cutting the boss in the center of the part you will have to use the From panel, extruding from an offset of 0.5 inch. Your model should look like Figure 32.31.

FIGURE 32.31

The tutorial model as of Step 8

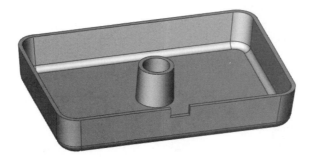

9. To create a Split Line, on the Front plane, draw a line from the bottom-right corner of the rectangular notch cut in Step 8 horizontally off the right side of the part. Make sure it goes past the part. Draw another short line from the bottom-right corner of the rectangular notch so that it makes a 100 degree angle with the horizontal line.

10. Use a Split Line to split all the faces that the lines project onto (should be a front, a back, two fillet faces, and a side for five total faces). Figure 32.32 shows the Split Line and the sketch.

FIGURE 32.32

Setting up a split

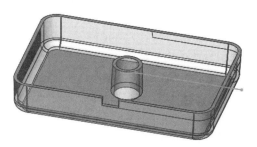

To create a Step Draft, initiate a Draft feature. Use the Step draft option. Select Perpendicular Steps. The draft angle should be 2 degrees. The direction of pull is the top thickness face of the box. Parting lines are the six edges of the split. Make sure all the yellow arrows are pointing to the same side of the split edges. Figure 32.33 shows the Step Draft in action.

FIGURE 32.33

The Step Draft feature in action

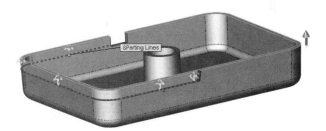

12. **Click OK to accept the feature.** Notice the drafted face steps out from the main part faces. Take a moment to examine the result of the Step Draft.

13. **To create Rib features, on the Front plane, create a sketch like that shown in Figure 32.34.** Initiate a Rib feature, and make it 0.075 inch wide at the base, with 1 degree of draft. Make sure you are using the Parallel to Sketch option (skyline).

FIGURE 32.34

Creating a skyline rib

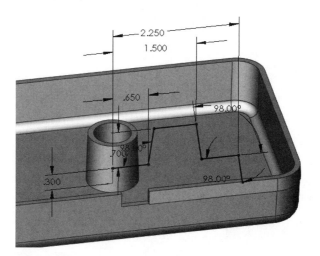

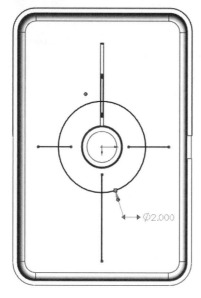

> **NOTE** You need to pay attention to the direction of the arrows for the draft (pointing up), and the selected faces (also pointing up). These arrows can have a mind of their own, and when you change one, it often changes the others without asking if that's what you want to do. You may have to individually select edges from the Parting Lines box and click Other Face to get all of the arrows pointing in the right directions.

14. Open a sketch on the horizontal face of the rib that is 0.3 inch above the Origin, as shown on the left side of Figure 32.33, and create the sketch shown on the right side of Figure 32.33.

15. **Create another Rib.** This time use the Perpendicular to Sketch (plan view) option. The thickness is again 0.075 inch at the base with 1 degree of draft. The part at this point should look like Figure 32.35.

FIGURE 32.35
_____

The part as of Step 15

16. Add the Mold Tools to your CommandManager (right-click a tab and select Mold Tools), or if you are not using the CommandManager, turn on the Mold Tools toolbar (by right-clicking on a toolbar and selecting Mold Tools).

17. To scale the part, add a Scale feature with a factor of 1.008. Scale about the Origin of the part.

18. To initiate the Parting Line tool., use the Top plane as the Pull Direction, and set the draft angle to 1 degree. Click the Draft Analysis button.

19. Notice a purple parting line that goes all the way around the part, but a warning message at the top of the Parting Line PropertyManager. The warning says that the parting line is complete, but you need to also create a shut-off surface. Figure 32.36 shows the Parting Line PropertyManager and the model at this point.

    You might also notice that the two side faces of the notches don't have draft. For now, go ahead creating the mold with the faces like this, and as an exercise later come back and add the draft and watch it propagate through the surface features into the mold blocks.

NOTE   You may need to deselect some edges around the rectangular notch. The edges
        selected for the Parting Line should be a clean single loop of edges that always sep-
arate the red faces from the green or yellow faces. Be careful that the Parting Line goes around
the Step Draft faces correctly.

FIGURE 32.36

The Parting Line PropertyManager and the model up to Step 19

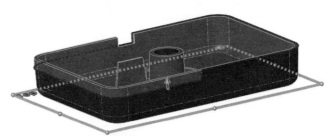

20. Click the green check to accept the Parting Line feature.

21. **To crate Shut-off faces, click the Shut-off Surface tool on the toolbar.** It should auto-
    matically find the hole in the middle of the part and understand where the shut-off needs
    to go. Click the All Contact icon at the bottom of the PropertyManager and then click the
    green check button to accept the feature.

22. **In the FeatureManager, expand the Surface Bodies folder.** Notice that it has sub-
    folders for Cavity and Core Surface Bodies.

23. **To create the Parting Surfaces, click the Parting Surface icon in the Command Manager.** Assign a distance of 2 inches, and make sure that it automatically picked up the Parting Line feature. The Mold Parameters option should be set to Perpendicular to Pull.

24. **Examine the preview of the Parting Surface.** Notice that it looks good, but not perfect. In this case, you will call it "good enough," although the angled lines around the rectangular cut out are not really "good enough." Ideally, you might remodel that face later, given it should all be theoretically planar anyway. Notice how the surface handles the stepped parting line created by the split line feature and the Step draft.

25. **Click the green check button to accept the feature.** The part at this point is shown in Figure 32.37.

FIGURE 32.37

The model as of Step 25

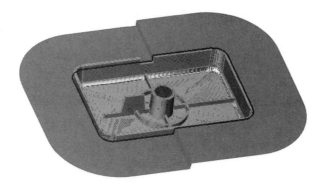

26. **Click the Tooling Split icon in the CommandManager.**

27. **Select the Top plane, and draw a centerpoint rectangle centered on the origin so that it is 6 inches by 8 inches, and the sketch fits within the bounds of the parting surface.** Make sure that you are looking at the part from the Top view.

28. **Exit the sketch by using the pencil icon in the ConfirmationCorner.** This enables the Tooling Split feature to continue.

29. **View the part from the side, and change the depth numbers at the top of the Tooling Split PropertyManager so that the block goes down .5 inch and up 1.5 inch.** Accept the feature when you are done.

30. **Right-click on the blue parting line in the graphics window and select Hide.** Also hide solid and surface bodies so you can see the inside of the block.

Look at the finished part provided on the CD-ROM if you need a reference. Use the controls on the Display Pane to hide and show bodies. Also use the Isolate option on right-mouse button menus for the bodies folder and the body in the graphics window.

Summary

SolidWorks provides a vast amount of plastics functionality. In this chapter, I've given you an introduction but there is far more for you to learn as you go. These features will become second nature after you have used them a couple of times. The power and flexibility is amazing when you think of the incredible range of parts that you can make with these features.

Chapter 33

Animating with MotionManager

S olidWorks has renamed the Animator product MotionManager, and it is now available in the base level of SolidWorks. The MotionManager enables you to create movies of parts and assemblies. These movies can show something as simple as a part rotating or as complicated as complex machinery in motion, including motion constrained by assembly mates, or motion driven by motors, springs, gravity, and contact.

This chapter does not cover Motion Analysis, formerly COSMOSMotion, because it is beyond the scope of the base SolidWorks package.

Overview

SolidWorks 2009 uses two different types of motion studies: Animation and Basic Motion. Animation uses key frames to drive the motion, and Basic Motion uses motors, springs, gravity (Physical Simulation), and collision (Physical Dynamics).

Understanding the terminology

The terminology used in this new product can be a little confusing. Here's an overview:

- **MotionManager.** Animator is now MotionManager. A more accurate way of saying this is that the MotionManager is the interface for the product formerly known as Animator. Animator as a separate product no longer exists. Its functionality has been absorbed into the base SolidWorks product.

- **Motion Analysis.** COSMOSMotion is now Motion Analysis. Motion Analysis is beyond the scope of this book.

- **Basic Motion.** Physical Simulation is now Basic Motion. Basic Motion uses motors, springs, gravity, and so on; it does not use key frames. It includes Physical Dynamics, which is the calculation of motion due to collisions.

- **Animation.** Assembly Motion is now Animation. Animation uses the *key frame* method, where the software interpolates between positions established by mates, free-hand drag, or positioning via Triad or XYZ values. Animation is not to be confused with *Dynamic Assembly Motion*, which is simply dragging parts in an assembly with the cursor to create motion.

 Another method that you can use to capture screen motion to a movie file is to choose View ➪ Screen Capture ➪ Record Video. The Radio Video tool also appears as a toolbar button on the Screen Capture toolbar. You can use Record Video to record whatever happens in the graphics window, including anything from using the Rollback Bar to running Basic Motion studies.

Formatting output

The MotionManager enables you to make animations within SolidWorks, and output movie files as `*.avi`, or as a series of `*.bmp` or `*.tga` still images. You can use it with the default (OpenGL) SolidWorks display, RealView display, or in conjunction with PhotoWorks to create more realistic rendered animations.

You can control the pixel size and frame rate of the recorded animation to help control finished file size, movie quality, and the amount of time it takes to record the animation. You can rotate or fly through single parts or assemblies. You can make assembly mechanisms move through animating mates, driving them with motors or manually positioning the parts in space.

One of the beautiful things about SolidWorks animations is that you can save them to an eDrawings file. You can send eDrawings to non-SolidWorks users for review, and the file format is small so animations are especially size efficient.

MotionManager interface

You can access the MotionManager interface in the lower left of the graphics window. The Model and Animation1 tabs allow you to toggle the interface on and off. The Model tab shows the normal SolidWorks interface. You can add tabs to create multiple motion studies. Figure 33.1 shows the lower-left corner of the SolidWorks window with each of the buttons activated. If you cannot see this interface, you may need to turn on the MotionManager. To do this, right-click on a toolbar and select MotionManager from the list of toolbars.

FIGURE 33.1

Accessing the MotionManager interface

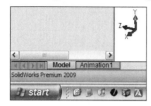 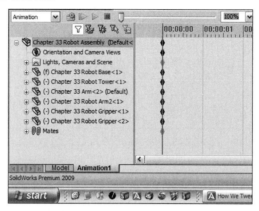

What can you animate?

You are able to animate the following:

- Distance mates
- Angle mates
- Part appearance (including display modes — shaded, wireframe, and so on)
- Part transparency
- Part visibility
- Part position
- View/zoom state
- Camera position and properties

When you animate colors and appearances, simple colors can fade from one color to another, but any appearance with a texture does not fade; it simply snaps to the next texture at the appropriate time. That is to say that you can fade red to blue, but you cannot fade marble to fabric.

You cannot animate the following:

- Changing part dimensions
- Changing PhotoWorks materials
- Configurations

Identifying elements of the MotionManager

The parts of the interface you will use the most are the key points, the design tree, and the time bar. The filters help you select or view limited sets of items, and the tabs at the bottom enable you to set up alternative studies. Playback speed enables you to change the rate of playback to either take in a long animation more quickly, or to see motion in one area in more detail. The timeline zoom in and out tools enable you to rescale the time interval on the timeline. Figure 33.2 identifies the major elements of the MotionManager.

FIGURE 33.2

The major elements of the MotionManager

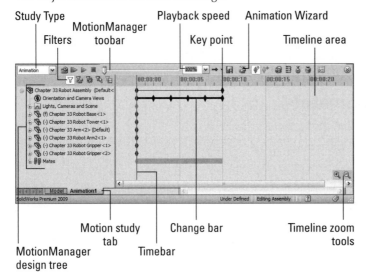

Using display options

When recording an animation to a movie file or a series of still images, you have several options for the type of display output to use. The first and easiest is the default SolidWorks display, without RealView. This is most appropriate for fast, technical presentations. You might want to use this to demonstrate the function of a particular mechanism or to simply rotate around a model to demonstrate the model in 3D rather than as a flat image or an eDrawing.

You can also turn on RealView and record the animation. If you do this, you should have appropriate appearances in use for individual parts. RealView appearances enable you to use reflective or textured materials on your parts.

The highest-quality images come through the PhotoWorks renderer. Using PhotoWorks takes much more time than the other options because each individual frame must be rendered just like a normal PhotoWorks rendering. PhotoWorks itself is beyond the scope of this book.

Planning an animation

It is often useful to plan any animation that is more involved than just a couple of moves on the screen. You can do this a couple of different ways. The easiest way is to write out a list of moves or positions you want display, with the approximate time of each position or action.

You might also use the storyboard technique professional video houses use. You create a series of images to represent the state of the animation at specific points in time. You can use static screen captures or hand sketches to do this, depending on the complexity of the geometry and animation.

Using the Animation Wizard

The easiest animations are those you can create with the Animation Wizard. Animation Wizard accommodates two types. The first is where a part or assembly is simply rotated on the screen, and the second uses an existing exploded view from an assembly. You can combine, reorder, reverse, copy, or move both types of animation sequences within a larger animation.

Creating a rotating animation

To create a rotating animation, first click the Animation1 tab at the bottom-left corner of the graphics window. This opens the MotionManager. Remember that you can turn the MotionManager itself on or off in the list of toolbars. (Choose Tools ⇨ Customize or View ⇨ Toolbars or right-mouse button (RMB) on any toolbar.)

 Click the Animation Wizard icon on the toolbar on top of the MotionManager. Figure 33.3 shows the dialog box that appears, and gives you the options to rotate model, collapse, explode, import from Basic Motion, or import from Motion Analysis. All options but rotate model are grayed out in this case is that the model loaded does not have an exploded view, or Basic Motion or Motion Analysis data.

After you select the appropriate type of animation and click Next, you select an axis of rotation, the number of rotations, and the direction. An important thing to note here is that the X, Y and Z axes do not refer to axes of the part; they refer to axes on the screen. Rotating about the X axis is like holding down the right-arrow key on the keyboard. The sample animation appears in the corner of the Animation Wizard, shown in Figure 33.4, shows what you can expect. It will change direction if you change the option.

FIGURE 33.3

The first page of the Animation Wizard: Select an Animation Type

FIGURE 33.4

The second page of the Animation Wizard: Select an Axis of Rotation

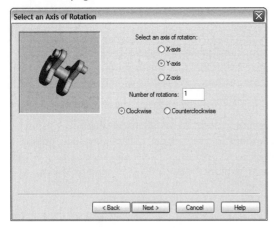

The final step in creating the rotating animation is to determine how long the animation will last, and at what point in the overall animation it should start. Figure 33.5 shows the Animation Wizard page to set these options.

NOTE Looping is only controlled during playback. The animation itself has a beginning and an end. If you want to play the finished movie with smooth looping, you should make sure that the start point and the end point of the animation are exactly the same.

FIGURE 33.5

The third page of the Animation Wizard: Animation Control Options

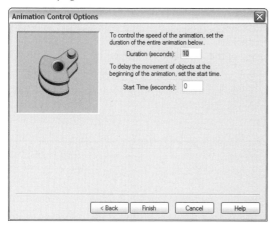

After you click Finish, MotionManager populates the timeline with key points along the timeline for the Orientation and Camera Views. Instead of rotating the part, the software rotates the view. It seems like a semantic difference, but when you start working with moving parts in assemblies while changing the view, the difference becomes important. Notice the heavy black line with diamonds on the row for the Orientation and Camera Views in Figure 33.6. Each diamond (key point) represents a view angle, and the line between them represents that MotionManager will interpolate the view between the key points, making the view transition smoothly. You will learn how to create key points later in this chapter.

FIGURE 33.6

Change bars in the MotionManager

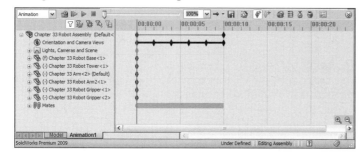

To play the animation, click the Play From Start or the Play button in the MotionManager toolbar, shown respectively in the image in the margin.

Creating an exploded view animation

The sample assembly on the CD-ROM is named `Chapter 33 Robot Assembly`, and is saved with an exploded view. You can create your own or use the one I have provided. If you use this file, create a new animation to practice with. To use the Animation Wizard to create an animated explode and collapse, first start with an assembly that has an exploded view and activate the Animation Wizard. Figure 33.3 shows the first page of the Animation Wizard where you select the animation type. Select Explode and click Next. Figure 33.7 shows the second page. Explode animations skip the second step, which is used by Rotate animations.

The second page of the Explode Animation Wizard

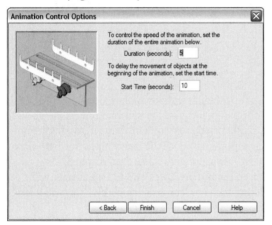

If you added the explode at the end of the rotate, your animation does both: rotate then explode, each in sequence. Later you will learn how to copy and reverse the key points for the explode to make it collapse and how to adjust key points to make parts move faster, slower, or simultaneously.

Animating the View

You are not limited to the Rotate Animation Wizard to changing the view. You can manually create key points or drive a camera along a path to create the view or transition between views that help you visualize your geometry.

Animating view changes

Animating view changes is a simple task in the MotionManager, and once you learn it, you will be able to apply what you learn to making parts and mechanisms in an assembly move in much the same way.

Again, start with the robot assembly. First clear the timeline of any key points. One way to do this is to simply choose File ➪ Reload to discard all changes, or you can right-click in the timeline area, choose Select All, and press Delete. Then set it to a Front view. An easy way to do this is to press the spacebar on the keyboard and double-click the Front view.

Orientation and Camera Views

The Orientation and Camera Views item in the MotionManager design tree is locked by default. You cannot manually change the view for the key point when this item is locked. To unlock it, right-click the Orientation and Camera Views entry, and deselect the Disable View Creation option. The icon changes from a black diamond with a red circle and line to a blue telescope.

The purpose of disabling the creation of new views is so you don't accidentally rotate the view and thus change the animation. I can tell you from experience that this is one of the most common mistakes I make when creating an animation.

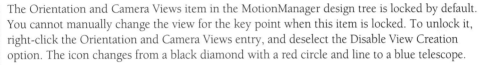

BEST PRACTICE **The best way to handle the Orientation and Camera Views option is to turn it off (allow view changes) only when you want to establish the view key points, then turn it off when you are done.**

To start this animation of the view, you need to turn off the Disable View Creation option, so that the blue telescope appears to the left of the entity in the design tree.

Introducing the Time Bar

The Time Bar is the vertical gray line in the timeline area that denotes the current time that you are editing in the animation. When you make a change to any element that can be animated, that change is applied at the time denoted by the Time Bar. To make a key point driven animation, the workflow usually involves moving the Time Bar, making a set of changes, moving the Time Bar, making another set of changes, and so on. I do the same thing here to demonstrate how it works.

I start by making sure the time bar is set to zero (all the way to the left), and then positioning the view I want to start the animation with. In this case, bring up the View Orientation box (spacebar) and double-click the view named 1.

I want the view to remain static for a couple of seconds when the animation starts. It might be too confusing to start the animation immediately with the view changing. To create this hesitation, I copy the first key point from the zero second mark to the two-second mark. It is as easy as it sounds. Click the key point in the same row as the Orientation and Camera Views, and then Ctrl+drag it to the right to the two-second mark. This causes the first two seconds of the view to be static.

Creating key points

Next, move the time bar to the five-second mark and bring up the View Orientation box again and activate view 2. This causes the view to swing around, and adds an additional key point to the timeline. The black bar between the two-second key point and the five-second key point indicates that MotionManager will interpolate the view orientation between the two defined points. The MotionManager now looks like Figure 33.8.

NOTE There is a bit of odd functionality here. If you have the time bar selected and press the spacebar, the time bar advances one second. If you need to access View Orientation instead of advancing a second, first click in the graphics window or the timeline area to clear the selection before pressing the spacebar.

FIGURE 33.8

The timeline at the five-second mark

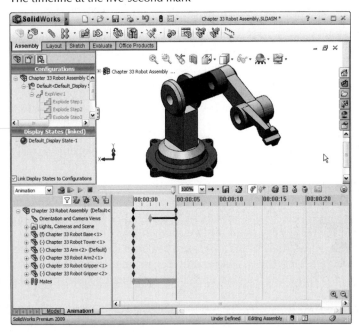

Zooming and free view manipulation

The next step is to zoom in to the grippers and simultaneously turn the view slightly to give a better view. Before changing the view, though, it would be nice to have another hesitation to give the viewer the chance to see what is there. To create the hesitation, click on the last key point in the Orientation and Camera Views row, and then Ctrl+drag it to the seven-second mark. Then move the time bar to the ten-second mark. Remember that the highlight color is now blue, not the green that long-time users are used to. Also remember that the workflow for copying a particular key is to select, then Ctrl+drag, not just Ctrl+drag. If you Ctrl+drag without the initial select, you may be copying other key points that were also selected at the time. The select operation serves two functions: first to deselect anything else, and second to select only the key point you are interested in.

> **NOTE** When creating an animation, you have to be very careful about making changes to anything, because those changes may be incorporated into the animation. If you just want to rotate the model to look at something, switch back to the Model tab near the lower-left corner of the SolidWorks window. The first tab always hides the MotionManager and you don't have to worry about changes to the views or positions of parts being recorded.

Once you have the time bar moved to the ten-second mark, zoom in on the grippers using whatever method you use to zoom, Shift+Z, middle mouse button (MMB) scroll, Zoom to Area, Zoom to Selection, or Zoom In/Out. When you are satisfied with the zoom, rotate the view slightly with the mouse, arrow keys, or any of the available toolbar tools. You may also want to pan the view slightly to get it positioned correctly. You need to be careful to make all the changes while the time bar is in a single location, or you may wind up with some very chopped-up view changes in the animation. The idea is to get a good partial side view of the grippers, such as that shown in Figure 33.9. Play the animation to see what you have created.

FIGURE 33.9

The timeline at the ten-second mark

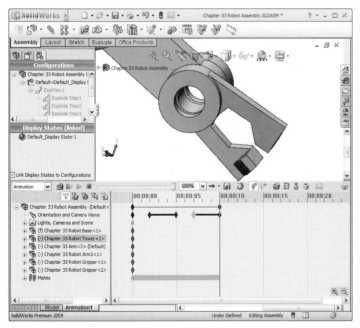

Using Interpolation modes

When you play the animation, it looks jerky, and not very smooth. When the MotionManager interpolates between key points, either for changing views or part positions, the default interpolation mode is linear. That means that it changes between points at a constant speed. This creates the jerkiness because the motion starts and stops abruptly.

To remedy this, MotionManager offers several interpolation modes. Right-click one of the key points that you have created, and select Interpolation modes at the bottom of the list that appears. Another menu flies out, as shown in Figure 33.10.

Selecting Interpolation modes

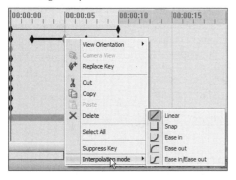

The icons for the modes should be self-explanatory. My only complaint is that the Ease out icon seems upside down. In any case, curves make smoother motion than lines. Ease in/Ease out create the smoothest motion; Ease in works best at the beginning of a change, and Ease out works best at the end of a change. Snap and Linear should be self-explanatory.

The default is linear, so if you want to change all four of the key points, you have to go through this selection four times, right? No, there is an easier way. You can box-select all four key points, then right-click on any of the selected key points, and change them all to say the Ease in/Ease out mode. Now play the animation again. Notice how much smoother the view changes are.

Correcting mistakes

When you start to use the MotionManager, you will probably make mistakes. MotionManager does you the favor of recording them all for you in the form of adding key points to the change line for either the part position or view orientation. One way to troubleshoot these types of mistakes is to drag the timeline through the key points, identifying which key points need to be removed. To remove a key point, just click on it and press Delete.

If you are making a long animation that covers a long period of time, say more than 30 seconds, the key points may be close together and difficult to distinguish from one another. You can use the zoom tools in the lower-right corner of the timeline area to zoom the timeline in or out. Zooming in makes the key points appear further away from one another, allowing you to select one that might be right on top of another.

Other mistakes or animation problems will also come up, such as parts that don't move correctly. In most of these situations, the fastest way to deal with them is to delete the problem key points and re-create them. Troubleshooting some errors tends to be fruitless and takes longer than re-creation.

Using paths to control cameras

 I introduced cameras in Chapter 5, so I will not go through the general details again. You might want to go back and brush up on some of the controls. The main controls you need for animations are the Target by selection, Position by selection and Set roll by selection, in addition to the Field of View settings.

The main weakness of the Rotate Animation Wizard is that it rotates about the screen axes. When I first saw the part rotate that way, I wondered how I could change it. It isn't as easy as maybe it ought to be, but once you understand the process, you can make it as simple as you need to make it. I will use the example of making the camera revolve around the axis of a part regardless of the orientation of the part as the example of how to drive a camera along a path. You can make this process as simple or as complex as you need to. I will start simple and make it gradually more complex.

To state the problem explicitly, rotating the view around the axis of the screen the way the Rotate Animation Wizard does it makes the part look like it is wobbling in space, or spinning while dangling from a string. It doesn't look like it is sitting on a turntable and the table is rotating, which I would guess is the effect most people are looking for. In order to spin the view around the part axis, make a path on a plane perpendicular to the axis, and draw some sort of a path on it.

Starting with the robot assembly from the CD-ROM (`Chapter 33 Robot Assembly.sldasm`), move to a top view, and open a 3D sketch. When doing prep work like this, it is better if you can work using the Model tab, instead of the MotionManager. This prevents you from creating any unnecessary key points for animatable items.

In the 3D sketch, from the Top view, draw a four-point closed loop spline, as shown in Figure 33.11. The reason I've created this in a 3D sketch is so that I can change the path to a non-planar path if I want to.

The path doesn't have to be perfectly circular; in fact, it might be better if it gets closer to the assembly on one side, making it rather kidney-shaped.

FIGURE 33.11

Creating a camera path

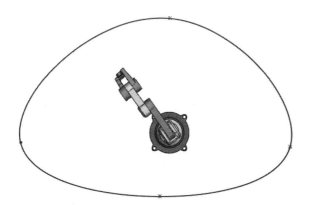

> **NOTE** To greatly simplify this task, you can create an offset plane, and sketch an ellipse or circle on the plane rather than using the 3D spline. The 3D spline is intended to give you the most control and flexibility.

The camera will be attached to this spline. You might also want to have a target point for the camera to follow as it goes around the path. I placed a sketch point inside the joint between the Tower and Arm parts. If the assembly or even a part origin is in a convenient location, you can also use this as a place to point the camera.

Once the path exists, exit the sketch and insert a new camera. You can insert a camera by right-clicking on the Lights, Cameras and Scene folder and selecting Add Camera. Remember that if the Lights, Cameras and Scene folder does not appear in the FeatureManager, you can turn it on by choosing Tools ➪ Options ➪ FeatureManager. Turn the option to Show. Figure 33.12 shows the PropertyManager for the Camera.

Using the fixed target method

To attach the camera to the spline and point it at the sketch point, make the following settings:

- **Aimed at target.** Select this radio button.
- **Target by selection.** Select this check box and select the 3D sketch point placed inside of the joint.
- **Position by selection.** Select this check box and select the spline.
- **Set roll by selection.** Select this check box and select Top plane.

FIGURE 33.12

The Camera PropertyManager

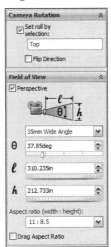

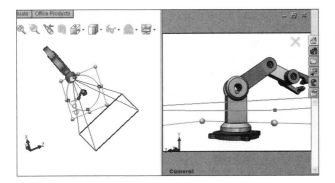

Notice when you insert the camera, the SolidWorks graphics window splits into two viewports. The left viewport is your view of the camera, the model, and their surroundings. The right viewport is the view through the camera.

You can set the camera angle now, but you should experiment a little first. In the left viewport, you can zoom the view up to a small window. Zoom to fit or otherwise zoom out until you can see the sketched spline. A yellow dot connects the lens of the camera to the spline. Drag the yellow dot around the spline slowly and observe the result in the right window. The image on the right in Figure 33.12 shows the arrangement of the viewports. As you drag the camera around the path, watch to make sure that the model stays in the field of view. Sections of the right viewport are grayed out to represent the visible field of view through the camera.

If portions of the model go out of the field of view, or you feel that the camera is too far away or too close to the model, you can move the camera or change the lens. To move the camera, exit the camera PropertyManager and edit the 3D sketch.

> **NOTE** Remember that when editing unconstrained 3D sketches, it is best to do it from orthogonal views. Any points you drag move in the plane of the screen. The best way to edit the size of the spline is to view it from the Top view, and drag out individual spline points.

Once you have exited the camera PropertyManager, to get back to it is not exactly the same as most other features in SolidWorks. One way is to right-click on it and choose Properties. The easiest way is to simply double-click the camera in the FeatureManager.

Using the sled method

If the first method was like filming an object on a turntable, this method is like walking around with a video camera on your shoulder. The first method attached the camera directly to the path, but in this method, you attach the camera to a dummy part, sometimes called a *sled*, and then move the sled around. The sled should be hidden when the animation is run and left visible for working purposes.

> **CAUTION** This functionality may or may not live up to your needs and expectations. You could politely call it "quirky," but it can be made to work within its limited range of capability, and works best when you do everything right the first time without needing edits. One of the cautions in the official SolidWorks documentation on the MotionManager is not to apply mates to the sled. This seems odd, especially given this particular application looks perfect for the Path mate, but I can vouch that the Path mate does not work well in this application.
>
> The SolidWorks documentation suggests that you use mates with the Use For Positioning Only option, so that the mate places the part, but is not added to the list of mates. I recommend you apply the mate but suppress it instead. If you need to put the part back to its original position, you can unsuppress and then resuppress the mate. The SolidWorks documentation recommends using the Move Component tool with the Along Entity setting, which is essentially the same as just dragging the part, but limiting the drag to a particular axis. This makes an easy task become a tedious one very quickly.

Take a look at this simple animation using a sled; it's one of the few that I actually got to work the way I wanted it to work. Open the Chapter 33 sled track assembly.

Start by creating a new motion study. Right-click on the Motion Study 1 tab and select Create New Motion Study. Do your new work in this new motion study rather than trying to edit the existing motion study.

Positioning the sled

Notice that the assembly has two parts: the track and the sled. In this animation, the sled goes around the three sides of the sled and then stops. The first thing to do is to position the sled in the track. I would make a coincident mate between the bottom of the side and the bottom inside face of the track. Figure 33.13 shows this arrangement.

FIGURE 33.13

Positioning the sled in the track

Moving the sled

 Next, create the motion of the sled around the track by using key points. Move the time bar to the next time you want to define the position of the sled, say one second, and then move the sled to the position it should be in at that time. You can use either simple dragging to get the part where it has to go, or you can use any of the options of the Move Component tool, shown in Figure 33.14.

FIGURE 33.14

Use the Move Component PropertyManager to move the sled.

When you move around the corners, remember that the sled is not going to follow an arc path; it interpolates linearly between key points. You can, however, make it rotate and translate at the same time. To do this from the end of a straight section, drag the sled with the left mouse button (LMB) to its new location, and then rotate the part by dragging with the right-mouse button to get it headed down the next straight section.

The assembly on the CD-ROM has an animation stored in it. You might want to check it out for reference.

Attaching the camera

Create a new camera by right-clicking the Lights, Cameras and Scene folder. Use the steps I outlined earlier in this chapter to attach the camera to the midpoint of the short side of the triangular sled, and target the pointy end of the sled. Be careful to not position or aim the camera such that it is half buried in the floor of the track or pointed at the floor. You want the camera to point in a direction parallel to the floor.

You may want to mate the bottom of the sled at a distance from the bottom of the track so the camera is not too close the floor.

Hiding the sled

Hiding the sled turns out to be more of a task than you might have imagined. Because you have to be able to see the sled to position it, and you have to have a portion of the sled in the field of view if you want to use it to control the camera target, you will have created the animation with the sled always visible. If you hide it, the MotionManager actually make it transparent in the background, and fades from opaque at the other end of the timeline. You need to move the time bar to the other end of the timeline and hide the part there, too.

Turning the camera on

Once you have created the animation from the bird's-eye point of view, and you can see the camera actually travel around the track, you will want to see the animation through the camera. To do this, first turn off Disable View Key Creation by right-clicking on the Orientation and Camera Views item, then right-click the camera in the MotionManager design tree and select Camera View. If you want to return to the bird's-eye view, just reverse the procedure.

In the end, using sleds has its own set of difficulties compared to simply moving the camera without attaching it to any thing. Neither is easy or convenient.

Animating with Key Points

In this chapter, I have already shown you a little about key points to introduce the idea, but here you will learn about how to use them in more detail. You can think of key points as snapshots at particular moments in time. If you said, "At the four-second mark, the wheel needs to be three inches from the wall," this statement describes a key point. To create a key point, drag the time bar to a new time, and make a change. Any of the animatable items I listed earlier in the chapter can create a key point.

Getting started

Consider this easy and useful example: a customer wants you to make a little animation of a holder for a stethoscope that he will show to a potential client in PowerPoint. The holder opens, the stethoscope slides out, and then the animation is reversed.

The assembly with the animation saved in it is on the CD-ROM as `Chapter 33 - scopecozy.sldasm`. The assembly and the completed animation timeline is shown in Figure 33.15.

FIGURE 33.15

Stethoscope animation setup

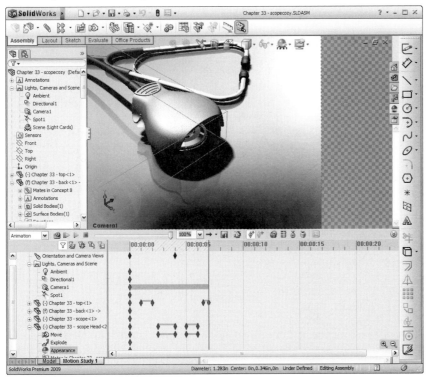

This animation uses RealView display, which the customer has said is good enough for his purposes. This cuts down the time significantly compared to using PhotoWorks to render the animation.

Your first task is to set up the camera. You could do this without a camera, but cameras are a convenient way to store a particular view, along with settings such as lens angle, perspective, camera position, and target. Plus, if you do decide to use PhotoWorks later, cameras are the only way to get depth of field for additional realism. Another advantage of the camera is that you are able to control the area in view more closely. If you don't use a camera, the area of view is just whatever is available in the view port. With the camera, you can specify a size and aspect ratio, and the available area is cropped appropriately.

Because the stethoscope model is cut into pieces to enable different parts of it to be positioned, you need to position the parts and the camera such that the break between the head and ear pieces is not visible. Leave enough open area so that when the stethoscope comes out, it will not run out of the area of view.

NOTE When adjusting the position of the camera, it is often easier to adjust the view itself than to manipulate the camera. In the Camera PropertyManager, turning off the Lock Camera Position Except When Editing option enables you to manipulate the view directly. This setting is on by default and will give you the camera with a red X icon if you try to rotate the view when the camera view is on. Switch to camera view and turn off Disable View Key Creation.

Using the time bar with key points

I like to start animations with some stillness. If you start an animation with motion, your viewer may not have the time to get settled. A second is usually enough time. Expand the Chapter 33 – Top part, click the key point for the Move row at the zero time mark, and Ctrl+drag it to the one-second mark. This means that the top will not move between zero and one second. Now move the time bar to two seconds and open the top by just dragging it up slightly. It should only open about half an inch.

Now move the time bar to the five-second mark. I want to create a mistake so you see one way to correct mistakes. At the five-second mark, move the stethoscope out of the holder three or four inches. Try to make sure you do not go far enough that the rubber tube runs into the plastic parts.

Notice that this creates a change bar that shows the position of the scope head part moving continually from time 00.00.00 to time 00.00.05. The motion is supposed to start at the three-second mark. I've shown you how to fix this in Figure 33.16.

Click on the key point for the motion of the scope head part. Then Ctrl+drag it from the zero-second mark to the three-second mark.

 If you run the animation at this point, you may see that the scope head does some unexpected movement, and a yellow line appears to the left of the change bar for the part. To fix this, click the Calculate button next to the Play button. I don't have a good answer for why this happens, but I have seen it on several animations.

FIGURE 33.16

Fixing a timeline problem

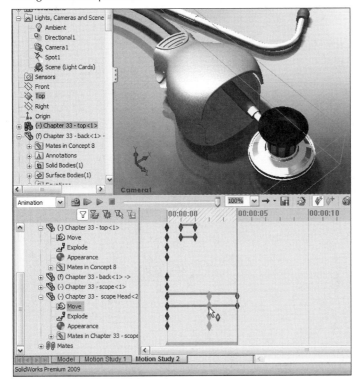

Copying and mirroring motion

The animation is essentially done at this point, except that now the stethoscope needs to go back into the holder and it has to close. You don't have to manually create all the steps to close the device, although you could if you wanted to. It is more efficient to simply copy and reverse the paths that you have already made.

To copy both sets of motion, the top opening and the head sliding out, drag a window around the key points to select them all, and then Ctrl+drag them to the six-second mark. Notice that this creates the situation shown in Figure 33.17. If you play the animation at this point, it is not at all what you want. It simply stacks the same motion on top of the original motion. You want it to be reversed.

FIGURE 33.17

Copying motion of parts

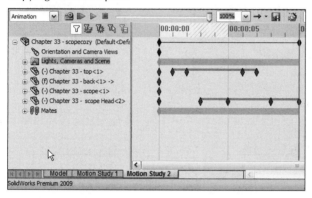

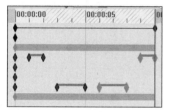

With the newly copied key points still selected, right-click on one of them and select Reverse Path. Notice that this now shows symmetrical key points.

Adjusting the speed of actions

The animation is getting close to complete, but now you notice that it would be better if the second half of the animation went by faster than the first half. To do this, move the key points on the right side of a change bar toward the left. You might want to move both key points for the top part closing so that it starts closer to the time when the scope head is back inside the holder. You could even make some of the motion overlap, so the top starts closing before the scope head is fully inside.

Again, if you see a strange effect like the scope head not going all the way back to where it belongs, trying pressing the Calculate button again. Calculate essentially rebuilds the animation after changes.

To make the motion a little smoother, right-click in empty space inside the time-line area, and choose Select All, then right-click one of the key points and select Interpolation Mode. Click the Ease in/Ease out option. Click Calculate again to watch the smoother animation.

If want variable speed, say for the scope head coming out of the holder (for example, it starts coming out slowly and then speeds up), you need to add at least one more key point. To do this, position the time bar to the left of the middle of the first scope head change bar, and click Place Key. This adds a key point in the existing change bar. This is shown in Figure 33.18. Then move the key point to the right. Make sure the new key point uses the Ease in/Ease out interpolation mode. Recalculate, and run the animation again.

FIGURE 33.18

Adding and moving a key point in an existing change bar

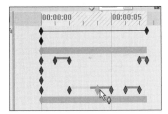

If you decide that the entire animation is too fast or too slow, you can also adjust this easily. Drag the right-most key point on the very top row with the Alt key depressed. This scales the entire animation up or down.

Getting output

Once the animation suits you, click the Save Animation toolbar button. This brings up the Save Animation to File dialog box, shown in Figure 33.19. The options for output formats are `*.avi`, or a `*.bmp` or `*.tga` series of still images. You could combine the still images to make an animated GIF to use on a Web site. Other types of output like Flash or QuickTime are not available directly from the SolidWorks software. Movie format converters are available on the Web for this purpose.

The options for the renderer are simply the SolidWorks screen or PhotoWorks. In this example, I used RealView and the SolidWorks screen renderer, which provides sufficient quality for my purposes. The main advantages of PhotoWorks over RealView are it offers a better choice of backgrounds, anti-aliasing, and more shadow control.

Other options

Image size and Aspect Ratio options are available only when you do not use a camera. Without the camera, you are at the mercy of the size and shape of the SolidWorks graphics window until you save the animation to a file.

FIGURE 33.19

Saving output data for your animation

The Schedule button enables you to schedule the output for a more convenient time. You would normally use this option when using the PhotoWorks, because rendered animations can take many hours to complete depending on render settings, length of animation, and the frames per second setting.

Frame information enables you to set the quality of the finished rendering. Low frame rates result in choppy motion. High frame rates will be much smoother, but the files may become unmanageably large. High-quality animations generally fall into the 25 to 30 frames per second (fps) range. The human eye cannot resolve faster rates, so it is usually pointless to go any higher than 30.

Test animations

Depending on the length of the animation and the other settings, test animations might run in the 10 fps range.

You might also consider using a specific range of time to test just a portion of the animation.

Unfortunately, many of the decisions that you make regarding animation quality settings directly relate to the time you have to produce the final movie file. The biggest time saver is to avoid PhotoWorks. If RealView suits your needs, you are well ahead on time.

Selecting a compressor

When you go to save the animation, the software prompts you to select a video compressor (codec). Typical options are the Microsoft Video and the Cinepak compressors. Sometimes when you record or play back a movie with a particular compressor, you get a lot of video garbage in the movie. If this happens, try another compressor. The used Microsoft Video for the first movie I recorded of this animation, and there was a lot of video noise. I switched to Cinepak and it worked perfectly.

Using Animations to Flex Parts

You cannot change part dimensions when animating. You cannot use features like the Flex to bend parts for an animation. If you can't do any of this, how do you make parts flex during an animation? This calls for another workaround, but it is the only way to actually make parts change shape with the MotionManager. You have to find a way to model the part such that you can make the changes using distance and angle mates in an assembly. That means that you have to do in-context modeling.

A lot of people treat in-context modeling as if it is some terrible infectious disease, but as I pointed out in Chapter 16, it is nothing to be afraid of if you know how to handle it. Still, when you're flexing parts with in-context tricks, it is best if you can keep it simple.

Figure 33.20 shows an assembly that uses this technique to twist the strap as the fork rotates. The assembly used to create this animation is on the CD-ROM, and is called `Chapter 33 yoke link.sldasm`. The finished movie file is also on the CD-ROM, and is called `Chapter 33 yoke link.avi`.

FIGURE 33.20

Twisting a strap during an animation

The main trick here is that the strap is made from three separate features. One feature is a revolve that fits the bottom shape of the pin. This feature is part of a part that moves with the fork and pin as they rotate. Another feature is an extrude made from an in-context feature. The in-context relation goes to a dummy part that remains stationary with respect to the rotating fork. And the final feature (really a pair of features) is a loft that goes from the ends of the rotate feature to the ends of the extrude feature.

As the fork part rotates, the in-context relation causes one feature to stay still while the other rotates, and the constant rebuilds the MotionManager does make it look like the strap is flexing.

You can use the same sort of idea to flex living hinges in plastic parts, or just about anything. A cleaner way to do this is to create planes in the in-context part, and then everything else is sketches. If you can drive the flex illusion with planes, you can get this trick to work in a wide range of situations. You usually wind up needing a loft feature, because no other feature is quite as flexible as a loft. It is possible to sometimes use other types of features, but I like the loft the best.

To create the actual motion in the MotionManager, you handle things just like in the other examples, but when you move the time bar, you double-click the angle mate and change the value. Driving animations with angle or distance mates is an effective way to get more exact motion.

In this case, the angle mate is the only thing driving the motion. There is some view orientation movement at the end of the movie, where I also copied the motion from the first half of the movie, and ran it again a little faster with different angle values closer up.

Animating with Basic Motion

Basic Motion is the functionality formerly known as Physical Simulation. It involves setting motors to turn parts, gravity to move parts and springs, and collisions to create animations that cannot be driven by mates or free motion. It uses a different solver than the rest of the animations in this chapter.

Basic Motion does not take into account effects such as momentum, bounce, resistance/friction, viscosity, reaction forces, and so on. To analyze for these effects, you will need to use Motion Analysis (formerly COSMOS Motion).

The study type selection box appears in the upper-left corner of the MotionManager. You will need to use Basic Motion, shown in Figure 33.21, for this example.

Using gravity and contact

Figure 33.21 shows an assembly that demonstrates the gravity and contact functions of Basic Motion. The problem is easy to set up. The part that is to move (ball) is underdefined, using only one mate to keep it in plane as it moves. The zigzag part uses a Fixed constraint. The assembly used in this example is on the CD-ROM and is called Chapter 33 zig zag.sldasm.

Setting up contact and gravity

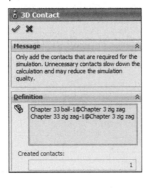

When you have added the physical simulation items, the MotionManager design tree looks like Figure 33.22. Editing items such as contact and gravity does not use the interface options that have been available in the rest of the SolidWorks software starting in the 2008 release. Left-click (select) does not bring up a context toolbar; you have to right-click and access the full right-mouse button menu.

Because this example goes by so quickly, you may wish to use the Playback Speed drop-down menu to get a better look at it. You can also set playback looping options with the drop-down menu to the right of the Playback Speed.

The MotionManager design tree with added items

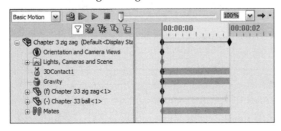

Using motors and springs

The use of motors does not necessarily require Basic Motion, but if you include springs, or contact or gravity problems, it does. Torsion springs require Motion Analysis, but linear springs only require Basic Motion. This example (on the CD-ROM as `Chapter 33 ratchet.SLDASM`) shows a motor driving a gear with a ratchet held to the gear teeth by a spring. I've added a swinging ball on a spring to show this isn't simple 2D functionality. (See Figure 33.23.)

FIGURE 33.23

A motor, gear, and ratchet assembly driven by Basic Motion

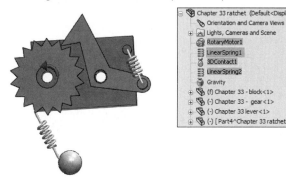

To set up this example, apply a counterclockwise motor to the inside circular edge of the gear, and select the block as the part to move relative to. In this case, I started the motor with a slow rpm (revolutions per minute), moved the time bar out a few seconds, and assigned a faster speed, so the motor speeds up over time.

The linear spring is easy to apply. Select the locations of both ends. In this case, I have circular bosses on the block and the ratchet to hold the spring.

Summary

Overall, the animation tools require some patience to get usable results. While the tools are not complex, they are not as reliable as you might wish. If you are realistic with your expectations, you are more likely to get usable results and avoid frustration.

Part VIII

Appendixes

The appendixes are a collection of information that doesn't fit well within the rest of the text. In particular, Appendix B is an immense collection of document and system settings.

Appendix A

Implementing SolidWorks

This appendix is intended to help anyone who is getting started with SolidWorks needs to rescue an existing but poorly implemented system. Everyone, from a single user to the CAD Administrator of a large installation, can benefit from reading this appendix.

Your success with SolidWorks does not only depend on the functionality and quality of the software, or even on how thoroughly you know the software. It also depends on how you maintain the system, license it, install it, and manage the design data, as well as how well your methods are accepted in the rest of the organization. SolidWorks becomes the interface between the engineering department and the manufacturing, IT, project management, and documentation departments. All these components come together to form the overall implementation and integration of SolidWorks into your business processes.

Licensing

Depending on how and where you buy SolidWorks, different licensing options may be available to you. The types of licenses available are educational, usb dongle, on-line activation, network license, temporary and home use licenses. SolidWorks does not allow the transfer of licenses between companies or individuals except if one company buys the entire assets of another.

IN THIS APPENDIX

Licensing

Training options

Implementation schemes

Hardware selection

Installation

Configuration and standardization

Data management

System maintenance

License activation

SolidWorks stand-alone software is licensed by a process called *activation*. The easiest way to activate the license is to connect the computer to the Internet after installing SolidWorks. A SolidWorks server holds the licensing database, which includes your SolidWorks serial number and contact data. After you have installed the software and open it, the Activation Wizard starts. Figure A.1 shows the first screen of the Activation Wizard.

FIGURE A.1

The Activation Wizard

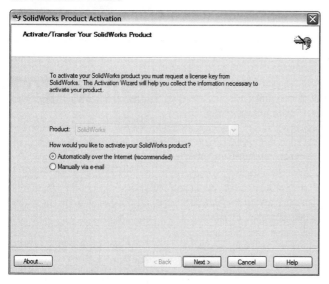

If your computer does not connect to the Internet, you can use the Activation Wizard to generate a file you can e-mail to SolidWorks. After determining which method you want to use for the activation (on-line or email), you must fill in your contact information. Using the Internet connection, SolidWorks then communicates with the activation server, and activates your machine to use the level of SolidWorks [you are registered for]: Standard, Office Professional, or Office Premium.

If the activation fails, SolidWorks may give you a [temporary] courtesy activation. Your reseller should be able to activate your license, or give you a reason why the activation failed. Each license is granted two activations that can be active at any time: one for the commercial use and another for the home use.

Think of activation as a floating license you can use across the Internet. Once you have activated your license on your computer, you can transfer it back to the license server and activate

SolidWorks on a different machine. SolidWorks is installed on several computers, and your license to use it is only activated on the computer you are using. Once you are finished working on this computer, the license is transferred back to the license server and available to you the next time you need it. This is very convenient.

Home license

The SolidWorks license agreement allows the primary user of a license at work to also use the license at home or on a laptop, providing that both are not in use at the same time. There are some complications when it comes to network licenses or licenses that require dongles (a hardware key that fits into a USB connection). Your reseller or support organization should be able to give you more details.

Alternatively, you can use license activation to run the software at home. Consult your employer to make sure they approve. Many employers support employees learning software or working on work projects at home. However, some may worry that you are working on the side with their license.

Network license

A network license works by running an application on a central server (this could be any computer, not necessarily a real server) that knows how many licenses it can dispense from a license file that SolidWorks provides to you. Each time you start SolidWorks on a computer connected to the server application, it takes one license away from the total available. This system can manage the different levels of SolidWorks, including add-ins. When you shut down SolidWorks, the license is added back to the available list.

A network license offers a fairly simple and straightforward way to install and manage SolidWorks. It is a convenient way for users to share licenses when there are fewer licenses than users. Assuming most of the users are not full-time users, this can be a good solution. If a user wants to run SolidWorks, but there are no available licenses, then the user receives a message saying so, and must wait until a license becomes available. You can add licenses to the network license by getting a new license file from SolidWorks or your reseller.

Dongle

A dongle is a hardware key that plugs into your computer via a USB connection, and allows software to run. Non-U.S. licenses of SolidWorks require dongles.

Levels of SolidWorks

SolidWorks comes in three levels: Standard, Professional, and Premium. Figure A.2 shows a detailed list of the functionality available in each level.

FIGURE A.2

Add-ins that are available with each level of SolidWorks software

	SolidWorks Standard	SolidWorks Professional	SolidWorks Premium
Mechanical CAD Capabilities			
SWIFT	✓	✓	✓
Getting Started	✓	✓	✓
User Interface	✓	✓	✓
Working with DWG	✓	✓	✓
Part Modeling	✓	✓	✓
RealView Graphics	✓	✓	✓
Advanced Surfacing	✓	✓	✓
Sheetmetal Design Tools	✓	✓	✓
Weldment Design	✓	✓	✓
Mold Design Tools	✓	✓	✓
Assembly Modeling	✓	✓	✓
Assembly Motion	✓	✓	✓
Large Assembly Mgt	✓	✓	✓
2D Drawing Creation	✓	✓	✓
Data Translation	✓	✓	✓
Design Reuse	✓	✓	✓
Bill of Materials	✓	✓	✓
Part Validation	✓	✓	✓
Design Automation of Repetitive Tasks	✓	✓	✓
Import/Export Capabilities	✓	✓	✓
Design Collaboration		✓	✓
Feature Recognition		✓	✓
Standard Hardware Libraries		✓	✓
Photorealistic Rendering		✓	✓
Design Standards Checking		✓	✓
Advanced Productivity Tools		✓	✓
Leverage Scanned Data			✓
Routed Systems			✓
ECAD to MCAD Integration			✓

Training Options

After the purchase of a new CAD system, training is extremely important. Productivity only comes when you combine good tools with appropriate skills. A lack of training often indicates the lack of an implementation plan, and generally leads to far lower productivity and a longer ramp-up time. Although training is valuable, you should try to get the best training possible for a reasonable price.

To make the best use of training, it is best for companies to immediately after the training get the trainees involved in projects using the new software. The biggest waste of time and money is to put the trainees back on the old software to finish another project. It is best to take project scheduling into account, and plan so that trainees have a new project to work on when they finish the training, especially if they have just completed classroom training with an instructor. The following sections cover some options for SolidWorks training.

998

Reseller training

When the reseller sells you the software, they may bundle in or simply add on the standard training. If you buy the training, make sure that the trainees are prepared for it. Their schedules need to be clear for the period of training, and not conflict with important deadlines or company meetings. Most important, make sure that all the trainees go through the SolidWorks tutorials before attending the class. They will get far more out of the class if they have some basic idea of what is going on before they get there. There is a lot to be said for being able to ask informed questions beyond the basic, "How do I start the software?" I taught SolidWorks training classes at resellers for about seven years, and the difference between a student who has done his homework and one who has not is immediately obvious.

Before signing up for the training, here are a few ideas.

Training as evaluation

If you are reading the appendix of this *SolidWorks Bible*, it is probably too late for this suggestion for your current SolidWorks purchase, but taking training as a part of the software purchase evaluation whenever you consider new software is a terrific way to help you make an informed decision about which software package to buy. Because of the time commitment involved, this is generally only an option if you come from a larger organization with a dedicated CAD Administrator. It is also best to have two people go through training to evaluate software rather than one; this way, they can trade and share ideas, and the company's decision does not rest on one person's opinions. Make a deal with the software resellers that as a part of the evaluation, you will get training on all the software packages being considered, and if you buy their software, you will pay for the training. This can also work the other way: you pay for the training up front, and if you buy the software, the cost of the training is treated as a credit toward the software purchase.

However you negotiate it, resellers may accept this option because they see that you are willing to invest in the evaluation process, and are serious about the purchase plans.

Using training as evaluation helps you to evaluate more than just the software; it also helps you to see what doing business with a particular CAD vendor or reseller is like. If they have to send you to another facility for training, you will want to take this into account. If the trainer is exceptionally knowledgeable, this is an obvious benefit. If you get to meet the support people, that is another benefit.

Quality of trainers

In the software reseller world, the sales department is given the highest priority. This means that the best technical people are generally devoted to sales demonstrations and contact with prospective customers. Following this line of thinking, any post-sales activity is usually a lower priority. For example, training and tech support are considered post-sales activity. Because sales organizations often see any technical function as pure overhead (even though it is the only thing on which the customer places value), they may cut corners when hiring technical staff.

Although you may be very impressed with the knowledge and abilities of the application engineer who does your initial software demonstration (which is typically a scripted and highly practiced performance), you should ensure that you become acquainted with the person who will be doing the training. This may be different person than you first encountered, depending on the size of the reseller organization.

SolidWorks Corporation gives a training certification test, and you should make sure that your trainer has been certified for training as a Certified SolidWorks Instructor (CSWI). Other certifications that the trainer should have include the Certified SolidWorks Professional (CSWP) and Certified SolidWorks Support Technician (CSWST). Of these, the CSWST is the most difficult to achieve. These technician certifications are far more involved than the CSWP, which is the customer certification.

Beyond the knowledge of clicking buttons and making menu selections, the trainer is a greater asset if he or she has experience in manufacturing or design in the real world. This way, the trainer can put the software examples into context and understand your questions more completely.

In summary, before getting training from your reseller, make sure that you are comfortable with the instructor. The main advantage of training with a live instructor is the instructor can react to your questions immediately.

SolidWorks training materials

The SolidWorks training materials generally get high marks for covering what you need to know. The *Advanced Assembly Modeling* book was always my favorite. Well illustrated and in color, the training books are generally written in a tutorial format, giving the instructor the steps to guide you through the demonstration. Given this layout, they could conceivably be used for self-paced learning, as well.

Unfortunately, these books are not available to the general public except through the reseller. You can try to buy them through your reseller without taking the class (which amounts to a $100 book versus a $1,500 class), but most resellers do not offer this option. You can try eBay, but books related to recent versions may be difficult to find.

Hiring a consultant

Reseller training fees are usually charged on a per-seat basis, and average approximately $300 per day per student. One user for one charge, two users for two charges, and so on. Hiring a consultant may give your company some flexibility, while still enabling you to get a live instructor and a flat rate. If you have a large SolidWorks installation and a number of users to train, this option could save you a significant amount of money. Consultants also offer other advantages, such as they come to your location, and they can customize material to include only the topics that you need, as well as include new material not covered by the standard SolidWorks books.

Specialty topics

Consultants are more likely to be specialists in a certain discipline such as machine design, plastics, or mold design, and so you stand a better chance of getting higher-quality information. If your company has special design practice requirements, it may be worthwhile to have a specialist consultant develop custom material for you. For example, if your company develops mixing equipment, and auger design is important to you, but the SolidWorks software does not have tools that apply directly to your design or manufacturing needs, then a consultant who has developed a process or an add-in custom application will be a worthwhile investment. High-end surfacing is another area where a consultant could do you some good, because there is a general lack of documentation on this topic for SolidWorks.

On-site training

On-site training generally sounds attractive to managers because you do not have to pay for a room, travel, or move computers. It seems more efficient, you have access to your people all day, and they can still reply to e-mails and phone calls. I have done a fair amount of on-site training, and have mixed opinions about it. While it is undoubtedly more convenient and less costly for the host company, the trainees are often far more distracted. I have even had classes that were put on hold because most of the trainees were called away to other tasks.

If you choose to do on-site training, try to set the class up in an area where there are minimal interruptions, and plan as though the trainees are not available for their normal duties at all.

Online or CD-based training

There are several vendors available that sell online or CD-based training. Check the SolidWorks Web site in the Partners area for links to specific suppliers. The advantages of this type of training are that you can go through them again and again, and then give the CDs to other users to go through at their leisure. Compared to reseller training, the cost is very low, and it does not require driving to the location, staying in a hotel, or clearing your schedule for a week. The CDs are often well indexed, with searches and hyperlinks, and video to demonstrate functions. Some also include self-testing for evaluation.

However, digital media cannot respond to questions the same way a live instructor can. A user must also be self-motivated to get much out of this kind of self-paced training.

Train the trainer

The *train the trainer* method can be a good option to help you save some training money and develop some in-house talent. This is particularly true if you have a strong SolidWorks user who is also inclined to being an instructor. The biggest challenge with this training scenario is finding materials for the trainer to teach from. The SolidWorks materials are not available for public sale, and developing your own curriculum is a daunting task.

If you are not familiar with this style of training, typically a couple of people attend the formal retail training, and then come back and train the rest of the users.

Local colleges

Local colleges may offer courses on SolidWorks. You can contact SolidWorks directly to get a list of the colleges in your area that are using SolidWorks software. Keep in mind that one of the difficulties with using a local college is that the educational version of the software is always one version behind the commercial software. This may or may not be a limiting factor for you. Generally there is not a big difference between the versions, although the jump from 2007 to 2008 is significant.

User groups

I am a huge proponent of user groups as a great way of disseminating SolidWorks knowledge. However, I would not rely on user groups for training. The meetings are a couple of hours a month at most and usually only cover a single topic each time. As a method of training, it would take years to get through the software in this way, but it is still a great source for information on specific topics.

 **See Appendix C for a larger listing of general help sources.**

Implementation Schemes

Choosing an implementation scheme that best fits your company is one of the first steps after making a new CAD purchase. How you choose to transition from one design software to another depends on many factors, including the skill of your users; how you manage your data; if you work on distinct projects or use teams; and if you do design or manufacturing, or both. The size of your company and the nature of how you work are likely to be the most influential factors.

Implementing new tools, processes, or procedures is usually a painful experience. Software in general, and CAD software in particular, tends to create a dedicated following, and switching allegiance is unthinkable for many users. Also, if you have a lot of time invested in learning a particular software, making a change can be a daunting and frustrating task. Different personalities deal with change differently, and if you are a CAD Administrator, although psychologist is not necessarily part of your job description, you need to be able to handle the resistance to change.

In any implementation scheme, it is imperative to have the backing of management, not just one level up, but often much higher than that, depending on the size of your organization. The directive that a change is going to be made needs to come from high enough up the ladder that there is no question about the commitment of the whole organization. End users will think harder before crossing senior management than they will before crossing the CAD Administrator. If the owner of the company has made the decision to buy the software, then you should also enlist him or her to help ensure that the implementation is successful. A failed design system implementation is much more costly than simply throwing away expensive software.

Recognizing that there is an infinite number of combinations of types of projects, sizes of organization, and so on, you may have to use your imagination to apply one of these scenarios to your situation. The following are some of the typical implementation schemes that I have worked with or helped develop at companies I have worked for or consulted with.

Planning

If you are responsible for a multi-seat installation of CAD software, then you need to plan any new software implementation. A flowchart, a timeline, or even a simple checklist is a good place to start with planning the implementation, depending on the size of your organization and the size of the task that you face. You should establish goals and dates, and try to understand the prerequisites and criteria for judging success at each step. You should also plan the costs associated with each step. Costs can include training, the learning curve, consulting, data conversion or archiving, new hardware, new infrastructure, or associated software.

Pilot project

If your organization tends to have several projects a year where a small number of users are involved in each project and the project has a finite length of perhaps a few months, then a pilot project may be a good option for your implementation scheme.

In the pilot project implementation scheme, you assign a small number of users (usually one to three) to a new project. The end of their training should coincide closely with the beginning of the project. Too often, users go to training but then have a gap until their first project with the new software begins, and they forget much of what they have learned.

The users selected for the pilot project should be users who can adapt easily to change, and who learn new software quickly. It may be useful to include a younger, enthusiastic user with an older, more experienced designer. Generally, having two people to encourage each another is a good tactic when setting up a team for this sort of project. One person can develop bad habits or become bogged down easily, while two people can work together to solve problems and learn from one another.

At the end of the pilot project, you have the opportunity to learn from difficulties and mistakes, to tweak the process for the next project, or to expand the project to the rest of the organization.

Phased approach

The phased approach works best when the company has several groups for different product lines (such as motors, brakes, and transmissions), or different disciplines (such as New Product Development, Production Engineering, Manufacturing Engineering, and so on). This approach tackles individual departments separately, by segmenting the immediate task. In the case where work between departments is sequential (passing from Development to Engineering to Manufacturing), the implementation process should obviously start at the top of the organization, and flow through the organization at the same speed that the newly created data flows through the organization.

One thing that the phased approach is *not* meant to do is to phase out the use of one CAD product while another is being phased in on the desktops of individual users. When changing CAD packages, it is best for each user to move completely to the new package. While there are always questions of practicality, such as what to do with unfinished projects or fix-up jobs in the old software, the company should move forward as quickly and cleanly as possible. Looking back or keeping the old software active can cause a lingering stagnation, which always puts an emphatic question mark at the end of the implementation. From an efficiency point of view, it is better to have a single user dedicated to changes and cleanup with the old software, rather than have several users splitting their time between the old and the new.

The phased approach allows you to learn from small mistakes and address the task in small pieces. Getting in over your head is a classic mistake of over-enthusiastic, poorly planned implementations.

This is also a good way to plan when there is more than just a CAD package being implemented. For example, when Product Data Management, or PDM, software is also being implemented, the complexity increases significantly. PDM software is arguably more complex to implement than CAD software, mainly because PDM affects your business processes on top of the large amounts of data that can be affected by the change. PDM is beyond the scope of this book, but it is related to the general discussion and cannot be completely avoided. I cover implementing general Data Management practices later in this appendix.

Typical phases used in the phased implementation can include the following:

- **Information gathering.** What was your condition when you started the implementation? If you ask five people in your organization to write down your documentation process, you may be surprised at how little they agree on what is currently happening. Getting everyone to agree on the initial state of affairs is key to agreeing on an improved process.

- **Process development.** Write the new process down. If you have flow-charting software, it is a good idea to use it and let people know what to expect, particularly management and IT (if you require desktop hardware/operating system support).

- **Pilot.** Run a live test partially to demonstrate that the process works and partially to work the problems out of the new process.

- **Rollout by department or discipline.** The software is rolled out according to the plan.

- **Evaluation.** Often called a *post mortem*, this involves evaluating how you did, and the strength of the new process.

Cold turkey

Cold turkey as an implementation scheme is probably not very useful unless you have a small group of users. Using the cold turkey method means that one day you just turn off the old software and turn on the new. It is probably best if it is planned in conjunction with the beginning of a new project, the hiring of a new employee, or some other culture-changing event. It is not a very sophisticated method, but in smaller groups it may make more sense than an involved schedule. It is advisable to have the training completed before you require the user to be productive with the software.

Hardware Selection

Hardware changes so quickly that my suggestions here have to be general rather than specific. Still, the overall requirements for SolidWorks have been about the same for several years. Basically, you need to get as much computer as you can afford.

Primary components

The main aspects of a new computer that you want to pay particular attention to are:

- CPU
- Video card
- Memory

CPU

The CPU is on top of the list because it is the least upgradeable. It is certainly possible to upgrade the CPU, but it is rarely economical to do so, because a new CPU in an otherwise old computer will not use the new CPU to its best advantage. Purchase the fastest CPU that you can afford. This is really the heart of your computer. The more complex your parts or assemblies, or the more intense computing that you do (such as Finite Element Analysis, or FEA, or photo rendering), the faster the CPU needs to be.

Multi-processor or multi-core

Any new computer you buy is going to be multi-core or multi-processor, with two, four, or eight cores. You may hear people say that SolidWorks is not multithreaded (this basically means that it can only do computations serially — one after another instead of in parallel), but this is not necessarily true. The response of SolidWorks to multi-core processors varies greatly, depending on what types of work you are doing. For loading assemblies, drawings, stress analysis, rendering, and some of the more complex multi-body solid or surface modeling operations, multi-core is extremely helpful.

If you use your computer for more than one task at a time, then a multi-core processor will be useful to you. For example, while you are waiting for SolidWorks to do an operation on a long FeatureManager or large assembly, you can also check your e-mail or fill in an Excel spreadsheet. This kind of multi-tasking definitely benefits from a multi-core processor. Drawings also benefit from multiple processors, as well as some advanced feature types. I suspect that multi-body parts are able to take advantage of the technology as well. This includes most surfaced parts, given most surface models are also multi-body models. However, if you are simply calculating a list of features in a single part, and each feature is dependent on the feature before it, then a multi-core processor may be of little advantage to you. Simple solid parts probably get the least benefit from multi-core arrangements.

AMD versus Intel

The AMD verse Intel battle has gone back and forth throughout the years. For the first edition of this book (*SolidWorks 2007 Bible*), AMD was making some of the fastest chips. Now, for the 2009 edition, everything is Intel. Your best bet is to check out a forum or user group to see what the current preferred hardware is if you are in the market for a new computer.

32x versus 64x systems

If you are getting a computer that you hope will last three years or more, then you will probably want to get a 64-bit-compatible processor. The main reason to move to the 64-bit system is to increase the available RAM. If you are working with very large assemblies or drawings, and you have problems with SolidWorks, or even with Windows shutting down because the memory limits of the system are exceeded, you are a good candidate for a 64-bit system.

CAUTION Be aware that some peripherals may not have drivers available for 64-bit use. If you are ordering new hardware or software, you should do a little research before spending the money to make sure everything is compatible.

XP or Vista

At the time of this writing, Microsoft has stopped selling XP, but will continue to support it for some time. Adoption of Vista has been relatively slow, especially for technical computing applications. The only statistics I have for the relative popularity of the two operating systems are Web statistics for my site and blog. They show Vista to be approximately 10 percent of the XP usage. WinNT, Linux, Win98, and Win2000 are down in the 2 to 5 percent range, with Mac in the 5 to 10 percent range.

If you are buying a new computer, there is currently no real reason to stay with XP. To maximize compatibility of your computer with hardware and software you might buy in the future, I suggest that you get Vista. Vista uses a lot of RAM, probably an additional gigabyte more than XP. For this reason, if you are going to go with Vista, you should go with Vista 64-bit. 32-bit Vista doesn't make much sense. By the time you get the Vista OS and SolidWorks loaded, you do not have a lot of resources left for loading large data sets. Of course, if you work for a larger organization, your IT department may have something to say about what OS you use.

The future is in 64-bit. All computers will eventually be 64-bit. It makes most sense to look to the future for new equipment.

Video card

For the past several years, it has been a safe bet to recommend an nVidia Quadro video card, something higher than the 500 model. The nVidia geForce cards also work but have some limitations. You should check the SolidWorks Web site, which has a link on the front page to video card test results. It all boils down to "Red is bad, Green is good." I have run into some users who have an unexplainable obsession with particular brands, and cannot accept that they work great for games but not for SolidWorks. The bottom line is that for SolidWorks, you should avoid the ATI Radeon, although the ATI FireGL works just fine.

Engineering and game applications use different graphic languages. SolidWorks uses Open Graphics Language, or GL, and works best with video cards that have good OpenGL drivers. Game cards use Direct X, which is a Microsoft graphics standard. Current trends in the CAD market are for CAD applications to start supporting Direct3D, leaving OpenGL behind. This is a point of contention with any CAD application that runs on the Mac OS, because Microsoft's Direct3D does not run in OSX. OSX uses OpenGL.

The video card comes in when you are moving shaded models on the screen, or when you are repainting after a rebuild. It is most extensively used for motion, transparency, and effects like RealView. High-end graphics cards for professional OpenGL applications can be extremely pricy, and often do not buy you a proportionate increase in speed. However, cards that use drivers with poor support for OpenGL can cause SolidWorks to crash frequently. It is considered a safe practice to buy a mid-line card, which provides much of the performance of the higher-end cards at a reasonable price.

If you have to save some money on one of the three major components, it may be okay to save on the graphics card. You can replace graphics cards on better computers much more easily than the CPU. Also, graphics cards range greatly in price from a couple of hundred dollars for a functional CAD card to a couple of thousand for bragging rights.

Memory (RAM)

For almost any purpose in SolidWorks, you need to start out with 2GB of RAM. Do not even try to settle for less than that. For complex parts and assemblies, you may need to go to 3 or 4GB. Windows cannot make use of more than 3GB of RAM. At this point, the memory limit is the only real reason for a SolidWorks user to move forward to 64-bit operating systems and applications. As I mentioned earlier, the Vista OS requires an additional gigabyte of RAM to run its more visual interface and services.

Fortunately, memory is the easiest and least expensive component to upgrade. If you buy too little RAM, then your computer uses the hard drive like RAM. However, the hard drive accesses data much more slowly than RAM, and this causes speed problems.

I have seen computers with 8GB to 16GB of RAM. Memory does not benefit you the same way a processor benefits you. With a processor, getting a faster processor results in shorter rebuild times. With memory, you only need enough to handle your OS, applications, and data. Any more than what is necessary is a waste, but if you have too little, your computer will crash. If you buy a computer with 16GB of RAM, but your SolidWorks parts, assemblies, and drawings only require 4GB, it might be good to have a cushion of, say, 6GB, but you could save that money and put it into a faster CPU.

Secondary components

Secondary components that affect a computer's speed (although not as much as the primary components) are:

- Hard drive
- Network card
- Motherboard

Hard drive

Two main distinctions in hard drives affect performance: drive speed and RAID configuration.

Drive speed

Drive speeds are measured in RPM (revolutions per minute), with the most common speeds being 5400, 7200, 10000, and 15000. The faster the drive spins, the faster it can access and write data.

RAID configuration

Redundant Array of Independent Disks, or RAID, can be configured in several ways for speed or for backup use. RAID0 (striped) writes data alternately between two physically separate disk drives essentially doubles the write speed. The downside of this option is that if either drive goes bad, your data may be inaccessible.

Network card

While it is recommended to work with local files, the network card speed does affect file transfer speeds. Network cards are commonly available in 10-, 100-, or 1000-Megabit-per-second transfer speeds.

Motherboard

Motherboards have many components and transfer-rate specs, such as Front Side Bus, or FSB, and Scalable Link Interface, or SLI, which allows you to use two video cards for increased performance.

Home-built computers

Some people are gifted with the ability to specify components that work well together and build their own computers. This is not an accidental gift. It usually comes from a fair amount of research to understand how the components interact and the compatibility of various setups.

Home-built computers are much more likely than pre-configured computers to have problems that are difficult to diagnose. The combination of IRQ conflicts, incompatible power supplies, latency problems, among others that the average lay user may not be familiar with can cause difficulties. It is safest to go with a brand that tests and warrantees their products.

Configured Systems

Systems configured by the vendor can be certified so that you are positive you are buying a system that works with the software you are buying the system for. HP and Dell both certify systems to work with SolidWorks.

Systems that you buy from a supplier, even when you specify components, are tested and "burned in", meaning they are run for a while to make sure none of the components are prone to early failure. If you do this kind of testing on a home-built computer, you are on the hook to replace it. While you may be able to exchange under warrantee, you will not be able to return components that you have installed and used.

Installation

The various types of installations of SolidWorks are fairly straightforward and easy enough for the average user to accomplish. You need to observe some general conditions before installing.

Before installing

The following points are really important, and (although reading and following instructions is not viewed as necessary by engineers and IT people) you really need to incorporate them.

Before installing SolidWorks, you need to make sure that you have Administrator rights on your computer.

Next, you need to make sure that your Windows installation is up to date. You can save yourself a lot of problems if you do this before installation. Also make sure that your computer has been scanned for viruses and defragmented before you start.

Finally, disable your anti-virus software and any application that may block access to the registry, such as anti-spyware and firewall software. Blocking applications such as these often prevent Solid Works from changing system files or accessing the registry to make needed changes or additions.

NOTE The anti-virus warnings are reportedly no longer necessary. I have installed successfully with anti-virus running many times. If you are having problems with crashes, it may be advisable to reinstall with the anti-virus disabled.

In particular, Norton AntiVirus seems to be the worst culprit when it comes to getting in the way. Do a search for Norton or Virus on the SolidWorks customer portal, and you will see many references where Norton is specifically blamed for all sorts of strange things happening in SolidWorks.

If you happen to make a mistake and install with your anti-virus application running, and you notice strange messages and crashes, disable the anti-virus application and reinstall using the Repair option on the installation. SolidWorks is not supposed to act strangely or crash randomly. If this is happening, there is a problem, because the software does not ship with massive and obvious problems immediately after installation. In my experience, most crashes and strange behaviors result from installation or system maintenance problems, not coding bugs in the software.

Installation Manager

The SolidWorks Installation Manager automatically takes care of several things. First, it checks your serial number and determines the software that you are entitled to. Next, it checks what is installed and displays a screen with the option to select or deselect software or service packs to download from the SolidWorks Web site. Finally, it initiates the installation of the downloaded data. The Installation Manager checks to see if you need any other system files for SolidWorks to work properly. If you do need these files, it will download and install them for you along with the rest of the software.

Installation Manager is installed as a separate application, and you can run it whenever you need to. You can also set it to automatically and periodically check for service pack updates. Installation Manager works on regular disc installations or on administrative image installations, which I are discuss later in this appendix.

Installing from discs

When a new version of SolidWorks is released, you can often choose to install from downloaded files. In the past, you would have to uninstall and reinstall from the DVD when it arrived in order to apply service packs. This is no longer the case. You can now update a downloaded installation with service packs.

Pay attention while installing

It is so easy to simply run the installation automatically and click Next, Next, Next . . . when installing, but you really need to pay attention. Close down your anti-virus application and other programs before installing. You should also clear out temporary file locations and defragment your drives. Read the notices as they come up, particularly the one about the Toolbox location (see Figure A.3). This has to do with Toolbox installation and could have a big impact on how Toolbox works on your system.

FIGURE A.3

A warning message displays, telling you that you are about to overwrite your Toolbox data.

 More information about the potential problems of using Toolbox is available in Chapter 17.

New installation or upgrade?

Definitely do a new installation. Most people want to have access to the old version as well as the new one for at least a period of time. Upgrading overwrites the existing old version. However, the best reason for doing a new installation is to simply perform the clean install, with no legacy software.

Level to install

Even though SolidWorks Office is no longer sold, it is still available as an installation option because many users have this level of the software. The only difference between Office and Professional is the installation of SolidWorks Workgroup PDM Client. Select the level that you purchased, which should be shown on the original box.

Customize

Customizing the components to install allows you to simply turn off certain files. For example, if you do not have a RealView-capable graphics card, it probably does not make sense to take up the extra space on your hard drive, and you can turn this option off. If you have the space, then you may want to install all of the software that you are entitled to. For example, you never know when you may need to use ScanTo3D to surface a point cloud.

Installation folders

This is where you really need to pay attention. By default, SolidWorks installs to your C:\ drive. However, I like to partition my drive so that C:\ is for operating system files and D:\ is for program files and data. When installing SolidWorks, I always append the version to the end of the folder name; for example, instead of just *SolidWorks*, it says *SolidWorks 2009*. This helps me to keep things organized when I have three versions on my computer and I need to add a Macros folder to one of them, or edit a particular symbols file.

Serial number and license server

With the standalone license, you must input a serial number. With the network license (sometimes called SNL for SolidWorks Network License), you must also enter a name for a license server. If you are using a network license, the server application should be installed on the license server prior to installing the clients.

SolidWorks Search

If you perform many searches on your computer for SolidWorks files, SolidWorks Search can save you some time. However, if you do not typically do this, I would not recommend installing SolidWorks Search. My experience has been that it slows down everything else and can even interfere with shutting down your computer.

Performance feedback

If you choose to participate in the Customer Experience Feedback Program, the software periodically sends information back to the SolidWorks Corporation. This includes information on the features used and the frequency of use; the cause of crashes; the system, processor, memory, and OS version; the SolidWorks version and serial number; active add-ins, the video card and driver; and which commands you have used. This information is meant to help SolidWorks evaluate problems such as random crashes, and understand how users use the software. This is likely SolidWorks Corporation's source of information for which features are used the most and which are used the least.

Other software

After the SolidWorks installation, you can install other software, such as eDrawings, SolidWorks Explorer, and DWG Editor. A reboot may also be required, and after the reboot, some of these additional applications may try to install themselves. It is best to let SolidWorks do what it needs to do to install all of the goodies. These should all be taken care of by the Installation Manager, but if you are bypassing the IM, these are not part of the core SolidWorks installation.

Administrative Image

The SolidWorks Administrative Image installation enables you to deploy a SolidWorks installation to multiple computers. It creates the installation in a central location so that computers on the network can install from the central location without the discs. You can also apply standardized settings to each installation. Creating an administrative image automates the task of installation greatly. This is similar to doing a normal installation, and you do it through the SolidWorks Installation Manager in much the same way that you would go about a normal installation. To learn more about the latest Administrative Image installation process, check out the SolidWorks Installation Guide, located on the Customer Portal, on the SolidWorks Web site.

Configuration and Standardization

I cover setting up the options in SolidWorks in detail in Appendix B. You can achieve standardization by using the Administrative Image installation or the Copy Settings Wizard.

Standardizing libraries, document templates, sheet formats, and Styles or Favorites are additional means to make documents created with SolidWorks more uniform throughout your organization. I cover each of these topics in their respective chapters, and they include discussions on how to propagate the data to other users by copying or sharing.

Data Management

Data Management is one of the most hotly debated topics in SolidWorks. However, little question exists that using a Product Data Management (PDM) or Product Lifecycle Management (PLM) system is the best way to go if you can afford it. PDM or PLM systems are beyond the scope of this book, but I will discuss manual file management techniques. Manual file management just means using Windows Explorer and any built-in functions in SolidWorks, such as SolidWorks Explorer.

Managing SolidWorks files is not like managing AutoCAD or Microsoft Office files. The external references in SolidWorks need to be maintained; so you can rename the files, but you have to do it in very specific ways. The most important rule is: *Do not use Windows Explorer to rename your files.* A secondary rule is that if you are creating assemblies of parts or drawings that reference parts or assemblies, *you should not put revision levels in your filenames.*

Of course, the main reason to understand rules like this is so that you know how and when to break them. Both these rules can be broken without harming your data, but only if you really know what you are doing. The beginning or casual user should adhere scrupulously to these rules. The best way to tell if you are a beginning or casual user is as follows: if you do not know *why* the two rules are so important, then the rules apply to you.

Filenames

When you model something round that rolls, it is very tempting to call it Wheel.SLDPRT. It is also tempting to call something that sits on the bottom Base.SLDPRT or something on top Cover.SLDPRT. This turns out to be poor practice. Descriptive names have the tendency to be duplicated the next time you make a similar part with a similar function. This kind of carelessness has caused me many problems. For example, I used to work for resellers, and had a lot of demonstration files on my computer. The demonstration files came from a variety of sources: some I had built, some were from customers, and some were from the SolidWorks Corporation. Once, during a file management presentation, I did a search on my computer for all of the parts named Cover. I found about 150 parts.

One session of SolidWorks cannot have two different files with the same filename open at the same time. You can have two different Base parts open at once, but they have to be in two different sessions of SolidWorks. If they are in different subassemblies that are used in the same top-level assembly, the first one to load will be used in both instances.

Rules of file management

The preceding example is a good argument for the first rule of SolidWorks File Management. The rules are as follows:

1. **Always use unique filenames.** Most people can see the logic of this, but when it comes to the next rule, many people cringe.

2. **Never use descriptive filenames.** Descriptive filenames are what intuitively come to mind when naming a part. The problem is that the same type of function in a similar part tends to create an identical descriptive filename. There is no way to guarantee that a purely descriptive filename will also be unique.

3. **Always use at least a sequential part of the filename.** I cannot tell you how many times I have heard people argue with fervor that they cannot read numbers, and the only way that they can tell this part from that one is to have a descriptive filename. I assure you that there are good reasons for these rules; I do not make them up.

   You will notice that even the files that are on the CD-ROM for this book have a sequential part in their filename, in that they are preceded by the chapter number, and then followed by the descriptive section of the name. This obeys the rules that I have just described.

   The filename is really meant for the computer to be able to keep track of the file; it is not intended primarily for human reference. A description of the part is for people to read, and nothing is harmed if two parts have identical descriptions. Descriptions can be displayed in the assembly FeatureManager; in fact, they can be displayed instead of the filename.

4. **Do not put the revision level in the filename.** This is the most controversial rule of file management. While this is common practice when files do not have external references, SolidWorks documents are very intolerant of this method. Changing the names of files breaks associative relationships between documents. You can do this if you are not building assemblies, or if you are not making drawings. For example, I may use a part called Part1 on Drawing1 and Assembly1. If I revise Part1, and rename it as Part1A using

Windows Explorer, the next time I open the drawing, it will unable to find the part. The same goes for the assembly. There are two ways to fix this simple problem:

■ With both Assembly1 and Drawing1 open, use the Save As command from SolidWorks to save Part1 as Part1A. In this case, the references to the assembly and drawing will be updated.

■ Use SolidWorks Explorer to rename Part1 to Part1A, and make sure that it updates the references.

These techniques make renaming the part possible, but if you have to do it on a larger scale, it quickly becomes impractical. For example, if you revise a bracket that is used in ten assemblies, you are going to spend a lot of time renaming parts.

Beyond filenames, there is the question of how, or indeed whether, files should be grouped into folders. Does it really make sense to break the files into folders simply to group them into smaller groups? The answer to that is ultimately reduced to a network speed issue. If Windows Explorer can refresh the screen in a reasonable amount of time with a thousand files, then there is no reason to break it down into smaller groups. If you use the Thumbnails views, then the refresh may be slower.

When doing PDM implementations, I recommend that you determine folder structure by one of two issues: permissions and searchability. Other than that, why do you really need to break up the files?

Compromise methods

If you find that strictly sequential numbers will not work for you or your company, a few compromise methods may work.

Intelligent numbering systems

Intelligent numbering systems have many drawbacks, but I have seen them work for companies. The intelligence usually breaks down at some point, and the system becomes more of an encumbrance than an improvement over a strictly sequential system.

Typically, intelligent or semi-intelligent numbering systems work by using some sort of a prefix to signify a defined type of document or part. The prefix may also signify a department for larger companies. Drawing numbers and part numbers are not always the same, because a part may require more than one drawing; for example, a casting that gets machined requires two drawings. Some companies will also change the part number of the machined casting. For example, you may have a number XX-YYYYY-ZZ, where XX denotes what type of part the number is documenting, such as electrical, sheet metal, casting, purchased, secondary operation, process flow document, and so on. YYYYY is a sequential number, assigned from a database or custom application. ZZ may be used as a dash number to signify secondary operations, components of an inseparable assembly, or versions of the same basic part number.

Hybrid naming system

Many people absolutely insist on a numbering system that allows them to scan a column of numbers and read some sort of descriptive language that has some significance. These are the people who often lack the imagination to understand that separating the filename (part number) and description can be both useful and beneficial.

If you accept that a descriptive name does not guarantee unique filenames, and at the same time insist that the filename contain descriptive information, then you are forced into a hybrid naming convention. This combines a sequential number and a descriptive name (or worse yet, a semi-intelligent number and descriptive name), and it has some detrimental effects. The first challenge from this method is determining how you structure the descriptive name so that anyone who makes a new descriptive name uses the same structure. Using the same structure is important for sorting (alphabetizing) and for scanning or keyword searching. Syntax structure governing descriptive names is notoriously (even hilariously) complicated.

The second real challenge from this method is that it makes the filename twice as long as it needs to be. As space inside the SolidWorks window is limited, having filenames with 20, 30, or more characters makes for inefficient use of space and time that you will spend expanding and shrinking windows.

Revision control

The issue of revision in the filename is so contentious and so many people have had to confront it, that several methods exist to deal with it:

- **The current revision is left without the revision in the filename.** When you create a new revision, you save the old revision using the Save As Copy command, and the revision is added to the filename. If you send any files out of the company, they are sent as an eDrawing with a revision in the filename. This has the advantage that the assembly will never reference the wrong part file. The downside of this method is the same as any other manual file management technique: the method is only as good as the discipline of the people using it. This is my preferred method of manual file management.

- **Only archive drawings, not models.** This can easily be done with either eDrawings or PDF documents. This works if you make drawings of your parts, and you are making drawings when you start the revision scheme on the models.

- **Configurations.** I have seen people use this method, although I cannot imagine how they made it work without losing a lot of current or past work, besides the fact that drawings do not have configurations. I do not recommend this method.

- **Use a PDM system.** Almost every objection that you can come up with for any of these manual techniques is resolved by a using a PDM system. In the end, that is the only answer that can give you a high level of confidence. The purchase of a simple PDM application is less expensive than a single documentation mistake.

Network files

If you are not using a PDM system and you are working with other SolidWorks users, you are almost certainly working with files across a network. Opening files across the network with SolidWorks is not a recommended practice, for three main reasons:

- **Performance.** Speed when working with files across the network can be incredibly slow. Just test it some time with a network file and a local file. Better yet, do it with a drawing or an assembly that references a lot of parts. Besides the speed of the network itself, other things such as firewall and anti-virus applications can significantly contribute to this problem. If an anti-virus program is scanning your SolidWorks files, you are probably losing 40 to 60 percent of your open and save time just to that.

- **File corruption.** When working across a network, your SolidWorks files are more likely to become corrupted. Search the knowledge base on the SolidWorks Web site for more specific information on this issue. I mention it here to discourage you from working across the network, if possible.

- **Undo.** The network does not have an Undo command for Delete or Move functions. Unless your IT department has provided for this, mistakes on the network can be permanent, requiring a time-consuming backup recovery.

If you have to share files with other users, then how do you do it if working across the network is not recommended? The ultimate solution is to manually imitate what PDM software automatically does. The best way to work on files is to work on them locally. PDM applications know this, and that is how they work. Copy the files locally to work on them. You gain all of the benefits of working locally, but you give up the ability to lock the network files so that other users cannot make changes to the files that you are already changing. This is automatically taken care of by the PDM system, and aside from changing permissions or physically moving files, there may not be a good manual equivalent.

Using a PDM application

Basically, everything under the File Management heading says that you should be using a PDM system to manage your files. It can be either inexpensive and easy to learn or costly and complex. Any PDM application is better than trying to manage SolidWorks files manually. If you own Solid Works Office Professional, then you own Workgroup PDM, which is a perfectly adequate tool for basic file management and revisioning. It is easy to learn, relatively easy to administer, and highly cost-effective. The details of Workgroup and Enterprise PDM are beyond the scope of this book.

Toolbox

I discuss Toolbox in Chapter 17. Usually by the time you start thinking about how to implement Toolbox, it is already too late. The time to think about it is before you install, but most users do not know that there are any potential problems before they have used the software for a while. Toolbox implementation is one of the more important decisions that you need to make. If you are trying to learn about Toolbox installation and setup, read Chapter 17 along with a test installation of SolidWorks and Toolbox.

Custom Properties tab

You can now set up a custom Custom Properties task pane tab to make it easier for users to enter formatted data into parts, assemblies and drawings. You can create different templates for the tab for different types of parts, different customers or any other purpose you might have.

Property Tab Builder

To create these new interfaces, you must use the Property Tab Builder, which you can find through your Start menu, at the path shown in Figure A.4.

FIGURE A.4

Finding the Property Tab Builder

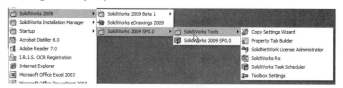

Within the Property Tab Builder, a built tab will look like Figure A.5.

FIGURE A.5

Building a Property Tab

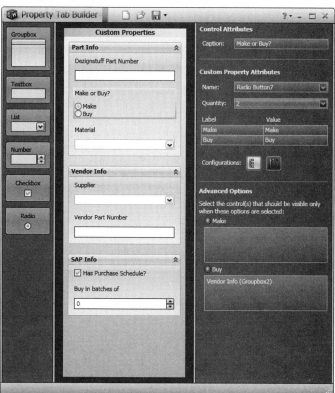

You can build tabs for part, assembly and drawing documents. You can create multiple templates per document type.

To get the tabs to show up in the Task Pane, save the tab as the appropriate template type (part, assembly or drawing) to a path that you have listed in Tools ➪ Options ➪ File Locations ➪ Custom Property Files. The next time you open a part, the tab is available to you on the Property Tab in the Task Pane, as shown in Figure A.6

FIGURE A.6

The resulting Custom Property interface

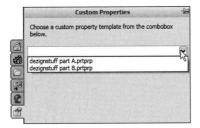

If you have multiple templates for one type of document, the Task Pane requires you to select one from a pull down list, shown in Figure A.6, on the left. This is drag and drop programming. Normally, interfaces like this are done through an API (application programming interface). This is very easy to set up, and makes your entry of custom property data as intuitive as you can make it.

System Maintenance

SolidWorks users need to be more computer savvy than other office workers. Engineers are more likely to exceed the limits of their computer than almost anyone else, and so they need to be able to handle any problems that arise.

I have found that companies that are large enough to have dedicated IT personnel have varied experiences. In some cases, the IT department acts as a support group that helps other people to do their jobs, which, in turn, increases revenue and pays everyone's salaries. In other companies, the world revolves around the IT department, and it is in a position of control rather than support. It has always been my policy when consulting and playing intermediary between IT and engineering to get IT to concede a little control or at least to develop an engineering department liaison who has enough access to the necessary people, places, and things to prevent engineering from losing work time due to IT system issues.

Here are some things that you need to do to maintain your system. Most are recommended anyway for general maintenance, but with the extra resources required by SolidWorks, maintenance is more critical for SolidWorks users.

- If you run anti-virus software, turn it off when installing software. Real-time scanning can also be extremely detrimental to performance, particularly when you are working across a network. Take a sensible approach to using anti-virus software. If running anti-virus software according to rigid company standard practices is costing you 20 to 50 percent of your SolidWorks work time, then you need to look at a different solution.

- Make sure that your video driver is approved on the SolidWorks Web site.

- Clear out the Windows temp folder locations regularly. The free application C-Cleaner can be useful for this.

- Regularly defragment your computer, as well as network locations of SolidWorks files.

- Back up your SolidWorks data, including libraries and customized files in your SolidWorks installation directory. Off-site backups are generally recommended in case of disasters such as fire or flood.

- Periodically make sure that the fan on your computer is functioning properly and is not clogged with dust or other debris.

- Keep the Microsoft updates current. Whether you do it manually or automatically does not matter as much as that you do it.

- Use System Restore and the emergency repair disk. This is basic computer maintenance common sense.

- If at all possible, keep your SolidWorks computer off of the Internet, or at least limit its exposure to the Internet. If you need to have the weather updates running on your taskbar or you just cannot live without a dancing dinosaur cursor, then do all of that on a separate computer that is older, cheaper, and less critical to how you make a living.

- If at all possible, avoid installing semi-professional software on your SolidWorks computer. Every time you install or uninstall software, something is added to, and possibly not removed from, the registry. This accumulates over time. There are ways to clean the registry, but the best way to clean it is to not clutter it up in the first place. This is a great use for your older multi-media computer.

- iTunes is a great application, and I love listening to music while I am working as much as anyone. You can already hear what I am going to say next. I use a retired home computer to play music, access the Internet, and install any questionable software on. This kind of computer can be purchased new for $500, and used for next to nothing. Use a KVM (keyboard, video, mouse) switch to share all of the peripherals (the keyboard, mouse, and monitor) between the two computers.

SolidWorks implementation is not just buying a new box of software and installing it. You need to think through many aspects before you embark on this endeavor. From training to hardware selection to file management to upgrades and system maintenance, you should have a plan in place for how you are going to deal with these requirements. The larger your organization, the more critical good planning is.

Appendix B

Tools, Options

IN THIS APPENDIX

System Options

Document Properties

A program with the complexity of SolidWorks is going to have a lot of settings. You can access most of these settings in the Tools ⇨ Options menu. These include system settings that affect only your local computer and document settings (template-based) that are saved with the file. You will not likely need to know all of the settings unless you are doing CAD administration or consulting work, or writing a SolidWorks Bible, but this reference will familiarize you with the most important settings. All settings shown in the figures are the recommended settings for general use. Recommendations always change with the situation, and so you should only use these recommendations as starting points.

In this appendix, the star icon denotes features that are new in SolidWorks 2009, and the rabbit icon denotes features that affect performance. Be aware that from version to version, the options may change names, change locations or be removed altogether. I have not documented settings that have been moved or removed.

System Options

System Options apply only to your local computer, but they apply to every document that you open. The settings are not saved with the files, so be aware that when changing the System Options, other users on different computers will not necessarily see things the way that you see them.

Settings that are saved with the file and used on other computers are called Document Properties, and are discussed later in this appendix.

General Settings Page

The General System Options are for items that affect all of the software. One of the most used settings on this page is showing the dimension names, but several others are important. Figure B.1 shows the list of options on this page.

FIGURE B.1

The System Options ⇨ General page

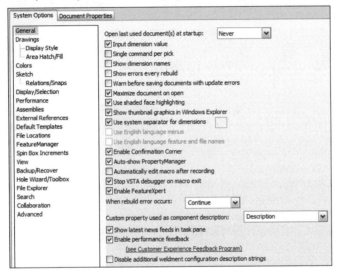

- **Open last used document(s) at startup:** The options are Never or Always. If you select Always, then when you start SolidWorks, it automatically opens the last document that you had open. Default is Never.

- **Input dimension value:** When you place driving dimensions in model sketches, the Modify dialog box appears so that you can change the dimension immediately, as shown in Figure B.2. The one place this does not work is when you set sketch entities to be automatically dimensioned, which is controlled by a setting at Tools ⇨ Options ⇨ Sketch ⇨ Enable On Screen Numeric Input On Entity Creation.

FIGURE B.2

The Modify dialog box

- **Single command per pick:** This option is often overlooked. It allows only one application of a tool for each selection, after which the tool is automatically turned off. For example, if you turn on the Single Command Per Pick option and you click the Line tool, then after you draw one line, the Line tool turns itself off. If you double-click the Line icon from the toolbar, then you can draw multiple lines as usual. For selections from the right-mouse button menu and drop-down menus, the setting is always followed and cannot be overridden. Default is off.

TIP This double-clicking function also works in other Windows applications such as PowerPoint, in various functions such as drawing figures, and in text boxes.

- **Show dimension names:** This option displays the dimension name in parentheses below the actual dimension. It is most useful when you use Design Tables, Link Values, or Equations. See Figure B.3. Deafult is off.

FIGURE B.3

Using the Show Dimension Names option

- **Show errors every rebuild:** Every time the model rebuilds, if any errors exist, then SolidWorks displays error messages, as shown in Figure B.4. This option can also be controlled in the What's Wrong dialog box that appears when errors exist in the active document. Default is off.

FIGURE B.4

A warning message for a sketch error

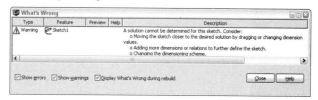

- **Warn before saving documents with update errors:** The effect of this option is particularly noticeable in assemblies, but also in individual parts. When you save a document with an error, SolidWorks asks whether or not you really want to save it, as shown in Figure B.5. Default is on.

The Update Error warning

> **TIP** The Don't ask me again toggle is a nice option if you find these messages annoying. The one caveat to this is that the setting often only pertains to the current session of SolidWorks. After SolidWorks is closed down and restarted, you may see the same prompt again. Messages that are permanently dismissed are listed and may be retrieved at Tools ⇨ Options ⇨ Advanced.

- **Maximize document on open:** This option causes all of the new windows in SolidWorks to be maximized within the SolidWorks window, even if the actual SolidWorks window is not maximized. Default is on.

- **Use shaded face highlighting:** When the model is shaded, any selected face turns entirely to the selection color (green by default). If this option is turned off, then only the edges of the face are highlighted. Default is on.

- **Show thumbnail graphics in Windows Explorer:** This setting turns the small SolidWorks icons in front of the filename shown in the Windows Explorer detail view into a very small preview of the part. This option creates a performance issue because the thumbnails take longer for Windows to process than the standard file type icons. See Figure B.6.

  If you are using the Vista Operating System, you do not have the opportunity to turn this option off, so you will not be able to see the standard icons for parts and assemblies if the part has a preview stored in the current version. Default is on.

FIGURE B.6

Thumbnail graphics in Windows Explorer

TIP If you want to display the preview of the part in Windows Explorer, then it is probably better to use the Views ⇨ Thumbnail setting in Windows Explorer rather than the SolidWorks setting. The SolidWorks setting creates small icons that are barely distinguishable, while the Windows Explorer setting shows icons that are clearly visible, as shown in Figure B.7.

FIGURE B.7

Using the Windows Explorer setting in Windows Explorer

TIP In Windows XP, you can set the size of the Windows Thumbnail icons in the Windows Registry at [HKEY_CURRENT_USER\Software\Microsoft\Windows\CurrentVersion\Explorer] ThumbnailSize = 32. Use a value between 32 and 256. Larger sizes will affect load time. In Windows Vi sta the thumbnail size can be set right from the Views menu in Windows Explorer.

CAUTION Editing the registry can be dangerous to your operating system and potentially to your hardware. Undertake this sort of change with extreme care and only if you understand what you are doing.

- **Use system separator for dimensions:** This setting establishes the character used to separate decimal values from whole number values. In Europe, a comma is most frequently used, while in the United States, a period is used. This setting depends on the Windows setting that is found in the Windows Control Panel. Deafult is on.

  When the setting is on, SolidWorks uses the default Windows setting, and the box to the right where you enter the separator character is disabled. When the setting is off, the box to the right is enabled.

- **Use English language menus:** This setting is active only when SolidWorks has been installed in a language other than English. English is always available, regardless of what language was installed.

- **Use English language feature and filenames:** Again, this setting is active only when a language other than English has been installed. This setting does not change the displayed names of existing documents and features; it only controls the default names assigned to new documents and features.

- **Enable Confirmation Corner:** All SolidWorks functions that use the Confirmation Corner (triangular area of the upper-right corner of the graphics window containing the green check mark and the red X) should also have a green check mark icon in the Property Manager or on the right-mouse button menu. Turning this option off could save some interface space, although it is not recommended. Default is on. See Figure B.8.

The Confirmation Corner

- **Auto-show PropertyManager:** This option automatically shows the PropertyManager for items such as sketch entities and dimensions. If this setting is off, then you need to manually select the PropertyManager tab to access settings for these items. Default is on.

NOTE Starting in SolidWorks 2009 you can detach the PropertyManager from the FeatureManager area and float it in the graphics window, or dock it to a number of places. It can even be put on a second monitor.

- **Automatically edit macro after recording:** This setting saves you from manually opening macros so that you can edit them immediately after recording them. Default is off.

- **Stop VSTA debugger on macro after recording:** VSTA stands for Visual Studio Tools for Applications.

- **Enable FeatureXpert:** This option enables the Mate, Fillet, and Draft Xperts. The Xperts are intended for two purposes, either for novice users or for situations where a large number of entities are involved and you want the system to sort out errors automatically. Default is on.

- **When rebuild error occurs:** The available options are Continue, Stop, or Prompt. Continue ignores the error and rebuilds what is can. Stop causes the rebuild to stop at the first error and allows you to correct the error before moving down the tree. Prompt asks you what to do if there is an error. Default is Prompt.

- **Custom property used as component description:** The available options are any custom property. This setting affects which custom property is used in the Save As and Open dialog boxes. You can use the drop-down menu to replace the word Description and the value that follows it with any custom property name and value, as shown in Figure B.9.

NOTE This does not apply to the Description used in the BOM.

- **Show latest news feeds in Task Pane:** When SolidWorks starts up, you can see RSS feeds (blog entries) in the Task Pane. You can get back to these on the SolidWorks Resources tab of the Task Pane. Default is on.

- **Enable performance feedback:** Performance feedback is data about how you use SolidWorks, how often it crashes, and what was happening when it crashed. This feedback is in the form of an e-mail, and works best with Outlook. Default is set during installation.

FIGURE B.9

The Description custom property is shown in the Save As dialog box.

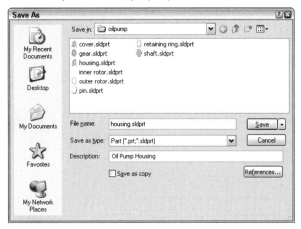

Drawings page

The Drawings page has many general settings that affect the display and default settings used on your computer. If you want to affect specific geometry or data types, then you may want to look on the Document Properties page. Figure B.10 shows the Drawings page of settings.

- **Eliminate duplicate model dimensions on insert:** Prevents duplicate dimensions when Insert, Model Items is used. This setting can be overridden by the Eliminate Duplicates toggle in the Model Items PropertyManager. Default is on.

- **Mark all part/assembly dimensions for import into drawings by default:** Model dimensions use a setting called "Mark for drawing" to determine if a dimension should be inserted when using Insert Model Items. This option marks all new dimensions with the Mark for drawing option by default. Default is on.

- **Automatically scale new drawing views:** This option automatically scales new drawing views, based on the size of the view geometry relative to the size of the sheet. Default is 2X.

- **Show contents while dragging drawing view:** When moving drawing views, it is often useful to see the view geometry. The downside of this option is obviously system performance, particularly on large assembly views. The alternative is to only show the rectangular view border when dragging. Default is on.

FIGURE B.10

The System Options ⇨ Drawings page

- **Display new detail circles as circles:** No, you are probably not the only one to whom this sounds like double-speak. A detail circle refers to any closed loop that is used to create a detail view. This option displays the loop as a circle, regardless of whether it is drawn as a hexagon, rectangle, ellipse, spline, or any other closed profile. Turning is off enables it to be shown as it was drawn. The behavior of this setting is affected by the Document Property drafting standard in use. Default is off.

- **Select hidden entities:** This option allows you to select edges that have been manually or automatically hidden by moving the cursor over them, and using the right-mouse button menu. Default is off.

- **Allow auto-update when opening drawings:** This option rebuilds drawings and associated models when you open the drawing. Default is on.

- **Disable note/dimension inference:** When placing or moving notes and dimensions, inference lines help you align to other notes or dimensions. Default is off.

- **Print out-of-sync water mark:** Detached drawings that have not been updated since the model was last changed can be printed with a watermark to make sure that users know that what was printed was not the latest available version. Default is on.

- **Show reference geometry names in drawings:** Reference geometry, such as planes and axes, may be assigned names that are important, or may just have generic default names such as Plane1. This option allows you to control whether or not these entities are shown on drawings. Default is off.

- **Automatically hide components on view creation:** If an assembly component is not visible when a view is created, then it will be set to hidden. This helps to reduce drawing rebuild times. Default is off

CAUTION This option can leave parts hidden when they should be shown, for example, when using exploded and section views.

- **Display sketch arc centerpoints:** This is the same as the setting under the Sketch heading. Sketched arc centerpoints (not edge centerpoints) can be shown or hidden using this setting. This setting only applies to drawings. Default is off.

- **Display sketch entity points:** This refers to endpoints, ellipse, parabola, and spline control points. When these points are off, it can be difficult to tell where the ends of sketch entities are in a chain of entities. Troubleshooting sketches can also become more difficult when the points are turned off. However, some people find the display of the points to be distracting. This setting only applies to drawings. Default is off.

- **Save tessellated data for drawings with shaded and draft quality views:** You can use tessellated data in View-only mode and in eDrawings. If this data is not saved, then the viewer and eDrawings will show blank views where shaded or draft quality views are called for. The setting has no effect on high-quality drawing views. Tessellated data increases drawing file size significantly. Default is on.

BEST PRACTICE Best practice for this setting is to turn it on. There is a constant trade-off between file size and performance (speed). Reading large files is slow compared to reading small files, but reading data is faster than re-computing the data.

- **Automatically populate View Palette with views:** The View Palette is located in the Task Pane, and you can use it to quickly drag-and-drop drawing views onto the drawing. Default is on. See Figure B.11.

- **Show sheet format dialog on add new sheet:** When starting a new drawing from a template without a format, SolidWorks prompts you to select a sheet format. Default is off.

- **Override quantity column name on Bill Of materials:** The default QTY column in the BOM can be difficult to manage, so SolidWorks offers the option to create your own column for quantity. Default is off.

- **Detail view scaling:** This option controls the default scale at which detail views will be created. This is most commonly set as shown. Default is 2.

- **Custom property used as Revision:** This option controls which custom property is used to drive the Revision Table. If it is blank, a property called Revision is used. Default is blank.

- **Keyboard movement increment:** You can nudge drawing views and annotations by pressing an arrow key on the keyboard. This setting controls the distance. Default is 10mm.

The View palette

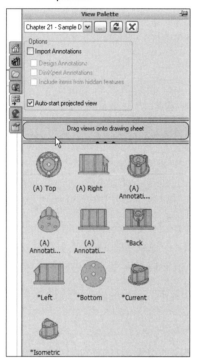

> **TIP**   SolidWorks tends to display many default values as ".39 in" or some multiple vari-
> ant. This is because SolidWorks thinks in metric units, and .39 inches corresponds
> to 10 millimeters.

Display Style

The Display Style page sets the defaults for display style, tangent edge display, and display quality, as shown in Figure B.12. These values apply only to newly created views, not views that already exist.

- **Display style for new views:** This setting applies to newly created views. It does not affect existing views. Default is Hidden Lines Removed.

- **Tangent edges in new views:** Edges between tangent faces display using the selected style. The Removed option does not typically work well with parts without sharp edges, although it would be a good way to display an image of only the silhouette outline of a part. Default is Visible.

FIGURE B.12

The System Options ➪ Drawings ➪ Display Style page

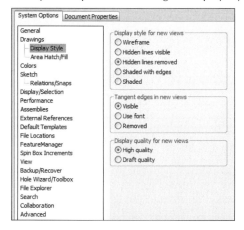

■ **Display quality for new views:** Draft quality views are created when the model is light-weight, and are typically used for large or complex assemblies to improve performance. Default is High Quality.

Area Hatch/Fill

This page allows you to set the defaults for hatching and area fills, as shown in Figure B.13.

FIGURE B.13

The System Options ➪ Drawings ➪ Area Hatch/Fill page

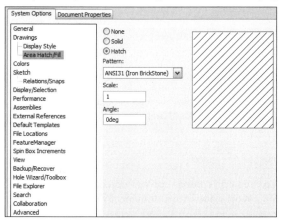

- **Area Hatch/Fill:** This setting determines the default hatch, scale, and angle for newly created hatch fills. Default is ANSI 31, scale:1, angle:0.

Colors

You can establish color schemes for various items on the interface by using the settings shown in Figure B.14.

FIGURE B.14

The System Options ⇨ Colors page

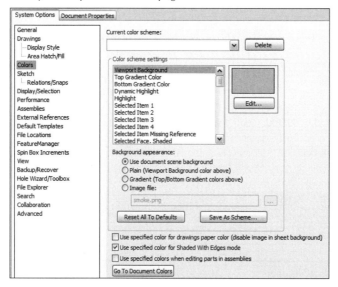

- **Current color scheme:** By default, SolidWorks installs with several color schemes, and you can make your own custom schemes and save those as well. You can use this drop-down menu to select a color scheme.

> **NOTE** Starting with SolidWorks 2008, the default color scheme is Blue on installation. For long time users, this changes the selection highlight color from green to a glowing blue for RealView users. The Green color scheme is closest to what the 2007 and prior settings were.

- **Entity colors:** Figure B.15 shows the list of entity colors that you can change. Some colors stand for multiple entities that may not be listed.

> **CAUTION** If you change the background to the same color as another object, then you may not be able to see the object. SolidWorks does not automatically change text color if it set to the same color as the background.

FIGURE B.15

List of entity colors that can be changed

| Viewport Background |
| Top Gradient Color |
| Bottom Gradient Color |
| Dynamic Highlight |
| Highlight |
| Selected Item 1 |
| Selected Item 2 |
| Selected Item 3 |
| Selected Item 4 |
| Selected Face, Shaded |

| Drawings, Paper Color |
| Drawings, Background |
| Drawings, Visible Model Edges |
| Drawings, Hidden Model Edges |
| Dimensions, Imported (Driving) |
| Dimensions, Non Imported (Driven) |
| Dimensions, Dangling |
| Dimensions, Not Marked for Drawing |
| Dimensions, Controlled by Design Table |
| Text |
| Sketch, Over Defined |

| Sketch, Over Defined |
| Sketch, Fully Defined |
| Sketch, Under Defined |
| Sketch, Invalid Geometry |
| Sketch, Not Solved |
| Sketch, Inactive |
| Grid Lines, Minor |
| Grid Lines, Major |
| Construction Geometry |
| Assembly, Edit Part |
| Assembly, Hidden Lines of Edit Part |

| Assembly, Hidden Lines of Edit Part |
| Assembly, Non-Edit Parts |
| Inactive Entities |
| Inactive Handles |
| Temporary Graphics |
| Temporary Graphics, Shaded |
| Active Selection Listbox |
| Surfaces, Open Edges |
| Edges in Shaded With Edges Mode |
| Feature Tree, Normal Item |
| Feature Tree, Selected Item |

| Temporary Graphics, Shaded |
| Active Selection Listbox |
| Surfaces, Open Edges |
| Edges in Shaded With Edges Mode |
| Feature Tree, Normal Item |
| Feature Tree, Selected Item |
| Annotations, Imported |
| Annotations, Non Imported |
| Assembly Interference Volume |
| Hidden Edge Selection Show Color |

■ **Background appearance:** You can select a document scene, from a plain color, a gradient color, or an image file background. Background images must be in one of the following formats: BMP, GIF, JPG, JPEG, TIF, WMF, and PNG. Not all compression formats are allowed.

 A free image application, such as IrfanView (www.irfanview.com), can be very helpful in changing formats, cropping images, or editing colors or resolutions.

TIP When you save SolidWorks files and preview them using thumbnail images, for example, through the Windows Explorer thumbnails, the Viewport Background color will be used as the image background, regardless of the Background Appearance setting. As a result, if the Background Appearance is set to Gradient using a grey top to a white bottom, and the Viewport Background is set to blue, then the thumbnail displays with a blue background. The default SolidWorks setting is a bright blue background. For this reason, I prefer to use white as a Viewport Background setting, although I normally use a gradient background.

■ **Reset All To Defaults:** If you create a visual mess that you cannot repair, then you can easily return the settings back to their defaults.

■ **Save As Scheme:** If you have multiple users on one Windows login or you just like a change of pace from day to day, then you can save your schemes. I use a scheme with a white background for capturing screen images and a gradient background for working.

■ **Use specified color for drawings paper color (disable image in sheet background):** One year, SolidWorks added an image of a crumpled sheet of paper that became the default image for the drawing sheet area. User outcry lead to the easy override of this by use of this setting. Default is off. (See Figure B.16.)

FIGURE B.16

Drawing paper color and drawing background

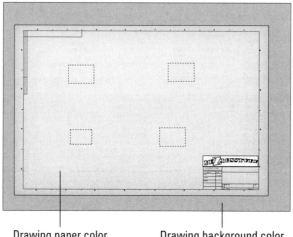

Drawing paper color   Drawing background color

- **Use specified color for Shaded With Edges mode:** The Shaded With Edges display mode can use either a single color for edges on all models (black is the default), or a contrasting shade (the same hue, but either lighter or darker). Default is on.

 **When displaying an assembly in Wireframe mode, it is most useful for each component to be displayed in its own color, rather than having all of the parts use the same color. The wireframe color can be related to the shaded color for a part through a document-specific setting, Document Properties ➪ Colors ➪ Apply Same Color to Wireframe, HLR, and Shaded. This setting is only available for part documents.**

- **Use Specified colors when editing parts in assemblies:** When editing parts in the context of an assembly, you can specify that the colors of parts being edited and parts not being edited to the colors specified in the object color list for Assembly, Edit Part and Assembly, Non-Edit Part. Default is off.

 **You can change the transparency of the parts by selecting System Options ➪ Display/Selection ➪ Assembly transparency for in-context edit.**

Sketch

You can control the default sketch behavior and display by using the settings shown in Figure B.17.

- **Use fully defined sketches:** If this setting is turned on, then you cannot exit a sketch or create a feature from a sketch unless the sketch is fully defined. Default is off.

- **Display arc centerpoints in part/assembly sketches:** Arc centerpoints can be useful to select for relations or dimensions, but they can also clutter your screen if there are too many of them. Default is on.

FIGURE B.17

The System Options ⇨ Sketch page

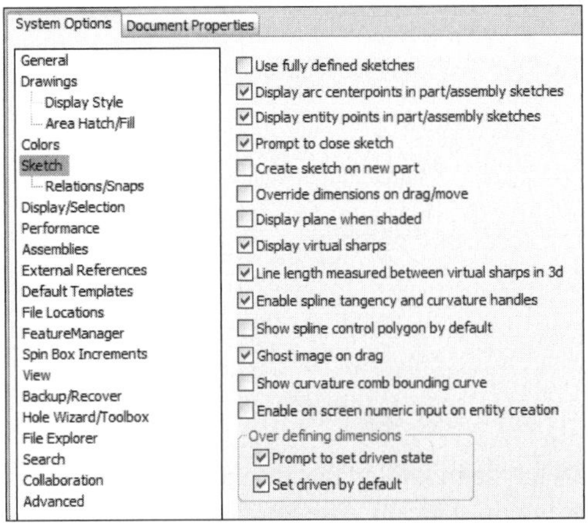

System Options	Document Properties

General
Drawings
   Display Style
   Area Hatch/Fill
Colors
Sketch
   Relations/Snaps
Display/Selection
Performance
Assemblies
External References
Default Templates
File Locations
FeatureManager
Spin Box Increments
View
Backup/Recover
Hole Wizard/Toolbox
File Explorer
Search
Collaboration
Advanced

☐ Use fully defined sketches
☑ Display arc centerpoints in part/assembly sketches
☑ Display entity points in part/assembly sketches
☑ Prompt to close sketch
☐ Create sketch on new part
☐ Override dimensions on drag/move
☐ Display plane when shaded
☑ Display virtual sharps
☑ Line length measured between virtual sharps in 3d
☑ Enable spline tangency and curvature handles
☐ Show spline control polygon by default
☑ Ghost image on drag
☐ Show curvature comb bounding curve
☐ Enable on screen numeric input on entity creation
Over defining dimensions
   ☑ Prompt to set driven state
   ☑ Set driven by default

- **Display entity points in part/assembly sketches:** *Entity points* means endpoints for all sketch entities, as well as control points for splines, ellipses, and parabolas. Endpoints are important to display because without them, you cannot know whether or not the length of the sketch entity has been defined. Figure B.18 shows a line segment with and without this setting. While the display looks cleaner without the big endpoints, the information conveyed by the color of the entity point is important. Default is on.

FIGURE B.18

Showing sketch entity points

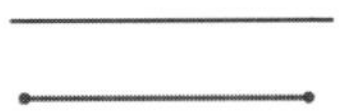

- **Prompt to close sketch:** If an open sketch profile can be closed using model edges, then SolidWorks prompts you to allow it to automatically convert edges to sketch entities as shown in Figure B.19. The software closes the sketch in the direction of the arrow, and allows you to reverse the direction in which to close the sketch. Default is off.
- **Create sketch on new part:** If you create a lot of new parts, then this may be a useful option. Default is off.

FIGURE B.19

A prompt appears, allowing you to automatically close the sketch.

CAUTION The Create Sketch on New Part option has been known to cause problems with third-party add-ins that create new parts automatically. The new sketch is placed on the Front (XY) plane.

- **Override dimensions on Drag/Move:** This is a great option for concept work. It allows you to drag fully defined sketches as if they were underdefined. It is also available through the menus at Tools ➪ Sketch Settings ➪ Override dims on Drag/Move. Default is off.

TIP You can use the Override Dimensions on Drag/Move setting in conjunction with the Instant3D tool. This enables dragging sketches and blind extrusion depths without editing sketches or features.

- **Display plane when shaded:** When you are editing a sketch and the model is displayed in a shaded mode, the sketch plane is translucent. This is often an aid that is used when training new users to help them visualize when they are in Sketch mode and which sketch plane they are using. The setting is often used with grid display, as shown in Figure B.20. Default is off.

FIGURE B.20

A shaded sketch plane with grid display

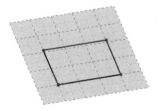

- **Display virtual sharps:** In the versions from SolidWorks 2007 pre-release to SP 2.0 when this appendix was written, this option did nothing. According to tech support, it is supposed to control the display of virtual sharps in the sketch. Default is on.

- **Line length measured between virtual sharps in 3D:** When you apply a dimension to a line in a 3D sketch with fillets on the ends of the line, the dimension goes to the virtual sharps rather than the endpoints of the line. Default is on.

- **Enable Spline Tangency and Curvature handles:** This setting makes the handles visible. Default is on.

- **Show spline control polygon by default:** The spline control polygon is the set of gray straight lines and dots that surround a spline. This control polygon is helpful in getting a smoothly shaped spline. Default is off.

- **Ghost image on drag:** This setting enables a ghosted image of where your sketch was originally placed when dragging. The ghost disappears when the sketch entity is dropped. Figure B.21 shows a sketch ghost. This is useful on all kinds of sketches, particularly complex sketches and splines. Default is on.

FIGURE B.21

A sketch ghost

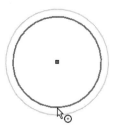

- **Show curvature comb bounding curve:** This option creates a curve that goes across the tops spines of the curvature comb. The bounding curve was at one time the default, but there were found to be problems with its display in areas where curvature changes drastically that could not be fixed easily, so SolidWorks removed it. Again, users cried out for it to be replaced regardless of the imperfection, so now we have it as an option. Default is off.

- **Enable on screen numeric input on entity creation:** This option only works when you are using click-click sketching, and does not work for click-drag. This is the option that basically disables Input Dimension Value when used in conjunction with the Add Dimensions option in the sketch entity PropertyManager and click-drag sketching. This is confusing and unnecessarily hamstrung by the programmers.

- **Prompt to set driven state:** When adding a dimension that overdefines a sketch, SolidWorks prompts you to set the dimension to a driven or reference dimension state (gray). The alternative is to leave it overdefining (red or pink). Default is on.

- **Set driven by default:** This setting automatically makes a dimension driven if it overdefines the sketch. Default is on.

Relations/Snaps

The settings shown in the Relations/Snaps page control sketch snapping behavior. Most of the Sketch Snaps can also be accessed using the Quick Snaps toolbar. Other snapping and automatic relation settings can also be accessed in the menus at Tools ⇨ Sketch Settings or Tools ⇨ Relations. See Figure B.22.

FIGURE B.22

The System Options ⇨ Relations/Snaps page

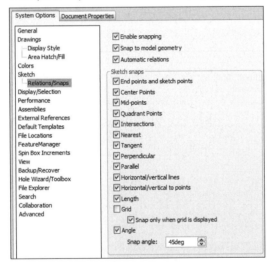

- **Enable snapping:** This option toggles all automatic relations, snapping, and inferencing. Items that are snapped to are controlled by the items selected in the Sketch snaps area. Default is on.

- **Snap to model geometry:** If this setting is off, then sketching does not interact with model geometry, such as edges and vertices, but it does interact with other sketch entities. Default is on.

■ **Automatic relations:** If this setting is turned off, then no automatic relations are created, although the inference symbols and relations still appear. Default is on.

 It is easy to tell which cursor symbols will result in an automatic sketch relation being applied. If the background of the symbol turns yellow, then the relation will be applied. If the background remains white, then no relation will be applied. For example, in Figure B.23, the horizontal relation will be applied, but the vertical relation is only implied.

FIGURE B.23

The horizontal relation is applied, but the vertical relation is only implied.

■ **Sketch snaps:** By default, all of these options are selected except for Grid. You can easily change the snap behavior through the Quick Snaps icon on the Sketch toolbar, as shown in Figure B.24. A sketch tool must be active for this icon to be activated.

FIGURE B.24

Quick Snap filters

```
· Point Snap
⊙ Center Point Snap
/ Midpoint Snap
◇ Quadrant Snap
✕ Intersection Snap
∠ Nearest Snap

⌒ Tangent Snap
H/V Point Snap

▦ Grid Snap
```

Display/Selection

The Display/Selection page allows you to set up your edge and in-context transparency settings, as shown in Figure B.25.

■ **Hidden edges displayed as:** This setting refers to edges that are not visible through the part. Default is Dashed.

■ **Allow selection in wireframe and HLV modes:** This option enables you to select hidden edges in display modes where they can be seen. HLV is short for Hidden Lines Visible. Default is on.

■ **Allow selection in HLR and shaded modes:** This option enables you to select hidden edges in display modes where they *cannot* be seen. On simple models where you want to be able to select edges without rotating the model or changing to Wireframe mode, this option can be useful. However, on complex models and assemblies, you may want to turn this option off. Default is off.

FIGURE B.25

The System Options ⇨ Display/Selection page

In releases prior to SolidWorks 2007, the Fillet feature automatically but temporarily *enabled* the Allow Selection in HLR and Shaded Modes option, even if it was turned off. This often made it extremely difficult to select edges or faces on a model with a lot of edges in the background (you were likely to get a hidden edge that you could not see). In SolidWorks 2007, the Fillet feature has a toggle to enable or disable this setting for that particular feature. See Figure B.26.

■ **Part/Assembly tangent edge display:** Edges created by fillets and other tangent features follow this display setting. There is a similar setting on the Drawings ⇨ Display Style page for new drawing views. Default is As Visible.

FIGURE B.26

The Fillet feature's Select Through Faces option for hidden edge selection

TIP This is a simple evaluation technique that is often employed to see which faces on a model are really tangent. Deviation Analysis is a more detailed method, but simply showing tangent edges in a font shows most of what you need to know at a glance. Edges that are not tangent can also be analyzed separately in more detail.

■ **Edge display in shaded with edges mode:** This setting hides edges that lie behind the solid or displays all edges in Shaded with Edges display mode, as shown in Figure B.27. HLR stands for Hidden Lines Removed. Default is HLR.

FIGURE B.27

Edge display in Shaded with Edges mode, showing the Wireframe option (left) and the HLR option (right)

■ **Assembly transparency for in context edit:** This setting forces either assembly transparency or opacity, or leaves transparency as-is when editing parts or assemblies in-context. In-context colors are controlled on the Colors page. Transparency often has a negative impact on graphics performance. Default is Force Assembly Transparency, 90%.

- **Highlight all edges of features selected in graphics view:** If this option is turned on, then all of the edges of a feature will be highlighted. Selected faces are highlighted according to the Use Shaded Face Highlighting setting on the General page. Default is off.

- **Dynamic highlight from graphics view:** When the cursor is over an entity such as a face, edge, or sketch element, the entire entity is highlighted and the cursor changes to show what type of entity would be selected if you clicked at that instant. Default is on.

- **Show open edges of surfaces in different color:** Open surface edges are edges that are not shared by two faces. The default color for this setting is medium blue by default and is driven by the Surfaces ⇨ Open Edges object type from the Colors page. Default is on.

- **Anti-alias edges/sketches:** Model edges, and most noticeably shaded model edges, can be anti-aliased to display more smoothly. Anti-aliasing means that angled lines, which typically display as jagged stair-steps, appear smoother. Sometimes this results in a slight blurring or even thickening of the edges. Default is on.

- **Display shaded planes:** When planes are displayed, they appear translucent—typically green from one side and red from the other. Colors are controlled in Document Properties ⇨ Plane Display. This setting may slow down some graphics cards. Default is on.

- **Enable selection through transparency:** Transparent parts in an assembly are invisible to the cursor if there is a shaded part under the cursor. If there is nothing under the cursor except for the transparent part, then it can be selected. You can override this setting by holding the Shift key while selecting the part. Default is on.

- **Display reference triad:** This refers to the reference triad in the lower left area of the screen. Default is on. See Figure B.28. The Triad can be used to reorient the view by clicking axes.

FIGURE B.28

The reference triad

- Display scrollbars in graphics view: Scrollbars and viewport splitter bars were removed from SolidWorks 2008, and then hurriedly put back in after users revolted. Now we have this option. If it is grayed out, close all documents and reaccess the setting. Default is off.

- **Display dimensions flat to screen, and Display notes flat to screen:** The alternative is to show the dimensions or notes parallel to the sketch plane in which they were applied. Default is off. See Figure B.29.

FIGURE B.29

Dimensions flat to screen and flat to the sketch plane

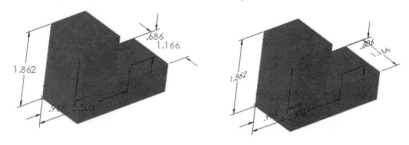

■ **Projection type for four view viewport:** The options are Third Angle or First Angle. This setting does not refer to drawings, only to viewports in the model or assembly window. In some cases SolidWorks will install with a standard you don't expect. Be sure to check this setting after installation, and make sure you understand the difference between first and third angle projections. See Figure B.30.

FIGURE B.30

Third and First Angle projection viewports

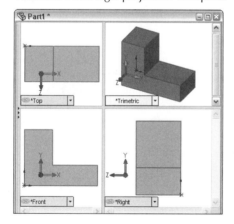
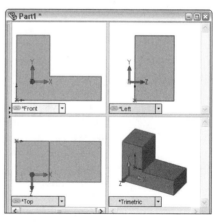

CAUTION This setting is not linked to dimensioning standards or the country in which the software is installed. Third Angle projection is used in the United States and is part of the ANSI standard, while the First Angle projection is used in Europe and is from the ISO standard. Sending a Third Angle drawing to a manufacturer where the standard is First Angle may at least cause some confusion, and could potentially cause incorrect parts to be manufactured.

Performance

All of these settings, shown in Figure B.31, affect an item's rebuild time, file size, or load time.

The System Options ⇨ Performance page

- **Verification on Rebuild (enable advanced body checking):** When SolidWorks rebuilds a model, it checks the geometry for errors. The errors it is checking for are faces within a given solid or surface body intersecting other faces of the same body anywhere except at an edge. To save on checking time (when the Verification on Rebuild option is off), each face of a body is checked only against adjacent faces within that body (faces with which it shares an edge). This is adequate for about 90 percent of models. When the Verification on Rebuild option is turned on, each face is checked against every other face in the body, which takes more time. The advantage of using this option is that you do not unknowingly create bad geometry. The rebuild time penalty varies, depending on the model, but adds between 5 percent and 60 percent to the rebuild time. The number of faces obviously affects the verification time (the number of faces is often greatly affected by the existence of small fillets), as does the number of bodies. If you are given two models with an equal number of faces, but one model is multi-body and the other is a single body, Verification On Rebuild creates less of a rebuild time penalty on the multi-body part, because faces do not have to be checked between bodies. Aside from longer rebuild times, a result of having this option turned on will be failed features when SolidWorks finds face intersection errors. Default is off.

BEST PRACTICE Best practice for the Verification on Rebuild option is to turn it on until it becomes too much of a burden in terms of long rebuild times. You should then only turn it on to check the model after critical points and when the model is complete. To make full use of this tool, turn it on, press Ctrl+Q, and run a Tools ⇨ Check analysis.

- **Ignore self-intersection check for some sheet metal features:** Sheet metal parts sometimes have an edge-on-edge condition that causes a self-intersection warning message to appear. This option suppresses the warning message when appropriate. Default is off.

- **High quality for normal view mode:** When a transparent model is not being rotated, zoomed, or panned, it is displayed in high quality transparency. For reference, low quality transparency causes a coarse "screen door" effect. This option is generally only turned off for low-end graphics cards and large assemblies. Default is on.

- **High quality for dynamic view mode:** When a transparent model is being rotated, zoomed, or panned, it is displayed in high quality transparency. Default is on.

TIP Some graphics cards may exhibit slowdowns if shaded (transparent) planes are in use (System Options ⇨ Display/Selection ⇨ Display Shaded Planes) with the high-quality transparency settings.

- **Curvature generation:** The options are Only on Demand and Always. This should always be left at its default setting, which is Only on Demand. Curvature can be displayed on a per-model or per-face basis. Because curvature display can slow down system performance, you should use this it sparingly, only when it is needed. The Always option generates the curvature display information behind the scenes, and makes it available more quickly, but at the expense of system memory and CPU time.

- **Level of detail:** Depending on the complexity of the assembly, and the performance of your graphics card, the *Less* end of the slider will cause small parts to be simplified into blocks when you rotate the view. Moving the slider toward *More* will prevent the simplification of parts, but may result in more choppy rotation. The label Off in the interface for this setting is conspicuously misplaced. The Help information for it is also misleading. Off refers to the decimation of detail being turned off, so that all of the detail is displayed (Help says that none of the detail is displayed). Default is about 75% of the way to the right. Figure B.32 shows a view with detail settings of More and Less.

- **Automatically load components lightweight:** Assembly components are loaded lightweight. This includes parts and subassemblies, unless the Always Resolve Sub-assemblies option is turned on. For a discussion on lightweight, see Chapter 14. Default is off.

- **Always resolve sub-assemblies:** When a top-level assembly is opened lightweight, subassemblies are resolved, although subassembly components are still lightweight. Default is off.

FIGURE B.32

A high level of detail compared to a low level of detail

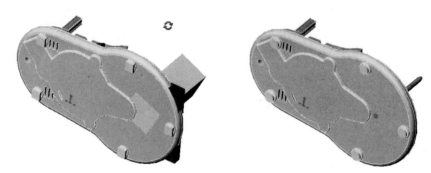

- **Check out-of-date lightweight components:** The options are Don't Check, Indicate, and Always Resolve. Out-of-date lightweight components are parts or assemblies that have changed since the last time they were resolved in the upper-level assembly. When they are in this state, they appear like the last version of the part or subassembly that was resolved. Obviously the Don't Check option is the most vulnerable to this kind of error, and Always Resolve is the most conservative approach.

  The Indicate option will put a special symbol on the components in the tree, indicating that the component is out of date. The symbol is a part icon with a lightweight feature, where the feather is blue with red stripes. Default is Don't Check

- **Resolve lightweight components:** The options are Prompt and Always. Some operations require data that, in turn, requires that lightweight components be resolved. In these cases, this option determines whether the user is prompted to approve the resolve or whether components are just resolved automatically. Default is Prompt.

- **Rebuild assembly on load:** The options are Prompt, Always, and Never. Sometimes when an assembly is opened, rebuild symbols will appear on some of the parts or features because referenced components have changed while the assembly was not open. In these cases, the assembly needs to be rebuilt to correctly represent the design. The best option for this setting will be determined by assembly size or complexity. Default is Prompt.

- **Mate animation speed:** When parts are mated in an assembly, it is a visualization aid to have them move into place so that you can see how the parts fit together. Pushing the slider all the way to the left turns off the animation. Default is Fast.

- **Update mass properties while saving document:** Solid mass properties take some time to compute, and can slow down rebuilding and saving times, particularly for larger assemblies with many parts. However, if you have BOMs or notes on drawings linked to part or assembly mass properties, then you may want to use this option. Default is off.

■ **Use shaded preview:** Most features allow a preview of the geometry. Although this can reduce performance on a marginal system, in most cases, it is a good way to visualize the finished feature, and it is also useful for troubleshooting. Loft and Sweep features allow a mesh preview in addition to the shaded preview. Default is on.

■ **Use Software OpenGL:** OpenGL, where GL stands for Graphics Language, is the standard that SolidWorks uses to drive the display of shaded 3D geometry. If your graphics card is not OpenGL compatible, then SolidWorks emulates the hardware acceleration with software. Software emulation is much slower than hardware acceleration. You can only change this option when there are no documents open. If your graphics card is not OpenGL compatible, then SolidWorks will turn on this option, and you will not be able to turn it off. The Use Software OpenGL option is often used for troubleshooting. If you are having trouble with SolidWorks crashing, then selecting the Use Software OpenGL option will either eliminate or indicate the graphics card or driver as the cause.

■ **No preview during open (faster):** When opening documents, SolidWorks displays a preview that can be panned, rotated, and zoomed. Disallowing this preview speeds up opening the documents. Default is off.

Assemblies

Figure B.33 shows the settings for assemblies, and is mostly comprised of large-assembly settings.

FIGURE B.33

The System Options ⇨ Assemblies page

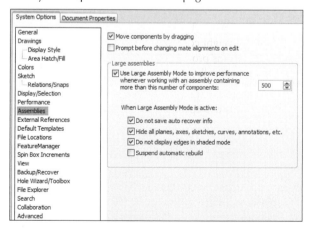

■ **Move components by dragging:** Without this option, you need to use the Move Component tool from the Assembly toolbar to move parts. The default setting (on) allows you to move underdefined components in an assembly by just using the Select cursor. Default is on.

- **Use Large Assembly Mode . . . :** Large Assembly Mode, or LAM, automatically initiates when the number of components in the active assembly exceeds the number that you enter here. You can also initiate LAM manually by selecting Tools ➪ Large Assembly Mode. LAM is saved with the document, and so the next time an assembly is opened, it is opened with the LAM settings. Default is on.

- **Do not save auto recover info:** This option overrides the Auto-recover setting on the Backup/Recover page. Default is on.

- **Hide all planes, axes, sketches, curves, annotations, etc.:** This option is the most frequent cause of confusion with LAM because it turns off all of the items in the View menu. To get the items back, just deselect Hide All Types in the View menu. Default is on.

- **Do not display edges in shaded mode:** This setting disables Shaded With Edges mode, using simple Shaded mode instead. This is because displaying edges reduces graphics performance. Default is on.

- **Suspend automatic rebuild:** In assemblies with many mates, patterns, or in-context features, rebuilding the assembly can take a fair amount of time. Suspending automatic rebuilds can save that time, but it may cause other problems if you are not careful such as out of date references. You can manually rebuild the assembly or override the setting by using the right-mouse button menu at the top of the assembly tree. Default is off.

External References

The External References page, shown in Figure B.34, contains some settings that you should be familiar with, particularly if you deal with assemblies, in-context relations, or other more involved assembly reference functions.

FIGURE B.34

The System Options ➪ External References page

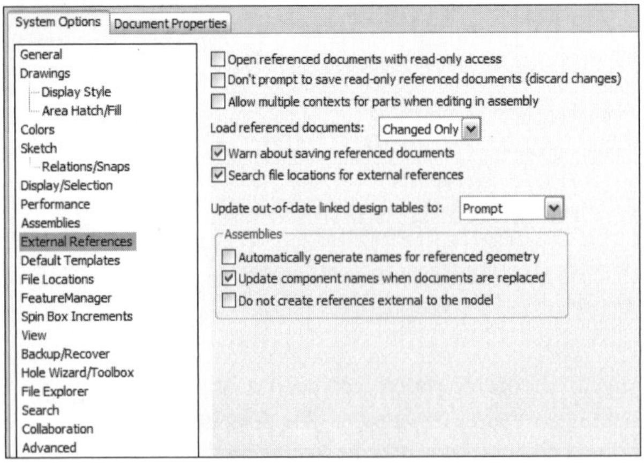

- **Open referenced documents with read-only access:** If you open an assembly, then all of the parts and subassemblies are opened with read-only access. If you open a drawing, then whatever is referenced by the drawing is also opened read-only. This option is typically used when many users are sharing files from folders directly over a network, especially if one user is working mainly on drawings, and another user is working on parts or assemblies. Using the Reload function allows you to change from read-only to read-write access, and vice versa. For more information, see the section of this appendix on Collaboration settings, as well as Appendix A. Default is off.

- **Don't prompt to save read-only referenced documents (discard changes):** If you open a large assembly as read-only, it is possible for changes to occur just in rebuilding the assembly, which, in turn, makes SolidWorks think that the parts have changed. In this case, when you exit the assembly, SolidWorks will prompt you to save the parts, even though they are read-only and cannot be saved. There is no way out of the loop, other than to just answer No to each prompt to save. This option can help keep you to avoid getting into that loop. Default is off.

- **Allow multiple contexts for parts when editing in assembly:** This option allows in-context references from one part to more than one assembly. Although it is usually considered very bad practice to use this option, there are times when you will need to. An example of an appropriate use for this option is if a plate has in-context references in both a subassembly and the top-level assembly. Remember that this is a System Option, and does not follow the document. In-context references are a major source of assembly performance problems. Default is off.

BEST PRACTICE Best practice for in-context references calls for moderation and avoiding circular references. For more information, see Chapter 16.

- **Load referenced documents:** The options are Prompt, All, None, and Changed Only. In this case, referenced documents refer to base parts, mirror parts, and so on. For example, if you open a part called Right Shoe, and Right Shoe was made by mirroring Left Shoe, and this option is set to All, then Left Shoe will automatically be opened as well. Default is Changed Only.

- **Warn about saving referenced documents:** When saving an assembly, this option enables or disables the prompt to save referenced documents. If you turn this option off, then referenced documents are automatically saved without prompting the user. This eliminates a dialog box that is usually unnecessary. Default is on.

- **Search file locations for external references:** The file locations referred to in this case are listed in System Options ⇨ File Locations ⇨ Referenced Documents. The Referenced Documents paths come first in the references search order. For more information on references search order, see Appendix A and the section of this appendix that discusses the System Options ⇨ File Locations page. Default is on.

- **Update out-of-date linked design tables to:** The options are Prompt, Model, and Excel File. This setting refers to linked design tables in two situations: design tables on drawings linked to model tables, and external design tables linked to the model. Default is Prompt.

- **Automatically generate names for referenced geometry:** When you turn this option on, it creates names for geometry used in mates, and thus requires write access to the parts being mated. The default setting is off, which is best unless you plan to replace parts using named entities. Naming is done through the Properties for each entity, such as face, edge, vertex, and so on. Default is off.

- **Update component names when documents are replaced:** This option should remain with the default setting (on) unless you use Component Properties to assign names to parts that are to be used in the assembly tree. Be aware that SolidWorks Routing disables this option. Default is on.

- **Do not create references external to the model:** This option applies to in-context references such as converted edges and feature end conditions. When you select this option, offset or converted sketch entities will be created without relations, and extrude "up to" features and offset surfaces will be created with broken references. This option is also available as a toolbar button on the Assembly toolbar, so it can be controlled on the fly. Default is off.

Default Templates

The default templates settings, shown in Figure B.35, help to determine how templates are used for automatically created files.

FIGURE B.35

The System Options ⇨ Default Templates page

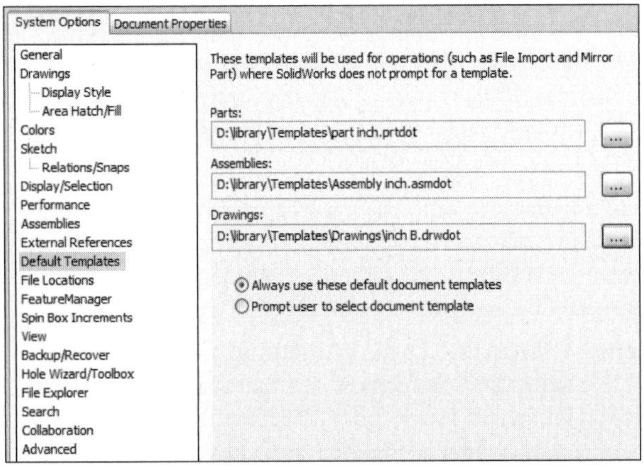

- **Default template paths:** You can specify the path to the template folder in the System Options, File Locations page.

- **Always use these default document templates** and **Prompt user to select document template:** These two options are actually a single toggle (one of them will always be on). When the system has to create a new document, this toggle determines how it will know which template to use. Situations where the system has to create a new document include imported parts, split parts, and mirrored parts. The Always Use these Default Document Templates option means that the above listed templates will be used automatically. If they are not available, then automatically generated default templates will be used (these are the original templates that exist with a new installation of SolidWorks). The Prompt User to Select Document Template option means that in those situations, the user will be prompted to select a template for each part that is generated. In imported assemblies with a lot of parts, it may be wise to opt for the automatic setting unless you need to specify different templates for different parts. Default setting is Always Use These Default Document Templates.

BEST PRACTICE Create a Library folder that includes items such as templates, blocks, library parts, and features, forming tools, and so on. This folder should be separate from your installation directory. This allows you to access the library between computers or multiple SolidWorks installations.

File Locations

Use the File Locations settings shown in Figure B.36 to establish libraries of different types of files, stored from version to version.

FIGURE B.36

The System Options ⇨ File Locations page

- **File Locations:** The list of file types for which SolidWorks can specify a specific library location is fairly extensive.

BEST PRACTICE Best practice for File Locations is to create a library folder somewhere other than the default SolidWorks installation folder. When you upgrade SolidWorks, change computers, change jobs, or share data with coworkers, this data is portable. File types that you can store this way include document and table templates, formats, logos, blocks, Design Library parts, library features, forming tools, special fonts, gauge tables, customized symbol files, material libraries, macros, and basically anything else on the list that you have improved from its default, installed state.

FeatureManager

The FeatureManager settings, shown in Figure B.37, determine how the FeatureManager reacts to various actions.

FIGURE B.37

The System Options ⇨ FeatureManager page

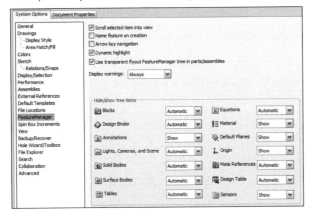

- **Scroll selected item into view:** When something is selected in the graphics window, the FeatureManager scrolls to display the selected feature. Of course, this happens only if the number of features in the FeatureManager is greater than the available window space can accommodate. Default is on.

- **Name feature on creation:** Although you may seldom want to rename *every* new sketch and feature as it is created, when you want to do so, this is the option to select. Immediately upon creation of a feature, you are put into Edit mode on the feature name. When I tried using this option, I found that I ended up with a lot of features named zzzz because I usually wanted to zoom out after creating a new feature. Default is off.

BEST PRACTICE It is certainly best practice to name key features and sketches with names that will be easy to identify later. Renaming features is not just for your own convenience, but is also useful if anyone downstream from you will need to edit your work.

TIP In addition to renaming features, you can use the Go To function in SolidWorks. Available from the right-mouse button menu, this function searches the FeatureManager for text that you enter. An even better functionality is the FeatureManager filter located at the top of the FeatureManager.

- **Arrow key navigation:** Under normal usage, the arrow keys rotate the model by an angle specified in System Options ⇨ View Rotation. However, when the Rollback bar in the FeatureManager has been selected and arrow key navigation is turned on, the up- and down-arrow keys control the Rollback bar. This allows you to more easily step through the features. One caveat with this is that if you are editing a part in-context, the down arrow will roll to the end in one keystroke. Default is off.

TIP On the topic of rollback management, the right-mouse button menu has several rollback options, such as Rollback, Roll to End, and Roll to Previous.

- **Dynamic Highlight:** This is not to be confused with the Dynamic Highlight from Graphics View option, found at System Options ⇨ Display/Selection. This option highlights faces, edges, vertices, sketch entities, and so on as you move the mouse over them in the graphics window. The other setting highlights items in the graphics window as you move the mouse over the features in the FeatureManager. Default is on.

- **Use transparent flyout FeatureManager in parts/assemblies:** There are many situations where the PropertyManager takes over the space where the FeatureManager should be, and you need to select something from the tree. When the flyout is activated, as shown in Figure B.38, it can be expanded by double-clicking the name of the feature at the top of the PropertyManager. Default is on.

FIGURE B.38

The flyout FeatureManager, activated through the PropertyManager

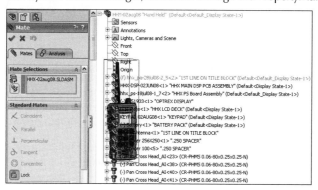

An alternative to displaying the flyout FeatureManager is splitting the FeatureManager, as shown in Figure B.39. An additional alternative to the flyout FeatureManager is to use the detachable

PropertyManager, which is what makes the flyout necessary in the first place. This is my preferred solution. To detach the PropertyManger, just drag the PropertyManager tab out of the FeatureManager area.

Splitting the FeatureManager

- **Display warnings:** The options are Always, Never, and All But Top Level. Never and All But Top Level may be options that you want to use when your boss is looking over your shoulder, but for real-world work, you should select the Always option so that you know when there is a problem. Default is Always.

BEST PRACTICE Best practice for displaying warnings is to set it to Always. Another best practice is to repair errors as soon as you can. Errors may cause more errors down the line, and they affect performance adversely because SolidWorks keeps trying to resolve the error.

- **Hide/show tree items:** These are folders and other items that can be shown at the top of the FeatureManager before the part features. Automatic means that the folder is not shown unless it has some content. Hide and Show are the other options.

NOTE I have noticed that the Automatic setting does not always work. For example, a Surface Body might exist, but the folder is not shown. For this reason, I simply set everything that I want to use to Show, and everything else to Hide. This way there is no guessing if the software is making good decisions or not.

Spin Box Increments

Figure B.40 shows the settings for the spin box increments. Spin boxes enable you to increase values by clicking on the arrows. Some spin boxes, such as the Dimension Modify spin box, also have a button that enables you to select from a list of increment values. The +-? symbol shown in the Modify box in Figure B.41 does this.

FIGURE B.40

The System Options ⇨ Spin Box Increments page

Whenever you click one of the spin arrows on a dimension or number setting, it increments by this value. The exceptions are features such as the tolerance for Fit Splines, where the increment values are determined by the scale of the geometry.

> **NOTE** The Modify dialog box shown in Figure B.41 contains a spin wheel below the number field. By clicking this wheel and dragging right or left, you can increase or decrease the value in the number field. You can also use the scroll wheel on your mouse to drive it. Holding the Ctrl key while dragging or scrolling increases the increment by a factor of ten. Holding the Alt key while dragging or scrolling decreases the increment by a factor of ten.

FIGURE B.41

A Modify dialog box with a spin wheel below the number field

View

The View Rotation options, shown in Figure B.42, are discussed below. View rotation can be done with the mouse, with the keyboard, and automatically by certain functions. The speed of rotation or increment of rotation is controlled by the settings on this page.

FIGURE B.42

The System Options ➪ View page

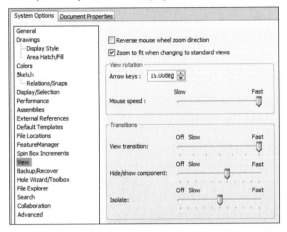

- **Reverse mouse wheel zoom direction:** Some SolidWorks users have a substantial background in some other software. Different software packages function differently when it comes to the Zoom function. The default function in SolidWorks is to zoom out (get smaller) when you roll the top of the scroll wheel away from you, and larger when the scroll wheel comes towards you.

- **Arrow keys:** This option determines how many degrees the view will rotate each time a user presses the arrow button. Default is 15.

- **Mouse speed:** By default, the SolidWorks mouse settings are the same as the Windows mouse settings for cursor speed. Default is Fast.

- **View transition:** When changing between named views or using a Shift-arrow (90-degree rotation) key combination, the view change animates to help prevent the user from becoming disoriented by an immediate and significant change of view. Moving the slider completely to the left (past the Fast setting) disables the view animation. Default is Fast.

- **Hide/show component:** When components in an assembly are shown or hidden, they fade in and fade out. You can use this option to control the speed of the fade. Default is about 60%.

■ **Isolate**: When you isolate parts in an assembly, this hides and shows parts. The hide/
show fades in or out, and this controls the speed. Default setting is 50%.

Backup/Recover

The Backup and Recover options have changed significantly for SolidWorks 2007. Figure B.43
shows the new settings.

The System Options ⇨ Backup/Recover page

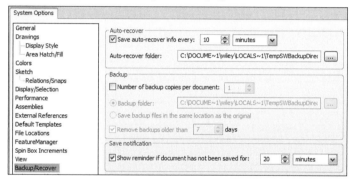

■ **Save auto-recover info every:** This setting allows you to specify that SolidWorks save
auto-recover information according to a number of changes or an amount of time. You
can also specify the folder to be used for the auto-recover data. Auto-recover information
is only used if SolidWorks crashes. The next time you launch SolidWorks after a crash, it
will offer you the chance to open the recovered files. The auto-recovered files are shown
in the Task pane. If SolidWorks exits normally, then the auto-recover information is
deleted at the end of the session. This setting can degrade performance, especially of large
parts or assemblies, because it periodically saves out data while you are working.

■ **Number of backup copies per document:** SolidWorks has separated the Auto-recover settings from the Backup settings so that they are now two clearly different functions. Backup
works differently from auto-recover in that backup occurs only during a save. The previously saved version is renamed (and moved to a new location if the Backup folder is specified). The backup functionality also includes the ability to purge backup files by age.

■ **Save notification:** This is the kind of setting that you will probably use after you have
crashed and lost a lot of work. It is a nice reminder that does not have to get in the way of
work, but not everyone has enough patience to deal with persistent (if polite) nagging.

Hole Wizard/Toolbox

The Hole Wizard and Toolbox operate from the same database of hole/hardware size data. The path shown on the page shown in Figure B.44 establishes where the database for these functions is located on your hard drive or network.

FIGURE B.44

The Hole Wizard/Toolbox settings page

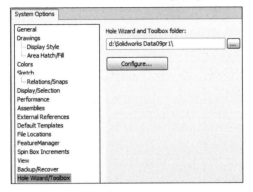

The ConFigure Button shown here displays some of the settings for establishing how Toolbox functions. More details can be found about the Toolbox product in Chapter 17.

File Explorer

The File Explorer is a part of the Task Pane. It can be shown by clicking the tab with the icon of the folder on it. This icon may be replaced if you are using a PDM product. The options for what you can display in the File Explorer are shown in Figure B.45. The File Explorer can be used as a substitute for Windows Explorer right within SolidWorks, as well as showing data with special significance to SolidWorks such as samples that install by default with SolidWorks, files already open in SolidWorks, and recently opened SolidWorks documents.

■ **Show in File Explorer view:** File Explorer is the Windows Explorer–like part of the Task Pane, as shown in Figure B.46. Notice that it has a folder for documents that are currently open in SolidWorks, as well as a recent documents list. The panel will disappear after you use it once, although you can click the push-pin icon to keep it displayed. This is a very useful panel.

FIGURE B.45

The System Options ⇨ File Explorer page

FIGURE B.46

The File Explorer panel

 The Task pane can be detached from its default location on the right side of the screen and either allowed to float or dock on the left side.

Search

The Search options are shown in Figure B.47. Windows Desktop Search is integrated into the new SolidWorks Search function. In order for this function to work properly, Windows Desktop Search must be installed (it is located on the SolidWorks CD-ROM), and then your drive or drives must be indexed, which will take some time.

FIGURE B.47

The System Options ⇨ Search page

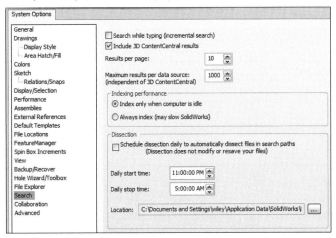

- **Search while typing:** With this option enabled, the search takes place immediately as you type the string to be searched instead of waiting for you to press Enter. This enables you to see results on partial strings as well as the complete search name. The SolidWorks Search feature is shown in Figure B.48. Default is off.

- **Include 3D ContentCentral results:** This option enables the local search to also search 3D ContentCentral website for parts as well. Default is on.

- **Results per page:** The search returns results in the Search panel of the Task pane, with easy-to-see previews, filenames, and path information, as shown in Figure B.49. You can also search on custom property information, as well as keywords. Default is 10.

The SolidWorks Search function

SolidWorks Search results

- **Maximum results per data source:** This setting allows you to specify limits, so that you are not overwhelmed with all of the available data. Default is 1000.

Indexing Performance

- **Index only when computer is idle:** This setting avoids slowing your computer down when it is in use. The default is on.
- **Always Index:** I can't imagine a situation in which I would want this setting to be on. It is off by default.

Dissection

Dissection is a process by which SolidWorks searches through the parts in your hard drive, and makes the features and sketches available to you as an automatically created library. To be honest, I have yet to see anyone actually use this. The vast majority of sketches and features I create will never be of use to me again. If I do find one that I will need again, I manually make a library feature of it.

The main thing you need to know about Dissection is how to turn it off. Just make sure the box in front of this Tools Options option is cleared (see Figure B.50).

In early versions of SolidWorks 2008, the setting was turned on by default, and people noticed that their computers started grinding away and flashing SolidWorks screens at 11 pm. It was very alarming even after you knew what it was and how to control it. In SolidWorks 2009, the setting is turned off by default.

FIGURE B.50

The Windows Desktop Search Indexing Status dialog box

Collaboration

You should consider using the Collaboration settings when setting up a PDM application or a manual document management system between multiple users. The Collaboration settings are shown in Figure B.51.

FIGURE B.51

The System Options ⇨ Collaboration page

- **Enable multi-user environment**: This option enables the rest of the collaboration options.

- **Add shortcut menu items for multi-user environment**: When you select this option, the items Make Read-Only and Get Write Access become available on the right-mouse button (shortcut) menu and the File menu.

> **TIP** There is no indication on the FeatureManager whether individual parts in an assembly are read-only or read-write. The only indication appears at the top of the screen, after the filename, where it is indicated in brackets, for example, as [Read-Only]. Another way to check is to look at the File ⇨ Find References lists; a read-only indicator appears after the filename.

- **Check if files opened read-only have been modified by other users**: This option will check open read-only documents, at the indicated interval, for changes.

Advanced

The Advanced page of Tools ➪ Options contains all of the messages that you have dismissed and asked SolidWorks not to remind you about again. These are the settings remembered between sessions. If you ever need to get one of these messages back, you can return to this page and click messages to show. Figure B.52 shows an Advanced page populated with several dismissed messages.

FIGURE B.52

The Tools ➪ Options ➪ Advanced page

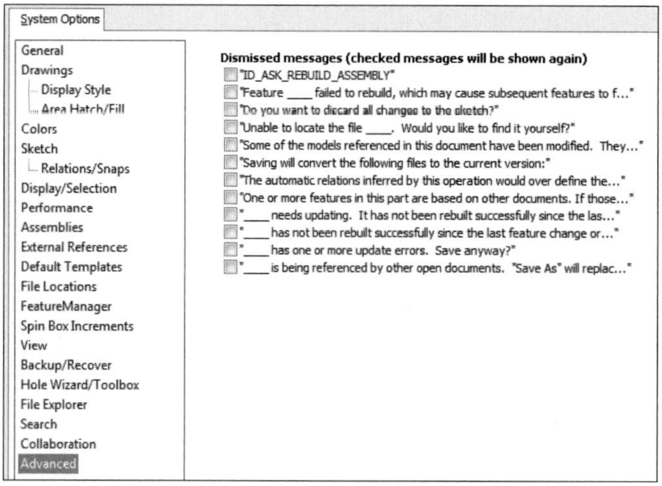

Document Properties

In this case, the term "Document Properties" refers to the settings that are specific to each individual document. This does not have anything to do with File Properties or Custom Properties. Document Properties settings are stored in templates and reused when you use the template to create a new document.

I often hear the question, "Can I change the template used by a document?" The answer is always "No." However, you can change the settings for individual documents to match the template you would have used if you could. Some tools exist that can help you take a list of settings and write them to a group of documents. These tools are available on the Internet for download. One that I am familiar with is an Excel spreadsheet with some VBA programming that handles this function.

If you have not had a look at the Document Properties pages of Tools ➪ Options in the last couple of releases, you really should refamiliarize yourself with all of the new options. On top of the new options, many existing options have been reorganized into a new layout in Document Properties.

The following list details each of the Document Properties settings and gives some insight about when and why you should use each setting.

Drafting Standard

In any company I have ever worked with, I have never seen anyone actually follow a standardized drafting standard to the letter. Companies always tend to takes bits and pieces of different standards and personal preference and put them together into a custom standard that makes sense for their own use. SolidWorks has finally recognized this and now allows you to create your own custom standard or select from one of the standardized standards.

The Drafting Standard page enables you to create your own standard, or load other custom standards from a file, as shown in Figure B.53.

FIGURE B.53

The Drafting Standard Page

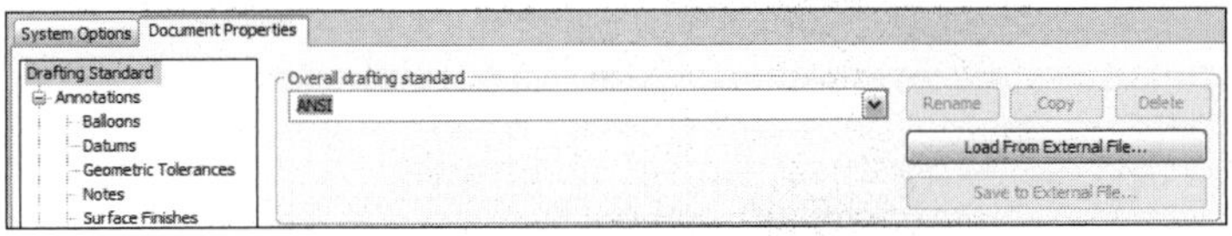

I think the move of reorganizing the Document Properties and adding prominence to standards capability, including custom standards is very helpful. There are more settings, they are more easily accessed, and of course the custom standard enables users to take better advantage of the software through improved flexibility.

Annotations

The Annotations page enables you to set options that are common to all annotation types. Figure B.54 shows the Annotations page of the Document Properties. Many of these options are reused for other items under the Drafting Standard heading.

- **Text**: This enables you to set the font and size for all annotations text. Notice that dimensions text settings are separate from the annotations text settings.

- **Attachments**: This enables you to set the type of arrow head to be used when an annotation is attached to various types of entities.

- **Bent Leaders**: Enables you to tell the software that all new annotations will or will not employ bent leaders by default, and what length those leaders will be.

- **Zeroes settings**: The "Standard" option means that the use of leading or trailing zeroes is to be determined by the drafting standard employed. The "Smart" option means that for metric dimensions, trailing zeroes are always removed for whole values (5.00 becomes 5), and shown for non-zero decimals (5.50 remains 5.50).

The annotation types listed under the Annotations page reuse most of the same options, represented below in Figure B.55 using the Balloons page.

The Annotations page of the Document Properties window

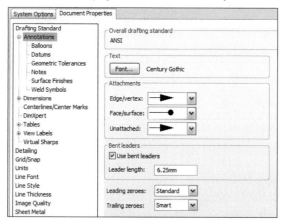

The Balloon options are representative of other annotation type options.

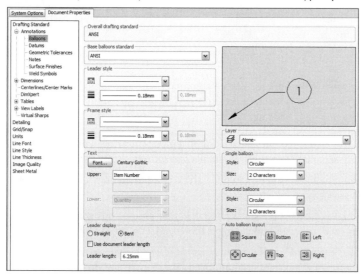

- **Leader Style:** Establishes the line type and line thickness used for annotation leaders.

- **Frame Style:** Establishes the line type and line thickness used for balloon border.

- **Text:** Allows you to override the overall annotations font for that particular type of annotation. With balloons, upper and lower refer to values in a split balloon.

- **Leader Display:** Allows you to override the overall annotations settings for bent or straight leaders and bent leader length.

- **Layer:** New annotations can be automatically placed onto layers as they are created.

- **Single/Stacked balloons:** Establish the default type of balloon used for either single or stacked balloons.

- **Auto balloon layout:** Establishes the default layout type when you invoke automatic ballooning.

Dimensions

Many of the options for dimensions are repeated from the other types above, so I will not duplicate definitions for them here. The options for dimensions are either self-explanatory or explained visually on the page, as Figure B.56 shows.

FIGURE B.56

Dimensions options

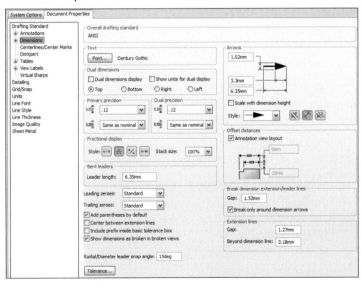

You can control options for the individual dimension type defaults for angle, arc length, chamfer, diameter, hole callout, linear, ordinate, and radius dimensions as well.

Centerlines/Center Marks

The options for centerlines and center marks are shown in Figure B.57.

FIGURE B.57

Options for centerlines and center marks

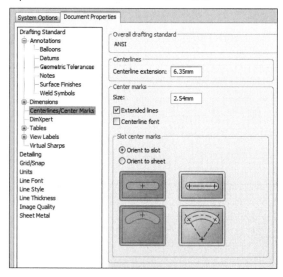

- **Centerline extension**: Refers to any lines extended beyond the "+" centermark. Extension distance refers to the distance past the arc or circular edge.
- **Center marks**: Size refers to the size of the "+".
- **Extended lines**: Refers to lines extended beyond the "+" centermark.
- **Centerline font**: Applies the centerline font to extended lines.
- **Orient to Slot/Sheet**: Means that the "+" will be oriented such that it is square with the sheet or with the slot. If the slot is at an angle, and you choose to orient the center mark to the slot, the "+" will also be at an angle.

DimXpert

The DimXpert options are different for part and drawing documents. They are far more extensive for part documents, so I show the part options in Figure B.58 and Figure B.59. DimXpert options help you set up how things like instance counts or slot callouts are displayed, in addition to helping with options to make tolerancing faster and easier.

FIGURE B.58

DimXpert options for part documents

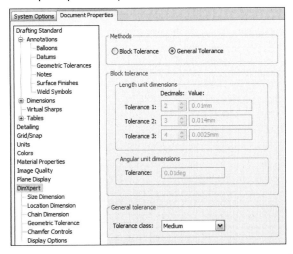

FIGURE B.59

DimXpert Display options

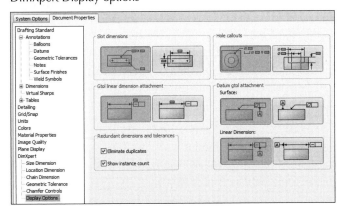

Tables

The options that you control through these pages are the defaults for layout and appearance for BOMs, General tables, Hole tables and Revision tables. Here Figure B.60 shows the Bill Of Materials options as a representation of the options available in the other table types.

FIGURE B.60

Bill of Materials options

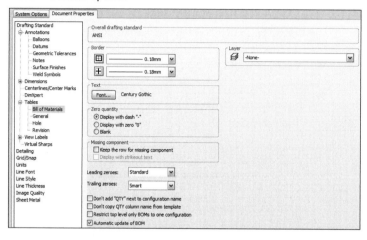

View Labels

Auxiliary, Detail and Section views use arrows and labels to identify and show the alignment and cuts used in the views. The options under View Labels page control the various elements involved, which should be self explanatory. Figure B.61 shows the Detail view label options, which are representative of the other types of views.

FIGURE B.61

Detail View Label options

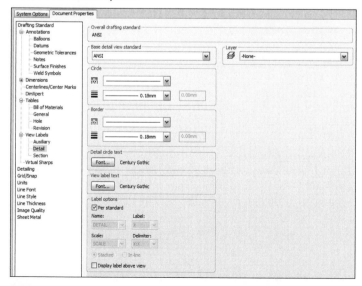

Virtual Sharps

Virtual Sharp display on a drawing (and in sketches) is controlled on this page. A virtual sharp is the corner where two edges would intersect if they were not interrupted by a fillet, chamfer or other item breaking the edge. The options for Virtual Sharp display are shown in Figure B.62.

Virtual Sharp Display Options

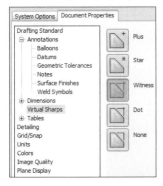

Detailing

Many of the Detailing options are also available by right-mouse button on the Annotations folder in the FeatureManager and select Details. The page also displays differently depending on if you are editing the properties of a part, assembly or drawing. Figure B.63 shows the available options for a drawing document.

Annotations Display Options

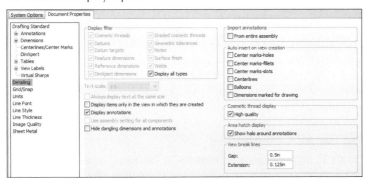

Display Filter

Select the entity types to be displayed in this particular document or template. Display All Types shows everything.

Of special note here is the Shaded Cosmetic Threads. The difference between normal Cosmetic Threads and Shaded Cosmetic Threads is shown in Figure B.64.

FIGURE B.64
_____

Shaded Cosmetic Thread

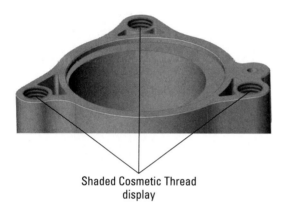

Shaded Cosmetic Thread
display

Text Scale

The Text Scale option is only available for parts and assemblies, and only when Always Display Text At The Same Size is OFF.

Always Display Text At The Same Size

This option causes annotations and dimensions to appear the same size on the screen regardless of zoom state. It is not active in drawings because drawings always need to show text at 1:1 size.

Display Items Only In The View In Which They Are Created

This setting is sometimes frustrating, hiding annotations unless the model is in exactly the view in which the annotation was created. It becomes very easy to lose annotations. On the other hand, if you are disciplined in how you create annotations (consider using Annotation Views), this can help reduce clutter in drawing and model views.

Use Assembly's Setting For All Components

This option makes it easier to see all the component annotations in the assembly using a single set of settings, regardless of differences between settings in individual component files. This is only available in assemblies.

Hide Dangling Dimensions And Annotations

SolidWorks has become increasingly "error-phobic" in recent releases, offering more and more options to make errors invisible. Best practice is definitely on the side of fixing problems as they come up, rather than masking them over.

- **Import annotations from entire assembly:** Places dimensions from all the parts in an assembly on the assembly drawing when views are created. Default is off.

- **Auto Insert on View Creation**: Determines which entity types you want to be automatically inserted from the model into drawings when the view is created. New for 2007 is the differentiation between center marks for holes and fillets. Defaults for all of these are off.

  - Center Marks – Holes
  - Center Marks – Fillets
  - Center Marks - Slots
  - Centerlines
  - Balloons
  - Dimensions Marked for Drawing

- **Cosmetic Thread Display, High Quality**: Cosmetic threads on the backside of a part will be hidden if this option is ON (see Figure B.65). For speed, turn this option OFF. Figure B.66 demonstrates that this setting only makes a difference for shaded model views on the drawing. For any wireframe mode, the hidden cosmetic thread is not shown unless the hidden lines of the view are visible.

- Area Hatch Display, Show Halo Around Annotations: A halo is simply a gap in the hatch pattern, as shown in Figure B.65.

- **View break lines:** When you create a broken view, the break lines by default have a .5 inch gap between them, and extend past the view border by .125 inch.

FIGURE B.65

Cosmetic Threads, High Quality and Draft Quality

Draft and high quality   Draft quality   High quality

FIGURE B.66

Show Halo Around Annotations turned ON and OFF

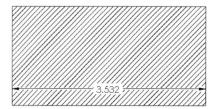 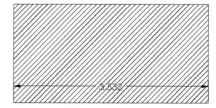

Grid/Snap

One of the first questions new users tend to ask is how to turn off the grid in sketches. This is a bit ironic, since the grid is most useful for new users mainly to help them keep track of when they are in or out of sketch mode. The Grid/Snap options are shown in Figure B.67.

FIGURE B.67

The Grid/Snap Options Page

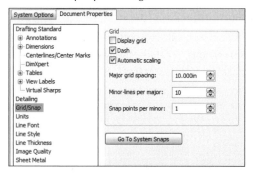

- **Display Grid**: This option turns on/off the display of the grid in the sketch.
- **Dash**: Minor grid lines, specified below, are dashed. If this option is OFF, the minor grid lines are solid.
- **Automatic Scaling**: As you zoom in and out, the minor grid goes from 10 divisions to 5 to 2, depending on your settings.

Units

The Units options page enables you to select either a predefined unit system or create custom settings including primary and dual length units, angular units as well as special units for mass properties / section properties. Units of force are included for the strength properties associated with COSMOSWorks Xpress. The Units options page is shown in Figure B.68.

The Units Options Page

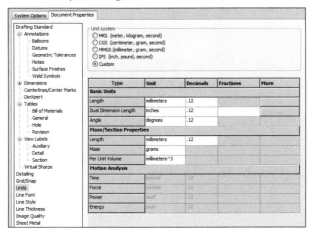

After the "how do I turn off the grid" question, the next most popular setting question is "how do I make SolidWorks remember that I want to use inches instead of mm?". Of course the answer is templates. Set the units the way you want them on a blank document (or delete all the features from an existing document) and save the file as a template. This applies to parts, assemblies and drawings.

Fractions

SolidWorks can use fractional dimensions, and convert decimals to fractions. To set up fractions, set the Denominator box to the smallest division that you will want to use, and check the Round To Nearest Fraction box. Be aware that when you do this, some values will be approximated.

The only units that will accept fractional values are all of the English units except Feet. Interestingly, you can use fractional mils (.001, thousandths of an inch) and microinches (.000001, millionths of an inch). Fractions are most appropriate for inches and feet and inches.

Line Font

Many types of edges, identified in Figure B.69, can have special line fonts assigned to them. You can even create custom line fonts, although the custom line styles are limited to being used in drawings, not in parts or assemblies. New line styles are created in the next section on Line Styles.

Line Font Options Page

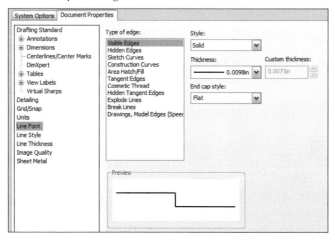

The one setting that is not self-explanatory on this page is the End Cap Style. This is new to SolidWorks 2007. In the past, thicker line types would have poorly jointed corners, as shown in Figure B.70 in the image to the left. This is using the Flat end cap style. The square end cap is shown to the right. If you use thick lines and see this happening, now you have a way to fix it.

Using End Cap Style To Make Thicker Lines Look Better

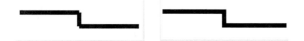

Line Style

The Line Style option page is where you can modify existing styles and even create new line styles. The instructions are right there on the page, it is a simple code to create special line styles. This is shown in Figure B.71.

Line Thickness

The thing to remember with line thickness is that the visual thickness has no relation to the actual thickness dimension that you assign to the line. You could assign the Thin line thickness to a value of 2 mm, and it would not change the way the Thin line displays. The options for this are shown in Figure B.72.

FIGURE B.71

The Line Style Options Page

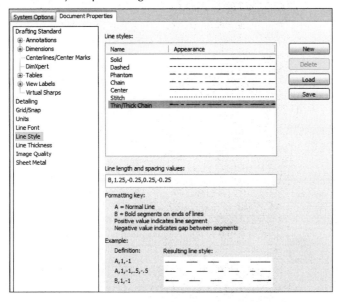

FIGURE B.72

Line Thickness options

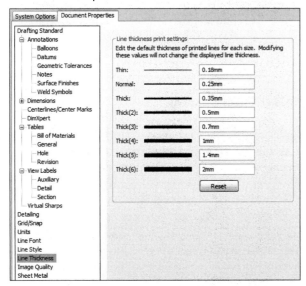

Colors

The Document Properties Colors options page enables you to specify colors for certain feature types in part and assembly documents. System Options Colors options specify colors for portions of the interface rather than part geometry. The Advanced button enables you to specify transparency and other effects.

Curvature

The curvature window is shown to the right in Figure B.73. This enables you to specify the color spread for various curvature values. Remember that curvature is the inverse of radius (c=1/r), so the smaller the radius the bigger the curvature.

FIGURE B.73

The Document Properties Colors Options Page

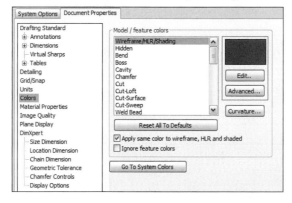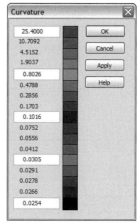

Apply Same Color To Wireframe, HLR and Shaded

This setting is only valid in part documents. This is probably one of the least appreciated options in SolidWorks. Many parts from SolidWorks Corporation do not use this setting, so when you open an assembly where the parts do not have this set, and turn the assembly to wireframe, all of the edges are black. This will make you feel like you are back 15 years ago modeling wireframes in AutoCAD.

Do yourself a favor and save your part templates to use this setting.

BEST PRACTICE Use the Apply Same Color To Wireframe, HLR and Shaded option to be able to differentiate parts in an assembly shown in wireframe by color. The alternative is a black-on-black wireframe display, which is guaranteed to make you grumpy quickly.

Image Quality

Image quality can have a definite affect on the performance of parts and assemblies. This setting is highly dependent on a couple of things, primarily your graphics card, but also including part complexity and number of parts in an assembly. The Image Quality options page is shown in Figure B.74.

FIGURE B.74

The Image Quality Options Page

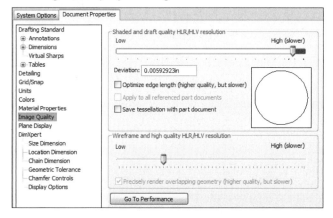

BEST PRACTICE The best practice recommendation for image quality is to set it as low as you can stand it. This may be at different levels for different parts.

The way SolidWorks (and indeed most 3D graphics applications) displays curved 3D geometry is to create a set of smaller flat triangular facets. This is called tessellation. If these triangles get too large, curved surfaces are not recognizable, they might look more like hexagons than circles, but if the triangular facets get too small, your graphics card may not be able to process them quickly enough. So image quality settings are definitely a compromise. The slider at the top of the window applies to shaded models.

Deviation

The Deviation setting measures how far from the real shape the displayed shape is. By making a curved edge into a series of straight lines, the number shown represents the maximum distance from the line to the curve. As the quality gets higher, the deviation gets lower.

Optimize Edge Length

SolidWorks is not explicit about this, but it is assumed that what is being "optimized" is the quality of the display, not the speed of the system.

Apply To All Referenced Part Documents

This setting is valid for assembly documents only. In an assembly, individual part display quality settings are used unless this option is ON. However, if you have your part quality settings high for good visualization, and the assembly setting low for good speed, you will need to change the part settings back to high after you have them open in the assembly. This becomes a bit of a frustration unless you can find a good middle ground or a macro that changes the settings for you quickly and easily.

Save Tessellation With Part Document.

This setting is valid for part documents only. This option toggles the tessellated display data being saved in the part file. This can have an impact on save time and file size. Do not get over excited about turning this option OFF; however, you need to remember that it is faster to read existing data than it is to recalculate it.

Wireframe And High Quality HLR/HLV Resolution

This slider works for wireframe display and drawings. Again, set it as low as you can stand it if you are having performance problems.

Plane Display

Planes in SolidWorks can be displayed either with just a rectangular outline or with a transparent shaded face. Each "side" of the plane can be viewed with different colors. Although immediately this might not seem useful, I find it very useful when working in detail on a larger part. It helps me keep my bearings. The slider shown in Figure B.75 enables you to change the transparency of the planes as well.

FIGURE B.75

The Plane Display Options Page

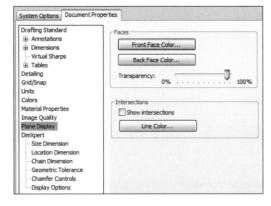

Plane intersections can also be shown by a dotted line of a specified color, but since you cannot select them or actually use them for anything other than visualization, I tend to turn them off.

Sheet Metal

The extent of the sheet metal drawings options is to enable you to control flat pattern colors and bend notes on drawings, as shown here in Figure B.76.

FIGURE B.76

The Sheet Metal option page

Appendix C

What's on the CD-ROM

The only file you see on this book's companion CD-ROM is a single zip file. Extract the contents of the file to your hard drive in a location that is easy to access.

The CD contains example and tutorial parts, assemblies, and drawings, as well as templates, macros, and tables as appropriate for each chapter. The files are organized within folders for each chapter and are named for the chapter and the function they demonstrate. Some of the files are starting points for tutorials, and some are finished models meant to be examined.

If you make changes to files, I recommend that you perform a Save As command to keep the original file intact. You also can retrieve originals from the CD again if needed.

> **CAUTION** I do not recommend that you open files directly from the CD or from the zip file, because SolidWorks will react with messages about read-only files.

System Requirements

Make sure that your computer meets the minimum system requirements listed in this section. If your computer doesn't match up to these requirements, you may have a problem using the contents of the CD.

For Windows XP Professional:

- Intel and AMD processors, single dual or quad cores.
- 1GB RAM minimum (2GB recommended).

IN THIS APPENDIX

Using the CD

System requirements

Troubleshooting

- Virtual memory twice the amount of RAM (recommended).
- A certified OpenGL workstation graphics card and driver. (Check the SolidWorks website for details, www.solidworks.com.)
- A mouse or other pointing device.
- Microsoft Internet Explorer 6 minimum (IE 7 recommended).
- A CD drive minimum (DVD drive recommended)

For Vista:

- 1 GB RAM minimum (2 GB recommended)
- Other minimum requirements are the same as for Windows XP Professional.

For more details about the system requirements for SolidWorks 2009 and a list of certified graphics cards and drivers, visit solidworks.com.

Some systems that run Windows XP Professional may not be compatible with Vista. For the latest information on system compatibility with Vista, visit microsoft.com.

Realistically, you will never be satisfied with minimum requirements. If you are using PhotoWorks, PhotoView 360 or any simulation (FEA) software, multiple processors or multiple cores are advantageous. Multi-body modeling makes use of multiple cores but also takes advantage of higher processor clock speeds. Maximum clock speeds are usually higher for lower number of cores, so higher speeds take precedence over number of cores for general solid modeling. You may get better performance per dollar with dual core processors than with quad core processors for functionality other than rendering and FEA.

You can only take advantage of more RAM up to the limit needed by your data sets. You can check your Windows Task Manager to see how much memory your largest or most complex models consume. For example, if your largest models use 3 GB of RAM, you should have at least 4 GB of RAM, but will probably not see a benefit from 16 GB. You should use 64 bit operating systems if you intend to use more than 3 GB of RAM.

Troubleshooting

If you have difficulty installing or using any of the material on the companion CD, try the following solutions:

- **Turn off any anti-virus software that you may have running.** Installers sometimes mimic virus activity and can make your computer incorrectly believe that it is being infected by a virus. (Be sure to turn the anti-virus software back on later.)
- **Close all running programs.** The more programs you're running, the less memory is available to other programs. Installers also typically update files and programs; if you keep other programs running, installation may not work properly.

- Contact the author. For problems with the content of the CD, visit the author's website (`www.dezignstuff.com`), blog (`www.dezignstuff.com/blog`), or send an email (matt@dezignstuff.com).

- **See the ReadMe file.** Please refer to the ReadMe file located at the root of the CD for the latest product information at the time of publication.

Customer Care

If you still have trouble with the CD, please call the Wiley Product Technical Support telephone number: (800) 762-2974. Outside the United States, call 1 (317) 572-3994. You can also contact Wiley Product Technical Support at `http://support.wiley.com`. John Wiley & Sons will provide technical support only for installation and other general quality control items. For technical support on the applications themselves, consult the program's vendor or author.

To place additional orders or to request information about other Wiley products, please call (800) 225-5945.

Index

Symbols and Numerics

A

F

M

U

Wiley Publishing, Inc.
End-User License Agreement

READ THIS. You should carefully read these terms and conditions before opening the software packet(s) included with this book ("SolidWorks 2009 Bible"). This is a license agreement ("Agreement") between you and Wiley Publishing, Inc. ("WPI"). By opening the accompanying software packet(s), you acknowledge that you have read and accept the following terms and conditions. If you do not agree and do not want to be bound by such terms and conditions, promptly return the Book and the unopened software packet(s) to the place you obtained them for a full refund.

1. **License Grant.** WPI grants to you (either an individual or entity) a nonexclusive license to use one copy of the enclosed software program(s) (collectively, the "Software") solely for your own personal or business purposes on a single computer (whether a standard computer or a workstation component of a multi-user network). The Software is in use on a computer when it is loaded into temporary memory (RAM) or installed into permanent memory (hard disk, CD-ROM, or other storage device). WPI reserves all rights not expressly granted herein.

2. **Ownership.** WPI is the owner of all right, title, and interest, including copyright, in and to the compilation of the Software recorded on the disk(s) or CD-ROM "Software Media." Copyright to the individual programs recorded on the Software Media is owned by the author or other authorized copyright owner of each program. Ownership of the Software and all proprietary rights relating thereto remain with WPI and its licensers.

3. **Restrictions on Use and Transfer.**

   (a) You may only (i) make one copy of the Software for backup or archival purposes, or (ii) transfer the Software to a single hard disk, provided that you keep the original for backup or archival purposes. You may not (i) rent or lease the Software, (ii) copy or reproduce the Software through a LAN or other network system or through any computer subscriber system or bulletin-board system, or (iii) modify, adapt, or create derivative works based on the Software.

   (b) You may not reverse engineer, decompile, or disassemble the Software. You may transfer the Software and user documentation on a permanent basis, provided that the transferee agrees to accept the terms and conditions of this Agreement and you retain no copies. If the Software is an update or has been updated, any transfer must include the most recent update and all prior versions.

4. **Restrictions on Use of Individual Programs.** You must follow the individual requirements and restrictions detailed for each individual program in the "What's on the CD-ROM" appendix of this Book. These limitations are also contained in the individual license agreements recorded on the Software Media. These limitations may include a requirement that after using the program for a specified period of time, the user must pay a registration fee or discontinue use. By opening the Software packet(s), you will be agreeing to abide by the licenses and restrictions for these individual programs that are detailed in the "What's on the CD-ROM" appendix and on the Software Media. None of the material on this Software Media or listed in this Book may ever be redistributed, in original or modified form, for commercial purposes.

5. **Limited Warranty.**

   (a) WPI warrants that the Software and Software Media are free from defects in materials and workmanship under normal use for a period of sixty (60) days from the date of purchase of this Book. If WPI receives notification within the warranty period of defects in materials or workmanship, WPI will replace the defective Software Media.

   (b) WPI AND THE AUTHOR(S) OF THE BOOK DISCLAIM ALL OTHER WARRANTIES, EXPRESS OR IMPLIED, INCLUDING WITHOUT LIMITATION IMPLIED WARRANTIES OF MERCHANTABILITY AND FITNESS FOR A PARTICULAR PURPOSE, WITH RESPECT TO THE SOFTWARE, THE PROGRAMS, THE SOURCE CODE CONTAINED THEREIN, AND/OR THE TECHNIQUES DESCRIBED IN THIS BOOK. WPI DOES NOT WARRANT THAT THE FUNCTIONS CONTAINED IN THE SOFTWARE WILL MEET YOUR REQUIREMENTS OR THAT THE OPERATION OF THE SOFTWARE WILL BE ERROR FREE.

   (c) This limited warranty gives you specific legal rights, and you may have other rights that vary from jurisdiction to jurisdiction.

6. **Remedies.**

   (a) WPI's entire liability and your exclusive remedy for defects in materials and workmanship shall be limited to replacement of the Software Media, which may be returned to WPI with a copy of your receipt at the following address: Software Media Fulfillment Department, Attn.: SolidWorks 2009 Bible, Wiley Publishing, Inc., 10475 Crosspoint Blvd., Indianapolis, IN 46256, or call 1-800-762-2974. Please allow four to six weeks for delivery. This Limited Warranty is void if failure of the Software Media has resulted from accident, abuse, or misapplication. Any replacement Software Media will be warranted for the remainder of the original warranty period or thirty (30) days, whichever is longer.

   (b) In no event shall WPI or the author be liable for any damages whatsoever (including without limitation damages for loss of business profits, business interruption, loss of business information, or any other pecuniary loss) arising from the use of or inability to use the Book or the Software, even if WPI has been advised of the possibility of such damages.

   (c) Because some jurisdictions do not allow the exclusion or limitation of liability for consequential or incidental damages, the above limitation or exclusion may not apply to you.

7. **U.S. Government Restricted Rights.** Use, duplication, or disclosure of the Software for or on behalf of the United States of America, its agencies and/or instrumentalities "U.S. Government" is subject to restrictions as stated in paragraph (c)(1)(ii) of the Rights in Technical Data and Computer Software clause of DFARS 252.227-7013, or subparagraphs (c) (1) and (2) of the Commercial Computer Software - Restricted Rights clause at FAR 52.227-19, and in similar clauses in the NASA FAR supplement, as applicable.

8. **General.** This Agreement constitutes the entire understanding of the parties and revokes and supersedes all prior agreements, oral or written, between them and may not be modified or amended except in a writing signed by both parties hereto that specifically refers to this Agreement. This Agreement shall take precedence over any other documents that may be in conflict herewith. If any one or more provisions contained in this Agreement are held by any court or tribunal to be invalid, illegal, or otherwise unenforceable, each and every other provision shall remain in full force and effect.